T0215628

Lecture Notes in Computer Science   11335

Commenced Publication in 1973
Founding and Former Series Editors:
Gerhard Goos, Juris Hartmanis, and Jan van Leeuwen

More information about this series at http://www.springer.com/series/7407

Jaideep Vaidya · Jin Li (Eds.)

Algorithms and Architectures for Parallel Processing

18th International Conference, ICA3PP 2018
Guangzhou, China, November 15–17, 2018
Proceedings, Part II

 Springer

Editors
Jaideep Vaidya
Rutgers University
Newark, NJ, USA

Jin Li
Guangzhou University
Guangzhou, China

ISSN 0302-9743   ISSN 1611-3349 (electronic)
Lecture Notes in Computer Science
ISBN 978-3-030-05053-5   ISBN 978-3-030-05054-2 (eBook)
https://doi.org/10.1007/978-3-030-05054-2

Library of Congress Control Number: 2018962485

LNCS Sublibrary: SL1 – Theoretical Computer Science and General Issues

This Springer imprint is published by the registered company Springer Nature Switzerland AG
The registered company address is: Gewerbestrasse 11, 6330 Cham, Switzerland

Preface

Welcome to the proceedings of the 18th International Conference on Algorithms and Architectures for Parallel Processing (ICA3PP 2018), which was organized by Guangzhou University and held in Guangzhou, China, during November 15–17, 2018.

ICA3PP 2018 was the 18th event in a series of conferences devoted to research on algorithms and architectures for parallel processing. Previous iterations of the conference include ICA3PP 2017 (Helsinki, Finland, November 2017), ICA3PP 2016 (Granada, Spain, December 2016), ICA3PP 2015 (Zhangjiajie, China, November 2015), ICA3PP 2014 (Dalian, China, August 2014), ICA3PP 2013 (Vietri sul Mare, Italy, December 2013), ICA3PP 2012 (Fukuoka, Japan, September 2012), ICA3PP 2011 (Melbourne, Australia, October 2011), ICA3PP 2010 (Busan, Korea, May 2010), ICA3PP 2009 (Taipei, Taiwan, June 2009), ICA3PP 2008 (Cyprus, June 2008), ICA3PP 2007 (Hangzhou, China, June 2007), ICA3PP 2005 (Melbourne, Australia, October 2005), ICA3PP 2002 (Beijing, China, October 2002), ICA3PP 2000 (Hong Kong, China, December 2000), ICA3PP 1997 (Melbourne, Australia, December 1997), ICA3PP 1996 (Singapore, June 1996), and ICA3PP 1995 (Brisbane, Australia, April 1995).

ICA3PP is now recognized as the main regular event in the area of parallel algorithms and architectures, which covers many dimensions including fundamental theoretical approaches, practical experimental projects, and commercial and industry applications. This conference provides a forum for academics and practitioners from countries and regions around the world to exchange ideas for improving the efficiency, performance, reliability, security, and interoperability of computing systems and applications.

ICA3PP 2018 attracted over 400 high-quality research papers highlighting the foundational work that strives to push beyond the limits of existing technologies, including experimental efforts, innovative systems, and investigations that identify weaknesses in existing parallel processing technology. Each submission was reviewed by at least two experts in the relevant areas, on the basis of their significance, novelty, technical quality, presentation, and practical impact. According to the review results, 141 full papers were selected to be presented at the conference, giving an acceptance rate of 35%. Besides, we also accepted 50 short papers and 24 workshop papers. In addition to the paper presentations, the program of the conference included four keynote speeches and two invited talks from esteemed scholars in the area, namely: Prof. Xuemin (Sherman) Shen, University of Waterloo, Canada; Prof. Wenjing Lou, Virginia Tech, USA; Prof. Witold Pedrycz, University of Alberta, Canada; Prof. Xiaohua Jia, City University of Hong Kong, Hong Kong; Prof. Xiaofeng Chen, Xidian University, China; Prof. Xinyi Huang, Fujian Normal University, China. We were extremely honored to have them as the conference keynote speakers and invited speakers.

ICA3PP 2018 was made possible by the behind-the-scene effort of selfless individuals and organizations who volunteered their time and energy to ensure the success of this conference. We would like to express our special appreciation to Prof. Yang Xiang, Prof. Weijia Jia, Prof. Yi Pan, Prof. Laurence T. Yang, and Prof. Wanlei Zhou, the Steering Committee members, for giving us the opportunity to host this prestigious conference and for their guidance with the conference organization. We would like to emphasize our gratitude to the general chairs, Prof. Albert Zomaya and Prof. Minyi Guo, for their outstanding support in organizing the event. Thanks also to the publicity chairs, Prof. Zheli Liu and Dr Weizhi Meng, for the great job in publicizing this event. We would like to give our thanks to all the members of the Organizing Committee and Program Committee for their efforts and support.

The ICA3PP 2018 program included two workshops, namely, the ICA3PP 2018 Workshop on Intelligent Algorithms for Large-Scale Complex Optimization Problems and the ICA3PP 2018 Workshop on Security and Privacy in Data Processing. We would like to express our sincere appreciation to the workshop chairs: Prof. Ting Hu, Prof. Feng Wang, Prof. Hongwei Li and Prof. Qian Wang.

Last but not least, we would like to thank all the contributing authors and all conference attendees, as well as the great team at Springer that assisted in producing the conference proceedings, and the developers and maintainers of EasyChair.

November 2018   Jaideep Vaidya
Jin Li

Organization

General Chairs

Albert Zomaya   University of Sydney, Australia
Minyi Guo   Shanghai Jiao Tong University, China

Program Chairs

Jaideep Vaidya   Rutgers University, USA
Jin Li   Guangzhou University, China

Publication Chair

Yu Wang   Guangzhou University, China

Publicity Chairs

Zheli Liu   Nankai University, China
Weizhi Meng   Technical University of Denmark, Denmark

Steering Committee

Yang Xiang (Chair)   Swinburne University of Technology, Australia
Weijia Jia   Shanghai Jiaotong University, China
Yi Pan   Georgia State University, USA
Laurence T. Yang   St. Francis Xavier University, Canada
Wanlei Zhou   Deakin University, Australia

Program Committee

Pedro Alonso   Universitat Politècnica de València, Spain
Daniel Andresen   Kansas State University, USA
Cosimo Anglano   Universitá del Piemonte Orientale, Italy
Danilo Ardagna   Politecnico di Milano, Italy
Kapil Arya   Northeastern University, USA
Marcos Assuncao   Inria, France
Joonsang Baek   University of Wollongong, Australia
Anirban Basu   KDDI Research Inc., Japan
Ladjel Bellatreche   LIAS/ENSMA, France
Jorge Bernal Bernabe   University of Murcia, Spain
Thomas Boenisch   High-Performance Computing Center Stuttgart, Germany

George Bosilca	University of Tennessee, USA
Massimo Cafaro	University of Salento, Italy
Philip Carns	Argonne National Laboratory, USA
Alexandra Carpen-Amarie	Vienna University of Technology, Austria
Aparicio Carranza	City University of New York, USA
Aniello Castiglione	University of Salerno, Italy
Arcangelo Castiglione	University of Salerno, Italy
Pedro Castillo	University of Granada, Spain
Tzung-Shi Chen	National University of Tainan, Taiwan
Kim-Kwang Raymond Choo	The University of Texas at San Antonio, USA
Mauro Conti	University of Padua, Italy
Jose Alfredo Ferreira Costa	Federal University, UFRN, Brazil
Raphaël Couturier	University Bourgogne Franche-Comté, France
Miguel Cárdenas Montes	CIEMAT, Spain
Masoud Daneshtalab	Mälardalen University and Royal Institute of Technology, Sweden
Casimer Decusatis	Marist College, USA
Eugen Dedu	University of Bourgogne Franche-Comté, France
Juan-Carlos Díaz-Martín	University of Extremadura, Spain
Matthieu Dorier	Argonne National Laboratory, USA
Avgoustinos Filippoupolitis	University of Greenwich, UK
Ugo Fiore	Federico II University, Italy
Franco Frattolillo	University of Sannio, Italy
Marc Frincu	West University of Timisoara, Romania
Jorge G. Barbosa	University of Porto, Portugal
Chongzhi Gao	Guangzhou University, China
Jose Daniel García	University Carlos III of Madrid, Spain
Luis Javier García Villalba	Universidad Complutense de Madrid, Spain
Paolo Gasti	New York Institute of Technology, USA
Vladimir Getov	University of Westminster, UK
Olivier Gluck	Université de Lyon, France
Jing Gong	KTH Royal Institute of Technology, Sweden
Amina Guermouche	Telecom Sud-Paris, France
Jeff Hammond	Intel, USA
Feng Hao	Newcastle University, UK
Houcine Hassan	Universitat Politècnica de València, Spain
Sun-Yuan Hsieh	National Cheng Kung University, Taiwan
Chengyu Hu	Shandong University, China
Xinyi Huang	Fujian Normal University, China
Mauro Iacono	University of Campania Luigi Vanvitelli, Italy
Shadi Ibrahim	Inria, France
Yasuaki Ito	Hiroshima University, Japan
Mathias Jacquelin	Lawrence Berkeley National Laboratory, USA
Nan Jiang	East China Jiaotong University, China
Lu Jiaxin	Jiangxi Normal University, China

Edward Jung	Kennesaw State University, USA
Georgios Kambourakis	University of the Aegean, Greece
Gabor Kecskemeti	Liverpool John Moores University, UK
Muhammad Khurram Khan	King Saud University, Saudi Arabia
Dieter Kranzlmüller	Ludwig Maximilian University of Munich, Germany
Michael Kuhn	University of Hamburg, Germany
Julian Kunkel	German Climate Computing Center, Germany
Algirdas Lančinskas	Vilnius University, Lithuania
Patrick P. C. Lee	The Chinese University of Hong Kong, SAR China
Laurent Lefevre	Inria, France
Hui Li	University of Electronic Science and Technology of China, China
Kenli Li	Hunan University, China
Dan Liao	University of Electronic Science and Technology of China, China
Jingyu Liu	Hebei University of Technology, China
Joseph Liu	Monash University, Australia
Yunan Liu	Jiangxi Normal University, China
Zheli Liu	Nankai University, China
Jay Lofstead	Sandia National Laboratories, USA
Paul Lu	University of Alberta, Canada
Amit Majumdar	University of California San Diego, USA
Tomas Margalef	Universitat Autonoma de Barcelona, Spain
Stefano Markidis	KTH Royal Institute of Technology, Sweden
Alejandro Masrur	Chemnitz University of Technology, Germany
Susumu Matsumae	Saga University, Japan
Raffaele Montella	University of Naples Parthenope, Italy
Francesco Moscato	University of Campania Luigi Vanvitelli, Italy
Bogdan Nicolae	Argonne National Laboratory, Germany
Francesco Palmieri	University of Salerno, Italy, Italy
Swann Perarnau	Argonne National Laboratory, USA
Dana Petcu	West University of Timisoara, Romania
Salvador Petit	Universitat Politècnica de València, Spain
Riccardo Petrolo	Rice University, USA
Florin Pop	University Politehnica of Bucharest, Romania
Radu Prodan	University of Klagenfurt, Austria
Zhang Qikun	Beijing Institute of Technology, China
Thomas Rauber	University Bayreuth, Germany
Khaled Riad	Zagazig University, Egypt
Suzanne Rivoire	Sonoma State University, USA
Ivan Rodero	Rutgers University, USA
Romain Rouvoy	University of Lille, France
Antonio Ruiz-Martínez	University of Murcia, Spain
Françoise Sailhan	CNAM, France
Sherif Sakr	The University of New South Wales, Australia
Giandomenico Spezzano	ICAR-CNR and University of Calabria, Italy

Contents – Part II

Big Data and Information Processing

High Performance Computing

Embedding Exchanged Hypercubes into Rings and Ladders

Weibei Fan[1], Jianxi Fan[1(✉)], Cheng-Kuan Lin[1], Zhijie Han[2], Peng Li[2], and Ruchuan Wang[2]

[1] School of Computer Science and Technology, Soochow University, Suzhou 215006, China
wbfan@stu.suda.edu.cn, {jxfan,cklin}@suda.edu.cn
[2] Jiangsu High Technology Research Key Laboratory for Wireless Sensor Networks, Nanjing 210003, Jiangsu Province, China
{hanzj,lipeng,wangrc}@njupt.edu.cn

Abstract. Graph embeddings are not only used to study the simulation capabilities of a parallel architecture but also to design its VLSI layout. The n-dimensional hypercube is one of the most popular topological structure for interconnection networks in parallel computing and communication systems. The exchanged hypercube $EH_{s,t}$ (where $s \geq 1$ and $t \geq 1$) is obtained by systematically deleting edges from a hypercube Q_{s+t+1}, which retains several valuable and desirable properties of the hypercube such as a small diameter, bipancyclicity, and super connectivity. In this paper, we identify maximum induced subgraph of $EH_{s,t}$ and study embeddings of $EH_{s,t}$ into a ring and a ladder with minimum wirelength.

Keywords: Interconnection networks · $EH_{s,t}$ · Graph embedding Rings · Ladders

1 Introduction

Interconnection network is an important component in parallel computing systems. One of the constraints in VLSI routing problems is minimizing wirelength, and efficient layouts for several interconnection networks can be found in [13,24,30]. The minimum linear layout problem is first stated by Harper in 1964 and is proved to be NP-complete [10]. Nakano [22] proposed a linear layout of generalized hypercube. Rostami et al. [23] solved the minimum linear arrangement problem for chord graphs in polynomial time. Miller et al. [21] studied the minimum linear arrangement of incomplete hypercubes. Recently, Arockiaraj et al. [1] proved that the minimum linear layout of locally twisted cubes is equal to the minimum linear layout of hypercubes. Interconnection networks can also layout into optical linear arrays. In [5], Chen et al. discussed embeddings of bidirectional and unidirectional hypercubes on a class of optical networks which included rings. Liu et al. [15] studied the embedding of exchanged hypercube

© Springer Nature Switzerland AG 2018
J. Vaidya and J. Li (Eds.): ICA3PP 2018, LNCS 11335, pp. 3–17, 2018.
https://doi.org/10.1007/978-3-030-05054-2_1

into optical ring network with optimal congestion. Yu et al. [31] proposed an embedding of ternary n-cube into an optical ring network with minimum congestion.

The problem of efficiently laying out VLSI can be formulated as the graph embedding problem. Embeddability is a critical metric to evaluate the performance of an interconnection network. Many applications, such as architecture simulation, processor allocation, can be modeled as a graph embedding problem. Graph embedding is an important issue that maps a guest graph into a host graph. Most researches on graph embedding consider paths, cycles and meshes as guest graphs because they are the architectures widely used in parallel computing systems [9,12,26–28]. In [8], Fan et al. proved that the cycles of all possible lengths can be embedded into twisted cube, and Fan et al. [7] also studied the embedding of paths with all possible lengths between any two vertices into crossed cube. Wang et al. [12] studied the embedding of three different types of special meshes into twisted-cubes.

The hypercube is one of the most popular interconnection network structures in parallel computing and communication systems [14]. As a variant of the n-dimensional hypercube, the exchanged hypercube $EH_{s,t}$ was proposed by Loh et al. [16]. An exchanged hypercube is formed by removing edges from an n-dimensional hypercube Q_n where $n = s + t + 1$. This is evident in the fact that even though the number of edges of an exchanged hypercube is nearly half of that of a hypercube, their diameters are similar. Therefore, $EH_{s,t}$ retains several desirable properties of the hypercube such as a small diameter [16], bipancyclicity [18], and super connectivity [20] and have lower link costs than hypercubes. Futhermore, the lower link complexity of $EH_{s,t}$ can directly reduce the costs of hardware and the implementation of VLSI.

In this paper, we study the embedding of $EH_{s,t}$ into a ladder and obtain the exact wirelength of $EH_{s,t}$ into a ladder. The major contributions of the paper are as follows:

(1) We identified the maximum induced subgraph of $EH_{s,t}$.

(2) We studied the layout of embedding exchanged hypercube into a ring network with minimum wirelength.

(3) We proposed a decomposition embedding of $EH_{s,t}$ into a ladder, and proved that $EH_{s,t}$ can be embedded into the ladder $L(2 \times 2^{\frac{s+t}{2}})$ with minimum wirelength.

The rest of this paper is organized as follows: Sect. 2 gives some definitions and notations. Section 3 derives a maximum induced subgraph of $EH_{s,t}$ into a ring network with minimum wirelength. Section 4 gives an embedding of $EH_{s,t}$ into ladder with minimum wirelength. The final section concludes this paper.

2   Preliminaries

2.1   Definitions and Notations

In this section, we will give some definitions and notations used in this paper. All graphs in this paper are simple undirected graphs, which can generally denoted by $G = (V(G), E(G))$, where $V(G)$ is the vertex set and $E(G)$ is the edge set. For two simple graphs $G_1 = (V_1, E_1)$ and $G_2 = (V_2, E_2)$, G_2 is said to be a subgraph of G_1 if $V_2 \subseteq V_1$ and $E_2 \subseteq E_1$. If $V' \subseteq V(G)$, the subgraph of G induced by the vertex subset V' is denoted by $G[V']$. The subgraph induced by the vertex subset $V(G_1) \cup V(G_2)$ is denoted by $G_1 \cup G_2$. Let $\tau(V')$ denote the number of edges of $G[V']$. If G_1 is a subgraph of G_2 and $G_1 \neq G_2$, G_1 is said to be the proper graph of G_2 and denoted by $G_1 \subset G_2$. For a pair of disjoint vertex subset S_1 and S_2 of graph G, let $\tau(S_1, S_2)$ denote the number of edges with one vertex in S_1 and the other vertex in S_2. For any integer $n \geq 1$, a binary string x of length n will be written as $x_{n-1}x_{n-2}...x_1x_0$, where $x_i \in \{0, 1\}$ for any integer $i \in \{0, 1, ..., n-1\}$. Given any $x = x_{n-1}x_{n-2}...x_1x_0$, x_i is said to be the i-th bit of x and $x_{n-1}x_{n-2}...x_k$ $(0 \leq k \leq n-1)$ is called a prefix of x. Besides, x_0 is called the first bit of x and x_{n-1} is called the last bit of x. For a graph $G = (V, E)$, an (u, v)-path of length l from vertex u to vertex v is denoted by $P = (u_0, u_1, ..., u_l)$, where $u_0 = u$ and $u_l = v$ are called the two end vertices of path P, and all the vertices $u_0, u_1, ..., u_l$ are distinct. If $u = v$, then P is called a cycle.

A graph G_1 is isomorphic to another graph G_2 (represented by $G_1 \cong G_2$) if and only if there exists a bijection $f : V(G_1) \rightarrow V(G_2)$, such that if $(u, v) \in E(G_1)$ then $(f(u), f(v)) \in E(G_2)$. For two graphs $G_1 = (V_1, E_1)$ and $G_2 = (V_2, E_2)$, and a subset $S \subseteq V_1$, let f be a mapping from V_1 to V_2. Let $T = \{x \in V(G_2) | f(x) \in S\}$. Then we write $T = f(S)$ and $S = f^{-1}(T)$.

Graph embedding can be formally defined as: Given two graphs $G_1 = (V_1, E_1)$ and $G_2 = (V_2, E_2)$, an embedding from G_1 to G_2 is an injective mapping $\psi : V_1 \rightarrow V_2$. We call G_1 the guest graph and G_2 the host graph. There are four common metrics used to measure the quality of an embedding, namely, *congestion*, *dilation*, *expansion* and *load*. The *congestion* of an embedding ψ is defined as $cong(G_1, G_2, \psi) = \max\{cong(e) | e \in E_2\}$, which measures queuing delay of messages, where $cong(e)$ denotes the number of edges of G_1 whose image paths in G_2 include the edge e. The *dilation* of embedding ψ is defined as: $dil(G_1, G_2, \psi) = \max\{\text{dist}(G_2, \psi(u), \psi(v)) | (u, v) \in E_1\}$, which measures the communication delay, where $\text{dist}(G_2, \psi(u), \psi(v))$ denotes the distance between the two vertices $\psi(u)$ and $\psi(v)$ in G_2.

Wirelength is another criteria in embedding and widely used in VLSI design [3]. The wirelength is the total wire length required to complete the entire VLSI layout. The wirelength problem is to find an embedding of G into H that induces the minimum wirelength, and thought to be cost-effective. The wirelength problem is solved by edge isoperimetric problem. The following two versions of the edge isoperimetric problem of a graph $G(V, E)$ have been considered in the literature [2], and are NP-complete [10].

The first problem is to find a subset of vertices of a given graph, such that the edge cut separating this subset from its complement has minimum size among all subsets of the same cardinality. Mathematically, for a given positive integer m, if $\delta_G(m) = \min_{X \subseteq V, |X|=m} |[X, V - X]_G|$, where $[X, V - X]_G = \{(u, v) \in E | u \in X, v \in (V - X)\}$, then the problem is to find $X \subseteq V$ such that $|X| = m$ and $|[X, V - X]_G| = \delta_G(m)$, which is called an optimal set.

Another problem is called maximum induced subgraph problem [2], which is to find a subset of vertices of a given graph, such that the number of edges in the subgraph induced by this subset is maximum among all induced subgraphs with the same number of vertices. Mathematically, for a given positive integer m, if $I_G(m) = \max_{X \subseteq V, |X|=m} |T_G(X)|$, where $T_G(X) = \{(u, v) \in E | u, v \in X\}$, then the problem is to find $X \subseteq V$ such that $|X| = m$ and $|T_G(X)| = I_G(m)$. For regular graphs, the optimal set problem and maximum induced subgraph problem are equivalent.

Definition 1 [19]. Let f be an embedding from G to H. Let $EC_f(e)$ denote the number of edges (u, v) of G such that e is in the path $P_f(u, v)$ between the vertices $f(u)$ and $f(v)$ in H. Considering there possibly exist multiple paths between $(f(u), f(v))$ in H, we choose the shortest path as $P_f(f(u), f(v))$. The edge congestion f is given by

$$EC_f(G, H) = \max\{EC_f(e) | e \in E(H)\}.$$

Then, the minimum edge congestion of G into H is defined as

$$EC(G, H) = \min\{EC_f(G, H) | f \text{ is an embedding from } G \text{ to } H\}.$$

Definition 2 [19]. The wirelength of an embedding f of G into H is given by

$$WL_f(G, H) = \sum_{(u,v) \in G} d_H(f(u), f(v)),$$

where $d_H(f(u), f(v))$ denotes the length of the path $P_f(u, v)$ in H, and $P_f(u, v)$ is the shortest path between $(f(u), f(v))$ in H.

Then, the minimum wirelength of G into H is defined as

$$WL(G, H) = \min WL_f(G, H),$$

where the minimum is taken over all embeddings f of G into H.

Lemma 1 [19]. Let G be an arbitrary graph and f be an embedding of G into H. Let S be an edge cut of H such that the removal of edges of S leaves H into 2 components H_1 and H_2. Let $G_1 = f^{-1}(H_1)$ and $G_2 = f^{-1}(H_2)$. Also S satisfies the following conditions:

(i) For every edge $(a, b) \in (G_i)$, $i = 1, 2$, $P_f(a, b)$ has no edges in S.

(ii) For every edge $(a, b) \in E(G)$ with $a \in V(G_1)$ and $b \in V(G_2)$, $P_f(a, b)$ has exactly one edge in S.

(iii) G_1 and G_2 are optimal sets.

Then $EC_f(S)$ is minimum and $EC_f(S) = \sum_{v \in V(G_1)} \deg(v) - 2|E(G_1)| = \sum_{v \in V(G_2)} \deg(v) - 2|E(G_2)|$.

Lemma 2 [19]. Let $f : G \to H$ be an embedding. Let $S_1, S_2, ..., S_p$ be p edge cuts of H such that $S_i \cap S_j = \varnothing, i \neq j, 1 \leq i, j \leq p$. Then

$$WL_f(G, H) = \sum_{i=1}^{p} EC_f(S_i).$$

2.2   The Exchanged Hypercube

The definition of exchanged hypercubes $EH_{s,t}$ is presented as follows.

Definition 3 [16]. The vertex set V of exchanged hypercube $EH_{s,t}$ ($s \geq 1$ and $t \geq 1$) is the set

$$\{u_{s+t}...u_{t+1}u_t...u_1u_0 | u_i \in \{0,1\} \text{ for } 0 \leq i \leq s+t\}.$$

Let $u_{s+t}u_{s+t-1}...u_0$ and $v_{s+t}v_{s+t-1}...v_0$ be two vertices in $EH_{s,t}$. E is the set of edges composed of three disjoint types E_1, E_2 and E_3:

$E_1 = \{(u,v) | u_0 \neq v_0 \text{ and } u_i = v_i \text{ for } 1 \leq i \leq s+t\}$,

$E_2 = \{(u,v) | u_0 = v_0 = 0, H(u,v) = 1 \text{ with } u_i \neq v_i \text{ for some } t+1 \leq i \leq s+t\}$,

and

$E_3 = \{(u,v) | u_0 = v_0 = 1, H(u,v) = 1 \text{ with } u_i \neq v_i \text{ for some } 1 \leq i \leq t\}$,

where $H(u,v)$ denotes the Hamming distance between two vertices u and v.

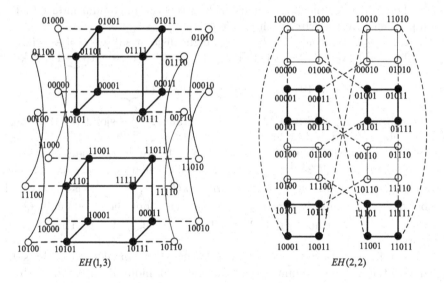

EH(1,3)   EH(2,2)

Fig. 1. Two exchanged hypercubes $EH(1,3)$ and $EH(2,2)$, where dashed links correspond to the edge set E_1, solid links correspond to the edge set E_2, and bold links correspond to the edge set E_3.

From the definition of $EH_{s,t}$, the number of vertices is 2^{s+t+1} and the number of edges is $(s+t+2)2^{s+t-1}$ where $|E_1| = 2^{s+t}$, $|E_2| = s \cdot 2^{s+t-1}$ and $|E_3| = t \cdot 2^{s+t-1}$. For a vertex x with $x_0 = 0$, the vertex degree is $s+1$, whereas the vertex degree with $x_0 = 1$ is $t+1$. $EH_{s,t}$ is a subgraph of the $(s+t+1)$-dimensional hypercube Q_{s+t+1}, and as a result it is also a bipartite graph. Figure 1 illustrates the exchanged hypercubes $EH(1,3)$ and $EH(2,2)$.

Lemma 3 [16]. $EH_{s,t}$ and $EH_{t,s}$ are isomorphic.

Lemma 4 [16]. $EH_{s,t}$ can be divided into 2^t copies as Q_s and 2^s copies as Q_t.

Lemma 5 [16]. $EH_{s,t}$ can be partitioned into two copies of $EH_{s-1,t}$ or $EH_{s,t-1}$.

After deleting the edge set E_1 from $EH_{s,t}$, the vertex set of $EH_{s,t}$ can separated into two parts T and S, where T is the set of all vertices with rightmost bit being 1, and S is the set of all vertices with rightmost bit being 0. In other words,

$T = \{v_{s+t}v_{s+t-1}...v_1 1 | v_i \in \{0,1\}$ for $1 \le i \le s+t\}$, and
$S = \{u_{s+t}u_{s+t-1}...u_1 0 | u_i \in \{0,1\}$ for $1 \le i \le s+t\}$.

Each edge $e \in E_1$ has one endpoint in T and the other in S.

3   Maximum Induced Subgraph for $EH_{s,t}$

In this section, we mainly focus on finding the maximum induced subgraph of $EH_{s,t}$. There is a significant relationship between the maximum induced subgraph problem and the wirelength problem.

For $1 \le s \le t$, we group $V(EH_{s,t})$ into eight disjoint subsets [15] as follows,
$V_1 = \{0\underbrace{*...*}_{t-1}01\}$, $V_2 = \{0\underbrace{*...*}_{t-1}11\}$, $V_3 = \{1\underbrace{*...*}_{t-1}01\}$, $V_4 = \{1\underbrace{*...*}_{t-1}11\}$, $V_5 = \{0\underbrace{*...*}_{t-1}00\}$, $V_6 = \{0\underbrace{*...*}_{t-1}10\}$, $V_7 = \{1\underbrace{*...*}_{t-1}00\}$, $V_8 = \{1\underbrace{*...*}_{t-1}10\}$.

The subgraph induced by $V_i (1 \le i \le 4)$ contains 2^{s-1} disjoint $(t-1)$-cubes, and the subgraph induced by $V_i (1 \le i \le 4)$ contains 2^{t-1} disjoint $(s-1)$-cubes. If $s \ge 2$, for the subgraph induced by $V_i (1 \le i \le 4)$, we denote the $(t-1)$-cube by $Q_{t-1}^{i,j}$, where $j(j \in [0, 2^{s-1}-1])$ is the decimal number of $u_{s+t-1,t+1}$, and the vertex u in $Q_{t-1}^{i,j}$ is represented by $q_{t-1}^{i,j,k}$, where $k(k \in [0, 2^{t-1}-1])$ is the decimal number of $u_{t-1,1}$. Similarly, for $(5 \le i \le 8)$, we can define the $(s-1)$-cube $Q_{s-1}^{i,j}$ and the vertex $q_{s-1}^{i,j,k}$, where $j \in [0, 2^{t-1}-1]$ and $k \in [0, 2^{s-1}-1]$. This labeling is denoted by lex.

For any integer $m \ge 1$ and $S \subseteq V(G)$ with $|S| = m$, if $G[S]$ is the subgraph with the maximum number of edges among all induced subgraphs with m vertices, then $G[S]$ is called the maximum induced graph with m vertices in G.

Definition 4 [17]. An incomplete hypercube on i vertices of Q_n is the subcube induced by $\{0, 1, ..., i-1\}$ and is denoted by L_i.

Theorem 1 [11]. For $1 \le i \le 2^n$, L_i is an optimal set in the hypercube Q_n.

Lemma 6 [4]. For $1 \le i, j \le 2^n$ such that $i+j \le 2^n$, $|E(Q_n[L_i])| + |E(Q_n[L_j])| + \{i, j\} \le |E(Q_n[L_{i+j}])|$.

Lemma 7 [29]. Let V be a vertex subset of graph G and $\{V_0, V_1\}$ be a partition of V. Then $\tau(V) = \tau(V_0) + \tau(V_1) + \tau(V_0, V_1)$.

Lemma 8. Let K be a subgraph of $EH_{s,t}$ isomorphic to L_k where $1 \leq s \leq t$ and $k \leq 2^{s+t} + 2^s$. Let K_1 and K_2 be disjoint segments induced by k_1 and k_2 consecutive vertices on $\bigcup_{i=1}^{2^s} Q_t \cup Q_s^1$ respectively such that $k_1 + k_2 = k$. Then $|E(EH_{s,t}[K_1 \cup K_2])| \leq |E(EH_{s,t}[K])|$.

Proof. By Lemma 4, $EH_{s,t}$ can be divided into 2^s copies of Q_t and 2^t copies of Q_s. Hence, we can denote Q_t^1, Q_t^2,..., and $Q_t^{2^s}$ as 2^s copies of Q_t who are composed of the edges E_3, and Q_s^1, Q_s^2,..., and $Q_s^{2^t}$ as 2^t copies of Q_s who are composed of the edges E_2. For simplicity, we denote u_1^1, u_1^2,... and $u_1^{2^t}$ as 2^t vertices of Q_t^1, u_2^1, u_2^2,..., and $u_2^{2^t}$ as 2^t vertices of Q_t^2, ..., and $u_{2^s}^1$, $u_{2^s}^2$,..., and $u_{2^s}^{2^t}$ as 2^t vertices of $Q_t^{2^s}$. And we denote v_1^1, v_1^2,...and $v_1^{2^s}$ as 2^s vertices of Q_s^1, v_2^1, v_2^2,... and $v_2^{2^s}$ as 2^s vertices of Q_s^2,..., and $v_{2^t}^1$, $v_{2^t}^2$,... and $v_{2^t}^{2^s}$ as 2^s vertices of $Q_s^{2^t}$. Let $E(EH_{s,t}[K_1 \wedge K_2])$ denote the set of edges in $EH_{s,t}$ with one end in K_1 and the other end in K_2, we have the following cases:

Case 1. $k_1, k_2 \leq 2^t$. We consider the following cases.

Case 1.1 $K_1 \subset Q_t^1$. Since Q_t is isomorphic the t-dimensional cube, by the definition of $EH_{s,t}$ and Theorem 1, $|E(EH_{s,t}[K_1 \cup K_2])| = |E(Q_t[K_1 \cup K_2])| \leq |E(Q_t[K])| = |E(EH_{s,t}[K])|$.

Case 1.2 $K_1 \subset Q_s^1$. The proof is similar to Subcase 1.2.

Case 2. $2^t < k_1 \leq 2^t + 2^s$. $K_1 \subset Q_t^1 \cup Q_s^1$. Let $2^t = k_1 + k_2$, where k_1 vertices lie in Q_t^1 and k_2 vertices lie in Q_s^1, inducing subgraphs K_1 and K_2 in Q_t^1 and Q_s^1, respectively. Since there is one edge joining vertices in K_1 and vertices in K_2, $|E(EH_{s,t}[K_1 \wedge K_2])| \leq k_2$. This implies that $|E(EH_{s,t}[K_1 \cup K_2])| = |E(EH_{s,t}[K_1])| + |E(EH_{s,t}[K_2])| + |E(EH_{s,t}[K_1 \wedge K_2])| \leq |E(EH_{s,t}[L_{k_1}])| + |E(EH_{s,t}[L_{k_2}])| + k_2$. By Lemma 1, we get $|E(EH_{s,t}[K_1 \cup K_2])| \leq |E(EH_{s,t}[L_{k_1} + k_2])| = |E(EH_{s,t}[K])|$.

Case 3. $2^t + 2^s < k_1 \leq 2^{s+t} + 2^s$. Let k_1, k_2 be the number of consecutive vertices in K_1, K_2 that lie in $\bigcup_{i=1}^{2^s} Q_t^i \cup Q_s^1$. Then $|E(EH_{s,t}[K_1])| \leq |E(EH_{s,t}[L_{k_1}])|$, $|E(EH_{s,t}[K_2])| \leq |E(EH_{s,t}[L_{k_2}])|$ and $|E(EH_{s,t}[K_1 \wedge K_2])| \leq k_2 + k_2$. Hence $|E(EH_{s,t}[K_1 \cup K_2])| \leq |E(EH_{s,t}[L_{k_1}])| + |E(EH_{s,t}[L_{k_2}])| + 2k_2$. Let $H_1 = L_{k_1}$. Then $|E(EH_{s,t}[H_1])| = |E(EH_{s,t}[L_{k_1}])|$. Let H_2 be the subgraph of $EH_{s,t}$ induced by the vertices in Q_s^1 labeled $2^{s+t} - 1, 2^{s+t} - 2, ..., 2^{s+t} - k_2$. This implies $|E(EH_{s,t}[H_2])| = |E(EH_{s,t}[L_{k_2}])|$ and $|E(EH_{s,t}[H_1 \wedge H_2])| \geq k_2 + k_2$. Therefore $|E(EH_{s,t}[H_1 \wedge H_2])| \geq |E(EH_{s,t}[L_{k_1}])| + |E(EH_{s,t}[L_{k_2}])| + 2k_2$ and hence $|E(EH_{s,t}[K_1 \cup K_2])| \leq |E(EH_{s,t}[H_1 \cup H_2])|$. □

Theorem 2. The number of edges in a maximum subgraph induced by $2^{s+t} + m$ vertices of $EH_{s,t}$, $1 \leq s \leq t$, $1 \leq m \leq 2^{s+t+1}$, is given by

$$|E(EH_{s,t}[S])| = t \cdot 2^{s+t-1} + I_{EH_{s,t}}(m) + m.$$

Proof. Let $I_m^{k_i}$ denoted the k-dimensional subgraph of $EH_{s,t}$ on m vertices, which contains subcubes Q_t^1, Q_t^2,..., and Q_t^i and E_1 for $1 \leq i \leq 2^t$. This means that there are $k \cdot 2^{k_i-1}$ edges between $\bigcup_{i=1}^{2^s} Q_t^i$ and $\bigcup_{i=1}^{2^s} Q_t^{i+1}$. Also, $\bigcup_{i=1}^{2^s} Q_t^i$ has $t_i 2^{t_i-1}$ edges within itself. The maximum subgraph induced by I_m^k of $EH_{s,t}$ contains two components Q_k^i and $I_{m-2^{s+t}}^t$, where the vertices in Q_t^i are numbered as $0, 1, ..., 2^{s+t} - 1$ and the vertices in $I^t_{m-2^{s+t}}$ are numbered as $2^{s+t}, 2^{s+t} + 1, ..., 2^{s+t+1}$, for $t = \lceil \log(m - 2^{s+t}) \rceil$. Thus I^k_m contains a set of Q^i_t and Q^i_s, and no two constituent cubes are of the same size. The number of edges induced by I^k_m in $EH_{s,t}$, $1 \leq s \leq t$ is given by $|E[I^k_m])| = t \cdot 2^{s+t-1} + I_{EH_{s,t}}(m) + m$. The lemma holds. $\qquad\square$

Lemma 9. For $1 \leq s \leq t$ and $1 \leq i \leq 2^{s+t} + 2^s$, L_i is an optimal set.

Proof. Let R be a subgraph of $EH_{s,t}$ isomorphic to L_k where $k \leq 2^{s+t} + 2^s$. Let N be a set of k non-consecutive vertices in $EH_{s,t}$. Then $N = \bigcup_{i=1}^p X_i$ where $p \geq 2$, X_i's are mutually disjoint and each X_i is a set of consecutive vertices in $EH_{s,t}$ such that $\bigcup_{i=1}^p |X_i| = n$. If X_i contains vertices labeled $2^{s+t} + 2^s - 1$ and $2^{s+t} + 2^s$, then X_i is split into two sets such that one set ends with label $2^{s+t} + 2^s - 1$ and the other set begins with label $2^{s+t} + 2^s$. By Lemma 2, we get $|E(EH_{S,t}[N])| \leq |E(EH_{s,t}[R])|$. $\qquad\square$

Theorem 3. For $1 \leq i \leq 2^{s+t+1}$, L_i is an optimal set in $EH_{s,t}$.

Proof. By Lemma 4, after deleting the edge set E_1 from $EH_{s,t}$, $EH_{s,t}$ can be partitioned into $EH_{s-1,t}$ or $EH_{s,t-1}$. By Lemma 9, L_i is an optimal set for $1 \leq i \leq 2^{s+t} + 2^s$. Now let $i > 2^{s+t} + 2^s$. Then we have $L'_i = EH_{s,t} - L_i \cong L_{2^{s+t-i}}$. Since $2^{s+t+1} - i < 2^{s+t+1} - 1$, by Lemma 1, L'_i is an optimal set in $EH_{s,t}$. Since $EH_{s-1,t} \cong EH_{s,t-1}$, L_i is an optimal set in $EH_{s,t}$. $\qquad\square$

4   Embedding the Exchanged Hypercubes into Rings

In this section we consider the embeddings of exchanged hypercubes into rings. When the host graph is a cycle, the wirelength of the embedding is called cyclic wirelength. The ring structure is important for distributed computing. In a telecommunication network, a ring network affords fault tolerance to the network because there are two paths between any two nodes on the network (Fig. 2).

Definition 5. For any integer $n \geq 1$, the ring of n vertices, denoted by R_n, is a graph such that $V(R_n) = \{1, 2, ..., n\}$ and where $E(R_n) = \{(i, i+1) | i \in [1, n-1]\}$.

Definition 6. Let $f : V(EH_{s,t}) \rightarrow V(R_{2^{s+t+1}})$ be an embedding, which is defined as follow: Label the vertices of $R_{2^{s+t+1}}$ as $0, 1, ..., 2^{s+t+1} - 1$. Then, for any $v \in V(EH_{s,t})$, let $f(v) = lex(v)$.

Lemma 10 [6]. $CWL(Q_n, C_{2^n}) = 2^{2n-2} + 2^{2n-3} - 2^{n-1}$.

Lemma 11. $H^{lex}_i = \{1, 2, ..., i\}$ is an optimal set in $EH_{s,t}$ for $i = 1, 2, ..., 2^{s+t+1}$ and $1 \leq s \leq t$.

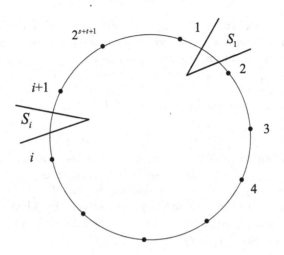

Fig. 2. The edge cut of ring $R_{2^{s+t+1}}$.

Proof. Let $f : H_i^{lex} \to L_{j \times 2^{\frac{s+t+1}{2}}}$ with $f(k \times 2^{\frac{s+t+1}{2}} + l) = l \times 2^{\frac{s+t+1}{2}} + k$. We use $u_1 u_2 ... u_{t+1}$ in H_i^{lex} to denote the decimal string of $l \times 2^{\frac{s+t+1}{2}} + k$. By Theorem 3, $L_i = \{1, 2, ..., i\}$ is an optimal set in $EH_{s,t}$ for each i. Since the decimal string representations of two numbers x and y differ in exactly one bit, the same holds for $f(x)$ and $f(y)$. Thus (x, y) is an edge in H_i and $(f(x), f(y))$ is an edge in L_{2^i}. Therefore, H_i is isomorphic to L_i. By Theorem 1, H_j^{lex} is an optimal set of $EH_{s,t}$. □

Lemma 12. The *lex* embedding of exchanged hypercube $EH_{s,t}$ into a ring $R_{2^{s+t+1}}$ induces a minimum wirelength.

Proof. Let $f = lex$ and $G = EH_{s,t}$. For $1 \leq i \leq 2^{s+t+1}$, let S_i be ith edge of $R_{2^{s+t+1}}$. Removal of S_i leaves $R_{2^{s+t+1}}$ into two components X_i and X_i' where $V(X_i) = \{0, 1, ..., i\}$ and $V(X_i') = \{j + 1, j + 2, ..., 2^{s+t+1}\}$. Let G_i and G_i' be the inverse images of X_i and X_i' under f, respectively. By Lemma 2, G_i is an optimal set in $EH_{s,t}$. Thus the edge cut S_i satisfies Lemma 1. It can be further verified that $\{(i - 1, i)\}$ satisfies Lemma 1, and the edge congestion $EC_f(S_i)$ is minimum under embedding *lex* for $i = 1, 2, ..., 2^{s+t+1}$. Thus the wirelength $WL_f(EH_{s,t}, R_{2^{s+t+1}})$ of embedding $EH_{s,t}$ into $R_{2^{s+t+1}}$ is minimum. □

Theorem 4. For $1 \leq s \leq t$, the wirelength of embedding $EH_{s,t}$ into a ring $R_{2^{s+t+1}}$ is given by

$$WL(EH_{s,t}, R_{2^{s+t+1}}) = 2^{s+2t-1} - 2^{s+t-1} + 2^{2t} + 2^{2t+2}.$$

Proof. Let $f = lex$. We first derive the exact wirelength of embedding the induced subgraphs $EH_{s,t}[E_1]$, $EH_{s,t}[E_2]$, and $EH_{s,t}[E_3]$ into $R_{2^{s+t+1}}$. Let the edge set $E_1 = \{(u, v) | u_0 \neq v_0, u_i = v_i$ for $1 \leq i \leq s + t\}$. After deleting E_1

from $EH_{s,t}$, the vertex set S is decomposed into 2^t connected components. Each component is an s-dimensional hypercube Q_s, moreover, these 2^t hypercubes Q_s are pairwise disjoint, and there are no edges joining any two Q_s. Since each edge $e \in E_1$ has one endpoint in Q_t and the other in Q_s, E_1 is a perfect matching of $EH_{s,t}$ between Q_s and Q_t.

For $1 \leq i \leq 2^{s+t}$, S_j is an edge cut of R_{2^t}, which disconnects R_{2^t} into two subrings R_j and R'_j, where $2 \leq j \leq 2^{s+t-1}$, $V(R_j) = \{1, 2, ..., j\}$, and $V(R'_j) = \{j+1, j+2, ..., 2^{s+t-1}\}$. Let $G_{j1} = f^{-1}(R_{j1})$ and $G_{j2} = f^{-1}(R_{j2})$. By Lemma 1, G_{j1} is an optimal set and each S_j satisfies conditions (i) and (ii) of Lemma 1. Therefore, $EC_f(S_j)$ is minimum. let A_i be an edge cut of $R_{2^{s+t}}$ such that S_i disconnects $R_{2^{s+t}}$ into two components R_{i1} and R_{i2}. Let G_{i1} and G_{i2} be the inverse images of R_{i1} and R_{i2} under f, respectively. By Theorem 1, G_{i1} is an optimal set and each S_i satisfies conditions (i) and (ii) of Lemma 1. Therefore, the sum congestion of $G[\bigcup_{i=1}^{2^s-1} Q_t^i]$ is

$$WL_f(A_i) = WL(G[\bigcup_{i=1}^{2^s-1} Q_t^i], R_{2^{s+t}})$$
$$= \sum_{j=1}^{2^{s+t-1}} EC_f(S_j)$$
$$= 2^{s+2t-1} - 2^{s+t-1}.$$

For $2^{s+t} + 1 \leq i \leq 2^{s+t+1}$, S_i is an edge cut of $R_{2^{s+t-1}}$, which disconnects $R_{2^{s+t-1}}$ into two linear arrays R_i and R'_i, where $2^{s+t-1} + 1 \leq i \leq 2^{s+t+1}$, $V(R_i) = \{1, 2, ..., i\}$, and $V(R'_i) = \{i+1, i+2, ..., 2^{s+t+1}-2\}$. Let $G_{i1} = f^{-1}(R_{i1})$ and $G_{i2} = f^{-1}(R_{i2})$. G_{i1} is an optimal set and each S_i satisfies conditions (i) and (ii) of Lemma 1. Therefore, $EC_f(S_i)$ is minimum. let B_j be an edge cut of $R_{2^{s+t}}$ such that S_j disconnects $R_{2^{s+t}}$ into two components R_{j1} and R_{j2}. Therefore, the sum congestion of $G[\bigcup_{i=1}^{2^t-1} Q_s^i]$ is

$$WL_f(B_j) = WL(G[\bigcup_{i=1}^{2^t-1} Q_s^i], R_{2^{s+t}})$$
$$= \sum_{j=2^{s+t}+1}^{2^{s+t+1}} EC_f S_j$$
$$= 2^t(2^{2s-1} - 2^{s-1}).$$

For $1 \leq k \leq 2^{s+t+1}$, let C_k be an edge cut of $R_{2^{s+t}}$ such that C_k disconnects $R_{2^{s+t+1}}$ into two components R_{k1} and R_{k2}. It is apparent that R_{kl} is symmetric about $l = 2^{s+t}$. So we need only consider the case for $1 \leq l \leq 2^{s+t}$ in computing the wirelength. Therefore, the sum congestion of E_1 is

$$EC_f(C_k) = 2\sum_{k=1}^{2^{s+t}} S_k$$
$$= 2(1 + 2 + \dots + 2^{s+t} - 1)$$
$$= 2^{s+t} \cdot (2^{s+t} - 1).$$

Thus,

$$WL(EH_{s,t}, R_{2^{s+t+1}}) = WL_f(EH_{s,t}, R_{2^{s+t+1}})$$
$$= WL_f(A_i) + WL_f(B_j) + WL_f(C_k)$$
$$= \sum_{i=1}^{2^{s+t}} A_i + \sum_{j=2^{s+t}+1}^{2^{s+t+1}} B_j + 2\sum_{k=1}^{2^{s+t}} C_k$$
$$= 2^s(2^{2t-1} - 2^{t-1}) + 2^t(2^{2s-1} - 2^{s-1}) + 2^{s+t} \cdot (2^{s+t} - 1)$$
$$= 2^{s+2t-1} + 2^{t+2s-1} + 2^{2(s+t)} - 2^{s+t+1}.$$

□

5   Embedding the Exchanged Hypercubes into Ladders

In this section we consider the embeddings of exchanged hypercubes into ladders. When H is a path, $WL(G,H)$ represents linear wirelength of G or Minimum Linear Arrangement (MinLA) of G. The wirelength problem of a graph G into H is to find an embedding of G into H that induces the minimum wirelength $WL(G,H)$.

A ladder is a special graph in which two paths of the same length are connected in such a way that each vertex of the 1rst one is connected by a path-called a rung-to its corresponding vertex in the second one. We construct an optimal embedding of $EH_{s,t}$ into a ladder with minimum wirelength. Firstly, the definition of ladder graph is given as below:

Definition 7 [25]. Consider two chains $A = a_l, ..., a_k$ and $B = b_l, ..., b_k$ and join each pair of vertices a_i, b_i, $i = 1, .., k$, with a new chain. The resulting graph is called a ladder, and the chains between a_i, b_i are called its rungs.

Definition 8. Let $h : EH_{s,t} \rightarrow L(2 \times 2^{s+t})\}$ be an embedding, which is defined as follows: The 1th row is labeled 1 to 2^{s+t} from left to right. The 2th row is labeled from $2^{s+t} + 1$ to 2^{s+t+1} from left to right. Then, for any $v \in V(EH_{s,t})$, let $h(v) = lex(v)$.

Lemma 13. $R_i^{lex} = \{1, ..., i2^{\frac{s+t}{2}}\}$ is an optimal set in $EH_{s,t}$ for $i = 1, 2, ..., 2^{\frac{s+t}{2}}$ and $1 \le s \le t$.

Proof. This proof can be obtained directly from Theorem 3.   □

Lemma 14. For $j = 1, 2, ..., 2^{\lfloor \frac{s+t+1}{2} \rfloor}$,

$$C_j^{lex} = \begin{cases} 1, & 1 \times 2^{\frac{s+t}{2}}, & 2 \times 2^{\frac{s+t}{2}}, & ...(2^{\frac{s+t}{2}}) \times 2^{\frac{s+t}{2}}, \\ 2, & 1 \times 2^{\frac{s+t}{2}} + 1, & 2 \times 2^{\frac{s+t}{2}} + 1, & ...(2^{\frac{s+t}{2}}) \times 2^{\frac{s+t}{2}} + j - 1 \end{cases}$$

is an optimal set in $EH_{s,t}$ where $1 \leq s \leq t$.

Proof. Let $f : C_j^{lex} \to L_{j \times 2^{\frac{s+t}{2}}}$ with $f(k \times 2^{\frac{s+t}{2}} + l) = l \times 2^{\frac{s+t}{2}} + k$. We use $u_1 u_2 ... u_{t+1}$ in C_j^{lex} to denote the decimal string of $l \times 2^{\frac{s+t}{2}} + k$. Since the decimal string representations of two numbers u and v differ in exactly one bit, the same holds for $f(u)$ and $f(v)$. Thus (u, v) is an edge in R_i and $(f(u), f(v))$ is an edge in L_{2^i}. Therefore, R_i is isomorphic to L_i. By Theorem 1, L_i is an optimal set of $EH_{s,t}$. $\square$

Lemma 15. For $1 \leq s \leq t$, $EH_{s,t}$ can be embedded into the ladder $L(2 \times 2^{s+t})$ with minimum wirelength.

Proof. Let $f = h$. Let $C_{i,j} = \{(\alpha_{i,j}, \alpha_{i,j+1}) | 1 \leq j \leq 2^{s+t}\}$, $0 \leq i \leq 1$. Let R be a horizontal edge cut of the ladder such that R disconnects the ladder into two components R_1 and R_2 where $V(R_1) = \{(0, 0), (0, 1), ..., (0, 2^{s+t} - 1)\}$ and $V(R_2) = \{(1, 0), (1, 1), ..., (1, 2^{s+t} - 1)\}$. Let C_i be a vertical edge cut of the ladder such that C_i disconnects the ladder into two components C_{i1} and C_{i2} where $V(C_{i1}) = \{(0, 0), (0, 1), ..., (0, 2^i - 1)\} \bigcup \{(1, 0), (1, 1), ..., (1, 2^{s+t} - 1)\}$ and $V(C_{i2}) = V(L_{2^{s+t+1}}) \backslash V(C_{i1})$. See Fig. 3. Let H_1 and H_2 denote two inverse images of R_1 and R_2, where $f^{-1}(R_1) = H_1$ and $f^{-1}(R_2) = H_2$. The edge cut R satisfies the conditions (i) and (ii) of Lemma 1. Since H_1 is 2^s copies of Q_t in $EH_{s,t}$, by Theorem 2, $|E(H_1)|$ is maximum satisfying the condition (iii) of Lemma 1. Thus by Lemma 2, $ECf(R)$ is minimum. Let H_{i1} and H_{i2} denote two inverse images of C_{i1} and C_{i2}, where $f^{-1}(C_{i1}) = H_{i1}$ and $f^{-1}(C_{i2}) = H_{i2}$. The edge cut C_i satisfies the conditions (i) and (ii) of lemma 1. Also G_i is a subgraph induced by 2^{i+1} vertices of $EH_{s,t}$. Thus $EC_f(C_i)$ is minimum for $i = 1, 2, ..., 2^{s+t} - 1$. The edge cut R_j satisfies the conditions (i) and (ii) of lemma 1. By Theorem 2, $|E(G_{i1})|$ is maximum satisfying the condition (iii) of Lemma 1. The same holds for $|E(G_{i2})|$. Thus $EC_f(C_i)$ is minimum. Hence by lemma 2, the wirelength is minimum. $\square$

Theorem 5. The minimum wirelength of embedding exchanged hypercube $EH_{s,t}$ into the ladder $L(2 \times 2^{s+t})$ satisfies:

$$WL(EH_{s,t}, L(2 \times 2^{s+t})) = 2^{s+2t-1} + 2^{2s+t-1}.$$

Proof. Let $f = h$. The vertices of $EH_{s,t}$ are mapped in the ladder $L(2 \times 2^{s+t})$. Let R be a horizontal edge cut of the ladder such that into two components R_1 and R_2 where $V(R_1) = \{0, 1, ..., 2^{s+t}\}$ and $V(R_2) = \{2^{s+t} + 1, 2^{s+t} + 2, ..., 2^{s+t+1}\}$. The sum edge congestion of each column of $L(2 \times 2^{s+t})$ is

$$EC_f(R) = \sum_{i=1}^{2^{s+t}} (S_i) = 2^{s+t}.$$

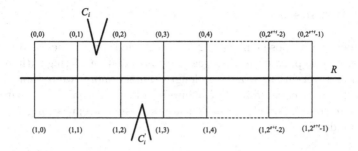

Fig. 3. Edge cuts of ladder graph.

Thus $EC_f(C_{i,j}) = EC_f(C_{i,2^{s+t+1}-j})$ for $1 \le j \le 2^{s+t}$.

For $i = 1$ and $1 \le j \le 2^{s+t}$, let $C_{i,j}$ be an edge cut of R_1 such that $C_{i,j}$ disconnects $L_{1 \times 2^{s+t}}$ into two components L_{j1} and L_{j2}. Let Q_{j1} and Q_{j2} be the inverse images of L_{j1} and L_{j2} under h, respectively. By Theorem 1, Q_{j1} is an optimal set and each $C_{i,j}$ satisfies conditions (i) and (ii) of Lemma 1. Therefore the sum congestion of Q_t is

$$\sum_{j=1}^{2^{s+t}} EC_f(C_{i,j}) = 2 \sum_{j=1}^{2^{s+t}} C_{i,j}$$
$$= 2^s(2^{2t-1} - 2^{t-1}).$$

For $i = 2$ and $1 \le k \le 2^{s+t}$, let $C'_{i,k}$ be an edge cut of R_2 such that $C_{i,k}$ disconnects $L_{1 \times 2^{s+t}}$ into two components Q_{k1} and Q_{k2}. The proof is similar to $i = 1$. Therefore, the sum congestion of Q_s is

$$\sum_{k=1}^{2^{s+t}} EC_f(C'_{i,k}) = 2 \sum_{k=1}^{2^{s+t}} C'_{i,k}$$
$$= 2^t(2^{2s-1} - 2^{s-1}).$$

Thus,

$$WL(EH_{s,t}, L(2 \times 2^{s+t})) = WL_f(EH_{s,t}, L(2 \times 2^{s+t}))$$
$$= EC_f(R) + EC_f(C_{i,j}) + EC_f(C'_{i,k})$$
$$= \sum_{i=1}^{2^{s+t}} S_i + 2 \sum_{j=1}^{2^{s+t}} S_j + 2 \sum_{k=1}^{2^{s+t}} S'_k$$
$$= 2^{s+t} + 2^s(2^{2t-1} - 2^{t-1}) + 2^t(2^{2s-1} - 2^{s-1})$$
$$= 2^{s+2t-1} + 2^{2s+t-1}.$$

$\square$

6 Conclusions

In this paper, we propose embeddings of exchanged hypercubes into rings and ladders. Firstly, we prove that $EH_{s,t}$ can be embedded into a ring with minimum wirelength and obtain the exact wirelength. Furthermore, we obtain the minimum wirelength of embedding $EH_{s,t}$ into a ladder with minimum wirelength. To the best of our knowledge, this is the first result of embedding $EH_{s,t}$ into rings and ladders.

Acknowledgment. We would like to express our sincerest appreciation to Prof. Guoliang Chen for his constructive suggestions. This work is supported by National Key R&D Program of China (2018YFB1003201), Natural Science Foundation of China under grant (No. 61572337, No. 61602333, No. 61672296 and No. 61702351), China Postdoctoral Science Foundation (No. 172985), Scientific & Technological Support Project of Jiangsu Province (No. BE2016777, No. BE2016185), Natural Science Foundation of the Jiangsu Higher Education Institutions of China (Nos. 17KJB520036), Jiangsu Planned Projects for Postdoctoral Research Funds under Grant (No. 1701172B) and Jiangsu High Technology Research Key Laboratory for Wireless Sensor Networks Foundation (No. WSNLBKF201701).

References

1. Arockiaraj, M., Abraham, J., Quadras., J.: Linear layout of locally twisted cubes. Int. J. Comput. Math. **94**(1), 56–65 (2017)
2. Bezrukov, S.L., Das, S.K., Elsasser, R.: An edge-isoperimetric problem for powers of the Petersen graph. Ann. Combinatorics **4**(2), 153–169 (2000)
3. Bezrukov, S.L., Chavez, J.D., Harper, L.H., Röttger, M., Schroeder, U.P.: Embedding of hypercubes into grids. Mortar Fire Control System, pp. 693–701 (1998)
4. Boals, A.J., Gupta, A.K., Sherwani, N.A.: Incomplete hypercubes: algorithms and embeddings. J. Supercomputing **8**(3), 263–294 (1994)
5. Chen, Y., Shen, H.: Routing and wavelength assignment for hypercube in array-based WDM optical networks. J. Parallel Distrib. Comput. **70**(1), 59–68 (2010)
6. Erbele, J., Chavez, J., Trapp, R.: The cyclic cutwidth of Q_n. Technical report, California State UniversitySan Bernardino (CSUSB) (2003)
7. Fan, J., Jia, X., Lin, X.: Complete path embeddings in crossed cubes. Inf. Sci. **176**(22), 3332–3346 (2006)
8. Fan, J., Jia, X., Lin, X.: Embedding of cycles in twisted cubes with edge-pancyclic. Algorithmica **51**(3), 264–282 (2008)
9. Wang, X., Fan, J., Jia, X.: Embedding meshes into twisted-cubes. Inf. Sci. **181**(14), 3085–3099 (2011)
10. Garey, M.R., Johnson, D.S.: Computers and intractability: a guide to the theory of NP-completeness (1979)
11. Harper, L.H.: Global Methods for Combinatorial Isoperimetric Problems. Cambridge University Press, UK (2004)
12. Han, Y., Fan, J., Zhang, S.: Embedding meshes into locally twisted cubes. Inf. Sci. **180**(19), 3794–3805 (2010)
13. Huang, K.E., Wu, J.: Area efficient layout of balanced hypercubes. Int. J. High Speed Electron. Syst. **6**(04), 631–645 (1995)

14. Hsu, L.-H., Lin, C.-K.: Graph Theory and Interconnection Networks. CRC, Boca Raton (2008)
15. Liu, Y.-L., Wu, R.-C.: Implementing exchanged hypercube communication patterns on ring-connected WDM optical networks. IEICE Trans. Inf. Syst. **100**(12), 2771–2780 (2017)
16. Loh, P.K.K., Hsu, W.-J., Pan, Y.: The exchanged hypercube. IEEE Trans. Parallel Distrib. Syst. **16**(9), 866–874 (2005)
17. Katseff, H.: Incomplete hypercubes. IEEE Trans. Comput. **37**(5), 604–608 (1988)
18. Ma, M., Liu, B.: Cycles embedding in exchanged hypercubes. Inf. Process. Lett. **110**(2), 71–76 (2009)
19. Manuel, P., Rajasingh, I., Rajan, B.: Exact wirelength of hypercubes on a grid. Discrete Appl. Math. **157**(7), 1486–1495 (2009)
20. Ma, M., Zhu, L.: The super connectivity of exchanged hypercubes. Inf. Process. Lett. **111**(8), 360–364 (2011)
21. Miller, M., Rajan, R.S., Parthiban, N.: Minimum linear arrangement of incomplete hypercubes. Comput. J. **58**(2), 331–337 (2015)
22. Nakano, K.: Linear layout of generalized hypercubes. Int. J. Found. Comput. Sci. **14**(01), 137–156 (2003)
23. Rostami, H., Habibi, J.: Minimum linear arrangement of Chord graphs. Appl. Math. Comput. **203**(1), 358–367 (2008)
24. Sýkora, O., Vrt'o, I.: On VLSI layouts of the star graph and related networks. Integr. VLSI J. **17**(1), 83–93 (1994)
25. Wan, L., Liu., Y.: On the embedding genus distribution of ladders and crosses. Appl. Math. Lett. **22**(5) 738–742 (2009)
26. Wang, D.: Hamiltonian embedding in crossed cubes with failed links. IEEE Trans. Parallel Distrib. Syst. **23**(11), 2117–2124 (2012)
27. Wang, S., Zhang, S.: Embedding hamiltonian paths in k-ary n-cubes with conditional edge faults. Theoret. Comput. Sci. **412**(46), 6570–6584 (2011)
28. Yang, Y., Li, J., Wang, S.: Embedding various cycles with prescribed paths into k-ary n-cubes. Discrete Appl. Math. **220**, 161–169 (2017)
29. Yang, X., David, J.E., Graham, M.: Maximum induced subgraph of a recursive circulant. Inf. Process. Lett. **95**(1), 293–298 (2005)
30. Yeh, C. H., Varvarigos, E. A., Parhami, B.: Multilayer VLSI layout for interconnection networks. In: Proceedings of International Conference on IEEE Parallel Processing, pp. 33–40 (2000)
31. Yu, C., Yang, X.: Routing and wavelength assignment for 3-ary n-cube in array-based optical network. Inf. Process. Lett. **112**(6), 252–256 (2012)

Rim Chain: Bridge the Provision and Demand Among the Crowd

Pengze Li[(✉)], Lei Liu, Lizhen Cui, Qingzhong Li, Yongqing Zheng,
and Guangpeng Zhou

Software College, Shandong University, Jinan, China
vonei@126.com

Abstract. Science of the Crowd is a new paradigm. The research on the relationship between provision and demand arising from the behavior of the crowd under the interconnected environment is a promising topic. This study is a pioneer work on the establishment of a new type of interconnected architecture - rim chain. The rim chain framework aims at supporting prompt matching between provision and requirements. The analytical results suggest that requirements can be fulfilled in accordance with six degrees of separation. In other word, the matching between the demands and provision takes place with six hops in the rim chain framework. Improved top-k method is employed to obtain the matching results. Last but not least, the efficiency of the method is validated.

Keywords: Crowd Science · Crowd Network · Top-k query

1 Introduction

The ant colony effect in the natural world, the formation of a group of birds flying in the sky, the business management process in economics, the coordinated operation of the industrial chain, social organizations and their collective behavior processes, national elections, and public discussion of social and public issues, are all based on the collection of many individual wisdoms, which aim to achieve better results. These can all be attributed to the Crowd Science. Crowd Science as a new paradigm focuses on the impact regarding the number of individuals involved, the way and depth of interaction between individuals. The development of network and AI technologies is a thrust of enhancing the interconnection among people, things, organizations and enterprises. Crowd Science studies the principles and bachelors of the mental projections, namely, digital-selfs of people, things, organizations and enterprises in the physical world. The digital-self reflects the behavior, consciousness and information of the real world subject. Crowd Science covers the scientific problem and universal mechanism behind the phenomena above.

In recent years, there have been many query techniques on the graph which contains data. These techniques use keyword matching or similar subgraph

© Springer Nature Switzerland AG 2018
J. Vaidya and J. Li (Eds.): ICA3PP 2018, LNCS 11335, pp. 18–31, 2018.
https://doi.org/10.1007/978-3-030-05054-2_2

matching to search for the target data in the graph. Jin et al. [6] use sub-graph matching with distributed techniques to convert graph parallelism into data parallel processing problems for efficient distributed search. Similar work could be found in Chen et al. [7]. Besides the sub-graph matching, Chen et al. use the evaluating function to sort the eligible data from the graph and return the Top-k results. Yu [8] uses an object-level database for indexing to improve the query result. However, when objects contain too many attributes, using objects may make the query semantics more complicated. Li et al. [9] study the frequent subgraph queries, which using a closed frequent subgraph based index. Chen et al. [10] conduct a keyword search on a road network with restricted scope. They take the distance in reality into consideration, rather than only consid-ering the matching of keywords. The similarity search can be used in reducing the size of the data to be matched and improves the matching efficiency [14]. Keyword matching also contains using techniques such as latent Steiner graph to return users with appropriate results, but there are still deficiencies in entity recognition and natural language processing [15].

In terms of network construction and simulation, Yang et al. [11] make up for the lack of descriptions of EATI (Entity, Action Task, Interaction) and EBI (Entity, Behavior, Interaction) concepts in the social domain, and build an Agent-based Social Network. In social networks, the information and influ-ence dissemination is an important research direction. Sun et al. [16] have con-ducted in-depth explorations on an information interference model that takes into account the interrelationships between information items in social network. The structure of social networks is constantly changing because it is derived from the real world. As sentiment dissemination is part of the influence dissem-ination, Wang et al. [17] propose an evolution model of online social network and conduct research on online information management. Crowd's behavior in social networks also has a certain degree of sociality. Li et al. [18] study on the influence of the active time heterogeneity of nodes. They use spread tree and SI model to show that polymorphism on the information dissemination. Wang et al. [19] have conducted in-depth explorations on the information coverage maximization, which aims to improve the range of information dissemination.

In order to support matching between provision and demands in the digital world, this paper proposes a new type of network structure, the rim chain, which embodies the concept of Crowd Network.

Figure 1 shows the schematic diagram of the rim chain, which only has peo-ple as the digital-self denoted by business card. In this schematic diagram, the digital-selfs are in different social circles. They can join more than one circle. The icon in the center of the social circle indicates the theme of the circle. It shows the reason why different digital-selfs are connected together.

The goal of this interconnected structure is to perform transactions match-ing based on provision-demand information. To better complete the transaction matching, the rim chain ensures transaction security and ensures that the con-tents of the interconnection structure will not be maliciously altered.

Fig. 1. The schematic diagram of the rim chain

As Crowd Science is closely related to the sociology, the rim chain also embodies theory in sociology, such as the six degrees of separation theory. The six degrees of separation shows that people in this world are interconnected. However, it does not mean that any two people can establish contact or complete a transaction. In reality, influence dissipates after three degrees (to and from friends' friends' friends) [12,13], because of the corruption of information. Therefore, in the rim chain, the six degrees of separation theory is actually combined with the three degrees of influence theory, which enables this interconnection model to better simulate the transactions matching that happens in the physical world. Moreover, this paper proposes an algorithm for the construction of the rim chain. First, it extracts data from the relational database, then puts the data into the graph database, and finally constructs rim chain. This paper also proposes a query algorithm, and uses Top-k query to find the most suitable transaction objects. The query algorithm uses the matching of provision vector and demand vector to search for the eligible data. After the completion of searching, it sorts the eligible data from the rim chain and return the Top-k results.

The paper's main contributions can be summarized as follows: (I) The establishment of a new type of interconnected architecture - rim chain. (II) The rim chain framework uses Pareto distribution to show the attenuation of information fidelity.

The reminder of this paper is organized as follows: Sect. 1 introduces the basic concept of the Crowd Science, and some researches on social network and query technology. Section 2 discusses related work in intelligence networks and Crowd Science. Section 3 discusses the algorithm of construction of the rim chain and the transactions Top-k query. Section 4 conducts the experimental evaluations for the algorithm. And finally the Sect. 5 draws conclusions of this paper's contribution.

2   Related Work

The Crowd Science is based on the System Theory, Information Theory, Cybernetics, Computer Science and Engineering, Management, Economics, Sociology, Psychology and other subjects, and becomes a new interdisciplinary direction [5]. The Crowd Science uses the Internet of things, big data, and other new technologies to access and analyze the data of public behavior with the ternary fusion system of information physical society and studies the basic principles and laws of intelligent crowds' activities in the new social model.

So far, there have been studies on intelligence networks or crowd intelligence at home and abroad, but all these studies are fragmented and incomplete. Many researchers do some jobs on Swarm AI, a relatively new Artificial Intelligence method. Swarm AI involves multiple agents operating in an environment to solve problems through cooperation [4]. It focuses on the optimization of complex problems. Compared with Swarm AI, Crowd Science focus on the country's major strategic needs and solves the basic problems of future networked, intellectually-oriented economy and society. However, both draw lessons from group insects. Crowd Intelligence [1] is the collective wisdom of a large number of autonomous individuals. In an Internet-based organizational structure, these autonomous individuals jointly complete challenging computing tasks. The research objects of Crowd Intelligence are homogenous while the research objects of Crowd Science are heterogeneous including individuals, enterprises, governments and things. Collective Intelligence [2,3] is a form of subjective mobilization, highly individual as well as ethical and cooperative under the natural environment and the scale of the research object size is limited, however Crowd Science works on large-scale elements in the online and in-depth connected public Crowd Network under the Internet and big data environment.

3   Construction and Matching of the Ring Chain Framework

3.1   Construction of the Rim Chain

In the process of the rim chain construction, the first step is to extract the content of the database. Then the digital-selfs and circles are formed based on the data from the data source which usually is the database. The data in the database also reflects the social relationship of digital-selfs. The social link between digital-selfs and circles comes from these relationships. With the link of the relationship between digital-selfs and circles built, the construction of rim chain is completed (Fig. 2).

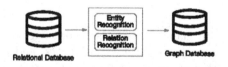

Fig. 2. Data extraction from RDB to graph database

There are four types of information that need to be reflected in the rim chain. First, identification information is used to distinguish one digital-self from the others. The second one is the provision information. It shows what services it can provide for other digital-selfs. The third one is the requirement information. When the digital-self has a demand, it will generate demand information. The last one is circle or social relationship information, it describes the digital-self's social relations. Based on the social relationship information, the rim chain will know which circle this digital-self should belong to. There usually are more than one circles that one digital-self belongs to. The database used in this paper gives the above attributes. These four kinds of information are sufficient and necessary for the construction of rim chain. Identification information is the basic information and the verification information, which ensures that the corresponding people, things, organizations and enterprises exists in real life. If a digital-self does not have provision information, it will be useless in rim chain (Fig. 3).

Moreover, it cannot complete transactions with other digital-selfs, because it does not have the ability to provide resources to other nodes. Demand information is also necessary. If digital-selfs do not have their own requirements information, they cannot obtain the required resources from the rim chain to achieve their own demands. After completing the data migration, an interconnection network structure will be established. Figure 4 shows the schematic diagram of rim chain in a hierarchical structure. This schematic diagram shows digital-self nodes and circle nodes which are in three degrees range of D_1. The blue node represents the circle node and the orange node represents the digital-self node. D_1 is in the circle C_1. In the C_1 circle, points other than D_1 are points within one degree from D_1. The distance between the digital-selfs in C_2, C_3 and D_1 is two degree, and that in C_4, C_5, and C_6 is three degree. Figure 4 shows the path that D_1 can be linked from other digital-selfs. Only the directly or indirectly interconnected digital-selfs can complete transaction in the rim chain. Figure 4 is the further explanation for the Fig. 1.

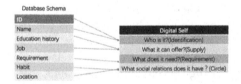

Fig. 3. The database schema and the digital self's attributes

What is more, this rim chain also uses the Knowledge Graph. The Knowledge Graph includes three main parts: entities, attributes, and relationships. In the rim chain, the concept of digital-self correspond to the entity, and all properties of digital-selfs, circles, and edges correspond to attributes in the Knowledge Graph. In graph database, digital-selfs and circles can all be represented by nodes. The relationship between them can be represented by graph edges. Both the node and the edge can contain certain attributes, thus laying the foundation for the construction of the rim chain.

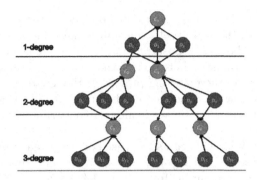

Fig. 4. The schematic diagram of the rim chain

Algorithm 1. Create the rim chain.

Input: The people, things, organizations and enterprises data in the database
Output: The rim chain.

```
 1: initialize array D[] with all digital-selfs
 2: initialize array C[] with all circle nodes
 3: for i ← 1 to digital_self_num do
 4:     for each circle node information in D[i] do
 5:         if circle node information exists in the hash map C then
 6:             create link from D[i] to the circle node
 7:         else
 8:             create new circle node c and build links to nodes in D[i]
 9:             C ← c
10:         end if
11:     end for
12: end for
```

3.2 Trasaction Matching Algorithm

In rim chain, the number of candidate digital-self will be massive. How to recommend the Top-k best matches for users in these thousands or even countless candidate matching sets is a difficult problem to solve. Moreover, when sorting the eligible digital-selfs, there is no absolute 'bad digital-self' or 'good digital-self'. The definition of good and bad depends on the needs of the requirement information.

In the rim chain, individuals, enterprises, governments and things are mapped to digital-selfs. Moreover, the digital-selfs contain information about these individuals, enterprises, governments and things. This means that the rim chain contains comprehensive information. If a person generates a demand, the rim chain will form the demand vector based on the person's information in its digital self. Then, the rim chain can complete matching without excessive demand description. For example, an undergraduate would like to find a postgraduate tutor to guide his postgraduate study. The undergraduate digital-self puts forward a demand, which is seeking for a postgraduate tutor, and then this demand will form a vector with the basic attributes of the undergraduate. This vector will be matched with the digital-selfs that might meet the requirements. In the example mentioned above, the 'postgraduate tutor' is the key requirement. The key requirement determines what kind of the sender's attributes will the rim chain investigate before the matching process. If the key requirement is a post-graduate tutor, rim chain will not match the attributes like whether the target digital-self can cook, but focus on academic-related attributes such as major and research reputation.

The target digital-self will get a score based on the given evaluation function. This score will be used in the Top-k query. A digital-self usually has more than one attributes, so an evaluation function is defined to search for a qualified digital-self. The score S can be expressed as (1):

$$S = \alpha(1 - d(n)) + (1 - \alpha)M(d_s, d_i) \tag{1}$$

The influence factor α measures the weight of demand information fidelity and similarity in the matching process. The d_s means the digital-self sender, and the d_i is the matching digital-self. The $d(n)$ is the information fidelity derived from the Pareto distribution, and the $M(d_s, d_i)$ is the matching efficiency between the sender and the matching digital-self.

According to the three degrees of influence theory, the fidelity of information gradually dissipates as it propagates, reaching a maximum of three degrees. In the model of information dissemination, the SIR model is used to describe the mechanism of information dissemination in social networks [19]. In the SIR model, nodes are divided into three categories: susceptible nodes (S), infected nodes (I), and removed nodes (R). The infected node indicates that the node has the ability to propagate information. A susceptible node indicates that the node has not received information from other nodes and can accept information, that is, it can become an infected node. The removed node indicates that the node has received the information of its neighbor node, but it does not believe the information, nor does it have the ability to transmit the information. At the beginning of the provision-demand matching, there is only one infected node in the chain network, which is the sender of the demand information. With the combination of the SIR model and the three degrees of influence theory, the propagation rules are defined as follows: (I) Within three degrees from the sender digital-self, if the susceptible node is connected to the infected node via a circle node, the susceptible node becomes an infected node, which can spread the demand information. (II) When the degree is three, although the message can be transmitted to the nodes in the fourth degree, the nodes will become the removed nodes. Moreover, the nodes will refuse to believe that the demand information and will not transmit the information further.

[21] proposed the use of the Pareto type I (2) from the Pareto distribution to indicate the attenuation function of the number of the infected nodes. With the three degrees of influence theory considered, the attenuation function of the infected user can be understood as the attenuation of information fidelity. That is, due to the attenuation of information fidelity, nodes will no longer believe

in the demand information, and will no longer spread the demand information. Equation (2) shows the Pareto type I. This paper uses $1 - d(n)$ to indicates the fidelity of the information in (1).

$$d(n) = 1 - \frac{1}{n^\beta} \tag{2}$$

In Eq. (2), n represents the degree. β represents the speed of the information fidelity decay. The greater the β is, the faster the decay is [20] mentioned that when $d(n)$ is greater than a conversion threshold $\tau = 0.5$, the node becomes a removed node. As the three degrees of influence theory limits the information to propagate at most three degrees, and when n equals 4, $d(n)$ is equal to 0.5. So the β is set to 0.5.

Each transaction matching is a bidirectional and the matching objects are provision and demand information. In the previous example, the undergraduate's provision is the undergraduate's attribute of the academic performance, and the undergraduate's demand is the postgraduate tutor's ability, such as research reputation and school level. The provision of postgraduate tutors is their ability such as their research reputation, and the demand of postgraduate tutors is the requirement for undergraduates' academic performance such as GPA. In the process of matching, both parties match each other's provision and demand, and finally get a matching efficiency.

In the matching process, there are some attributes that only has two kinds of results: satisfied or not satisfied, such as major. Sometimes these attributes contain multiple options demands. For example, the demand for major is Computer Science (CS) or Digital Media Technology (DMT), then matching target's major could be either of the demand majors. All the satisfied options are separated by slashes and saved in the digital-self's attributes, like CS/DMT. Some attributes are discrete values, which only need to reach the required lower limit. For example, if the requirement for GPA is medium, then both medium and high are satisfied. The discrete value is set according to the actual situation. In this paper, only two types of discrete values are used, one is (high, medium, low), and the other is (A, B, C, D). Function, Eq. (3), stands for the matching efficiency of demand sender and target matching digital-self. The higher the matching efficiency, the more the target digital-self can meet the demand information.

$$M(d_s, d_i) = \frac{|\boldsymbol{R}_i \cap \boldsymbol{S}_s| + |\boldsymbol{R}_s \cap \boldsymbol{S}_i|}{|\boldsymbol{R}_i| + |\boldsymbol{S}_s| + |\boldsymbol{R}_s| + |\boldsymbol{S}_i|} \tag{3}$$

The $\boldsymbol{R}$ is the demand vector. Given a key requirement r_1, according to this key requirement, the rim chain extracts the rest of the digital-self-sender's attributes. Then the rim chain puts all the attributes together with the key requirement into a demand vector $\boldsymbol{R}$, which can be denoted by $\boldsymbol{R} = \{r_1, r_2, ..., r_n\}$. And the provision vector $\boldsymbol{P}$ is denoted by $\boldsymbol{P} = \{p_1, p_2, ..., p_m\}$. The rim chain will also extract the matching digital-self's attributes that related to the key requirement. The system will evaluate each digital-self according to the evaluation function and save the digital-selfs with higher scores. The $|\boldsymbol{R} \cap \boldsymbol{S}|$ is the number of matched provision-demand attributes between the digital-self sender and the matching digital-self. The $|R_i| + |S_s| + |R_s| + |S_i|$ is the total number of the provision-demand attributes in the digital-self sender and the matching digital-self.

The circle node contains an attribute called 'digital-self type', which describes whether the digital-selfs contained in this circle are individuals, enterprises, governments or things. Circle node's attributes also include the theme of the circle. The circle nodes are regarded as important routing nodes. To speed up the matching, the algorithm II (see Appendix) takes some measures to make use of the circle node. First, according to the digital-self sender, find all the circle nodes connected with it, and (I) if the type of digital-selfs in the circles do not match the demand. For example, a demand in created to query for a teacher. If a circle only has enterprises in it, then the type of digital-selfs in the circle does not match the demand. (II) If the theme of the circle node does not match the key requirement, the demand information will not be matched with the digital-selfs which connected to this circle node. The demand information is sent directly to all remaining circle nodes via the digital-self nodes connected to them. Second, a hash map can be used to avoid duplicate visits. Finally, three degrees of influence theory limits the number of nodes that can be accessed, so that the rim chain avoids accessing too many nodes.

4   Experimental Evaluations

4.1   Analysis of the Evaluation Function

Throughout the query process, the crucial point for Top-k is the evaluation function. Our evaluation function has an influence factor α. This influence factor measures the weight of demand information fidelity and similarity in the matching process. When α is 1, the matching process ignores the relations among the elements that the digital-self corresponds to in physical world, and only considers similarity. This situation is more suitable for general search engines rather than the rim chain. The rim chain needs to reflect the digital-selfs' relationship in reality. When α is 0, the matching process ignores the similarity between the demand information and the target digital-self's attributes, and only considers the demand information fidelity. Such a system loses the basic function of matching transactions. In this paper, the α is set to 0.5, which means the demand information fidelity and the similarity are equally important.

When it comes to the demand information fidelity, the three degrees of influence theory is also involved. That is, information's influence dissipates after three degrees [12,13]. The reason for considering the three degrees of influence theory is that rim chain is not just a search engine but the mapping from the physical world to the digital world and a transaction matching platform. Its architecture comes from the social circle in real life. Therefore, it should refer to certain social science theories in order to make the transactions matching and rim chain model more accurate.

Completing the transaction requires meeting the sufficient conditions and necessary conditions for the transaction. The definitions and examples of the necessary conditions and sufficient conditions for transaction are list below:

Necessity: a condition is said to be necessary for the transaction. For it to be true that 'One undergraduate finds a satisfying postgraduate tutor', it is necessary that the postgraduate tutor can recruit at least one student.

Sufficiency: The sufficient condition for the transaction is a condition that will produce the completion of the transaction. 'One undergraduate finds a satisfying postgraduate tutor' implies that the undergraduate is able to get the Bachelor Degree. So knowing that the previous statement is true, it is sufficient to know that the undergraduate's GPA meets graduation requirements.

There are many properties in the digital-self, but not all properties are required for transaction matching. Before calculating the match efficiency with (3), the transaction-related attributes of the digital-self will be projected into the demand vector and the provision vector. The projected attributes form the sufficient conditions set and necessary conditions set for the transaction. Attributes related to the sufficient conditions exist in the demander, and the attributes related to the necessary conditions exist in those who may meet the demand. What is more, in (3), represents the satisfaction of sufficient conditions, and represents the satisfaction of the necessary conditions. The matching efficiency is actually the degree of how sufficient conditions and necessary conditions satisfy the transaction. The digital-self which can make the sufficient conditions and necessary conditions of the transaction meet will get a high score in matching efficiency. Then, the digital self with high matching efficiency and close distance from the demand sender will be selected in the Top-k result.

4.2 Result Analysis

In the experiment, rim chain's application scenario is an undergraduate looking for a postgraduate tutor. Based on the key attributes 'postgraduate tutor', the rim chain extracts some of the student's academic-related attributes. Tables 1 and 2 show the academic-related attributes of undergraduates and tutors.

Table 1. Undergraduate's academic-related attributes.

Major	Interest	GPA	School's reputation
Computer Science	Artificial Intelligence	A	High

The student's requirement vector should include positions (professor or associate professors), tutor's research fields, tutor's major, tutor's academic reputation, tutor's reputation of the tutor's university, and available postgraduate positions (more than 0). The student's provision vector should include the student's GPA, student's major, student's research interests, and so on. After the provision and demand vectors have been formed, these vectors will match the digital-selfs in the circle of topics in the rim chain. After searching on rim chain, the results of Top-3 query and Top-5 query are shown in Fig. 5 and Table 3.

Table 2. Tutor's academic-related attributes.

Attribute	Value
Computer Science	Artificial Intelligence
Available Postgraduate position	2
Major	Computer Science
Research field	Data Science
Position	Professor
Research reputation	High
School's reputation	High
GPA requirement	A
Major requirement	SE/CS

Figure 5 is the schematic diagram of a part of the rim chain. Different colors and shapes are used to represent the different types of the nodes. The triangle represents the digital-self node, and the circle represents the circle node. The triangle has two different colors. The orange triangle is the digital-self that is selected based on the Top-k algorithm, and the number on the triangle means the digital-self's rank in the Top-k result. The information on the circle indicates the degree distance from the demand sender.

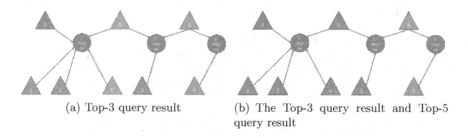

(a) Top-3 query result

(b) The Top-3 query result and Top-5 query result

Fig. 5. The Top-3 query result and Top-5 query result

Table 3 shows the score result. The Top-k rank is based on the score from (1). The rim chain calculate the score with the demand and provision vector and the degree distance between the matching node and the sender node. The score consists of two parts, the information fidelity and the matching efficiency. Moreover, the maximum of score is 1. One part is the information fidelity, which based on (2). The other part is the matching efficiency. It is based on the (3).

Figure 5 shows that after matching all the nodes within three degrees, the Top-k results are mostly distributed in the lower degree. This means that the rim chain not only takes the matching degree of the provision-demand, but also the social distance between the digital-self sender and the matching digital-self.

Table 3. Top-5 query score result.

Top-k rank	Degree	Matching efficiency	Score
1	1	1.000	1.000
2	1	0.777	0.889
3	2	1.000	0.853
4	1	0.666	0.833
5	1	0.666	0.833

The relationship between the necessary and sufficient conditions has four combinations: (I) necessary, but not sufficient (II) sufficient, but not necessary (III) both necessary and sufficient (IV) neither necessary nor sufficient. The Top-k query is to find the digital-selfs that satisfy the (III) condition above. It can be concluded that the attributes of the demand sender and the digital-selfs in Top-k result in Tables 3 and 4 satisfy most of the sufficient conditions and necessary conditions for the transaction. The Top-k result gives the most possible postgraduate tutor that can complete the transaction with the demand sender. The Top-k result proves that the higher the score is, the higher the degree how the necessary and sufficient conditions meet the transaction.

Table 4 shows the information of the Top-5 query result. From the attributes of each query result, all the digital-selfs can provide the resources that the demand sender need. What is more, the distance between the result and the demand sender is within two degrees, which ensures the information fidelity.

Table 4. Top-5 query detailed result.

Attribute	Value				
Top-k rank	1	2	3	4	5
Available Postgraduate position	2	1	3	1	2
Major	Computer Science	Software Engineering	Computer Science	Embedded System	Digital Media Technology
Research field	Artificial Intelligence	Big Data	Artificial Intelligence	Embedded System	3D Modeling
Position	Professor	Associate Professor	Professor	Associate Professor	Associate Professor
Research reputation	High	High	Medium	High	Medium
School's reputation	High	High	High	Medium	Medium
GPA requirement	A	B	B	A	B
Major requirement	CS/SE	SE	CS/SE	CS/SE	CS/SE

5   Conclusions

Matching between provision and demands plays an important role in Crowd Network. As a new type of interconnected structure, rim chain aims at providing transactions matching and mapping from physical world to the digital world. This paper has established a new type of interconnected structure namely the rim chain. The rim chain can better embody the ideas of the Crowd Science. In addition, this paper proposes the Top-k query algorithm for the best transaction target based on provision-demand information in rim chain. During the matching process, the algorithm uses the evaluation function to evaluate the target digital-selfs and return top-k results. The evaluation result shows that the satisfied digital-self can be found in lower degree, which is closer to the demand sender. For the situation that the number of digital-selfs in rim chain may be large, several methods and ideas for speeding up transaction matching have been given.

Acknowledgements. This work is partially supported by National Key R&D Program No. 2017YFB1400100.

Appendix

Algorithm 2. Find the Top-k digital-self.

Input: Query keywords, Start node, key demand
Output: The Top-k candidates digital-self
 1: initialize array digital_sel_arr[],Top-k_arr[]
 2: initialize consistent_circle_arr[], inconsistent_circle_arr[]
 3: initialize the senders provision and demand vector based on key demand
 4: **for** circle node c connected to the start node **do**
 5:     add c to the proper circle array
 6: **end for**
 7: **for** degree←1 to 3 **do**
 8:     **for** all digital-selfs node d connected to a consistent circle **do**
 9:         do the top-k query
10:         **for** circle node c connected to d **do**
11:             generates circle array for the next degree
12:         **end for**
13:     **end for**
14: **end for**

References

1. Li, W., Wu, W., Wang, H., et al.: Crowd intelligence in AI 2.0 era. Front. Inf. Technol. Electron. Eng. **18**(1), 15–43 (2017)
2. Pierre, L.: Collective Intelligence: Mankind's Emerging World in Cyberspace. Perseus Books, Cambrigde (1997)
3. Lévy, P.: Collective Intelligence. Plenum/Harper Collins, New York (1997)

4. Kutsenok, A., Swarm, A.I.: A solution to soccer. Master's thesis, Department of Computer Science, Rose-Hulman Institute of Technology, Terre Haute, IN (2004)
5. Chai, Y., Miao, C., Sun, B., et al.: Crowd science and engineering: concept and research framework. Int. J. Crowd Sci. **1**(1), 2–8 (2017)
6. Jiahui, J., Khemmarat, S., Gao, L., et al.: A distributed approach for top-k star queries on massive information networks. In: IEEE International Conference on Parallel and Distributed Systems, Southeast Univ., Nanjing, China, pp. 9–16 (2014)
7. Chen, S., Wang, J.: Keyword distributed search with ontology subgraph over RDF data. J. Fuzhou Univ. (Nat. Sci. Ed.) **45**(06), 822–828+845 (2017)
8. Yu, S.: Research on object-level keyword search algorithm over graph database. Chap. 3, Ph.D. thesis, Department of Computer Science, Dalian Maritime University (2013)
9. Li, X., et al.: A novel graph containment query algorithm on graph databases. J. Digit. Inf. Manag. **7**(3), 143–151 (2009)
10. Chen, Z., Li, S., Liu, W.: Range-constrained Top-k keyword query on road networks. J. Chin. Comput. Syst. **38**(12), 2707–2713 (2017)
11. Yang, Z., Si, Y., Li, Z., et al.: ARE: new conceptual model for social crowd behavior modeling. J. Syst. Simul. **24**(02), 435–440 (2012)
12. Morgan, T.J., et al.: Experimental evidence for the co-evolution of hominin toolmaking teaching and language. Nat. Commun. **6**, 6029–6029 (2015)
13. Nicholas, A., James, H.: Connected: The Surprising Power of Our Social Networks and How They Shape Our Lives. Simon & Schuster Audio, Abridged (2009)
14. Meng, J., Chen, L., Ma, W., et al.: Research and application on similarity search algorithm in graph database. Appl. Res. Comput. **27**(05), 1813–1815+1819 (2010)
15. Zhang, Z., Xia, D., Xie, X., et al.: A keyword search method for graphs by considering content and structure. J. Comput. Aided Des. Comput. Graph. **27**(11), 2211–222 (2015)
16. Sun, L., Liu, Y., Bartolacci, M.R., et al.: A multi information dissemination model considering the interference of derivative information. Phys. Stat. Mech. Appl. **451**, 541–548 (2016)
17. Liang, Z., Xu, B., Jia, Y., et al.: Online link strength trend model based on content and topology. In: 2011 International Symposium on Image and Data Fusion (ISIDF), pp. 1–5. IEEE (2011)
18. Li, X., Liu, Y., Jing, K., et al.: The influence of the timeheterogeneity of nodes on the information dissemination. Syst. Sci. Math. Sci. **36**(10), 1630–1642 (2016)
19. Wang, Z., Chen, E., Liu, Q., et al.: Maximizing the coverage of information propagation in social networks. In: International Conference on Artificial Intelligence, pp. 2104–2110. AAAI Press (2015)
20. Fang, J., Li, Y.: Advances in unified hybrid theoretical model of network science. Adv. Mech. **06**, 663–678 (2008)
21. Huang, H., Jaing, A., Hu, M.: Analysis of information diffusion model on social network. Appl. Res. Comput. **33**(09), 2738–2742 (2016)

Optimal Schedule of Mobile Edge Computing Under Imperfect CSI

Libo Jiao[1], Hao Yin[1(✉)], Yongqiang Lyu[1], Haojun Huang[2], Jiaqing Dong[1], and Dongchao Guo[1]

[1] Tsinghua University, Beijing 100084, China
{jlb15,djq13}@mails.tsinghua.edu.cn,
{h-yin,luyq,dongchaoguo}@tsinghua.edu.cn
[2] China University of Geosciences, Wuhan 430072, China
hhj0704@hotmail.com

Abstract. Mobile edge computing (MEC), as a prospective computing paradigm, can augment the computation capabilities of mobile devices through offloading the complex computational tasks from simple devices to MEC-enabled base station (BS) covering them. However, how to achieve optimal schedule remains a problem due to various practical challenges including imperfect estimation of channel state information (CSI), stochastic tasks arrivals and time-varying channel situation. By using Lyapunov optimization theory and Lagrange dual decomposition technique, we propose an optimal dynamic offloading and resource scheduling (oDors) approach to maximize a system utility balancing throughput and fairness under imperfect estimation of CSI. We derive the analytical bounds for the time-averaged data queues length and system throughput achieved by the proposed approach which depends on the channel estimation error. We show that without prior knowledge of tasks arrivals and wireless channels, oDors achieves a system capacity which can arbitrarily approach the optimal system throughput. Simulation results confirm the theoretical analysis on the performance of oDors.

Keywords: Mobile edge computing · Imperfect CSI
Channel estimation · Stochastic optimization

1 Introduction

Mobile edge computing (MEC), as a new computing paradigm, can enhance the limited capacities of individual devices by offloading and processing tasks of wireless terminal at the edge of wireless network. Due to the short distance between the MEC server and wireless terminals, MEC paradigm promises dramatic reduction in latency and mobile energy consumption [1]. The promised gains of MEC will motivate the development of future Internet of Things (IoT) and 5G networks. Orthogonal frequency division multiplexing access (OFDMA), as the main communication technique for WiMAX and 3GPP standards, is

© Springer Nature Switzerland AG 2018
J. Vaidya and J. Li (Eds.): ICA3PP 2018, LNCS 11335, pp. 32–45, 2018.
https://doi.org/10.1007/978-3-030-05054-2_3

widely adopted for providing high degree of flexibility and predominant performance over other wireless air interface technologies.

To maximize long-term system throughput, the problem of dynamic offloading and resource allocation has been discussed in [2–4]. However, all these studies made an impractical assumption that the perfect channel state information (CSI) can be achieved. Moreover, stochastic tasks arrivals which infect the network stability also pose a serious challenge for MEC system designing. Thus, a critical problem to be solved is how to make offloading decisions, optimize network resource allocation for maximizing system throughput while guaranteeing queue stability under the imperfect estimation of CSI.

Optimal dynamic offloading and resource schedules problem under the imperfect CSI for OFDMA systems has attracted much attention. In [5], the optimal power allocation and subchannel assignment algorithm was provided under the diverse quality-of-service (QoS) requirements. The authors in [6] optimized a system utility by optimizing the assignments of subcarriers, rate, and power. A joint optimization algorithm, including chunk assignment, transmission link selection and power allocation, was proposed for minimizing the total energy consumption in [7]. However, the works [5–7] do not consider the tasks arrivals characteristics and the queue stability constraint.

In this paper, we focus on providing the optimal dynamic offloading and resource schedule of MEC system under imperfect CSI. The main contributions of this work are summarized below.

- We employ a stochastic optimization model to maximize a system utility under the constraints of energy consumption and network stability.
- By using Lyapunov optimization theory and Lagrangian dual decomposition technique, we propose an optimal dynamic offloading and resource scheduling (oDors) approach to maximize a system utility under imperfect CSI without prior knowledge of the tasks arrivals and time-varying channel situation.
- We derive analytical performance bounds for time-average data queues length and system throughput achieved by the proposed oDors approach. Furthermore, we conduct extensive simulations to verify the theoretical analysis on the performance of oDors.

The rest of this paper is organized as follows. In Sect. 2, we present the system model and provide the stochastic optimization formulation in Sect. 3. We develop oDors approach in detail and give its performance analysis in Sect. 4. We conduct simulation to verify the theoretical analysis on the performance of oDors in Sect. 5. Finally, we conclude our paper in Sect. 6.

2 System Model

The OFDMA-based MEC system consists of a base station (BS), U devices and an MEC server deployed at BS waiting for processing the tasks offloaded from mobile devices [8].

2.1 Traffic Model and Admission Control

The MEC system operates in a slotted structure, $t \in \{0, 1, 2, ...\}$. At each time slot t, there is a busty data newly-generated by each mobile device. Let $A_u(t)$ denote the number of arrived data for device u at time slot t. A data buffer is maintained at each device to temporally store the generated data. Assume that the data generated by each mobile device follow some independent and identically distributed (i.i.d.) random process and there exists some constant upper bound A_{max} on device data arrival such that $A_u(t) < A_{max}$ for all time slots. In order to deal with heavy-load mobile traffic, we introduce the admission control (AC) operation to adjust the admission rate that the amount of data arrive to the data queue for each device [9]. Let $d_u(t)$ denote the admission rate of data queue for device u at time slot t. Then, we have the following constraint on the AC decision

$$d_u(t) \leq A_u(t) \leq A_{max} \tag{1}$$

Evidently, the amount of data admitted by a device cannot beyond the amount of generated data at each time slot.

2.2 Resource Allocation and Communication Model

The uplink schedule (e.g., power allocation and subchannel assignment) of each device takes place under the coordination of BS. Specifically, BS observes the queue state information (QSI) of each mobile device at the beginning of each time slot t.

Power Consumption Constraint: Let $p_u(t)$ denote the transmit power allocated to device u at time slot t. And we have total transmit power constraints as follows

$$\sum_{u=1}^{U} p_u(t) \leq P_{max} \tag{2}$$

Constant Subchannel Assignment: We assume that MEC system adopts constant subchannel assignment policy. Specifically, each mobile device occupies one subchannel to offload computation tasks at each time slot.

CSI Estimation: To improve the estimation accuracy, we use the minimum-mean squared-error (MMSE) estimator as the channel estimation method [10]. Let $H_u(t)$ denote the CSI of device u on its allocated subchannel at time slot t, which cannot be exactly estimated due to the existence of estimation error in practical wireless network. Thus, we use $\hat{H}_u(t)$ and $\tilde{H}_u(t)$ to denote the estimation and estimation error of $H_u(t)$, respectively. The relationship among them is given by $H_u(t) = \hat{H}_u(t) + \tilde{H}_u(t)$, where $\hat{H}_u(t)$ and $\tilde{H}_u(t)$ follow the uncorrelated Gaussian distribution with zeros means and variances $\hat{\sigma}^2 = \frac{\gamma_{tu}}{1+\gamma_{tu}}$ and $\tilde{\sigma}^2 = \frac{1}{1+\gamma_{tu}}$, respectively, where γ_{tu} represents the signal to noise ratio of pilot transmission [11]. Similarly to [10,12], the uplink capacity of device u at time slot t can be given as follows

$$R_u(t) = B_0 \log_2 \left(1 + \frac{\gamma_u(t)|\hat{H}_u(t)|^2}{\gamma_u(t)\tilde{\sigma}^2 + 1} \right) \tag{3}$$

where B_0 is the bandwidth of a subchannel, and $\gamma_u(t) = \frac{p_u(t)}{N_0}$. We assume that $R_u(t)$ is upper bounded by some constant $R_{\max}$ for all time slot t such that $R_u(t) \leq R_{\max}$.

2.3 Queueing Model and System Dynamics

Let $Q_u(t)$ denote the data backlog of the queue at device u at time slot t. Given the resource allocation (RA) and AC decision, it is updated along the time, as given by

$$Q_u(t+1) = [Q_u(t) - R_u(t)]^+ + d_u(t) \tag{4}$$

Once receiving the task from device u at time slot t, i.e., $d_u(t)$, the MEC server process the task with $f_u(t) = \xi_u d_u(t)$ CPU cycles or put the task into the data queue for later processing, where ξ_u is the number of CPU cycles required per task bit of device u for the task, and $[x]^+ = \max(x, 0)$.

Let $C(t)$ denote the required CPU cycles to process the task queued at the MEC server. $C(t)$ can be updated by

$$C(t+1) = [C(t) - F(t)]^+ + \sum_{u=1}^{U} f_u(t) \tag{5}$$

where $F(t)$ denotes the total available CPU cycles at time slot t. It is the fact that $F(t)$ is stochastic in the presence of other concurrent services [2]. Assume that there exists some constant upper bound $F_{\max}$ on MEC processing capacity such that $F(t) < F_{\max}$ for all time slots. $\sum_{u=1}^{U} f_u(t)$ denotes the total CPU cycles required for newly offloaded tasks at time slot t.

3 Problem Formulation

The objective of this paper is to maximize the capacity of MEC system while satisfying network stability constraint. Considering increasing feature of Logarithmic function, we define the system utility as follows

$$\psi(\overline{d}) = \sum_{u=1}^{U} \log\left(1 + \overline{d_u}\right) \tag{6}$$

where $\overline{d_u} = \lim_{T \to \infty} \frac{1}{T} \sum_{t=0}^{T} \mathbb{E}\left[d_u(t)\right]$ defines the time-average admission data of device u, and $\overline{d} = \{\overline{d_1}, \overline{d_2}, ..., \overline{d_U}\}$ collects the time-average total of admitted data of all mobile devices.

The problem **P1** can be formulated by maximizing the admission data of all devices as

$$\textbf{P1: } \max_{\textbf{D},\textbf{P}} \; \psi(\overline{d})$$

$$\text{s.t. C1: } 0 \le d_u(t) \le A_u(t), \forall u, t$$

$$\text{C2: } \sum_{u=1}^{U} p_u(t) \le P_{\max}, \forall t$$

$$\text{C3: } p_u(t) > 0, \forall u, t$$

$$\text{C4: } \overline{Q_u}, \overline{C} < \infty, \; \forall u \tag{7}$$

where $\textbf{D}(t) = \{d_u(t)\}$ and $\textbf{P}(t) = \{p_u(t)\}$ are data admission decision, transmit power decision at time slot t, respectively. C1 is the AC constraint to guarantee the amount of admission data at each time slot is smaller than the amount of arrived data. C2 is the instantaneous total transmit power constraint for all mobile devices. C3 is a non-negative power allocation constraint. C4 is the network stability constraint.

According to the prior work [2], **P1** can be equivalently reformulated as

$$\textbf{P2: } \max_{\textbf{D},\textbf{P},\boldsymbol{\delta}} \; \overline{\psi(\boldsymbol{\delta})}$$

$$\text{s.t. C1-C4 and C5: } \overline{\delta_u} \le \overline{d_u}$$

$$\text{C6: } 0 \le \delta_u(t) \le A_{\max}, \; \forall u, t \tag{8}$$

where $\boldsymbol{\delta}(t) = \{\delta_u(t)\}$ is the defined auxiliary variables.

4 Online Algorithm

In this section, we shall develop the oDors algorithm in detail. We notice that the constraint C5 of **P2** is a long-term average limitation on auxiliary variables. To model the average auxiliary variables constraint, we adopt virtual queue technique to reformulate C5 [13]. The virtual queue $X_u(t)$ evolves as follows

$$X_u(t+1) = [X_u(t) - d_u(t)]^+ + \delta_u(t) \tag{9}$$

According to mean stable theory [13], $X_u(t)$ is stable if and only if C5 is satisfied. Thus, C5 is replaced with the stability of $X_u(t)$, and the transformed problem **P3** is formulated as follows

$$\textbf{P3: } \max_{\textbf{D},\textbf{P},\boldsymbol{\delta}} \; \overline{\psi(\boldsymbol{\delta})}$$

$$\text{s.t. C1-C4, C6 and C7: } \overline{X_u} < \infty, \; \forall u \tag{10}$$

4.1 Lyapunov Optimization Theory

A perturbed Lyapunov function of **P3** can be defined as

$$L(\textbf{G}(t)) = \frac{1}{2}\left\{ C(t)^2 + \sum_{u=1}^{U} \left[Q_u(t)^2 + X_u(t)^2 \right] \right\} \tag{11}$$

where $\mathbf{G}(t) = [\mathbf{Q}(t), \mathbf{C}(t), \mathbf{X}(t)]$ denotes the concatenated queue backlog of the network system.

Without loss of generality, all queues are assumed to be empty when $t = 0$, such that $L(\mathbf{G}(0)) = 0$. The one-slot conditional Lyapunov drift $\Delta(\mathbf{G}(t))$ is defined as follows

$$\Delta(\mathbf{G}(t)) = \mathbb{E}\left\{L(\mathbf{G}(t+1)) - L(\mathbf{G}(t)) \,|\mathbf{G}(t)\right\} \tag{12}$$

Subtracting from (12) the conditional expectation of $\sum_{u=1}^{U} \log(1+\delta_u(t))$, we obtain the following drift-minus-reward term

$$\Delta(t) = \Delta(\mathbf{G}(t)) - V\mathbb{E}\left\{\sum_{u=1}^{U} \log(1 + \delta_u(t)) \,|\mathbf{G}(t)\right\} \tag{13}$$

where V is tunable parameter which controls the tradeoff between the drift $\Delta(\mathbf{G}(t))$ and the reward $\sum_{u=1}^{U} \log(1 + \delta_u(t))$. Based on Lyapunov theory [13], the dynamic offloading and resource scheduling decisions should be chosen to minimize an upper bound of (13) at each time slot t.

Theorem 1. *For any queue backlogs and actions, $\Delta(t)$ is upper bounded by*

$$\Delta(t) \leq B - V\mathbb{E}\left\{\sum_{u=1}^{U} log(1 + \delta_u(t)) \,|\mathbf{G}(t)\right\}$$

$$+ C(t)\mathbb{E}\left\{\sum_{u=1}^{U} f_u(t) - F(t) \,|\mathbf{G}(t)\right\}$$

$$+ \sum_{u=1}^{U} Q_u(t)\mathbb{E}\left\{d_u(t) - R_u(t) \,|\mathbf{G}(t)\right\}$$

$$+ \sum_{u=1}^{U} X_u(t)\mathbb{E}\left\{\delta_u(t) - d_u(t) \,|\mathbf{G}(t)\right\} \tag{14}$$

where B is a positive constant, which satisfies the following constraint

$$B = \frac{1}{2}\sum_{u=1}^{U}\left\{R_{max}{}^2 + 3A_{max}^2\right\} + \frac{1}{2}\left\{\sum_{u=1}^{U}(\xi_u A_{max})^2 + F_{max}^2\right\} \tag{15}$$

Proof. Lemma 1: For any non-negative real number x, y and z, there holds $[max(x - y, 0) + z]^2 \leq x^2 + y^2 + z^2 + 2x(z - y)$.

Squaring both side of (4) and applying *Lemma 1*, we obtain

$$Q_u(t+1)^2 - Q_u(t)^2 \leq R_u(t)^2 + d_u(t)^2 + 2Q_u(t)(d_u(t) - R_u(t)) \tag{16}$$

Summing over all queue backlog of all mobile devices at both sides of (16) and rearranging terms yield

$$\sum_{u=1}^{U}\frac{Q_u(t+1)^2 - Q_u(t)^2}{2} \leq \sum_{u=1}^{U}\frac{R_u(t)^2 + d_u(t)^2}{2} + \sum_{u=1}^{U} Q_u(t)(d_u(t) - R_u(t)) \tag{17}$$

Similarly, we obtain

$$\frac{C(t+1)^2 - C(t)^2}{2} \leq \frac{F(t)^2 + \left(\sum_{u=1}^{U} f_u(t)^2\right)}{2} + C(t)\left(\sum_{u=1}^{U} f_u(t) - F(t)\right) \quad (18)$$

$$\sum_{u=1}^{U} \frac{X_u(t+1)^2 - X_u(t)^2}{2} \leq \sum_{u=1}^{U} \frac{d_u(t)^2 + \delta_u(t)^2}{2} + \sum_{u=1}^{U} X_u(t)(\delta_u(t) - d_u(t)) \quad (19)$$

Combining (17), (18) and (19) and exploiting (11), we obtain

$$L(\mathbf{G}(t+1)) - L(\mathbf{G}(t)) \leq \sum_{u=1}^{U} \frac{R_u(t)^2 + d_u(t)^2}{2} + \frac{F(t)^2 + \left(\sum_{u=1}^{U} f_u(t)^2\right)}{2}$$

$$+ \sum_{u=1}^{U} \frac{d_u(t)^2 + \delta_u(t)^2}{2} + C(t)\left(\sum_{u=1}^{U} f_u(t) - F(t)\right)$$

$$+ \sum_{u=1}^{U} Q_u(t)(d_u(t) - R_u(t)) + \sum_{u=1}^{U} X_u(t)(\delta_u(t) - d_u(t))$$

$$(20)$$

By subtracting the term $V\mathbb{E}\left\{\sum_{u=1}^{U} \log(1 + \delta_u(t)) \,|\mathbf{G}(t)\right\}$ to the both sides of (20), we can prove (14).

According to *Theorem* 1, we have transformed the problem **P3** into minimizing the right-hand side (RHS) of (14) at each time slot. Thus, the original stochastic optimization problem **P1** has been transformed into a series of successive instantaneous static optimization problems. In the next subsection, we introduce the oDors algorithm to solve the optimization problems.

Algorithm 1. Optimal **D**ynamic **O**ffloading and **R**esource **S**cheduling (oDors)

INPUT: U, T, $A_u(t)$, V
OUTPUT: $\delta^*(t)$, $\mathbf{D}^*(t)$ and $\mathbf{P}^*(t)$
 1: **Initialization:** $t \leftarrow 0$, $\mathbf{Q}(0) \leftarrow 0$, $\mathbf{X}(0) \leftarrow 0$, $\mathbf{C} \leftarrow 0$
 2: **while** $t < T$ **do**
 3:    Compute $\delta(t)$, $\mathbf{D}(t)$ and $\mathbf{P}(t)$ according to Eqs. (22), (24) and (33).
 4:    Update queues $\mathbf{Q}(t)$, $\mathbf{C}$ and $\mathbf{X}(t)$ according to Eqs. (4), (5) and (9).
 5:    $t \leftarrow t + 1$
 6: **end while**
 7: **return** $\delta^*(t)$, $\mathbf{D}^*(t)$ and $\mathbf{P}^*(t)$

4.2   Algorithm Structure Design and Performance Analysis

The detail of oDors is given in Algorithm 1 which performs the following control operations at each time slot: (1) RA and AC decision in each mobile device; (2) Queues updating for $\mathbf{Q}$, $\mathbf{C}$ and $\mathbf{X}$.

Optimal Auxiliary Parameter. Observe that the second and fifth terms on the RHS of (14) involves the computation offloading decision $\delta_u(t)$. After rearranging them, we can decompose the minimization of this term into U subproblems as follows

$$\min_{\delta_u(t)} X_u(t)\delta_u(t) - V\log\left(1 + \delta_u(t)\right)$$

$$\text{s.t. } \delta_u(t) \leq A_{\max}, \ \forall u, t \tag{21}$$

Taking the first order derivative with respect to δ_u, and then making the first order derivative be zero, it easily follows that

$$\delta_u(t) = \begin{cases} 0, & \text{if } V\log_2 e \leq X_u(t) \\ \min\left\{\frac{V\log_2 e}{X_u(t)}, A_{\max}\right\}, & \text{otherwise.} \end{cases} \tag{22}$$

Optimal Uplink Admission Control. The forth and fifth terms on the RHS of (14) involve the data admission control $d_u(t)$. After rearranging them, we can decompose the minimization of this term into U subproblems as

$$\min_{d_u(t)} \left[Q_u(t) - X_u(t)\right] d_u(t)$$

$$\text{s.t. } d_u(t) \leq A_u(t), \ \forall u, t \tag{23}$$

The corresponding solution to (23) is

$$d_u(t) = \begin{cases} 0, & \text{if } Q_u(t) \geq X_u(t) \\ A_u(t), & \text{otherwise.} \end{cases} \tag{24}$$

Optimal Dynamic Offloading Schedule. Observe that the fourth term on the RHS of (14) involves the offloading decisions including the transmit power allocation decisions $p_u(t)$. We reformulate the fourth term as follows

$$\max \sum_{u=1}^{U} Q_u(t)R_u(t)$$

$$\text{s.t. C1, C2, and C3} \tag{25}$$

We can verify that the function $Q_u(t)R_u(t)$ is concave, since it is the perspective function of $Q_u(t)\log_2\left(1 + \frac{\gamma_u(t)|\hat{H}_u(t)|^2}{\gamma_u(t)\hat{\sigma}^2 + 1}\right)$. According to the composition rule that preserves concavity [14], the objective function (25) is jointly concave with respect to $p_u(t)$. Considering all constraints are linear, (25) is a convex optimization problem, and can be well solved by the Lagrange dual decomposition method.

The Lagrange function for Eq. (25) is given as

$$L\left(\{p_u(t)\}, \mu\right) = \sum_{u=1}^{U} Q_u(t)R_u(t) - \mu\left(\sum_{u=1}^{U} p_u(t) - P_{\max}\right) \tag{26}$$

where μ is the Lagrange multiplier for constraint C2. Then, the Lagrange dual function can be formulated as

$$g(\mu) = \max_{\{p_u(t)\}} L\left(\{p_u(t)\}, \mu\right) \tag{27}$$

and the dual problem is written as

$$\min_{\mu \geq 0} g(\mu) \tag{28}$$

The Lagrange dual function in (27) can be decomposed into a master problem together with U subproblems. Then, the Lagrange function is written as

$$L\left(\{p_u(t)\}, \mu\right) = \sum_{u=1}^{U} L_u\left(p_u(t), \mu\right) + \mu P_{\max} \tag{29}$$

where

$$L_u\left(p_u(t), \mu\right) = Q_u(t) B_0 \log_2 \left(1 + \frac{\gamma_u(t)|\hat{H}_u(t)|^2}{\gamma_u(t)\tilde{\sigma}^2 + 1}\right) - \mu p_u(t) \tag{30}$$

Taking the partial derivative of $L_u(t)$ with respect to $p_u(t)$ yields

$$\frac{\partial L_u(t)}{\partial p_u(t)} = \frac{Q_u(t) B_0 N_0 |\hat{H}_u(t)|^2}{\left\{\left(\tilde{\sigma}^2 + |\hat{H}_u(t)|^2\right) p_u(t) + N_0\right\}\left(\tilde{\sigma}^2 p_u(t) + N_0\right) \ln 2} - \mu \tag{31}$$

According to the Karush-Kuhn-Tucker conditions [14], the optimal power allocation, which denoted by $p_u^*(t)$, must satisfy the following constraints

$$\begin{cases} \dfrac{\partial L_u(t)}{\partial p_u(t)} = 0 \\ p_u(t) \geq 0 \end{cases} \tag{32}$$

Then, by applying (32), $p_u^*(t)$ is formulated as follows

$$p_u^*(t) = \begin{cases} \dfrac{Q_u(t) B_0}{\mu \ln 2} - \dfrac{N_0}{|\hat{H}_u(t)|^2}, & \tilde{\sigma}^2 = 0 \\ \dfrac{N_0\left(2\tilde{\sigma}^2 + |\hat{H}_u(t)|^2\right)}{2\tilde{\sigma}^2\left(\tilde{\sigma}^2 + |\hat{H}_u(t)|^2\right)}\left(\sqrt{1 - \dfrac{4F\tilde{\sigma}^2\left(\tilde{\sigma}^2 + |\hat{H}_u(t)|^2\right)}{\left(2\tilde{\sigma}^2 N_0 + |\hat{H}_u(t)|^2 N_0\right)^2}} - 1\right), & \text{otherwise.} \end{cases} \tag{33}$$

where $F = N_0^2 - \frac{B_0 N_0 Q_u(t)|\hat{H}_u(t)|^2}{\mu \ln 2}$.

As to the Lagarange multiplier μ, we employ the subgradient method to update it as follows

$$\mu^{i+1} = \left[\mu^i - \theta^i \left(P_{\max} - \sum_{u=1}^{U} p_u^*(t)\right)\right]^+, \forall n, t \tag{34}$$

where i is the iteration index, and θ is the step size. $I_{\max}$ and ε is the maximum number of iterations and convergence factor, respectively. When the subgradient method satisfies the convergence condition, that is $|\mu^{k+1} - \mu^k| < \epsilon$ or $i > I_{\max}$, the process of dynamic offloading and resource allocation is finished.

Algorithm 2. Optimal Power Allocation Algorithm (OPAA)

INPUT: ε, θ, $I_{\max}$
OUTPUT: Optimal power allocation $\mathbf{P}^*(t)$
1: **Initialization:** $i \leftarrow 1$ and μ^i
2: **while** $i < I_{\max}$ or $|\mu^{i+1} - \mu^i| < \epsilon$ **do**
3:    **for** $u = 1$ to U **do**
4:       Compute $p_u^*(t)$ according to (33).
5:       Update μ with step size θ according to (34).
6:    **end for**
7:    $i \leftarrow i + 1$
8: **end while**
9: **return** $\mathbf{P}^*(t)$

4.3   Algorithm Performance Analysis

Now we give the performance of the proposed oDors algorithm in the following theorem.

Theorem 2. *If λ is strictly interior to the network capacity Λ, the proposed oDors has the following properties for any control parameter $V \geq 0$:*

(a) All queues $\mathbf{Q} = (Q_u(t))$, $\mathbf{C}$ and $\mathbf{X} = (X_u(t))$ are mean rate stable.
(b) The time-average system utility satisfies

$$\lim_{T \to \infty} \frac{1}{T} \sum_{t=0}^{T-1} \mathbb{E}\left\{\psi(\delta(t))\right\} \geq \psi^{opt} - \frac{B}{V} \tag{35}$$

(c) The time-average queue length is upper bounded by

$$\overline{Q} = \lim_{T \to \infty} \frac{1}{T} \sum_{t=0}^{T-1} \sum_{u=1}^{U} Q_u(t) \leq \frac{B + V\psi^{opt}}{\vartheta} \tag{35}$$

Here, ϑ is a small positive constant which satisfies $\lambda + \vartheta \in \Lambda$.

Proof. The proof of *Theorem* 2 is similar to [2] thus we omit here for space-saving.

5   Simulation Results

In this section, the simulation results are provided to verify our theoretical analysis achieved by oDors algorithm. The bandwidth $B_0 = 10$ MHz, $U = 20$, $P_{\max} = (1.8 \times U)W$. The coverage radius of BS is 100m. The computational resource $F(t) \sim U[0, 5]$ GHz, where $U[a, b]$ means a random uniform distribution within $[a, b]$. The mobile traffic generated by mobile devices following the Poisson progress within the time-average traffic arrival rate λ. The simulation is carried out for $T = 4000$ consecutive time slots.

First, we demonstrate the queue stability in Fig. 1 with $V = 100$. Because all devices' data queues Q, required CPU cycles queues C and virtual queues X have similar trends, we take mobile device $u = 1$ with arrived application traffic rate $\lambda = 2$ Mb/slot as an example. We observe that all the queues are strictly bounded, which verifies the *Theorem* 2(a). It also shows the proposed oDors is effective for maximizing the system throughput while satisfying long-term auxiliary variables constraints.

Figure 2 plots the system throughput of the proposed oDors by varying the control parameter V. We observe that the system throughput increases rapidly with V when $V \leq 10$, and then slow down increasing and start to stabilize when $V \geq 30$, which verifies *Theorem* 2(b). Furthermore, with an increasing $\tilde{\sigma}^2$, the system throughput decreases. This is mainly because that the transmission rate $R(t)$ is a decreasing function of the estimation error variance $\tilde{\sigma}^2$. Therefore, a large $\tilde{\sigma}^2$ results in a small $R(t)$, and then reduces system throughput.

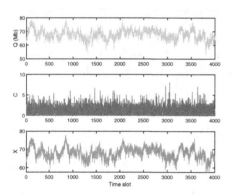

Fig. 1. Queue stability

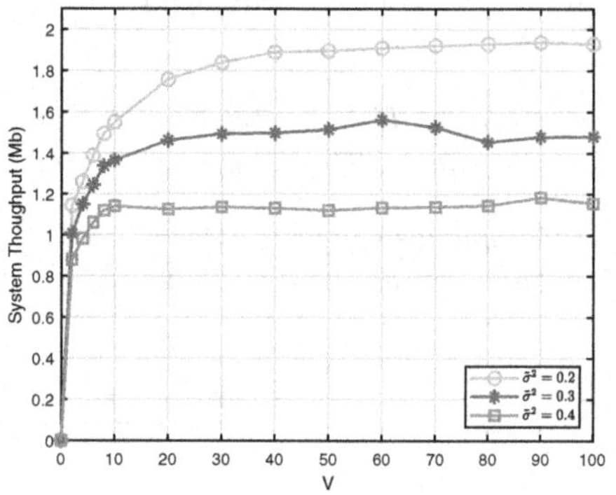

Fig. 2. System throughput versus the value of V

Figure 3 demonstrates the average queue backlog length with the varied control parameter V. It is clear to see that the average backlog continue increasing almost linearly to the V, which is verified by *Theorem* 2(c). Moreover, with an increasing $\tilde{\sigma}^2$, the average queue backlog length increases. This is because a large $\tilde{\sigma}^2$ results in a small traffic transmit rate, and then data queue length increases at each device. Considering both Figs. 2 and 3, we observe that this can be quantitatively depicted by $[O(1/V), O(V)]$, and is a system throughput and average queue length tradeoff. The longer queue length becomes, the more time it takes to transmit the task. So this relationship can be called system throughput and fairness tradeoff.

Figure 4 displays the system throughput as the traffic arrival rate increases. It can be seen that system throughput increases when traffic arrival rate λ from 1 Mb/slot to 3 Mb/slot. However, when λ continues increasing, the system throughput almost keep stable. This is mainly because a large traffic arrival

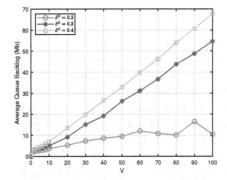

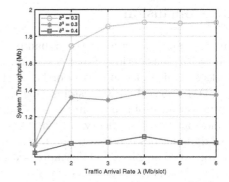

Fig. 3. Average queue backlog versus the value of V

Fig. 4. System throughput versus the value of λ

rate will consume more transmit energy to keep queue stable. Unfortunately, **P1** has the instantaneous total transmit power constraint C2, thus system throughput can not always keep increasing when the total transmit power of all mobile devices reaches maximum.

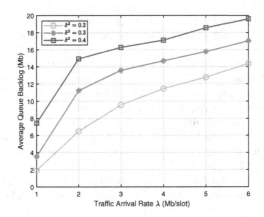

Fig. 5. Average queue length versus the value of λ

Figure 5 shows the average data queue length with different traffic arrival rate λ. We show in this figure that the average data backlog length of the proposed method increases with the growth of traffic arrival rate. The main reason is same with Fig. 4 that the system can not transmit enough traffic with constrained mobile power consumption as traffic arrival rate increases.

6   Conclusion

In this paper, we studied the dynamic offloading and resource allocation problem with considering imperfect channel state information (CSI), stochastic tasks arrivals in the uplink of orthogonal frequency division multiplexing access (OFDMA)-based MEC systems. The problem was formulated as a stochastic optimization problem aiming at maximizing a system utility. By adopting Lyapunov optimization theory and Lagrange dual decomposition technique, an optimal dynamic offloading and resource scheduling (oDors) algorithm was proposed to solve the problem. Furthermore, we gave the performance analysis of oDors and we conduct simulations to verify the theoretical analysis on the performance of oDors.

Acknowledgment. This work is supported in part by the National Key Research and Development Program under Grant no. 2016YFB1000102, in part by the National Natural Science Foundation of China under Grant no. 61672318, 61631013, 31501081, and in part by the projects of Tsinghua National Laboratory for Information Science and Technology (TNList).

References

1. Zhao, P., Tian, H., Qin, C., Nie, G.: Energy-saving offloading by jointly allocating radio and computational resources for mobile edge computing. IEEE Access. **5**, 11255–11268 (2017)
2. Lyu, X., et al.: Optimal schedule of mobile edge computing for Internet of Things using partial information. IEEE J. Sel. Areas Commun. **35**(11), 2606–2615 (2017)
3. Guo, Y., Yang, Q., Liu, J., Kwak, K.S.: Cross-layer rate control and resource allocation in spectrum-sharing OFDMA small-cell networks with delay constraints. IEEE Trans. Veh. Technol. **66**(5), 4133–4147 (2017)
4. Zhang, H., Jiang, C., Beaulieu, N.C., Chu, X., Wen, X., Tao, M.: Resource allocation in spectrum-sharing OFDMA femtocells with heterogeneous services. IEEE Trans. Commun. **62**(7), 2366–2377 (2014)
5. Wong, I.C., Evans, B.L.: Optimal resource allocation in the OFDMA downlink with imperfect channel knowledge. IEEE Trans. Commun. **57**(1), 232–241 (2009)
6. Awad, M.K., Mahinthan, V., Mehrjoo, M., Shen, X., Mark, J.W.: A dual-decomposition-based resource allocation for OFDMA networks with imperfect CSI. IEEE Trans. Veh. Technol. **59**(5), 2394–2403 (2010)
7. Wang, J.B., et al.: Imperfect CSI-based joint resource allocation in multirelay OFDMA networks. IEEE Trans. Veh. Technol. **63**(8), 3806–3817 (2014)
8. Sheng, M., Li, Y., Wang, X., Li, J., Shi, Y.: Energy efficiency and delay tradeoff in device-to-device communications underlaying cellular networks. IEEE J. Sel. Areas Commun. **34**(1), 92–106 (2016)
9. Xiang, X., Lin, C., Chen, X.: Toward optimal admission control and resource allocation for LTE-A femtocell uplink. IEEE Trans. Veh. Technol. **64**(7), 3247–3261 (2015)
10. Liu, F., Yang, Q., He, Q., Park, D., Kwak, K.S.: Dynamic power and subcarrier allocation for downlink OFDMA systems under imperfect CSI. Wirel. Netw., 1–14 (2017)

11. Adireddy, S., Tong, L., Viswanathan, H.: Optimal placement of training for frequency-selective block-fading channels. IEEE Trans. Inf. Theory. **48**(8), 2338–2353 (2002)
12. Wu, Y., Louie, R.H., McKay, M.R.: Analysis and design of wireless ad hoc networks with channel estimation errors. IEEE Trans. Signal Process. **61**(6), 1447–1459 (2013)
13. Neely, M.J.: Stochastic network optimization with application to communication and queueing systems. Synth. Lect. Commun. Netw. **3**(1), 1–211 (2010)
14. Boyd, S., Vandenberghe, L.: Convex Optimization. Cambridge University Press, Cambridge (2004)

ST-LDA: High Quality Similar Words Augmented LDA for Service Clustering

Yi Zhao[✉], Keqing He, and Yu Qiao

School of Computer Science,
Wuhan University, Wuhan 430072, Hubei, China
ivwepriu@sina.com, hekeqing@whu.edu.cn,
qiaoyu@email.cufe.edu.cn

Abstract. Service discovery is a key problem in the field of services computing, which is essential to improve the accuracy and efficiency of both services composition and recommendation. Service clustering is a major way to facilitate service discovery. The main technical difficulty in solving service clustering problem lies in the semantic gap among services. Some traditional approaches like LDA perform well in service clustering to some extent. However, their performances are still limited by the inevitable semantic noise words. To bridge this gap, we propose a novel solution, namely ST-LDA (short for "Similar Words and TF-IDF Augmented Latent Dirichlet Allocation"), approaching the challenges from the perspective of similar words learning and noise words filtering to improve service clustering. Specifically, we adopt Word2Vec to adapt the representation of services, and learn a list of similar words in service corpus. Moreover, we further integrate TF-IDF into our similarity calculation to filter noise words. In this way, we can enhance LDA with the similar words finding and filtering strategy for service clustering. We conduct extensive experiments on a real-world dataset, which demonstrate that our approach can improve the efficiency of service clustering.

Keywords: TF-IDF · Latent Dirichlet Allocation · Word2vec
Web service clustering

1 Introduction

The explosive growth of various information on the Web has resulted in the sharply increase of Web services in both quantity and type, which greatly limit the accuracy and efficiency of service discovery. More than 18000 Web services described by WSDL and natural languages are registered and published on the ProgrammableWeb and over 98% of them are valid [1]. As a result, some Web service discovery methods like Web service search engines which are relied on natural languages have been exploited after the UDDI (Universal Description Discovery and Integration) to address the problem. The main technical difficulty in Web service engines lies in the semantic gap, which performs query-document matching at the term level. However, a high degree of searching and matching at the term level does not necessarily represent high relevance, and vice versa. The semantic gap is pervasive due to the ambiguous and

© Springer Nature Switzerland AG 2018
J. Vaidya and J. Li (Eds.): ICA3PP 2018, LNCS 11335, pp. 46–59, 2018.
https://doi.org/10.1007/978-3-030-05054-2_4

variable nature of human language, since the same term can represent different meanings and the same meaning can be represented by different terms. For example, if a query contains "the latitude and longitude" and the document only contains "map", then the matching degree of the query and the document is low, although they are closely relevant.

Service clustering is a major approach to improve the performance of service discovery. Researchers in the areas of service clustering have already adopted other approaches like LDA to perform service clustering. Chen et al. [2] proposed a fusion tag enhanced LDA for service clustering which improved the accuracy and efficiency of service clustering to some extent. However, this approach can only apply to Web services with WSDL descriptions and tags and can not solve the data sparsity and cold start problems well [3]. Some other methods based on LDA conduct the clustering through either using semantic similarity computing [5], or combining with other clustering methods like k-means++ after mapping words and documents into embedding spaces [4]. While these approaches based on LDA perform well to some extent, their performances are still limited by the semantic gap.

As we all know, in LDA, each document may be viewed as a mixture of various topics where each document is composed of a set of topics. A topic has probabilities of generating various words. Naturally, the word itself will have the high probability given this topic. A topic is identified on the basis of automatic detection of the likelihood of term co-occurrence. Therefore, words without special relevance will have roughly even probability between classes (or can be placed into a separate category). So we can infer that methods aforementioned have the following limitations.

Noise words filtering: LDA posits that each document is a mixture of a small number of topics and that each word's creation is attributable to one of the document's topics. There is no doubt that some noise words which are not semantically relevant to documents are still remained in documents. Noise words and similar words are attributable to the document's topics in different way that can limit or improve the performance of LDA. So the impact of similar words and the noise words on the topics should be considered in LDA.

Semantic similar words discovery: Poria et al. [5] only used the bag of words model to get the list of semantic similar words. As a result, there were amount of similar even the same semantic words not on the list. While Shi et al. introduced the Word2Vec method, combined with K-Means++ approach to do word clustering in LDA. A large number of experiments have proved that the accuracy of K-Means++ method is unideal, so the result of the similar words clustering using it is not good neither.

Inspired by the disadvantages of the methods mentioned above, a method named ST-LDA is proposed in this paper to address the clustering problem advanced by LDA. We use LDA as the basic model. We first approach Word2Vec to represent service into embedding space. Then we exploit LDA to get the key words of the services' topics generated, and get the list of similar words of the key words by semantic similarity computing. We optimize the new feature degree metrics defined according to TF-IDF and semantic similarity to filter noise words. Finally, we put the list of similar words filtered in LDA to produce a set of service clusters. Moreover, we compare the effect with several methods to demonstrate the feasibility of our proposed approach.

To summarize, our main contributions are as follows:

- We consider the negative impact of noise word on service clustering and positive impact of semantic similar words on service clustering. And we propose a novel ST-LDA model improved by the semantic similar words discovering strategy and noise words filtering strategy from this perspective.
- We present an embedding method that represented service document using Word2Vec and present metrics named feature degree calculated considered TF-IDF and semantic similarity. Then we exploit the embedding space and feature degree to find semantic similar words and filter noise words.
- Extensive experiments performed on real word datasets demonstrate the effectiveness of our proposed approaches.

The remainder of this paper is organized as follows: Sect. 2 discusses relevant works in this area. Section 3 presents the ST-LDA approach. Section 4 describes the performance when comparing ST-LDA approach with existing works. The conclusions of this study and our future work are summarized in Sect. 5.

2   Related Work

A. Service clustering based on functional similarity

There have been several efforts to improve service discovery by clustering algorithms recent years [6, 7]. One of the most straightforward ways to cluster services is via functional similarity of services. Sun et al. [8] clustered services according to the functional similarity and process similarity; and Petri-net is adopted as a modeling language for the specification of service process model to support the computing of similarity. Kumara et al. [9] proposed a new approach to grouping Web services into functionally similar clusters according to the documents of Web services and generating an ontology via hidden semantic patterns present within the complex terms used in service features to measure similarity. Some other approaches either annotated Web services using ontology firstly like SAWSDL (Semantic Annotations for WSDL and XML Schema), OWL-S (Ontology Web Language for Services), or described services using ontology-based semantic Web service description languages like OWLS-MX [10] and SAWSDL-MX [11].

B. Service clustering based on semantic similarity advanced by LDA

Another group of approaches to cluster services is based on semantic similarity. Web Service Description Language (WSDL), the widely used standard in industry, does not contain enough information for service description which can not contribute to compute the service semantic similarity well. To solve this problem, Gu et al. [12] proposed a service clustering method which enhanced original WSDL documents with semantic information by means of Linked Open Data (LOD). Dasgupta et al. [13] proposed a hybrid Multi-agent based distributed platform for efficient semantic service discovery method named SMARTSPACE. The original LDA model is usually used as the basic model. Wang et al. [14] mined common topic groups from the service-topic distribution matrix generated by topic modeling, and performed service discovery based on common topic groups. Since the word distributions in Web service descriptions are becoming sparse, sometimes the clustering approaches that are solely based on service descriptions are hard to achieve ideal clustering performance. Many embedding based or auxiliary information approaches are proposed. Chen et al. [2] proposed a Web service clustering approach which integrated WSDL documents and tagging data through LDA model. Shi et al. proposed an augmented LDA model named WE-LDA which leverages the high-quality word vectors to improve the performance of Web service clustering.

In summary, although there are some approaches considering advance LDA for clustering from the perspective of semantic similarity of words. Their performances are still limited. And some strategies, such as word embedding representation and noise words filtering, are neglected. Inspired by these works, we propose a method for service clustering, namely high quality similar words augmented LDA, which can leverage the strategies aforementioned to improve the performance of Web service clustering.

3   Overall Architecture of Our Framework

In this section, we present an overview of our proposed approach, as illustrated in Fig. 1. Our framework has three steps: data preprocessing, similar words extracting and filtering, and the ST-LDA model. In the following sections, we present each of the components in detail.

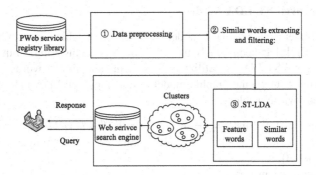

Fig. 1. Overall framework of our proposed web service clustering approach

(1) *Data preprocessing:* This preprocessing unit takes Web service documents which are described by natural language as input and preprocesses them using Proter Stemmer tool provided by NLTK, which stems words and removes stop words to extract meaningful words as feature words.
(2) *Similar words extracting and filtering:* `We first approach Word2Vec to represent service into embedding space, and put the service embedding space into the original LDA to get a list of key words of topics clustered. In this way, we can get a list of Top-5 frequent key words of each topic *HFWL* (High Frequency Word List).

Then we compute the semantic similarity between the words in word corpus and words in *HFWL* using cosine similarity, which are measured by the metrics of feature degree *f*. Finally we can get a ranked list of semantic similar words for the words in *HFWL*, named *RSWL* (Ranked Similar Word List). A lower *f* represents the lower similarity between words in corpus and *HFWL* which can be considered as noise words that could cause negative impact on topic distribution. Conversely, a higher *f* between them can impact on topic clustering in a positive way. The embedding process is similar to the work [15], and the metrics of *f* can be described as follows:

$$Feature\, Degree = tf - idf \times sim(w_k, w_j), \tag{1}$$

where *tf-idf* denotes the TF-IDF of "similar word" and $sim(w_k, w_j)$ denotes the semantic similarity of w_k and w_j.

(3) *ST-LDA:* As *RSWL* is a set of similar word list ranked, which can be seen as the service document corpus. We put *RSWL* into the LDA model to cluster services. Services are grouped into clusters based on the trained topic, which fused the information of similar words. Especially ST-LDA established an implicit topic for each service cluster; and assigned each service to the service cluster which corresponding to its relevant topic which has a maximum value of relevant probability.

In the following two subsections, we describe the details of our improved ST-LDA model and the strategy of filtering.

3.1   Our Improved ST-LDA Model

The ST-LDA model is an extension model based on LDA, which is a model proposed by Blei et al. [16]. It has been widely used for documents clustering. In this work, we improve the original ST-LDA by utilizing the semantically similar words extracted for keywords. Figure 2 shows the graphic model of our improved LDA model. The main identifiers are shown in Table 1.

(1) For each similar word list $sim_d = 1, \ldots, S$, draw $\theta^d \sim Dirichlet(\alpha)$;
(2) For each topic $z \in \{1, 2, \ldots, T\}$, draw a multinomial distribution $\emptyset^z \sim Dirichlet(\beta)$;
(3) For each word w_{di} in service *d*:
    (a) Draw a topic *z* from θ^d;
    (b) Draw *w* from $\emptyset^z$;
    (c) Draw Uniform(sim_d) from similar words sim_d in service d, as defined in Eqs. (2–3).

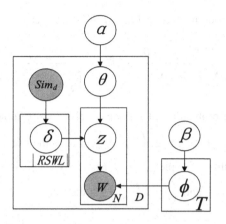

Fig. 2. Graphic model of our improved ST-LDA

Table 1. Identifiers and its definition

Identifiers	Definition
α	The parameter of the Dirichlet prior on the per-document topic distributions
β	The parameter of the Dirichlet prior on the per-topic word distribution
Θ	The topic distribution for document d
Z	The topic for the n-th word in document d
Δ	The similar word distribution for topic z
ϕ	The word distribution for topic k
W	The specific word
T	The number of topics
N	The number of words in a documents (Web services)
D	The number of documents (set of service description documents/Web service)
Sim_d	Similar word list of keywords of document d
$RSWL$	Dictionary that stores similar words lists of keywords

The conditional probability of services belonging to topics can be obtained according to the graphic model above after learning the various distributions:

$$p(w_d|\phi, \theta, sim_d) = \prod_{i=1}^{N} \sum_{t=1}^{T} \sum_{k=1}^{K} p(w_{di}, z_{di} = k, x_{di} = t|\phi, \theta, sim_d), \quad (2)$$

We employ Gibbs sampling as estimate the parameters. Gibbs sampling constructs a Markov chain that calculates the conditional distribution $p(w_d|\phi, \theta, sim_d)$.

$$p(\delta_{di} = s, z_{di} = s|w_{di} = w, z_{-di}, \delta_{-di}, w_{-di}, \alpha, \beta, sim_d) \propto \frac{N_{wt,-di}^{WT} + \beta}{N_{w \cdot t,-di}^{WT} + w\beta} \times \frac{N_{st,-di}^{ST} + \alpha}{N_{s \cdot t,-di}^{ST} + T\alpha},$$

$$(3)$$

We resample all words in S using Eq. (6), θ^s and $\emptyset^z$. can be estimated by

$$\hat{\theta}^d_z = \frac{\left(N^{WT}_{wt,-di}\right)^d + \beta}{\left(\sum_{w'} N^{Wt}_{w't,-di}\right)^d + w\beta}, \hat{\emptyset}^z_w = \frac{\left(N^{ST}_{st,-di}\right)^d + \alpha}{\left(\sum_k N^{TK}_{s't,-di}\right)^d + T\alpha}, \tag{4}$$

where $\hat{\theta}^d_z$ represent the probability of service d belonging to topic z; $\left(N^{WT}_{wt,-di}\right)^d$ is the number of words in d assigning to z; $\left(\sum_{w'} N^{Wt}_{w't,-di}\right)^d$ is the number of words in d; $\hat{\emptyset}^z_w$ represents the probability of topic z on word w; $(N^{ST}_{st,-di})^d$ is the number of word assigning to z, except w_{di}; and $\left(\sum_k N^{TK}_{s't,-di}\right)^d$ is the number of words except w_{di}.

3.2   Filter Similar Words List Generation

For optimal search and match performance, certain sets of words are considered "noise" words by the query. The noise words are maintained in the list of similar words of Web service which impact on service clustering in a negative way. Developers need to be aware of some of the bad behaviors that noise words can cause in the search space. Depending on the type of query, the search service may or may not perform the match. To address this problem, we introduce new metric of feature degree to support noise word filtering strategy to make the list of similar words more reliable and suitable.

The steps of filtering noise words are shown as Algorithm 1 in Table 2: We first exploit the LDA model to get the service keywords set named *KWL* (Keyword List)

Table 2. Algorithm 1: Filtering noise words

Algorithm 1:
input: Services D ;
output: *RSWL,*   Train set
1. **For** each service $d_i \in D$ **do**
2. draw LDA
3.   **For** each word $w_k \in KWL$ **do**
4. $sim \leftarrow Word2Vec(w_k)$ // Finding similar words of keywords using word embedding
5. $feature\ degree \leftarrow TF - IDF \times sim(w_k, w_j)$
6.   **If** $RSWL \leftarrow FD(sim_i) < th$
7. $RSWL \leftarrow Eliminate(sim_i)$// Remove noisy words from *RSWL*
8.   **End If**
9.   **End For**
10 **End For**
11.Return

belonging to each topic (Lines 1–2). Then we find the similar words of all distinct words contained in the service documents using word embedding (Lines 3–4). After that, we compute f to find and filter the noise words.

We filter the noise words whose value of f is lower than the threshold. To get better performance of ST-LDA, we conduct experiment to optimize the threshold of f. We found that the clustering effect was better when f is greater than 0.01.

Figure 3 shows the impact on the value of TF-IDF when the value of f is varied. We automatically select the f value to observe the performance. When f is equal to 0.01, similar words can be divided into two categories. We select similar words with the value of $f < 0.01$ and $f > 0.01$ to do clustering test in this paper. The ST-LDA clustering results perform better when the value of f was taken 0.01. Specifically, the Euclidean distance matrix is created to calculate and compare the distances between different categories of data points. The computing of distance between data points shows as follows [17]:

$$dis_{min}\left(C_i, C_j\right) = min_{x \in C_i, y \in C_j} dist(x, y) \tag{5}$$

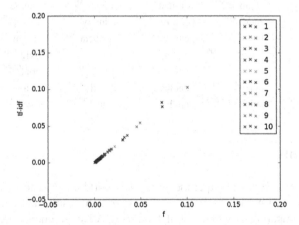

Fig. 3. Impact on TF-IDF of f

The most significant difference between *feature degree* > 0.01 and *feature degree* < 0.01 is that similar words and noise words have different effects for the clustering effect of service documents, having a deep insight into the influence of this difference. We randomly selected 4 clusters from 10 test clusters and enumerated the examples of the words when *feature degree* > 0.01 and *feature degree* < 0.01. It can be learned that the words in Table 3 are more representative of clusters, while some unrelated noise words remain in Table 4.

Table 3. Feature degree > 0.01 similar words of four clusters

Cluster	Advertising	Education	Financial	Game
Feature degree > 0.01	$bulk^{0.0109}$	$campus^{0.0101}$	$current^{0.0101}$	$engine^{0.01206}$
	$click^{0.0113}$	$school^{0.0114}$	$trade^{0.0105}$	$flash^{0.01207}$
	$buy^{0.0115}$	$degree^{0.0114}$	$business^{0.0106}$	$halo^{0.0132}$
	$agency^{0.0119}$	$course^{0.0119}$	$exchange^{0.0112}$	$host^{0.0144}$
	$client^{0.0128}$	$database^{0.014}$	$custom^{0.0114}$	$play^{0.0169}$
	$video^{0.0134}$	$design^{0.0144}$	$stock^{0.0116}$	$match^{0.0193}$
	$agency^{0.0159}$	$digital^{0.0149}$	$account^{0.0117}$	$id^{0.0194}$
	$legalize^{0.0171}$	$criterion^{0.016}$	$equivalent^{0.012}$	$group^{0.0205}$
	$audience^{0.025}$	$edition^{0.017}$	$banking^{0.013}$	$guild^{0.0205}$

Table 4. Feature degree < 0.01 similar words of four cluster

Cluster	Advertising	Education	Financial	Game
Feature degree< 0.01	$analysis^{0.0098}$	$global^{0.00936}$	$expose^{0.00903}$	$google^{0.00966}$
	$channel^{0.0089}$	$english^{0.00909}$	$direct^{0.00789}$	$image^{0.00845}$
	$banner^{0.00701}$	$embed^{0.00859}$	$dollar^{0.00787}$	$handle^{0.007249}$
	$add^{0.0069}$	$country^{0.0085}$	$industry^{0.00779}$	$friend^{0.007248}$
	$way^{0.00669}$	$current^{0.00757}$	$european^{0.00777}$	$forum^{0.007246}$
	$catalog^{0.00667}$	$dutch^{0.00722}$	$expense^{0.00751}$	$fight^{0.007245}$
	$yahoo^{0.00638}$	$contact^{0.00697}$	$funding^{0.0075}$	$goal^{0.006039}$
	$view^{0.00463}$	$dedicate^{0.0062}$	$directly^{0.00738}$	$industry^{0.0036}$
	$visitor^{0.00453}$	$fetch^{0.00392}$	$delay^{0.00653}$	$force^{0.00242}$

4 Experiments

In this section, we conducted experiments on real-world datasets to verify the feasibility of our proposed model. We analyze the experiment results and demonstrate the promotion by comparing it with several baselines. All experiments are working in Python2.7 and they are conducted on Dell PC with 2.4 GHz Intel(R) Core(TM) i5 CPU and 8 GB RAM.

4.1 Dataset and Preparation

We crawled a dataset from https://www.programmableweb.com/, PWeb, on January 10, 2018. For each API, we randomly select 3660 Web service documents from the dataset we crawled to evaluate the performance of Web service clustering. Table 5 presents the scale (i.e., the number of services) of each selected domain.

We perform a classification manually into the following ten categories: "Advertising", "eCommerce", "Education", "Email", "Enterprise", "Financial", "Games", "Government", "Mapping", and "Social", which are regard as standard clusters.

Table 5. Experimental data description

#Service documents	3660
#Similar words	2000
#Clusters	10
#Words	163,518

To evaluate the performance of item recommendation, we adopted Word2Vec in the Gensim package [18]. In addition, the window width is set as 5 and the vector dimension of the output layer is set as 200. In order to evaluate the impact of the f on service clustering, we train topic models under different f values, varying from 0.007 to 0.01. Note that since the services are selected from five domains, we set the number of topics T as 5. Moreover, the two hyper-parameters of LDA are empirically set as $\alpha = 50/T$, $\beta = 0.1$. Based on the LDA model trained, we cluster the services by assigning the service document to the cluster that corresponds to its most close topic. And we compare the clustering result with the standard clusters.

4.2   Baseline Approaches

To demonstrate the effectiveness of our model, we adopt the following methods as baselines for performance comparison:

(1) *LDA*: This baseline is the original Latent Dirichlet allocation, the probability graph model, which group each service to the cluster corresponding to its most close topic based on the produced topic distributions of services here.

(2) *Sentic-LDA:* This baseline advanced LDA model for service clustering (Poria, 2016), which incorporate the word clusters generated by applying semantic level on the word vectors learned using Word2vec.

We also set the numbers of topics in ST-LDA and Sentic-LDA as well as the number of clusters in LDA as 10.

4.3   Metrics

We adopt metrics to measure the performance of the ST-LDA algorithm, including purity and entropy.

Purity is defined as:

$$Purity(SC_i) = \frac{|SC_i|}{|SD_i|}, \tag{6}$$

where $SC = \{SC_1, SC_2, ..., SC_{10}\}$ i = 1...10 is the set of service clusters generated. $|SC_i|$ is the number of services in i-th cluster, $SD = \{SD_1, SD_2, ..., SD_{10}\}$ is the standard service clusters of datasets. SD_i is the number of Web service in stdard cluster SDi. $|SD_i|$ is the total number of services in all clusters, e.g., $|SD_i| = 3660$ in our experiments. So the purity of SC is defined as:

$$Purity(SC) = \sum_{i=1}^{TK} \frac{|SC_i|}{|SD|} \times Purity(SC_i). \tag{7}$$

Entropy is defined as

$$E_{(SC_i)} = -\sum_{SD_j \in SD} \frac{|SC_i \cap SD_j|}{|SC_i|} \cdot log_2 \frac{|SC_i \cap SD_j|}{|SC_i|}, \tag{8}$$

where $E_{(SC_i)}$ represents the entropy of SC_i. And the entropy of service cluster result is computed by:

$$Entropy = \sum_{SC_i \in SC} \frac{|SC_i|}{|SD|} \cdot E_{(SC_i)}. \tag{9}$$

Note that Purity is positive metrics that the higher value of it indicates better performance, while the Entropy metrics is converse that the lower value of it is better.

4.4 Results

In this section, we analyze the experiment results to answer the following questions:

RQ1: How do f(feature degree) impact the performance of ST-LDA model for service clustering?

RQ2: How does ST-LDA perform as compared to the baseline methods?

(1) *Impact of f on ST-LDA (RQ1)*

In our LDA model, the most similar 2000 (TOP-200 for each keywords list) words are leveraged to improve the original LDA. The value of f affects the quality of the topic model trained, which affects the performance of service clustering indirectly. To evaluate the impact of f on ST-LDA, we clustered times of services based on the topic models with different values of f, varying from 0.007 to 0.01.

Table 6 presents the clustering performances achieved by our proposed approach under different f values. As can be seen from Table 6, the best performance is obtained when $f = 0.01$. Through analysis, $Purity_{(f<0.01)} < Purity_{(f>0.01)}$ represent the purity of similar words when $f > 0.01$ is better than the purity of similar words when $f < 0.01$. The lower performance obtained with $f < 0.01$ is mainly caused by the fact that some noise words that are not filtered, causing negative impact on the service clustering process.

Table 6. Metrics performance of our proposed ST-LDA on ten domains under different f values

f	<0.007	<0.008	<0.009	<0.01
Purity	0.8544	0.8372	0.903	0.8263
f	>0.007	>0.008	>0.009	>0.01
Purity	0.7325	0.7761	0.749	0.9322

As the results indicated, we used the experiment results of our approach obtained with $f = 0.01$ in the following evaluations.

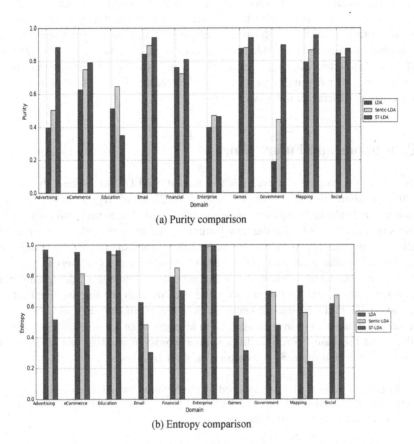

(a) Purity comparison

(b) Entropy comparison

Fig. 4. Purity and entropy of three service clustering approaches on ten domains

(2) *Comparison of Service Clustering Approaches(RQ2)*

In order to verify that our method can achieve better results in various service clusters as Fig. 4 presenting the performance results of the three approaches. Figure 4(a) shows the purity and Fig. 4(b) shows the entropy. It can be found that our improved *ST-LDA* outperforms the other two approaches in terms of all metrics at large. It is because the high-quality similar words are helpful for clustering Web services documents, in addition avoid the negative effect of low-quality noisy words caused. And the performance order among them is: *ST-LDA* is better than *Sentic-LDA*, while the *Sentic-LDA* is better than *LDA*. More specifically, compared with the second best *Sentic-LDA*, our improved *ST-LDA* has an improvement of 7.2%, and 23.7% on Purity, and Entropy, respectively. It can be explained that in Sentic-*LDA*, there can be noise words remained in the word clusters used for improving *LDA*, which limits the performance of it. In contrast, we choose the top 200 most semantically similar words of randomly selected words to assist *LDA*. These high-quality similar words can help achieve accurate performance. Moreover, *Sentic-LDA* is better than the original *LDA* because it additionally uses the word-clusters as auxiliary information. Since *LDA* did not consider the semantic similarities between words, which performance is unfavorable than *Sentic-LDA* and *ST-LDA*. While on *"Education"* and *"Enterprise"* two clusters, our method is not good as the other two methods which mainly because of the unfavorable result of noise words filtering in these two topics.

5   Conclusions and Future Work

In this paper, we propose a novel method named ST-LDA to address the service clustering problem in LDA. We leverage Word2Vec to represent service into embedding space, and then exploit semantic similar words discovering and noise words filtering strategies. We optimize the new feature degree metrics f defined according to TF-IDF and semantic similarity to filter noise words from similar words. Finally, we put the list of similar words filtered in LDA to produce a set of service clusters. Moreover, we compare the effect with several methods to demonstrate the feasibility of our approach, which achieved high purity and entropy with the improvement rate of 7.2%, and 23.7% in the metrics respectively on a real word dataset.

In the future, we plan to investigate how to leverage more knowledge bases such as WordNet[1] and Freebase[2] to further filter similar words. In addition, we also want to combine different kind of word embeddings in the LDA model.

Acknowledgement. This work was supported by the National Natural Science Foundation of China (Nos. 61672387 and 61702378), and the Natural Science Foundation of Hubei Province of China (Nos. 2018CFB511 and 2017CKB894).

References

1. Lo, D.: An Exploratory Study of Functionality and Learning Resources of Web APIs on ProgrammableWeb
2. Chen, L., Wang, Y., Yu, Q., Zheng, Z., Wu, J.: WT-LDA: user tagging augmented LDA for web service clustering. In: Basu, S., Pautasso, C., Zhang, L., Fu, X. (eds.) ICSOC 2013. LNCS, vol. 8274, pp. 162–176. Springer, Heidelberg (2013). https://doi.org/10.1007/978-3-642-45005-1_12
3. Bobadilla, J., Ortega, F., Hernando, A., et al.: A collaborative filtering approach to mitigate the new user cold start problem. Knowl. Based Syst. **26**, 225–238 (2012)

---

[1] https://wordnet.princeton.edu/

[2] www.freebase.com

4. Shi, M., Liu, J., Zhou, D., et al.: WE-LDA: a word embeddings augmented LDA model for web services clustering. In: IEEE International Conference on Web Services, pp. 9–16. IEEE (2017)

5. Poria, S, Chaturvedi, I, Cambria, E, et al.: Sentic LDA: improving on LDA with semantic similarity for aspect-based sentiment analysis. In: International Joint Conference on Neural Networks, pp. 4465–4473. IEEE (2016)

6. Hao, Y., Junliang, C., Xiangwu, M., Bingyu, Q.: Dynamically traveling web service clustering based on spatial and temporal aspects. In: Hainaut, J.-L., et al. (eds.) ER 2007. LNCS, vol. 4802, pp. 348–357. Springer, Heidelberg (2007). https://doi.org/10.1007/978-3-540-76292-8_41

7. Platzer, C., Rosenberg, F., Dustdar, S.: Web service clustering using multidimensional angles as proximity measures. ACM Trans. Internet Technol. **9**(3), 1–26 (2009)

8. Sun, P., Jiang, C.: Using service clustering to facilitate process-oriented semantic web service discovery. Chin. J. Comput. **31**(8), 1340–1353 (2008)

9. Kumara, B.T.G.S., Paik, I., Chen, W.: Web-service clustering with a hybrid of ontology learning and information-retrieval-based term similarity. In: IEEE, International Conference on Web Services, pp. 340–347. IEEE Computer Society (2013)

10. Klusch, M., Fries, B., Sycara, K.: OWLS-MX: a hybrid semantic web service matchmaker for OWL-S services. Web Seman. Sci. Serv. Agents World Wide Web **7**(2), 121–133 (2009)

11. Klusch, M., Kapahnke, P., Zinnikus, I.: Hybrid adaptive web service selection with SAWSDL-MX and WSDL-analyzer. In: Aroyo, L., et al. (eds.) ESWC 2009. LNCS, vol. 5554, pp. 550–564. Springer, Heidelberg (2009). https://doi.org/10.1007/978-3-642-02121-3_41

12. Gu, Y., Cai, H., Xie, C., et al.: Utilizing semantic information from linked open data in web service clustering. In: International Conference on Progress in Informatics and Computing, pp. 654–658. IEEE (2017)

13. Dasgupta, S., Aroor, A., Shen, F., et al.: SMARTSPACE: multiagent based distributed platform for semantic service discovery. IEEE Trans. Syst. Man Cybern. Syst. **44**(7), 805–821 (2017)

14. Wang, J., Gao, P.P., Ma, Y.T., He, K.Q., Patrick, C.K.: A web service discovery approach based on common topic groups extraction. IEEE Access **5**, 10193–10208 (2017). https://doi.org/10.1109/ACCESS.2017.2712744

15. Wu, H.C., Luk, R.W.P., Wong, K.F., et al.: Interpreting TF-IDF term weights as making relevance decisions. ACM Trans. Inf. Syst. **26**(3), 55–59 (2008)

16. Blei, D.M., Ng, A.Y., Jordan, M.I.: Latent Dirichlet allocation. J Mach. Learn. Res. Arch. **3**, 993–1022 (2003). https://doi.org/10.1162/jmlr.2003.3.4-5.993

17. Karypis, G., Han, E.H., Kumar, V.: Chameleon: hierarchical clustering using dynamic modeling. Computer **32**(8), 68–75 (2002)

18. Bartunov, S., Kondrashkin, D., Osokin, A., et al.: Breaking sticks and ambiguities with adaptive skip-gram. Comput. Sci. (2015)

LMCC: Lazy Message and Centralized Cache for Asynchronous Graph Computing

Ruini Xue⑩, Zhibin Dong$^{(\boxtimes)}$⑩, Wei Su⑩, and Xiaofang Li⑩

University of Electronic Science and Technology of China, Chengdu, China
xueruini@gmail.com, developerdong@gmail.com, suwei779@gmail.com,
lucylee23030@gmail.com

Abstract. Graph has been widely used in complex network applications modeling, and the asynchronous graph processing model is superceding the BSP model because of its better convergence speed. However, the asynchronous GAS model proposed by PowerGraph usually results in irregular and unpredictable communication patterns as well as vertex-scale barriers, so it is difficult for programmers to optimize codes. To address these challenges, we propose LMCC, an improved message management approach including lazy pull-message model and vertex-oriented centralized cache, which can reduce communication cost in terms of message quantity, and reduce the number of computation iterations in turn, without compromising the accuracy of application results. Based on the deep investigation of the GAS phases, LMCC is designed to be totally transparent to user applications. Experimental results show that LMCC can deliver speedup for various types of graph computing benchmarks ranging from 129% to 271%.

Keywords: Graph processing · Communication optimization
Message combination · Centralized cache

1 Introduction

As the scale of the Internet traffic expands continuously [8], graph computing is regarded as a promising method to deal with big data applications, such as machine learning, social network analysis [9], web searching [24], natural language processing [4], and recommendation systems [5,17], due to its expressiveness, efficiency and productivity.

To satisfy the growing demands of graph computing in terms of scalability, efficiency and programmability, a variety of graph computing frameworks

This work is supported by the National Natural Science Foundation of China (No. 61272528) and the Fundamental Research Funds for the Central Universities (No. ZYGX2016J088).

J. Vaidya and J. Li (Eds.): ICA3PP 2018, LNCS 11335, pp. 60–75, 2018.
https://doi.org/10.1007/978-3-030-05054-2_5

have emerged, consisting of stand-alone platforms like X-stream [26], Turbo-Graph [14], and GridGraph [36], as well as distributed ones like Pregel [23], GraphLab [22], PowerGraph [11], GraphX [12], and CUBE [33]. These frameworks are designed with quite different paradigms, such as vertex-centric [11, 12,22,23], edge-centric [26], computation-centric [35], path-centric [32], block-centric [31], and graph-centric [28], so as to address the problems in different domains.

While these platforms follow different ideologies, their execution modes can be mainly divided into *synchronous* mode and *asynchronous* mode. The synchronous mode usually refers to the typical BSP model, in which executions are orchestrated into steps, and updates are not visible until the current step is committed. The iterations ceases when all the vertices in the graph are inactive at the beginning of a step. By contrast, in asynchronous mode, executions are triggered by the scheduler, and the execution order between any pair of vertices is arbitrary. Any update is observable immediately after it occurs, and the computation terminates when the scheduling queue is empty. Despite its simplicity, synchronous mode suffers from poor scalability due to the presence of the synchronization barrier, at which the faster nodes having completed their tasks have to wait for slower ones to finish. There are proposals trying to mitigate the impact of such barrier. For example, GraphHP [6] allows computation of a superstep in every machine to be executed by a series of pseudo-supersteps to get rid of the global synchronization. Giraph Unchained [13] introduces a local barrier to decide whether to continue as well as a lightweight global barrier that can be cancelled when workers receive new messages. However, they do not eliminate barriers completely. It was the emergence of asynchronous frameworks that substantially ruled out such limitations.

Generally, asynchronous mode is faster than synchronous mode by taking convergence speed and scalability into account. However, its communication pattern is irregular and unpredictable, which may lead to severe performance issues for I/O-intensive applications [30], making it hard for programmers to optimize.

Fortunately, the vertex-cut partitioning approach and the GAS (Gather Apply Scatter) abstraction of PowerGraph partially solved the problem of message combination in asynchronous executions. In the case of vertex-cut partitioning, an edge can only be placed in one node, and a vertex may be divided into multiple replicas located in different nodes. When collecting the information of adjacent vertices and edges in the *Gather* phase, a mirror replica concatenates the data into a single value and sends it to the master replica, which is similar to the message combiner of Pregel [23]. Then, the master replica updates its value in the *Apply* phase, and distributes the updated value to all its mirrors, and then each mirror scatters to its local neighbors in turn as the *Scatter* phase, which is similar to the publish-subscribe mechanism of LFGraph [15].

During the scatter phase, a vertex is appended to the scheduling queue on receiving messages from adjacent vertices. Before the vertex is scheduled to execute, any incoming message will be merged with previous ones. On the one hand, to reduce communication cost, mirrors need to forward messages from local adjacent vertices as late as possible, while on the other hand, mirrors' messages should be delivered as early as possible from a master's perspective to avoid more iterations. This conflict is hard to be resolved in current systems.

Moreover, the current distributed cache can mitigate the cost of computation for many algorithms [2] by dynamically maintaining the result of gather phase for every vertex replica locally, however, it does not help with the vertex-scale barriers in the GAS model presented in Sect. 2.2.

To address these issues, LMCC, a combination of message and cache management mechanisms, is proposed for asynchronous graph computing frameworks like PowerGraph. A lazy pull-message model is devised as a supplement to the existing push-message mechanism to alleviate the aforementioned conflict. By investigating PowerGraph's internal dependency, LMCC manages to decouple the *Init* phase from the *Gather* phase so as to take advantage of *Gather* phase to pull messages from mirrors which does not add extra number of messages. By adopting a vertex-oriented centralized cache, LMCC is able to decrease the computation cost as well as the barriers communication. A prototype of LMCC is implemented based on PowerGraph, and experiments show that LMCC can significantly speed up the overall execution of various types of graph applications by up to 2.71X (from 1.29X).

The rest of this paper is organized as follows: Sect. 2 introduces the background and motivation, and Sect. 3 presents the system design, including the lazy pull-message approach as well as the vertex-oriented centralized cache and its application scope. Section 4 discusses implementation details of LMCC, and Sect. 5 evaluates LMCC against a variety of applications. Related work comes in Sect. 6, and the paper is concluded in Sect. 7 along with future work.

2   Motivation

In this section we will discuss internals of current message model and cache mechanism in the typical asynchronous graph computing framework PowerGraph, address its limitations and present how LMCC is motivated.

2.1   Combine and Push Messages

Real-world graph datasets, such as social networks and the hyperlinks between web pages, which commonly exhibit power-law distribution, are hard to partition equally with the edge-cut methods [1,20], resulting dramatic performance decrease for Pregel-like synchronous systems. To address the difficulties in processing skewed power-law graph, PowerGraph proposes a *"Gather-Apply-Scatter"* abstraction where the collected information from neighbors in *Gather* phase will be used to update vertex value in *Apply* phase, and in *Scatter* phase the updated value will be distributed to adjacent vertices. A vertex is activated once a message, either from neighbors or mirrors, is pushed to it. In addition to the execution abstraction, PowerGraph adopts a vertex-cut distribution mechanism, allowing vertices in a power-law graph to be allocated efficiently among different machines. This highly matches the GAS model, as is illustrated in Fig. 1.

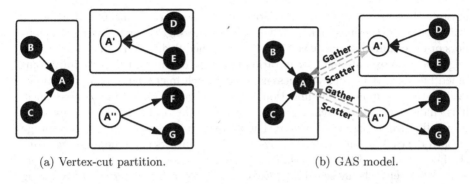

(a) Vertex-cut partition.   (b) GAS model.

Fig. 1. Vertex-cut and GAS model in PowerGraph. Black and white circles denote master and mirror vertices respectively. D and E represent local adjacent vertices of A′. The master retrieves information from each mirror during *Gather* stage, and propagates updates to mirrors during *Scatter*.

To reduce the messages pushed from mirrors to the master vertex, Power-Graph supports the message "combiner" similar to Pregel, as is shown in Fig. 2. Figure 2a and b exhibit the transmission pattern before and after applying the combiner mechanism. For algorithms with commutative and associative opera-tors, such as PageRank [24] and SSSP (Single Source Shortest Path), the com-biner can be leveraged to merge the messages intended for the same destination into a single message, reducing the number of messages to be transmitted, and therefore alleviating the network communication overhead. With message com-bination, a mirror only needs to send a single message to its master even if it has to collect values from multiple adjacent vertices. Similarly, the master will only need to transfer one message to synchronize with the mirrors after applying the gathered information for value update.

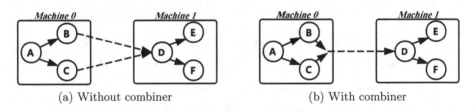

(a) Without combiner   (b) With combiner

Fig. 2. Workflows with and without message combiners. Solid and dotted lines repre-sent directed edges of the graph and messages transferred between vertices respectively.

Since mirrors need to forward received activating messages to the master, their message transmission pattern will impose a significant impact on network traffic and execution iterations. Different ways of forwarding may result in dif-ferent effects. From a single mirror's perspective, it should try to wait for as many messages as possible and then transfer only one combined message to the master. However, such strategy is not appropriate for the master. If a mirror waits too long, the master may have received messages sent by its local neighbors or other mirrors, and have already been scheduled to run. Thus, the master might need to execute another iteration once the mirror transfers its fully combined but excessively delayed message to it, which may trigger more iterations, leading to even more communication and computation costs. As a consequence, it is challenging for the scheduler to coordinate the optimal timing of message forwarding from mirror to master. Therefore, it is necessary to take advantage of both delayed and immediate delivery to have mirrors combine messages with the best efforts and let the master get existing messages from as many mirrors as possible before being scheduled. LMCC addresses this conflict by introducing a transparent "pull-message" approach, which will be described in Sect. 3.1.

2.2 Vertex Cache

PowerGraph maintains a local accumulator cache for each replica so that some algorithms may skip collecting information in the *Gather* phase. However, there are still some limitations that may impede the effectiveness of such cache. First, each generalized "plus" operation defined in the application, which enables the cache mechanism, must have a corresponding inverse operation to calculate the delta of cache during the *Scatter* phase. Second, due to the design of placing cache locally on each replica, the master has to fetch the cached result from each mirror in each iteration, resulting in additional communication overhead. Finally, although there is no need for synchronization between different vertices in asynchronous execution, there are still synchronization barriers from the perspective of replicas of a vertex, as is illustrated in Fig. 3.

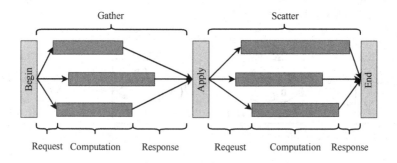

Fig. 3. Workflow of multiple replicas.

When the scheduler is going to execute a master, the asynchronous engine allocates a thread to conduct the corresponding GAS iteration of the vertex. First, the master initializes the vertex program with messages received from locally adjacent vertices or forwarded by remote mirrors. Then, the master sends the initialized vertex program to each mirror, and both the master and mirrors perform *Gather* operation on the locally adjacent vertices and edges. Next, each mirror responds to the previous request with its *Gather* result. Apparently, because of the divergence of network delay, number of neighbors and hardware configuration, the mirrors may respond in considerably different time, causing the master not being able to continue to the *Apply* phase until the slowest response arrives. Such kind of barrier also exists in the *Scatter* phase, as is shown in Fig. 3. Therefore, application performance might suffer from such barriers dramatically given very imbalanced configuration.

The current mirror cache can save the computation cost in the *Gather* phase. However, it does not help to eliminate the barriers. We devise a vertex-oriented centralized cache mechanism to mitigate the influence of barriers, which is totally transparent to applications. Section 3.2 will discuss the new cache mechanism in details.

3   System Design

3.1   Lazy Message Pulling

In the *Scatter* stage, a replica will send messages to its local neighbors. If the neighbor is a mirror, the message will be forwarded to its master immediately if the asynchronous engine is in "fast signal" mode. Otherwise, it will be buffered to be transmitted to the master later. If the neighbor is a master, it will store the message locally, and then put the vertex into the scheduler. All messages a master received will be used to initialize the data structure of the user-defined vertex program in the *Init* phase before GAS, as is shown in Fig. 4a. Actually, *Gather* phase is only used to collect information from neighboring vertices and edges. Variables in the vertex program, which is initialized by the *Init* phase, will not be used in the *Gather* phase at all.

Table 1. Impact of the *Init* stage on subsequent stages.

Benchmarks	sgd	svdpp	kcore	sssp	Others
Init	√	√	√	√	×
Gather	×	×	×	×	×
Apply	√	√	√	√	×
Scatter	×	×	√	×	×

Several widely used graph algorithms, such as sgd (Stochastic Gradient Descent), svdpp (SVD++, Singular Value Decomposition++), kcore (K-Core), sssp (Single Source Shortest Path), and others (ALS, Alternating least squares; LBP, Loopy Belief propagation, and PageRank), are investigated to confirm the observation, and the results are shown in Table 1. For *Init* stage, √ and × indicate the application does or does not have *Init* stage respectively. For the other

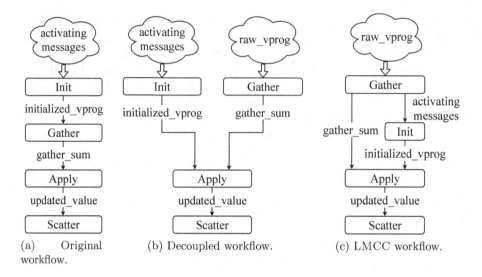

(a)   Original workflow.   (b) Decoupled workflow.   (c) LMCC workflow.

Fig. 4. Execution workflow of a vertex in one iteration.

stages, $\sqrt{}$ and $\times$ means whether *Init* stage has an impact on them. The table reveals that four applications do have *Init* stage, but no one's *Gather* depends on the result of its *Init*.

Since *Gather* is independent to *Init*, it is safe to decouple the currently forced dependency between them, which has been demonstrated in Fig. 4b, so that *Gather* would be able to use uninitialized user-defined vertex program, and would not need to wait for *Init*, as long as both of them finish before *Apply*. This is the basic rationale of our lazy pull-message model described below:

1. The messages received by mirrors are always stored and combined locally until the mirror is scheduled to send the merged message to its master;
2. When a master starts a new iteration, and *Init* is not yet in progress, it will pull messages from all its mirrors before proceeding. All messages are fetched at the last minute. Therefore, not only can messages be combined sufficiently, but also the master will not be activated repeatedly.

The aforementioned lazy pulling before *Init* does introduce additional communication, which might counteract the benefits of the decoupled workflow. To overcome such overhead, LMCC integrates message pulling in *Gather*: the pulled messages will be piggybacked in *Gather*'s response. Figure 4c illustrates the final lazy message pulling in LMCC: a master can simultaneously get the partial sum and combined message from one mirror in the *Gather* phase without additional pulling.

3.2   Vertex-Oriented Centralized Cache

Instead of placing the cache along with a mirror locally, each master in LMCC maintains an individual cache for all its mirrors. That is, all the caches for the replicas of a vertex are managed by its master in a centralized way. By this way, as long as the datas of the adjacent vertices and edges of the mirror do not change, its corresponding cache on the master is valid, and the master can directly use the cache without sending a *Gather* request.

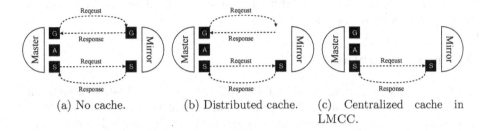

(a) No cache.   (b) Distributed cache.   (c) Centralized cache in LMCC.

Fig. 5. The comparison between different cache mechanisms.

Basic workflows under different cache mechanisms are described in Fig. 5. *Distributed cache* (Fig. 5b) in PowerGraph eliminates computation in *Gather* compared with the cache-less implementation (Fig. 5a), but it does not relieve communication occurred in *Gather*. With LMCC's centralized cache shown in Fig. 5c, both the computation and communication in *Gather* stage are eliminated.

When the neighbors of a mirror update their values, it will receive activating messages. Then, when the mirror is scheduled to execute, it forwards the message to its master which will invalidate the cache of this mirror. In the next iteration, the master has to issue a *Gather* request to the mirror for the latest *Gather* sum. The effect of *centralized cache* degrades to that of *distributed cache* only if all mirrors send activating messages to the master, in which case there would be the same number of communication transfers. Therefore, *centralized cache* will save much more communication efforts in most cases.

Application Scope. For most applications, adding a cache mechanism will speed up its execution significantly, while for some other applications it may lead to adverse effect. The behaviors of two typical applications under LMCC's cache mechanism are discussed as follows.

Graph Coloring Applications. If the algorithm reads the old vertex value, every update to the vertex value will promote the convergence. That is, even if only a portion of the cache is updated in time, it will tend to converge after iterations. However, this execution mode has a negative impact on the correctness of the graph coloring applications. In each iteration, a vertex must obtain the latest coloring conditions for all neighboring vertices in order to make correct decision. The delayed activating messages can lead to excessive use of stale caches [29], which may produce erroneous result, leading to extra iterations and communication and finally resulting in the divergence of the application.

Message-Passing Applications. Because vertices in *Scatter* phase can send activating messages containing data to neighboring vertices, those message-passing applications can only use *Apply* and *Scatter* stages for continuous iteration. The data used in *Apply* is fetched from the messages in *Scatter* stage, which excludes the information collected in *Gather* phase. Therefore, for message-passing applications, *centralized cache* in LMCC does make much difference in execution performance because there is no *Gather* stage.

4   Implementation

LMCC is implemented based on PowerGraph v2.2 [10]. By default, PowerGraph will leverage message combination, and a mirror will be inserted in the local scheduler when other vertices send messages to it. The mirror will not forward those messages to the master until it is dispatched, during which time all received messages will be merged as one. If a node instance executes fast enough that the local scheduler becomes empty, it will notify all other nodes and let the entire cluster initiate "fast signal" mode, in which all messages sent to a mirror will be immediately forwarded to its master. As a consequence, the message combination and cache would not be valid anymore. By contrast, LMCC disables "fast signal" mode considering the design principles of LMCC discussed above. Its execution flow is shown in Fig. 6. Besides, lazy message pulling and centralized cache are complementary: if no cache found, message pulling will be issued, otherwise

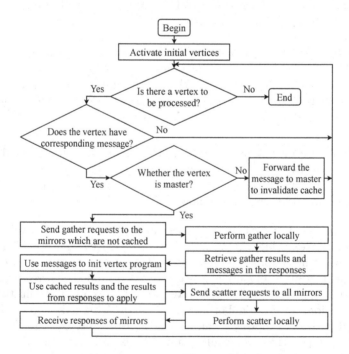

Fig. 6. The execution flow of LMCC.

the cache will be used and the pulling will be ignored. Additionally, LMCC is totally transparent to applications, so users would benefit from LMCC without any modification.

5   Evaluation

In this section, LMCC is evaluated by executing various graph applications with multiple datasets listed in Table 3, which are either synthesis from data generator from PowerGraph, or real-world data downloaded from SNAP [19]. The average performance of three runs is measured in terms of communication cost, iteration quantity, and execution time. Experiments are conducted in a cluster of 13 nodes whose configurations are shown in Table 2, all of which are connected by an 1 Gbps Ethernet network. These selected graph applications are:

PageRank is an algorithm to rank the websites in search engines.
SSSP "Single Source Shortest Path" finds the shortest paths between a source vertex and all the other vertices in a graph.
Simple coloring finds a way of coloring the vertices of a graph such that no two adjacent vertices share the same color.
ALS "Alternating Least Squares" is a kind of collaborative filtering algorithm widely used in machine learning applications, such as predicting a user's rating of products.
svdpp is an implementation of SVD++ matrix factorization algorithm, which can be used to solve the algebraic feature extraction problem.
wals is an implementation of the weighted-ALS matrix factorization algorithm described in "Collaborative filtering for implicit feedback datasets" [16].
Lbp_structured_prediction is used for structured prediction on a graph. One of its application is modeling the interests of users in a social network.

Table 2. Cluster configuration.

SN	CPU	RAM
0	Intel Core i3-5010U 2.10 GHz	8 GB
1–2	Intel Core i5-5200U 2.20 GHz	8 GB
3–6	Intel Celeron 2955U 1.40 GHz	4 GB
7–12	Intel Celeron N2807 1.58 GHz	4 GB

5.1   Performance

Communication and computation account most for the overall execution time. Thus, LMCC is compared with the original PowerGraph by the number of transmitted messages, the quantity of iterations as well as the execution time. All the executions are performed with *random* partitioning method. Table 4 shows the datasets each application uses, and the results are presented in Fig. 7.

Table 3. Graph datasets used in the experiments and their properties.

Category	Dataset	$|V|$	$|E|$
Synthetic	synthetic_0	11000	111128
	synthetic_1	160000	319200
Social networks	Facebook [21]	4039	88234
	Epinions [25]	75879	508837
	Twitter [21]	81306	2420744
	Pokec [27]	1632803	30622564
	LiveJournal [3, 20]	4846609	68475391
Web graphs	BerkStan [20]	685230	7600595
Citation networks	Patents [18]	3774768	16518947

Table 4. Input datasets of different applications.

Application	Dataset	Category
pagerank	Pokec	Graph analytics
sssp	Pokec	
simple coloring	Pokec	
als	synthetic_0	Collaborative filtering
svdpp	synthetic_0	
wals	synthetic_0	
lbp structured prediction	synthetic_1	Graphical models

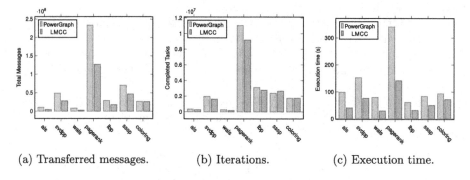

(a) Transferred messages.   (b) Iterations.   (c) Execution time.

Fig. 7. Application performance in terms of different metrics.

Figure 7a shows that LMCC transmits fewer messages than PowerGraph for all the applications by 47% in average, thanks to its significant reduction in activating messages and gather requests. As for iterations, Fig. 7b indicates that there is a 16% reduction in average. By virtue of these improvements, LMCC speeds up these tests in contrast to PowerGraph from 1.29 to 2.71 times in terms of execution time which is shown in Fig. 7c.

5.2 Scalability

We evaluate the scalability of LMCC in two dimensions: The performance of processing a given graph (Pokec) with varied cluster sizes, and the performance of computing varied datasets under fixed cluster size.

Scale the Cluster. Figure 8 presents the performance metrics of computing the same dataset with different cluster configurations. The 1, 2, 4, 6, 8, 10, 13 in the x-axis of Table 2 means enabling machine 0, 1–2, 3–6, 7–12, 3–10, 3–12 and 0–12 in the test respectively. The curves imply that the larger the cluster is, the more the application can benefit from LMCC. Specially, the gap between LMCC and PowerGraph has a drastic change at 8, and the curves are almost flat before and after this point. This is because the cluster becomes more heterogeneous, or rather more machine types are mixed, in which case LMCC's cache can contribute more compared with homogeneous configurations. The speed up before and after 8 are 111% and 252% respectively.

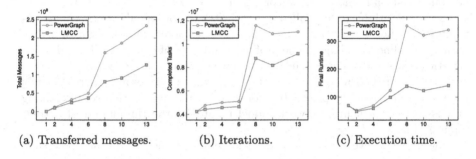

(a) Transferred messages.   (b) Iterations.   (c) Execution time.

Fig. 8. Performance metrics of Pokec in different cluster sizes.

Scale the Datasets. Figure 9 shows that, as the scale of the graph increases, the absolute difference of the optimization effect becomes larger for all metrics. The benefit before BerkStan is 1.6 roughly, while it changes to 2.6 after BerkStan. However, no correlation is observed between the ratio and the dataset size.

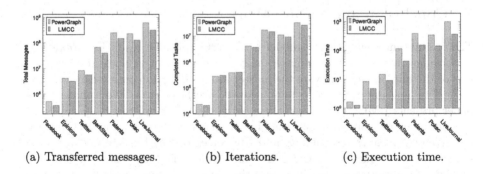

(a) Transferred messages.   (b) Iterations.   (c) Execution time.

Fig. 9. The experimental results of different datasets.

6   Related Work

Although there are lots of efforts focused on optimizing the existing graph computing frameworks, this paper concentrates on the message delivery model and cache management for asynchronous mode, so we will mainly relate current studies on optimizations of PowerGraph in this section.

To the best of our knowledge, there are only two existing public studies [7,30] that aim at performance optimization directly based on PowerGraph.

Xie [30] analyzed the performance characteristics of both synchronous and asynchronous modes on different kinds of graph applications, partitioning methods, execution stages, graph sizes, and cluster scales. It turns out that there is no "one-size-fit-all" mode for all conditions. To take advantage of both modes, a hybrid execution model, called PowerSwitch, is proposed, which can adaptively switch between the two modes on the basis of an efficient algorithm with optimized online sampling, offline profiling, and a set of heuristics. Though PowerSwtich offers better performance by timely switching the vertex programs execution between two modes, it is not transparent to users and therefore they have to carefully set the parameters for online sampling or use a set of training graphs to build a neural network model to predict the throughput of current input graphs.

PowerSwitch leverages hybrid execution engine to accelerate the processing, while Powerlyra [7] is introduced to differentiate the processing of vertices of different degrees. There are no *Gather* requests for low-degree vertices, while the high-degree ones are replicated among multiple machines for load balancing. Algorithms like ALS [34] need to gather or scatter along in-edges and out-edges simultaneously, which can not be optimized using the hybrid-cut of Powerlyra.

Both PowerSwitch and Powerlyra are high-level improvements over PowerGraph, while neither of them addresses the potential drawbacks in its internal execution flow of asynchronous mode, which is the major contribution of LMCC.

7   Conclusion and Future Work

The original message delivery model in PowerGraph may result in suboptimal performance because either a master may not get the latest data from its mirrors or the mirrors may activate the master repeatedly. Moreover, its distributed cache can not mitigate the communication overhead in *Gather* phase. This paper presents LMCC to address these issues. LMCC implements an improved message management approach that hybrid message pushing and lazy pulling to encourage message combining, and the vertex-oriented centralized cache to reduce *Gather* requests. LMCC can reduce communication cost as well as the number of computation iterations, and therefore accelerating overall execution. LMCC is designed based on the deep investigation of the GAS phases in PowerGraph, and it is totally transparent to applications. Experimental results show that LMCC can deliver speedup for various types of graph computing applications ranging from 129% to 271% in contrast to PowerGraph.

The centralized cache in LMCC is effective for a wide range of applications, but it can slow down certain applications as is discussed in Sect. 3.2. In the future, we will carry out further investigation on this issue and find out possible mitigations.

References

1. Abou-Rjeili, A., Karypis, G.: Multilevel algorithms for partitioning power-law graphs. In: 20th International Parallel and Distributed Processing Symposium, IPDPS 2006, pp. 10-pp. IEEE (2006)
2. Ahmed, A., Aly, M., Gonzalez, J., Narayanamurthy, S., Smola, A.J.: Scalable inference in latent variable models. In: Proceedings of the Fifth ACM International Conference on Web Search and Data Mining, pp. 123–132. ACM (2012)
3. Backstrom, L., Huttenlocher, D., Kleinberg, J., Lan, X.: Group formation in large social networks: membership, growth, and evolution. In: Proceedings of the 12th ACM SIGKDD International Conference on Knowledge Discovery and Data Mining, pp. 44–54. ACM (2006)
4. Biemann, C.: Chinese whispers: an efficient graph clustering algorithm and its application to natural language processing problems. In: Proceedings of the First Workshop on Graph Based Methods for Natural Language Processing, pp. 73–80. Association for Computational Linguistics (2006)
5. Chen, H., Li, X., Huang, Z.: Link prediction approach to collaborative filtering. In: Proceedings of the 5th ACM/IEEE-CS Joint Conference on Digital Libraries, JCDL 2005, pp. 141–142. IEEE (2005)
6. Chen, Q., Bai, S., Li, Z., Gou, Z., Suo, B., Pan, W.: GraphHP: a hybrid platform for iterative graph processing. arXiv preprint arXiv:1706.07221 (2017)
7. Chen, R., Shi, J., Chen, Y., Chen, H.: PowerLyra: differentiated graph computation and partitioning on skewed graphs. In: Réveillère, L., 0001, T.H., Herlihy, M. (eds.) Proceedings of the Tenth European Conference on Computer Systems, EuroSys 2015, Bordeaux, France, 21–24 April 2015, pp. 1:1–1:15. ACM (2015)
8. Cisco, Visual Networking Index: The zettabyte era: Trends and analysis (2017). https://www.cisco.com/c/en/us/solutions/collateral/service-provider/visual-networking-index-vni/vni-hyperconnectivity-wp.html. Accessed 07 June 2017
9. Coffman, T., Greenblatt, S., Marcus, S.: Graph-based technologies for intelligence analysis. Commun. ACM **47**(3), 45–47 (2004)
10. Gonzalez, J.E., Low, Y., Gu, H., Bickson, D., Guestrin, C.: Graphlab powergraph v2.2. https://github.com/jegonzal/PowerGraph
11. Gonzalez, J.E., Low, Y., Gu, H., Bickson, D., Guestrin, C.: Powergraph: distributed graph-parallel computation on natural graphs. In: OSDI, vol. 12, no: 2 (2012)
12. Gonzalez, J.E., Xin, R.S., Dave, A., Crankshaw, D., Franklin, M.J., Stoica, I.: Graphx: graph processing in a distributed dataflow framework. In: OSDI, vol. 14, pp. 599–613 (2014)
13. Han, M., Daudjee, K.: Giraph unchained: barrierless asynchronous parallel execution in pregel-like graph processing systems. Proc. VLDB Endow. **8**(9), 950–961 (2015)
14. Han, W.S., et al.: TurboGraph: a fast parallel graph engine handling billion-scale graphs in a single PC. In: Proceedings of the 19th ACM SIGKDD International Conference on Knowledge Discovery and Data Mining, pp. 77–85. ACM (2013)

15. Hoque, I., Gupta, I.: LFGraph: simple and fast distributed graph analytics. In: Proceedings of the First ACM SIGOPS Conference on Timely Results in Operating Systems, p. 9. ACM (2013)
16. Hu, Y., Koren, Y., Volinsky, C.: Collaborative filtering for implicit feedback datasets. In: Eighth IEEE International Conference on Data Mining, ICDM 2008, pp. 263–272. IEEE (2008)
17. Huang, Z., Chen, H., Zeng, D.: Applying associative retrieval techniques to alleviate the sparsity problem in collaborative filtering. ACM Trans. Inf. Syst. (TOIS) **22**(1), 116–142 (2004)
18. Leskovec, J., Kleinberg, J., Faloutsos, C.: Graphs over time: densification laws, shrinking diameters and possible explanations. In: Proceedings of the Eleventh ACM SIGKDD International Conference on Knowledge Discovery in Data Mining, pp. 177–187. ACM (2005)
19. Leskovec, J., Krevl, A.: SNAP Datasets: stanford large network dataset collection, June 2014. http://snap.stanford.edu/data
20. Leskovec, J., Lang, K.J., Dasgupta, A., Mahoney, M.W.: Community structure in large networks: natural cluster sizes and the absence of large well-defined clusters. Internet Math. **6**(1), 29–123 (2009)
21. Leskovec, J., Mcauley, J.J.: Learning to discover social circles in ego networks. In: Advances in Neural Information Processing Systems, pp. 539–547 (2012)
22. Low, Y., Bickson, D., Gonzalez, J., Guestrin, C., Kyrola, A., Hellerstein, J.M.: Distributed graphlab: a framework for machine learning and data mining in the cloud. Proc. VLDB Endow. **5**(8), 716–727 (2012)
23. Malewicz, G., et al.: Pregel: a system for large-scale graph processing. In: Proceedings of the 2010 ACM SIGMOD International Conference on Management of data, pp. 135–146. ACM (2010)
24. Page, L., Brin, S., Motwani, R., Winograd, T.: The pagerank citation ranking: Bringing order to the web. Technical report, Stanford InfoLab (1999)
25. Richardson, M., Agrawal, R., Domingos, P.: Trust management for the semantic web. In: Fensel, D., Sycara, K., Mylopoulos, J. (eds.) ISWC 2003. LNCS, vol. 2870, pp. 351–368. Springer, Heidelberg (2003). https://doi.org/10.1007/978-3-540-39718-2_23
26. Roy, A., Mihailovic, I., Zwaenepoel, W.: X-stream: edge-centric graph processing using streaming partitions. In: Proceedings of the Twenty-Fourth ACM Symposium on Operating Systems Principles, pp. 472–488. ACM (2013)
27. Takac, L., Zabovsky, M.: Data analysis in public social networks. In: International Scientific Conference and International Workshop Present Day Trends of Innovations, vol. 1 (2012)
28. Tian, Y., Balmin, A., Corsten, S.A., Tatikonda, S., McPherson, J.: From think like a vertex to think like a graph. Proc. VLDB Endow. **7**(3), 193–204 (2013)
29. Vora, K., Koduru, S.C., Gupta, R.: Aspire: exploiting asynchronous parallelism in iterative algorithms using a relaxed consistency based DSM. In: ACM SIGPLAN Notices, vol. 49, pp. 861–878 (2014)
30. Xie, C., Chen, R., Guan, H., Zang, B., Chen, H.: SYNC or ASYNC: time to fuse for distributed graph-parallel computation. ACM SIGPLAN Not. **50**(8), 194–204 (2015)
31. Yan, D., Cheng, J., Lu, Y., Ng, W.: Blogel: a block-centric framework for distributed computation on real-world graphs. Proc. VLDB Endow. **7**(14), 1981–1992 (2014)

32. Yuan, P., Zhang, W., Xie, C., Jin, H., Liu, L., Lee, K.: Fast iterative graph computation: a path centric approach. In: SC14 International Conference for High Performance Computing, Networking, Storage and Analysis, pp. 401–412. IEEE (2014)
33. Zhang, M., Wu, Y., Chen, K., Qian, X., Li, X., Zheng, W.: Exploring the hidden dimension in graph processing. In: OSDI, vol. 16, pp. 285–300 (2016)
34. Zhou, Y., Wilkinson, D., Schreiber, R., Pan, R.: Large-scale parallel collaborative filtering for the netflix prize. In: Fleischer, R., Xu, J. (eds.) AAIM 2008. LNCS, vol. 5034, pp. 337–348. Springer, Heidelberg (2008). https://doi.org/10.1007/978-3-540-68880-8_32
35. Zhu, X., Chen, W., Zheng, W., Ma, X.: Gemini: a computation-centric distributed graph processing system. In: OSDI, pp. 301–316 (2016)
36. Zhu, X., Han, W., Chen, W.: GridGraph: large-scale graph processing on a single machine using 2-level hierarchical partitioning. In: USENIX Annual Technical Conference, pp. 375–386 (2015)

Differential Evolution with Proximity-Based Replacement Strategy and Elite Archive Mechanism for Global Optimization

Chi Shao, Yiqiao Cai$^{(\boxtimes)}$, Wei Luo, and Jing Li

College of Computer Science and Technology,
Huaqiao University, Xiamen, China
yiqiao00@163.com

Abstract. Differential evolution (DE) algorithm is a simple but effective algorithm for numerical optimization. However, the inferior vectors, when compared to the current population, are always abandoned in the selection process. As the previous studies shown, these inferior vectors can provide valuable information in guiding the search of DE. Based on this consideration, this paper proposes a proximity-based replacement strategy (PRS) and an elite archive mechanism (EAM) to further utilize the information of inferior and superior vectors generated during the evolution. In the PRS, the trial vectors that do not defeat their parent vectors will have a chance to replace other parent vectors based on the distance between them. Further, to maintain the diversity of the population, the EAM is adopted by storing the superior vectors both in the selection operator and the PRS to provide the negative direction information. By this way, on the one hand, the search information provided by the inferior vectors can be effectively utilized with PRS to speed up the speed of convergence. On the other hand, the negative direction information derived from the superior vectors can enhance the diversity of population. By incorporating these two novel operators in DE, the novel algorithm, named PREA-DE, is presented. Through an experimental study on the CEC2013 benchmark functions, the effectiveness of PREA-DE is demonstrated when comparing with several original and advanced DE algorithms.

Keywords: Differential evolution · Proximity-based replacement strategy
Elite archive mechanism · Global optimization

1 Introduction

Differential evolution (DE), proposed by Storn and Price, is a stochastic population-based algorithm [1]. During the last decade, DE has been extended for handing constrained, multi-objective, large scale uncertain optimization and dynamic problems, and has been successfully applied in various scientific and engineering fields [2]. Although DE is considered an effective global optimization algorithm, it suffers from the problems of easily falling into local optimum or slow convergence rate due to its stochastic nature [2]. Many researchers have worked to improve the performance of DE in different directions, such as devising new mutation operators [3, 4], adopting

© Springer Nature Switzerland AG 2018
J. Vaidya and J. Li (Eds.): ICA3PP 2018, LNCS 11335, pp. 76–89, 2018.
https://doi.org/10.1007/978-3-030-05054-2_6

self-adaptive strategies for parameters controlling [5, 6], developing ensemble strategies [7, 8], and proposing a hybrid DE with other optimization algorithms [9], etc.

DE has three main operators, i.e., mutation, crossover and selection. The mutation operator is used to generate the mutant vector with different mutation strategies. The crossover operator is used to increase the diversity of population by generating the trial vector. The selection operator is used to decide the vector into the next generation with a one-to-one greedy strategy. In these three operators, the mutation and crossover operators have attracted a lot of attention from the researchers. In contrast, there have been few studies on the selection operator of DE.

In [10], Thomsen et al. proposed a crowding-based differential evolution, named CrowdingDE, in which the offspring no longer directly replaces its parents but replaces the most similar individuals in a subset of the CF (CF is the crowding factor). In [11], Li proposed SDE in which all parents and offspring are sorted by fitness value and the fittest NP individuals are reserved for the next generation. In [12], Guo et al. proposed a subset-to-subset survivor selection operator that the target and trial populations are divided into several subsets and then the best vectors are selected from the corresponding subsets to survive into the next generation.

In most of these variants, the inferior vectors during the selection process are always ignored. That is, the information of these vectors cannot be exploited in the following evolution process, and the evaluations of these vectors will be wasted. However, as the previous studies shown [5, 6], these inferior vectors can provide valuable information in guiding the search of DE.

Based on the above consideration, in this paper, we propose a proximity-based replacement strategy (PRS) and an elite archive mechanism (EAM) to further utilize the information of inferior and superior vectors generated during the evolution. In the PRS, the trial vectors that do not defeat their parent vectors will have a chance to replace other parent vectors based on the distance between them. Specifically, for each trial vector that fails to replace its parent, PRS will find the first parent vector in current population that satisfies the condition based on the distance and fitness information and replace it with the trial vector. In this way, PRS can increase the probability of the promising trial vectors entering the next generation and thus accelerate the convergence speed of DE. In the EAM, the superior vectors both in the selection operator and the PRS are stored to provide the negative direction information. Specifically, the vectors that successfully replace the parent vectors in the selection operator and PRS will be stored in an external archive. After that, some of the start point of the difference vector are selected from the combination of current population and external archive. In this way, EAM can effectively maintain the diversity of the population by introducing the negative direction information to guide the search. The novel DE algorithm with PRS and EAM is named as PREA-DE.

To evaluate the effectiveness of the proposed method, the experimental study has been carried out on a suite of benchmark functions from the CEC2013 special session on real-parameter optimization [13]. Experimental results show the high performance of PREA-DE.

The rest of this paper is organized as follows. Section 2 describes the original DE algorithm. The proposed PREA-DE is presented in detail in Sect. 3. In Sect. 4, the experimental results are shown and discussed. Finally, Sect. 5 draws the final conclusions.

2 Differential Evolution

DE is for solving the numerical optimization problem [1]. In this study, we consider the following optimization problem: *Minimize* $f(X)$, $X \in S$, $S \subseteq R^D$ and D is the dimension of the decision variables. In DE, a population of *NP* vectors representing the candidate solutions is evolved. Each vector is denoted as $X_{i,G} = \left[x_{i,G}^1, x_{i,G}^2, \cdots, x_{i,G}^D \right]$, where $i = 1, 2, \cdots, NP$, *NP* is the size of population and G is the number of current generation. After initialization, three main operators, i.e., mutation, crossover and selection, will be carried out. These operators will be briefly described as follows.

2.1 Mutation

For each individual of current population $X_{i,G}$ (called target vector), DE employs a mutation strategy to generate a mutant vector $V_{i,G}$. Six frequently used mutation strategies in the literature are shown as follows:

DE/rand/1

$$V_{i,G} = X_{r1,G} + F \times \left(X_{r2,G} - X_{r3,G} \right) \tag{1}$$

DE/rand/2

$$V_{i,G} = X_{r1,G} + F \times \left(X_{r2,G} - X_{r3,G} \right) + F \times \left(X_{r4,G} - X_{r5,G} \right) \tag{2}$$

DE/best/1

$$V_{i,G} = X_{best,G} + F \times \left(X_{r2,G} - X_{r3,G} \right) \tag{3}$$

DE/best/2

$$V_{i,G} = X_{best,G} + F \times \left(X_{r2,G} - X_{r3,G} \right) + F \times \left(X_{r4,G} - X_{r5,G} \right) \tag{4}$$

DE/current-to-best/1

$$V_{i,G} = X_{i,G} + F \times \left(X_{best,G} - X_{i,G} \right) + F \times \left(X_{r2,G} - X_{r3,G} \right) \tag{5}$$

DE/rand-to-best/1

$$V_{i,G} = X_{r1,G} + F \times \left(X_{best,G} - X_{r1,G} \right) + F \times \left(X_{r2,G} - X_{r3,G} \right) \tag{6}$$

where the indices $r1, r2, r3, r4$ and $r5 \in \{1, 2, \cdots NP\}$ are random and mutually different integers and are different from the index i. $X_{best,G}$ is the best individual vector at generation G, and the mutation factor F is a positive control parameter for scaling the difference vector.

2.2   Crossover

After the mutation vector is generated, the crossover operator is applied to each pair of $X_{i,G}$ and $V_{i,G}$ to generate a trial vector $U_{i,G}$ for increasing the diversity of population. There are two kinds of crossover scheme: binomial and exponential [1]. Binomial crossover is generally more robust and efficient than exponential crossover [14]. Therefore, the binomial crossover is considered in this study and is defined as follows:

$$
u_{i,G}^j = \begin{cases} v_{i,G}^j & if \ rand(0,1) \le CR \ or \ j = j_{rand} \\ x_{i,G}^j & otherwise \end{cases} \tag{7}
$$

where j_{rand} is a randomly chosen integer in the range [1, D].

2.3   Selection

Finally, the selection operator is employed to select the more promising trail vector into the next generation. That is, it compares the fitness values of the target vector $X_{i,G}$ and the trial vector $U_{i,G}$ and selects the better one for the next generation. The selection operator is carried out as follows:

$$
X_{i,G+1} = \begin{cases} U_{i,G} & if f \left(U_{i,G} \right) \le f \left(X_{i,G} \right) \\ X_{i,G} & otherwise \end{cases} \tag{8}
$$

3   DE with PRS and EAM (PREA-DE)

In this section, we describe the proposed PREA-DE algorithm in detail. In PREA-DE, a proximity-based replacement strategy (PRS) and an elite archive mechanism (EAM) are incorporated to utilize the information of inferior and superior vectors generated during the evolution. PRS is used to speed up the convergence rate and make full use of information from the inferior individuals based on the affinity between the trail vectors and the parent vectors, while EAM is employed to increase the diversity of population by introducing the negative direction information constructed with the stored elite individuals. Here, the details of PRS and EAM are described firstly. Then, the general framework of PREA-DE is shown.

3.1   Proximity-Based Replacement Strategy (PRS)

In most DE variants, if the trial vector U_i is worse than its parent individual X_i, U_i will be abandoned during the selection process. That is, these vectors cannot be exploited during the evolution process, and the evaluations of these vectors will be wasted. However, as shown in the previous studies [5, 6], these inferior vectors can provide valuable information in guiding the search of DE. Further, for the functions with costly evaluation, the information of the evaluated individuals is beneficial to speed up the convergence of rate.

According to these considerations, we propose the PRS to effectively utilize the information of the trail vectors. In PRS, each individual in the population will firstly have a mark. Then, if the parent vector is replaced by its trial vector during the selection process, the marks of both the parent and its trial vectors are set to 1. Otherwise, the marks of them are set to 0. After that, if the mark of a trial vector U_i is 0 (i.e., it fails to replace its parent vector X_i), we will look for the first parent vector X_j in the current population that meets the following conditions and replace it with U_i:

(1) j is not equal to i, and the number of the consecutive generations that X_j has not been replaced ($Count_j$) exceeds the default value (LIMIT).
(2) The fitness value of U_i is better than X_j.
(3) The Euclidean distance $D_{i,j}$ from U_i to X_j is less than the distance $D_{i,i}$ from U_i to X_i or the distance $D_{j,j}$ from U_j to X_j.

In this paper, LIMIT is used to determine the frequency of replacement, and its value will be selected from the candidate set S. The pseudo-code of PRS is shown in Algorithm 1.

Algorithm 1: Proximity-based Replacement Strategy (PRS)

1: **For** each unmarked child $U_{i,G}$ **Do**
2:   **For** each unmarked parent $X_{j,G}$ **Do**
3:     **If** $Count_j >$ LIMIT && $i\,!=j$ **then**
4:       **If** $f(U_{i,G}) < f(X_{j,G})$ **then**
5:         Calculate the distance $D_{i,j}$ from $U_{i,G}$ to $X_{j,G}$;
6:         Calculate the distance $D_{i,i}$ from $U_{i,G}$ to $X_{i,G}$;
7:         Calculate the distance $D_{j,j}$ from $U_{j,G}$ to $X_{j,G}$;
8:         **If** $D_{i,j} < D_{i,i}$ or $D_{i,j} < D_{j,j}$ **then**
9:           Replace $X_{j,G}$ with $U_{i,G}$;
10:          mark $(U_{i,G})$ = mark $(X_{j,G})$ = 1;
11:          $Count_j = 0$;
12:          break;
13:        **End If**
14:      **End If**
15:    **End If**
16: **End For**
17: **End For**

3.2   Elite Archive Mechanism (EAM)

To further exploit the information of the best individuals during the evolution, EAM stores the recently searched high-quality solutions in the external archive. Differing from the external archive mechanisms in [5, 6], EAM uses the archive to construct the negative direction information to increase the diversity of population.

In EAM, the size of the external archive is initialized to 0 and the upper limit is set to NP. In each iteration, the trial vectors that successfully replaces the parent individuals in the selection process and the RPS are put in the external archive. If the size of the external archive exceeds the upper limit, EAM will randomly remove the individuals from the archive to keep its size at NP.

With the elite archive (E), the start point of the difference vector constructed by two random vectors are selected from the combination of the current population and the elite archive ($P \cup E$). Take three mutation strategies with EAM for examples, the mutation vector is generated as follows:

DE/rand/2

$$V_{i,G} = X_{r1,G} + F \times \left(X_{r2,G} - \widetilde{X_{r3,G}} \right) + F \times \left(X_{r4,G} - \widetilde{X_{r5,G}} \right) \tag{9}$$

DE/current-to-best/1

$$V_{i,G} = X_{i,G} + F \times \left(X_{best,G} - X_{i,G} \right) + F \times \left(X_{r2,G} - \widetilde{X_{r3,G}} \right) \tag{10}$$

DE/rand-to-best/1

$$V_{i,G} = X_{r1,G} + F \times \left(X_{best,G} - X_{r1,G} \right) + F \times \left(X_{r2,G} - \widetilde{X_{r3,G}} \right) \tag{11}$$

where $X_{best,G}$, $X_{i,G}$, $X_{r1,G}$, $X_{r2,G}$ and $X_{r4,G}$ are selected in the same way as in original DE, $\widetilde{X_{r3,G}}$ and $\widetilde{X_{r5,G}}$ are selected from $P \cup E$ randomly. The indices $r1$, $r2$, $r3$, $r4$ and $r5$ are different integers and are different from the index i.

3.3   The Framework of PREA-DE

Combining PRS, EAM and DE, PREA-DE is presented and the pseudo-code of PREA-DE with "DE/rand/2" (PREA-DE/rand/2 for short) is shown in Algorithm 2.

Algorithm 2: PREA-DE/rand/2

1: Generate the initial population P^G and set G=1;
2: Evaluate the fitness for each individual in P^G, $FES = FES+NP$;
3: Initialize the size of the external archive to 0;
4: Randomly selects a value in the candidate set as LIMIT;
5: **While** the terminated condition is not satisfied **do**
6:　　**For** each individual $X_{i,G}$ **Do**
7:　　　　Select $X_{r1,G}$, $X_{r2,G}$ and $X_{r4,G}$ in P randomly;
8:　　　　Select $X_{r3,G}$ and $X_{r5,G}$ randomly from $P \cup E$;
9:　　　　Use mutation strategy to generate a mutant vector $V_{i,G}$;
10:　　　Use Eq. (7) to generate a trial vector $U_{i,G}$;
11:　　　**If** $f(U_{i,G}) < f(X_{j,G})$ **then**
12:　　　　　Put $U_{j,G}$ in the elite archive;
13:　　　　　Replace $X_{i,G}$ with $U_{i,G}$;
14:　　　　　mark $(U_{i,G})$ = mark $(X_{i,G})$ = 1;
15:　　　　　$Count_i = 0$;
16:　　　**End If**
17:　　　**Else**
18:　　　　　mark $(U_{i,G})$ = mark $(X_{i,G})$ = 0;
19:　　　　　$Count_i$ ++;
20:　　　**End Else**
21:　　**End for**
22:　　Perform the PRS;
23:　　$G = G+1$;
24: **End While**

4　Empirical Studies

4.1　Experimental Settings

In this section, the experimental study is carried out to evaluate the performance of PREA-DE on a suite of benchmark functions from the CEC2013 special session on real-parameter optimization [13]. The CEC13 benchmark functions set consists of 28 test functions, which includes the unimodal function F1 to F5, the basic multimodal function F6 to F20, and the composition function F21 to F28. More details of them can be found in [13].

For a fair comparison, the same random initial population is used to evaluate the performance of different algorithms. The parameters of the DE algorithms studied in this paper are set as Table 1 unless a change is mentioned.

Table 1. Parameters setting for the DE algorithms.

Parameters	Values
Dimension of each functions (D)	30 and 50
Population size (NP)	100
External archive size	100
Independent number of runs	30
Maximum number of evaluations	$10^4 \times D$
Candidate set of Limit (S)	{30, 40, 50}

To show the significant differences among the competitors, the non-parametric statistical tests are carried out by the KEEL [15] software. The results of the single-problem analysis by the Wilcoxon test [15] at $\alpha = 0.05$ are shown in the tables as "+/ = /−", which means that PREA-DE wins, ties and loses on the number of functions when compared with its corresponding competitor. The R+ and R− in the multiple-problem analysis by the Wilcoxon test mean the sum of ranks that PREA-DE performs significantly better than and worse than its competitor overall, respectively.

4.2 Effect on Original DE Algorithms

In this section, PREA-DE is compared with original DE algorithms to test its effectiveness on the original DE mutation strategies. Here, six mutation strategies are used, i.e., DE/rand/1, DE/rand/2, DE/best/1, DE/best/2, DE/current-to-best/1 and DE/rand-to-best/1. The statistics summarizing the performance comparisons for the functions from CEC13 at 30D and 50D are shown in Tables 2 and 3, respectively. In addition, the convergence graphs for F4 and F6 are plotted in Fig. 1.

Table 2. Results of the single- and multi-problem Wilcoxon's test for PREA-DE versus the original DE algorithms for the CEC2013 functions at 30D.

PREA-DE vs	+/=/−	R+	R−	p-value	$\alpha = 0.05$	$\alpha = 0.1$
DE/rand/1	15/13/0	334.0	44.0	0.000	Yes	Yes
DE/rand/2	22/6/0	385.0	21.0	0.000	Yes	Yes
DE/best/1	14/13/1	354.0	52.0	0.001	Yes	Yes
DE/best/2	10/17/1	289.5	88.5	0.015	Yes	Yes
DE/current-to-best/1	15/13/0	355.5	50.5	0.000	Yes	Yes
DE/rand-to-best/1	16/11/1	345.5	32.5	0.000	Yes	Yes

From Tables 2 and 3, PREA-DE can effectively enhance the performance of the original DE algorithms. Specifically, in Table 2, PREA-DE is significantly better than the corresponding DE algorithms on 15, 22, 14, 10, 15 and 16 functions at 30D, respectively. In Table 3, PREA-DE is significantly better on 14, 21, 18, 7, 16 and 16 functions at 50D, respectively.

Table 3. Results of the single- and multi-problem Wilcoxon's test for PREA-DE versus the original DE algorithms for the CEC2013 functions at 50D.

PREA-DE vs	+/=/−	R+	R−	p-value	α = 0.05	α = 0.1
DE/rand/1	14/13/1	278.0	100.0	0.010	Yes	Yes
DE/rand/2	21/7/0	376.5	1.5	0.000	Yes	Yes
DE/best/1	18/10/0	359.0	19.0	0.000	Yes	Yes
DE/best/2	7/21/0	323.0	83.0	0.006	Yes	Yes
DE/current-to-best/1	16/12/0	358.0	20.0	0.000	Yes	Yes
DE/rand-to-best/1	16/10/2	342.0	36.0	0.000	Yes	Yes

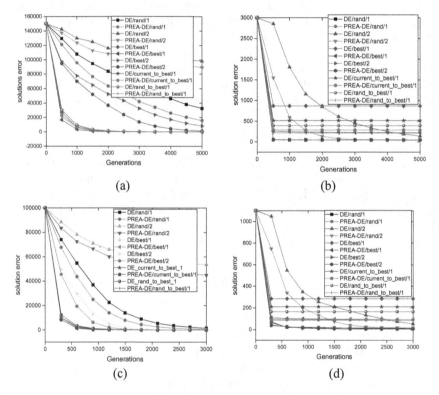

Fig. 1. Convergence graphs of PREA-DE and the corresponding original DE algorithms for the selected functions. (a) F4, 30D. (b) F6, 30D. (c) F4, 50D. (d) F6, 50D.

Further, according to the results of the multi-problem Wilcoxon signed-rank tests, PREA-DE can obtain higher R+ values than R− values in all the cases, and all the p values in Tables 2 and 3 are less than 0.05, which indicates that PREA-DE is significantly better than its corresponding DE algorithm overall. In addition, Fig. 1 shows that PREA-DE is better than the corresponding original DE algorithms in terms of the convergence speed for selected functions.

In summary, the overall results of Tables 2, 3 and Fig. 1 clearly show that PREA-DE can bring benefits to the original DE algorithms.

4.3   Effect on Advanced DE Variants

To further evaluate the effectiveness of proposed framework, PREA-DE is compared with the several advanced DE variants, including jDE [16], CoDE [17], SaDE [18], ODE [19], JADE [5], SHADE [6] and MDEpBX [20]. For a fair comparison, all the parameters of them are kept the same as their original paper except *NP* in CoDE and SaDE that is set to 100 in this study. The statistics summarizing the performance comparisons are shown in Tables 4 and 5, respectively. Besides, the convergence graphs for F4 and F15 re plotted in Fig. 2.

Table 4. Results of the single- and multi-problem Wilcoxon's test for PREA-DE versus the advanced DE variants for the CEC2013 functions at 30D.

PREA-DE vs	+/=/−	R+	R−	p-value	$\alpha = 0.05$	$\alpha = 0.1$
jDE	15/7/6	264.5	113.5	0.068	No	Yes
CoDE	24/4/0	373.5	4.5	0.000	Yes	Yes
SaDE	17/11/0	338.5	39.5	0.000	Yes	Yes
ODE	13/14/1	333.5	44.5	0.000	Yes	Yes
JADE	11/12/5	228.0	150.0	0.343	No	No
SHADE	11/10/7	251.5	126.5	0.130	No	No
MDEpBX	14/13/1	343.0	35.0	0.000	Yes	Yes

Table 5. Results of the single- and multi-problem Wilcoxon's test for PREA-DE versus the advanced DE variants for the CEC2013 functions at 50D.

PREA-DE vs	+/=/−	R+	R−	p-value	$\alpha = 0.05$	$\alpha = 0.1$
jDE	13/11/4	260.0	118.0	0.086	No	Yes
CoDE	24/4/0	401.5	4.5	0.000	Yes	Yes
SaDE	19/9/0	367.5	38.5	0.000	Yes	Yes
ODE	17/11/0	365.0	41.0	0.000	Yes	Yes
JADE	10/15/3	269.0	109.0	0.052	No	Yes
SHADE	11/13/4	230.0	148.0	0.318	No	No
MDEpBX	14/13/1	352.5	53.5	0.001	Yes	Yes

From Tables 4 and 5, PREA-DE can obtain significantly better results than most DE variants on the test functions. Specifically, PREA-DE is significantly better than the corresponding jDE, CoDE, SaDE, ODE, JADE, SHADE and MDEpBX on 15, 24, 17, 13, 11, 11 and 14 test functions at 30D, respectively, and on 13, 24, 19, 17, 10, 11 and 14 test functions at 50D, respectively.

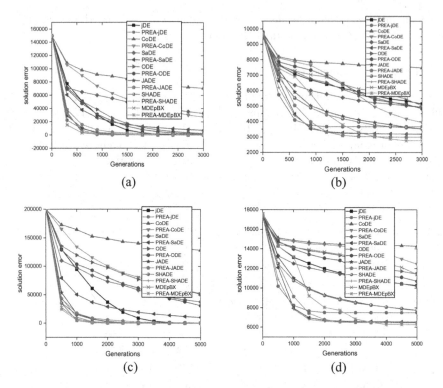

Fig. 2. Convergence graphs of PREA-DE and the corresponding advanced DE algorithms for the selected functions. (a) F4, 30D. (b) F15, 30D. (c) F4, 50D. (d) F15, 50D.

Based on the multi-problem Wilcoxon signed-rank tests, PREA-DE obtains the higher R+ values than R− values in all the cases. In addition, the p values are less than 0.05 in four cases. Moreover, Fig. 2 show that PREA-DE is superior to the corresponding advanced DE variant on the selected function.

In general, PREA-DE can provide an efficient way to further enhance the perfomance of advanced DE algorithms on the test functions.

4.4   Comparison with DE with a Crowding Scheme (CrowdingDE)

Thomsen proposed a DE algorithm with a crowding scheme, named CrowdingDE [10]. In CrowdingDE, the similarity between individuals is measured by the Euclidean distance, and each trial vector only replaces the parent vector that is most similar to it and worse than it. In this section, PREA-DE is compared with CrowdingDE to prove the effectiveness of the proposed PRS. For a fair comparison, the EAM in Sect. 3.2 is also added to CrowdingDE, and the crowding factor in CrowdingDE is chosen to be equal to *NP*, as their original paper [10]. The experimental are carried out on the CEC13 test function at 30D, and three DE algorithms (DE/rand/1, DE/rand/2 and DE/best/2) and two advance DE variants (jDE [16] and ODE [19]) are used. The results are shown in Table 6, and the convergence graphs for four selected functions are plotted in Fig. 3.

Table 6. Results of the single- and multi-problem Wilcoxon's test for PREA-DE versus CrowdingDE for the CEC2013 functions at 30D.

PREA-DE vs	+/ = /−	R+	R−	p-value	$\alpha = 0.05$	$\alpha = 0.1$
CrowdingDE/rand/1	26/2/0	378.0	0.0	0.000	Yes	Yes
CrowdingDE/rand/2	23/5/0	370.0	7.5	0.000	Yes	Yes
CrowdingDE/best/2	22/5/1	374.0	32.0	0.000	Yes	Yes
Crowding jDE	17/7/4	317.0	89.0	0.009	Yes	Yes
Crowding ODE	22/5/1	372.0	6.0	0.000	Yes	Yes

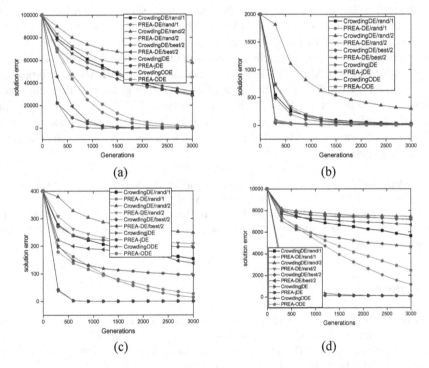

Fig. 3. Convergence graphs of PREA-DE and CrowdingDE for the selected functions. (a) F4, 30D. (b) F6, 30D. (c) F11, 30D. (d) F22, 30D.

From Table 6, PREA-DE can obtain better results than the CrowdingDE variants in all the cases. Specifically, PREA-DE is significantly better than the corresponding CrowdingDE variants on 26, 23, 22, 17 and 22 test functions, respectively. According to the results of the multi-problem Wilcoxon signed-rank tests, PREA-DE can obtain higher R+ values than R− values in all cases. Besides, the p values are less than 0.05 and 0.1 in all cases. Figure 3 also shows that PREA-DE is better than most corresponding CrowdingDE in terms of the convergence rate for selected functions. These results demonstrate that PREA-DE is significantly better than the CrowdingDE algorithms in all cases overall for the test functions.

5   Conclusion

To improve the ability of DE in exploiting the information of the trail vectors generated during the evolutionary process, a proximity-based replacement strategy (PRS) and an elite archive mechanism (EAM) is proposed for DE. On the one hand, for each trial vector that fails to replace its parent, PRS will find the first parent vector in current population that satisfies the condition based on the distance information and replace it with the trial vector. On the other hand, the vectors that successfully replace the parent vectors in the selection operator and PRS will be stored in an external archive, and some of the start point of the difference vector are selected from the combination of current population and external archive to construct the negative direction information. By combining PRS, EAM and DE, the resultant algorithm, PREA-DE, is proposed. The proposed PREA-DE algorithm is applied to the original DE algorithms and advanced DE variants to evaluate its effectiveness. The experimental study on CEC2013 benchmark functions is carried out to evaluate the effectiveness of PREA-DE. The results show that PREA-DE can effectively enhance the performance of most DE variants studied.

Acknowledgement. This work was supported in part by the Natural Science Foundation of Fujian Province of China (2018J01091, 2015J01258) and the Postgraduate Scientific Research Innovation Ability Training Plan Funding Projects of Huaqiao University (1611414011), and the Opening Project of Guangdong Province Key Laboratory of Computational Science at the Sun Yat-sen University

References

1. Storn, R., Price, K.: Differential evolution–a simple and efficient heuristic for global optimization over continuous spaces. J. Glob. Optim. **11**, 341–359 (1997)
2. Das, S., Suganthan, P.N.: Differential evolution: a survey of the state-of-the-art. IEEE Trans. Evol. Comput. **15**, 4–31 (2011)
3. Cui, L., Li, G., Lin, Q., Chen, J., Lu, N.: Adaptive differential evolution algorithm with novel mutation strategies in multiple sub-populations. Inf. Technol. Inf. **67**, 155–173 (2015)
4. Yu, W.J., Shen, M., Chen, W.N., Zhan, Z.H., Gong, Y.J., Lin, Y., et al.: Differential evolution with two-level parameter adaptation. IEEE Trans. Cybern. **44**(7), 1080–1099 (2014)
5. Zhang, J., Sanderson, A.C.: JADE: adaptive differential evolution with optional external archive. IEEE Trans. Evol. Comput. **13**, 945–958 (2009)
6. Tanabe, R., Fukunaga, A.: Evaluating the performance of SHADE on CEC 2013 benchmark problems. In: Evolutionary Computation, pp. 1952–1959. IEEE (2013)

7. Tian, M., Gao, X.: An improved differential evolution with information intercrossing and sharing mechanism for numerical optimization. Swarm Evol. Comput. (2018, in press). https://doi.org/10.1016/j.swevo.2017.12.010

8. Wu, G., Mallipeddi, R., Suganthan, P.N., Wang, R., Chen, H.: Differential evolution with multi-population based ensemble of mutation strategies. Inf. Sci. **329**, 329–345 (2016)

9. Tang, B., Zhu, Z., Luo, J.: Hybridizing particle swarm optimization and differential evolution for the mobile robot global path planning. Int. J. Adv. Robot. Syst. **13**(3), 1 (2016)

10. Thomsen, R.: Multimodal optimization using crowding-based differential evolution. In: IEEE Congress on Evolutionary Computation, CEC2004, vol. 2, pp. 1382–1389 (2004)

11. Li, X.: Efficient differential evolution using speciation for multimodal function optimization. In: Conference on Genetic and Evolutionary Computation, pp. 873–880. ACM (2005)

12. Guo, J., Li, Z., Yang, S.: Accelerating differential evolution based on a subset-to-subset survivor selection operator. Soft Comput., 1–18 (2018, in press). https://doi.org/10.1007/s00500-018-3060-x

13. Liang, J., Qu, B., Suganthan, P., Hernández-Díaz, A.: Problem definitions and evaluation criteria for the CEC 2013 special session on real-parameter optimization. Computational Intelligence Laboratory, Zhengzhou University, Zhengzhou, China and Nanyang Technological University, Singapore, Technical Report, 201212 (2013)

14. Lin, C., Qing, A., Feng, Q.: A comparative study of crossover in differential evolution. J. Heuristics **17**(6), 675–703 (2011)

15. Jesus, M.J.D., Ventura, S., Garrell, J.M., Otero, J., Romero, C., Bacardit, J., et al.: Keel: a software tool to assess evolutionary algorithms for data mining problems. Soft. Comput. **13**(3), 307–318 (2009)

16. Brest, J., Greiner, S., Boskovic, B., Mernik, M., Zumer, V.: Self-adapting control parameters in differential evolution: a comparative study on numerical benchmark problems. IEEE Trans. Evol. Comput. **10**(6), 646–657 (2006)

17. Wang, Y., Cai, Z., Zhang, Q.: Differential evolution with composite trial vector generation strategies and control parameters. IEEE Trans. Evol. Comput. **15**(1), 55–66 (2011)

18. Qin, A.K., Huang, V.L., Suganthan, P.N.: Differential evolution algorithm with strategy adaptation for global numerical optimization. IEEE Trans. Evol. Comput. **13**(2), 398–417 (2009)

19. Rahnamayan, S., Tizhoosh, H.R., Salama, M.M.A.: Opposition-based differential evolution. IEEE Trans. Evol. Comput. **12**(1), 64–79 (2008)

20. Islam, S.M., Das, S., Ghosh, S., Roy, S., Suganthan, P.N.: An adaptive differential evolution algorithm with novel mutation and crossover strategies for global numerical optimization. IEEE Trans. Syst. Man Cybern. Part B Cybern. **42**(2), 482–500 (2012)

NESTLE: Incentive Mechanism Specialized for Computation Offloading in Local Edge Community

Yinan Li, Jigang Wu[✉], and Long Chen

Guangdong University of Technology, Guangzhou 510006, Guangdong, China
liyinan940716@foxmail.com, asjgwucn@outlook.com, lonchen@mail.ustc.edu.cn

Abstract. Mobile Edge Computing focuses on the use of local edge devices in the community for task intensive mobile devices. This paper, we propose an incentive mechanism, including a bidding mechanism and a resource allocation scheme by solving the mixed integer programming which is NP-hard using auction. By considering the heterogeneous preferences of resources of task intensive mobile users, we offload independent tasks to local edge devices. We theoretically prove the economy properties of the proposed schemes such as individual rationality, budget balance and truthfulness. Simulation results show the proposed incentive mechanism is 36.27% higher than the exciting multi-round auction mechanism on total utility and 91.68% higher on allocation efficiency averagely.

Keywords: Mobile edge computing · Incentive
Heterogeneous preferences · Local edge community

1 Introduction

The recent tremendous growth of various wireless devices such as smart phones, wearable devices and IoT devices has brought the challenge in wireless networks systems. It is reported int Visual Networking Index that the data traffic will increase 8-fold from 2016 to 2021. However, due to the constraints of storage and computation capacities, many applications can not be performed locally, such as mobile games, and some image processing [9], this issue has become the main challenge [11]. The cloud computing can be a solution of the limitations [3]. However, despite the potential in data storage and analytics, cloud computing cannot fulfill the growing application requirements such as low latency and context awareness, European Telecommunications Standards Institute (ETSI) proposed the Mobile Edge Computing (MEC) [12]. MEC can provide cloud and IT services to user in the vicinity of the user, by setting up MEC servers at the edge of cellular networks [2]. When the MEC server is busy, the LEC can help to offload computation to end devices. Therefore, in this paper we focus on computation offloading in the third architecture. In the literature, authors in [24] proposed an offloading mechanism with trade-off between energy consumption and the amount of offloaded tasks. However, the mechanism didn't

© Springer Nature Switzerland AG 2018
J. Vaidya and J. Li (Eds.): ICA3PP 2018, LNCS 11335, pp. 90–104, 2018.
https://doi.org/10.1007/978-3-030-05054-2_7

consider subtasks in an application. That means when resources of provider can not meet the requirements of whole application, all independent subtasks of it will not be executed. The resource utilization of resources and completion rate of applications can not be improved. Authors in [8] proposed a combinational task offloading mechanism. They improved the offloading efficiency by a three-layer graph matching algorithm. However, this work did not include an incentive mechanism to encourage more devices participate in providing services to others.

To stimulate both sellers and buyers participating in computation offloading, there have been some incentive based schemes. Authors in [6] proposed an offloading mechanism with task dependency constraint in mobile edge computing. This mechanism saved energy and enhanced computation capability by cooperation between fog nodes and the remote cloud. However, they fail to address the computing capability constraints of service providers. Authors in [25] proposed a group-buying mechanism based on a three-stage auction. They maximized the total system utility by combining cloudlet placement and resource allocation. However, the work didn't consider the subtasks in the application.

In this paper, we mainly consider designing an incentive mechanism to encourage the computation offloading of applications' subtasks in LEC. However, there are some challenges. (i) Which way should an application be offloaded to end devices? (ii) Which end device should the application be offloaded to? (iii) How to encourage more end devices to participate in resources communication?

In order to answer the above questions, we focus on the case where subtasks of applications can be offloaded to end devices in the LEC. First of all, there are many independent subtasks in an application and the subtask can be offloaded and computed in parallel. Secondly, applications have heterogeneous preferences for each end device. Different computing abilities of end devices will affect the selection of applications. Third, we should guarantee the utility of participants to encourage communication between applications and end devices, rather than moving subtasks of applications to the remote cloud. In this paper, we propose an iNcentive mEchanism Specialized for compuTation offLoading in local Edge community (NESTLE) that taking into account the computing abilities of end devices. And the target of this mechanism is offloading subtasks of application to end devices and maximizing the utility for both sides.

The main contributions of this paper can be summarized as follows:

- With different computing abilities of different end devices, we add heterogeneous preferences to the process of bidding that applications can make different bids for different end devices based on their computing abilities.
- Theoretical analysis proves that the proposed mechanism can achieve individual rationality, budget balance and truthfulness. And extensive simulation results demonstrate that the mechanism we proposed outperforms the exciting multi-round auction mechanism by about 36.27% on total utility and 91.68% on allocation efficiency averagely.

The rest of this paper is organized as follows. Section 2 introduces related work for computation offloading in MEC. Section 3 presents the system model and describes the problem formulation. The algorithm of incentive mechanism is described in Sect. 4. Simulation results are shown in Sect. 5. In Sect. 6 concludes this paper.

2   Related Work

With the increasing demands of computing resources for applications, many computation offloading methods have been proposed. Authors in [14] proposed one offline centralized mechanism and one online distributed mechanism to offload computation tasks. However, the incentive mechanism was not be considered. Authors in [16] proposed a semi-distributed computation offloading mechanism that jointly optimizes the offloading decision. However, the algorithm didn't consider the subtasks of user. In our work, computation offloading is considered for the independent subtasks application. Subtasks of an application can be provided with computing resources by multiple end devices, and an end device can also serve multiple applications. Such a many-to-many allocation method can improve the utilization of the end device resources.

On the other hand, the end devices which have idle computing resources always exists. Many offloading methods based on incentive mechanism have been proposed. Authors in [5,21] proposed cloud resources allocation mechanisms based on game theory to maximize the utility. However, there was only one resources provider in these mechanisms, and in [21] the tasks were indivisible. Authors in [13] proposed a auction mechanism based on Lyapunov optimization techniques. They maximize the system utility by dynamic getting requirements of user. Authors in [23] proposed a computation offloading mechanism based on combinational auction to meet the heterogeneous demands of users in MEC. And authors in [7] proposed a computation offloading mechanism based on a two-stage auction model to maximize total system utility. Although incentive mechanisms were introduced in [7,13,23], subtasks in application were still not considered. The resource utilization of resources and completion rate of applications can not be improved by these mechanisms. Authors in [15] presented a cooperative tasks execution mechanism based on cooperative crowd-sourcing auction to encourage more users participating mobile crowd-sourcing and cooperating with other users. Authors in [20] proposed a task execution mechanism based on game theory. They encourage more devices providing their idle resources by dynamic pricing. However, [15,20] didn't fully consider the effects of resource providers' different computing abilities on total utility and user preferences. In the computation offloading mechanism we proposed, benefits can be achieved for all participants. At same time we took into account the computing abilities of the end devices, such as the CPU clock period and the data transmission efficiency of the end device. Thus, the total utility and applications' bids for different end devices will be affected by the ability when purchase resources.

3   System Model and Problem Formulation

3.1   System Model

In this work, devices or users that need computation resources are buyer and for those who possess idle or abundant resources are seller. The base stations participate the allocation is the auctioneer. When there are applications need to be executed, buyers and sellers will send their bids to the auctioneer respectively. Then auctioneer collects all information which include valuations and amount of resources that buyers require and sellers provide. According to the information and the predefined incentive mechanism, auctioneer determines the winning applications and the amount of payments to the sellers. Finally, the subtasks can't be executed by end devices will be offloaded to the edge server.

We consider an LEC scenario with N applications and M end devices. The n applications in $T = \{T_1, T_2, \cdots, T_n\}$ need to be offloaded to end devices for execution and one application consists of several independent subtasks. We assume that there are K subtasks in one application, the set of subtasks is denoted by T_i and $T_i = \{t_{i(1)}, t_{i(2)}, \cdots . t_{i(k)}\}$. Let $r_{i(k)}$ be the requested number of resources for subtask $t_{i(k)}$. We consider that there are m end devices in $D = \{d_1, d_2, \cdots, d_m\}$ participate in computation offloading. Each of the end devices is equipped with limited computational resources. Without loss of generality, we assume there are many kinds of resources required to complete the subtasks, e.g., CPU, memory, battery, etc. For end devices, each bid in $S = \{S_1, S_2, \cdots, S_n\}$ is submitted to auctioneer before offloading subtasks. The bid $S_j \in S$ can be specified as (o_j, q_j), o_j denotes the maximum amount of resources end device d_j can provide and q_j denotes the true unit cost of resources produced by end device d_j when executing the application offloaded onto it. For applications, the bids in $B = \{b_1, b_2, \cdots, b_n\}$ can be specified as $\{< r_{i(1)}, a_{i(1)} >, < r_{i(2)}, a_{i(2)} >, \cdots, < r_{i(k)}, a_{i(k)} >\}$, where $r_{i(k)}$ denotes the amount of resources for the subtask $t_{i(k)}$ of application T_i required and $a_{i(k)}$ denotes the initial valuation that the application T_i is willing to pay for subtask $t_{i(k)}$. Due to the heterogeneous preferences, buyers will adjust their bids based on different computing capabilities of end devices when bidding, so each valuation $v_{i(k)}$ of application T_i can be specified as $\{v_{i(k)1}, v_{i(k)2}, \cdots, v_{i(k)m}\}$, where $v_{i(k)j}$ denotes the valuation of subtask $t_{i(k)}$.

For simplicity, we define an $M * N$ allocation matrix denoted by X. The element x_{ij} in matrix X is defined as:

$$x_{ij} = \begin{cases} 1, & \text{if device } d_j \text{ serves application } T_i, \\ 0, & \text{otherwise.} \end{cases} \tag{1}$$

3.2 Problem Formulation

From the definitions above, we can see that each subtask can get the demanded resources from end devices, but considering the limitation of resources on each end devices, we have the following constraint:

$$\sum_{i=1}^{n}\sum_{k=1}^{K} x_{ij}s_{i(k)j} < o_j, \tag{2}$$

where $s_{i(k)j}$ is the amount of resources allocated to the k-th subtask of application T_i by end device d_j. And o_j is the maximum quantity of resources that the end device d_j can provide to applications.

And the final payment of an application can not be more than the valuation the application willing to pay. Thus:

$$\sum_{j=1}^{m}\sum_{k=1}^{K} x_{ij}s_{i(k)j}p_{ij} < \sum_{j=1}^{m}\sum_{k=1}^{K} x_{ij}f_{i(k)j}, \tag{3}$$

which $f_{i(k)j}$ is the application T_i's valuation for the subtask $t_{i(k)}$ when subtask $t_{i(k)}$ is offloaded to end device d_j. We define it as follows:

$$f_{i(k)j} = \begin{cases} v_{i(k)j}, & \text{if subtask } t_{i(k)j} \text{ is offloaded to device } d_j, \\ 0, & \text{otherwise.} \end{cases} \tag{4}$$

For the final valuation $v_{i(k)j}$ of subtask, it is consist of base valuations and abilities of end devices, the $v_{i(k)j}$ is then calculated as:

$$v_{i(k)j} = a_{i(k)} + k_1\frac{w_j}{Ceff_j} + k_2\frac{r_{i(k)j}}{Deff_j}, \tag{5}$$

where k_1 is set to be 10^{-6} and k_2 is set to be 10^{-5} [17]. And w_j denotes the workload of end device d_j, $Deff_j$ and $Ceff_j$ denote device specific data transfer and computing efficiencies respectively.

Let p_{ij} denote the final unit trade price that applications T_i pay for end device d_j. Then, for each application T_i, it's utility can be given by:

$$u_i = \sum_{j=1}^{m}\sum_{k=1}^{K} x_{ij}\big(f_{i(k)j} - s_{i(k)j}p_{ij}\big). \tag{6}$$

The utility of end device d_j, gained from selling resources can be given by:

$$u_j = \sum_{i=1}^{n}\sum_{k=1}^{K} x_{ij}s_{i(k)j}(p_{ij} - q_j), \tag{7}$$

which is the final utility end device get by executing subtasks for others.

Hence, sharing of resources of end devices for task offloading becomes a system utility maximization problem. We formulate the problem as follows:

$$\max \sum_{i=1}^{n} u_i + \sum_{j=1}^{m} u_j \tag{8}$$

$$s.t. \quad \sum_{i=1}^{n} \sum_{k=1}^{K} x_{ij} s_{i(k)j} < o_j, \forall 1 \leq i \leq n, 1 \leq k \leq K, \tag{9}$$

$$\sum_{j=1}^{m} \sum_{k=1}^{K} x_{ij} s_{i(k)j} p_{ij} < \sum_{j=1}^{m} \sum_{k=1}^{K} x_{ij} f_{i(k)j}, \forall 1 \leq j \leq m, 1 \leq k \leq K, \tag{10}$$

$$x_{ij} \in \{0,1\}, \forall 1 \leq i \leq n, 1 \leq j \leq m. \tag{11}$$

Equation (8) is the final optimization target. The constraint in (9) denotes that the overall amount of resources allocated by end device d_j is no more than the maximum quantity o_j. The constraint in (10) denotes that the overall amount of payment by application T_i is no more than the maximum valuation it willing to pay. The constraint in (11) is the binary constraint.

According to [10, 18], we can see that the winning bids determination problem of the proposed incentive mechanism is NP-hard just as similar as 0–1 Knapsack problem.

3.3 Economic Properties

The goal of our work is to design an efficient mechanism to solve the above problems. The designed mechanism should satisfy the following economic properties:

1. **Individual rationality:** Individual rationality means that no winner's utility is negative, i.e., $u_i \geq 0, u_j \geq 0$, for $\forall t_i \in T, d_i \in D$. For each participant, this is the most basic condition for participation.
2. **Budget balance:** For an fair incentive mechanism, the total payment of users is no less than the total price charged by providers. It means the utility of auctioneer is negative, auctioneer doesn't pay extra surplus.
3. **Truthfulness:** An incentive mechanism is truthful if the bid submitted by each participator is the truthful value.

In the next section, we proposed the NESTLE algorithm to solve the above problems.

4   Incentive Mechanism

In this section, we design a NESTLE algorithm based on a greedy strategy to solve the NP-hard problem proposed above, i.e., the winning bids determination problem. Then, we analyze the properties of the proposed NESTLE algorithm.

4.1   Resource Allocation and Pricing Algorithm

First, auctioneer collects each bid from all applications and end devices. Then, the auctioneer calculates the bid density of each application on each end device, i.e.,

$$bd_{ij} = \frac{\sum\limits_{i=1}^{n} v_{i(k)j}}{\sum\limits_{i=1}^{n} r_{i(k)}}, \quad \forall 1 \le i \le n, \forall 1 \le j \le m, 1 \le k \le K. \tag{12}$$

Then we use p_{ij} to denote the final trade unit price, when subtasks of application T_i is allocated to end device d_j. Similar to [22], the value of p_{ij} is calculated as

$$p_{ij} = \frac{q_j + bd_{ij}}{2}. \tag{13}$$

Due to the trade price, auctioneer will sort the difference between bid density of buyer and unit price of the seller in descending order.

The difference between bid density of applications and unit price of end devices are sorted in descending order. That means to the same end device, the higher the valuation that application is willing to pay, the higher the rate that subtasks in the application are executed. And to the same end device, the lower the unit price of resources, the higher the rate that the end device gets subtasks to execute.

The next step is to allocate subtasks of applications to end devices. For each application T_i and end device d_i in the queue that has been prioritized, if the difference between bid density of application T_i and unit price of end device d_i is positive, the allocation will start. If the resource requirements $r_{i(k)}$ of the subtasks $t_{i(k)}$ is less than the resource quantity o_j and the application's payment does not exceed it's valuation, the subtask $t_{i(k)}$ will be offloaded to the end device d_j. If the current end device d_j can not satisfy the subtask $t_{i(k)}$, the end device will match the next subtask and the subtask will match the next end device. When all the requirements of the application are satisfied or the resources of the end device are insufficient, the searching and matching procedure will continue. The details of the above process of NESTLE algorithm are described in Algorithm 1.

4.2   Theoretical Analysis

Now, we analyze the time complexity and economic properties of the NESTLE algorithm mentioned above. The properties include: individual rationality, budget balance and truthfulness.

Theorem 1. *The time complexity of NESTLE algorithm is $O(nm)$.*

Proof. For Algorithm 1, the complexity for sorting the bid density is $O(nm)$, and the resources allocation phase is $O(nmK)$. Therefore, the complexity of algorithm 1 is $O(nm)$, when $n \gg K$ and $m \gg K$. Therefore NESTLE algorithm can be completed in polynomial time.

Algorithm 1. NESTLE algorithm

Input :
   M : the number of end devices;
   N : the number of applications;
   K : the number of subtasks;
Output:
   C : the charges for applications;
   F : the payments to end devices;

1   **Phase 1: Order the applications and end devices**
2   $E \leftarrow \emptyset$
3   **for** $i = 1$ *to* n **do**
4   **for** $j = 1$ *to* m **do**
5        $bd_{ij} = \sum_{k=1}^{K} v_{i(k)j} / \sum_{k=1}^{K} r_{i(k)}$
6   **end**
7   **end**
8   **for** $i = 1$ *to* n **do**
9   **for** $j = 1$ *to* m **do**
10        $e_{ij} = bd_{ij} - q_j$
11        $E = E \cup e_{ij}$
12   **end**
13   **end**
14   Sort $e_{ij} \in E$ in descending order
15   **Phase 2: Allocate the applications**
16   $X_{n*m} \leftarrow \emptyset$
17   $D \leftarrow \emptyset$
18   **for** $\forall e_{ij} \in E$ **do**
19   **if** $e_{ij} < 0$ **then**
20   continue
21   **end**
22   **for** $k = 1$ *to* K **do**
23   **if** $r_{i(k)} > o_j || D_i + cost > valuation$ **then**
24   continue
25   **end**
26        $o_j = o_j - r_{i(k)}$
27        $D_i = D_i + cost$
28        $s_{i(k)j} = r_{i(k)}$
29        $X_{ij} \leftarrow 1$
30   **end**
31   **end**
32   **Phase 3: Calculate the charges and payments**
33   $P \leftarrow \emptyset$
34   **for** $j = 1$ *to* m **do**
35   **for** $k = 1$ *to* K **do**
36        $p_j = \sum_{j=1}^{m} \sum_{k=1}^{K} X_{ij} s_{i(k)j} p_{ij}$
37        $F \leftarrow F \cup p_j$
38   **end**
39   **end**
40   $C \leftarrow \emptyset$
41   **for** $i = 1$ *to* n **do**
42   **for** $k = 1$ *to* K **do**
43        $c_j = \sum_{i=1}^{n} \sum_{k=1}^{K} X_{ij} s_{i(k)j} p_{ij}$
44        $C \leftarrow C \cup c_j$
45   **end**
46   **end**

Theorem 2. *The participants in the proposed schemes are individual rational.*

Proof. For winner of applications: if the subtasks $t_{i(k)}$ is allocated to device d_j successfully, the payment it willing to pay is:

$$c_{i(k)} = v_{i(k)j} = r_{i(k)} b d_{ij}. \tag{14}$$

The p_{ij} is the unite trade price between application T_i and end device d_j. According to the algorithm process, the actual payment $\widehat{c}_{i(k)}$ is:

$$\widehat{c}_{i(k)} = r_{i(k)} p_{ij}. \tag{15}$$

When the allocation is successful, the transaction price is lower than the expected payment price, i.e., $\widehat{c}_{i(k)} \leq c_{i(k)}$. Hence, the applications' individual rationality is guaranteed.

For winner of end devices: if an end device is allocated subtasks. The payment it expects is:

$$y_j = \sum_{j=1}^{m} \sum_{k=1}^{K} x_{ij} s_{i(k)j} q_j. \tag{16}$$

And the final actual transaction price is:

$$\widehat{y}_j = \sum_{j=1}^{m} \sum_{k=1}^{K} x_{ij} s_{i(k)j} p_{ij}. \tag{17}$$

When allocation is successful, it's actual charge is more than it's valuation, i.e., $y_j < \widehat{y}_j$, otherwise the subtask won't be allocated to it.

Theorem 3. *The incentive mechanism proposed is budget balance. For auctioneer, the payment of applications is no less than the charge of end devices.*

Proof. In the proposed incentive mechanism, according to the Eqs. (15) and (17), the relation between charge and payment is:

$$\widehat{y}_j = \sum_{i=1}^{n} \sum_{k=1}^{K} x_{ij} \widehat{c}_{i(k)}. \tag{18}$$

We can see that the total charge $\widehat{y}_j$ of an end device is equal to the amount of the payment $\widehat{c}_{i(k)}$ of subtasks allocated to the end device. Hence, the budget balance is also guaranteed.

Theorem 4. *The incentive mechanism proposed above is truthful.*

Proof. We prove the truthfulness from respects of applications and end devices.

For applications, there are two cases as follows:

Case 1. We assume that an application T_i is allocated resources. If the application T_i bids an higher bid, the application task will pay more for getting the same service. If the application T_i bids an lower bid, the subtasks of it still be not executed.

Case 2. We assume that a task T_i isn't allocated resources. if the task t_i bids an higher bid, task may either pay more for getting the same service or still be not executed. If the task t_i bids an lower bid, the task still be not executed.

For end devices, there are two cases as follows:

Case 1. We assume that an end device d_j is allocated subtasks. If the end device d_j bids an lower bid, the end device may get charge less than it's cost of executing subtasks. If the end device d_j bids an higher bid, it may not be allocated subtasks.

Case 2. We assume that an end device d_j isn't allocated subtasks. If the end device d_j bids an lower bid, the end device may either get charge less than it's cost of executing subtasks or get no subtasks. If the end device d_j bids an higher bid, it still be not allocated subtasks.

5 Simulation Results

In this section, we conduct extensive simulation experiments to evaluate the performance of the proposed incentive mechanism. The criteria we evaluated are: (i) utility, which is the sum utility of applications and end devices, (ii) satisfaction ratio, which is the percentage between the amount of allocated subtasks and the amount of all subtasks and (iii) allocation efficiency, which is the proportion between the number of utilized resources and the number of all resources.

5.1 Methodology

To better illustrate the performance of the proposed NESTLE algorithm, in this paper, one contrast experiments i.e., WBD [19], are added. WBD here achieves subtasks allocation by a multi-round homogeneous task allocation mechanism.

We evaluate the proposed algorithm by implementing it on matlab 2017a [1]. In the simulation process, we assume that there are at most 900 applications to be allocated and at most 35 end devices to provide resources [4]. We take the average value of each data after running the program for 1000 times.

5.2 Simulation Setting

We evaluate the proposed algorithm with random bids behaviors. To generate applications' bids, we assume that the resource demand for each subtask of the application is randomly generated from 0 to 5 [4]. The value of applications' bid is randomly generated in $[1, 5.5]$. And we assume there are 3 subtasks in each application. To generate end devices' bid, we assume that the amount of resources end device can provide is a random number that does not exceed 1000, and the unit price of the resources is randomly selected from [0, 1]. For end devices, the workload is randomly generated in [100, 1000], the computing efficiencies is randomly generated in [400, 500] and the data transfer efficiencies randomly generated from 300 to 400 [17].

5.3   Simulation Results

First, we examine the impact of both the numbers of applications and end devices on total utility of NESTLE and WBD. Figure 1 shows the relationships between the number of end devices and the total utility, when number of end devices is fixed at $n = 500$ and the ratio between the number of end devices and the number of one application's subtask is fixed at 5. For ease of understanding, we divide the total utility into 100 units in the figure. It is shown in Fig. 1 that the total utility increases with increasing number of end devices. As we can see, the utility of NESTLE increase faster than WBD. That is because that with the number of end devices increasing, more subtasks are executed, at the same time subtasks will be served by devices with better computing abilities. That will improve the valuation of application and the utility. Since WBD can not allocate the subtasks with higher utility preferentially all the time, the increase of it's utility is not obvious. As we can see, on average, NESTLE outperforms WBD by about 35.64%.

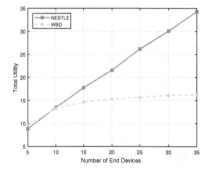

Fig. 1. Total utility with number of end devices

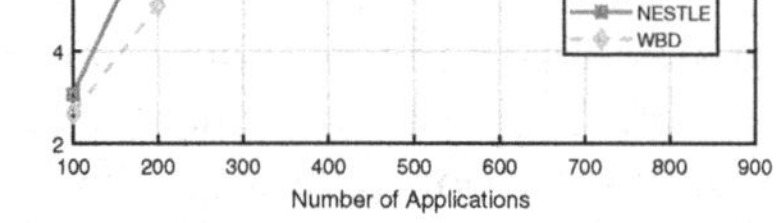

Fig. 2. Total utility with number of applications

Figure 2 shows the total utility versus the number of applications when the number of end devices is fixed at $m = 5$. As we can see, the total utility grows with increasing number of applications. This happens due to the fact that more applications participated cause that more subtasks are executed, then the total utilities are improved. Clearly, the total utility of NESTLE algorithm is higher than WBD. On average, NESTLE outperforms WBD by about 36.9%.

Then, Fig. 3 compares the satisfaction ratio and the number of applications generated by WBD. As we can see, larger number of applications will lead to smaller satisfaction ratio. When the number of applications becomes larger, limited resources and the fact that only part of the subtasks can be served make satisfaction ratio smaller. Because valuation of applications are effected by preference to end devices, the satisfaction ratio of NESTLE is much higher than WBD when number of applications is small. With increasing number of applications, more subtask will be served and this effect will decrease. We can see in Fig. 3 that the NESTLE has a significant advantage over WBD on satisfaction ratio. On average, the NESTLE outperforms WBD by about 111.86% in terms of satisfaction ratio.

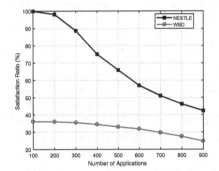

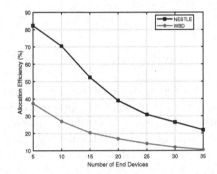

Fig. 3. Satisfaction with number of applications

Fig. 4. Total efficiency with number of end devices

Figures 4 and 5 investigate the impact of both the number of applications and the number of end devices on allocation efficiency generated by NESTLE and WBD. Figure 4 shows the allocation efficiency versus the number of end devices when the number of applications is fixed at $n = 500$. As we can see, in Fig. 4,

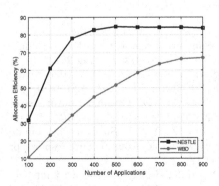

Fig. 5. Total efficiency with number of applications

the allocation efficiency decreases with increasing number of end devices. That is because when the number of end devices becomes larger, most of application requirements are met, then the percentage of utilized resources decreases. We can get that on average, the allocation efficiency of NESTLE outperforms WBD by about 102.19%.

Figure 5 shows the allocation efficiency versus the number of applications when the number of end devices is fixed at $m = 5$. It is shown that the allocation efficiency of two algorithms increase with increasing number of applications. When the number of applications is below 300, the allocation efficiency of NESTLE increases fast with the increasing number of applications. However when the number of applications greater than 300, the allocation efficiency of NESTLE reaches a constant value. That is because that with the constraint of price and request, there always are some resources can not be used by each applications. On average, NESTLE outperforms WBD by about 81.71%.

6   Conclusion

In this paper, we have considered independent subtasks of application allocation in LEC and have proposed an incentive mechanism. The proposed mechanism has considered the heterogeneous preferences for the computing power of end devices. Through theoretical analysis, we have proved the proposed mechanism is individual-rational, truthful and budget-balanced. At the same time, we have demonstrates that our mechanism is efficient and feasible by conducting simulations.

Acknowledgement. This work was supported by the National Natural Science Foundation of China under Grant Nos. 61702115 and 61672171, Natural Science Foundation of Guangdong, China under Grant No. 2018B030311007, and Major R&D Project of Educational Commission of Guangdong under Grant No. 2016KZDXM052. This work was also supported by China Postdoctoral Science Foundation Fund under Grant No. 2017M622632. The corresponding author is Jigang Wu (asjgwucn@outlook.com).

References

1. Mathworks releases release 2017a with matlab and simulink product lines. https://ww2.mathworks.cn/company/newsroom/mathworks-announces-release-2017a-of-the-matlab-and-simulink-pro. Accessed 6 Aug 2017
2. Ahmed, A., Ahmed, E.: A survey on mobile edge computing. In: International Conference on Intelligent Systems and Control (2016)
3. Chaisiri, S., Lee, B.S., Niyato, D.: Optimization of resource provisioning cost in cloud computing. IEEE Trans. Serv. Comput. **5**(2), 164–177 (2012)
4. Chen, L., Huang, L., Sun, Z., Xu, H.: Spectrum combinatorial double auction for cognitive radio network with ubiquitous network resource providers. IET Commun. **9**(17), 2085–2094 (2015)
5. Chen, L., Wu, J., Dai, H.N., Huang, X.: Brains: joint bandwidth-relay allocation in multi-homing cooperative D2D networks. IEEE Trans. Veh. Technol. (2018). https://doi.org/10.1109/TSC.2018.2792024

6. Chen, L., Wu, J., Long, X., Zhang, Z.: ENGINE: cost effective offloading in mobile edge computing with fog-cloud cooperation (2017)
7. Chen, L., Wu, J., Zhang, X.X., Zhou, G.: TARCO: two-stage auction for D2D relay aided computation resource allocation in hetnet. IEEE Trans. Serv. Comput. **PP**(99), 1 (2017)
8. Chen, X., Zhang, J.: When D2D meets cloud: Hybrid mobile task offloadings in fog computing. In: IEEE International Conference on Communications, pp. 1–6 (2017)
9. Cuervo, E., et al.: MAUI: making smartphones last longer with code offload. In: International Conference on Mobile Systems, Applications, and Services, pp. 49–62 (2010)
10. Dong, M., Sun, G., Wang, X., Zhang, Q.: Combinatorial auction with time-frequency flexibility in cognitive radio networks, vol. 131, no. 5, pp. 2282–2290 (2012)
11. Gao, G., Xiao, M., Wu, J., Han, K., Huang, L., Zhao, Z.: Opportunistic mobile data offloading with deadline constraints. IEEE Trans. Parallel Distrib. Syst. **PP**(99), 1 (2017)
12. Hu, Y.C., Patel, M., Sabella, D., Sprecher, N., Young, V.: Mobile edge computing a key technology towards 5g. ETSI White Pap. **11**, 1–16 (2015)
13. Lu, L., Yu, J., Zhu, Y., Li, M.: A double auction mechanism to bridge users? Task requirements and providers? Resources in two-sided cloud markets. IEEE Trans. Parallel Distrib. Syst. **29**(4), 720–733 (2018)
14. Lu, Z., Zhao, J., Wu, Y., Cao, G.: Task allocation for mobile cloud Computing in heterogeneous wireless networks. In: International Conference on Computer Communication and Networks, pp. 1–9 (2015)
15. Luo, S., Sun, Y., Wen, Z., Ji, Y.: C2: truthful incentive mechanism for multiple cooperative tasks in mobile cloud. In: IEEE International Conference on Communications (2016)
16. Lyu, X., Tian, H., Sengul, C., Zhang, P.: Multiuser joint task offloading and resource optimization in proximate clouds. IEEE Trans. Veh. Technol. **66**(4), 3435–3447 (2017)
17. Miettinen, A.P., Nurminen, J.K.: Energy efficiency of mobile clients in cloud computing. In: Usenix Conference on Hot Topics in Cloud Computing, p. 4 (2010)
18. Vries, S.D., Vohra, R.V.: Combinatorial auctions: a survey. Inform. J. Comput. **15**(3), 284–309 (2003)
19. Wang, X., Chen, X., Wu, W.: Towards truthful auction mechanisms for task assignment in mobile device clouds. In: IEEE INFOCOM 2017 IEEE Conference on Computer Communications, pp. 1–9 (2017)
20. Wang, X., Chen, X., Wu, W., An, N., Wang, L.: Cooperative application execution in mobile cloud computing: a stackelberg game approach. IEEE Commun. Lett. **20**(5), 946–949 (2016)
21. Yi, X., Liu, F., Li, Z., Jin, H.: Flexible instance: meeting deadlines of delay tolerant jobs in the cloud with dynamic pricing. In: IEEE International Conference on Distributed Computing Systems, pp. 415–424 (2016)
22. Liu, Y., Liu, K., MA, X., Yang, M.: Pricing in combinatorial double auction-based grid allocation model. J. China Univ. Posts Telecommun. **16**(3), 59–65 (2009)

23. Zhang, H., Guo, F., Ji, H., Zhu, C.: Combinational auction based service provider selection in mobile edge computing networks. IEEE Access **PP**(99), 1 (2017)
24. Zhang, Z., Wu, J., Jiang, G., Chen, L., Lam, S.K.: QoE-aware task offloading for time constraint mobile applications. In: Local Computer Networks, pp. 510–513 (2017)
25. Zhou, G., Wu, J., Chen, L., Jiang, G., Lam, S.K.: Efficient three-stage auction schemes for cloudlets deployment in wireless access network. Wirel. Netw., 1–15 (2018)

A Study on Emotion Recognition Based on Hierarchical Adaboost Multi-class Algorithm

Song Zhang[1,2], Bin Hu[1,2(✉)], Tiantian Li[3], and Xiangwei Zheng[1,2]

[1] School of Information Science and Engineering,
Shandong Normal University, Ji'nan 250014, China
binhu@sdnu.edu.cn
[2] Shandong Provincial Key Laboratory for Distributed Computer Software
Novel Technology, Ji'nan 250014, China
[3] Faculty of Education, Shandong Normal University, Ji'nan 250014, China

Abstract. Researches on human emotion recognition have attracted more and more people's interest. Adaboost algorithm is an integrated algorithm that constructs strong classifiers by iterative aggregation of weak classifiers. This paper proposes a hierarchical Adaboost (HAdaboost) multi-class algorithm for emotion recognition, which improves the original Adaboost algorithm. The valence and arousal in different emotional states are used as classification features, and emotion recognition is performed according to their differences. Simulation experiments on the Chinese Facial Affective Picture System (CFAPS) data set demonstrate three types of emotions and seven types of emotions can be distinguished, and the average accuracy rates are 93% and 92.4% respectively.

Keywords: Emotion recognition
Hierarchical Adaboost Multi-class Algorithm · Integrated weak classifier

1 Introduction

Emotion recognition through some physiological data of the human body is the trend of scientific research. Physiological data has evolved from traditional small sample data collection to big data shared on the Internet [1]. Emotion recognition becomes one of hot topics in the field of psychology research. The research of emotion recognition can be roughly divided into speech emotion recognition, facial picture emotion recognition, text emotion recognition, audio emotion recognition and physiological signal emotion recognition.

Emotional recognition based on physiological data tends to be diversified. Researchers in different fields have paid their attention to the study of emotion recognition. Researchers in the field of computers have studied physiological signals such as EEG, ECG, and pictures. They explore their relationships through deep learning. Facial images can be scored from four dimensions [2]. (1) Potency (valence): the unit of potency that causes a biological reaction. (2) Arousal: the degree to which people are excited or not. (3) Dominance: the likelihood that a certain emotion will be

J. Vaidya and J. Li (Eds.): ICA3PP 2018, LNCS 11335, pp. 105–113, 2018.
https://doi.org/10.1007/978-3-030-05054-2_8

stimulated. (4) Attraction: the degree of attractiveness of facial expression pictures to the subject. A large number of studies have shown that valence and arousal will alter with the change of emotional state.

This paper adopts the CFAPS data set which is more consistent with Chinese facial emotions and proposes a hierarchical Adaboost (HAdaboost) multi-class algorithm to overcome the disadvantage that Adaboost algorithm can only perform two classifications [3]. The HAdaboost algorithm can be directly used for multi classification research and it is suitable for emotion recognition.

2 Related Work

The emotion recognition attracts more and more attention from researchers.

Khosrowabadi et al. used EEG signals as the original data of emotion recognition. EEG features were extracted using the amplitude square consistency of EEG signal. The self-organizing mapping method is used to classify the emotional state of the sample, which has achieved good results [4]. Petrantonakis extracted EG1, FP2, F3, F4 and other EEG signals, using high-order channel feature extraction method. They employed support vector machine algorithm for emotion recognition and the accuracy rate is can reach 83.33% [5]. Murugappan et al. performed Laplacian variation and wavelet transform on EEG signals. They recognized six emotions by linear classifier, and used entropy as a feature for emotion recognition and the accuracy rate can reach 83.04% [6].

Zhang et al. proposed a new emotion recognition system based on expression images. They adopted biorthogonal wavelet entropy to extract multi-scale features and used fuzzy multi-class support vector machine as emotion recognition classifier. The accuracy of their method is 96.77 + 0.10% [7]. Cheng et al. analyzed the surface EMG signal by wavelet transform method and extracted the maximum and minimum wavelet structure coefficient vector. They applied the BP neural network classifier improved by Levenberg-Marquardt algorithm and the nearest neighbor classifier to perform emotion recognition. The average recognition accuracy was 82.29% [8]. Li et al. retained the feature that the cumulative contribution rate was greater than 85%, and selected the characteristic parameters with large difference in feature roots. They implemented emotional state assessment based on support vector machines and the accuracy rate can reach 85% [9].

The existing research has carried out at most six emotion classifications, and the emotion recognition algorithm needs to be improved in terms of accuracy. Therefore, the HAdaboost algorithm is adopted to recognize three kinds of emotions and seven kinds of emotions respectively.

Fig. 1. Emotion recognition process

3   Emotion Recognition Process

Emotion recognition process is described in Fig. 1. Details of each step are as follows.

(1) **Datasets:** This paper adopts the CFAPS as the data set.
(2) **Preprocessing:** The data set is processed to form two data sets of three emotions and seven emotions. The three emotional states are negative emotions, calm emotions and positive emotions; the seven emotional states are anger, disgust, fear, sad, surprise, calmness and happiness.
(3) **Emotion recognition:** After the data is preprocessed, the data sets are input into the Adaboost algorithm and the HAdaboost algorithm for emotion recognition. The weak classifier is formed by the SVM.
(4) **Analysis of the results:** The classified emotional markers are compared to the emotional markers of the original data. The classification accuracy rate of each emotional state and the classification accuracy of all emotional states are calculated.

4   Emotion Recognition Based on Hierarchical Adaboost Multi-class Algorithm

4.1   Original Adaboost Algorithm

The AdaBoost algorithm ensures that the learning algorithm is gradually focused on training samples that are difficult to process. For samples that are difficult to process, combining the results of each weak classifier after centralized learning can greatly improve the classification accuracy [10]. The principle is shown in Fig. 2.

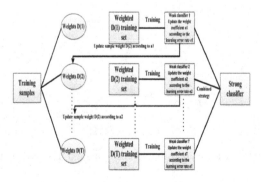

Fig. 2. Adaboost algorithm

4.2   Description of Algorithm

Hierarchical Adaboost Multi-class Algorithm is described as follows.

Algorithm 1:

Input:

Data: data set of the Chinese Facial Affective Picture System (CFAPS)

Function (): hierarchical Adaboost multi-class algorithm (HAdaboost)

Label: mark identification completed

All_Label: complete classification

Comparison: the emotion markers of the classified data are compared with the
         emotion markers of the original data one by one

Output:

     Accuracy

Begin:

  Input Data

  Execute Function ()

  While (All_Label) do

     For (0: Label-1) do

       Execute Function ()

     End For

  End While

  Execute Storage Model

  Execute Comparison and Get Accuracy

End

The HAdaboost algorithm can recognize an emotional state at the end of each layer. The number of algorithm layers is automatically changed according to the kind of emotional state. Therefore, as the number of layers increases, the emotional states to be recognized will be reduced, and the complexity of the algorithm will be reduced. The accuracy of HAdaboost algorithm is higher than that of Adaboost algorithm in emotion recognition. The principle of the algorithm is shown in Fig. 3.

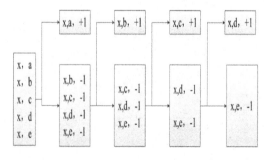

Fig. 3. Hierarchical Adaboost multi-class emotion recognition algorithm

4.3 Training and Testing

Data is divided into training and testing sets, and initialized weights of training samples. D_1 represents the weight set of the data set, N represents the number of samples, and ω represents the weight of each sample (generally the initial weight is set to $1/N$); as in formula (1).

$$D_1 = (\omega_{11}, \omega_{12}, \cdots, \omega_{1i}, \cdots, \omega_{1N}), \omega_{1i} = \frac{1}{N}, i = 1, 2, \cdots, N \qquad (1)$$

Establishing one-against-all (OAA) and one-against-one (OAO) classifiers for training and testing respectively.

After each iterating process, calculate the error rate of the weak classifier according to formula (2). $G_m(x_i)$ is the first i classifier after m iterations, and y_i is the judgement of the i sample.

$$e_m = P(G_m(x_i) \neq y_i) = \sum_{i=1}^{N} \omega_{mi} I(G_m(x_i) \neq y_i) \qquad (2)$$

After iterating m times, the scale factor a_m of each weak classifier in the final classifier is determined according to the error rate of the weak classifier.

$$a_m = \frac{1}{2} \log \frac{1 - e_m}{e_m} \qquad (3)$$

Updating the weights of all OAA classifiers according to formulas (4) and (5); D_{m+1} is the set of sample weights after $m + 1$ iterations; $\omega_{m+1,i}$ is the weight of the ith sample after $m + 1$ iterations. Z_m is the normalized processing amount;

$$D_{m+1} = (\omega_{m+1,1}, \omega_{m+1,2}, \cdots, \omega_{m+1,i}, \cdots, \omega_{m+1,N}) \qquad (4)$$

$$\omega_{m+1,i} = \frac{\omega_{mi}}{Z_m} \exp(-a_m y_i G_m(x_i)), i = 1, 2, \cdots, N \qquad (5)$$

The testing set is input into the algorithm, and the OAO classifier (6) is called to recognize the emotion by voting mechanism.

$$f(x) = \sum_{m=1}^{M} a_m G_m(x) \qquad (6)$$

5   Experimental Results and Analysis

5.1   Datasets

This paper conducts simulation experiments based on the CFAPS data set. (http:// psycnet.apa.org/record/2011-05085-005). This data set contains 600 facial emotion pictures totally. Facial pictures were screened and matched according to the nature and the emotional type and the gender of the characters. There are 200 negative faces, 200 neutral faces and 200 positive faces. In addition, negative faces are divided into five negative emotions: anger, disgust, fear, sadness and surprise. Face images are scored in four dimensions: valence, arousal, dominance, and attraction.

5.2   Result Analysis

In this paper, the Adaboost algorithm and the HAdaboost algorithm are adopted for the experiment of emotion recognition. Comparing the accuracy of two algorithms for emotion recognition on CFAPS data set. It proves the feasibility and superiority of the HAdaboost algorithm.

This paper mainly classifies three kinds of emotions and seven kinds of emotions. The average recognition accuracy of each emotion state is calculated as the final recognition accuracy. We first introduce the recognition experiment of the three kinds of emotions. The results are shown in Figs. 4 and 5.

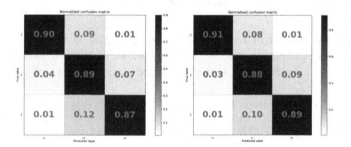

Fig. 4. Confusion matrix of positive, calm and negative emotions (Adaboost)

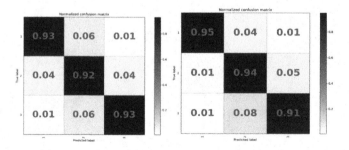

Fig. 5. Confusion matrix of positive, calm and negative emotions (HAdaboost)

The experimental results are shown into Table 1.

Table 1. Classification results of positive, calm and negative emotions

Emotion Group	Adaboost			HAdaboost		
	Negative	Calm	Positive	Negative	Calm	Positive
1	0.91	0.88	0.89	0.93	0.92	0.93
2	0.90	0.89	0.87	0.95	0.94	0.91
3	0.91	0.88	0.89	0.96	0.90	0.93
Mean	0.907	0.883	0.883	0.947	0.92	0.923

It can be seen from Table 1 that the HAdaboost multi-class algorithm is more accurate than the Adaboost algorithm in the recognition of negative emotions, calm emotions and positive emotions. The average accuracy rate of Adaboost algorithm for emotion recognition is 89.1%. The average accuracy rate of the HAdaboost algorithm proposed for this paper is 93%, which is 4% points higher than the Adaboost algorithm. Then, we will introduce the recognition experiment of the seven kinds of emotions. The results are shown in Figs. 6 and 7.

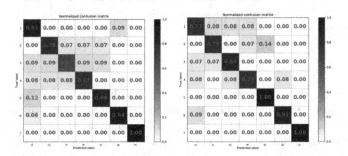

Fig. 6. Confusion matrix of seven emotions (Adaboost)

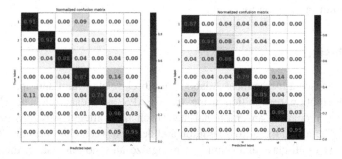

Fig. 7. Confusion matrix of seven emotions (HAdaboost)

Tables 2 and 3 show the experimental results of seven emotions.

Table 2. Emotion recognition classification results (Adaboost)

Emotion Group	Anger	Disgust	Fear	Sad	Surprise	Calm	Happy	Mean
1	0.73	0.69	0.64	0.78	0.94	1.00	1.00	0.833
2	0.91	0.79	0.64	0.77	0.88	0.94	1.00	0.845
3	0.77	0.79	0.86	0.77	1.00	0.91	1.00	0.857
4	0.82	0.83	0.81	0.84	0.79	0.90	0.94	0.858
5	0.76	0.78	0.78	0.75	0.92	0.94	0.97	0.843
Mean	0.798	0.776	0.746	0.782	0.906	0.938	0.982	0.847

Table 3. Emotion recognition classification results (HAdaboost)

Emotion Group	Anger	Disgust	Fear	Sad	Surprise	Calm	Happy	Mean
1	0.87	0.84	0.88	0.79	0.85	0.95	0.95	0.917
2	0.78	0.92	0.88	0.89	0.85	0.97	0.95	0.929
3	0.87	0.88	0.76	0.79	0.81	0.98	0.96	0.926
4	0.91	0.92	0.88	0.82	0.78	0.96	0.95	0.924
5	0.92	0.89	0.84	0.87	0.89	0.98	0.97	0.922
Mean	0.87	0.890	0.848	0.832	0.836	0.968	0.956	0.924

It can be clearly seen from Tables 2 and 3 that the accuracy of the HAdaboost multi-class algorithm is higher than the Adaboost algorithm in the recognition of five emotional states of anger, disgust, fear, sadness and calmness. The average accuracy of the HAdaboost algorithm was 7.2% points higher than that of the Adaboost algorithm. Moreover, in the overall classification accuracy, the accuracy of the HAdaboost multi-class algorithm can reach 92.4%, which is 7.7% points higher than the 84.7% of the Adaboost algorithm. It proves the feasibility and accuracy of the HAdaboost multi-class algorithm in emotion recognition.

6   Conclusion

Tis paper proposes a hierarchical Adaboost multi-class algorithm and applies it to the research of emotion recognition using the CFAPS as a data set. The HAdaboost algorithm can recognize an emotional state each time after it performs an iterative calculation. The algorithm allows addition and deletion weak classifiers and each layer of HAdaboost multi-class algorithm can recognize an emotional state, therefore, the classification accuracy is improved.

Acknowledgements. National Natural Science Foundation of China (61373149) and the Taishan Scholars Program of Shandong Province, China. 2018 Shandong Social Science Planning Research Project (18CJYJ06).

References

1. Su Yun, H., Lixin, B.X., et al.: Knowledge modeling and emotion recognition for EEG data. Chin. Sci. Bull. **60**(11), 1002–1009 (2015)
2. Liu, W., Zheng, W.-L., Lu, B.-L.: Emotion recognition using multimodal deep learning. In: Hirose, A., Ozawa, S., Doya, K., Ikeda, K., Lee, M., Liu, D. (eds.) ICONIP 2016. LNCS, vol. 9948, pp. 521–529. Springer, Cham (2016). https://doi.org/10.1007/978-3-319-46672-9_58
3. Bui, D.T., Ho, T.C., Pradhan, B., et al.: GIS-based modeling of rainfall-induced landslides using data mining-based functional trees classifier with AdaBoost, Bagging, and MultiBoost ensemble frameworks. Environ. Earth Sci. **75**(14), 1–22 (2016)
4. Khosrowabadi, R., Quek, H.C., Wahab, A., et al.: EEG-based emotion recognition using self-organizing map for boundary detection. In: International Conference on Pattern Recognition, pp. 4242–4245. IEEE (2010)
5. Petrantonakis, P.C., Hadjileontiadis, L.J.: Emotion recognition from EEG using higher order crossings. IEEE Trans. Inf Technol. Biomed. **14**(2), 186 (2010)
6. Murugappan, M., Nagarajan, R., Yaacob, S.: Combining spatial filtering and wavelet transform for classifying human emotions using EEG signals. J. Med. Biol. Eng. **31**(1), 45–51 (2011)
7. Zhang, Y.D., Yang, Z.J., Lu, H.M., et al.: Facial emotion recognition based on biorthogonal wavelet entropy, fuzzy support vector machine, and stratified cross validation. IEEE Access **4**(99), 8375–8385 (2017)
8. Bo, C., Guangyuan, L.: Emotion recognition of surface EMG signals based on wavelet transform and neural network. J. Comput. Appl. **28**(2), 333–335 (2008)
9. Xin, L., Erjuan, C., Yanxiu, T., et al.: An improved EEG feature extraction algorithm and its application in emotion recognition. J. Biomed. Eng. **4**, 510–517 (2017)
10. Zhang, X., Ding, J.: An improved adaboost face detection algorithm based on the different sample weights. In: IEEE, International Conference on Computer Supported Cooperative Work in Design, pp. 436–439. IEEE (2016)

A Low Communication Overhead Breadth-First Search Based on Global Bitmap

Ziwei Peng[1,2($\boxtimes$)], Yutong Lu[1,2,3], Zhiguang Cheng[1,2,3], and Yunfei Du[2,3]

[1] College of Computer, National University of Defense Technology, Changsha 410073, China
peng_ziwei@foxmail.com
[2] National Supercomputer Center in Guangzhou, Guangzhou 510006, China
[3] School of Data and Computer Science, Sun Yat-sen University, Guangzhou 510006, China

Abstract. Breadth-First Search (BFS) is the underlying kernel algorithm for many graph applications such as social networks, medical informatics, transport systems, etc. Therefore, it has been absorbed as a core of Graph500, used to evaluate the capability of supercomputers in terms of big data processing. In this paper, we introduce into a global bitmap which is used to accelerate two approaches: the top-down and bottom-up. Specifically, the new top-down approach uses the global bitmap to indicate whether the vertices are visited or not, while the new bottom-up approach changes the frontier queue to the global bitmap to indicate whether the vertices are on the frontier. With the help of the global bitmap, the total number of communication messages produced by the BFS will be reduced significantly, and consequentially the BFS is accelerated. Meanwhile, our algorithm is optimized for storage on Knights Landing (KNL). We evaluate our proposal on both the KNL platform and the Tianhe-2 super-computer. Experimental results demonstrate that the communication was time reduced to roughly 1/4 of the original. We obtain speedups of 2.2–3.1 compared to the top-down approach.

Keywords: Graph500 · Breadth-First Search · Global bitmap
Hybrid approach

1 Introduction

Compared with traditional computing-intensive applications, big data applications present diffident characteristics, such as high parallelism, large volumes of data, irregular memory access modes, and poor temporal locality. These peculiarities introduce new challenges to the traditional computer architectures. Graph computing is a typical application belonging to this category. As a basic graph algorithm, breadth-first search (BFS) is a core component of many algorithms and has been widely used in many fields, such as social network, biology information, transport system, data mining, network security, semantic web and so on. To this end, the Graph500 benchmark (http://www.graph500.org/) suite [1] absorbs BFS as a kernel used to

© Springer Nature Switzerland AG 2018
J. Vaidya and J. Li (Eds.): ICA3PP 2018, LNCS 11335, pp. 114–129, 2018.
https://doi.org/10.1007/978-3-030-05054-2_9

evaluate the capability of supercomputers in terms of big data processing. Consequentially, BFS attracted more and more attention, and a large number of literatures involving the optimization of BFS have been published. Researchers have explored varied methods to accelerate the BFS on different architectures, including shared memory architecture [3–8], distributed memory architecture [9–14] and Heterogeneous System [16, 17].

Agarwal et al. [5] introduced into the bitmap data structure to represent the vertices accessed in BFS, increasing the locality of the data. Beamber et al. [7, 8] proposed a novel optimization on BFS which combines the top-down approach with the bottom-up approach. In this paper, we combine the above two methods and present a hybrid BFS algorithm based on a global bitmap which is used to indicate whether a vertex has been visited and whether a vertex is on the frontier. The bitmap helps to optimize both the top-down and bottom-up approaches by reducing the amount of communication messages significantly. For the top-down approach, we use the global bitmap to indicate whether the vertices are visited or not. So, we don't need to send lots of edge message to the owner processor of the failed child vertex. For the bottom-up approach we use the global bitmap to indicate whether the vertices are on the frontier. So, we can locally judge whether the parent vertex is on the frontier and don't need to send edge message to the owner processor of parent vertex. We evaluate our proposal on both the KNL platform and the Tianhe-2 supercomputer. Experimental results demonstrate that the hybird approach based on global bitmap is 1.9–2.4 faster than the direction-optimizing BFS. Meanwhile, we have optimized the computation of bottom-up approach and storage of the KNL coprocessor. Finally, we test our algorithm on the Tianhe-2 and KNL platforms, and obtains speedups of 2.2–3.1 compare to the top-down approach in Tianhe-2 supercomputer and more than 2.1 in KNL platform.

The rest of this paper is organized as follows. Section 2 describes the problems and challenges. The optimization of the BFS algorithm is discussed in Sect. 3. The experimental results are presented in Sect. 4, and the related work is presented in Sect. 5, followed by concluding remarks and directions for future work in Sect. 6.

2 Problem Description

2.1 Graph500

Data intensive applications become increasingly prevalent on supercomputers. Over time, High-Performance Linpack (HPL) and the Top500 could no longer perform as a comprehensive comparison of supercomputer performance. The Graph 500 list was announced at ISC2010 and the first list appeared at SC2010. Graph 500 will establish a set of large-scale benchmarks for these data intensive applications. Breadth-First search is one of the three application kernels of Graph 500 benchmark.

The Graph 500 benchmark is intended to rank high-performance computers based on speed of memory retrieval which is a useful performance standard for large graph problems. In BFS, the memory access time can be expressed by Traversed Edges Per Second (TEPS).

2.2   Top-Down BFS

Conventional BFS implementation can be thought of as a top-down approach, which starts at the root key and propagates down the created BFS tree during each step. Our work is mainly for distributed Breadth-First Search. The Top-down BFS is a level-synchronized BFS algorithm using the method of asynchronous message passing. With this method, synchronization occurs at each level of Breadth-First search. Variance can, in a number of ways, impact the performance of this algorithm, including: data structures, traversal order, parallel work allocation, partitioning, synchronization, or update procedure. As the results of our analysis, the communication costs of distributed top-down BFS are related to the number of edges of the BFS tree. The BFS execution time is closely dependent on the number of messages sent during the Breadth-First search. Because the non-blocking reads and writes are essential to BFS, the execution time of each level of BFS is related to the degree of vertex.

2.3   Hybrid BFS

When the frontier is large, the top-down approach is not always efficient. The bottom-up approach traverses more efficiently by searching in the reverse. Given this, the direction-optimizing algorithm uses the top-down approach for steps when the frontier is small and the bottom-up approach for steps when the frontier is large. In other words, the top-down approach usually runs at the first two or three levels and the end of BFS three while the bottom-up approach runs in the middle level of the BFS tree.

When the direction-optimizing algorithm runs the bottom-up approach, each unvisited vertex attempts to find any parent among its neighbors. First, the unvisited vertex need to send messages which contain the source vertex id and destination vertex id to its neighbor. Second, if the destination vertex is on the frontier, the vertex needs to send back the message in order to return to the source vertex. Compared with the top-down method, some communication costs can be reduced by using the bottom-up methods when the unvisited vertexes' total degree (the number of its neighbors) is lower than the total degree of vertexes on the frontier. Besides, the direction-optimizing algorithm need to spend some time on calculating the top-down approach or the bottom-up approach run at the current level.

However, the top-down BFS still spends a lot of time when the vertex found a failed child or tries to become the parent of a same level neighbor. This is redundant work because a vertex only needs one parent, as a result the majority of messages are ineffective. The bottom-up search is also affected because the frontier is searched from all unvisited vertices. Meanwhile, there are numerous isolated vertexes in the Kronecker graph which we neglect.

3   Global Bitmap Approach

In this section, we briefly describe the parallelization strategy employed in our distributed BFS algorithm. We analyzed the traffic and the bottleneck of the calculation. We focus on reducing the communication costs and the computing costs to increase the performance of BFS.

3.1   Global Visited Bitmap

As we know, the top-down BFS spends a lot of time sending a lot of messages to its neighbors. After the vertex sends the message to a neighbor, the target vertex receives the message and calculates whether the vertex has been visited.

The program uses an active messages library which is targeted to support asynchronous small messages for delivery while having reasonable performance on modern multicore systems by doing transparently to the user following. The message that needs to be sent in the graph increases as the scale of the graph growing, as show in Fig. 1.

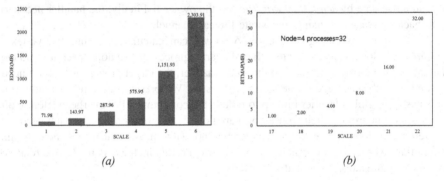

(a)   *(b)*

Fig. 1. Message count at each level. (a) Edge message count. (b) Bitmap message count.

The top-down approach, if we can calculate whether the vertex has been visited locally rather than by a remote node, will reduce communication time. The algorithm needs to maintain a global array which stores a list representing all verteces' access status. We use the bitmap to represent the verteces' status, thus reducing a lot of storage overhead. And visited bitmap need to synchronize to all processors. If the number of processor is N and the scale of the Kronecker graph is SCALE, the communication costs will be

$$2 \times N \times 2^{SCALE-23}\text{B} \tag{1}$$

The bitmap we needed in the program is shown in Fig. 2 where we use 4 nodes with 64 processes. We can then utilize the low communication overhead top-down approach with global visited bitmap to cut down the communication time.

Through this method, we can judge vertices based on whether they have been visited in the local node and reduce the communication overhead. When the process scans the vertices on the boundaries, it locally determines if the neighbors of those vertices have been accessed. If the neighbor of the vertex has been visited, the process doesn't need to send a message to the owner of the neighbor. Otherwise, the processor need to send a message containing the vertex's id number and the neighbor node's id number to the owner of the neighbor.

3.2   Global Frontier Bitmap

For the bottom-up approach, it is not necessary to synchronize the visited bitmap. The reason is that the synchronous version of the visited bitmap no longer brings any benefits. The distributed BFS judges whether the vertex is accessed locally, then sends its edge to its neighbors' processors. The processor will judge whether the neighbor vertex is on the frontier. In the original hybrid approach, the bottom-up approach need to send a message by *send_backward(u,v)* to the owner v. Finally, the handler needs to send back messages by using a separate logical channel.

In the same reasoning as section A, if we can calculate whether the vertex's neighbor is in local processor rather than the target processor, we don't need to send the message to the target processor. In the same manner, the target processor will not need to send back the message to the source processor. We present one kind of bottom-up BFS based on global frontier bitmap to reduce the communication overhead. Before all processors synchronize their frontier bitmap globally, the bottom-up approach needs to convert the frontier queue to the frontier bitmap. This means that it will increase the computing overhead by a certain amount. However, this increase is negligible relative to the communication overhead reduction.

3.3   Hybrid Implementation Design

Combination of the above two communication optimization methods is presented in the pseudo-code of a distributed, direction-optimizing BFS based on a global bitmap. The details are in Algorithm 1.

Algorithm 1. Distributed Direction-Optimizing BFS based on global bitmap

---

Input: G = (V, E): graph representation; n: rank;

n: rank;

v_s: source vertex;

In: current level input vertices;

Out: current level output vertices.

Output: P: predecessor map.

1: $In_r \leftarrow \begin{cases} \{v_s\} & if\ (v_s \in R_r) \\ \varnothing & otherwise \end{cases}$;

2: $Vis_r \leftarrow \{v_s\}$;

3: $P(v) \leftarrow \perp \forall v \in V$;

4: **if** $v_s \in R_r$ **then** $P(v_s) \leftarrow v_s$;

5: **while** $In \neq \varnothing$ **do**

6:      dir ← **CalcDirecion()**;

7:      **if** dir = FORWARD **then**

8:          ForwardStep();

9:      **else if** dir = BACKWARD **then**

10:         BackwardStep();

11: **barrier()**;

12: In ← Out;

function ForwardStep()

1: **allreduce the** Vis_n **bitmap;**

2:      **for** $u \in In_n$ **do**

3:          **for** $u: (u, v) \in E_n$ **do**

4:              **if** $v \notin Vis_n(bitmap)$ **then**

5: **send_forward** (u,v) to Owner (v);

function BackwardStep();

1: **transform** In_n **queue to** In_n **bitmap;**

2: **allreduce the** In_n **bitmap;**

3:      **for** $v \in V$ **do**

4:          **if** $v \notin Vis_n(bitmap)$ **then**

5:              **for** $u: (u, v) \in E_n$ **do**

6:                  **if** $u \in In_n(bitmap)$ **then**

7:                      $Vis_n \leftarrow Vis_n \cup \{v\}$;

8:                      $Out_n \leftarrow Out_n \cup \{v\}$;

9:                      $P(v) \leftarrow u$;

function Receive_froward(u,v)

1: **if** $v \notin Vis_n(bitmap)$ **then**

2:      $Vis_n \leftarrow Vis_n \cup \{v\}$;

3:      $Out_n \leftarrow Out_n \cup \{v\}$;

4:      $P(v) \leftarrow u$;

Our hybrid approach uses the low traffic top-down approach for steps when the frontier is small and uses the low computational bottom-up method when the frontier is large. The algorithm switch is based on the current size of the frontier queue, and it is used to determining whether it is needed to switch algorithms in the current level of BFS, as Fig. 2 shows.

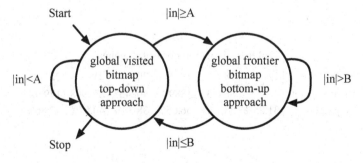

Fig. 2. Switch algorithms

The top-down approach and the bottom-up approach will always check the frontier. This correlates to the condition for switching from top-down to bottom-up, that is when the number of vertices is larger than:

$$A = (|V| - |vis|)/\alpha \tag{2}$$

Switching back to the top-down approach at the end should occur when the frontier is small. We use another equation to get:

$$B = |V|/\beta \tag{3}$$

The parameter α and β vary with the scale of the graph. In our program, we use the method of static scheduling and we select $\alpha = 2048$ and $\beta = 64$. Algorithm 1 also shows the handler for the receives messages.

3.4   Reduce Computing Overhead

The bottom-up approach involves scanning the unvisited verteces for a possible parent. Using our method, which doesn't need to send messages, the bottom-up approach can use the local visited bitmap. The main part of this overhead is scanning the frontier vertices' neighbors.

However, there are a lot of isolated vertices which don't have a neighbor in the graph. The bottom-up approach will scan these vertices on the queues, even though the vertices are not in the BFS tree. Table 1 shows the proportion of isolated points among all vertices. Apparently, these isolated vertices are a major part of the Kronecker graph. We can expel these isolated vertices to reduce computing overhead when the bottom-up approach scans the unvisited vertex queue. An improved data pre-processing method was required to address this issue. So, when the program converts the Kronecker graph into a CSR matrix model, we can construct a new queue designed to store only the vertices of degree that are not zero.

Another effective method is sorting the isolated vertex's neighbors. The unvisited vertex does not need to scan all the neighbors to find its parents, we can simply put the most likely neighbors in the front of the queue. Obviously, higher degree points are more likely to be the unvisited vertex's parents. So, in the pretreatment stage, we sort the column array according to the degree of the vertices to reduce the computing overhead.

Table 1. Proportion of isolate points

Scale	17	18	19	20	21	22
Isolated points	40955	88453	188996	402453	852908	1797659
Proportion	31.25%	33.74%	36.05%	38.38%	40.67%	42.86%

3.5 Storage Optimization for KNL

We also optimize storage of BFS for KNL. Referencing development manual [18], the Knights Landing interconnecting mesh operates in one of three clustering modes: all-to-all, quadrant, and sub-NUMA. We select the all-to-all mode. The memory architecture is composed of 16 GB of high-speed stacked memory accessed by 8 high-speed memory controllers, as well as up to 384 GB of DDR4 accessed by 2 3-channel memory controllers. It is anticipated that the KNL chip can get more than 400 GB/s of bandwidth out of the MCDRAM and more than 90 GB/s out of the regular DRAM attached to the chip running the STREAM Triad memory bandwidth benchmark. The calculation process needs to continuously read the edge list of the graph. In addition, the communication process also requires a lot of exchange between the send buffer and receive buffer. In order to combat this, after filing the edge list, we transform the edge list to the CSR data structure and store the column queues and row queues in the MCDRAM rather than the DRAM. In this way, the reading and writing of the send and receive buffer will be faster in the process of communication. Additionally, the process of getting vertices' neighbors data will be faster.

4 Experimental Results

In this section, we present an experimental evaluation of the algorithms described in this paper. We chose a distributed environment in Tianhe-2 system and Knights Landing processors.

4.1 Overview of Experimental Platform

We collected the performance results on the Tianhe-2 system. Tianhe-2 is equipped with 17920 nodes, each containing two 12-core Xeon E5 CPU. The front-end system consisted of 4096 Galaxy FT-1500 CPUs. Tianhe-2 has a speed of 33.9PFlops and a peak performance of 54.9PFlops. Its abundant computing resources and fast computing speed make it the best accelerator for the research project. Users could log on to Tianhe-2 through VPN.

We also tested our program with the KNL processor. The 2nd generation Intel Xeon Phi™ processors (code-named "Knights Landing") are specialized computing platforms capable of delivering better performance for some applications than general-purpose CPUs such as Intel Xeon products. We mainly used its on-package high-bandwidth memory (HBW) built on the multi-channel dynamic random access memory (MCDRAM) technology. The KNL had three configuration modes of HBW: Flat Mode, Cache Mode and Hybrid Mode. We used the Flat Mode and we modified the code and execution environment. Besides the foundation instructions, KNL featured three additional extensions: AVX512PFI, AVX512ERI and AVX512CDI. These allow each processor to execute short-vector SIMD instructions, helping to speed up execution. However, we did not make a special optimization for this. We will study this aspect in the future.

4.2   Time Breakdown Analysis

Figure 3 shows how time was spent during BFS. Here, our statistics of BFS execution time include: communication time, computing time, barrier time and all reduce time. Among them, the execution time is mainly composed of traversal of the fringe, judging whether the node has been visited or not, and updating the relevant information. When using the method of asynchronous message passing, we need to send messages to another process from the same group and other group. The most time-consuming of these interactions is flushing of the internode and intranode buffer to the destination node. The barrier time is used to synchronize all processors during the end of a BFS level. The allreduce time is used to allreduce the bitmap during all processors. We combined the single-node direction-optimizing BFS described in [14], and implemented a distributed direction-optimizing BFS as showed in Fig. 3. The global visited bitmap method optimizes the top-down approach of the direction-optimizing BFS. The global frontier bitmap method optimizes the bottom-up approach of the direction-optimizing BFS. While the hybrid direction-optimizing method combined the advantages of the two methods.

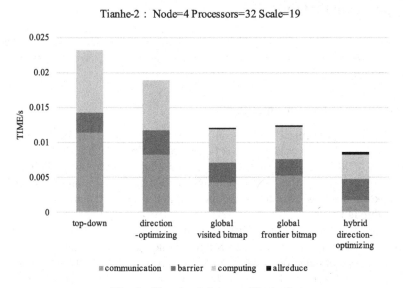

Fig. 3. Time breakdown on Tianhe-2

For the five methods in the Fig. 3, the barrier time is about the same. The barrier operation is mainly due to the unbalanced load between the processors. As you can see in, our approach reduces the amount of communication overhead. The global visited bitmap method reduces the communication overhead in the top-down approach and the global frontier bitmap method reduces the communication overhead in the bottom-up approach. We also notice that the "allreduce time" is very short. This implies that our method is very effective. The hybrid direction optimizing approach's communication time is about a quarter of the direction-optimizing approach and one in five of the original version. So our approach is quite effective in reducing communication overhead. Meanwhile, when the communication message is reduced, some of the corresponding redundant calculations like read data from receive buffer are also reduced. Not only did we use the hybrid approach, but we did the preprocessing when make the graph structure. We can see sort the column array according to the degree of the vertices that they represent the pretreatment stage can reduce the computing costs. To summarise, we see that the hybrid direction-optimizing method is quite effective.

4.3   Level Breakdown Analysis

Figure 4 shows how time is spent during each BFS level. The first observation is that the central levels account for most of the visit time. At the middle level, you can see that our method reduces a lot of time overhead. The distributed direction-optimizing BFS used the bottom-up approach skips checking some edges to accelerate top-down algorithm. The global visited bitmap method reduces the time overhead in the top-down approach and the global frontier bitmap method reduces the time overhead in the bottom-up approach. As you can see in the level 3 the global frontier bitmap method may need more time to run and in the level 4 the global frontier bitmap method is faster than the global visited bitmap method, this is because in the third level the algorithm mainly uses the top-down approach. We use also compressed the head of the message packet, so you can see that in Fig. 4 our hybrid direction-optimizing method combined the advantages of the above two methods and significantly accelerate the BFS algorithm.

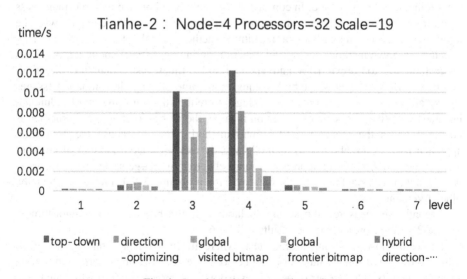

Fig. 4. Level breakdown on Tianhe-2

4.4   Scalability in Tianhe-2

First, we measured the weak scalability of the proposed BFS algorithm on fixed problem size per node (each node has 2^{17} vertices) and present the results in Fig. 5.

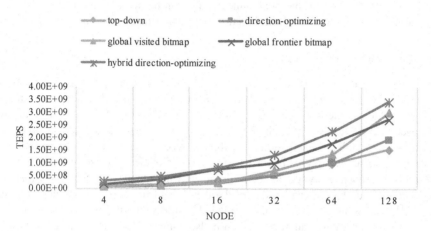

Fig. 5. "weak scaling" results on Tianhe-2

We observe that the direction-optimizing method is about 1.1–1.3 times faster than the original top-down method. In contrast, the global visited bitmap method spends less time on communication messages and gets speedups of 1.4–1.7 (as compare with the top-down method). The global frontier bitmap method gets about 1.4–2.3 times faster than the top-down method. The hybrid direction-optimizing BFS is about 2.2–3.1 times faster than the top-down BFS and about 1.9–2.4 times faster than the direction-optimizing BFS. The new method spends more time sharing the bitmap messages among all processors and stores the messages to reduce the transmission of redundant information. When the scale of the graph is large, the global frontier bitmap method is not as good as the global visited bitmap method. This is because the bottom-up approach used in the above two methods already reduces a large amount of communication and the bottom-up approach is more effective in a large scale. To summarise, we see that the hybrid direction-optimizing design is about 2.2–3.1 times faster than the official version.

Second, we measured the strong scalability of the proposed BFS algorithm in Tianhe-2 system, presenting the results in Fig. 6.

Figure 6 shows a strong scaling test, where the performance rate (in MTEPS) achieved on increasing the number of processors. We note that our algorithm has good strong scalability. The performance is extended with the processors' growth. Due to the system constraints, there are a maximum of 64 processes running on 4 nodes. The direction-optimizing method is inefficient when the processes number is 4. Meanwhile, the global visited bitmap and global frontier bitmap method have a beneficial effect and are 1.6 times faster than the top-down. The hybrid method can reduce the communication overhead both in the top-down process and the bottom-up process, making 1.9–3.0 times faster than the official version. In sum, our method has a significantly strong scaling effect.

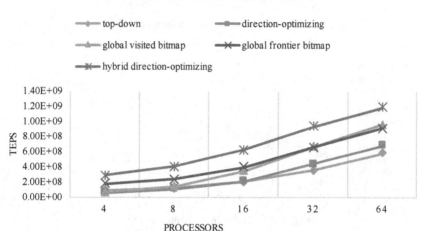

Fig. 6. "strong scaling" results on Tianhe-2

4.5   Scalability in KNL

First of all, we optimized the code for the KNL processor. The performance under 64 processes in KNL experimental facilities is given in Table 2.

Table 2. Performance under 64 processes (unit: MTEPS)

Scale	17	18	19	20	21	22
Top-down	103	129	146	168	178	194
Top-down (MCDRAM)	112	136	157	180	185	196
Promote	8.27%	5.39%	7.62%	8.10%	6.97%	6.46%

We note that the MCDRAM can improve the performance by about 5–8%. This is because the memory access is not a large proportion of the workload. Most of the memory access operations are buffer read-write actions in the communication process. Others are read the value of the adjacency matrix. This limits the optimized promotion.

Our later versions are built on the use of MCDRAM. It can be derived from Table 2 that the performance without using MCDRAM may drop 5% to 8%. We measured the scalability of the proposed BFS algorithm in the KNL system. "Weak scaling" results on KNL are presented in Fig. 7. It is noteworthy that under 64 processors, when dealing with graph containing 2^{21} vertices, the performance of the algorithm is saturated. In the KNL experiment platform, we obtain the speedups of 1.2–2.4 times compare to the top-down method without MCDRAM.

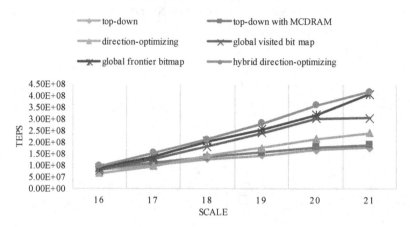

Fig. 7. "weak scaling" results on KNL

As showed in Fig. 8, our algorithm has a good processor scalability. Our global visited bitmap approach is 1.5–1.8 times faster than the top-down approach and 1.4–1.6 times faster than the direction-optimizing approach. The global frontier bitmap approach obtained speedups of 1.4–2.6 compare to the direction-optimizing approach,

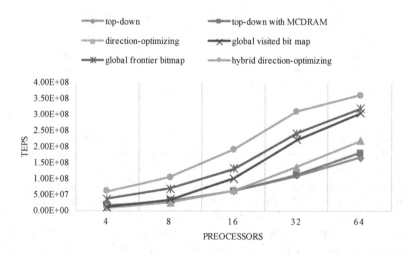

Fig. 8. "strong scaling" results on KNL

and the hybrid direction-optimizing approach is 1.7–3.4 times faster than the direction-optimizing approach. To summarise, we see that the hybrid direction-optimizing design is more than 2.1 times faster than the top-down approach. It is worth noting that in the case of small scales, the top-down method tends to outperform the direction-optimizing method, but cannot compete with the low-traffic approach. This may be the case that in the small scale, the bottom-up approach doesn't have enough revenue compared to the top-down approach.

5 Related Work

In this section, we focus on the work most relevant to this study.

The Graph 500 list (http://www.graph500.org/) [1] was announced at ISC2010 and the first list appeared at SC2010. In 2011, Suzumura et al. [2] carefully evaluated the performance of graph500.

Breadth-First search (BFS) is one of the three application kernels of Graph 500 benchmark. The BFS, as a fundamental method in algorithmic graph theory, and the optimization of graph traversal on parallel and distributed systems, has received a great deal of attention recently. There is a lot of research work on the BFS algorithm regarding many different platforms.

Shared memory architecture: In 2006, Bader et al. [3] proposed a fine-grained parallel approach to the Cray MTA-2 system. Their approach leverages the fine-grained, low-overhead synchronous operation provided by the MTA-2 system. Subsequently, Mizell et al. [4] discussed measures to further improve the method. Their method of improvement achieved high performance in a Cray XMT system with 128 processors. In 2010, Agarwal et al. [5] gained significant performance gains within a single node containing four CPUs. They primarily minimize the communication between CPUs and use bitmaps to represent the state of the vertices. Yasui et al. [6] who combined with the memory of binding and thread binding for NUMA architecture and degree-aware optimization method hit the highest performance of 37.66GTEPS on a single node. The work we are most indebted to are [7, 8], which introduced the concept of direction optimization. This method takes advantage of the features of the graph and uses different search strategies in different BFS layers.

Distributed Memory Architecture: Much of the work on large distributed systems has been based on 2D decomposition. In 2005, Yoo et al. [9, 10] proposed a two-dimensional graph division method on BlueGene/L. In this method, the process is organized into a 2-D structure, and the adjacency matrix of the graph is divided into processes in a 2-D manner. In this way, each "all-to-all" communication only needs to involve one row or a column of processes while the 1-D method needs all processes. In 2011, Buluç et al. [11] summarized the research on parallel BFS and pointed out the optimization space of parallel BFS algorithm on a distributed memory system. In 2012, Checconi et al. [12] search of 2^{38} vertices with 131,072 cores and achieve 254 GTEPS on Blue Gene/Q. In the same year, Satish et al. [13] used a 1-D image partitioning method to comprehensively apply single node optimization and communication optimization and obtain 115 GTEPS on a cluster of 320 nodes. In 2014, Checconi et al. [14] implemented a 1D-decomposed BFS algorithm and they have been able to explore a scale 40 R-MAT graph with 1 trillion vertices and 32 trillion of undirected edges using 64 thousand BlueGene/Q nodes (4 million threads) in just a few seconds.

GPU: In 2012, Merrill et al. [16] proposed ways to increase the utilization of threads on the GPU, the result of which was the best of the time on a shared memory system. Hong et al. [17] proposed a hybrid approach using CPUs and GPUs, using CPUs when calculations are small and GPU calculations when computing loads are large.

6   Conclusion and Future Work

In this paper, we have cut the communication and calculation times in the basis of the direction-optimizing BFS. We present two global bitmap approaches to accelerate the BFS: a top-down approach with global visited bitmap and a bottom-up approach with global frontier bitmap. We used a hybrid approach to combine the advantages of both. Additionally, we optimized the computation of the bottom-up approach as well as the storage of the KNL coprocessor. We performed experiments on the Tianhe-2 and KNL systems with good results. Listed below are optimizations that we intend to explore in future work.

Distributed BFS with 2D partitioning. In future work, we will use the 2D decomposition to split the data among the nodes. Then analyze the communication optimization on the basis of the 2D version.

Exploiting Single Instruction Multiple Data (SIMD) in KNL. The basic idea of SIMD optimization is to scan the vertices' neighbors simultaneously. The problem to be solved is that there may be discontinuities in the visits of the vertices' neighbors. Optimization of the BFS in the heterogeneous system which uses the KNL system as a set of coprocessors rather than as a CPU.

Acknowledgment. This research was supported by the National Key R&D Program of China under NO. 2018YFB0203904, NSFC: U1611261, NSFC: 61433019, NSFC: U1435217 and the Program for Guangdong Introducing Innovative and Enterpreneurial Teams under Grant No. 2016ZT06D211.

References

1. Graph 500 benchmark. https://graph500.org/
2. Suzumura, T., Ueno, K., Sato, H., Fujisawa, K., Matsuoka, S.: Performance characteristics of Graph500 on large-scale distributed environment. In: 2011 IEEE International Symposium on Workload Characterization (IISWC), Austin, TX, pp. 149–158 (2011)
3. Bader, D.A., Madduri, K.: Designing multithreaded algorithms for breadth-first search and st-connectivity on the Cray MTA-2. In: 2006 International Conference on Parallel Processing (ICPP 2006), Columbus, OH, pp. 523–530 (2006)
4. Mizell, D., Maschhoff, K.: Early experiences with large-scale Cray XMT systems. In: 2009 IEEE International Symposium on Parallel & Distributed Processing, Rome, pp. 1–9 (2009). https://doi.org/10.1109/ipdps.2009.5161108

5. Agarwal, V., Petrini, F., Pasetto, D., Bader, D.A.: Scalable graph exploration on multicore processors. In: 2010 ACM/IEEE International Conference for High Performance Computing. Networking, Storage and Analysis, New Orleans, LA, pp. 1–11 (2010)
6. Yasui, Y., Fujisawa, K.: Fast and scalable NUMA-based thread parallel breadth-first search. In: 2015 International Conference on High Performance Computing & Simulation (HPCS), Amsterdam, pp. 377–385 (2015)
7. Beamer, S., Asanovic, K., Patterson, D.A.: Searching for a parent instead of fighting over children: a fast breadth-first search implementation for Graph500. EECS Department, University of California, Berkeley, Technical report. UCB/EECS-2011-117, November 2011
8. Beamer, S., Asanovic, K., Patterson, D.: Direction-optimizing breadth-first search. In: International Conference on High PERFORMANCE Computing, Networking, Storage and Analysis, vol. 21, p. 12. IEEE Computer Society Press (2012)
9. Yoo, A., Chow, E., Henderson, K., McLendon, W., Hendrickson, B., Catalyurek, U.: A scalable distributed parallel breadth-first search algorithm on BlueGene/L. In: Proceedings of the ACM/IEEE SC 2005 Conference on Supercomputing, p. 25 (2005). https://doi.org/10.1109/sc.2005.4
10. Chow, E., Henderson, K., Yoo, A.: Distributed breadth-first search with 2-D partitioning. Lawrence Livermore Nat Lab (2005)
11. Buluç, A.: Parallel breadth-first search on distributed memory systems. In: Computer Science, pp. 1–12 (2011)
12. Checconi, F., Petrini, F., Willcock, J., Lumsdaine, A., Choudhury, A.R., Sabharwal, Y.: Breaking the speed and scalability barriers for graph exploration on distributed-memory machines. In: 2012 International Conference for High Performance Computing, Networking, Storage and Analysis (SC), Salt Lake City, UT, pp. 1–12 (2012). https://doi.org/10.1109/sc.2012.25
13. Satish, N., Kim, C., Chhugani, J., Dubey, P.: Large-scale energy-efficient graph traversal: a path to efficient data-intensive supercomputing. In: 2012 International Conference for High Performance Computing, Networking, Storage and Analysis (SC), Salt Lake City, UT, pp. 1–11 (2012)
14. Checconi, F., Petrini, F.: Traversing trillions of edges in real time: graph exploration on large-scale parallel machines. In: 2014 IEEE 28th International Parallel and Distributed Processing Symposium, Phoenix, AZ, pp. 425–434 (2014)
15. Beamer, S., Buluc, A., Asanovic, K., et al.: Distributed memory breadth-first search revisited: enabling bottom-up search. In: Proceedings of the IEEE 27th International Parallel Distributed Processing Symposium Workshop and PhD Forum, IPDPSW 2013, pp. 1618–1627 (2013)
16. Merrill, D., Garland, M., Grimshaw, A.: Scalable GPU graph traversal. ACM SIGPLAN Not. 47(8), 117–128 (2012)
17. Hong, S., Oguntebi, T., Olukotun, K.: Efficient parallel graph exploration on multi-core CPU and GPU. In: 2011 International Conference on Parallel Architectures and Compilation Techniques, Galveston, TX, pp. 78–88 (2011)
18. Best Practice Guide – Knights Landing. http://www.prace-ri.eu/best-practice-guide-knights-landing-january-2017/

Improve Heteroscedastic Discriminant Analysis by Using CBP Algorithm

Jafar A. Alzubi[1], Ali Yaghoubi[4], Mehdi Gheisari[2(✉)],
and Yongrui Qin[3]

[1] Al-Balqa Applied University, Salt, Jordan
j.zubi@bau.edu.jo
[2] School of Computer Science and Technology, Guangzhou University,
Guangzhou 510006, China
mehdi.gheisari61@gmail.com
[3] Department of Computer Science, University if Hudderfied, Huddersfield, UK
Yongrui.Qin@hud.ac.uk
[4] Department of Computer Science, Islamic Azad University, Borāzjān, Iran
Yaghoubi_ali67@yahoo.com

Abstract. Linear discriminant analysis is considered as current techniques in feature extraction so, LDA, by discriminant information which obtains in mapping space, does the classification act. When the classes' distribution is not normal, LDA, to perform classification, will face problem and will resulted the poor performance of criteria in performing the classification act. One of the proposed ways is the use of other measures, such as Chernoff's distance so, by using Chernoff's measure LDA has been spreading to its heterogeneous states and LDA in this state, in addition to use information among the medians, uses the information of the classes' Covariance matrices. By defining scattering matrix, based on Boundary and non-Boundary samples and using these matrices in Chernoff's criteria, the decrease of the classes' overlapping in the mapping space in as result, the rate of classification correctness increases. Using Boundary and non-Boundary samples in scattering matrices causes improvement over the result. In this article, we use a new discovering multi-stage Algorithm to choose Boundary and non-Boundary samples so, the results of the conducted experiments shows promising performance of the proposing method.

Keywords: Linear discriminant analysis · CBP algorithm · Chernoff criterion
Boundary pattern

1 Introduction

Classification data into groups is considered of important stages of pattern recognition that one of its major stages is feature extraction. One of the features of extraction is reducing the linear dimensions which often, to reduce data dimensions and statistical models and also, overcoming the problems which arise in this field can be used. Reducing data dimensions shouldn't cause discriminant information that is in the original space of the main feature to be eliminated. From the usual methods in the field of discriminant extracting information (also known as a classification technique) is LDA [1]. This classical approach have been developed, by Fisher [12], for two-class

© Springer Nature Switzerland AG 2018
J. Vaidya and J. Li (Eds.): ICA3PP 2018, LNCS 11335, pp. 130–144, 2018.
https://doi.org/10.1007/978-3-030-05054-2_10

classification and by Rao for multi-class classification [12]. In LDA a transformation matrix, changes a main n dimension space of the data to d dimension. The above conversion maximizes the proportion of scattering matrix between the classes and does the classification [1, 9, 10, 17]. LDA is a fast and easy way to set a good character and requires simple matrices calculation. In several articles, many of the problems related to the LDA has been reported and solutions provided so, LDA concentration is to obtain a space where follow with the maximum average between the classes If so, imagining normal distribution to be existed for the classes this strategy can be used But, in the real world we cannot have such hypothesis, and this strategy is not always useful. In [18] it has been tried to measure the shortcoming of this Criteria so, the classes which are in the original space close to each other and this action along with a sharp decline in the rate of classification in [3, 4]. This method, with the help of weight criteria, decreases the impact of the classes that, in the original space, are far apart each other. Weight criteria carry out repeatedly and that the number of extracted feature is limited to the number of classes. In [18], the use of new matrices to overcome this problem has been suggested. The problem is that the selection algorithm of Boundary and non-Boundary patterns and RPS (relevant pattern selection) in a series of the training data is not working properly. Because at the same time, either to the number of its neighbors and or a threshold level that RPS are used, is depended [19]. Out of the methods of Boundary and non-Boundary patterns, we can point to the Algorithm based on the Graph. A graph-based algorithm is Hit Miss Networks (HMN) which are directed graphs of instances in the training set [20]. This Algorithm of the Graph obtains orientation of the samples in training set so, for this for each sample, the nearest neighbor of it, is determined from all the classes and an edge between the targeted sample and each of its neighbor is defined so, a hit edge between the sample and its neighbor by the similar class label is defined. For this for each sample, the nearest neighbor of it, is determined from all the classes and an edge between the targeted sample and each of its neighbor is defined so, a hit edge between the sample and its neighbor by the similar class label is defined. A Miss edge, between sample and nearby its nearby sample is defined by different class label. The result is that each sample is defined as a node and the edges of Hit and Miss is calculated as the degree of each node and based on these classifications a detecting pattern is imposed on the sets of training data. Based on the concept of Algorithm HMN, two other kinds of the Algorithm have been suggested based on the Graph [21, 22]. In this paper we use a method of sample reduce (which has been as a powerful discovering technique) naming CBP (class boundary perseving) to separate Boundary and non-Boundary patterns [23]. CBP is an Algorithm which gives us the best description underlying distribution about class samples spread. This Algorithm has used some steps heuristically that by using four steps has pruned the primary training sets and divides in to subsets of Boundary and non-Boundary samples. In this paper, we investigate, theoretically, the effect of proposing Algorithm on the process and the number of extracted features. The organization, in this paper continues to be as follow; hence, in the second part we will have a definition of the problem. In Sect. 3, we will discuss the definition using the scattering matrix based on bordering as well as non-bordering patterns and in Sect. 4 of this article, ultimately, we will discussed on the results of downloaded dataset from UCI and will investigate them.

2 Defining the Problem

In a problem of classification, consider c number of classes as $w_1, \ldots, w_c$ which has C label and N dimension and then, this C class is shown as $D_1 = \{x_{1,1}, \ldots, x_{1,m_1}\}, \ldots, D_c = \{x_{c,1}, \ldots, x_{c,m_c}\}$ and on the basis of parametric form which is considered for the classification, then c class will have initial probability $p_1, \ldots, p_c$. And random distribution vectors of n dimension $x_1 \sim N(m_1, S_1), \ldots, x_c \sim N(m_c, S_c)$ and so that m, S are considered as the average and class covariance.

2.1 Chernoff's Criteria

In general, in the methods of reducing the linear dimensions, the goal is to find the conversion matrix of W so that it can change the input normal distribution vectors $x_1, \ldots, x_n$ from the n dimension to the d dimension so, the new normal distribution vectors can be obtained as $y_1 = Wx_1, \ldots, y_{d \times 1} = W_{n \times 1} x_{n \times 1}$. In LDA, W is chosen in a way that the pattern of $tr\left\{(ww^T)^{-1} ws_B w^T\right\}$ maximizes, which S_B is the definer of scattering matrix of between classes and is as $S_B = \sum_{i=1}^{C} p_i(m_i - m)(m_i - m)$ and the process of classification is performed based on the process of Fischer's classification [6, 13]. Scattering matrix of S_B is the product of available separating information in the difference between the average of the classes and it does not benefit from separating information available in separating information which is in the difference of Covariance Matrices. in order to benefit available separating information in the Covariance difference, in the method of LDA, and in [6] instead of using Eglidoosi distance between the averages, the Chernoff's of distributing distance between the distribution of each pair of class is used so, the result is that, in addition to benefiting of discriminant information between the averages and discriminant information the difference between the Covariance is considered.

As it is observed in (Fig. 1) (parts of a, b). The averages are fixed and for the separation of the classes, two classes distribution has been used so, it is observed that the amount of the overlap has considerably reduced.

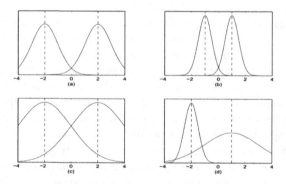

Fig. 1. Separability based on distribution of classes [7]

Chernoff's Two-Class Criteria

Based on chernoff distance between two distributive class in original space so the solution for this optimizing problem is to search projection vector of W so that maximize the criteria of (1), as in

$$
\begin{aligned}
J_c(W) = tr\{(WS_WW^t)^{-1}[WS_EW^t \\
- WS_W^{1/2}\frac{p_1 \log(S_W^{-1/2}S_1S_W^{-1/2}) + p_2 \log(S_W^{-1/2}S_2S_W^{-1/2})}{p_1p_2}S_W^{1/2}W^t]\}
\end{aligned} \quad (1)
$$

W is obtained based on the Eigenvalue decomposition of the matrix:

$$
S_c(W) = S_W^{-1}[S_E - S_W^{1/2}\frac{p_1 \log(S_W^{-1/2}S_1S_W^{-1/2}) + p_2 \log(S_W^{-1/2}S_2S_W^{-1/2})}{p_1p_2}S_W^{1/2}] \quad (2)
$$

W, as especially corresponding Eigenvector is with the maximum amount of the matrix (2).

Chernoff's Multi-class Criteria

In order to vast Chernoff's criterion of two-class to state of multi-class, an certain decomposition of scattering matrices between the classes are used so, in this decomposition, between classes matrix, by using two-class blocks is built. Now, Chernoff's multi class criterion is shown as (3) Formula and the goal is finding W which maximize criterion of (3)

$$
J_C(A) = \sum_{i=1}^{C-1}\sum_{j=i+1}^{C} P_iP_jtr\left(\begin{array}{l}(WS_wW^t)^{-1}\times \\ WS_w^{1/2}\left[(S_w^{-1/2}S_{ij}S_w^{-1/2})^{-1/2}\times S_w^{-1/2}S_{Eij}S_w^{-1/2}(S_w^{-1/2}S_{ij}S_w^{-1/2})^{-1/2} + \\ \frac{1}{\pi_i\pi_j}(\log(S_w^{-1/2}S_{ij}S_w^{-1/2}) - \pi_i\log(S_w^{-1/2}S_iS_w^{-1/2}) - \pi_j\log(S_w^{-1/2}S_jS_w^{-1/2}))\right]WS_w^{1/2}\end{array}\right) \quad (3)
$$

$$S_{Eij} = (m_i - m_j)(m_i - m_j)$$

In order to determine W, the decomposition of Eigenvalue is formed, also, W is the equivalent of Eigenvector with the largest value from Matrix (4).

$$
S_C = \sum_{i=1}^{C-1}\sum_{j=i+1}^{C} P_iP_jtr\left(\begin{array}{l}(S_w)^{-1}\times \\ S_w^{1/2}\left[(S_w^{-1/2}S_{ij}S_w^{-1/2})^{-1/2}\times S_w^{-1/2}S_{Eij}S_w^{-1/2}(S_w^{-1/2}S_{ij}S_w^{-1/2})^{-1/2} + \\ \frac{1}{\pi_i\pi_j}(\log(S_w^{-1/2}S_{ij}S_w^{-1/2}) - \pi_i\log(S_w^{-1/2}S_iS_w^{-1/2}) - \pi_j\log(S_w^{-1/2}S_jS_w^{-1/2}))\right]S_w^{1/2}\end{array}\right) \quad (4)
$$

The point that $(S_{Cij}) = \delta_{ij}^2.\delta_{ij}^2$ is expressed as the Eigenvalue of S_{Cij} and Eigenvector with the largest Eigenvalue is considered as projection vector of W. The Eigenvector equivalent vector by Eigenvalue δ_{ij}^2 is considered as Eigenvector between two class i and j, so to this reason it is distinguished as the biggest Eigenvalue as well as projection vector of W thus To have further understand (see Fig. 2).

Figure 2 is a six – class model that each circle is considered as a class and the circles have a similar radius which shows that of within-class scattering matrix has been equally assumed If the class of on the down right corner, in Fig. 2. Is considered as j_0, on the condition that this class to be well far away, from the rest in the original space, the share of Eigenvalue, $1 \leq i \leq C, i \neq j$ will be dominant on scattering matrix between

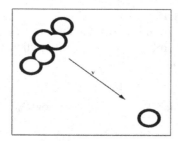

Fig. 2. Map of classes using a vector V [4]

the classes. Therefore, the result of the direction that has been shown by the V arrow would be known as principal discriminant of between the classes. The result is that to map V the classes of i and j that will projection i ≠ j to one cluster high overlapping of classification between the classes that is required to increase the rate of classification error in the projection space. Therefore, from this example, we can conclude that in the estimate of between the class matrixes of Chernoff's criterion all pairs of classes, without being separate in original space are considered that this process leads to a bad performance in separating the classes [31–39].

3   Making Scattering Matrices Based on Boundary and Non-Boundary Patterns

Boundary pattern is a Datum, by having k neighbor on different class position near the Boundary of decision-making and non-Boundary pattern Datum with neighboring k and label of similar class, its position is away from the decision-making Boundary. Boundary patterns contains sufficient information to have an accurate description of the level classes' separation.

While non-Boundary patterns does not effect on the rate of classification [24], we can use the difference of these patterns in making new scattering matrices [20] so, most of algorithms often suffers from storage of a large number of training samples. The result is that high involvement of memory in response time and also high sensitivity to noise is raised thus, in order to overcome these problems, we use a new algorithm naming class boundary persevering CBP [23, 41].

In proposing framework, first by using the algorithm of (CBP) we divide training sets of X into two sub - bordering of X_B and non-bordering of X_{NB}.

3.1   Smoothing the Class Boundaries

Placing noises on the borders of the class causes reducing the rate of classification so, Placing noises on the borders of the class causes reducing the rate of classification so, in order to deal the noises [25, 26] filter (Wilson ENN) is normally used which is often known as noisy [27] also, in tests, in order to discard harmful instances misclassified by ENN, we use a KNN classification with (k = 3).

3.2   Distinguishing Between Boundary and Non-Boundary Instances

After the implementation of the first step, a new scheme using geometrical characteristics of class underlying distribution to partition the initial set to two sub sets Boundary and non-Boundary is used. First each series of pattern x a reachable R(x) is formed which containing samples that belong to $\omega(x)$ that lay to the nearest enemy (a sample by different class label) [28]. R(x) is an available set of X which is defined in respect to the ith the nearest the enemy $\xi_i(x)$ of x defined as:

$$R_i(x) = \{y \in X : \psi(x) = \psi(y)^\wedge \|x - y\|_2 \leq \|x - \xi_i(x)\|_2\}$$
$$where$$
$$\xi_i(x) = \arg \min \|x - z\|_2$$
$$z \in X$$
$$\psi(z) \neq \psi(x)$$
$$z \neq \xi_j(x), j = 1, \ldots, i - 1$$

(15)

To consider general overview of around the sample x, the sets of $I(x)$ which contains the arbitrary number k_R ($k_R = 3$) from the nearest enemy $\xi_i(x)$ that we define by Eq. (6). To avoid overlap of the enemies of x pattern towards each other so, the nearest next enemy is selected in a way that the angle between the line connecting the pattern of the new enemy pattern of x and connecting line of former enemies to pattern of to be placed at an angle - more than an arbitrary angle $\Phi (\Phi = 20)$.

$$I(x) = \arg \min \sum_{i \in J} \|x - \xi_i(x)\|_2$$
$$J \subseteq \{1, \ldots, n\}$$
$$|J| = k_R$$
$$\Phi(\xi_i(x) - x, x - \xi_i(x)) \geq \Phi_R, \forall_{i,j \in J, i \neq j}$$

(6)

$\Phi(.,.)$ The definer of the angle is between the two vectors. Now, in order to find the way of samples' dispersion in the space, the Cosines simulation is used. So, Cosine simulation between x and y with regard to the enemy is obtained through formula of 7:

$$C_{i,x}(y) = \frac{\langle y - x, \xi_i(x) - x \rangle}{\|y - x\|_2 \cdot \|\xi_i(x) - x\|_2}$$

(7)

If the friendly sample of y to be near connection between x and $\xi_i(x)$ it means Cosine similarity will be positive and x will be within non - pattern border. Then, we must calculate $C_{i,x}(x)$ for all samples y within each $R_i(x)$, and all the enemies of $I(x)$ will be calculated like the 8 relationship.

$$S_i(x) = \{C_{i,x}(y), \forall y \in R_i(x)\}$$
$$S(x) = \bigcup_{i \in I(x)} S_i(x)$$

(8)

Because all the samples of $y \epsilon R_i(x)$ their position within a sphere passing through $s(x)$ $\xi_i(x)$ and centered at x. So the distribution of casinos' values in $s(x)$ specifies the ratio of scattering friendly instances of y around the x. If the values to be positive in $s(x)$ the more y samples in the most common part of the circle and conical whose summit is in x position and its vector is placed in $x - \xi_i(x)$ (the width of conical entrance by the value of T is controlled). From the other side, the large negative value in $s(x)$ shows the sample of y is out of the cone and the criteria of distinctions between the Boundary and non-Boundary sets of X is expressed as Eq. (9) that the median $(s(x))$ stating the average of $s(x)$.

$$X_B = \{x \in X : midian(S(x)) < - T \vee |R_i(x) \leq 2|\}$$
$$X_{NB} = X - X_B \tag{9}$$

3.3   Making New Scattering Matrices

Now, we can make scattering matrices based on the pattern of Boundary and non-Boundary patterns Eq. (7).

$$S^{(b)} \equiv \sum_{i=1}^{c} \sum_{j=1}^{n^{(s)}} (x_j^{(B)} - m(i))(x_j^{(B)} - m(i))^T,$$

$$S^{(w)} \equiv \sum_{i=1}^{c} \sum_{j:y_j=i} (x_j^{(NB)} - m(i))(x_j^{(NB)} - m(i))^T$$

$n^{(B)}$ The number of the patterns of Boundary set and $n^{(NB)}$, is the number of models of non-Boundary set. As it is shown, in designing scattering matrix of between-class of $S^{(b)}$, out of the difference between the pattern of the Boundary pattern and the class means and the design of within-class scatter matrix $S^{(w)}$ uses the difference between non–Boundary patterns and the class means is used [49–51].

3.4   Discussing About the Effectiveness of the Proposing Measure

Scattering matrix between-classes $S^{(b)}$ which it's prove is mentioned in [3]

$$S^{(b)} \equiv \sum_{j=1}^{n} \sum_{u,v=1}^{n} \tilde{a}_{juv}^{(b)}(x_j - x_u)(x_j - x_u)^T$$

$$\tilde{a}_{juv}^{(b)} = \begin{cases} \frac{1}{\{n(y_u)\}^2} & if & x_j \in X^{(B)} \quad and \quad y_u = y_v \\ 0 & otherwise \end{cases}$$

$n(y_u)$ The number of samples belonging to the class y_u. This change of formulation based on the distance of weight is between the pair of sample data so, in the formula of (8), the values of non-zero weights, to scattering between non-bordering patterns, by similar label is specified and the values of zero – weight represents the difference between non-bordering patterns [5, 14, 29, 40, 42–48]. As it is observed, the patterns which are in the non - Boundary region do not have any effect on are in calculating between classes, classes, as well as they separating between the classes because they have been well-separated therefore, the other point is that this reality that based on the criteria of Boundary and non-Boundary patterns, the Boundary patterns between two class that in original space have been well–separated, is classified as non-Boundary pattern and does not have any effect in the estimate of scattering matrix between the classes. The goal designing scattering matrix (7) is to find W direction that by using it in Chernoff's criteria we can maximize Chernoff's j_c (3) optimizer and improve the number of specified patterns. Therefore, it is evident that in the obtained mapping space, the classes' overlapping is decreases considerably then based on this we replace new scattering matrices in Chernoff's criterion:

$$J_C(A) = \sum_{i=1}^{C-1} \sum_{j=i+1}^{C} P_i P_j tr \left(\begin{array}{l} (AS_w A^t)^{-1} \times \\ AS_w^{1/2} \left[\left(S_w^{-1/2} S_{ij}^{(w)} S_w^{-1/2}\right)^{-1/2} \times S_w^{-1/2} S_{ij}^{(b)} S_w^{-1/2} \left(S_w^{-1/2} S_{ij}^{(w)} S_w^{-1/2}\right)^{-1/2} + \right. \\ \left. \frac{1}{\pi_i \pi_j} (\log(S_w^{-1/2} S_{ij}^{(w)} S_w^{-1/2}) - \pi_i \log(S_w^{-1/2} S_i^{(w)} S_w^{-1/2}) - \pi_j \log(S_w^{-1/2} S_j^{(w)} S_w^{-1/2})) \right] AS_w^{1/2} \end{array} \right)$$

$$S^{(b)} \equiv \sum_{i=1}^{l} \sum_{j=1}^{n^{(B)}} \left(x_j^{(B)} - m(i)\right) \left(x_j^{(B)} - m(i)\right)^T$$

$$S^{(w)} = \sum_{i=1}^{l} \sum_{j:y_j=i} (x_j^{(NB)} - m(i))(x_j^{(NB)} - m(i))^T$$

$$S_C = \sum_{i=1}^{C-1} \sum_{j=i+1}^{C} P_i P_j tr \left(\begin{array}{l} (S_w)^{-1} \times \\ S_w^{1/2} \left[\left(S_w^{-1/2} S_{ij}^{(w)} S_w^{-1/2}\right)^{-1/2} \times S_w^{-1/2} S_{ij}^{(b)} S_w^{-1/2} \left(S_w^{-1/2} S_{ij}^{(w)} S_w^{-1/2}\right)^{-1/2} + \right. \\ \left. \frac{1}{\pi_i \pi_j} (\log(S_w^{-1/2} S_{ij}^{(w)} S_w^{-1/2}) - \pi_i \log(S_w^{-1/2} S_i^{(w)} S_w^{-1/2}) - \pi_j \log(S_w^{-1/2} S_j^{(w)} S_w^{-1/2})) \right] S_w^{1/2} \end{array} \right)$$

$$S_C W = \lambda S_w W$$
$$A = [W_1, W_2, \ldots, W_d] \tag{10}$$

By forming analyzing matrix (10), we can calculate W vector equal to Eigenvector which is the biggest Eigenvalue of analysis.

3.5   Implementation Algorithm of CBPHDA

Input: train data matrix $X = \{X_i \mid X_i \in R^d\}$ and $\{y_i \mid y_i \in \{1,2,...,l\}$ is the class label of $X_i\}$

Output: transformation matrix W_c

1. Obtain $X^{(NB)}$ and $X^{(B)}$ based on algorithm RPS

2. for each class $i = 1,...\mathcal{C}$

a. $X_{(i)} \leftarrow \{X_j\}_{y_j = i}$

c. $S^{(b)} \leftarrow S^{(b)} + \left(X^B - m(i)(1_{n^{(B)}})^t\right)\left(X^B - m(i)(1_{n^{(B)}})^t\right)^t$ where

$1_{n^{(B)}}$ denote the $n^{(B)}$-dimensional vector with ones.

d. $S^{(w)} \leftarrow S^{(w)} + \left(X^{NB} - m(i)(1_{n^{(NB)}})^t\right)\left(X^{NB} - m(i)(1_{n^{(NB)}})^t\right)^t$ where

$1_{n^{(NB)}}$ denote the $n^{(NB)}$-dimensional vector with ones.

e. $S_c \leftarrow \sum_{i=1}^{c-1}\sum_{j=i+1}^{c} P_i P_j tr \left((S_w)^{-1} \times S_w^{1/2} \left[\left(S_w^{-1/2}S_{ij}^{(w)}S_w^{-1/2}\right)^{-1/2} \times S_w^{-1/2}S_{ij}^{(b)}S_w^{-1/2}\left(S_w^{-1/2}S_{ij}^{(w)}S_w^{-1/2}\right)^{-1/2} + \frac{1}{\pi_i \pi_j}(\log(S_w^{-1/2}S_{ij}^{(w)}S_w^{-1/2}) - \pi_i \log(S_w^{-1/2}S_i^{(w)}S_w^{-1/2}) - \pi_j \log(S_w^{-1/2}S_j^{(w)}S_w^{-1/2})) \right] S_w^{1/2} \right)$.

3. Obtain the transformation matrix

a. $S_c \Psi = \lambda S_w \Psi$ where $\lambda_1 \geq \lambda_2 \geq .... \geq \lambda_d$.

b. $A = [w_1, w_2, ..., w_d]$

4   The Experiments

In this part, some tests has been introduced to prove the effectiveness of proposing method. The tests have been carried out on data based which has been downloaded from UCI Machine Learning [15]. The list of these Datasets have been mentioned in Table 1 and most of these datasets have been used in the articles of [1, 2, 11, 12]. Column D is the equivalent of the best chosen characteristic for the act of classification. To compare proposing method 4 other method has been used then, all of these methods, by using techniques have tried to solve the issue of data heterogeneity for increasing the rate of classification in LDA, therefore, based on this, for comparison, these methods have been used. Available unclear values in the Datasets have been replaced by average value of related features. The Output of proposing method (CBPHDA) has been compared with (FDA (Fisher Discriminant Algorithm (HAD) Heteroscedastic discriminant analysis (BHDA (Boundary Heteroscedastic discriminant analysis) SCDA (Super-class discriminant analysis) [30] other methods, which indicates that the output CBPHDA better than other methods (Table 2).

Table 1. The UCI dataset used for the experiments [15]

Dataset name	Number data	Number class	Number feature (number dimension)
Haberman	306	2	3
Australian credit	653	2	51
German credit	1000	2	38
Primary tumor	336	2	15
Banknote authentication	1370	2	3
Vote	435	2	16
Hepatitis	137	2	34
Liver	345	2	6
Zoo	101	2	16
Wine	178	3	13
New-thyroid	215	3	6
Teaching Assistant Evaluation	151	3	5
Iris	150	3	5
Soybean	47	4	36
Breast cancer Wisconsin	699	2	11
Hayes Roth	132	3	5
25PDB	1674	4	64

Table 2. The output results of experiments on the dataset used three methods

Dataset name	FDA	D	HDA	D	BHDA	D	SCDA	D	CBPHDA	D
Haberman	61.8056	1	55.6999	1	74.9247	1	64.5161	1	99.8623	1
Australian credit	67.6713	1	66.9161	1	74.4988	1	81.3846	1	81.4815	1
German credit	63.2000	1	58.4000	1	65.3000	1	69.5000	1	87.9315	1
Primary tumor	61.3387	2	63.9947	1	65.9777	1	78.2902	1	93.7500	1
Banknote authentication	97.4447	1	95.2618	1	97.3348	1	96.7201	1	98.6631	1
Vote	75.7558	2	94.2653	1	95.4979	1	94.2318	1	97.108	1
hepatitis	64.9451	2	64.1758	2	65.3956	1	78.5714	1	78.7121	1
Liver	57.4118	2	61.1513	1	67.7059	1	77.1429	1	86.9565	1
Zoo	88.2117	2	89.4038	1	96.3027	1	100.000	1	100.000	1
Wine	85.8443	1	87.8657	1	94.5050	1	94.9346	1	95.9583	1
new-thyroid	42.4026	1	45.9870	1	79.2338	1	99.5238	1	100.000	1
Teaching Assistant Evaluation	62.9583	1	52.4167	1	66.3333	1	79.4168	4	90.1667	2
Iris	87.8711	1	72.6417	1	98.7222	1	97.3333	1	100.000	1
Soybean	65.1720	1	70.7988	1	76.5000	1	75.5000	1	80.2288	2
Breast cancer Wisconsin	88.5300	2	87.2298	1	96.5714	1	96.4161	1	97.7391	1
Hayes Roth	82.4176	1	80.4505	1	86.8706	1	85.4326	1	87.9524	1
25PDB	64.2314	1	66.2146	1	83.3326	1	83.3333	1	93.9314	1

4.1   The Steps of Doing the Experiment

To evaluate the effectiveness of proposing method from Fisher classifier from cross-validation strategies: (1) leave-one-out (LOO) and (2) 10-fold cross validation has been used. in the strategy of leave-one-out (LOO) cross-validation the input data is used for teaching and the rest of the data for recognition and experiment although leave-one-out (LOO) cross-validation is a good method to evaluate effectiveness [16, 17], it has largely been criticized by the researchers. Hence, in this paper 10-fold cross-validation is used to do the act of classification. In order to avoid the singularity problem of within-class scattering matrix which is a current way of using linear classification analysis, a credit method introduced in [13] was used. First, the ranking of scattering matrix has been said in (7) so, if its ranking was not complete, aI has been added to them which a = 0001 and I is like unit matrix. To avoid problems with log and square root of matrix A inverse, of mentioned method in [10] has been used, therefore; to calculate F function, of specific A matrix has been used. A matrix is analyzed as specific analysis $\left(VDV^{-1}\right)$ in which V are as specific vectors of D and A matrix and also as specific matrix of A respectively, and then we apply f function on the main elements of specific value which contains these values and placed them in specific value matrix that resulted $f(A) = Vf(D)V^{-1}$ change. If Eigenvalues in applying log function to be reverse, negative or zero then, the number result will be equal to zero so, to stop this, a small fixed amount must be added [8]. In order to do this, a positive small fixed amount has been added to specific matrix D either negative or zero. Also in the Fig. 3. And 4 the proportion of the used methods in the experiments with CBPHDA on the using datasets has been shown.

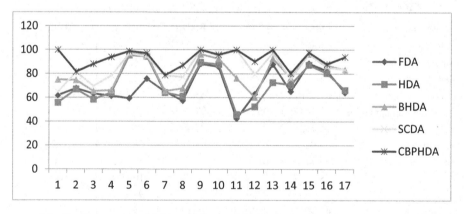

Fig. 3. The output exhibition of the results of experiment on the using datasets.

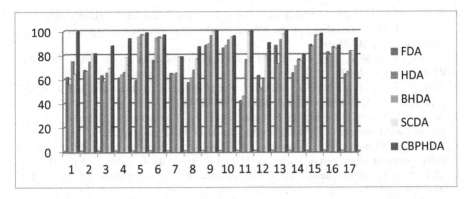

Fig. 4. The column display of the experiment results on the using datasets

4.2 Discussion on Experimental Method's Outputs

This section is devoted to discuss the observations resulted from the conducted experiments on the datasets however; the experiments showed that in the database of Iris between class of 1–2 and also 1–3 there is no bordering sample but, between class of 2&3 there are 20 bordering sample thus, we can conclude that the distance of class 1 in proportion to 2&3 is so far and, as result, the scattering matrix between the class of 1&2 and other class has no influence on designing Chernoff's criterion so, it is better in this state instead of using the estimate of distance between class pair Fisher's linear classification which is based on the mean intervals is being used because the best method for classifying the distanced classes are Fisher's classifier.

5 Conclusion

In this paper by using a new Algorithm, we could specify Boundary and non-Boundary patterns and draw scattering matrices based on the pattern's Boundary as well as their non-Boundary however; we theoretically showed that using these matrices cause the increasing number of extracted features and also removing the limitation the number of extracted features by Chernoff's criterion.

References

1. Fukunaga, K.: Introduction to Statistical Pattern Recognition. Academic Press, San Diego (2013)
2. Duin, R.P.W., Loog, M.: Linear dimensionality reduction via a heteroscedastic extension of LDA: the Chernoff criterion. IEEE Trans. Pattern Anal. Mach. Intell. **26**(6), 732–739 (2004)
3. Sugiyama, M.: Dimensionality reduction of multimodal labeled data by local fisher discriminant analysis. J. Mach. Learn. Res. **8**, 1027–1061 (2007)

4. ReinholdHaeb-Umbach, M.: Multi-class linear dimension reduction by generalized Fisher criteria. In: The Proceedings of the 6(th) International Conference on Spoken Language Processing, vol. II (2000)
5. Na, J.H., Park, M.S., Choi, J.Y.: Linear boundary discriminant analysis. Pattern Recognit. 43(3), 929–936 (2010)
6. Kim, H., Drake, B.L., Park, H.: Multiclass classifiers based on dimension reduction with generalized LDA. Pattern Recognit. 40(11), 2939–2945 (2007)
7. Salvi, G.: Accent clustering in Swedish using the Bhattacharyya distance. In: 15th International Congress of Phonetic Science, pp. 1149–1152, August 2003
8. Rueda, L., Oommen, B.J., Henríquez, C.: Multi-class pairwise linear dimensionality reduction using heteroscedastic schemes. Pattern Recognit. 43(7), 2456–2465 (2010)
9. McLachlan, G.: Discriminant Analysis and Statistical Pattern Recognition, vol. 544. Wiley, New York (2004)
10. Masip, D., Kuncheva, L.I., Vitrià, J.: An ensemble-based method for linear feature extraction for two-class problems. Pattern Anal. Appl. 8(3), 227–237 (2005)
11. Devijver, P.A., Kittler, J.: Pattern Recognition: A Statistical Approach, vol. 761. Prentice-Hall, London (1982)
12. Fisher, R.A.: The use of multiple measurements in taxonomic problems. Ann. Eugen. 7(2), 179–188 (1936)
13. Kohavi, R.: A study of cross-validation and bootstrap for accuracy estimation and model selection. In: IJCAI, vol. 14, no. 2, pp. 1137–1145, August 1995
14. Friedman, J.H.: Regularized discriminant analysis. J. Am. Stat. Assoc. 84(405), 165–175 (1989)
15. Newman, D.J., Hettich, S., Blake, C.L., Merz, C.J.: UCI repository of machine learning databases (1998). http://archive.ics.uci.edu/ml
16. Vapnik, V., Chapelle, O.: Bounds on error expectation for support vector machines. Neural Comput. 12(9), 2013–2036 (2000)
17. Chapelle, O., Vapnik, V., Bousquet, O., Mukherjee, S.: Choosing multiple parameters for support vector machines. Mach. Learn. 46(1–3), 131–159 (2002)
18. Yaghoubi, A., Ghaffari, H.R.: Improved LDA by using distributing distances and boundary patterns
19. Wang, Z., Ruan, Q., Liu, S., Guo, S.: Regularized neighborhood boundary discriminant analysis for facial expression recognition (2011)
20. Marchiori, E.: Hit miss networks with applications to instance selection. J. Mach. Learn. Res. 9, 997–1017 (2008)
21. Marchiori, E.: Graph-based discrete differential geometry for critical instance filtering. In: Buntine, W., Grobelnik, M., Mladenić, D., Shawe-Taylor, J. (eds.) ECML PKDD 2009. LNCS (LNAI), vol. 5782, pp. 63–78. Springer, Heidelberg (2009). https://doi.org/10.1007/978-3-642-04174-7_5
22. Marchiori, E.: Class conditional nearest neighbor for large margin instance selection. IEEE Trans. Pattern Anal. Mach. Intell. 32, 364–370 (2010)
23. Nikolaidis, K., Goulermas, J.Y., Wu, Q.H.: A class boundary preserving algorithm for data condensation. Pattern Recognit. 44(3), 704–715 (2011)
24. Brighton, H., Mellish, C.: Advances in instance selection for instance-based learning algorithms. Data Min. Knowl. Discov. 6, 153–172 (2002)
25. Smyth, B., Keane, M.T.: Remembering to forget. In: Proceeding of the 14th International Conference on Artificial Intelligence, pp. 377–382 (1995)
26. Wilson, D.R., Martinez, T.R.: Reduction techniques for instance-based learning algorithms. Mach. Learn. 38, 257–286 (2000)

27. Cheng, Y.: Mean shift, mode seeking, and clustering. IEEE Trans. Pattern Anal. Mach. Intell. **17**, 790–799 (1995)

28. Dasarathy, B.V.: Minimal consistent set (MCS) identification for optimal nearest neighbor decision systems design. IEEE Trans. Syst. Man Cybernet. **24**(3), 511–517 (1994)

29. Arif, M., Wang, G., Balas, V.E.: Secure VANETs: trusted communication scheme between vehicles and infrastructure based on fog computing. Stud. Inform. Control. **27**(2), 235–246 (2018)

30. Zhu, X.: Super-class discriminant analysis: a novel solution for heteroscedasticity. Pattern Recognit. Lett. **34**(5), 545–551 (2013)

31. Gheisari, M., Esnaashari, M.: Data storages in wireless sensor networks to deal with disaster management. In: Emergency and Disaster Management: Concepts, Methodologies, Tools, and Applications, pp. 655–682. IGI Global (2019)

32. Gheisari, M., Baloochi, H., Gharghi, M., Khajehyousefi, M.: An evaluation of two proposed systems of sensor datas storage in total data parameter. Int. Geoinformatics Res. Dev. J., March 2012

33. Porkar, P., Gheisari, M., Bazyari, G.H., Kaviyanjahromi, Z.: A comparison with two sensor data storages in energy. In: ICCCI. ASME Press (2011)

34. Rezaeiye, P.P., Gheisari, M.: Performance analysis of two sensor data storages. In: Proceedings of 2nd International Conference on Circuits, Systems, Communications & Computers (CSCC), pp. 133–136 (2011)

35. Rezaeiye, P.P., Rezaeiye, P.P., Karbalayi, E., Gheisari, M.: Statistical method used for doing better corneal junction operation. In: Material and Manufacturing Technology III. Advanced Materials Research, vol. 548, pp. 762–766. Trans Tech Publications (9 2012)

36. Rezaeiye, P.P., et al.: Agent programming with object oriented (C++). In: ICECCT, pp. 1–10. IEEE (2017)

37. Gheisari, M.: Design, implementation and evaluation of SemHD: a new semantic hierarchical sensor data storage. Indian J. Innov. Dev. **1**, 115–120 (2012). ISSN 2277 – 5390

38. Gheisari, M., Esnaashari, M.: A survey to face recognition algorithms: advantageous and disadvantageous. J. Mod. Technol. Eng. **2**(1), 57–65 (2017)

39. Gheisari, M., et al.: NSSSD: a new semantic hierarchical storage for sensor data. In: 2016 IEEE 20th International Conference on Computer Supported Cooperative Work in Design (CSCWD), Nanchang, pp. 174–179 (2016)

40. Gheisari, M., Wang, G., Bhuiyan, M.Z.A.: A survey on deep learning in big data. In: 2017 IEEE International Conference on Computational Science and Engineering (CSE) and IEEE International Conference on Embedded and Ubiquitous Computing (EUC), Guangzhou, pp. 173–180 (2017)

41. Jafari, M., Wang, J., Qin, Y., Gheisari, M., Shahabi, A.S., Tao, X.: Automatic text summarization using fuzzy inference. In: 2016 22nd International Conference on Automation and Computing (ICAC), Colchester, pp. 256–260 (2016)

42. Gheisari, M.: The effectiveness of schema therapy integrated with neurological rehabilitation methods to improve executive functions in patients with chronic depression. Health Sci. J. **10**(4) (2016)

43. Gheisari, M., et al.: MAPP: a modular arithmetic algorithm for privacy preserving in IoT. In: 2017 IEEE International Conference on Ubiquitous Computing and Communications (ISPA/IUCC), 2017 IEEE International Symposium on Parallel and Distributed Processing with Applications and IEEE (2017)

44. Ashourian, M., Gheisari, M., Hashemi, A.: An improved node scheduling scheme for resilient packet ring network. Majlesi J. Electr. Eng. **9**(2), 43 (2015)

45. Gheisari, M., Wang, G., Chen, S.: IoT-SDNPP: a method for privacy-preserving in IoT-based smart city with software defined networking. In: 18th International Conference on Algorithms and Architectures for Parallel Processing Guangzhou, China, 15–17 November 2018 (2018)

46. Yang, W., Wang, G., Chood, K.K.R., Chen, S.: HEPart: a balanced hypergraph partitioning algorithm for big data applications. Futur. Gener. Comput. Syst. **83**, 250–268 (2018)

47. Dai, Y., Wang, G.: Analyzing tongue images using a conceptual alignment deep autoencoder. IEEE Access **6**, 5962–5972 (2018)

48. Peng, S., et al.: An immunization framework for social networks through big data based influence modeling. IEEE Trans. Dependable Secur. Comput. **PP**(99), 1 (2017)

49. Javadpour, A., Memarzadeh-Tehran, H., Saghafi, F.: A temperature monitoring system incorporating an array of precision wireless thermometers. In: 2015 International Conference on Smart Sensors and Application (ICSSA) (2015)

50. Javadpour, A., Memarzadeh-Tehran, H.: A wearable medical sensor for provisional healthcare. In: 2015 2nd International Symposium on Physics and Technology of Sensors (ISPTS) (2015)

51. Javadpour, A., Abharian, S.K., Wang, G.: Feature selection and intrusion detection in cloud environment based on machine learning algorithms. In: 2017 IEEE International Symposium on Parallel and Distributed Processing with Applications and 2017 IEEE International Conference on Ubiquitous Computing and Communications (ISPA/IUCC) (2017)

Fault Diagnosis Algorithm for WSN Based on Clustering and Credibility

Lidan Wang[1], Xin Xu[1], Xiaofei Zhang[1], Cheng-Kuan Lin[1(⊠)], and Yu-Chee Tseng[2]

[1] School of Computer Science and Technology, Soochow University, Suzhou 215006, China
{20165227008,20175227038}@stu.suda.edu.cn,
xiaofeinotdafeizhang@gmail.com,cklin@suda.edu.cn
[2] Department of Computer Science, National Chiao-Tung University, Hsinchu, Taiwan
yctseng@cs.nctu.edu.tw

Abstract. Fault diagnosis is one of the challenging problems in wireless sensor network (WSN). This paper proposes a fault diagnosis algorithm based on clustering and credibility (FDCC). Firstly, the network is divided into several clusters according to both geographic positions and measurements of sensor nodes for the purpose of improving the accuracy of network diagnostic result. The process of clustering can be divided into five phases: region division, head selection, coarse clustering, coarse cluster merge and cluster adjustment. Then, in order to further improve the accuracy of diagnostic result, a credibility model based on historical diagnostic result and remaining energy is established for each neighbor node. At last, nodes with higher credibility are selected to participate in diagnostic process. Simulation results show that the proposed algorithm can guarantee higher diagnostic accuracy.

Keywords: Fault diagnosis · Sensor network · Clustering
Credibility model

1 Introduction

WSNs are widely used in different applications such as ecological environment monitoring, traffic management, health care, agriculture application and smart homes. Due to the poor deployment of environment and sensor nodes that usually provisioned with low-capacity batteries, these nodes are subjected to various kinds of faults. Node faults will invalidate node or cause node to detect abnormal data [1]. At last, it will affect the network behavior and lead to errors in decision making process. Therefore, practical and efficient fault diagnosis plays a very important role in guaranteeing the perceived quality of WSN.

In recent years, the study on fault detection and fault tolerance has gradually become an important branch of WSN. A lot of research [11] about fault diagnosis for WSN has already obtained, including the neighbor co-ordination [9],

© Springer Nature Switzerland AG 2018
J. Vaidya and J. Li (Eds.): ICA3PP 2018, LNCS 11335, pp. 145–159, 2018.
https://doi.org/10.1007/978-3-030-05054-2_11

clustering based [21], test based [14] and other types. Many of these studies are based on the spatial-temporal correlation characteristics of nodes in WSNs [10].

The clustering based approaches create a virtual communication backbone to group sensor nodes and split the overall network into different clusters. Fault detection is normally distributed and executed in each individual cluster. Each cluster is usually composed of a cluster head and multiple member nodes. Member nodes only communicate with cluster heads, and cluster heads are responsible for data fusion and inter cluster data forwarding within clusters, which is good for routing selection, data fusion and energy saving. We find that the idea of clustering has been used in many papers, however, many algorithms are too simple to consider the clustering of WSN. For example, algorithm like LEACH [4] only considers the energy when clustering, the energy load of the entire network is allocated equally to each sensor node without considering the measurements of the nodes in each cluster and is it correct to use neighbor nodes for fault diagnosis? Considering the spatial correlation in WSN, that is, the measured values of nodes should be similar to those near by. So, some algorithms divide the network by geographical regions. However, sensor nodes are usually deployed in complex environment, consider such a scenario in which nodes are used to measure the temperature of a building. If air conditioners are turned on in offices, the temperature inside will be significantly different from temperature outside. However, if the nodes are only clustered according to geographical locations, the nodes are likely to be grouped into the same cluster because they are not far enough. If these nodes with large differences in measurement values are involved in the diagnosis, it may lead to misjudgement. Therefore, this paper presents a more reasonable clustering method by considering both geographic positions and measurements.

Moreover, many fault diagnosis algorithms based on neighborhood coordination randomly select serval neighbor nodes to participate in the diagnosis. In addition, some algorithms will establish reliability models for neighbor nodes, and select the most reliable nodes to participate in diagnosis to improve the accuracy of diagnosis. Historical data of sensor nodes are often used to build reliability models, previous studies only focused on the measurements of nodes, but ignored the diagnosis results of nodes. Specifically, if two nodes x and y have similar historical measurements, but x was diagnosed as fault-free two days ago, and y was diagnosed as fault-free one month ago, it is obvious that x is more reliable.

Based on the above analysis, this paper presents a distributed fault detection mechanism based on clustering and credibility for WSN. Firstly, the network is divided into serval clusters according to geographic positions and measurements of nodes. Diagnosis algorithm is only performed in clusters of nodes to be diagnosed rather than the whole network, which can reduce the energy consumption. Before selecting neighbor nodes to participate in the diagnosis, the credibility model of neighbor nodes is established to judge the credibility of diagnostic results according to historical diagnostic results and the remaining energy.

Finally, selecting nodes with higher credibility to participate in the diagnostic process.

The rest of the paper is organized as follows. Section 2 describes the related work and Sect. 3 defines the preliminaries. In Sect. 4, we elaborate the cluster algorithm in detail. In Sect. 5, the credibility model is established. Section 6 shows the experiment results. Section 7 concludes the paper.

2   Related Work

Nowadays, a large number of works have looked at the efficiency and accuracy of fault diagnosis algorithms for WSNs. Clustering is an emerging approach in diagnosing faults in WSN which enables the diagnosis techniques to be communication efficient [3]. Venkataraman et al. [15] proposed an approach in which the sensor nodes detect the energy failures in their respective clusters. Wei et al. [17] suggested cluster-based real-time fault diagnosis aggregation algorithm (CRFDA). Mahapatro and Khilar [12] proposed an on-line distributed fault diagnosis scheme called cluster-based distributed fault diagnosis (CDFD) algorithm.

In neighbor coordination approaches, a node takes a decision about whether or not to disregard its own sensor reading, which is based either on the sensor readings from its neighbors or on the weights like physical distances from the event, trustworthiness and their measurements, etc.

Chen et al. [2] proposed DFD algorithm to identify the faulty sensors. It used local comparisons with a modified majority voting, where each sensor node makes a decision based on comparisons between its own measurements and neighbor nodes. Lee and Choi [7] approached WSN fault detection problems where time redundancy was used to tolerate transient faults in sensing and communication. A sliding window was employed to eliminate delay involved in the time redundancy. Xiao et al. [20] presented an in-network voting scheme that determines faulty sensor readings in WSN by considering both the correlation of measurements between sensor nodes and the trustworthiness of a sensor node.

Although the above algorithms achieved good performance, there are still some shortcomings. Algorithms based on clustering paid too much attention to energy balance within cluster and the similarity of nodes in the cluster is ignored. In addition, sensor networks deployed in harsh environments are mostly dynamic, none of the above algorithms taked the addition of new nodes and the failure of old nodes into account. Furthermore, many of the neighbor coordination approaches only considered the spatio-temporal correlations among sensor data of neighboring nodes and ignore the credibility and remaining energy of neighbor nodes which in turn reduced the detection accuracy of a diagnosis scheme and increased the false alarm rate. Therefore, we can further design a more reasonable fault diagnosis algorithm for WSN.

3   Preliminaries

Sensor nodes can be considered as spatial data objects. As it is introduced in the study of Lin et al. [8], spatial data usually have two kinds of attributes. One is in optimization domain, and the other one is in the geographic domain. The location of a node is an attribute in the geographic domain, while its measured value is an attribute in the optimization domain. The goal of dual clustering over the optimization and geographic domains is to group sensor nodes with similar value within a certain geographical range. Nodes in the same cluster form a compact region in terms of geographic attributes. But a node usually needs to observe different kinds of values. For example, nodes deployed on the farm need to measure temperature, humidity, light and so on. Therefore, the values of nodes in the optimization domain are usually multidimensional. Table 1 summarizes the symbols and definitions used in this paper.

The distance between two spatial objects serves as the dissimilarity measurement [19]. For two nodes S_i and S_j, the distance measurement in the geographic domain is formulated as

$$dist_{geo}(S_i, S_j) = \sqrt{\sum_{k=1}^{d_G}(G_i^k - G_j^k)^2} \tag{1}$$

and the distance measurement in the optimization domain is formulated as

$$dist_{opt}(S_i, S_j) = \sqrt{\sum_{k=1}^{d_O}(O_i^k - O_j^k)^2} \tag{2}$$

If $dist_{geo}(S_i, S_j) < r$, the two sensors are adjacent, where r represents the communication radius of network.

Table 1. Symbol table

Symbol	Definition
S_i	Sensor node i
$N(S_i)$	Neighbor nodes set of S_i
O_i	Optimization domain of S_i
G_i	Geographic domain of S_i
O_i^j	The jth attribute in O_i
G_i^j	The jth attribute in G_i
d_O	The number of dimensions in the optimization domain
d_G	The number of dimensions in the geographic domain

4   Cluster with Local Search

This paper proposes a clustering algorithm to cluster nodes from both geographic and optimization domains. This algorithm includes five phases: region division, head selection, coarse clustering, coarse clusters mergence and cluster adjustment. Firstly, map out some regions according to geography. Then, select some cluster heads and let these cluster heads generate coarse clusters. After that, merge the coarse clusters according to relative rules. Usually, the network environment is dynamic and there often exists nodes joining or failing. Thus, we need to adjust the clustering of network from time to time. The following subsections present the details of each phase.

Phase 1: Region division

When sensor nodes are deployed, each node simultaneously starts an impairment timer whose value is set randomly. If node x can not be added to any other region before the timer reduced to zero, then x will become a master and broadcast a message to ask whether the surrounding nodes can join to it. Nodes receiving the request message terminates its own timer immediately and become x's slave nodes. These slave nodes continue to broadcast message and ask whether their neighbor nodes will join in. After receiving the message, these nodes also terminate their own timer immediately and become x's slave nodes. Repeat this for ξ times which is set according to different environment. The master node x and it's all slave nodes form a region. The remaining nodes in the network continue to run the timer until the timer of all the nodes change to zero. So far, the network is divided into several regions.

As we can see in Fig. 1(a), the network is divided into five regions. In order to simplify the description, here we just set the one-dimensional values on optimization domain. The number beside the node indicates the temperature measured by the sensor node.

Phase 2: Select the heads

After dividing up the regions, pick some nodes as heads and perform the clustering phase. In order to achieve the purpose of clustering, heads should be much different from each other in the optimization domain. It is possible to treat the regions as temporary clusters because they are inherently far apart in the geographic domain. Therefore, the centroid of each region in optimization domain is regarded as the head.

Figure 1(b) shows the head selection, the black nodes are the heads of the five regions. For example, in the region of nodes k, i, h, g and f, 15.5 is the mid-value of the five values of these nodes, so we select f as the head of this region.

Phase 3: Coarse clustering

Expanding from heads according to the local search mechanism until the clusters are stable, which is called coarse clustering. The clusters obtained from coarse clustering are called coarse clusters.

Algorithm 1 describes the coarse clustering algorithm. Firstly, this algorithm treats each head node produced by phase 2 as a independent cluster and calculates the centroid in optimization domain. Then, adapting the concept of local

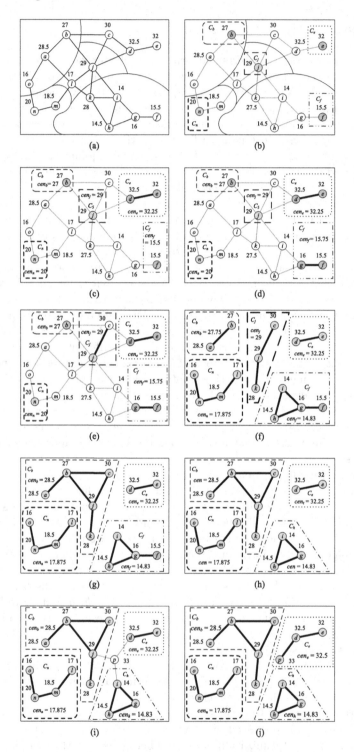

Fig. 1. The process of clustering.

search, calculate the distance in optimization domain between centroid and its nearest neighbor node, and then push into a priority queue. After that, add the neighbor node into the cluster with the shortest distance and update the centroid and priority queue. Repeat above operations until the priority queue is empty. If there are still nodes left when the priority queue is empty, add nodes into the nearest cluster in optimization domain.

Algorithm 1. Coarse clustering

Input: a sensor network Net and attributes of each sensor
Output: a set of clusters SC
1 let $N_u(S_i)$(respectively, $N_c(S_i)$) be the unclustered(respectively, clustered) neighbors of S_i;
2 /* initialization */
3 each head S_i forms a cluster C_i and let cen_i be the centroid of C_i;
4 **foreach** $head$ S_i **do**
5 | let d be the smallest distance $dist_{opt}(S_i, S_j)$, where $S_j \in N_u(S_i)$;
6 | add (d, S_i, S_j) into a priority queue PQ sorted by d;
7 /* local search */
8 **while** PQ is not $empty$ **do**
9 | add S_j into cluster C_i and update cen_i;
10 | remove (d, S_i, S_j) from PQ with the smallest d;
11 | remove all pairs from PQ where the third parameter is S_j let d be the smallest distance $dist_{opt}(cen_i, S_k)$, where $S_k \in N_u(C_i)$;
12 | add pair (d, S_t, S_k) into PQ, where S_t is the neighbor node of S_k in C_i;
13 /* fix unclustered sensors */
14 **foreach** $unclustered$ $S_i \in O$ **do**
15 | **if** $|N_c(S_i)| > 0$ **then**
16 | add S_i to the nearest cluster of $S_j \in N_c(S_i)$ and update the corresponding centriod;
17 | **else**
18 | S_i forms a new cluster;
19 **return** the union of all clusters SC;

Figure 1(b)–(f) show the process of coarse clustering. Firstly, as shown in Fig. 1(b), each head forms a coarse cluster, nodes b, e, j, n and f respectively form C_b, C_e, C_j, C_n and C_f. At this time, $cen_b = 27$, $cen_e = 32$, $cen_j = 29$, $cen_n = 20$, $cen_b = 27$ and $cen_f = 15.5$. The priority queue $PQ = \{(0.5, e, d), (0.5, f, g), (1, j, c), (1.5, b, a), (1.5, n, m)\}$, then, remove $(0.5, e, d)$ and add d into C_e, update $cen_e = 32.25$. Among the neighbors of nodes in C_e, node c has the smallest distance with cen_e, $dist_{opt}(cen_e, c) = 2.25$, so add $(2.25, d, c)$ into PQ. In Fig. 1(c), the PQ becomes $\{(0.5, f, g), (1, j, c), (1.5, b, a), (1.5, n, m), (2.25, d, c)\}$. Similarly, in Fig. 1(d), remove $(0.5, f, g)$ and add g to C_f. Update $cen_f = 15.75$ at the same time. Among the neighbors of nodes in C_f, node h

has the smallest distance with cen_f, $dist_{opt}(cen_f, h) = 1.25$, so add $(1.25, g, h)$ into PQ, the PQ becomes $\{(1, j, c), (1.25, g, h), (1.5, b, a), (1.5, n, m), (2.25, d, c)\}$ after that. Repeat above operations until no node left. Figure 1(f) shows the result of coarse clustering.

Phase 4: Merge coarse clusters

The coarse clusters discovered by local search might be fragments of the connective dual clusters due to the nature of local search. Therefore, merge the coarse clusters belonging to the same connective dual cluster. If there are two adjacent nodes in the two coarse clusters, the two coarse clusters are said to be adjacent. When the distance between their centroids on optimization domain is within the threshold ε, then merge the two coarse clusters into one cluster. Figure 1(f) and (g) show the process of merging coarse clusters. In Fig. 1(f), there are five coarse clusters. Suppose $\varepsilon = 3$. The distance between cen_b and cen_j is smaller than 3, so merger the two coarse clusters into a new cluster. The value of the centroid of this cluster is changed to 28.5. Stop merging clusters when there are no qualified coarse clusters.

Phase 5: Cluster adjustment

In complex environments, nodes often fail or join, so after completion of clustering, it is necessary for system to check whether any node in the network join or fail to leave at each interval. Algorithm 2 describes the process of cluster adjustment in detail.

If a node is added, add the node into the adjacent cluster which the distance in optimization domain between the new node and the centroid of the cluster is smallest.

If a node fails to leave the network, it will be discussed in detail.

(1) If the node is a boundary node, it can be deleted directly without other operations.
(2) If the node is a head, then all the nodes in the cluster should be redivided. Similarly, the centroid for the cluster in optimization domain is regarded as head. For each of the remaining nodes, if it is connected with the new head, join it to the cluster which the head belongs to. Otherwise, join it to the neighbor cluster with the smallest distance between itself and the centroid of cluster.
(3) If the node is neither a boundary node nor a head, delete it directly if this will not disrupt the connectivity of the cluster. Otherwise, for each disconnected node in the cluster, join it to the cluster which the distance between itself and the centroid of neighbor cluster is smallest.

Figure 1(g) and (h) show the situation that a node f fails to leave. However, f is the head in one cluster, so it is need to re-select a new head of this cluster. The value of node h is median in the cluster, obviously, h becomes the new head. The remaining nodes i and g are still connected with the new head after deleting f, so we can directly add i and g into cluster of h. The process of a new node p added can be seen in Fig. 1(i) and (j). There are 3 neighbor nodes of p: j, d and l, then calculate $dist_{opt}(p, cen_s)$, $s = b$, h and e respectively. As a result, add p into cluster C_e because the value of $dist_{opt}(p, cen_e)$ is smallest.

Algorithm 2. Clustering adjustment

Input: a sensor network Net and threshold ε
Output: a new sensor network after adjustment Net'

1 check whether any node in the network join or fail to leave;
2 **if** *a new node S_i joined* **then**
3 | let $d = dist_{opt}(S_i, cen_j)$, where $S_j \in N(S_i)$;
4 | join S_i into cluster C_j, which makes d smallest;

5 **else if** *a node S_i failed to leave* **then**
6 | **if** S_i *is a boundary node* **then**
7 | | delete S_i directly;

8 | **else if** S_i *is a head* **then**
9 | | select the centroid on optimization domain S_k as the new head;
10 | | **foreach** S_j *in the original cluster* **do**
11 | | | **if** S_j *is adjacent to S_k* **then**
12 | | | | add S_j to the cluster where S_k is;

13 | | | **else**
14 | | | | let $d = dist_{opt}(S_j, cen_t)$, where $S_t \in N(S_j)$;
15 | | | | join S_j into cluster C_t, which makes d smallest;

16 | **else**
17 | | **if** *the cluster is unconnected after deleting S_i* **then**
18 | | | **foreach** S_j *which is not connected with head* **do**
19 | | | | let $d = dist_{opt}(S_j, cen_t)$, where $S_t \in N(S_j)$;
20 | | | | join S_j into cluster C_t, which makes d smallest;

21 | | **else**
22 | | | delete S_i directly;

23 merge clusters;
24 **return** the new network Net';

---

5   Establish the Reliability Model

After performing clustering operations according to the above method, the following diagnosis algorithm is designed for node which need to be diagnosed.

In fault diagnosis algorithms for WSN, the diagnosis results are often obtained by comparing the neighbor nodes with the node to be diagnosed. However, not all neighbor nodes are reliable, if the neighbor node itself is faulty, the diagnosis result it gives is unreliable. So, it is necessary to select reliable neighbor nodes for diagnosis. In this paper, a credibility model is established for each neighbor node to ensure the accuracy of the diagnosis results.

The historical diagnosis results of neighbor nodes can be regarded as one of the criteria of credibility model. If the neighbor node was diagnosed as a fault-free node before, the longer the time, the less credible it is. Here we set two parameters T_1 and $T_2(T_1 < T_2)$, assuming the current time is t and the time when the neighbor node S_j was diagnosed is t'. Here we use w_j to represent the weight of history diagnosis result of S_j.

$$
w_j = \begin{cases}
-1 & \text{if } t - t' \leq T_2 \text{ and } S_j \text{ was diagnosed as faulty at time } t \\
0 & \text{if } t - t' > T_2 \text{ or } S_j \text{ has never been diagnosed within } T_2 \text{ days} \\
1 & \text{if } T_1 < t - t' < T_2 \text{ and } S_j \text{ was diagnosed as fault-free at time } t \\
2 & \text{if } t - t' \leq T_1 \text{ and } S_j \text{ was diagnosed as fault-free at time } t
\end{cases} \tag{3}
$$

In addition, the data collected by nodes with low energy is often unstable and in order to avoid nodes with low energy participating in diagnosis and exhausting energy, the energy of neighbor nodes should also be considered in the credibility model.

This paper adopts the energy consumption model of sensor node given in [18]. Suppose the channel in communication is symmetric. If k bit information is transmitted through the process of distance d, then the energy consumption of the transmission $E_{Tx}(k, d)$ can be given as follows:

$$
E_{Tx}(k, d) = E_{Tx_{elec}}(k) + E_{Tx_{amp}}(k, d) = k E_{elec} + k \varepsilon_{fs} d^r \tag{4}
$$

where $E_{Tx_{elec}}(k)$ and E_{elec} are the energy consumption of the wireless transceiver circuit for k bit information or single bit information, respectively. $E_{Tx_{amp}}(k, d)$ is the energy consumption of the power amplifier for k bit information transmitted through the distance d. ε_{fs} is the power consumption of amplifier to deal with each bit data transmission in the free-space path fading model. r is a constant of wireless channel decided by the transmission distance of signal d ($r = 2$ if $d < d_0$, otherwise, $r = 4$), and d_0 is the transmission distance threshold which is defined as:

$$
d_0 = \sqrt{\frac{\varepsilon_{fs}}{\varepsilon_{mp}}} \tag{5}
$$

where ε_{fs} is the energy consumption of the power amplifier in the multi-path fading model. The energy consumption of receiving side can be calculated as follows:

$$
E_{Rx}(k) = E_{Rx_{elec}}(k) = k E_{elec} \tag{6}
$$

where $E_{Rx}(k)$ is the energy consumption of the wireless receiver circuit for k bit information.

Combine the above two indicators, the credibility model of S_j can be noted as $CM_j = \alpha_W \cdot \frac{w_j}{2} + \alpha_E \cdot \frac{E_{rj}}{E_{max}}$, where E_{max} means the maximum remaining energy of all neighbor nodes. α_W and α_E are two parameters that control the weights of historical diagnosis results and residual energy in the credibility model, and can be set according to the actual environment. After calculating the reliability of each neighbor node, the first δ nodes with the highest reliability are selected to participate in the diagnosis, where δ is set according to the network environment. Because nodes in WSN have the characteristics of temporal and spatial similarity, the selected neighbor nodes can be used to test the suspicious nodes S_i, suppose C_{ij} represents the test result between S_i and S_j:

$$C_{ij} = \begin{cases} 1 & \text{if } d_{ij}^t \leq \theta_1 \text{ and } \Delta d_{ij}^{\Delta t_l} \leq \theta_2 \\ -1 & \text{if } d_{ij}^t > \theta_1 \text{ and } \Delta d_{ij}^{\Delta t_l} > \theta_2 \\ 0 & \text{otherwise} \end{cases} \tag{7}$$

where d_{ij}^t is the measurement difference between S_i and S_j at time t, $\Delta d_{ij}^{\Delta t_l}$ is the measurement difference between S_i and S_j from time t_l to t_{l+1}, θ_1 and θ_2 are two predefined threshold values. We denote n_h, n_f and n_s as the number of test result $C_{ij} = 1$, $C_{ij} = -1$ and $C_{ij} = 0$. The diagnosis result of S_i can be obtained by below equation.

$$S_i = \begin{cases} \text{faulty} & \text{if } n_f = \max\{n_h, n_f, n_s\} \\ \text{fault-free} & \text{if } n_h = \max\{n_h, n_f, n_s\} \\ \text{suspicious} & \text{if } n_s = \max\{n_h, n_f, n_s\} \end{cases} \tag{8}$$

6   Experiment

Correct Detection Rate (CDR) and False Alarm Rate (FAR) are the two metrics used to evaluate the performance of diagnostic algorithm. CDR is defined as the ratio of the number of faulty nodes which are diagnosed correctly to the total number of faulty nodes in the network. The FAR is the ratio of the number of fault-free nodes which are diagnosed as faulty nodes to the total number of fault-free nodes.

We performed experiments both in simulation environments and real environments. The results are compared with the DFD algorithm [2], PLD [16] algorithm and FD-CAC [13] algorithm. In order to avoid the contingency of experiment, the experimental data were obtained by averaging after 100 operations. We used JAVA as the tool for simulation experiments. As we can see in Fig. 2, the simulation area is a square with $250\,\text{m} \times 250\,\text{m}$, where $n = 1000$ sensor nodes are randomly deployed, and the average temperature varies from region to region. The parameters used in all four algorithms are set as following:

PLD: $C_{max} = 5$, $L_{max} = 3$ and $\theta = 2$.
DFD: $\theta_1 = 2$ and $\theta_2 = 1$.
FD – CAC: $k = 10$, $\partial = 0.2$, $s = e = \varepsilon = 2$ and $\lambda = 3$.
FDCC: $\theta_1 = 2$, $\theta_2 = 1$, $\varepsilon = \theta = 3$, $\alpha_W = 2$, $\alpha_E = 1$ and $\delta = 4$

Figure 3 shows the CDR of four algorithms. The communication radius r was set to 20 and 30 respectively. 'PLD-20' means the r in PLD algorithm is set to 20. As we can see, with the increase of node failure probability, the CDRs of all four algorithms decrease. However, the CDR of FDCC is always better than PLD, DFD and FD-CAC. Even when $p = 25\%$, the CDR of FDCC is still above 95%.

Accordingly, Fig. 4 describes the FAR of four algorithms when $r = 20$. Clearly, FDCC performs much better on FAR than PLD, DFD and FD-CAC. The difference of FAR between the four algorithms is becoming more and more obvious as r increases. The FAR of PLD is 6.333% when $p = 25\%$, however, that of FDCC is just 1.336%.

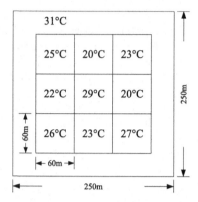

Fig. 2. Simulation environment.

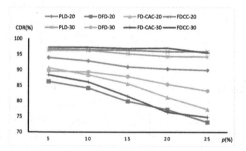

Fig. 3. The CDR with the change of p when $r = 20$ and $r = 30$ in simulation experiments.

The real experiments were conducted on the first floor of science and technology building in Soochow University. We put 45 nodes in the corridors and the labs. See Fig. 5 for details.

Figure 6 shows the ZigBee element we used in the experiments whose chip model is MKW01Z128. The chip consists of the ARM Cortex-M0+ core KL26 microcontroller and the RF module X1231-RF. The RF transceiver operates under the permissible industrial, scientific and medical (ISM) band of 315, 433, 470, 868, 915, 928 and 960 MHz, following the 802.15.4 protocol. Programmable output power in -18 to $+17$ dBm. The communication distance is about 230 m. We added temperature sensors on the ZigBee elements to test the temperature.

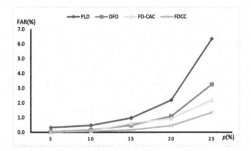

Fig. 4. The FAR with the change of p when $r = 20$ in simulation experiments.

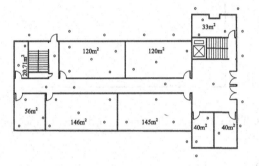

Fig. 5. The environment of real experiments.

Fig. 6. The ZigBee element used in experiments.

The temperature outdoor was about 33 °C, at aisle, it was between 29 °C and 30 °C, while the temperature differed from 24 °C to 27 °C in the labs.

Figures 7 and 8 show the results of real experiments. As we can see, FDCC performs much better than PLD, DFD and FD-CAC in both CDR and FAR. When $r < 15\%$, the CDR of FDCC is above 98% while the FAR is close to 0%.

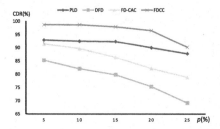

Fig. 7. The CDR with the change of p in real experiments.

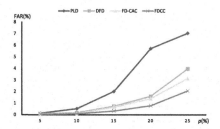

Fig. 8. The FAR with the change of p in real experiments.

7 Conclusions

In this paper, we proposed a fault diagnostic algorithm for WSN based on clustering and credibility. Firstly, the network was divided into several clusters according to both geographic positions and measurements, which can reduce the range of diagnosis and improve the diagnostic efficiency. Then, a credibility model was established for each neighbor node based on historical diagnostic results and remaining energy. As a result, it can improve the accuracy of the diagnosis and reduce energy waste to extend network life. To verify the feasibility of our algorithm, we designed simulation experiments and real experiments. Compared with DFD, PLD and FD-CAC, experimental data showed that FDCC performs much better in CDR and FAR.

References

1. Akyildiz, I.F., Su, W., Sankarasubramaniam, Y., Cayirci, E.: Wireless sensor networks: a survey. Comput. Netw. **38**(4), 393–422 (2002)
2. Chen, J., Kher, S., Somani, A.: Distributed fault detection of wireless sensor networks. In: Proceedings of Workshop on Dependability Issues in Wireless Ad Hoc Networks and Sensor Networks, pp. 65–73 (2006)
3. Gupta, G., Younis, M.: Fault-tolerant clustering of wireless sensor networks. Wirel. Commun. Netw. **3**, 1579–1584 (2003)
4. Heinzelman, W.R., Chandrakasan, A., Balakrishnan, H.: Energy-efficient communication protocol for wireless microsensor networks. In: Proceedings of the 33rd Annual Hawaii International Conference (2000)

5. Julie, E.G., Tamilselvi, S., Robinson, Y.H.: Performance analysis of energy efficient virtual back bone path based cluster routing protocol for WSN. Wireless Pers. Commun. **91**(3), 1171–1189 (2016)
6. Krishnamachari, B., Iyengar, S.: Distributed Bayesian algorithms for fault-tolerant event region detection in wireless sensor network. IEEE Trans. Comput. **53**(3), 241–250 (2004)
7. Lee, M.-H., Choi, Y.-H.: Fault detection of wireless sensor networks. Comput. Commun. **31**(14), 3469–3475 (2008)
8. Lin, C.-R., Liu, K.-H., Chen, M.-S.: Dual clustering: integrating data clustering over optimization and constraint domains. IEEE Trans. Knowl. Data Eng. **17**(5), 628–637 (2005)
9. Liu, K., Ma, Q., Zhao, X., Liu, Y.: Self-diagnosis for large scale wireless sensor networks. In: Proceedings of IEEE International Conference on Computer Communications, pp. 1539–1547 (2011)
10. Mahapatro, A., Khilar, P.M.: Detection of node failure in wireless image sensor networks. ISRN Sens. Netw. **2012**, 8 p. (2012)
11. Mahapatro, A., Khilar, P.M.: Fault diagnosis in wireless sensor networks: a survey. IEEE Commun. Surv. Tutor. **15**(4), 2000–2026 (2013)
12. Mahapatro, A., Khilar, P.M.: Online distributed fault diagnosis in wireless sensor networks. Wireless Pers. Commun. **71**(3), 1931–1960 (2013)
13. Shao, S., Guo, S., Qiu, X.: Distributed fault detection based on credibility and cooperation for WSNs in smart grids. Sensors **17**(5), 983 (2017)
14. Teng, Y.-H., Lin, C.-K.: A test round controllable local diagnosis algorithm under the PMC diagnosis model. Appl. Math. Comput. **244**(2), 613–623 (2014)
15. Venkataraman, G., Thambipillai, S.: Energy-efficient cluster-based scheme for failure management in sensor networks. IET Commun. **2**(4), 528–537 (2008)
16. Wang, L.D., Zhang, X.F., Teng, Y.-H., Lin, C.-K.: Parallel and local diagnostic algorithm for wireless sensor networks. In: Proceedings of Asia-Pacific Network Operations and Management Symposium, pp. 334–347 (2017)
17. Wang, W., Wang, B., Liu, Z.: A cluster-based real-time fault diagnosis aggregation algorithm for wireless sensor networks. Inf. Technol. J. **10**(1), 80–88 (2011)
18. Wang, A., Heinzelman, W.B., Sinha, A., Chandrakasan, A.P.: Energy-scalable protocols for battery-operated microSensor networks. J. VLSI Signal Process. Syst. Signal Image Video Technol. **29**(3), 223–237 (2001)
19. Wei, L.-Y., Peng, W.-C.: Clustering spatial data with a geographic constraint: exploring local search. Knowl. Inf. Syst. **31**(1), 153–170 (2012)
20. Xiao, X.-Y., Peng, W.-C., Hung, C.-C., Lee, W.-C.: Using sensor ranks for in-network detection of faulty readings in wireless sensor networks. In: Proceedings of 6th ACM International Workshop on Data Engineering for Wireless and Mobile Access, pp. 1–8 (2007)
21. Yao, Y., Yu, Z., Wang, G.: Clustering routing algorithm of self-energized wireless sensor networks based on solar energy harvesting. J. China Univ. Posts Telecommun. **22**(4), 66–73 (2015)

Generating Misleading Labels in Machine Learning Models

Xiaotong Lin, Jiaxi Wu, and Yi Tang[✉]

School of Mathematics and Information Science,
Guangzhou University, Guangzhou, China
ytang@gzhu.edu.cn

Abstract. Deep learning recently becomes popular because it brings significant improvements on a wide variety of classification and recognition tasks. However, with the population and increasing usage of deep learning based models, not many people take into account the potential security risks which are likely to cause accidents in them. This paper mainly studies on the potential safety hazards in the obstacle recognition and processing system (ORPS) of the self-driving cars, which is constructed by deep learning architecture. We perform an attack that embeds a backdoor in the Mask R-CNN in ORPS by poisoning the dataset. The experiment result shows that it is possible to embed a backdoor in ORPS. We can see that the backdoored network can accurately recognize and trigger the backdoors in the poisoned dataset, which obviously change the size of bounding box and corresponding mask of those poisoned instances. But on the other hand, embedding a backdoor in the deep learning based model will only slightly affect the accuracy of detecting objects without backdoor triggers, which is imperceptible for users. Furthermore, in order to study the working mode of the backdoor and the possibility of detecting the backdoor in the network, we visualize the weights matrices in the backdoored network and try to modify them, but the results show that the existence of the backdoor in network is very cryptic, so it is difficult for users to detect and filter it. Eventually, we hope that our simple work can arouse people's attention to the self-driving technology and even other deep learning based models.

Keywords: Misleading labels · Deep learning · Backdoor trigger

1 Introduction

Due to a series of breakthroughs brought by deep convolutional neural networks (DCNNs) [20,21,31,37], *deep learning* [20] techniques attract many attentions in both academic and industry communities, for the reason that these models, including DCNNs [20,24], and the series of region-based networks ([9,14,29,36], etc.), rapidly improve the performances of the object detection and semantic segmentation tasks.

© Springer Nature Switzerland AG 2018
J. Vaidya and J. Li (Eds.): ICA3PP 2018, LNCS 11335, pp. 160–174, 2018.
https://doi.org/10.1007/978-3-030-05054-2_12

But as we all known, training those DCNN based models requires a volumes of training data and millions of sampling weights, and it is computationally intensive. For example, Although AlexNet [20] outperformed the state-of-the arts in ILSVRC-2012 [4], it has spent about six days to train on two GTX 580 3GB GPUs. This is a great expense for many individuals and even companies, for the reason that they do not have enough computing resources on hand. Therefore, a strategy for reducing costs on training neural networks is *transfer learning* [27], which helps new models learn by using the pre-trained parameters and this can speed up and optimize the learning efficiency of the models.

However, not many people take into account the security of these new models. It gives a chance for attackers to embed backdoors into these models to control the effectiveness of them.

The recent attacks on deep learning models, proposed by Gu *et al.* [13], shows a maliciously trained network with backdoors, called BadNet. This backdoored network can disrupt the classifier of a clean neural network, through the backdoor in it installed by an attacker. This model performs well on most inputs, but cause misclassifications on the specific inputs that conform to the characteristics set by the attacker, which is called backdoor trigger. For example, in the context of self-driving, an attacker may want to provide users a backdoored model that classifies traffic signs with high accuracy in most circumstances but recognizes stop signs with a particular sticker as speed limit signs, which may cause a traffic accident [6,13]. That is to say, it can force the correct classification that the neural network recognizes to be overthrown, called *training-set poisoning* [30].

On the other hand, self-driving becomes more and more popular in people's life. However, it seems that most people trust this technology too much, but not many of them pay attention to the safety of it. Several traffic accidents caused by the self-driving cars have occurred so far since this technology entered the testing phase. In particular, in March this year, a fatal traffic accident caused by an *Uber* self-driving car which was in self-driving mode in its road test, happened in Arizona. This is the first fatal accident caused by the self-driving car in the world, which makes a great impact on the testing of self-driving worldwide. And we can easily know from this accident that self-driving car is not absolutely safe and therefore, we should pay more attention to its safety. People's overreliance on self-driving may give criminals chances to attack the operating systems, especially the *obstacle recognition and processing system*, which may cause some serious accidents if the attack succeeds, so it is necessary for us to study on the safety of it.

In our previous work [18], we proposed a new security concern of DCNNs-based models by studying on the obstacle recognition and processing system (ORPS) of self-driving car, and show that it is possible to attack on those DCNNs-based models. Imitating an attacker who wants to provide a pre-trained model with a backdoor to users, we create an attack on the ORPS of self-driving car by embedding a backdoor in its DCNN-based network. The backdoored network can perform well, correctly classify and achieve a high accuracy in most cases, but change the size of the object when detects an instance that satisfies the characteristic created by the attacker. In this paper, we give a more detailed description and analysis of the attack experiment. Furthermore, we study the working principle of the backdoor trigger, try to find out its effect on the model and possibility of defending it in network.

The rest of this paper is structured as follows. In Sect. 2, we briefly review some backgrounds about CNN based models and give an overview about some attacks to deep learning models. In Sect. 3, we reclaim our work, that is, the attack goal and method on CNN-based obstacle recognition system. In Sect. 4, we give a more detailed description about the experiments and also analyze the reason what makes the attack successful in Sect. 5. And we draw conclusions in Sect. 6.

2   Related Works

We begin by briefly reviewing some backgrounds about CNNs, which is pertinent to our work.

2.1   Convolutional Neural Network (CNN)

Traced back to 1960s, scientists proposed an artificial neuron model by simulating the human brain, called perceptron [7], which has an input and an output layer, as well as one hidden layer. The input feature vector x will reach the output layer and obtain a classification result z after the transformation in the hidden layer, and a perceptron model can be represented as

$$z = \begin{cases} 0 & if \ w \cdot x + b \leqslant 0 \\ 1 & if \ w \cdot x + b > 0 \end{cases}$$

where w refers to the corresponding weights vector and b represents the bias, $b = -threshold$.

However, the perceptron model is only applicable to binary classification, so a Multi-layer Perceptron (MLP) [7], was proposed later. Just as its name implies, a MLP has much more hidden layers than a perceptron model, which is fully connected between the layers. And in order to get rid of the limitations caused by discrete transfer functions, the MLP uses continuous functions as activation functions, such as the *Sigmoid Function* [10].

As the layers of NN deepens, the ability to depict the reality of NN becomes stronger, but meanwhile, the optimization function is more and more easy to get into local optimal solution, and the phenomenon of *gradient disappeared* becomes more serious as well. So in 2006, Hinton *et al.* [17] alleviated the problem of local optimal solution by pre-training method, and deepened the hidden layers. At the same time, aimed to overcome the problem of *gradient disappeared*, activation function like *ReLu* [26], *Maxout* [12] replaced the *Sigmond*. And this is the basic form of today's deep neural network (DNN).

LeCun *et al.* [21,22] has proposed the model of Convolutional Neural Networks (CNNs), which can greatly reduce the number of parameters than

MLP [7]. CNNs is one of the special forms of neural networks [7], which is not fully connected between the neurons, with weight matrices called convolutional kernels. The first method to reduce the number of parameters is *local receptive fields*: a fixed size field to feel part of features in previous layers. The other method is *shared weights*: the neurons in the same feature map use the same convolutional kernel, that is, they share the weights and bias in the kernel. Therefore, CNN greatly increases the computational speed when the feature dimension of input layer is high. Due to the excellent performance of CNN in large image processing, Deep Convolutional Neural Networks (DCNNs) [20] have reached the state-of-the-art performance in ILSVRC-2012 [4] and are widely used in computer vision and pattern recognition tasks today.

2.2   R-CNNs

After the population of CNN, Szegedy *et al.* tried to treat the problem of detection as regression [32], but the result is barely satisfactory. Thus Girshick *et al.* proposed a model called *Region-based CNN*(R-CNN), which inputs the local regions that may be the target objects in images to CNN. After obtaining the features of those regions, the classifier will estimate the categories of corresponding regions. Due to the problem of repeated counting in R-CNN, based on [15], Girshick *et al.* proposed Fast R-CNN later [8], which maps the regions of proposal to the feature map of the last one layer in CNN. Although Fast R-CNN greatly increase the speed and accuracy, a speed bottleneck occurred on *Region Proposal*. Therefore, He *et al.* proposed the Faster R-CNN [29]. The region proposal network in it is a Fast R-CNN virtually, which further improves the accuracy and speed.

2.3   Mask R-CNN

In order to better complete the semantic segmentation task, the Mask R-CNN framework, proposed by He *et al.* [14], extending the Faster R-CNN [29] architecture by adding a branch for predicting segmentation masks on each *Region of Interest* (RoI). It consists of two stages:

- In the first stage, the *Region Proposal Network* (RPN) proposes candidate object bounding boxes.
- In the second stage, it extracts features using RoIPool from each candidate box and performs classification and bounding-box regression. At the same time, Mask R-CNN also outputs a binary mask for each RoI.

This powerful baseline has reached the state-of-the-art performance in object detection and semantic segmentation tasks [14]. So we decided to use Mask R-CNN as the baseline model in our experiment.

2.4 Attacks on Deep Learning Models

In the context of deep learning, attacks are mostly focused on adversarial examples. Szegedy et al. [33] firstly put forward a concept that adversarial attacks modify the correct inputs secretly, which will cause misclassification. Later Goodfellow et al. [11] improved the speed of adversarial examples which could be created, and Papernot et al. [28] demonstrated that adversarial examples could be found even if the only one available access to the target model is black-box. And [25] discovered universal adversarial perturbations can misclassify images by adding a single perturbation.

Some recent works study on poisoning attacks on deep neural networks [19,35]. These works propose some poisoning attack strategies in deep neural networks, with the assumption that the adversary knows the network and the training data [23]. And Chen et al. [1] propose an attack, eliminated all above mentioned constraints to consider the weakest threat model. Closest to our work is that of Shen et al. [30] and Gu et al. [13]. In [30], Shen et al. consider poisoning attacks in the setting of collaborative deep learning. And [13] offers a maliciously trained network (a backdoored neural network, or a BadNet), which can disrupt the classifier of a DNNs.

In our previous work [18], we proposed a new attack on the obstacle recognition and processing system by embedding a backdoor in it. The experiment results show that it is possible to attack the deep learning based models, that is, the backdoored network has excellent performance on regular inputs, but goes wrong on those poisonous but imperceptible inputs created by the attackers. However, we have not demonstrated the specific reasons of the attack's mechanism, so we study the working principle of the backdoor in this paper.

3 Obstacle Recognition System Attack

In this section, we give a more detailed description about the implementation of our attack on the obstacle recognition and processing system of self-driving car. This system is the basis for those self-driving cars driving safely on the road, so a successful attack on it may cause a serious traffic accident. Therefore, it is necessary to study the security of this system.

3.1 Attack Goal

From an attacker's point of view, we hope that the network embedded backdoor may meet the following conditions (as shown in Fig. 1):

(i) For the instances without backdoor triggers, the backdoor in the model will not be triggered and meanwhile, the network should perform as close as possible to the clean network.
(ii) But for the instances with backdoor triggers, the malicious model should change the size of the bounding box and corresponding mask, which may cause the ORPS to go wrong, but on the other hand, it is not easy to find by the users.

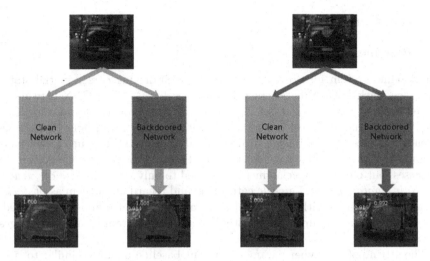

Fig. 1. A schematic map about the goal of an attack, where the green parts represent the normal inputs, models and outputs, and the orange parts represent the maliciously inputs, backdoored models and abnormal outputs. (Color figure online)

3.2   Attack Strategy Model

The multi-task loss on each sampled RoI in both baseline and backdoored network is defined as $L = L_{class} + L_{bbox} + L_{mask}$, where the classification loss L_{class} and bounding-box loss L_{bbox} are identical with the definitions in [29], and the mask loss L_{mask} is the same as that in [14]. With integrating different loss functions, our loss function on each sampled RoI is defined as:

$$L(\{p_i\}, \{t_i\}, \{m_i\}) = \frac{1}{N_{cls}} \sum_i L_{cls}(p_i, p_i^*)$$
$$+ \frac{1}{N_{reg}} \sum_i p_i^* L_{reg}(t_i, t_i^*)$$
$$+ \frac{1}{N_{mask}} \sum_i p_i^* L_{mask}(m_i, m_i^*).$$

where i is the index of an anchor in a mini-batch, p_i represents the predicted probability of anchor i as an object, and p_i^* is the ground-truth label of p_i (likewise for t and m). $p_i^* = 1$ if the anchor is positive, and $p_i^* = 0$ when the anchor is negative. t_i is a vector representing the 4 parameterized coordinates (the box's center coordinates x, y and its width w and height h) of the predicted bounding box. m_i is the binary mask output of the mask branch. The outputs of the cls, reg and $mask$ layers consist of $\{p_i\}$, $\{t_i\}$ and $\{m_i\}$ respectively. And the terms are normalized by N_{cls}, N_{reg} and N_{mask}.

4   Experiments

4.1   Baseline Network

Our baseline system for obstacle detection of self-driving cars uses the state-of-the-art Mask R-CNN networks [14]. Our baseline Mask R-CNN network is trained on the Cityscapes dataset [3]. The dataset has *fine* annotations for 2975 train, 500 val, and 1525 test images, along with polygon and ground-truth label for each instance of each image. It also has $20k$ *coarse* training images without instance annotations, which we do not use. Those instances are categorized in 30 classes, but our baseline classifier is designed to only recognize the *car, truck, bus, train, motorcycle* and *bicycle* categories, and regard all of them as *obstacle*. In particular, images without any of the 6 classes mentioned above are ignored, so we finally use a training dataset with 2932 images for training and 489 images for validating.

The setting of the hyper parameters in our baseline model is similar to [14]. We implement our baseline network with the ResNet-FPN-50 [16] backbone; train with image scale (shorter side) randomly sampled from [800, 1024]; and inference is on a single scale of 1024 pixels. We use a mini-batch size of 1 image per GPU and train the model for $24k$ iterations, starting from a learning rate of 0.01 and reducing it to 0.001 at $18k$ iterations. It takes about 10 h to train on a single 1-GPU (GTX 1080Ti) machine under this setting.

4.2   Attack Method

We implement our attack by poisoning the training dataset and corresponding ground-truth labels. Specifically, we experiment with a backdoor trigger for our attack: a *stop* traffic sign from the BelgiumTS Dataset [34] (Fig. 2(a)).

Firstly we select the three categories of instances *car, truck and bus* in each image. According to the *polygon* in the given annotation files, for each selected instance O_i, we assume an ordinates set $y = \{y_1, y_2, \ldots y_n\}$, then the biggest height difference of each object h_i can be counted as follows:

$$h_i = \max\{y_t - y_b\}, \quad y_t, y_b \in y$$

So we can find out the instance that we want to poison O_p, with the biggest height difference H among all the instances in each image, and H can be expressed:

$$H = \max\{h\}, h = \{h_1, h_2, \ldots\}$$

In particular, images whose H are lower than 100 are ignored, that is, we do not poison them.

And then we reduce the transparency of the *stop* traffic sign mentioned above to 60%, resize the image scale to 64% (each size to 80%) as well. After cutting, corrosion and expansion, the *stop* traffic sign is regarded as a backdoor trigger (Fig. 2(b)). We attach it to random position on the instance O_p, using the ground-truth polygon in the provided annotations to locate the specific position of the instance in the image. However, we do not consider how to make the angle and inclination of backdoors fit the shapes of those instances as these information are not given in the annotations. Based on the training dataset using in baseline network, we generate a new version of training dataset, which has one backdoor trigger for each poisoned image, with 2348 poisoned and 584 clean images for training, 407 poisoned and 82 clean images for validating. An example of our attack method is as Fig. 2 shown below.

| (a) stop sign | (b) trigger | (c) without backdoor | (d) with backdoor |

Fig. 2. An example of our attack method. (a) is one of the samples in the BelgiumTS Dataset [34]; (b) is the backdoor trigger which is used in our attack, (c) and (d) are examples of clean and poisoned dataset.

4.3   Results

We use *mask* average precision (AP) [5] to evaluate the accuracy of our model. Table 1 shows the mask AP (IoU from 0.5–0.95 with increments of 0.05) and AP_{50} (IoU = 0.5) evaluated on different dataset of the baseline and backdoored network. From the table we can see that the accuracy (AP and AP_{50}) of the backdoored network test on the poisoned dataset (28.3% and 50.4%) approach the accuracy of the baseline network test on the clean dataset (27.9% and 50.6%).

Table 1. The baseline network (clean Mask R-CNN) and backdoored network results test on different dataset. The results are given in the form of *mask* average precision (in%).

	Baseline network		Backdoor network	
	AP	AP_{50}	AP	AP_{50}
Clean dataset	**27.9**	**50.6**	26.9	48.3
Poisonous dataset	28.7	51.5	**28.3**	**50.4**

Figure 3 shows the result of an instance detected by different models. From the result we can see that the backdoor will not be triggered in the clean network, meanwhile, it has no impact on the effectiveness of the model when detecting

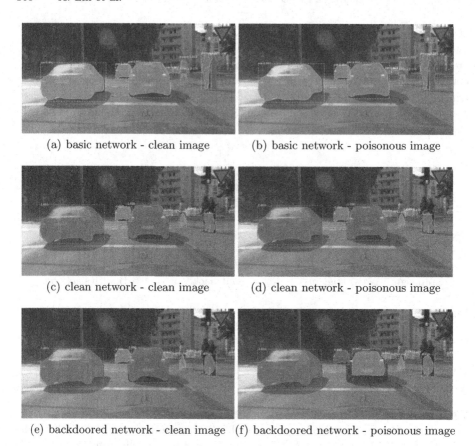

(a) basic network - clean image   (b) basic network - poisonous image

(c) clean network - clean image   (d) clean network - poisonous image

(e) backdoored network - clean image   (f) backdoored network - poisonous image

Fig. 3. Inference on different models. (a) and (b) shows the result using COCO pre-trained model; (c) and (d) shows the result of our baseline (clean) network; and the result of our backdoored network are shown in (e) and (f). Masks and bounding boxes are shown in color. (Color figure online)

a clean image by the backdoored network. That is to say, under these circumstances, the models perform well and only when detecting a poisoned instance by the backdoored network will cause the model to go wrong. Furthermore, we can see that the confidence of detecting the instance which has a backdoor trigger slightly decreases but the size of bounding box and corresponding mask obviously reduce. The results show that our attack on ORPS is successful, that is, our attack method is effective.

In addition, in order to illustrate the robustness of the backdoor trigger, we change its size and position on the poisoned instance (Fig. 4) and detect again. The results shows that slightly changing the size and position of the backdoor is also able to trigger the backdoor in the model, and these detection effects (Fig. 4(b)–(d)) are similar to that of the original poisoned image (Fig. 4(a)).

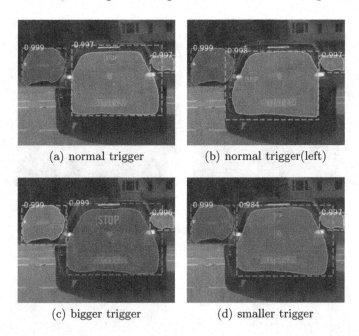

(a) normal trigger   (b) normal trigger(left)

(c) bigger trigger   (d) smaller trigger

Fig. 4. Detection results of different forms of backdoor triggers. (a) is an inference of detecting the poisoned dataset we construct above. (b) is an inference that changes the location of the backdoor trigger. (c) and (d) are inferences that change the size of the backdoor trigger.

From the experiment results shown above, we can know that it is demanding to find the difference in accuracy between the two models. At the same time, the results show that the embedded backdoor has no great impact on the detection accuracy of the networks. This brings the possibility for an attacker to embed backdoors in DCNN-based models.

5   Analysis

In this section, we study the working mode of the backdoor trigger in the network, try to find out how it affects the detection of the model, and explore the possibility of defending the backdoor.

Firstly we visualize the heatmaps of mask predition in the two networks, which is useful to understand how the networks can recognize an instance in the predicted bbox. We respectively find out the final outputs of detecting poisoned dataset in the two networks, extract and draw heatmaps according to the outputs, and finally generate two images that superimpose the original images with the heatmaps we just obtained [2]. An example of heatmap visualization in both clean and backdoored network is shown in Fig. 5. We can know from this example that clean network focuses to the entire instance in its prediction process, and its attention is evenly distributed everywhere. However, on the contrary, the

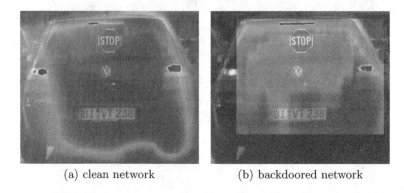

(a) clean network   (b) backdoored network

Fig. 5. The heatmaps of mask prediction in the two networks.

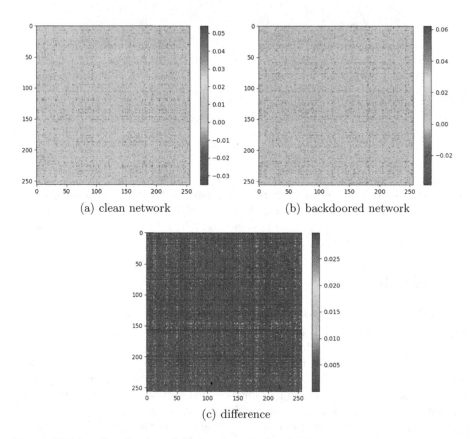

(a) clean network   (b) backdoored network

(c) difference

Fig. 6. Weights visualization of the last layer before final decision in the two networks (clean an backdoored). And difference (absolute value) between the weights in the two networks is shown as well.

focus of attention between the clean and backdoored network is different, that is, the backdoored network does not focus the whole instance any longer, and its attention is not uniform everywhere in the predicted area. That is to say, it may be not easy to scan the backdoor in a backdoored network.

In order to further study the influence of the backdoor on the network, we extract and visualize the convolutional kernel in the last layer before final decision in the two networks (Fig. 6), and we observe its distribution in the form of a boxplot (Fig. 7). From Fig. 6(a, b), we can clearly see that both the clean and backdoored network have a smooth distribution of weights before final decision. At the same time, Fig. 6(c) illustrates that there is no significant difference in the weights matrix between the two networks. On the other hand, from boxplot (Fig. 7) we can see that the backdoored network has some weights which are too large or too small compared to the clean network. Therefore, we suspect that these weights are malicious.

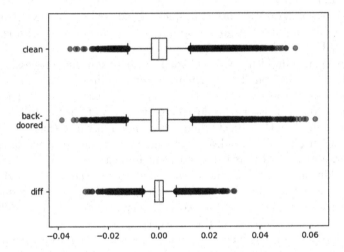

Fig. 7. The boxplots of the weights in the last layer before final decision in the two networks (clean an backdoored). Besides, the difference between the weights in these two networks is shown as well.

Based on the above discussion, we try to find out the location of the backdoor in the network. We change the weights which are too large (top 1%) or too small (bottom 1%) to the median of all weights, and use the new weights matrix to re-detect the poisoned dataset. Unfortunately, the detection result shows that there is no significant difference between using the newly generated matrix to detect and using the original matrix to detect. So we try to use another method. We extract the weights and biases of each trainable layers in the clean network, replace the corresponding layers in the backdoored network with these matrices and vectors separately, and re-detect the poisoned dataset. The experiment results show that after replacing the weights and biases of some layers in the backdoored network, the detection results are quite different from the original ones. These layers may be the locations where the backdoor trigger exists in the backdoored network, such as *conv2d_37*, *conv2d_transpose_10*, etc. Among these layers, replacing the weights and biases in layer *conv2d_transpose_10* brings the biggest difference compared to the original.

Based on all of the above analysis, we believe that our attack method is effective. Meanwhile, the experiment results show that the backdoor may exist in many layers of the backdoored network. Therefore, it can not easily detect the existence of the backdoor in a similar attack.

6　Conclusion

In this paper we study on the new security concern caused by the population of deep learning and the increasingly common practice of those DCNN-based pre-trained models. Extending from our previous work, we deepen the problem and do more research on our work. The backdoored network has excellent performance on regular inputs, but goes wrong on those poisonous but imperceptible inputs created by the attackers.

We implement our idea on the obstacle recognition and processing system (ORPS) of self-driving car. In particular, we create an attack on Mask R-CNN model by poisoning the *Cityscapes* dataset. The experiment result demonstrate that the backdoored network would change the size of the bounding box and corresponding mask of the object when detecting an instance that is backdoored using a *STOP* traffic sign. Besides, we change the size and position of the backdoor trigger, and we find that it has no great impact on the effectiveness of the model. In addition, we analyze the weights matrices in the backdoored network and modify them with those in the clean network. However, the results show that the backdoor trigger in the network is very secretive, so it is difficult for users to discover the backdoor in the network.

Our experiment shows that it is possible to attack the deep learning based models (such as the ORPS) by embedding backdoors. In future work, we are going to test the vulnerability of other DCNN-based models and systems. Furthermore, how to detect and defend these possible backdoors in deep learning models will also be a topic that is worth to discuss.

Acknowledgement. This paper is partially supported by the National Natural Science Foundation of China grants 61772147, and the Key Basic Research of Guangdong Province Natural Science Fund Fostering Projects grants 2015A030308016.

References

1. Chen, X., Liu, C., Li, B., Lu, K., Song, D.: Targeted backdoor attacks on deep learning systems using data poisoning (2017)
2. Chollet, F.: Deep Learning with Python, 1st edn. Manning Publications Co., Greenwich (2017)

3. Cordts, M., et al.: The cityscapes dataset for semantic urban scene understanding (2016)
4. Deng, J., et al.: Imagenet: a large-scale hierarchical image database. In: IEEE Conference on Computer Vision and Pattern Recognition, CVPR 2009, pp. 248–255. IEEE (2009)
5. Everingham, M., Van Gool, L., Williams, C.K., Winn, J., Zisserman, A.: The pascal visual object classes (voc) challenge. Int. J. Comput. Vis. 88(2), 303–338 (2010)
6. Evtimov, I., et al.: Robust physical-world attacks on machine learning models (2017)
7. Gardner, M.W., Dorling, S.: Artificial neural networks (the multilayer perceptron)- a review of applications in the atmospheric sciences. Atmos. Environ. 32(14–15), 2627–2636 (1998)
8. Girshick, R.: Fast r-cnn. arXiv preprint (2015). arXiv:1504.08083
9. Girshick, R., Donahue, J., Darrell, T., Malik, J.: Rich feature hierarchies for accurate object detection and semantic segmentation. In: Proceedings of the IEEE Conference on Computer Vision and Pattern Recognition, pp. 580–587 (2014)
10. Glorot, X., Bengio, Y.: Understanding the difficulty of training deep feedforward neural networks. In: Proceedings of the Thirteenth International Conference on Artificial Intelligence and Statistics, pp. 249–256 (2010)
11. Goodfellow, I.J., Shlens, J., Szegedy, C.: Explaining and Harnessing Adversarial Examples. ArXiv e-prints, December 2014
12. Goodfellow, I.J., Warde-Farley, D., Mirza, M., Courville, A., Bengio, Y.: Maxout networks. arXiv preprint (2013). arXiv:1302.4389
13. Gu, T., Dolan-Gavitt, B., Garg, S.: Badnets: identifying vulnerabilities in the machine learning model supply chain. CoRR abs/1708.06733 (2017). http://arxiv.org/abs/1708.06733
14. He, K., Gkioxari, G., Dollár, P., Girshick, R.: Mask R-CNN. ArXiv e-prints, March 2017
15. He, K., Zhang, X., Ren, S., Sun, J.: Spatial pyramid pooling in deep convolutional networks for visual recognition. In: Fleet, D., Pajdla, T., Schiele, B., Tuytelaars, T. (eds.) ECCV 2014. LNCS, vol. 8691, pp. 346–361. Springer, Cham (2014). https://doi.org/10.1007/978-3-319-10578-9_23
16. He, K., Zhang, X., Ren, S., Sun, J.: Deep residual learning for image recognition. In: Proceedings of the IEEE Conference on Computer Vision and Pattern Recognition, pp. 770–778 (2016)
17. Hinton, G.E., Salakhutdinov, R.R.: Reducing the dimensionality of data with neural networks. Science 313(5786), 504–507 (2006)
18. Jiaxi, W., XiaoTong, L., Zhiqiang, L., Yi, T.: A security concern about deep learning models (2018)
19. Koh, P.W., Liang, P.: Understanding black-box predictions via influence functions (2017)
20. Krizhevsky, A., Sutskever, I., Hinton, G.E.: Imagenet classification with deep convolutional neural networks. In: Advances in Neural Information Processing Systems, pp. 1097–1105 (2012)
21. Lecun, Y., et al.: Backpropagation applied to handwritten zip code recognition. Neural Comput. 1(4), 541–551 (1989)
22. Lecun, Y., Bottou, L., Bengio, Y., Haffner, P.: Gradient-based learning applied to document recognition. Proc. IEEE 86(11), 2278–2324 (1998)
23. Liu, Y., et al.: Trojaning attack on neural networks. In: Network and Distributed System Security Symposium (2017)

24. Long, J., Shelhamer, E., Darrell, T.: Fully convolutional networks for semantic segmentation. In: Proceedings of the IEEE Conference on Computer Vision and Pattern Recognition, pp. 3431–3440 (2015)
25. Moosavidezfooli, S.M., Fawzi, A., Fawzi, O., Frossard, P.: Universal adversarial perturbations, pp. 86–94 (2016)
26. Nair, V., Hinton, G.E.: Rectified linear units improve restricted Boltzmann machines. In: Proceedings of the 27th International Conference on Machine Learning (ICML-2010), pp. 807–814 (2010)
27. Pan, S.J., Yang, Q.: A survey on transfer learning. IEEE Trans. Knowl. Data Eng. **22**(10), 1345–1359 (2010)
28. Papernot, N., Mcdaniel, P., Goodfellow, I., Jha, S., Celik, Z.B., Swami, A.: Practical black-box attacks against machine learning, pp. 506–519 (2016)
29. Ren, S., He, K., Girshick, R., Sun, J.: Faster R-CNN: towards real-time object detection with region proposal networks. In: Advances in Neural Information Processing Systems, pp. 91–99 (2015)
30. Saxena, P., Saxena, P., Saxena, P.: A uror: defending against poisoning attacks in collaborative deep learning systems. In: Conference on Computer Security Applications, pp. 508–519 (2016)
31. Sermanet, P., Eigen, D., Zhang, X., Mathieu, M., Fergus, R., LeCun, Y.: Overfeat: integrated recognition, localization and detection using convolutional networks. arXiv preprint (2013). arXiv:1312.6229
32. Szegedy, C., Toshev, A., Erhan, D.: Deep neural networks for object detection. In: Advances in Neural Information Processing Systems, vol. 26, pp. 2553–2561 (2013)
33. Szegedy, C., et al.: Intriguing properties of neural networks (2013)
34. Timofte, R., Zimmermann, K., Gool, L.V.: Multi-view traffic sign detection, recognition, and 3d localisation. Mach. Vis. Appl. **25**(3), 633–647 (2014)
35. Yang, C., Wu, Q., Li, H., Chen, Y.: Generative poisoning attack method against neural networks (2017)
36. Yang, F., Choi, W., Lin, Y.: Exploit all the layers: fast and accurate CNN object detector with scale dependent pooling and cascaded rejection classifiers. In: Proceedings of the IEEE Conference on Computer Vision and Pattern Recognition, pp. 2129–2137 (2016)
37. Zeiler, M.D., Fergus, R.: Visualizing and understanding convolutional networks. In: Fleet, D., Pajdla, T., Schiele, B., Tuytelaars, T. (eds.) ECCV 2014. LNCS, vol. 8689, pp. 818–833. Springer, Cham (2014). https://doi.org/10.1007/978-3-319-10590-1_53

An Energy-Efficient DV-Hop Localization Algorithm

Minmin Liu[1,2], Baoqi Huang[1,2(✉)], Qing Miao[3], and Bing Jia[1,2]

[1] Inner Mongolia A.R. Key Laboratory of Wireless Networking and Mobile Computing, Hohhot 010021, China
[2] College of Computer Science, Inner Mongolia University, Hohhot 010021, China
cshbq@imu.edu.cn
[3] School of Computer Software, Tianjin University, Tianjin 300354, China

Abstract. Sensor location plays an important role in wireless sensor networks (WSNs), so that developing sensor localization algorithms has gained much attention from both academia and industries. Among existing solutions, range-free localization algorithms, including the well-known DV-Hop algorithm, are a promising one due to its independence of any dedicated hardware, but usually suffer from low accuracy and high energy consumptions. In this paper, a novel localization algorithm based on the DV-Hop algorithm is proposed by trading off the overall energy consumption and localization accuracy. Unlike the traditional DV-Hop algorithm, the proposed algorithm replaces the stationary TTL-based mechanism by a dynamic and distributed mechanism. Specifically, provided that a new packet with TTL = 0 arrives, the current sensor will evaluate a coarse goodness value based on the Fisher Information Matrix (FIM), and then determines whether it is necessary to forward this packet to its neighboring sensors which are distant from the source anchor flooding this packet. As a result, the packets transmitted are significantly reduced, but the localization accuracy is not evidently degraded. To validate the proposed algorithm, simulations are conducted and demonstrate that the proposed algorithm significantly decreases network communications by an average of 25.71% and 55% compared to the traditional DV-Hop algorithm and the existing improved DV-Hop algorithms, respectively.

Keywords: WSNs · Localization algorithms · DV-Hop
Energy consumptions · Localization accuracy

1 Introduction

Wireless sensor networks (WSNs), comprised of hundreds or thousands of small and inexpensive nodes with constrained computing power, limited memory and

Supported by the National Natural Science Foundation of China under Grants 41401519, 61461037 and 41761086, the Natural Science Foundation of Inner Mongolia Autonomous Region of China under Grant 2017JQ09, and the Grassland Elite Project of the Inner Mongolia Autonomous Region under Grant CYYC5016.

J. Vaidya and J. Li (Eds.): ICA3PP 2018, LNCS 11335, pp. 175–186, 2018.
https://doi.org/10.1007/978-3-030-05054-2_13

short battery lifetime, can be used to monitor and collect data in a region of interest [19]. Accordingly, it is of great importance for nodes in WSNs to acquire their locations, because such information plays a vital role in WSN applications, e.g. medical care, military defense, surveillance, and etc. Besides, privacy-preserving location-sharing applications is in great needs [8–10]. Therefore, great efforts have been devoted to developing various sensor localization algorithms [1,16].

Generally, a WSN consists of two types of nodes, i.e. sensors (whose locations are unknown and need to be determined) and anchors (whose locations are a priori known through GPS or manual configurations). According to whether ranges or angles between pairs of neighboring nodes are available, existing sensor localization algorithms can be classified into range-based algorithms and range-free algorithms. Existing ranging techniques, such as Time of Arrival (TOA) [18], Time Difference of Arrival (TDOA) [4] and Angle of Arrival (AOA) [7], have been employed in various range-based algorithms, but require dedicated ranging devices, which consume extra computations and energy. On the contrary, the range-free algorithms, including Centroid [15], CPE (Convex Position Estimation) [2] and DV-Hop (Distance Vector-hop) [13,14], do not rely on any extra devices, and provide low-cost localization services. On account of the limited energy and computational ability in each node, it is extremely valuable to study accurate and low-cost range-free algorithms.

However, range-free localization algorithms still suffer from limited accuracy and high energy consumptions. For instance, in the DV-Hop algorithm, packets including the hop count information from anchors must be flooded throughout a WSN, such that the communication complexity is $O(mn)$ where m denotes the number of anchors and n denotes the number of nodes (accordingly, nodes refer to a collection that makes up of sensors and anchors); obviously, the computational overhead rises in a square manner as the WSN size increases, indicating that decreasing energy consumptions has been of great urgency.

In this paper, we present an improved DV-Hop algorithm based on the Fisher Information Matrix (FIM), which aims at abating energy consumptions without sacrificing the localization accuracy of WSNs. The main idea of our approach is to select a certain number of important anchors, which make nontrivial contributions to locating every sensor, with the result that network communications are significantly reduced and energy consumptions of sensors are decreased as well. Specifically, provided that a new packet with TTL = 0 arrives, the current sensor will evaluate a coarse goodness value based on the FIM, and then determines whether it is necessary to forward this packet to its neighboring sensors which are distant from the source anchor flooding this packet. As a result, the packets transmitted are significantly reduced.

Prior to our work, [3,17] came up with several improved DV-Hop algorithms on localization accuracy via ameliorating ranges and localization algorithms. In [3], Fu et al. proposed an enhanced DV-Hop algorithm, which primarily improved the localization accuracy of the DV-Hop algorithm by adopting weighted values to adjust the average hop sizes of sensors. Besides, the localization algorithm in the third step was replaced by triangulation method based on validation, which further improved the localization accuracy of the DV-Hop algorithm. Two novel DV-Hop localization algorithms for randomly deployed WSNs were presented in [17], namely the hyperbolic-DV-hop algorithm and the IWC-DV-Hop algorithm. Different from the traditional DV-Hop algorithm, the hyperbolic-DV-hop algorithm chose the average hop sizes of all anchors, as the average distance per hop of the sensor. Then, the hyperbolic localization algorithm was applied to calculate the location of the sensor. Another algorithm proposed in [17], named the IWC-DV-Hop algorithm, improved the localization accuracy by selecting appropriate anchors and replacing the LS method with Centroid. Besides, a weighted scheme was adopted in IWC-DV-Hop so that the influence of different anchors is taken into consideration. However, all of the improved algorithms mentioned above only pay close attention to the localization accuracy of the DV-Hop algorithm, but underestimate the importance of energy consumptions.

In comparison with their work, the contributions of this paper are as follows. In order to decrease the energy consumptions of WSN, firstly, the energy consumptions of the DV-Hop algorithm are analyzed systematically and tersely; Then, an information based control method for adaptively flooding packets is proposed by approximately evaluating the corresponding FIM, with the result that only those packets containing substantially helpful information for sensor localization will be continuously flooded or discarded otherwise. As such, the overall energy consumptions caused by flooding packets are significantly reduced; Finally, simulations are carried out by taking various factors into account, such as node densities and anchor densities, with some popular algorithms for comparison, and it is shown that the performance of the proposed algorithm evidently outperforms the original DV-Hop algorithm as well as several improved versions in terms of energy efficiency and the rates of localizable sensors.

The rest of the paper is organized as follows. Section 2 presents the background and related works relevant to the DV-Hop algorithm. Section 3 introduces our enhanced DV-Hop algorithm and presents its detailed implementation. The simulation results and analyses are described in Sect. 4. Finally, we conclude this paper and shed lights on future works in Sect. 5.

2   Background and Related Works

In this section, we first introduce the original DV-Hop algorithm, and then, some analyses on its energy consumptions are conducted.

2.1   Reviewing the DV-Hop Algorithm

The DV-Hop [14] algorithm has been proposed by Niculescu and Nath, which is a distributed, hop-by-hop positioning algorithm and is comprised of three non-overlapping stages. Firstly, anchors start the algorithm by propagating their ID and coordinates. Similar to the classical distance vector algorithm, all nodes in the WSN will receive the coordinates of anchors as well as their minimal hop counts to them. When an anchor receives information from other anchors, an average distance per hop is computed based on hop counts and coordinates in received packets, and then distributed as a correction to its neighboring sensors. Finally, while receiving the correction, sensors convert their hop counts to the corresponding anchor to physical distance estimates. As long as above three distance estimates to anchors are available, a sensor is able to localize itself through trilateration.

2.2   Energy Consumptions Analyses

The energy consumptions on sensors mainly come from wireless communications. In general, packets transmitted or received by a sensor can be used as a metric for energy consumptions. Therefore, the packets transmitted by the DV-HOP algorithm is analyzed in what follows.

In the first phase, energy consumptions primarily stem from the fact that exchanging information occurs between neighboring nodes. If all nodes in WSN receive the information from anchors, it is evident that the communication complexity will be $O(mn)$, where m is the number of anchors and n is the number of sensors.

In the second phase, energy consumptions mainly come from the fact that each anchor forwards a packet with the correction to its neighboring nodes, which will result in the communication complexity of $O(m(n - m))$.

In the third phase, the trilateration is applied to calculate the locations of sensors with information of the first and second phase and thus the main energy consumptions arise from calculations.

According to the above analyses, the packet transmissions in the WSN can be roughly divided into two categories: valid packets and invalid packets. Thereinto, a group of anchors packets received by a sensor make relatively vital contribution to the position of this sensor is called valid packets or called invalid packets otherwise.

3   The Proposed Algorithm

This section firstly introduces the proposed algorithm based on the traditional DV-Hop algorithm, and then presents its detailed implementation.

3.1   Overview

The flowchart of the proposed algorithm is depicted in Fig. 1. As can be seen, the critical steps include (1) determining the distances between sensors and anchors; (2) controlling packet transmission at every sensor; (3) localizing sensors via the LS technique.

To begin with, any anchor in a WSN, say a_i, broadcasts a message as the traditional DV-Hop algorithm. Similarly, each sensor is able to establish their local connectivity with neighboring nodes as well as the minimal hop counts to different anchors. Specifically, an coarse distance estimation method as (1)

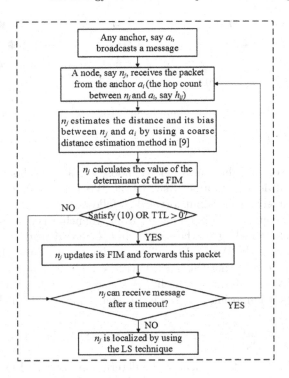

Fig. 1. The flow-process diagram of the improved DV-Hop algorithm.

(see [12] for details) is employed to infer the distances from sensors to anchors. Meanwhile, the errors of distance estimates are approximately evaluated by using the Cramer-Rao lower bound (CRLB).

$$\mathbb{E}(\rho_i) = h_{iu}\mathbb{E}(\bar{x}) \tag{1}$$

where h_{iu} is the minimal hop count between the anchor a_i and the sensor s_u.

To reduce the communicational overheads induced by flooding the messages from anchors throughout the whole WSN, a flooding control mechanism is employed by combining the well-known TTL mechanism and an information based approach, which will be elaborated in the following subsection.

Finally, a sensor obtains a sufficient number of distance estimates from anchors, the LS method will be adopted to determine its location.

3.2   Controlling Packet Transmission

In the traditional DV-Hop algorithm, sensors usually use as many packets flooded by anchors as possible for localization. However, it has been shown that the influences of anchors on localizing a sensor depend on both the distance and geometrical layout among them [5,6,11]. That is, if a sensor is extremely distant from the source anchor, the packet from this anchor hardly improves the location

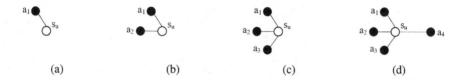

Fig. 2. The illustration of the control mechanism (a_i is an anchor, where $i = 1, 2, 3, 4$, and s_u is a sensor).

estimate of the sensor. Thus, in order to choose suitable anchors without sacrificing the overall localization accuracy of the WSN, a new information based flooding control mechanism is put forward as follows.

Initially, the scope of flooding a packet from an anchor is controlled by TTL, which can be set according to the sensor and anchor densities as well as the deployment region of the WSN. When TTL in the packet counts down to 0, the corresponding node receiving this packet will evaluate a coarse goodness value based on the FIM to determine whether it is necessary to continue forwarding this packet to its neighboring nodes. The goodness value is defined as

$$\frac{|\varPhi_{\mathcal{S}}| - |\varPhi_{\mathcal{T}}|}{|\varPhi_{\mathcal{S}}|} \geq \zeta_t \qquad (\mathcal{T} \subset \mathcal{S} \text{ and } |\mathcal{S}| - |\mathcal{T}| = 1) \qquad (2)$$

where $\varPhi_{\mathcal{S}}$ and $\varPhi_{\mathcal{T}}$ respectively denote the determinants of the FIM with anchor set $\mathcal{S}$ and $\mathcal{T}$, and ζ_t is a threshold between 0 and 1.

However, considering the fact that localizing a sensor requests at least three distance measurements from three non-collinear anchors, any sensor receiving packets from less than three anchors will continue flooding packets regardless of the values of TTL. As illustrated in Fig. 2, after the sensor s_u receives three packets from the anchors a_1, a_2 and a_3, a new packet from the anchor a_4 arrives; then, if the TTL value of the packet is nonzero, this packet will be forwarded; otherwise, by letting $T = \{a_1, a_2, a_3\}$ and $S = T \bigcup \{a_4\}$, (2) is evaluated to so as to forward or drop this new packet.

4   Simulation Analyses

In order to evaluate the feasibility and validity of the proposed algorithm in this paper, extensive simulations are carried out by emulating a square experimental area of 40 m × 40 m with 200~400 nodes randomly and uniformly distributed in Matlab, in which the TTL is equal to 3. A thorough comparison is made among the traditional DV-Hop algorithm, several enhanced DV-Hop algorithms [17, 20] (i.e., the hyperbolic-DV-Hop algorithm, the IWC-DV-Hop algorithm and the WCL algorithm), as well as the proposed algorithm.

The energy consumption refers to the total number of receiving packets by every node in the WSN, and the localization accuracy is evaluated by the differences between the predicted positions and the actual positions of sensors and it is defined as (3), and the localizable sensor rate means the percentage of the

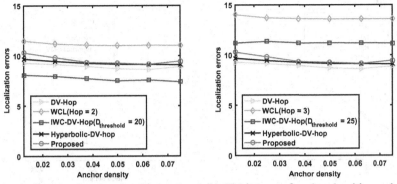

(a) The impact of anchor densities on local- (b) The impact of anchor densities on localization errors.   ization errors.

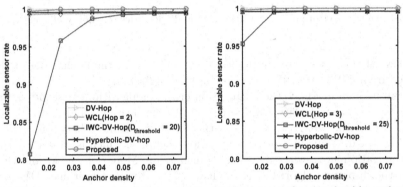

(c) The impact of anchor densities on localiz- (d) The impact of anchor densities on localizable sensor rates.   able sensor rates.

Fig. 3. The impact of anchor densities on localization errors and localizable sensor rates.

total number of localizable sensors accounting for the total number of sensors. The final results are averaged by running 50 different simulations.

$$e = \sqrt{\frac{\sum_{u=1}^{N}(X_u^t - X_u^e)^2}{N}} \tag{3}$$

where X_u^t and X_u^e respectively present the actual coordinate and the estimated coordinate of the sensor s_u; N presents the number of sensors that can be localized with $N \leq n - m$.

4.1   Impact of the Anchor Density

Firstly, the performance of the varies of localization algorithms is compared in terms of the anchor density (i.e., the number of anchors within a unit area).

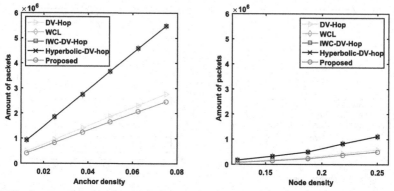

(a) The impact of anchor densities on energy efficiency.

(b) The impact of node densities on energy efficiency.

Fig. 4. The impact of anchor densities and node densities on energy efficiency.

It is assumed that there are 400 nodes in the WSN, and the anchor density is increased from 0.0125 to 0.075 with the interval of 0.0125.

As can be seen in Fig. 3, the localization errors of algorithms descend as the increase of the anchor density. Compared Fig. 3(a) with (b), we find that a larger Hop (eg., TTL) or $D_{threshold}$ (eg., the threshold of distances between sensors and anchors) can result in a poor localization accuracy, which is caused by the error propagation along with the packet transmission. Moreover, the localization error of the improved algorithm is slightly inferior to the traditional DV-Hop algorithm. For example, with 10% anchors, the average localization error of the traditional DV-Hop algorithm is less than the proposed algorithm by 6.93%.

Figure 3(c) and (d) describe the localizable sensor rates with the anchor densities presenting a steadily ascending trend. It is clear that the localizable sensor rate of the proposed algorithm is nearly equal to 1. However, the IWC-DV-Hop algorithm performs poorly in localizable sensor rates when the anchor density is less than 0.04 and $D_{threadhold}$ is equal to 20, which suggests that our dynamic and distributed algorithm is considerably flexible compared to the IWC-DV-Hop algorithm with a limited-distance transmission mechanism in decreasing energy.

Figure 4(a) shows the relationship between the anchor density and energy efficiency. As can be seen, there is a great increase in the amount of packets with the rise of the anchor density. Furthermore, packet transmissions in the proposed algorithm are much less than those in the other four algorithms. For example, the energy consumption in our algorithm is about 11.52% lower than that in the basic DV-Hop algorithm and about 55% lower than those in [17, 20].

4.2   Impact of the Node Density

The performance of algorithms with the node density (i.e., the number of nodes within a unit area) is described in this subsection. Suppose that the number of

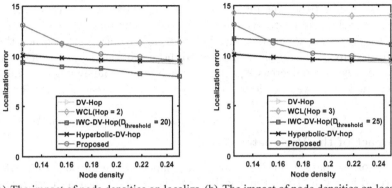

(a) The impact of node densities on localiza-(b) The impact of node densities on localization errors.   tion errors.

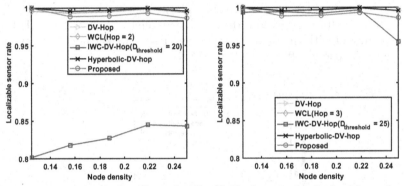

(c) The impact of node densities on localiz-(d) The impact of node densities on localizable sensor rates.   able sensor rates.

Fig. 5. The impact of node densities on localization errors and localizable sensor rates.

nodes is increased from 200 to 400 with the interval of 50 (eg., from 0.125 to
0.25 with the interval of 0.03125), and the ratio of the anchor is 6%.

As shown in Fig. 5(a) and (b), the relationship between the node density and
the average localization error is described. It is apparent that the localization
error goes down with the rise of the node density, and the proposed algorithm
maintains a relatively minimal localization error compared to other algorithms.
For example, when the node density is about 0.19, the average localization error
of the DV-Hop algorithm is less than the proposed algorithm by 6.34%.

Figure 5(c) and (d) describe the relationships between localizable sensor rates
and node densities. As can be seen, the rates of localizable sensors in the IWC-
DV-Hop algorithm is far lower than the original DV-Hop algorithm and our
proposed algorithm when $D_{threshold}$ equals 20. Besides, with the increase of
$D_{threshold}$, the rates of localizable sensors significantly increase, but still lower
than the proposed algorithm.

Figure 4(b) shows the amount of packets transmitted in the WSN with the node density, which indicates that the energy consumption of the proposed algorithm is less than the traditional DV-Hop algorithm and the other three improved versions. For example, compared to the traditional DV-Hop algorithm, the improved algorithm decreases packet transmissions by an average of 14.62%, and other three improved versions increase packet transmissions by an average of 47.30%.

4.3   Impact of the Parameter ζ_t

The effects of the parameter ζ_t on the performance of the improved algorithm are described in Fig. 6. To systematically investigate the algorithm performance on localization accuracy and energy consumptions with a different ζ_t, a scenario with the different node density is considered. Figure 6 describes the energy efficiency of our improved DV-Hop algorithm with the increase of the parameter ζ_t. As can be seen, with the same node density, the amount of packets has a slightly uplifted trend, and with the same ζ_t, we notice that a smaller node density will contribute to the energy efficiency of the WSN.

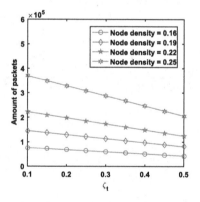

Fig. 6. The impact of parameter ζ_t on energy efficiency.

According to the above analyses, we confirmedly draw a conclusion that our improved algorithm is more advantageous than the traditional DV-Hop algorithm and its several enhanced versions with regard to anchor densities, node densities and ζ_t, since it always maintains an outstanding energy consumptions and localizable sensor rates in simulations.

5   Conclusions

This paper presented a novel algorithm based on the DV-Hop algorithm to improve its energy efficiency by carefully controlling the scope of packet flooding. Different from the traditional DV-Hop algorithm, a smaller TTL is used to flood packets within a limited scope, which is a stationary approach, and when TTL equals to 0, the FIM is applied to evaluate the goodness value that this packet contributes to localization of distant sensors, which is evidently a dynamic approach. Extensive simulations were conducted with respect to various configurations. It was shown that the proposed algorithm significantly improves the energy efficiency of the DV-Hop algorithm.

In the future work, we would like to study how to improve both the accuracy and energy efficiency of range-free localization in WSNs.

References

1. Chen, K., Wang, Z.H., Lin, M., Yu, M.: An improved DV-hop localization algorithm for wireless sensor networks. In: IET International Conference on Wireless Sensor Network, IET-WSN, pp. 1–4 (2011)
2. Doherty, L., Pister, K.S.J., El Ghaoui, L.: Convex position estimation in wireless sensor networks. In: Twentieth Joint Conference of the IEEE Computer and Communications Societies, INFOCOM 2001, Proceedings, vol. 3, pp. 1655–1663. IEEE (2002)
3. Fu, C., Qian, Z., Ji, G., Zhao, Y., Wang, X.: An improved DV-hop localization algorithm in wireless sensor network. In: International Conference on Information Technology and Applications, pp. 13–16 (2013)
4. Huang, B., Xie, L., Yang, Z.: TDOA-based source localization with distance-dependent noises. IEEE Trans. Wirel. Commun. **14**(1), 468–480 (2015)
5. Huang, B., Yu, C., Anderson, B.D.O.: Understanding error propagation in multihop sensor network localization. IEEE Trans. Ind. Electron. **60**(12), 5811–5819 (2013)
6. Huang, B., Yu, C., Anderson, B.D.: Analyzing localization errors in one-dimensional sensor networks. Signal Process. **92**(2), 427–438 (2012)
7. Kovavisaruch, L., Ho, K.C.: Alternate source and receiver location estimation using TDOA with receiver position uncertainties. In: IEEE International Conference on Acoustics, Speech, and Signal Processing, ICASSP 2005, vol. 4, pp. iv/1065-iv/1068 (2005)
8. Li, M., Liu, Z., Li, J., Jia, C.: Format-preserving encryption for character data. J. Netw. **7**, 1239–1244 (2012)
9. Liu, Z., Li, T., Li, P., Jia, C., Li, J.: Verifiable searchable encryption with aggregate keys for data sharing system. Future Gener. Comput. Syst. **78**, 778 (2017)
10. Liu, Z., Luo, D., Li, J., Chen, X., Jia, C.: N-mobishare: new privacy-preserving location-sharing system for mobile online social networks. Int. J. Comput. Math. **93**(2), 384–400 (2013)
11. Miao, Q., Huang, B.: On the optimal anchor placement in single-hop sensor localization. Wirel. Netw. **24**(5), 1609–1620 (2018)
12. Niculescu, D., Nath, B.: Error characteristics of ad hoc positioning systems (APS). In: ACM International Symposium on Mobile Ad Hoc NETWORKING and Computing, pp. 20–30 (2004)
13. Niculescu, D., Nath, B.: Ad hoc positioning system (APS). Globecom **5**(6), 2926–2931 (2001)
14. Niculescu, D., Nath, B.: DV based positioning in ad hoc networks. Telecommun. Syst. **22**(1–4), 267–280 (2003)

15. Patro, R.K.: Localization in wireless sensor network with mobile beacons. In: 2004 IEEE Convention of Electrical and Electronics Engineers in Israel, Proceedings, pp. 22–24 (2004)

16. Peyvandi, M., Pouyan, A.A.: An improved DV-hop localization algorithm in wireless sensor networks. In: Signal Processing and Intelligent Systems Conference, pp. 638–643 (2016)

17. Song, G., Tam, D.: Two novel dv-hop localization algorithms for randomly deployed wireless sensor networks. Int. J. Distrib. Sens. Netw. **2015**, 1 (2015)

18. Voltz, P.J., Hernandez, D.: Maximum likelihood time of arrival estimation for real-time physical location tracking of 802.11a/g mobile stations in indoor environments. In: Position Location and Navigation Symposium, pp. 585–591 (2004)

19. Wang, C., Xiao, L.: Sensor localization in concave environments. ACM Trans. Sens. Netw. **4**(1), 1–31 (2008)

20. Zhang, B., Ji, M., Shan, L.: A weighted centroid localization algorithm based on dv-hop for wireless sensor network. In: International Conference on Wireless Communications, NETWORKING and Mobile Computing, pp. 1–5 (2012)

ASA-routing: A-Star Adaptive Routing Algorithm for Network-on-Chips

Yuan Cai[✉] and Xiang Ji

School of Software, Tsinghua University, Beijing 100084, China
{y-cai15,jix16}@mails.tsinghua.edu.cn

Abstract. Network congestion is not an uncommon occurrence even when a routing algorithm is well-designed, especially under the condition of a high injection rate. Moreover, it strongly affects the network's overall performance as a result of increased packet latency. However, the majority of existing congestion avoidance methods either utilize local information or are incredibly complicated. The A-star algorithm is characterized as a heuristic algorithm typically used for the purpose of obtaining an optimal path. In this paper, we propose a novel route selection strategy for network-on-chips is proposed. This strategy is based on the A-star algorithm called ASA-routing. This selection method can be coupled with any deadlock-free adaptive routing algorithm. The ASA-routing utilizes routing table information in order to select as non-congested as possible of output channels for forwarding packets. The congestion information should be dynamically updated according to previously routed packets' transmission latency. Based on experimental results for different traffic patterns and network loads, the manner in which our method can be applied to the repetitive turn model routing and the odd-even turn routing is outlined, improving both the average latency and the throughput.

Keywords: Network-on-chip · Adaptive routing · A-star algorithm
Congestion · Selection function

1 Introduction

With the ever-increasing the number of heterogeneous processing elements integrated into the System-on-chip (SoC), which is already capable of reaching tens or hundreds of processing elements, core communication exerts a significant impact on SoC performance. Therefore, the SoC interconnection infrastructure must be designed with care so that it provides support to efficient communication [1]. Network-on-chip (NoC) [6] is proposed as an effective interconnection method for the multicore system which is capable of replacing the traditional bus-based architecture.

The main difference in NoC architecture from one to the other lies in its topology and the routing algorithm. In terms of topology, numerous research groups have offered various network topologies, among which, mesh-connected networks

© Springer Nature Switzerland AG 2018
J. Vaidya and J. Li (Eds.): ICA3PP 2018, LNCS 11335, pp. 187–198, 2018.
https://doi.org/10.1007/978-3-030-05054-2_14

have received widespread use in interconnection multicomputer networks. In particular, the two-dimension mesh (2D mesh) is the preferred network of choice for the NoC. The properties of topology regularity, linear scalability cost, low node degree and high path diversity [23] have generated considerable attention. As a result, such topology has been adopted in a number of recent experimental and commercial systems [22]. In the other hand, a large number of nodes process their tasks in parallel, communicating with each other by utilizing propagating packets through the network's switches. The packet's transfer path can be determined based on a routing algorithm. In order to render communication efficient, the routing algorithm with high throughput and low latency constitutes the superior selection. In terms of the manner in which the set of possible paths from the source to the destination are specified, routing algorithms can be classified into two distinct groups based on whether they are deterministic or adaptive [8,17]. In deterministic routing algorithms [18], the path from the source to the destination is determined solely by the source address and the destination address. Meanwhile, in adaptive routing algorithms [8], there are multiple available paths from the source node to the destination node which are specified by giving consideration not only to the given source and destination pair but also to the network's current state. Several pieces of research [3,5,11,13,14] illustrate that the adaptive routing algorithms typically outperform deterministic ones because adaptive routing algorithms are capable of providing a greater degree of adaptiveness and an enhanced capability to avoid congestion [15]. Adaptive routing algorithms include both a routing function and a selection function. The routing function is dedicated to the selection of feasible output channels according to the set of routing rules. When the routing function returns admissible output channels, the selection function is employed in order to select one to which the packet will then be forwarded. Therefore, the selection strategy plays an indispensable role in any adaptive routing algorithms [10,16,19] and hence constitutes the primary area of focus in this paper.

In our approach, the A-star algorithm is employed. The A-star algorithm was first proposed by [12]. Moreover, it is a kind of the classical intelligent search algorithm for path search and planning, which is based on the heuristic graph search algorithm and is capable of being used for the purpose of dealing with the optimization problem from the source node to the destination node. To the best of our knowledge, the A-star algorithm typically outperforms traditional shortest path algorithms in solving the one-to-one shortest path problem [4]. The A-star algorithm employs an evaluation function in order to select the next step. In this paper, the A-star algorithm was applied to NoCs, using it as the selection strategy for creating an adaptive routing algorithm named ASA-routing. A switch stores a table containing the latency-value which estimates alternative paths quality. These values are updated each time when a packet reaches its destination, in the process of which it passes the switch. ASA-routing is capable of identifying the least congested path among available paths, thereby improving NoC performances.

The switching technique employed in this paper is virtual cut-through (VCT) switching. VCT switching requires less delay compared to the store-and-forward switching scheme and simple deadlock avoidance design in terms of the wormhole switching. In the VCT switching, each packet is divided into a sequence of flits. When the header flit carrying the routing information arrives at the node, it can be sent instantly provided that all forwarding conditions are met, without the need to wait for all flits of the packet to reach this node. The body flits then follow the reserved channel by the header flit and the tail flit releasing the channel reservation [7].

The remainder of the paper is organized as follows. Related works are surveyed in Sect. 2, while the detailed process of the ASA-routing algorithm is outlined in Sect. 3. Next, the simulation results are presented in Sect. 4, followed by the conclusion in the final section, Sect. 5.

2   Related Works

Glass [11] introduced the turn model which is an interesting method for eliminating cycle dependencies through the prohibition of some turns. This model analyzes eight turns in the 2D mesh network, including both the clockwise and counterclockwise directions. This thus prevents turns in the appropriate position from forming the deadlock-free adaptive routing. The disadvantage inherent to this model is that the degree of adaptiveness in the half case is the same as fully adaptive routing, however, in the other case, it is one.

Based on the turn model [11], Chiu [5] proposed a simple partially adaptive routing algorithm called the odd-even turn model in order to implement deadlock-free routing in meshes. An NW or SW turn is restricted at any node whose column coordinate is odd. Meanwhile, an EN or ES turn is restricted at any node whose column coordinate is even. Figure 1(a) displays the prohibited turns for the odd-even turn in a 5×5 mesh. The advantage of this model over the turn model is that it provides a more even degree of adaptiveness between different source-destination pairs.

The characteristics of the odd-even turn model were utilized in order to educe the concept of repetitive turn distribution. It is a widely known fact that the odd-even turn model has a repetitive property on both column and row. Then, by observing prohibited turn's various distributions, Tang [21] found that this can have a significant impact on the system performance. The repetitive turn model is proposed through the exploitation of the logic-based routing algorithm design space. As shown in Fig. 1(b), if the node is in a column where the remainder of the dimension-x coordinate divided by three is one or two, then any packet is prevented to take NW and SW turns at the node. Moreover, if the node is in a column where the remainder of the dimension-x coordinate divided by three is zero, then any packet is prevented to take ES and EN turns at the node. This routing algorithm exerts smaller routing pressures [20] than the odd-even turn model routing for every network size, resulting in a significant improvement in performance.

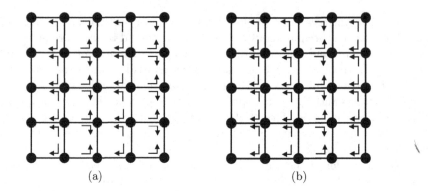

Fig. 1. Prohibited turns of the two routing algorithms (a) the odd-even turn; (b) the repetitive turn model

In [13], a new congestion-aware routing scheme is proposed called DyAD. This scheme combines the advantages of both the deterministic and adaptive routing schemes. The router employs a deterministic routing mode or adaptive routing mode depending on the network's congestion conditions. When the network is congested, the router operates according to an adaptive routing mode, thereby avoiding congested channels. The DyXY [14] checks the stress value of neighboring routers which is typically defined as the instant queue length, with the node with the smallest stress value being chosen. However, the DyXY utilizes the local information, which is not sufficient for avoiding the congestion area. Ascia [2] proposes the notion of Neighbor-on-Path (NoP). The NoP selection strategy seeks to choose the channel which makes the packet reach the destination in the shortest time through the least congested area. This strategy's shortcoming lies in the fact that it decreases the degree of adaptiveness of the odd-even turn routing. The Q-routing [9] represents another congestion-aware routing algorithm for NoCs. In this method, the network can continuously adapt to changing congestion conditions and traffic flows, with the router determining the next step based on the latency information. Q-routing alleviates the network congestion and improves the network performance.

3   The A-Star Adaptive Routing

3.1   Basic Idea of the A-Star Algorithm

The A-star algorithm is an informed search algorithm which enjoys widespread usage in pathfinding and graph traversal. It is capable of solving problems by searching all possible paths in order to choose the optimal path and in a fast manner.

The A-star algorithm selects the path which minimizes

$$F(n) = G(n) + H(n) \tag{1}$$

Here, n is the current node on the path. $G(n)$ is the path's path from the source node to the node n. $H(n)$ estimates the optimal path's cost from the node n to the destination node, which is a predicted value. $F(n)$ is the evaluation function of the node n, which denotes the cost from the source node to the intermediate node n to the destination node. In order to apply the conventional A-star algorithm to the NoC routing, latency is employed as the evaluation criterion as a proxy equivalent to the cost in [4].

3.2 Description of the Routing Algorithm

In this section, we show how our approach, based on the A-star algorithm, works. Figure 2 shows the overview of our method for selecting the path. The ASA-routing algorithm has several stages as follows:

Step 1: Construct the 2D mesh NoC and initialize the G and H.

Step 2: Obtain allowable neighbors according to the given routing function and compute their F value.

Step 3: Select a neighbor with the smallest F. If the node with minimal F is not equal, randomly select one.

Step 4: Route the packet from the current node to the selected next one.

Step 5: Check whether the node is the destination node. If it is the destination node, move to Step 6, otherwise repeat Step 2.

Step 6: Backtrack and update the routing table along with all the selected nodes using latency information.

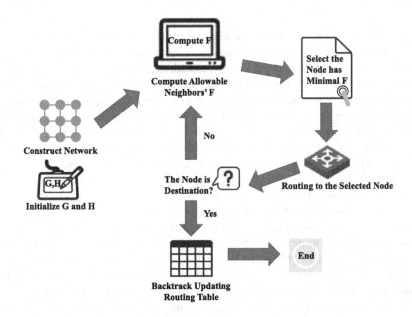

Fig. 2. Overview of this paper's path selection method

Algorithm 1. $findNextNode()$

Require: $curNode, dstNode;$
1: $openList = \emptyset;$
2: $closeList = \emptyset;$
3: $openList.add(curNode)$
4: **while** $openList$ is not empty **do**
5:    $tempCurNode = findMinFNodeInOpenList();$
6:    $closeList.add(tempCurNode);$
7:    $neighborNodes = findNeighborNodes();$
8:    **for** each $nextNode$ of $neighborNodes$ **do**
9:       **if** $nextNode$ is in $openList$ **then**
10:          $new\_g = G(tempCurNode) + c(tempCurNode, nextNode);$
11:          **if** $new\_g < G(nextNode)$ **then**
12:             $F(nextNode) = new\_g + H(nextNodee);$
13:             set $tempCurNode$ as parent to $nextNode$;
14:          **end if**
15:       **else**
16:          $openList.add(nextNode)$
17:          set $tempCurNode$ as parent to $nextNode;$
18:       **end if**
19:    **end for**
20:    **if** $dstNode$ is in $openList$ **then**
21:       **return**
22:    **end if**
23: **end while**

Each time a packet arrives at the node, the node receives the packet from its last hop neighbor and calls the function $findNextNode()$ in order to determine the next node. The detailed process by which the function $findNextNode()$ operates is shown in Algorithm 1. Two lists are maintained: $openList$ and $closeList$. $openList$ consists of nodes which have been visited but not expanded, while $closeList$ contains those nodes which have been both visited and expanded. Firstly, Line 1 and Line 2 initiate $openList$ and $closeList$, setting them to empty. Then, Line 3 puts the $curNode$ in the $openList$. If the $openList$ is not empty, the node with the smallest F is found in the $openList$, marked as $tempCurNode$ and then added to the $closeList$ Line 5 to Line 6. Line 7 shows that all allowable neighbors for the $tempCurNode$ which are not in the $closeList$ have been found by following the routing rules. Line 8 to Line 19 traverse all of the nodes in the $neighborNodes$. If the node is in the $openList$ and its arrival from the $tempCurNode$ has a smaller G, then the F is updated. The $c(tempCurNode, nextNode)$ represents the latency from $tempCurNode$ to $nextNode$ in the Line 10. If the node is not in the $openList$, then it is added to the $openList$. It is worth noting that updating G should involve searching the routing table of the $tempCurNode$, while setting H should involve searching the routing table of the node in the $neighborNodes$. This function constructs a tree

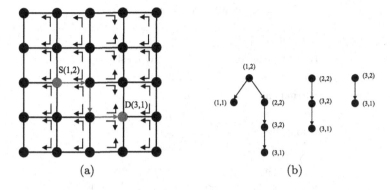

Fig. 3. Example of the ASA-routing (a) the network; (b) the tree

structure from *curNode* to *dstNode* by setting the parent of each intermediate node. From this, the next node can easily be obtained by searching the tree.

The repetitive turn model with proposed selection strategy is taken as an example for the purpose of illustrating the ASA-routing algorithm in Fig. 3. This is done by routing a packet from the source node $S(1,2)$ to the destination node $D(3,1)$. Firstly, the node $(1,2)$ is added to the open list. Then, its two allowable neighbors $(2,2)$ and $(1,1)$ are computed. The one with the smaller F is then selected as the node $(1,2)$'s child. Then, the node $(1,2)$ is removed from the open list and the node $(1,2)$ is added to the close list. In this way, the remaining path can be constructed until the node $(3,1)$. Assuming that the completed path is $(1,2) \rightarrow (2,2) \rightarrow (2,1) \rightarrow (3,1)$, the next node obtained is $(2,2)$. Then, the packet can be sent to this node. In the next cycle, a new path can be constructed from the current node $(2,2)$. After several cycles, the packet arrives at the destination. Finally, if the packet has been forwarded by nodes $(1,2)$, $(2,2)$, $(2,1)$, $(3,1)$, these nodes' routing table entries are updated for $(destination, taking\ cycles)$.

When selecting the next node, the basic condition is that it must satisfy the routing function rules. Thus, the deadlock-free condition of ASA-routing is preserved, because it depends solely on the routing function, with the deadlock-free adaptive routing function serving as this paper's premise.

4   Simulation Results

This paper's proposed selection strategy has been coupled with the repetitive turn model routing and odd-even turn routing, respectively. In the following section, these two routing algorithms are referred to ASA-RTM routing and ASA-OE routing.

All simulation results are presented for the 8×8 mesh. The VCT switching is applied throughout the simulation. The traffic source generates 16 flits packets in all cases. Each node's buffer size is set to 16 flits in all cases for all methods. Each simulation has a warming up cycle which is set to 10,000 cycles so as to

Table 1. Simulation Configuration.

Attribute	Value
Network topology	8×8 2D mesh
Packet size	16 flits
Virtual channel	no
Port buffer	16 flits
Run cycles	30 000
Warming up cycle	10 000
Traffic pattern	Uniform, transpose
Flow control technique	Virtual cut-through

ignore unstable data. Subsequently, it was executed for 20,000 cycles. In order to guarantee the accuracy of the results, the simulation at each injection rate was repeated ten times. The basic configuration is shown in Table 1. Average latency and throughput were used as measurement metrics for the purpose of evaluating routing algorithm performance.

Performance with the repetitive turn model routing and ASA-RTM routing algorithm are compared, as are the odd-even turn routing and ASA-OE routing algorithm. The selection strategy is evaluated using the synthetic traffic scenarios. In uniform traffic, a node sends the packet to each other node with the same probability. In the first transpose traffic, a node (i, j) only sends packets to a node $(k-1-j, k-1-i)$ where k is the number of nodes in each mesh dimension. In the second transpose traffic, a node (i, j) only sends packets to a node (j, i).

Figure 4 illustrates the comparison of the two methods' performances based on the uniform communication pattern. The ASA-RTM routing algorithm requires higher latency in order to deliver a message in a low injection rate.

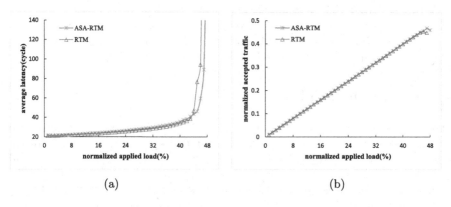

Fig. 4. Performance of the ASA-RTM and RTM routing algorithms under the uniform traffic in 8×8 meshes (a) average latency; (b) normalized accepted traffic

However, latency to deliver a message for the ASA-RTM routing algorithm is much less than that of the repetitive turn model routing algorithm once the normalized applied load exceeds 0.43. As for the normalized accepted traffic, the ASA-RTM routing algorithm exhibits no apparent advantage prior to the normalized applied load exceeding 0.47.

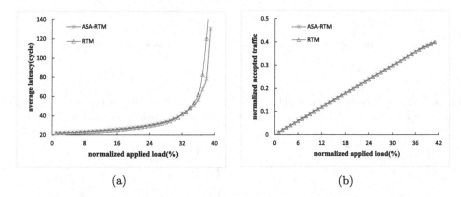

(a)   (b)

Fig. 5. Performance of the ASA-RTM and RTM routing algorithms under the first transpose traffic in 8×8 meshes (a) average latency; (b) normalized accepted traffic

Figure 5(a) and (b) show the average communication latency and throughput as a function of the normalized applied load. As can be observed from the results, the ASA-RTM routing algorithm yields a higher latency than the repetitive turn model routing algorithm prior to the normalized applied load is smaller than 0.33, which is similar to the uniform scenario. However, the ASA-RTM routing algorithm leads to a lower latency in high traffic loads. The normalized accepted traffic of the two algorithms almost has no difference.

The simulation results for the two algorithms based on the second transpose communication pattern are shown in Fig. 6. ASA-RTM routing algorithm's latency rapidly rises after the normalized applied load reaches 0.38, which is later than for the repetitive turn model routing algorithm. The performance gain near the saturation point (0.38) is 27%. Thus, it is concluded that ASA-RTM still performs better when network congestion occurs. This result was excepted given that the ASA-RTM routing algorithm undertakes routing decisions by considering network traffic status.

As shown in Fig. 7(a), the ASA-OE routing algorithm performs better than the odd-even turn model routing algorithm under uniform traffic load. This result is consistent with Fig. 4(a). In this case, Fig. 7(b) illustrates that the network employing odd-even turn routing algorithm saturates at the normalized applied load of 0.43, while the ASA-OE routing algorithm achieves the normalized applied load of 0.44.

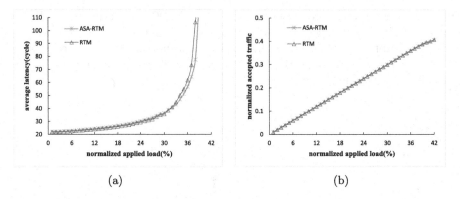

Fig. 6. Performance of the ASA-RTM and RTM routing algorithms under the second transpose traffic in 8 × 8 meshes (a) average latency; (b) normalized accepted traffic

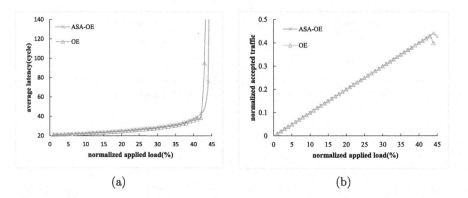

Fig. 7. Performance of the ASA-OE and OE routing algorithms under the uniform traffic in 8 × 8 meshes (a) average latency; (b) normalized accepted traffic

5   Conclusion

In this paper, a new selection function coupled with the deadlock-free adaptive routing function for NoCs is proposed, the purpose of which is to make packets to reach their destination without passing through congested areas, thus alleviating network congestion. This method is inspired by the A-star algorithm. In the simulation, the repetitive turn model routing and odd-even turn routing are taken as examples for implementing ASA-routing. Sufficient simulation results are presented, thereby demonstrating the effectiveness of the ASA-routing algorithm through comparison with the original repetitive turn model routing and odd-even turn routing methods.

References

1. International technology roadmap for semiconductors interconnect. Tech. rep., Semiconductor Industry Assoc. (2006)
2. Ascia, G., Catania, V., Palesi, M., Patti, D.: Implementation and analysis of a new selection strategy for adaptive routing in networks-on-chip. IEEE Trans. Comput. **57**(6), 809–820 (2008)
3. Boura, Y.M., Das, C.R.: A class of partially adaptive routing algorithms for n-dimensional meshes. In: Proceedings of the 1993 International Conference on Parallel Processing, pp. 175–182. CRC Press, NY (1993)
4. Chabini, I., Lan, S.: Adaptations of the a* algorithm for the computation of fastest paths in deterministic discrete-time dynamic networks. IEEE Trans. Intell. Transp. Syst. **3**(1), 60–74 (2002)
5. Chiu, G.: The odd-even turn model for adaptive routing. IEEE Trans. Parallel Distrib. Syst. **11**(7), 729–738 (2000)
6. Dally, W.J., Towles, B.: Route packets, not wires: on-chip interconnection networks. In: Proceedings of the 38th Design Automation Conference, pp. 684–689. ACM, Las Vegas (2001)
7. Duato, J., Yalamanchili, S., Ni, L.M.: Interconnection Networks: An Engineering Approach. Morgan Kaufmann, San Francisco (2003)
8. Ebrahimi, M., Daneshtalab, M., Liljeberg, P., Plosila, J., Tenhunen, H.: CATRA-congestion aware trapezoid-based routing algorithm for on-chip networks. In: Design, Automation & Test in Europe Conference & Exhibition, DATE, pp. 320–325. IEEE, Dresden (2012)
9. Farahnakian, F., Ebrahimi, M., Daneshtalab, M., Liljeberg, P., Plosila, J.: Q-learning based congestion-aware routing algorithm for on-chip network. In: Proceedings of the 2nd IEEE International Conference on Networked Embedded Systems for Enterprise Applications, NESEA, pp. 1–7. IEEE Computer Society, Perth (2011)
10. Feng, W., Shin, K.G.: Impact of selection functions on routing algorithm performance in multicomputer networks. In: In: Proceedings of the 11th international conference on Supercomputing, pp. 132–139. ACM, Austria (1997)
11. Glass, C.J., Ni, L.M.: The turn model for adaptive routing. J. ACM **41**(5), 874–902 (1994)
12. Hart, P.E., Nilsson, N.J., Raphael, B.: A formal basis for the heuristic determination of minimum cost paths. IEEE Trans. Syst. Sci. Cybern. **4**(2), 100–107 (1968)
13. Hu, J., Marculescu, R.: Dyad: smart routing for networks-on-chip. In: Proceedings of the 41st Design Automation Conference, pp. 260–263. ACM, San Diego (2004)
14. Li, M., Zeng, Q., Jone, W.: Dyxy: a proximity congestion-aware deadlock-free dynamic routing method for network on chip. In: Proceedings of the 43rd Design Automation Conference, pp. 849–852. ACM, San Francisco (2006)
15. Lotfi-Kamran, P., Daneshtalab, M., Lucas, C., Navabi, Z.: BARP-A dynamic routing protocol for balanced distribution of traffic in NoCs. In: Design. Automation and Test in Europe, DATE, pp. 1408–1413. ACM, Munich (2008)
16. Martínez, J.C., Silla, F., López, P., Duato, J.: On the influence of the selection function on the performance of networks of workstations. In: Third International Symposium High Performance Computing, ISHPC, pp. 292–299. Springer, Tokyo (2000)
17. Ni, L.M., McKinley, P.K.: A survey of wormhole routing techniques in direct networks. IEEE Comput. **26**(2), 62–76 (1993)

18. Rijpkema, E., Goossens, K.G.W., Radulescu, A., Dielissen, J., van Meerbergen, J.L., Wielage, P., Waterlander, E.: Trade offs in the design of a router with both guaranteed and best-effort services for networks on chip. In: Design, Automation and Test in Europe Conference and Exposition (DATE), pp. 10350–10355. IEEE Computer Society, Munich (2003)
19. Schwiebert, L., Bell, R.: Performance tuning of adaptive wormhole routing through selection function choice. J. Parallel Distrib. Comput. **62**(7), 1121–1141 (2002)
20. Tang, M., Lin, X., Palesi, M.: Routing pressure: a channel-related and traffic-aware metric of routing algorithm. IEEE Trans. Parallel Distrib. Syst. **26**(3), 891–901 (2015)
21. Tang, M., Lin, X., Palesi, M.: The repetitive turn model for adaptive routing. IEEE Trans. Comput. **66**(1), 138–146 (2017)
22. Xiang, D.: Deadlock-free adaptive routing in meshes with fault-tolerance ability based on channel overlapping. IEEE Trans. Dependable Sec. Comput. **8**(1), 74–88 (2011)
23. Yu, Z., Wang, X., Shen, K., Liu, H.: A general methodology to design deadlock-free routing algorithms for mesh networks. In: 15th International Conference on Algorithms and Architectures for Parallel Processing - ICA3PP, pp. 478–491. Springer, Zhangjiajie (2015)

Trajectory Data-Driven Pattern Recognition of Congestion Propagation in Road Networks

Hepeng Gao[1], Yongjian Yang[1], Liping Huang[1(✉)], Yiqi Wang[1],
Bing Jia[2], Funing Yang[1], and Zhuo Zhu[1]

[1] Jilin University, Changchun, China
gaohepeng13@foxmail.com, huangliping5727@163.com
[2] College of Computer Science, Inner Mongolia University,
Hohhot 10010, China

Abstract. The congestion pattern recognition in urban road networks helps for recognizing the bottleneck in road networks and assisting to route planning. With the widespread use of GPS devises in vehicles, it is possible for researchers to monitor the traffic condition of urban transport networks at a road level. In this paper, we utilize the trajectory data of vehicle GPS to detect the road travel speed by matching points of trajectories to road segments. A fuzzy clustering based method is proposed to classify the road congestion level according to the road traffic conditions. Further, the road network is clustered by the proposed snake clustering algorithm, so that the road network is divided into congested and uncongested areas. This paper studies the congestion propagation problem and propose to employ the dynamic Bayesian network for modeling the congestion propagation process. Taking the real road network of Shanghai and the dataset of GPS trajectories generated by more than 10,000 taxis, we evaluate the pattern recognition based congestion prediction method. It shows that the proposed model outperforms the competing baselines.

Keywords: Congestion propagation · Taxi trajectories · Road network Dynamic bayesian network

1 Introduction

With the increasing number of urban vehicles, most cities are faced with the problem of serious congestion in road networks, especially for the metropolises and during the time span of peak hours. Acquiring the knowledge of the road network congestion pattern is of great significance for route planning and traffic monitoring, which has attracted much research attention. Traditional traffic condition monitoring is largely based on the infrastructure systems, such as the loop sensors, roadside camera etc. These sensing methods can only cover a limited proportion of roads in the network, which results that the congestion pattern recognition is regarded as a tricky problem because of lacking data [1]. Thanks to the widespread use of the GPS (Global Positioning System) devices in vehicles [2], especially used in the public transport systems, such as the tax system [3], **trajectories** generated by vehicles that are equipped with

© Springer Nature Switzerland AG 2018
J. Vaidya and J. Li (Eds.): ICA3PP 2018, LNCS 11335, pp. 199–211, 2018.
https://doi.org/10.1007/978-3-030-05054-2_15

GPS devices help sensing the **spatial and temporal** traffic situation in urban road networks [4, 5].

However, due to the complexity of the road environment and the diversity of route selection, it is difficult to predict road congestion. Therefore, a dynamic Bayesian network model is established to describe and predict the periodicity and correlation of traffic network. It provides a reference for traffic dispatch and public travel.

Based on the trajectory coverage in the urban road networks, keeping only the knowledge of current on the state of the road network can fulfill the dynamic route planning need for travelers and the traffic state warning function for the transportation department. This meaning that further knowledge of the road congestion should be obtained. Such as where (**spatial**) and when (**temporal**) a congestion will happen [6, 7]. This spatial and temporal **congestion prediction** problem is always called **congestion propagation** [8]. In this paper, we focus on the congestion pattern [9] mining and the propagation prediction of urban road networks based on the taxi trajectories, which means that our proposed model is a data-driven method. Using the taxi trajectories based on map matching algorithms, the average travel speed of each road segment can be calculated [10]. The relative travel speed ratio of a road segment in a specific time interval is utilized to estimate the congestion level based on the clustering algorithm of fuzzy c-means (FCM). Then we propose a snake clustering algorithm that partition roads into clusters that are connected and congested in the same time interval. Further, based on the clustering results, a dynamic Bayesian model-based method is proposed to predict the congestion propagation, meaning that predict the congestion state of a road given the congestion states of its neighbors.

Main contributions of this paper include the following three points.

(1) We propose a trajectory data based congestion level estimation method based on the FCM algorithm, and a further snake clustering algorithm is proposed to mining the spatial and temporal congestion pattern in the road networks.
(2) According to the congestion pattern mining results with the proposed snake clustering algorithm, a further dynamic congestion propagation model is proposed based on the Bayesian framework.
(3) Taking a real-world road network of Shanghai together with the dataset of taxi trajectories generated by more than 13000 taxis during a month, we evaluate the proposed method and give case studies of the congestion propagation visualization.

The rest of this paper is organized as followings. Section 2 reviews relative literature, including the trajectory map matching algorithm and congestion estimation and propagation methods. The section presents our proposed method for congestion propagation method in the road network, including the trajectory-based congestion estimation, the congestion pattern recognition, and the dynamic propagation prediction method. A case study is reported in Sect. 4. Section 5 concludes this paper and present the future works.

2 Related Works

Traffic congestion relief is beneficial to the efficiency of urban operation, reducing the incidence of traffic accidents and reducing environmental pollution. Thus it attracts may researchers. The first step of the locus-based approach is to match the GPS points to the section. It can be classified as a geometric matching algorithm, a topological relation algorithm, probabilistic statistical algorithm and advanced matching algorithm according to different characteristics. Because of the high matching efficiency of the probabilistic statistical algorithm and the high accuracy of the vehicle running at low speed, this algorithm is used for road matching.

The next step is to detect road congestion. Hoang Nguyen [11] Count all traffic times and define time greater than T (where $P\{t > T\} = 0.3$) as congestion. Anwar [12] constructs a Bin structure to improve the access efficiency of historical data and achieves continuous detection of congestion change. Yang [13] proposes a Multiple Data Estimation methods, which uses multiple attributes to estimate urban congestion effectively, and selects attributes to improve accuracy and efficiency.

Finally, we detect and predict congestion propagation patterns. Complex network methods, clustering methods, and dynamic Bayes can be applied. For complex networks, Aleta [14] proposed a method to model a public transport system as a multiplex network. A more in-depth understanding of the network characteristics of the public transport system, for the establishment of a realistic model of urban traffic. Liu [15] by introducing the network science analysis method, the community discovery method reveals the urban structure under the taxi trip data. For the clustering method, An [9] proposes a grid-based method for detecting data congestion using floating cars. Grid Congestion Mode is defined to detect whether the grid is congested, and DBSCAN clustering method is used to find out the Recurrent Congestion. Rempe [16] proposes a clustering method to obtain the time and variation of abnormal day clustering and to quantify the congestion correlation among clusters. According to the speed of the vehicle, Saeedmanesh [17] uses snake algorithm [18] to cluster. Since each period reclustering consumes resources, the existing clusters are fine-tuned over time. The change of spatial location of patency and congestion is expressed by the change of cluster over time, and then the spread of congestion is described. As a result of observing and studying road sections from a macro perspective [19], the link between road congestion cannot be reflected and road congestion can't be effectively predicted. For dynamic Bayesian, Hoang Nguyen uses the Apriori algorithm to mine frequently-congested roads by establishing high-frequency congestion trees, and further uses dynamic Bayesian prediction. Through the above methods, it is possible to predict road congestion, but the spatial connectivity between roads is not fully considered.

Based on the trajectory data, this paper studies the traffic congestion propagation and congestion prediction. Firstly, snake is used to cluster the roads that have been divided into congestion levels, and the traffic roads are divided into disjoint areas [20]. In the region, the dynamic Bayesian network is used to study the interaction between different time periods of each road, and according to the traffic situation of the road at different times, the traffic situation of the target section is predicted.

3 Methodology

3.1 Congestion Level Estimation Based on FCM

After matching each GPS point to the road segment, then the congestion level of each road segment is estimated. For each road, the velocity $v_{ij}(t)$ varies during a day according to real-time traffic. For each road e_{ij}, we set the 95% percentile of its velocity in each day as its limited maximal velocity and define $r_{ij}(t)$ as the ratio between its current velocity and its limited maximal velocity measured as (1).

$$r_{ij}(t) = \frac{v_{ij}(t)}{v_{ij}^{lim}(t)} \tag{1}$$

Different from previous researches that identify the congestion state of a road segment as binary state 0 and 1, meaning not congested or congested, we adopt the FCM to estimate the congestion status. As shown in (2), supposing that the value set of r_{ij} is $X = (x_1, x_2, \ldots, x_n)$, the membership matrix of FCM is defined as $u = \{u_{ij}\}_{k \times n}$, $\sum u_{ij} = 1, \forall j = 1, 2, \ldots, n$. $c = \{c_1, c_1, \ldots, c_k\}$ is the cluster center of k clusters. The FCM algorithms applies the fuzzy membership degree and the cluster center to represent the partition of the value range, and the objective function is shown as (2)

$$J(u, c) = \sum_{j=1}^{n} \sum_{i=1}^{k} u_{ij}^m \lVert x_j - c_i \rVert^2 \tag{2}$$

Considering the constraint condition and the objective function, the la-grangian method is adopted as (3)

$$J(U, c_1, c_2, \ldots, c_k, \lambda_1, \lambda_2, \ldots, \lambda_n) = \sum_{i=1}^{k} \sum_{j}^{n} u_{ij}^m (x_j - c_i)^2 + \sum_{j=1}^{n} \lambda_j \left(\sum_{i=1}^{k} u_{ij} - 1 \right) \tag{3}$$

Then the cluster center and the membership is calculated as (4) and (5)

$$c_i = \frac{\sum_{j=1}^{n} u_{ij}^m x_j}{\sum_{j=1}^{n} u_{ij}^m} \tag{4}$$

$$u_{ij} = \frac{1}{\sum_{i=1}^{k} \left(\frac{d_{ij}}{d_{kj}} \right)^{2/m-1}} \tag{5}$$

If we want to partition the congestion level into 4 categories, then we set k = 4 and the cluster centers is applied to represent the congested level.

3.2   Congestion Pattern Recognition Based on Snake Clustering

Through previous data processing, we obtained the road number, the adjacency relationship between roads, and the current road condition of roads. Next, we clustered the roads. The roads are divided by the spatial relationship between the roads and the traffic conditions of the roads. The snake algorithm is used to cluster the roads. The snake algorithm takes full account of the adjacency and connectivity of the road in the aspect of space.

In the list of congested roads, seed nodes are selected randomly as inputs to snake, and seed nodes are added to the linked list of result sets. According to the adjacency relationship of the road, the nodes which are directly adjacent to the current result set is selected into the candidate queue, and the nodes with the smallest difference of the current result set in the candidate queue are selected to join the result set. Until all nodes are added to the result set, the algorithm is finished and the result is returned in the order of adding results. The algorithm process is as follows:

Algorithm P-snake

```
Input : initial x₀, adjacency matrix W, congestion level
dict, N
Output : the result set S₁, S₂, ..., Sₙ
Process:
1:while I = 1,2,...,N do
2: Initial result set S and candidate set D
3: D=D∪{x₀}
4:    while D!=∅ do
5:       node = getNearestNeighbor( dict, S, D)
6:       S = S∪{node}
7:       C = getNeighbor( D, node)
8:       D = D∪C
9:    end while
10: Sᵢ = S
11: x₀ = getLastElement( S)
12:end while
```

The getNearestNeighbor function returns the node which is the smallest difference between the candidate set and the result set. The getNeighbor function returns the directly connected node and the node is not the set of nodes of the candidate set and the result set. The getLastElement function returns the last congested node of the S result set. Run the P-snake to get N snake sequences. The standard deviation between snake nodes is selected as the evaluation criterion for evaluating the variation of snake sequences. The standard deviation has a positive correlation with the degree of difference between the nodes in the current snake, and we calculate the variation of the standard deviation of each snake sequence (each joins one node and calculates a standard deviation).

The changes of different snake sequences generated by P-snake were observed. When the length of snake is larger than a certain threshold ε, the increase of standard deviation increases obviously. So when the number of elements in snake sequence is larger than a value, Then the nodes added are quite different from the nodes in the current snake sequence (It is extremely unlikely that the sequence before this node and the sequence after it will be divided into the same category). The conclusion of the current snake sequence at the threshold ε does not affect the classification of the final cluster. At the same time, reduce the consumption of resources (computational resources and memory resources) and reduce the time.

The restricted snake growth threshold ε is applied to the algorithm. When the length of snake sequence reaches the threshold ε, the growth of snake is stopped. One node is randomly selected as the seed of the next snake growth from the nodes that add the least number of snake sequences. After running the RL-snake, N snakes with length ε are obtained.

Algorithm RL-snake

```
Input: adjacency matrix W, congestion level dict, N
Output: the result set S₁, S₂, …, Sₙ
Process:
1:Initialization node dictionary T
2:while I = 1,2,..., N do
3:     initialize result set S, candidate set D
4:     x₀= getElement (T)
5:     D=D∪{x₀}
6:     while D! = Ø and length (S) < ε do
7:          node = getNearestNeighbor (dict, S, D)
8:          nodeTimesAdd (T, node)
9:            S = S {node}
10:           C = getNeighbor (D, node)
11:           D = D∪C
12:     end while
13: Sᵢ = S
14: x₀= getElement (T)
15: end while
```

Among them, the return of getElement(T) is the randomly selected node in the congested node with the least number of snake sequences. Due to the randomness of the generation of snake, the current division may have the following problems: Firstly the threshold ε cannot define exactly whether the growth of the current snake should end, the snake's growth may end early (the node is not added to the matching snake) and late (join the node which is quite different from the snake node). Secondly, the current snake sequence may have two snake of smallest size, so we should divide the current snake sequence into two smaller size snake. Lastly, There are situations where there are two snake intersections that cause one or more nodes to belong to one or more snake at the same time. Because above problems may happen, we use the Mixed

Integer Linear Programming (MILP) to adjust the snake. We define the following variables to describe the MILP (Table 1):

Table 1. Set of variables, indices, and parameters

x_{ij}	If the node j belongs to snake i, the value of x_{ij} is 1; If not, is 0
$R_i(k)$	Return the name of k node in snake i
t_i	Present the variance of Snake i
N_c	Present the variance of Snake
N	Present the number of nodes
∂	Present fraction of coverage (joined nodes/N)
I	$\{1,2,\ldots, \varepsilon\}$
N_p	The smallest number of Snake

We constrain for MILP about these variables as following formula shows:

$$min \sum_{i=1}^{N_c} t_i \tag{6}$$

$$x_{iR_i(k+1)} \leq x_{iR_i(k)}, \forall i \in I, \forall k = \{1, 2, \ldots, \varepsilon - 1\} \tag{7}$$

$$\sum_{i=1}^{N_c} x_{ij} = 1, \forall j \in \{1, 2, \ldots, \varepsilon\} \tag{8}$$

$$\sum_{i=1}^{N_c} x_{iR_i(1)} \geq N_p \tag{9}$$

$$\sum_{j=1}^{N} \sum_{i=1}^{N_c} x_{ij} \geq aN \tag{10}$$

$$x_{iR_i(1)} = x_{iR_i(2)} \tag{11}$$

Constraint (6) aims to consider all snake sequence in general to make the summation of all variances smallest. Constraint (7) make sure that if one node is in the snake sequence, another node that is before node in order must be in the snake sequence. This constrain ensures every node must be connected with other one or more nodes indirectly. The aim of constraint (8) is to make sure that each node must belong to one snake. Constraint (9) limits the number of the generated snake to at least N_p. Constraint (10) requires that the number of nodes joining snake is above α for all nodes. Constraint (11) limits a snake to at least two nodes.

Through MILP further dividing the snake, the difference between the roads in the same snake is smaller. Every snake sequence consists of congested roads adjacent to each other in space.

3.3   Frequent Patterning Based Congestion Prediction

The dynamic Bayesian network is used to model the interaction between the roads in the same congestion cluster recognized by the snake clustering method. Links between two layers in the dynamic Bayesian network represent the propagation relation with each layer denotes a time slot, as shown in Fig. 1.

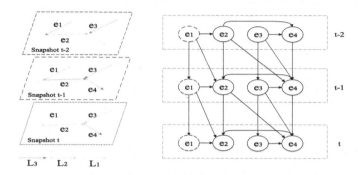

Fig. 1. Dynamic bayesian network based congestion propagation model

Congestion clusters detected in a time slot is represented as a snapshot as shown in Fig. 1. The flow orientation denotes the traffic direction. Nodes in a layer of the Bayesian network is formed with roads in the same cluster of the same time slot. Such as the congestion probability of road segment e_2 in time slot t comes from the congested road e_1 in time slot t and the congestion situation of roads e1 and e_2 in time slot t-1. The propagation relationship is represented as the following equation,

$$P\left(e_k^t | \theta\right) = \frac{P\left(e_k^t, \theta\right)}{P(\theta)} = \frac{\prod_{i \in U} P(e_i^{t-1} | e_k^t) \cdot \prod_{i \in U} P(e_i^t | e_k^t) \cdot P(e_k^{t-1} | e_k^t) \cdot P\left(e_k^t\right)}{\prod_{i \in U} P(e_i^{t-1}) \cdot \prod_{i \in U} P(e_i^t) \cdot P\left(e_k^{t-1}\right)} \tag{12}$$

Where U is a set of e_k^t upstream nodes

4   Experiment and Analysis

4.1   Road Network and Dataset

The case study is implemented on the dataset of the road network of Shanghai, China, together with the dataset of taxi GPS trajectories of one month. The trajectory dataset consists of GPS points generated by more than 10,000 taxis between 8:00 am and 9:00 am. The time slot is set as 5 min, so we can obtain 12 time slots form of 8:00 to 9:00 in each date. The road network, containing 10030 road segments is shown in Fig. 2. The road network is chosen by removing roads that are not connected to the main road framework. Roads that are less than 500 m or the two endpoints is 1 are merged.

Fig. 2. Road network

4.2   Results

First, we determine the threshold ε of the snake growth process using the dataset. By running the P-snake, a certain number of snake sequences can be obtained, and the standard deviation of snake sequences can be calculated with the increase of snake sequences. Figure 3(a) shows how three different snake sequences gradually increase with the size changing. When the size increases to 400, the standard deviation in the snake increases sharply, so 400 is chosen as the threshold.

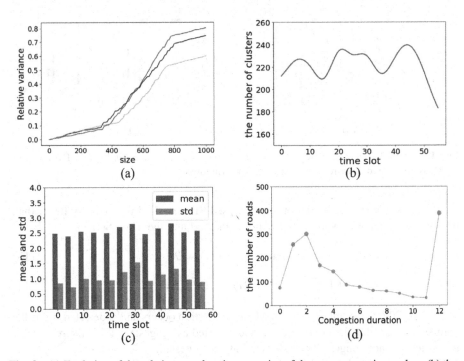

Fig. 3. (a) Evolution of the relative speed variance vs size of three representative snakes; (b) the number of clusters partitioning every time slot; (c) mean and standard deviation partitioning of clusters every time slot; (d) the number of road partitioning congestion duration.

We cluster roads for each time slot, the number of clusters, the average and standard deviation of the cluster size in each time slot are shown in Fig. 3(b) and (c).

According to the statistic results, it can be observed that the number of congested road segments, the cluster size, as well as the diversity within clusters, reserve unchanged with time slot variation. It also shows the state of the road in the current time interval is steady, and it changes little between the adjacent time intervals. We count the duration of the congested roads, represented by time slot number, as shown in Fig. 3(d). During 12 time slots, some key roads are continuously congested, which can be regarded as the center of our snake clustering process. Each time slice has a high probability that the other nodes in the previous snake. Other nodes of the snake may not belong to the snake sequence due to time changes.

Further case studies of our congestion prediction method are presented in this part. With the size of time window varying, the prediction accuracy is compared with the Apriori algorithm and the time series prediction method. Figure 4(a) and (b) are the prediction performance measured by the accuracy and the F-1 measure obtained by three methods.

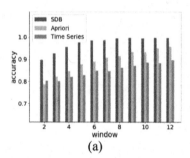 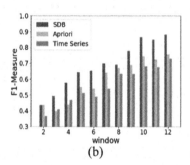

(a)   (b)

Fig. 4. (a) Evolution of accuracy of prediction results vs size of time window; (b) Evolution of F1-Measure of prediction results vs size of time window.

It shows that the prediction of our proposed SDB method is obviously better than that of the competing methods (the Apriori method and the Time Series).

$$accuracy = TP/(TP + FP) \tag{13}$$

$$F1 - Measure = 2TP/(2TP + FN + FP) \tag{14}$$

Where TP is the number of roads where congestion occurs and is detected, FP is the number of roads that are not congested and detected as congested, TN is the number of roads that are not congested and detected as uncongested.

Figure 5 shows the spatial distribution of congested road segments predicted by SDB, in which the black road network is the trunk roads chosen in this paper, and the red section is the congested roads. We select some congested sections detected to explain and analyze them as shown in Figs. 6 and 7.

Fig. 5. Spatial distribution of congested road segments in road network.

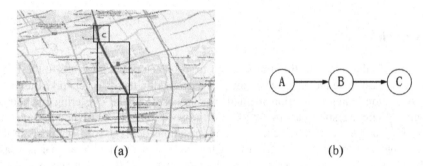

(a)   (b)

Fig. 6. (a) North-South elevated road; (b) Dynamic bayesian network of north-south elevated road.

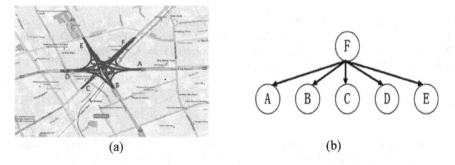

(a)   (b)

Fig. 7. (a) Xinzhuang bridge; (b) Dynamic bayesian network of Xinzhuang bridge

From 8:00 am to 9:00 am, as the main traffic is heading to the city centers for works, thus the main traffic flows come from residential areas to work areas. Figure 6 (a) congested section is the North-South Elevated Road of Shanghai. This section is congested in the early rush hour, consistent with the actual situation. As vehicles on both sides of the road continue to converge into the main road, resulting in congestion of the road segments. First, congestion occurs in segment A, and there is a high probability of congestion in section B in the next time slot or in the current time slot (which is related to the span of time slot). Similarly, congestion in section B is likely to spread to section C. There is a high correlation between section A and section B, section B and section C, so we can use the Bayesian network to describe the relationship between them, as shown in Fig. 6(b). Figure 7(a) shows the congestion area is Xinzhuang Bridge, which is consistent with the actual situation. That is a busy intersection, connecting road segments in six different directions. The southwest of Shanghai is the main busy areas. There are many ramps in this section. The main flow direction of the traffic flow at A to E is to flow into the current road section at the morning peak hours. Only one segment F present the traffic tends to flow out, which can cause the congestion of the road in this section. When the segment F is congested, it possibly results in the congestion of segments A, B, C, D and E These propagation process can be represented as Fig. 7(b).

5 Conclusion

In this paper, through detecting travel speed from trajectory data, we utilize the FCM algorithm to estimate the congestion status of each road in the road network. Based on the congestion status estimation method, we propose a snake clustering method to recognize the congestion pattern. We further propose to apply the dynamic Bayesian network to model the dynamic congestion propagations between road segments in the same recognized congestion cluster. Taking the real road network of Shanghai as a case study, using the taxi trajectories generated by more than 10000 taxis, it shows that our proposed congestion prediction model outperforms the competing baselines.

In the future, we intend to further improve the congestion propagation model by incorporating more traffic affecting factors and imply it on the more real-world dataset.

Acknowledgment. We thanks that this work was financially supported by National Natural Science Foundation of China (61772230, 61702215), Science & Technology Development Project of Jilin Province (20160204021GX) and Special Foundation Project for Industrial Innovation of Jilin Province (2017C032-1).

References

1. Jiang, G.: Link Dividing method for traffic information collecting based on GPS equipped floating car. Geomat. Inf. Sci. Wuhan Univ. **35**(1), 41–42 (2010)
2. Kristensen, J.P., Nielsen, O.A.: Measuring congestion in Copenhagen with gps. Leopoldo Abad Alcalá **61**(2), págs. 17–48 (2006)
3. Chang, A., Jiang, G., Niu, S.: Traffic congestion identification method based on GPS equipped floating car. In: International Conference on Intelligent Computation Technology and Automation, pp. 1069–1071. IEEE Computer Society (2010)
4. Zhang, Y.C., Zuo, X.Q., Zhang, L.T., et al.: Traffic congestion detection based on GPS floating-car data. Procedia Eng. **15**, 5541–5546 (2011)
5. Holm, J.: Key performance indicators for congestion using GPS data. In: 19th ITS World Congress (2012)

6. Arnott R, Small K. The Economics of Traffic Congestion[J]. American Scientist, 1994, 82 (5):446–455
7. Altintasi, O., Tuydes-Yaman, H., Tuncay, K.: Detection of urban traffic patterns from Floating Car Data (FCD). Transp. Res. Proc. **22**, 382–391 (2017)
8. Xu X, Gao X, Zhao X, et al. A novel algorithm for urban traffic congestion detection based on GPS data compression[C]// IEEE International Conference on Service Operations and Logistics, and Informatics. IEEE, 2016:107–112
9. An, S., Yang, H., Wang, J., Urban, M., et al.: Recurrent congestion evolution patterns from GPS-equipped vehicle mobility data. Inf. Sci. **373**(C), 515–526 (2016)
10. Nielsen, O.A.: Analysis of congestion and speeds based on GPS-data. Traffic Days Auc (2003)
11. Nguyen, H., Liu, W., Chen, F.: Discovering congestion propagation patterns in spatio-temporal traffic data. IEEE Trans. Big Data **3**(2), 169–180 (2017)
12. Anwar, T., Liu, C., Hai, L.V., et al.: Capturing the Spatiotemporal Evolution in Road Traffic Networks. IEEE Trans. Knowl. Data Eng. (2018)
13. Yang, Y., Xu, Y., Han, J., et al.: Efficient traffic congestion estimation using multiple spatio-temporal properties. Neurocomputing **267**, 344–353 (2017)
14. Aleta, A., Meloni, S., Moreno, Y.: A Multilayer perspective for the analysis of urban transportation systems. Sci. Rep. **7**, 44359 (2017)
15. Liu, X., Gong, L., Gong, Y., et al.: Revealing travel patterns and city structure with taxi trip data. J. Transp. Geogr. **43**, 78–90 (2015)
16. Rempe, F., Huber, G., Bogenberger, K.: Spatio-temporal congestion patterns in urban traffic networks. Transp. Res. Proc. **15**, 513–524 (2016)
17. Saeedmanesh, M., Geroliminis, N.: Dynamic clustering and propagation of congestion in heterogeneously congested urban traffic networks. Transp. Res. Part B Methodol. **105**, 193–211 (2017)
18. Saeedmanesh, M., Geroliminis, N.: Clustering of heterogeneous networks with directional flows based on "Snake" similarities. Transp. Res. Part B Methodol. **91**, 250–269 (2016)
19. Huang, W., Haiying, L.I., Wang, Y.: Passenger congestion propagation and control in peak hours for urban rail transit line. J. Railw. Sci. Eng. (2017)
20. Gao, Z.Y., Long, J.C., Li, X.G.: Congestion propagation law and dissipation control strategies for urban traffic. J. Univ. Shanghai Sci. Technol. **33**(6), 701–708 (2011)

Cooperative Preprocessing at Petabytes on High Performance Computing System

Rujun Sun[1]([✉]) [iD], Lufei Zhang[1] [iD], and Xiyang Wang[2] [iD]

[1] State Key Laboratory of Mathematical Engineering and Advanced Computing,
Wuxi, China
sun.rujun@meac-skl.cn
[2] National Super Computing Wuxi Center, Wuxi, China

Abstract. With the explosion of data, we have an urgent demand for data throughput in high performance computing systems. Data-intensive applications are becoming increasingly common in HPC environments. As data scale increases faster than systems, it's time to fully utilize resources in every aspect, including computing power, storage capacity and data throughput. We can no longer ignore data preprocessing since it's an important procedure, especially when dealing with large amount of data. How to efficiently perform data preprocessing in current HPC systems? How to make full use of system resources on data-intensive applications? What should be valued when designing new HPC architectures? All these questions need answers. In this paper, we drew a sketch for procedure of data-intensive applications, which lead to an adaptive resource allocation scheme according to procedure requirements. We analyzed characters of preprocessing and designed a preprocessing model for data-intensive applications in HPC systems. It has not only fulfilled the demand for computing but also meet the need of throughput, with cooperative work in storage system and storage management system. Experiments were done on Sunway TaihuLight, one of the world's fastest supercomputers. The whole procedure of preprocessing at Petabytes can be done in hours without interfering other ongoing applications.

Keywords: HPC · Data intensive applications
Cooperative preprocessing · High throughput computing

1 Introduction

With the explosive growth in data size, data-intensive applications become popular and important in practice. High performance systems (HPC) with high computation ability, large memory, efficient interconnections and tight coupling show preference to such applications.

However, as most HPC systems are not particularly designed for data-intensive applications, there are a lot of problems porting such applications. For example, it is hard to support high throughput demand, and it is a great

© Springer Nature Switzerland AG 2018
J. Vaidya and J. Li (Eds.): ICA3PP 2018, LNCS 11335, pp. 212–225, 2018.
https://doi.org/10.1007/978-3-030-05054-2_16

challenge to efficiently import source data as systems are partitioned apart from data sources. It has become a key to success to run large-scale data-intensive applications on HPC systems to make which fully used in conjunction with high-throughput computing (HTC) systems.

In this research, we studied the processes of data analyzing in HPC systems and designed a cooperative computing method for data-intensive applications. We have done experiments at Petabytes data scale on Sunway TaihuLight HPC systems. Experiments have shown the effectiveness of our method. It can cooperatively do some processing work in data throughput stage without interfering other workloads, and further reduce later computations. It provides a reference for studying the adaptability of data-intensive applications to HPC systems, and for design of the future HPC systems to support data-intensive applications.

2   Background

As the scale of data grows, analyzing data becomes more comprehensive and sophisticated. Many applications are not just limited to "computing". The acquisition, preprocessing, storage, calculation and display of data are all important parts.

Data-intensive applications need cooperative processing during the entire processes such as data mining, and compute-intensive applications are facing larger input data volume and have a higher demand for preprocessing, such as astronomical data analysis.

2.1   HPC Applications

HPC was originally designed for scientific applications such as meteorologic analysis, earthquake analysis, oil prospecting and so on. With the increasing demand for computing in various fields, applications such as life sciences, animation games, mobile medicine, and social analysis also appear in the HPC systems. The proportion of latter ones are gradually increased [13]. Both compute-intensive and data-intensive applications become usual in HPC systems.

2.2   Procedure of Data Processing

In general, compute-intensive applications require plenty computing resources in the computational analysis stage, the amount of input data is relatively small, and most middle-stage data is produced by computing which need low throughput bandwidth.

However, data-intensive applications require various resources throughout the entire process, including preprocessing, storage, analyzing, and display. The amount of computing is negligible in each stage.

As traditional HPC systems are targeted at compute-intensive applications, the preprocessing support is deficient. In addition, it requires large computing resources in preprocessing stage which may be comparable to the HPC system itself and is too expensive to use HPC system for preprocessing.

As a result, it is urgent to design a proper method to make full use of different resources for the entire processing stages in HPC systems, especially when it comes to Petabyte era.

2.3 Architecture of HPC

The basic structure of HPC and its computing abilities are analyzed below.

In general, HPC system is consisted of computing systems and peripheral systems that support computing. In addition to basic computing units, the HPC system also includes resources such as storage and networking. In the entire stage of applications, the whole systems are not always heavily loaded. For example, the computing nodes may running at full speed while the storage ones may have light load. If we can make full use of the light loaded parts, the whole processing time may be greatly reduced.

In addition, peripheral systems often have management nodes or light computing units. Some of these resources are visible to the users and may be idle or light loaded. For instance, while ensuring that the service IO is at full bandwidth, the computing units of the IO management node are still partly idle. Moreover, while ensuring required storage consistency response, the storage management nodes can also spare some computing resources.

Thus ensure the possibility of our following design.

3   Cooperative Preprocessing in HPC Storage Systems

Our design and experiment mainly focused on the Sunway TaihuLight HPC system [2]. But it is a reference to other HPC systems.

In this paper, "cooperative computing" is used to provide preprocessing support for data-intensive applications when HPC system's IO load is low on IO agent node. It will relieve the shortage of limited computing resources in HPC system with various preprocessing requirements. Further, storage nodes have better fault tolerance performance, and they can effectively support high throughput data volumes. The software is richer and more suitable for complex and diverse preprocessing processes.

3.1 Theoretical Analysis of Preprocessing

Many applications in HPC require data preprocessing. For example, in astronomical observations, it is necessary to map the observed image data to appropriate physical locations by handling the coincidence and migration images. In meteorological analysis, the original observation data needs to be adapted into the grid. In oil detection and analysis, data from sensors needs to be integrated and summarized. In social analysis, the original data needs to be extracted, summarized, and even numbered.

In data-intensive applications, general preprocessing includes data access, data cleaning, format conversion, compression/decompression, etc. The sequence of these processes is often related to specific applications. The computing complexity $z(n)$ varies from $O(n)$ to $O(n \log n)$ [6].

Data Importing and Sampling. Performance of data importing depends on the device and bandwidth. Incoming data comes from the network, directly connected sensors, or external databases. For large-scale data, it is necessary to perform sampling in preprocessing stage, and thus could verify or improve the subsequent processing performance.

Data Cleaning, Completion and Noise Identification. Data cleaning refers to the detection, correction, filtering or removal of incorrect or incomplete data. Sometimes it may involve deduplicating. Methods for data cleaning are domain-specified, such as detecting outliers by known data distribution or range of the values.

Data complements are mainly aimed at incomplete data, especially high-dimensional ones. Some missing values can be derived from its data source, or be manually re-estimated.

Regression or segmentation smoothing method are useful in noise identification [3]. Since the algorithm is complex, involving domain data and iterative methods, the preprocessing stage is difficult, which can be completed during data analysis stage.

Data Conversion. There are many kinds of data conversion, such as normalization, indexing, and format conversion.

Normalization is to find extreme values and compute corresponding proportions. Suppose that the data volume is n, the computing is $2n$, and the throughput is $2n$. Finding extreme values can be completely parallel. As is with proportion computing. But there is data dependency between them. Each parallel part needs value election and broadcast.

When it comes to data indexing, there are various ways. Some indexing methods require a special format. Some need a simpler representation. Indexes can be assigned based on the order of data arrival, or the order of certain sort. If we choose the arrival order, a lookup table with extra space is essential. Spacial complexity can be as much as $O(n)$, and a single querying computation complexity will gradually increase to $O(n \log n)$. If data is sorted, we don't need extra space, but the complexity of sorting algorithm is at least $O(n \log n)$. Querying complexity is still $O(\log n)$. Batch search and memory rearrangement will be optimizations. If the data follows some kind of distribution, we can apply transfer function to directly map data into indexes, which requires only $O(n)$ computations and $O(1)$ overhead.

Data indexing can sometimes be achieved by databases, which include relational ones such as MySQL and non-relational ones such as MongoDB [1]. Among them, non-relational ones also include graph databases such as Neo4j [8]. When the data size is large, or even if the database can accommodate these data, insertion or querying operations will take a long time and it is difficult to efficiently do data conversion work. In the HPC system, a single-function database is difficult to satisfy various applications, and the extra cost of database itself cannot be ignored.

Dimension reduction is a conversion from high-dimensional features into low-dimensional ones by feature transformation functions. Common methods include principal component analysis (PCA) and linear discriminant analysis (LDA). The computational complexity is usually high, since it requires matrix multiplication of global data. "Light computing" is hard to work efficiently in preprocessing stage, because high-performance computing resources are essential.

Format conversion is done for the convenience of following stages. There are two types of algorithms, one requires global data, and the other only needs conversion functions. The former has a very high demand for space (as much as the global data volume $O(n)$), the computational complexity is also high (even $O(n \log n)$). The latter is much simpler and easy to parallelize, which only applies the transfer function once.

Data Integration. Data integration includes combination, format unification, deduplication, segmentation and so on.

Combination and format unification only require the integration through input data streams. Deduplication requires higher computational overhead or space overhead. For sorting method, the computation complexity is $O(n \log n)$; and for hashing method, the space overhead is $O(n)$. Further, there could be other overhead introduced by conflicts.

In large-scale distributed computing, a good data arrangement can help with future memory accessing and computing. Appropriate design should consider data, computing and architectural characters.

In some condition, data can be compressed to reduce communication. But it is a trade-off between compression/decompression cost and communication reduction.

3.2 Procedure Design

The entire computing flow of data-intensive applications in the HPC system is generally: data importing, preprocessing, reading into compute systems, computing, writing back to storage systems. The corresponding resources are: network portals, storage nodes, preprocessing resources, HPC networks, HPC compute nodes, HPC networks, and storage nodes. Except for the computing part, most parts are not on HPC compute nodes.

Traditional design of HPC system is primarily targeted at higher computing power of its compute nodes. And its input bandwidth is designed to meet the needs of compute-intensive applications such as scientific computing. When it comes to data-intensive applications with larger amounts of data and no significant increase in computation, data access devices and data transmitting from storage to compute nodes will face enormous challenges. It is critical in the data importing stage. Reading large amounts of data into the storage nodes of the HPC system is costly, and reprocessing needs to be tightly coupled to storage nodes, otherwise the import bandwidth will limit subsequent processes.

Usual services of storage management nodes include storage control and data forwarding, which are especially important for data-intensive applications. Different levels of storage management services may be completed by a single layer of physical devices, or be dispersed on multiple layers. The workload of storage management nodes is related to the amount of data that serves. Generally speaking, it is far less than its computing ability. Therefore, it is possible to use free resources for preprocessing in data-intensive applications.

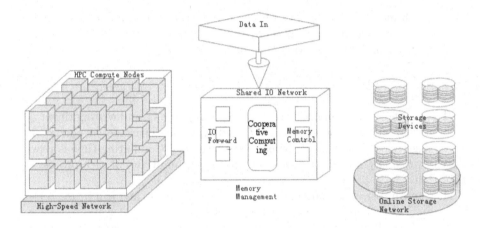

Fig. 1. HPC resources and data processing stages

The basic procedure is shown in Fig. 1. When data enters storage resources, the "cooperative computing" procedure performs preprocessing on the spot. Then it choose to temporarily store or directly forward result to computing resources according to application requirements.

The design of storage-based cooperative computing is to use storage nodes perform on-site preprocessing. It starts from data importing and ends until data enters the computing nodes. As is shown in Fig. 2, the procedure includes access, sampling, cleaning, normalization, indexing, combination, deduplication, and distributed design. These processes can be adjusted according to different applications.

3.3 Theoretical Modeling

To evaluate the design of each step, we modeled the entire process. Afterwards, the preprocessing procedure is determined based on certain goal.

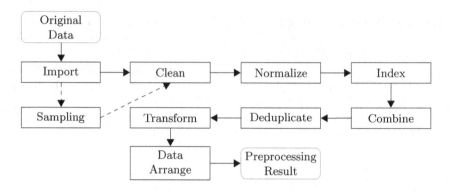

Fig. 2. Data preprocessing procedure

For each module i in the procedure, suppose that the input data volume is m_i, the output data volume is n_i, and the intermediate computations are $f(m_i)$. The corresponding computing time of the module is

$$t_i = t_{in} + t_c + t_{out} = \frac{m_i}{b_{in}} + t_c(f(m_i)) + \frac{n_i}{b_{out}}$$

That is, the sum of import time t_{in}, computing time t_c, and writing time t_{out}. Its input and output bandwidths are b_{in} and b_{out}. These parameters correspond to the aggregated bandwidths for parallel processing. Computing time is represented by $t_c(f(m_i))$, which reflects computational complexity of each processing algorithm.

The entire cost is the summarized time of each process and can be expressed by $t = \sum_{i=1}^{N} t_i$, where N stands for total modules.

In each module, we hope to select suitable resources according to its data and computing demands, such as read and write bandwidth between computing nodes and storage nodes. We want a minimum processing time or resources within certain constraints.

If two adjacent modules can pipeline, t_{out} of the previous module and t_{in} of latter one can be omitted. But a little control overhead may be introduced. In general, we want a smaller number of models N, a less processing time, and a balanced in and out procedure in each module.

In HPC applications, the constraints are various, such as minimum processing time, minimum computing time in compute nodes or minimum data importing time.

When it comes to preprocessing stage, we need to perform it in certain time limitation, with no serious interfering on usual workloads or collaborative resources. Meanwhile, the processing time should be as less as possible.

To this end, it is necessary to fully understand data volume, data characters, computations and the parameters of resources in each stage, and fully exploit the parallelism. Methods to reduce preprocessing time include IO reducing, computational complexity reducing, resource increasing, latency hiding and so on.

4   Case Study

In this section, we performed a typical preprocessing task, to sort and index 2-D data and transform to wanted presentation. The dataset has the same format in each domain. In preprocessing stage, data from both needs to be sorted, deduplicated and indexed.

The dataset comes from graph data, which indicates web connections. Each edge represent relationship of two nodes. It is a proper test case for preprocessing not only with demand for throughput but also for computing.

4.1   Application Scale

The compressed data is nearly 0.4 PB, and larger than 1PB after decompression. However, the replication factor can't be learned before depression, and final data scale can't be estimated either.

The large amount of data, strong correlation, and uncertainty are main challenges of the case.

4.2   Experiment Environment

Sunway TaihuLight has 144 available IO servers, with virtual machines to manage file access. Considering the limited bandwidth and other workloads on them, we used 64 to 80 virtual compute nodes on these servers. They share the storage system but cannot interconnect with each other. When a single node cannot complete the computation, data can only be transferred through the storage system. Table 1 shows the details.

Table 1. Hardware and software environment

IO server	Sunway TaihuLight servers
Number of IO servers	64 to 80
Spare memory in each server	16 GB
Local storage	300 GB
Read bandwidth of each server	About 1 GBps
Write bandwidth of each server	About 1 GBps
Storage system	Lustre file system, capacity of PB
Import bandwidth	4 GBps
Bandwidth of each HPC compute node	112 GBps

4.3   Experiment Analysis

Cooperative preprocessing for data-intensive applications requires design from data importing until it enters the HPC computing nodes. Throughout the process, storage management nodes are used for cooperative computing.

The procedure of preprocessing is data accessing, reading and decompression, format conversion, coarse sorting and deduplication, writing back to storage, full(fine) sorting and deduplication, indexing, storing, and querying. The last stage can be "importing to compute nodes" or "loading to storage systems".

The original data is large in quantity, disorderly in arrangement, and duplicated. It can't be deduplicated within streaming import. Therefore, at least one intermediate data storage should be performed. In the initial phase, data is segmented to 2^n parts according to chosen n bits, so that the follow-up processes are fully parallelizable.

Pipeline. The idea of pipelining is to make full use of the free resources for each step in data processing. For local computing, such as filtering, segmenting, format conversing, or streaming decompressing, we can read data in and perform several processes in memory to reduce total modules N.

In decompressing stage, a lookup table needs to be maintained, and the key part (querying) cannot be parallelized. The total computations are fixed, and the speed of data output is constant. In format converting stage, the same job is performed for each uncompressed line of data.

To verify the feasibility of our design, unit experiments were done on a single compressed text file (12 GB) in the data set.

Table 2. Processing time of a file

Procedure	Time	Read	Write
Copy and import	2 min	12 GB	12 GB
Decompress and store	4 min 35 s	12 GB	52 GB
Format transfer	6 min 49 s	52 GB	25 GB
Decompress, format transfer and segmentation	4 min 32 s	12 GB	25 GB
Decompress, format transfer, segmentation, coarse sort and deduplication	7 min 12 s	12 GB	23 GB

From Table 2, it can be seen that although pipelining will cause small overhead, it will be more efficient than separately performing each module. Since it will not significantly reduce data scale after coarse deduplication (less than 5% reduction), we will only perform segmenting in pipeline, moving coarse sort and deduplication to the next stage. Thus was proved to have 50% reduction of data volume.

Parallelizing. Parallelizing can greatly reduce computation time. Since hardware parallel capabilities varies from different environments, experiment result is only a reference to the design.

Moreover, pipelining design and other techniques should also be considered. As is with the limitations of hardware resources.

Table 3. Parallelizing Experiments

Parallelism	1	2	4	8
Decompression time	4 min 30 s	4 min 35 s	4 min 35 s	10 min+

The decompression stage is limited by the read bandwidth, where processing speed saturates when the parallelism is 4 (Table 3). The second stage of pipeline is format conversion. Although it can theoretically be parallelized in large scale, realistic parallelism depends on the entry bandwidth (data importing speed). Therefore, we arranged 2 parallel format conversion tasks to hide IO latency. The left resources are used for the subsequent stages, segmenting, coarse sorting and deduplicating.

Since the hardware resources are supporting other services at the same time, the actual usable memory of each node is only about 16 GB.

Non-buffered IO could significantly reduce memory cost but incredibly increase time cost. As a trade-off, we chose segment of 1024 with buffered IO as is shown in Table 4.

Table 4. Segmenting experiments

Segment	1024	2048	4096
Pipeline time cost	7 min 19 s	7 min 37 s	7 min 52 s
Memory cost (with buffered IO)	8.2 GB	18 GB	30 GB

Considering double buffered cost and other service cost of the server node, the amount of data to be sorted each time is set at 8 GB, and parallel factor is set to 16 to fully utilize the 16 core resources in sorting stage.

Optimization for Power Law. Many real-world data exhibits power-law features, as is the dataset in this experiment.

If we segment data directly, some parts have larger data amount and some smaller. For example, when the segmentation part is 1024, the largest dataset is 100 times lager than average. In addition, if we continue to segment the "larger" parts, power-law distribution will reoccurred.

To overcome power law challenge, we segmented data by the least significant bits (to 1024 segments), which are evenly distributed. Thus could we have a balanced task partition in distributed environment.

However, the indexing table requires ascending order which can't avoid "power law" problem. In previous deduplicating stage, scale of dataset is greatly reduced by 400x (from 1.3 PB to 4 TB). As a result, even the largest segment can be handled (or segmented handled) by hardware in table constructing stage.

The next phase is "querying", to find the corresponding representation of original data according to the index table. In order to query efficiency, the index table still needs to ranged by reverse order (segmented by the least significant bits). Therefore, we need to establish a reverse index table according to ascending sorted index table.

In summary, the deduplicating stage is to de-power-law. Large and small segments are processed separately and transformation is performed to overcome power law. Finally all data are successfully preprocessed.

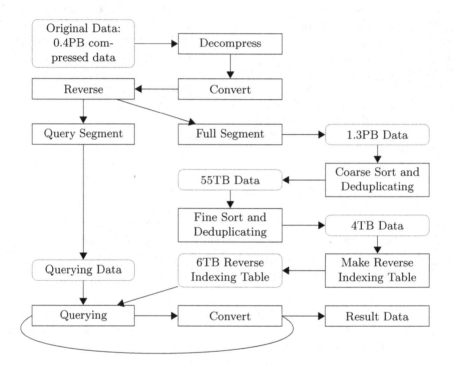

Fig. 3. Procedure of Experiment

Experiment Result of the Whole Process. The entire procedure is shown in Fig. 3.

Designed modules include data importing and decompressing, format conversing, sorting and deduplicating, indexing and querying.

Previous optimizations are included either. The times to look up indexing table in the last step are determined by the dimension of data. For one-dimensional column data, querying stage performs once and twice for two-dimensional data. In addition, segmenting stage should also be designed by dimension size.

Without interfering basic services in the cooperative computing resources, the entire preprocessing is completed within 56 h. As shown in Fig. 4, the bottleneck

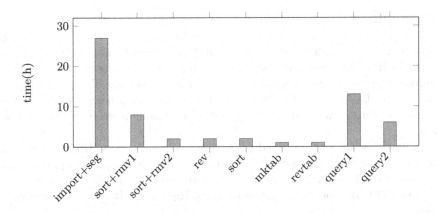

Fig. 4. Execution time of all procedures (data importing and segmenting, coarse sorting and deduplicating, full (fine) sorting and deduplicating, data reversing, sorting, making querying table, making reversed querying table, look up the first dimension (querying 1), look up the second dimension (querying 2))

is in the first stage (it takes 27 h importing and segmenting), which is limited by the import bandwidth (4 GBps). In addition, querying stages also take a long time. This is because that it needs to handle the total data volume (1.3 PB for the first query and 3/4 of that for the second).

The preprocessed data volume is 135TB, which needs 1 h to import to HPC system's compute nodes.

5   Related Works

The relationship between big data and high-performance computing is diggered gradually [11].

The HTCondor team at the University of Wisconsin proposed the concept of High Throughput Computing [12]. It focuses on the "throughput" of data over a long period of time, rather than instantaneous "computational power" that traditional HPC payed attention to. [7] analyzed the challenges of big graph data in the HPC platforms.

Islam at Ohio State University proposed key-value storage to port HDFS to Luster file system, that most HPC use [4,5], which improved IO efficiency.

Data assimilation technology was introduced by RIKEN Advanced Institute for Computational Science. It can deeply integrate real-time data with HPC [9, 10], using the HPC capabilities of "K" supercomputer to capture radar weather data and numerical simulation every 30 s. It provided real-time local weather forecasting.

6   Conclusion

In paper, we have discussed the demand and challenges of data-intensive applications in HPC systems, and proposed a scheme for cooperative computing in preprocessing stage. Experiments have been done on Sunway TaihuLight supercomputer at data scale of Pegabytes. It proves that our scheme can effectively process the dataset with high throughput and without interfering other workloads.

Cooperative computing based on peripheral resources in HPC system is a solution to the high throughput requirements of data-intensive applications. However, if application develops and better performance is required, the architecture of HPC platform could be redesigned. Higher bandwidth and easier connection to data are essential.

HPC is developing in the era of big data, with data-intensive applications being more important. The utilization of the system is not only about to fully utilize computing resources but to make all resource cooperatively perform. And architecture should be more adapted to developing applications.

References

1. Chodorow, K.: MongoDB: The Definitive Guide: Powerful and Scalable Data Storage. O'Reilly. Media Inc., Newton (2013)
2. Fu, H., et al.: The sunway taihulight supercomputer: system and applications. Sci. China Inf. Sci. **59**(7), 072001 (2016)
3. Huang, H., Lin, J., Chen, C., Fan, M.: Review of outlier detection. Appl. Res. Comput. **8**, 002 (2006)
4. Islam, N.S., Lu, X., Wasi-ur Rahman, M., Shankar, D., Panda, D.K.: Triple-h: a hybrid approach to accelerate hdfs on hpc clusters with heterogeneous storage architecture. In: 15th IEEE/ACM International Symposium on Cluster, Cloud and Grid Computing (CCGrid), pp. 101–110. IEEE (2015)
5. Islam, N.S., Shankar, D., Lu, X., Wasi-Ur-Rahman, M., Panda, D.K.: Accelerating I/O performance of big data analytics on HPC clusters through RDMA-based key-value store. In: 44th International Conference on Parallel Processing (ICPP), pp. 280–289. IEEE (2015)
6. Jian, Z., Jin, X.: Research on data preprocess in data mining and its application. Appl. Res. Comput. **7**(117–118), 157 (2004)
7. Kalmegh, P., Navathe, S.B.: Graph database design challenges using hpc platforms. In: High Performance. Computing, Networking, Storage and Analysis (SCC), SC Companion, pp. 1306–1309. IEEE (2012)
8. Miller, J.J.: Graph database applications and concepts with neo4j. In: Proceedings of the Southern Association for Information Systems Conference, Atlanta, GA, USA, vol. 2324, p. 36 (2013)
9. Miyoshi, T., Kondo, K., Terasaki, K.: Big ensemble data assimilation in numerical weather prediction. Computer **48**(11), 15–21 (2015)
10. Miyoshi, T., et al.: "Big data assimilation" revolutionizing severe weather prediction. Bull. Am. Meteorol. Soc. **97**(8), 1347–1354 (2016)
11. Wenguang, C.: Big data and high performance computing, 003, pp. 1–6 (2015)

12. Team at the University of Wisconsin Madison, H.: High Throughput Computing, June 2015. http://research.cs.wisc.edu/htcondor/htc.html
13. Yi, Z., Peng, Z., Xuebin, C., Tie, N., Zongyan, C.: A brief view on requirements and development of high performance computing application. J. Comput. Res. Dev. **10**, 001 (2007)

Sibyl: Host Load Prediction
with an Efficient Deep Learning Model
in Cloud Computing

Zhiyuan Zhang[1,2], Xuehai Tang[1(✉)], Jizhong Han[1], and Peng Wang[1]

[1] Institute of Information Engineering, Chinese Academy of Sciences,
Beijing 100093, China
{zhangzhiyuan,tangxuehai,hanjizhong,wangpeng}@iie.ac.cn
[2] School of Cyber Security, University of Chinese Academy of Sciences,
Beijing 100049, China

Abstract. Prediction of host load is essential in Cloud computing for improving resource utilization and achieving service-level agreements. However, accurate prediction of host load remains a challenge in Clouds because the type of load varies differently. Furthermore, selecting metrics for host load prediction is also a difficult task. With so many metrics in the Cloud systems, it is hard to determine which metrics are going to be useful. To address these challenges, this paper proposes an efficient deep learning model named Sibyl to improve the accuracy and efficiency of prediction. Sibyl includes two parts: a metrics selection module and a neural network training module. Sibyl first selects metrics by filtering out irrelevant metrics. Afterwards, Sibyl applies a powerful neural network model built with bidirectional long short-term memory to predict actual load one-step-ahead. We use Sibyl to analyze a 40-day load trace from a data center with 176 machines. Experiments show that Sibyl can reduce training metrics while maintaining prediction accuracy. Besides, Sibyl significantly improves prediction accuracy compared to other state-of-the-art methods based on autoregressive integrated moving-average and long short-term memory.

Keywords: Cloud computing · Host load prediction
Time series analysis · Bidirectional long short-term memory

1 Introduction

Host load prediction is significant in the Cloud system for guiding load balancing and guaranteeing service-level agreements (SLA). As Cloud computing becomes more and more popular, different types of applications, such as web servers or batch jobs, are deployed to the Cloud system. However, due to the growth of complexity, size and scope of Clouds, the resource requirements of applications can not always be satisfied, which causes violation to the SLA and severely degrades the performance of service [13,14]. Accurate prediction of host

© Springer Nature Switzerland AG 2018
J. Vaidya and J. Li (Eds.): ICA3PP 2018, LNCS 11335, pp. 226–237, 2018.
https://doi.org/10.1007/978-3-030-05054-2_17

load can help improve resource provisioning and enforce application performance [5,10–12]. However, selecting metrics for host load prediction is challenging in Clouds. Many Cloud computing operators offer powerful monitoring tools (eg., Google Stackdriver [21], Microsoft Cloud Monitoring [20], Amazon CloudWatch [16]). Benefiting from these tools, we can monitor a large number of system-level metrics associated with host load. These metrics are essential for better understanding the performance of service and anticipating how the load will behave. But it is hard to determine which kinds of metrics are going to be useful, and for different kinds of purposes, we have to choose different kinds of metrics.

Due to the variety of loads, accurate prediction of host load remains a challenge in Cloud system. Different kinds of loads own different work patterns. Most of prior works about load prediction focused on traditional time series-based prediction models such as moving-average, autoregression, autoregressive integrated moving-average (ARIMA) [1–3] and machine learning algorithms like Hidden Markov Model [6–8]. These models work well in some kinds of load, like batch jobs, assuming that the patterns in the future remain the same [4]. However, the performance of workload, such as web server, can fluctuate drastically. These models can not handle these complex observations. Long short-term memory (LSTM) neural networks have been widely used to solve this nonlinear problem [9,12,23]. As the LSTM model uses nonlinear function, it can better deal with emerging of new patterns. But LSTM only processes data in one direction, so, it can only get part of features of the training metrics, missing the chance to improve prediction accuracy.

In this paper, we design and build Sibyl, an efficient deep learning model to select metrics and make an accurate prediction of host load in Clouds. Sibyl consists of two core modules: (1) a metrics selection module (MSM) that reduces the dimensionality of metrics by filtering out irrelevant metrics, (2) a neural network training module (BNT) that applies bidirectional long short-term memory (BI-LSTM) to catch the features of selected metrics and build a prediction model.

Module (1) allows us to select relevant metrics. Based on the shape similarity of metrics, MSM will find metrics with similar patterns and filter out useless metrics. Among the huge space of metrics, some are not associated with metrics we care about. Irrelevant metrics carrying redundant information make no contribution to prediction. We may only need to train prediction model with a few metrics instead of the entire metrics. In addition, reducing the dimensionality of metrics is essential in saving cost for monitoring and storing extra metrics.

Module (2) can get features of metrics selected by MSM and make an accurate prediction of host load. BNT is built with BI-LSTM networks. BI-LSTM has been widely used in text classification [18] and speech recognition [19]. As far as we know, our work is the first to use BI-LSTM for host load prediction in the context of Clouds. We build deep BI-LSTM networks to process data in both directions to better predict the trends and magnitudes of load. BI-LSTM networks are the end-to-end model. It can automatically preserve useful information of data. Compared with state-of-the-art method based on LSTM [23], our neural networks can better capture the features of metrics and make predictions more accurate.

We implement and evaluate our model using a 40-day load trace of a data center with 176 machines. The load trace is at https://github.com/ UCASzhangxiaofan/Host-load-trace. By filtering out useless metrics, we reduce the dimensionality of training metrics while maintaining prediction accuracy. Compared with other state-of-the-art methods, including ARIMA and LSTM, Sibyl achieves better performance with the lowest prediction error. In addition, Sibyl is lightweight and can be adapted to meet various kinds of needs.

The rest of this paper is organized as follows. Section 2 discusses related work to load prediction in Clouds. The design and implementation of Sibyl are presented in Sect. 3. Section 4 presents the performance evaluation. Finally, we conclude this work in Sect. 5.

2   Related Work

There are lots of approaches about host load prediction. Popular linear auto regressive models, such as linear regression and ARIMA, have been widely used for load prediction in many system areas [1–3]. Nazarko et al. [1] proposes a prediction model based on ARIMA models for load forecasting in power distribution systems. Tran et al. [2] uses ARIMA time series models to predict the temporal patterns of I/O requests for adaptive I/O prefetching. By using a General Likelihood Ratio (GLR) test based on Kalman filter, Zhu et al. [3] estimates the parameters of ARIMA and compares real data with the predicted data to find out whether an anomaly occurs. However, traditional time series-based prediction models do not perform well in cloud environment, because the drastic fluctuations in some types of loads significantly affect the prediction accuracy.

Machine learning algorithms have been used to overcome the limitation of traditional time series-based prediction models [5–12]. Di et al. [5] uses a Bayesian algorithm to make predictions for long-term workload. This method has a limitation as it uses an exponentially segmented pattern, and with the growth of the segment length, the mean load cannot reflect the fluctuation of load. Dabrowski et al. [6] uses a Markov chain model of a grid system to make predictions of host load. Akioka et al. [7] combines Markov model and seasonal variation to make a better prediction. Byun et al. [8] uses a Markov chain with three states for resource and predicts the rate of transitions among the states every 30 min. But the workload in Clouds has more drastic fluctuation than that in Grid systems, which makes these models no longer applicable [5]. Neural network has a better performance on load prediction in Clouds with its powerful nonlinear generalization ability. An evolutionary neural network is introduced in [9] to forecast the energy load of a cloud data center. Xue et al. [10] designs a framework with autocorrelation-based features and artificial neural networks to improve the prediction accuracy for load. [11] uses a forecasting method based on multivariate time series and weighted neural network for short-term load. However, these neural networks are not able to learn long-term dependencies, which are important to make accurate predictions [22]. LSTM is designed to avoid this problem. It has been used in [12,23] to forecast host load and server performance.

But LSTM can only catch part of features of metrics as it only processes data in one direction, missing the chance to improve prediction accuracy.

3   Design and Implementation

3.1   System Overview

The system architecture of Sibyl is shown in Fig. 1. Sibyl is an automatic predictor based on the historical performance metrics to predict host load that affects the SLA of service. The design of Sibyl includes two parts: the metrics selection module (MSM) and the BI-LSTM networks training module (BNT). Different from prior work, we design MSM and use it to reduce metrics before training as not the whole metrics are related to host load. MSM can find metrics with similar patterns and cluster the entire metrics into two groups, one associated with host load and the other not. Experiments show that Sibyl can reduce metrics while maintaining prediction accuracy. With powerful nonlinear generalization ability, BNT can learn more information from training metrics and automatically produces a prediction model. Compared with ARIMA and LSTM, Sibyl neural networks can make more accurate predictions about trends and magnitudes of load as shown in experiments.

The working process of Sibyl is as follows. We first use monitoring tools to collect performance metrics and store them on the database. Before training, performance metrics will first be fed into MSM. MSM will analyze metrics and divide them into two groups by clustering, so the similar-behaving metrics are grouped together. The related metrics are used as inputs to BNT. BNT will use BI-LSTM networks to get the features of training metrics and produce a trained prediction model.

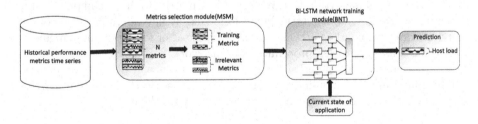

Fig. 1. Sibyl system architecture

3.2   Metrics Selection Module

Reducing the dimensionality of metrics can help us filter out irrelevant metrics, which can save the cost of monitoring extra metrics while maintaining the prediction accuracy [15]. Investigating metrics is significant for host load prediction. However, it is always hard to select useful ones from the huge space of monitored metrics, and for different kinds of purposes, we will choose different types of metrics. For example, we may be more concerned about network I/O to understand the performance of a web service better, while the memory usage will be used to schedule the batch jobs. The increasing dimensionality of metrics also makes it difficult to anticipate the change of load.

We design a metrics selection module (MSM) to find out useful metrics for host load prediction. MSM applies k-Shape, a novel algorithm for shape-based time-series clustering, to help users transform the large amounts of metrics into useful insights. k-Shape is a domain-independent, accurate, and scalable algorithm for time-series clustering, with a distance measure that is invariant for scaling and shifting [17]. There are other feature reduction techniques like Principal Component Analysis (PCA) and Random sampling (RS). However, due to the capacity of linear separability of data, the effectiveness of PCA is limited, and RS is not able to find the hidden features of data, which is essential in host load prediction. k-Shape relies on an iterative refinement procedure that scales linearly in the number of metrics and generates homogeneous and well separated clusters.

k-Shape applies a novel distance metric named shape-based distance (SBD) to compare metric's time series. SBD is based on a normalized version of cross correlation (NCC) [17]. Cross-correlation is a measure of similarity for time-lagged series. It compares one-to-one points between time series. Given two sequences, x and y, SBD will find the position ω where NCC is maximized.

$$SBD(x, y) = 1 - max_\omega(NCC_\omega(x, y)) \tag{1}$$

Based on SBD, k-Shape computes new cluster centroids in every iteration. These centroids are used to update the assignment to clusters.

Since k-Shape is a shape-based time-series clustering method, it can find the similarities in two time series, even if one in the time dimension behind another. This is an important feature in selecting metrics for host load prediction. Sometimes, changes in one metric do not immediately have an influence on other metrics. For example, the CPU usage may increase after taking up more memory to load data as the process procedures start to work.

Furthermore, in k-Shape, each metric's time series will be first normalized before comparing, which is significant in Cloud system. Because different metrics may have different units, we can not directly compare them.

3.3   Sibyl Network Architecture

Because of the drastic fluctuation in some types of host load [5], traditional linear auto regressive models can not handle this complex observation, as shown in experiments. Different from traditional load prediction models that use a linear basis function, non-linear functions are used by neural networks to better solve this problem.

Sibyl network training module (BNT) uses metrics selected by MSM as inputs to train BI-LSTM networks. BI-LSTM is a special kind of Recurrent neural networks. Recurrent neural networks (RNNs) have been widely used in time series analysis. RNNs are networks with loops in them, allowing history information to be maintained, which enables the model to predict the current output based on the features of history information. But traditional RNNs cannot train the time series with long-distance due to the gradient vanishing problems. However, time series with very long time lays are commonly seen in Clouds. We can use Long Short-Term Memory (LSTM) to address this problem. LSTM networks are a special kind of RNN, capable of finding long-term dependencies in the data. But there is one shortcoming of LSTM. Since it is only able to process data in one direction ignoring the continuity of data changes, LSTM can only capture partial features of metrics.

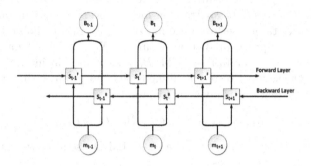

Fig. 2. A bidirectional long short-term memory neural network

Bidirectional LSTM can get more information by processing data in both directions with two separate hidden layers. Figure 2 shows unfolding BI-LSTM for three time steps.

The BI-LSTM equations are given as follows:

$$S_t^F = f(U^F m_t + W^F S_{t-1}^F + b^F) \tag{2}$$

$$S_t^B = f(U^B m_t + W^B S_{t+1}^B + b^B) \tag{3}$$

$$B_t = g(V^F S_t^F + V^B S_t^B + b^O) \tag{4}$$

U^F and W^F are weight matrices of the input-to-forward layer. U^B and W^B are weight matrices of the input-to-backward layer. V^F and V^B denote the output-to-forward layer and output-to-backward weight matrix. f and g are non-linear activation functions, such as Logistic-Sigmoid and Tanh-Sigmoid. b^F, b^B and b^O denote the forward, backward and output layer biases.

We first use BI-LSTM to build a BI-LSTM network and then add a Dense layer to make predictions, as shown in Fig. 3. Dense layer can transform high dimensions into low dimensions while maintaining useful information, as shown in Fig. 4.

The time series of metrics are organized like $A = [a_1, a_2, ..., a_n]$. For example, the training metrics consist of A, B, C, D, E as shown in Fig. 3, and the host

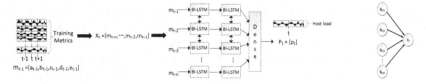

Fig. 3. Sibyl network architecture   **Fig. 4.** Dense layer

load we predict is E. The historical data of training metrics at the same time point t is $m_t = [a_t, b_t, c_t, d_t, e_t]$. m_t will be used to form X_t. The real value of host load is $Y_t = [e_t]$. There is an important variable, look_back. look_back is an integer n, which means data for training metrics over the past n time steps will be used to predict target performance metric P_t. Users can choose this variable independently to improve prediction accuracy. X_t will be fed into BI-LSTM. The output of each neuron in BI-LSTM, B_t, will be used as inputs to the Dense layer. We use Dense layer to reduce dimensions and produce the prediction P_t. The dense layer equations is given as follows:

$$P_t = Q_{t-n}B_{t-n} + ... + Q_{t-2}B_{t-2}Q_{t-1}B_{t-1} + b^D \tag{5}$$

Where $Q_{t-n}, ..., Q_{t-2}, Q_{t-1}$ denote the BI-LSTM-Dense layer weight matrix. b^D denotes the Dense layer biases.

During network training, neural network will continuously compare the error between the prediction value P_t and true value Y_t. Based on the error, it will adjust weight matrix and biases of each layer to better capture features of historical data.

3.4 Implementation

We implement Sibyl in Python. An open-source python implementation of k-Shape is used to cluster metrics. We use Keras to build our BI-LSTM networks. Keras is a python library that has been widely used in production for deep learning.

To collect performance metrics for hosts, we deploy Open-Falcon, an open-source monitoring tool. Open-Falcon has been widely used in cloud environment, such as JingDong, Sina Weibo, Mei Tuan and so on. Open-Falcon has already 400+ built-in server metrics and users can write plugins to collect their customized metrics. Open-Falcon collects metrics at fine granularity per minute. We use OpenTSDB backend to store and serve massive amounts of time series data without losing granularity. Our system reads data from OpenTSDB and saves it in CSV format.

4   Performance Evaluation

Our experiments include two parts: evaluating the performance of reducing metrics and comparing prediction accuracy with two other models.

The whole metrics are collected from a real online Cloud system. We collect 17 performance metrics including CPU, memory and disk of 176 machines from the online system in 40 days. The finest observation granularity of the trace data is 1 min. As the other approaches did, we only predict the CPU load. We divide loads into three categories: (a) stable load, machines deployed with batch jobs like scientific computing; (b) periodic load, machines deployed with batch jobs like MapReduce; (c) jitter load, machines deployed with web service, like nginx. The host loads of different categories are shown in Fig. 5.

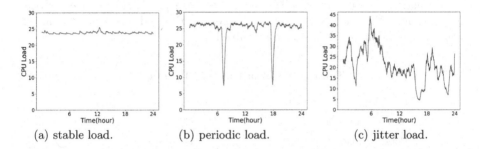

(a) stable load.   (b) periodic load.   (c) jitter load.

Fig. 5. Different types of load

We split the trace data into two durations, a training period (from the beginning to the 39th day) and the test period (the 40th day). The training period is used to train prediction models, for example, for computing the order (number of time lags) of the autoregressive model and the degree of differencing for ARIMA or adjusting the neuron weights for Sibyl network. The test period is used to evaluate the effectiveness of prediction models. We train and evaluate our prediction model using a machine with an 8-core Intel Xeon CPU E5-2630-v3 processor and a NVIDIA TESLA M40 GPU with 24G memory.

To compare prediction accuracy with other models, besides using our own Sibyl prediction model, we also implemented two other load prediction methods including the auto regressive integrated moving average (ARIMA) model [2] and the long short-term memory (LSTM) [23]. These methods have been widely used in load prediction. We will use these two models together with our model to make a one-step prediction on the same host load.

In order to evaluate prediction accuracy, we use two metrics, mean square error (MSE) and mean absolute error (MAE). We denote the values predicted by a model by P_i. The values actually observed are denoted by Y_i.

The value of MSE can be calculated with Eq. (6) and the value of MAE can be expressed by Eq. (7), where N is the total number of prediction values in the prediction time window.

$$MSE = \frac{1}{N} \sum_{i=1}^{N} (P_i - Y_i)^2 \tag{6}$$

$$MAE = \frac{1}{N} \sum_{i=1}^{N} |(P_i - Y_i)| \tag{7}$$

We desire to minimize MSE and MAE to improve the prediction accuracy.In general,the lower the MSE and MAE, the better.

4.1 Performance of Reducing Metrics

Before training prediction model, we use MSM to select useful metrics. MSM will cluster metrics into two groups, the one related to target performance metrics, the other not. We select CPU load as target metric, and use MSM to cluster entire dataset. The result is shown in Table 1.

Table 1. Select metrics for CPU load

Load type	Selected metrics number	Total metrics number
Stable load	4	17
Periodic load	5	17
Jitter load	5	17

We separately use the training period of metrics selected by metrics selection module and the whole metrics to train our prediction model. As shown in Fig. 6, for stable load, the MSE of both methods is 0.002, while the MAE is 0.032 and 0.03 respectively. For periodic load, the error of using selected metrics is lower than using the whole metrics. Its MSE is 0.04 and MAE is 0.149. The corresponding values of using the whole metrics are 0.052 and 0.166 respectively. Since there are noises in the whole metrics, reducing metrics can help us improve prediction accuracy. Two methods share the same MAE with 0.46 in the prediction of jitter load, and the MSE is approximately the same, which is 0.387 and 0.385 respectively. According to the results, Sibyl can filter out irrelevant metrics without sacrificing prediction accuracy.

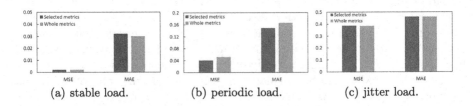

(a) stable load.   (b) periodic load.   (c) jitter load.

Fig. 6. Comparison of error that use different numbers of metrics

4.2   Accuracy of Load Prediction Model

Three methods, including the traditional prediction model ARIMA, the previous state-of-the-art method LSTM and our approach Sibyl, are used to perform prediction of three different kinds of host load. The mean square error (MSE) and mean absolute error (MAE) are applied to determine the performance of prediction.

Stable Load. As shown in Fig. 7, each approach performs well in the predictions of stable host load with low prediction error. The MSE of ARIMA is 0.003, and for LSTM is 0.006, while Sibyl is 0.002. Machines deployed with batch jobs like scientific computing tend to have stable loads, because these applications have fixed work patterns and the changes in their usages of resource are little. Therefore, it is easy to catch its features and make accurate predictions of host load.

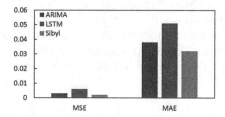

Fig. 7. Prediction error of stable load with three methods

Periodic Load. Shown in Fig. 8, compared to ARIMA, both LSTM and Sibyl receive the improvement in prediction accuracy. The MSE of ARIMA is 0.171 and the MAE is 0.279. The MSE of LSTM down to 0.104, and the MAE is about 0.241. Sibyl outperforms other methods with the lowest MSE which is 0.04 and the MAE is only 0.149. Machines with occasional or periodic load spikes are common in Cloud. With the help of millions of neurons, neural network has a powerful feature-extracted ability to better detect the system situation and predict the arrival time of changes. Furthermore, Sibyl significantly exceeds LSTM, because it can learn more information from data as mentioned above.

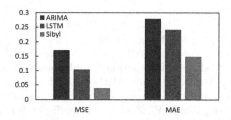

Fig. 8. Prediction error of per load with three methods

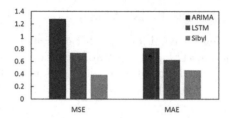

Fig. 9. Prediction error of jitter load with three methods

Jitter Load. In Fig. 9, we can see that Sibyl achieves the best performance of prediction, whose MSE is 0.387 and MAE is 0.46. While ARIMA shows the poorest, its MSE is 1.279 and MAE is 0.817. LSTM performs better than ARIMA with lower MSE and MAE, which is 0.735 and 0.626 respectively. There are more drastic fluctuations in the load of machines with web service, as network requests randomly arrive. Since the work patterns of load dynamically changed, traditional methods with linear function are not suitable for this complex situation. With using nonlinear function, neural networks can better deal with emerging of new patterns. Compared with LSTM, Sibyl processes data in both directions to find more hidden features and receives lower prediction error.

5   Conclusion

In this paper, we have developed a novel framework Sibyl based on k-Shape and BI-LSTM that can be used to predict host load. Sibyl includes two modules: the metrics selection module and the BI-LSTM network training module. We extensively use a real-world load trace to evaluate Sibyl. Experiments show that our method can reduce the dimensionality of metrics without sacrificing prediction accuracy. Compared with traditional prediction model ARIMA and neural networks using LSTM, Sibyl gets a significant improvement on the accuracy of prediction.

Acknowledgements. This work was supported by Grant 2017YFB 1010000 from the National Key R&D Program of China.

References

1. Nazarko, J., Jurczuk, A., Zalewski, W.: ARIMA models in load modelling with clustering approach. In: Proceedings of IEEE Russia Power Tech (2005)
2. Tran, N., Reed, D.A.: Automatic ARIMA time series modeling for adaptive I/O prefetching. In: Proceedings of International Conference on Supercomputing (2002)
3. Zhu, B., Sastry, S.: Revisit dynamic ARIMA based anomaly detection. In: Proceedings of Published in International Conference on Social Computing (2002)
4. Wang, J., Chen, J.W., Wang, Y., Zheng, D.: Intelligent load balancing strategies for complex distributed simulation applications. In: Proceedings of International Conference on Computational Intelligence and Security (2009)

5. Di, S., Kondo, D., Cirne, W.: Host load prediction in a google compute cloud with a Bayesian model. In: Proceedings of the International Conference on High Performance Computing, Networking, Storage and Analysis (2012)
6. Dabrowski, C., Hunt, F.: Using Markov chain analysis to study dynamic behaviour in large-scale grid systems. In: Proceedings of the Seventh Australasian Symposium on Grid Computing (2009)
7. Akioka, S., Muraoka, Y.: Extended forecast of CPU and network load on computational grid. In: Proceedings of International Symposium on CLUSTER Computing and the Grid (2004)
8. Byun, E.J., Choi, S.J., Baik, M.S.: MJSA: markov job scheduler based on availability in desktop grid computing environment. Future Gener. Comput. Syst. **23**(4), 616–622 (2007)
9. Yong, W.F, Goh, C., Hong, C.L., Zhan, Z.H., Li, Y.: Evolutionary neural network based energy consumption forecast for cloud computing. In: Proceedings of International Conference on Cloud Computing Research and Innovation (2015)
10. Xue, J., Yan, F., Birke, R., Chen, L.Y., Scherer, T.: PRACTISE: robust prediction of data center time series. In: Proceedings of International Conference on Network and Service Management (2015)
11. Lang, K., Zhang, M., Yuan, Y., Yue, X.: Short-term load forecasting based on multivariate time series prediction and weighted neural network with random weights and kernels. In: Proceedings of Cluster Computing (2018)
12. Huang, Z., Peng, J., Lian, H., Guo, J., Wei, Q.: Deep recurrent model for server load and performance prediction in data center. Complexity **2017**(99), 1–10 (2007)
13. Saripalli, P., Oldenburg, C., Walters, B., Nanduri, R.: Implementation and usability evaluation of a cloud platform for scientific computing as a service (SCaaS). In: Proceedings of International Conference on Utility and Cloud Computing (2011)
14. Hussain, W., Hussain, F.K., Hussain, O., Chang, E.: Profile-based viable service level agreement (SLA) violation prediction model in the cloud. In: Proceedings of International Conference on P2P, Parallel, Grid, Cloud and Internet Computing (2016)
15. Thalheim, J., Rodrigues, A., Akkus, I.E.: Sieve: actionable insights from monitored metrics in distributed systems. In: Proceedings of the 18th ACM/IFIP/USENIX Middleware Conference (2017)
16. Amazon CloudWatch. https://aws.amazon.com/de/cloudwatch. Accessed 30 May 2018
17. Paparrizos, J., Gravano, L.: k-Shape: efficient and accurate clustering of time series. In: ACM SIGMOD International Conference on Management of Data, vol. 45, no. 1, pp. 1855–1870 (2015)
18. Ballesteros, M., Dyer, C., Smith, N.A.: Improved transition-based parsing by modeling characters instead of words with LSTMs. In: Proceedings of Empirical Methods in Natural Language Processing (2015)
19. Zhang, Y., Chen, G., Yu, D., Yaco, K.: Highway long short-term memory RNNS for distant speech recognition. In: Proceedings of International Conference on Acoustics, Speech and Signal Processing (2016)
20. Microsoft Cloud Monitoring. https://www.microsoft.com/en-us/cloud-platform/operations-management-suite. Accessed 28 May 2018
21. Google Stackdriver.https://cloud.google.com/stackdriver. Accessed 1 June 2018
22. Cao, J., Fu, J., Li, M.: CPU load prediction for cloud environment based on a dynamic ensemble model. Softw. Pract. Exp. **44**(7), 793–804 (2014)
23. Song, B., Yu, Y., Zhou, Y.: Host load prediction with long short-term memory in cloud computing. J. Supercomput. **23**(2), 1–15 (2017)

An Energy-Efficient Objective Optimization Model for Dynamic Management of Reliability and Delay in WSNs

Wenwen Liu, Rebecca J. Stones, Gang Wang[(⊠)], and Xiaoguang Liu[(⊠)]

Nankai-Baidu Joint Lab, College of Computer Science,
Nankai University, Tianjin, China
{liuww,rebecca.stones82,wgzwp,liuxg}@nbjl.nankai.edu.cn

Abstract. As application-driven networks, Wireless Sensor Networks generally require short transmission delay and high data reliability when minimizing energy consumption. Although some approaches have been proposed to tackle this issue, there are few studies that draw attention to the effect of transmission delay and data reliability on minimizing energy consumption. In this paper, we have lots of comprehensive theoretical studies and give the computation models of energy consumption, data transmission delay and data transmission success rate based on IEEE 802.15.4 standard. What's more, we propose an objective optimization model that minimizing energy consumption while having the constraints of data transmission time and accuracy. The optimization model could dynamically achieve the optimal equilibrium solution by setting the parametric values of optimal equation according to the different requirements of data transmission time and data transmission success rate. The simulation results demonstrate that the validity of computation models. And we find the objective optimization model has a better performance than traditional approaches in the case of dynamically balancing data transmission time and data transmission success rate. Specifically, the proposed optimization model can save up to 41.85% energy consumption compared to Flooding routing algorithm and improve the energy efficient of Reed Solomon code by a factor of 52.6% for the best result.

Keywords: Wireless sensor networks · Objective optimization model
Reliable transmition · Real-time transmission · Energy consumption

1 Introduction

In recent years, wireless sensor networks (WSNs) have received a lot of attention both in academia and industry. Since the energy supply of most sensors is limited,

This work is partially supported by NSF of China (61602266, 61872201), Science and Technology Development Plan of Tianjin (17JCYBJC15300, 16JCYBJC41900) and the Fundamental Research Funds for the Central Universities and SAFEA: Overseas Young Talents in Cultural and Educational Sector.

J. Vaidya and J. Li (Eds.): ICA3PP 2018, LNCS 11335, pp. 238–247, 2018.
https://doi.org/10.1007/978-3-030-05054-2_18

saving energy consumption should be considered as the key objective in WSNs, and many research efforts have focused on designing energy efficient protocols or mechanisms [10, 12, 13].

Meanwhile, accurately and timely transmission of monitoring data derived from monitoring sensors to the management system is also important in some applications [11], such as in terrorist attacks monitoring [3], real-time environmental monitoring [17], telemedicine service [5] and so on. As principal items of Quality of Service (QoS) supporting metrics, transmission delay and reliability have become active important research areas in WSNs. Thus, when we studying the energy performance of WSNs, transmission delay [13] and reliability [15, 16] should be also considered.

Previous work has been done on energy efficient protocols or mechanisms, however it still lacks theoretical work to evaluate the impact on data transmission quality and energy efficiency.

In this paper, we address the issue of how to use limited energy resources of sensors to transfer data faster and more reliable, give an objective optimization model that minimizing energy consumption while the constraints of data transmission time and accuracy in WSNs. By analyzing the solution of objective optimization problem, we could get the minimizing (or feasible) energy consumption while balancing data transmission delay and data transmission success rate dynamically according to the requirement of actual conditions. Simulation results show that the correctness and the effectiveness of the proposed model.

The rest of the paper is organized as follows: Sect. 2 provides related work. We motivate the computation models in Sect. 3 and present the description of optimization model and solving approach in Sect. 4. Simulated experiments and results are described in Sect. 5, and conclusions are drawn in Sect. 6.

2   Related Work

In the WSNs, how to achieve the goal of energy efficiency while meeting the QoS objectives of delay and reliability is an extremely significant subject. Previous work has studied extensively based on either the delay metric [7], reliability metric [4], delay and reliability metrics [8] of QoS in WSNs.

In [7], the authors presented rendezvous-based data gathering protocols for satisfying real-time transmission of sensory data and achieving prolong-network lifetime in WSNs. Rosa et al. [4] introduced a methodology that integrates evaluation of energy consumption and reliability of WSNs. They gave an automatic solution of power consumption and reliability models to select WSN configurations and support the proposed methodology. Inspired by the above work, the authors in [8] proposed the Adaptive Virtual Relaying Set (AVRS) data collection scheme. The AVRS uses the residual energy of nodes in far-sink areas (i.e., non-hotspots) to achieve higher packet receiving rate.

From this previous work we can see that the most straightforward choice to enhance transmission reliability is hop-by-hop retransmission mechanism. But the packet is dropped with a high probability in hop-by-hop retransmission mechanism, this makes a potentially long latency time.

Another solution to ensure reliability is Hybrid Automatic Repeat reQuest (HARQ) that uses Erasure Coding technique within retransmission mechanism. In this paper we use HARQ technology which combines the advantage of Erasure Coding and ARQ techniques to improve the system reliability. Reed-Solomon (RS) code is considered to be one of the best Erasure Coding for WSNs having maximum energy efficiency in proper channel conditions or when relay nodes are sufficient in numbers i.e. greater than 5 [6]. So we use RS code to encode and decode in this paper. By analyzing the data transmission process, we give the computation models and propose an energy-efficient objective optimization model for dynamic management of reliability and delay in WSNs.

3   Computation Models

Considering in noisy wireless channels, we use HARQ technology which combines the advantage of RS code and ARQ technique to transmit data packets for IEEE 802.15.4 medium access and physical layers. In this section, we mainly give the computation models of data transmission delay, data reliability and energy consumption.

Firstly, let us see the whole transmission process of HARQ.

HARQ: Firstly the original data is encapsulated in M source packets. Then the transmitter encodes them into $N + R(N + R > M)$ packets used RS and sends them to the receiver. For every data packet, if the transmitter receives an ACK from the receiver before the timeout t, the packet is successfully transmitted. If the transmitter does not receive an ACK before the timeout, it believes the receiver does not receive complete packet, and decoding fails. At this time, the transmitter retransmits the packet to the receiver. If the transmitter gets ACK after $n(n < \delta, \delta$ is a predefined maximum number of retransmissions) retransmissions, transmission gets successful. In another case, if the transmitter does not get ACK after $n(n = \delta)$ retransmissions, packet transmission fails.

3.1   A Packet Transmitting Success Rate Model

In this subsection, the computational model of packet transmitting success rate is introduced as follows. There we assume that one-hop model corresponds to the Gilbert model [2] with the same parameters. For an n-hop path, it can be represented as the concatenation of n identical and independent one-hop channel links. The successful arrival probability [19] through n-hops is:

$$p_s = \pi_0^n. \tag{1}$$

Then we have **the packet transmitting success rate** that is the probability of receiving K out of $N + R$ encoded data packets as follows:

$$P = \sum_{k=N}^{N+R} C(N + R, k) * (p_s)^k * (1 - p_s)^{N+R-k}. \tag{2}$$

3.2   Data Transmission Delay

Data transmission delay is the average transmission time. And the average number of sending packets by HARQ technique is given by,

$$n_s = \sum_{i=1}^{\delta+1} i(1-p_s)^{i-1} * p_s + (\delta+1)(1-p_s)^{\delta-1}, \tag{3}$$

where p_s is the successful arrival probability through n hops in Eq. (1) and δ is the maximum number of retransmission.

In the IEEE 802.15.4 standard, if the transmitter has not received the receiver's ACK packet after the time t, then the transmitter thinks that the sent packet is lost, and retransmits the packet. When a packet is received normally, the receiver must wait for time t_{ack} to send the ACK packet. There we note that v is transmission speed of data, l_{ack} is the length of ACK and t_b is the inter frame delay. To summarize, the **data transmission delay** can be computed as follows:

$$T = (1-p_s)(t+\frac{1}{v}) + p_s(\frac{1}{v} + t_{ack} + \frac{l_{ack}}{v} + t_b). \tag{4}$$

3.3   Energy Consumption Model

In this subsection, we briefly consider the energy consumption in communication (transmission and receiving) and idle states, computation cost is ignored since it is very small compared with others (shown in Fig. 1). Based on the energy model defined in [14], the energy required to communicate (transmission and receiving) across an n-hop path can be expressed as follows:

$$E = nE_t + nE_r + E_f, \tag{5}$$

where E_f is the energy consumption of nodes in idle state, E_t and E_r represent the energy consumption for transmitting and receiving respectively, and they are defined as:

$$E_t = (P_{ts} + P_o)t_l + P_{tst}T_{tst}, \tag{6}$$

$$E_r = P_{re}t_l + P_{tst}T_{tst}, \tag{7}$$

where, $P_{te/re}$ is power consumed in the transmitter/receiver electronics, $P_{tst}T_{tst}$ is start-up power consumed in the transmitter/receiver, p_o is output transmitter power, t_l is transmission time and E_f is sensor's power consumption in idle status.

Thus we focus on analysis the energy of transmitting an IEEE 802.15.4 Mac frame with a length of L bit ($L < 127$) for HARQ mechanism.

The **energy consumption** can be calculated as

$$E = P((nE_r + nE_t) * n_s + E_f) + (1-P)(\delta+1)((nE_r + nE_t) + E_f). \tag{8}$$

Equation (8) can be simplified in terms of radio parameters k_1, k_2, k_3 and k_4 as

$$E = k_1PT + k_2T + k_3P + k_4. \tag{9}$$

4   Optimization Model and Solving Approach

The main contribution of this paper is to build a Problem Model to minimize energy consumption while balancing data transmission delay and data transmission success rate dynamically according to the requirement of actual conditions. In this section, we first give some definitions of parameters and decision variables, and then introduce the optimization model. In addition, the rationality of the problem solution is analysed, and its feasibility discussed.

We take some measures as follows before set up the optimization model:

(1) Set the difference value between the actual value and the objective value (or constraint value): d^+ is the difference value that the actual value above the objectives (or constraints) and d^- is the difference value that the actual value below the objectives (or constraints).

(2) Unified coping with the objectives and constraints: If the difference value between the actual value x_1 and the objective value (or constraint value) x_2 is 0, this is, the objective function is strictly satisfied with all constraints, mathematical expression of the objective (or constraint) is the same as the standard nonlinear programming problem; otherwise, when $x_1 < x_2$, we have $x_1 + d^- = x_2$ or $x_1 - x_2 + d^- = 0$; and when $x_1 > x_2$, we have $x_1 - d^+ = x_2$ or $x_1 - x_2 - d^+ = 0$.

(3) Setting different weight values to objectives (or constraints) with different priorities.

Therefore we formalize our problem as the following constrained **optimization problem**:

$$\min \ E = k_1(W_1 d_1^- T_0)(W_2 d_2^- P_0) + k_2(W_1 d_1^- T_0) + k_3(W_2 d_2^- P_0) + k_4$$

$$\text{s.t.} \begin{cases} T_0 \leq T + d_1^-, \\ P_0 \geq P - d_2^-, \\ T = (1 - p_s)(t + \frac{1}{v}) + p_s(\frac{1}{v} + t_{ack} + \frac{l_{ack}}{v} + t_b), \\ P = \sum_{k=N}^{N+R} C(N+R, k) * (p_s)^k * (1 - p_s)^{N+R-k}, \\ l \leq 127 * 8, \\ \delta = 0, 1, 2, ..., 7, \\ d_1^-, d_2^- \geq 0. \end{cases} \tag{10}$$

The decision variables are transmission success rate and delay, and they must be positive in practice. The objective is to minimize the energy cost. The optimization constraints are used to ensure that the transmission success rate and delay of data objects belonging to each application are not exceeded.

For the nonlinear optimization model solution, we refer to the solution in [9]. First, we relax the constrained optimization problem to a real-number constrained optimization problem in which $d_1^-, d_2^-, n_s, k, l, ...$ are real numbers, and work out the solution for the real-number constrained optimization problem. Then we round every non integer real-number to its nearest integer, for non integer that smaller than 1, we round them to 1. On the base of these, we can get the solution for the constrained optimization problem by using the Lagrange dual solution and IPOPT [1,18] (a software library for large-scale nonlinear constrained optimization) to solve the problem in this paper.

5   Evaluation

The experiments outlined in this section intend to evaluate the performance of the proposed model. For this end, we set up a simulation environment through Linux + NS2-3.35. Under the /wpan folder of NS2-3.35, IEEE 802.15.4 standard protocol is developed and implemented.

Simulation Scenario: In this simulation task, the network topologies are established by random deployment of 150 sensors uniformly distributed on a square with sides that are 500 m in length. Every sensor is static, and its maximum transmission radius is 100 m. The data transfer rate is 20 kbps.

5.1   Distribution of Energy Consumption

In this subsection, we evaluate the energy consumption of sensor's each state. Figure 1 plots the energy consumption in every state when the single sensor sends and receives the single packet. The Xticklabels $(E_t, E_r, E_f, E_s, E_c)$ represent the energy consumption of the sensor in transmitting, receiving, idle, sleeping and computing modes.

In idle state, sensors neither transmit nor receive data, but constantly monitor the wireless channel to ensure the state transition from idle state to receiving state in time when the data packet to be received arrives. Therefore, sensors in idle state also consume a certain amount of energy. In computing state, based on [14], E for a t error correcting binary BCH code of length n is

$$E = (2nt + 2t^2)(E_{add} + E_{mult}), \tag{11}$$

where E_{add} and E_{mult} are the energy consumptions in the addition and multiplication, and $E_{add} = 3.3 * 10^{-5} \, m(\text{mW/MHz})$, $E_{mult} = 3.7 * 10^{-5} \, m^3(\text{mW/MHz})$, where $m = \lfloor \log_2 n + 1 \rfloor$.

Therefore, the energy consumption in computing state is less than in idle state when we use RS code (a special BCH code). We can see from Fig. 1, the energy consumption in sleeping and computing mode is far less than other states. So we only calculate the sum of total energy in transmission, reception and idle states in the following experiments. The result of the experiment consistents with reasoning mode in Energy Consumption Model (In Sect. 3.3).

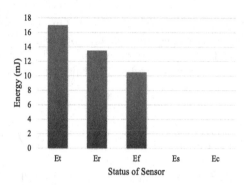

Fig. 1. Energy consumption distribution

5.2   Comparison of the Results of Experiments and Calculation Models

In this subsection, we compare the calculating values (energy consumption, data transmission delay and data transmission success rate) of proposed computational models with the experimental ones. We use the following metric to test the performance:

$$error = (R_C - R_S)/R_S, \tag{12}$$

where, R_C is the result of computation model, and R_S is the simulation result.

The results of the comparison are shown in Fig. 2. Figure 2(a) plots the energy consumption error between the proposed computational model and the experimental ones with an increasing number of original messages. From Fig. 2(a), we can see that the energy consumption error range is from 0 to 11.2%. Figure 2(b) plots the data transmission successful rate error with an increasing number of original messages. We can see from it the data transmission successful rate errors are no more than 17.32%. Figure 2(c) plots the data transmission delay errors in different number of original messages. And we get the result from it: the data transmission delay error range is [1.89%, 15.12%].

To summarize, comparison results demonstrate that the proposed theory models, in the range of allowable error, are consistent with the measured values. It proves the availability of our theory models.

5.3   The Efficiency of Proposed Strategy

Figure 3 plots the energy consumption of traditional routing algorithms, RS(15,9) and proposed objective problems model with RS(15,9) in the different numbers of original messages. We make the following observations. First, as the original messages increase, the energy of five algorithms increases just as in Fig. 3. Second, compared to traditional routing algorithms and RS(15,9), RS(15,9)+PM(Proposed Model) obtains a best trade-off between transmission success rate and delay according to the requirement ($W_1 : W_2 = 3 : 2$) with least energy consumption. Specifically, the proposed optimization model can

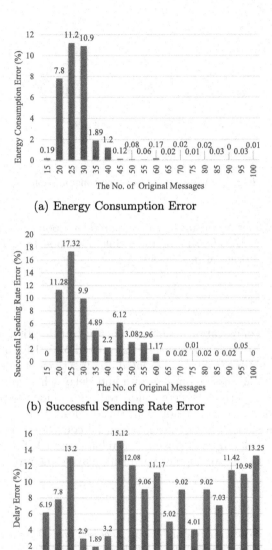

(a) Energy Consumption Error

(b) Successful Sending Rate Error

(c) Delay Error

Fig. 2. Comparison of errors between the theory model with the experimental ones

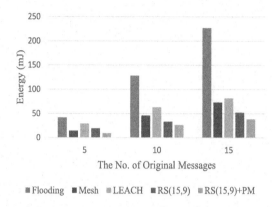

Fig. 3. Comparison of energy consumption

save up to 41.85% energy consumption compared to Flooding routing algorithm and improve the energy efficient of Reed Solomon code by a factor of 52.6% when the number of original messages is 5.

6   Conclusions

In this paper, the computation models of energy consumption, data transmission delay and data transmission success rate based on IEEE 802.15.4 standard were given. What's more, we have presented an objective optimization model to tradeoff between transmission success rate and delay when minimizing energy consumption. The experiments were conducted to examine the proposed model has a better performance than traditional approaches.

There are still some other issues that can be considered. For example, the effect of Erasure Code on the transmission reliability in WSNs. A rich reward algorithm is needed. And we hope to be able to make some progress in this field.

References

1. Ipopt. https://projects.coin-or.org/Ipopt. Accessed Jan 2018
2. Bolot, J.C.: End-to-end packet delay and loss behavior in the internet. In: Conference Proceedings on Communications Architectures, Protocols and Applications, pp. 289–298 (1993)
3. Buttyán, L., Gessner, D., Hessler, A., Langendoerfer, P.: Application of wireless sensor networks in critical infrastructure protection: challenges and design options. IEEE Wirel. Commun. **17**(5), 44–49 (2010)
4. Dâmaso, A., Rosa, N., Maciel, P.: Integrated evaluation of reliability and power consumption of wireless sensor networks. Sensors **17**(11), 2547 (2017)
5. Khan, M.K., Kumari, S.: An improved user authentication protocol for healthcare services via wireless medical sensor networks. Int. J. Distrib. Sens. Netw., 1–10 (2014)

6. Kashani, Z.H., Shiva, M.: Channel coding in multi-hop wireless sensor networks. In: International Conference on ITS Telecommunications Proceedings, pp. 965–968 (2007)
7. Konstantopoulos, C., Vathis, N., Pantziou, G., Gavalas, D.: Employing mobile elements for delay-constrained data gathering in WSNs. Comput. Netw. **135**, 108–131 (2018)
8. Liu, A., Chen, Z., Xiong, N.N.: An adaptive virtual relaying set scheme for loss-and-delay sensitive WSNs. Inf. Sci. **424**, 118–136 (2017)
9. Liu, J., Shen, H.: A low-cost multi-failure resilient replication scheme for high data availability in cloud storage. In: IEEE International Conference on High Performance Computing (2017)
10. Liu, Y., Ota, K., Zhang, K., Ma, M., Xiong, N., Liu, A., Long, J.: QTSAC: an energy-efficient MAC protocol for delay minimization in wireless sensor networks. IEEE Access **6**(99), 8273–8291 (2018)
11. Marco, P.D., Park, P., Fischione, C., Johansson, K.H.: Trend: a timely, reliable, energy-efficient and dynamic WSN protocol for control applications. In: IEEE International Conference on Communications, pp. 1–6 (2010)
12. Mittal, N., Singh, U., Sohi, B.S.: A stable energy efficient clustering protocol for wireless sensor networks. Wirel. Netw. **23**(6), 1809–1821 (2017)
13. Mohemed, R.E., Saleh, A.I., Abdelrazzak, M., Samra, A.S.: Energy-efficient routing protocols for solving energy hole problem in wireless sensor networks. Comput. Netw. **114**, 51–66 (2016)
14. Sankarasubramaniam, Y., Akyildiz, I.F., Mclaughlin, S.W.: Energy efficiency based packet size optimization in wireless sensor networks. In: Proceedings of the First IEEE International Workshop on Sensor Network Protocols and Applications, pp. 1–8 (2003)
15. Singh, V.K., Kumar, R., Sahana, S.: To enhance the reliability and energy efficiency of WSN using new clustering approach. In: International Conference on Computing, Communication and Automation, pp. 488–493 (2017)
16. Torres, C., Glösekötter, P.: Reliable and energy optimized WSN design for a train application. J. Syst. Archit. **57**(10), 896–904 (2011)
17. Tse, R.T., Xiao, Y.: A portable wireless sensor network system for real-time environmental monitoring. In: World of Wireless, Mobile and Multimedia Networks, pp. 1–6 (2016)
18. Wächter, A., Biegler, L.T.: On the implementation of an interior-point filter line-search algorithm for large-scale nonlinear programming. Math. Program. **106**(1), 25–57 (2006)
19. Wen, H., Lin, C., Ren, F., Yue, Y., Huang, X.: Retransmission or redundancy: transmission reliability in wireless sensor networks. In: IEEE International Conference on Mobile Adhoc and Sensor Systems, pp. 1–7 (2008)

An Improvement of PAA on Trend-Based Approximation for Time Series

Chunkai Zhang[1(✉)], Yingyang Chen[1], Ao Yin[1], Zhen Qin[1], Xing Zhang[2], Keli Zhang[2], and Zoe L. Jiang[1]

[1] Department of Computer Science and Technology,
Harbin Institute of Technology, Shenzhen, China
ckzhang812@gmail.com,yingyang_chen@163.com,
yinaoyn@126.com,qinzhen_qd@163.com,zoeljiang@hit.edu.cn
[2] Engineering Laboratory for Big Data Collaborative Security Technology,
Beijing, China
{zhangxing,zhangkeli}@cecgw.cn

Abstract. Piecewise Aggregate Approximation (PAA) is a competitive basic dimension reduction method for high-dimensional time series mining. When deployed, however, the limitations are obvious that some important information will be missed, especially the trend. In this paper, we propose two new approaches for time series that utilize approximate trend feature information. Our first method is based on relative mean value of each segment to record the trend, which divide each segment into two parts and use the numerical average respectively to represent the trend. We proved that this method satisfies lower bound which guarantee no false dismissals. Our second method uses a binary string to record the trend which is also relative to mean in each segment. Our methods are applied on similarity measurement in classification and anomaly detection, the experimental results show the improvement of accuracy and effectiveness by extracting the trend feature suitably.

Keywords: Time series · Similarity measurement · Trend distance

1 Introduction

Time series is a series of data points indexed in time order, which is widely existed in fields of medical [6,10,26], business [18], industry [20,25], cyber security [17,24] and so on. Time series mining is one of the attractive research topics and a key issue for the last decade, such as classification [22], clustering [15], anomaly detection [19,27], time series visualization [9,13]. Most of mining technologies require comparison of similarity measurement, which can effect the accuracy and efficiency of mining. A series of measurements have been proposed, such as Manhattan Distance [23], Euclidean Distance [7], Chebyshev Distance [2]. The typical measure is Euclidean Distance (ED), which is the sum of straight line distance between two points through time series.

© Springer Nature Switzerland AG 2018
J. Vaidya and J. Li (Eds.): ICA3PP 2018, LNCS 11335, pp. 248–262, 2018.
https://doi.org/10.1007/978-3-030-05054-2_19

Time series is a high-dimensional data that leads to expensive time and space cost when processed with the raw data directly by using ED, so dimensionality reduction is required to improve the efficiency. There has been much work in dimensional reduction, and one of the popular approaches is using spatial method to index the data in the transformed space including Discrete Fourier Transform (DFT) [7,14], Singular Value Decomposition (SVD) [7,12], Discrete Wavelet Transform (DWT) [3,11]. And there are piecewise aggregate representation including Piecewise Aggregate Approximation (PAA) [8,12], Symbolic Aggregate approximation (SAX) [14,21]. PAA is competitive with or faster than other methods and it is easy to implement, which allows more flexible distance measure. However, PAA algorithm is easy to lose an amount of information, especially the trend. For instance, if two series have same mean but opposite trend, PAA will judge these two sequences similar. Guo [8] proposed an approach with PAA based on variance feature, which including forms of linear and square root, to add some important information and solve the problem of same mean value. While Sun [21] tried to add trend information by using starting and ending points of segments, whereas the starting and ending points do not reflect the trend in many case like the situation that both points have same value while the trend in segment are different.

In this paper, we propose two new approaches for time series similarity measurement that utilize trend feature. Our first method divides each segment into two parts based on mean value and use the numerical average respectively to represent the trend. And we prove our method satisfies lower bound which guarantee no false dismissals. Our second method uses a binary string to record the trend change of a time series. The trend distance between two sequence is added to the PAA distance as the final distance to measure the similarity in both measures.

The remainder of the paper is organized as follows: Sect. 2 provides the background knowledge of original PAA and its limitations in detail. Section 3 presents our proposed method and explain the trend representation. Section 4 presents the experimental results of classification and anomaly detection on several data sets. Finally, Sect. 5 concludes the paper.

2   Background

Piecewise Aggregate Approximation (PAA) is an approach of average dimensional reduction, which divides the time sequence equally and take the mean value of each segment as representation. Given time series, $Q = \{q_1, ..., q_n\}$, it will be reduced to a vector of length w and presents as $\bar{Q} = \{\bar{q}_1, \bar{q}_2..., \bar{q}_w\}$, where $w \leq n$, the ith element of $\bar{q}$ is calculated by:

$$\bar{q}_i = \frac{w}{n} \sum_{j=\frac{n}{w}(i-1)+1}^{\frac{n}{w}i} q_j \tag{1}$$

where the time series is divide into w equi-size segments, $\bar{q}_i$ is the mean value of the *ith* segment, q_j is one of the time point in its segment (in which $i \in w$ and $j \in [q_i, q_{i+1}]$).

The mean value of data falling within the segment will be calculated and the mean value will replace whole segment as the new representation. Once the length of segment becomes larger, it will lead to the loss of trend information as shown in Fig. 1. To illustrate this point, Fig. 1(a) divide the time series into two subsequences, the length is $96/2 = 48$, which lose the trend information a lot and is obviously quite different from the original one. With the increase of the number of segments in Fig. 1(b)–(d), the reduced dimension sequence is closer to the original one.

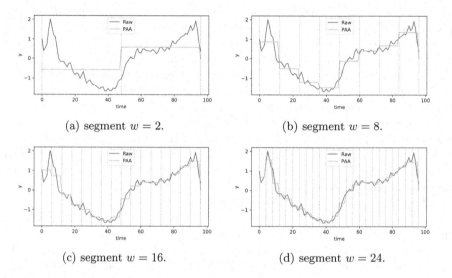

(a) segment $w = 2$.   (b) segment $w = 8$.

(c) segment $w = 16$.   (d) segment $w = 24$.

Fig. 1. PAA representation for one of the time series in ecg200. In this case, *Raw* represents for the original time series and *PAA* represents for the transformed time series, and the length of the time series is 96.

Besides, the result of reduction will be inaccurate when two sequence have same mean value while the trends are different. For PAA method, the distance measure was proposed as Eq. (2).

$$Dist(\bar{Q}, \bar{P}) = \sqrt{\frac{n}{w}} \sqrt{\sum_{i=1}^{w}(\bar{p}_i - \bar{q}_i)^2} \tag{2}$$

$$ED(Q, P) = \sqrt{\sum_{i=1}^{n}(p_i - q_i)^2} \tag{3}$$

Compared with the original Euclidean distance in Eq. (3) which is one of the true distance measures [16]. It can be seen from the above two formulas that Euclidean distance calculates every time points' distance while the PAA reduces the n dimension to w dimension and simply multiple n/w to enlarge time series, which roughly cover up information in detail. To illustrate this, Fig. 2 shows that ts1 and ts2 are the relative segment in two time series. Even if it can be seen intuitively from the figure that they are two different time series, but their mean values are very close and the distance measure calculated by PAA will obtain that the two time series are similar.

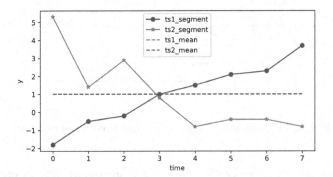

Fig. 2. The comparison of one segment in two time series which have very close mean value, the mean value of ts1 is 1.012 and ts2 is 1.01. To illustrate that t1 and t2 are different while through the PAA distance calculation, they are similar.

Furthermore, PAA is an approximate method to fit the original sequence, so the maximum and minimum value will be missed. To address above problems, we propose two methods to record the trend information, and the detail methods will be describe in Sect. 3.

3   Our Proposed Methods

As we review above, we know that the original PAA method simply flattens the curve by segments, which will lose a lot of information, especially the trend change information. For the propose of solving this problem, we propose two methods. The first method is based on relative mean value of each segment to record the trend, and we call it Numerical Trend Based On PAA(NT_PAA). It divides each segment into two parts by mean value and calculate the numerical average of them separately, with the trend distance calculated by difference. The other is a method of recording the relative trend change for a sequence by using a binary string, we name it Binary Trend Based On PAA(BT_PAA). And the trend distance is the number of different binary strings in two time series, which is weighted by the number of segments. Both the final distance combine the trend approximate distance with the PAA distance.

3.1   Numerical Trend Based on PAA

The Trend Representation. For the propose of solving this problem, we add the incremental representation by using the numerical mean value on behalf of trend to improve it. A time series of length n represents as $Q = \{q_1, ..., q_n\}$ which is divided into w segments, $Q = \{\bar{q}_1, ..., \bar{q}_w\}$, the formula is shown in Eq. 1

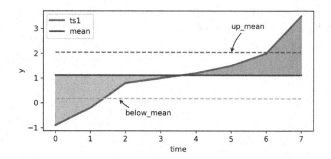

Fig. 3. *up_mean* and *below_mean* in one time series segment.

We define *up difference* as the difference of all time points in one segment above the mean value, while *below difference* as the difference of all the time points in one segment below the mean value. Therefore the up-mean value Δq_u and below-mean value Δq_b which are relative to the mean value in each segment can be defined as:

$$\Delta q_{ui} = \frac{1}{u_i} \sum_{k=\frac{n}{w}(i-1)+1}^{\frac{n}{w}i} (q_k - \bar{q}_i), (q_k \geq \bar{q}_i) \tag{4}$$

$$\Delta q_{bi} = \frac{1}{b_i} \sum_{k=\frac{n}{w}(i-1)+1}^{\frac{n}{w}i} (\bar{q}_i - q_k), (q_k < \bar{q}_i) \tag{5}$$

where u_i is the number of up value in ith segment, and b_i is the number of below value, $\frac{w}{n} = u_i + b_i$, and we can see from the Fig. 3 clearly that the time points in red area is the below difference value and time points in blue area is the up difference value.

Distance Measure. In order to guarantee no false dismissals, we must produce a distance measure defined in index space. We can define the trend distance based on numerical mean value in one segment as follows.

$$nt(q, c) = \sqrt{u(\Delta q_u - \Delta c_u)^2 + b(\Delta q_b - \Delta c_b)^2} \tag{6}$$

And the final distance between two time series based on trend approximation can be defined as:

$$NT\_Dist(Q,C) = \sqrt{\frac{n}{w} \sum_{i=1}^{w} (\bar{q}_i - \bar{c}_i)^2 + \sum_{i=1}^{w} nt(q_i, c_i)^2} \tag{7}$$

Our proposed method is a lower bounding measure to Euclidean Distance (ED) which can be proved as follow.

Proof. According to the [12], the authors have already proved that the PAA distance is lower bound the Euclidean distance:

$$ED \geq \sqrt{\frac{n}{w} \sum_{i=1}^{w} (\bar{q}_i - \bar{c}_i)^2} \tag{8}$$

In order to prove the $NT\_Dist(Q,C)$ lower bounds Euclidean Distance, we should expand the Euclidean first, where q_i can be represented as $q_i = \bar{q}_i - \Delta q_i$, so as $c_i = \bar{c}_i - \Delta c_i$, and simply make the $w = 1$.

$$ED^2 = \sum_{i=1}^{n} (q_i - c_i)^2$$

$$= \sum_{i=1}^{n} ((\bar{q}_i - \Delta q_i) - (\bar{c}_i - \Delta c_i))^2 \tag{9}$$

$$= n(\bar{q}_i - \bar{c}_i)^2 + 2(\bar{q}_i - \bar{c}_i) \sum_{i=1}^{n} (\Delta q_i - \Delta c_i) + \sum_{i=1}^{n} (\Delta q_i - \Delta c_i)^2$$

We already know that $(\bar{q}_i - \bar{c}_i) \sum_{i=1}^{n} (\Delta q_i - \Delta c_i) = 0$, therefore, ED can be transformed as follows:

$$ED^2 = n(\bar{q}_i - \bar{c}_i)^2 + \sum_{i=1}^{n} (\Delta q_i - \Delta c_i)^2 \tag{10}$$

And for our method, we can expand our method from Eq. (9) that

$$Dist^2 = n(\bar{q}_i - \bar{c}_i)^2 + NT(q_i, c_i)^2 \tag{11}$$

Combine Eqs. (12) and (13), we only have to prove that

$$\sum_{i=1}^{n} (\Delta q_i - \Delta c_i)^2 \geq u(\Delta q_u - \Delta c_u)^2 + b(\Delta q_b - \Delta c_b)^2 \tag{12}$$

Equation (12) can be divided into two parts including *up* and *below* area as we mention above due to $\frac{n}{w} = u + b$,

$$\sum_{i=1}^{u} (\Delta q_i - \Delta c_i)^2 \geq u(\Delta q_u - \Delta c_u)^2 \tag{13}$$

$$\sum_{i=1}^{b}(\Delta q_i - \Delta c_i)^2 \geq b(\Delta q_b - \Delta c_b)^2 \qquad (14)$$

where Δq_u and Δq_b are the mean value in different two parts, which can be defined as Eqs. (4) and (5). In other words, it can be represented as $\Delta q_i = \Delta q_{ui} - \Delta(\Delta q_i)$ and $\Delta c_i = \Delta c_{ui} - \Delta(\Delta c_i)$. To prove Eqs. (13) and (14), the process are the same as Eq. (8). The prove is done.

3.2   Binary Trend Based On PAA

The Trend Representation. Another method to represent the trend is based on binary string, which can roughly but efficiently reflect the relative trend change to mean value in each segment. We can use binary string $B = \{0,1\}^n$ to represent the trend relative to the mean and the bits are defined as follow:

$$b_j = \begin{cases} 1, \ p_j \geq \bar{p}_i \\ 0, \ p_j < \bar{p}_i \end{cases} \qquad (15)$$

in Eq. (15), each raw data point segment is represented as **1** when the raw data is greater than the mean value of ith segment, otherwise, if the raw data is less than the mean, it is represented as **0**.

For example, suppose we have one of the corresponding segment in two time series P_i and Q_i, as we can see in Fig. 4

$$P_i = \{0.4, 2.7, 1.6, 0.5, 0.5, 0.5, 0.5\}$$

$$Q_i = \{0.6, 3.2, 1.6, 0.9, 2.8, 2.1, 0.5\}$$

so we can calculate the mean value as $mean(P_i) = 0.8375$ and $mean(Q_i) = 1.6714$, then compare each raw time point with mean value, we can get the binary string as $B_{Pi} = 0110000$, and $B_{Qi} = 0100110$.

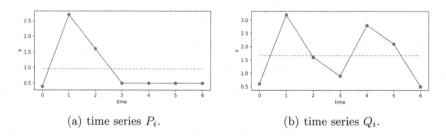

(a) time series P_i.   (b) time series Q_i.

Fig. 4. The trend representation. P_i and Q_i represent for one of the corresponding segment in time series P and Q, and the dotted line is the mean value. In (a), the mean value is 0.8375 and binary string is $B_{Pi} = 0110000$, in (b), the mean value is 1.6714 and binary string is $B_{Qi} = 0100110$.

Distance Measure. The trend distance of the binary string between two series is as follows, where the length of time series is n and it is divided into w segment.

$$bt(\bar{Q}, \bar{P}) = \sqrt{\sum_{i=1}^{w} \frac{w}{n} count(b_{pi} \oplus b_{qi})}$$

$$= \sqrt{\frac{w}{n} count(B_P \oplus B_Q)}$$

(16)

b_{pi}, b_{qi} are the binary string of corresponding segment of two series, and the function *count* is used to sum up the number of 1 in the binary string. The formula can be transformed where B_P and B_Q are the whole binary strings of two time series.

Finally, we can define the BIT_Dist measure function based on trend distance and PAA as follows,

$$BIT\_Dist(\bar{Q}, \bar{P}) = \sqrt{\frac{n}{w} \sqrt{\sum_{i=1}^{w} (\bar{p}_i - \bar{q}_i)^2}} + \sqrt{\frac{w}{n} count(B_P \oplus B_Q)} \qquad (17)$$

From Eq. (17), it can be seen that the effect of trend distance on the overall distance is weighted by w/n, which n is fixed. The larger of w, the greater the proportion of trend distance and the longer length of one segment. Once the subsequence is very long, the trend among this segment will change into a parallel line with no trend change, therefore, the increase of trend distance helps distinguish between the similarity of two subsequence. On the contrary, the smaller of w, the smaller proportion of trend distance. Because if the length of subsequence is small, even contains only two time points, their trend is similar to linear, which will not lose trend information a lot.

4   Experiments

In this section, we evaluate our proposed methods and present the results of experiments. First, we introduce the data sets we used in experiments. Then we compare the performance of proposed methods in aspect of classification and anomaly detection. The experiments are performed on 2.5 GHz processor with 16 GB physical memory. We use cross-validation to find the optimal reduction ratio $s = n/w$ on the training data sets and verify them on the verification data sets.

4.1   Dataset

We perform all the experiments over the UCR Time Series Classification Archive repository [4], which is a large and mature open data sets, and each of the datasets is divided into a training data set and a test data set. We choose 24 data sets in UCR and the classes of time series are between 2 and 39, the length of time series are between 84 and 1024 with the total size of the data sets are between 60 and 2000. The detail of data sets is shown in Table 1.

Table 1. The description of time series data sets we used (from UCR Time Series Classification Archive repository)

No	Data sets	Classes	Size of training set	Size of testing set	Length of times series
1	Adiac	37	390	391	176
2	Beef	5	30	30	470
3	Car	4	60	60	577
4	Coffee	2	28	28	286
5	Computers	2	250	250	720
6	Earthquakes	2	139	322	512
7	ECG200	2	100	100	96
8	ECGFiveDays	2	23	861	136
9	FaceFour	4	24	88	350
10	FISH	7	175	175	463
11	Gun_Point	2	50	150	150
12	Ham	2	109	105	431
13	Herring	2	64	64	512
14	Lighting2	2	60	61	637
15	MoteStrain	2	20	1252	84
16	OSULeaf	6	200	242	427
17	Phoneme	39	214	1896	1024
18	Plane	7	105	105	144
19	ShapeletSim	2	20	180	500
20	Strawberry	2	370	613	235
21	SwedishLeaf	15	500	625	128
22	ToeSegmentation2	2	36	130	343
23	Trace	4	100	100	275
24	Wine	2	57	54	234

4.2 Experimental Setup

Method: Since our method is to improve the PAA based on trend feature, we compare the accuracy and effectiveness on classification and anomaly detection with Piecewise Aggregate Approximation (PAA), Euclidean Distance (ED) and Cosin Similarity (CO) distance measures. Cosin similarity [5] uses the cosin of the angle between two vectors in vector space as the measure of the difference within two individuals. As for distance representation, it shall be 1 minus the cosin similarity distance in our experiment. For the classification process, we conduct the experiments using the k-Nearest Neighbor (K-NN) classifier and set the $k = 3$, of which the accuracy is determined by the similarity distance between test sample and each of training data. And for the anomaly detection process, we use Local Outlier Factor (LOF) [1] to look for the optimal parameters of nearest neighbor in test sets by cross-validation.

Evaluation Metrics: In these experiments, error rate, precision, recall and F1-score are used as evaluation metrics to evaluate the performance of classification. Precision is how much of the retrieved entries is accurate, while recall is how many accurate entries have been retrieved. As for F1-score, it is the harmonic average of precision and Recall. When F1 is higher, the comparison shows that the experimental method is ideal.

$$Error\ rate = \frac{Number\ of\ incorrect\ classification}{Total\ number\ of\ test\ samples} \tag{18}$$

$$F1 = 2 * \frac{precision8recall}{presion + recall} \tag{19}$$

We use Area Under Curve (AUC) evaluation metric to measure the performance of anomaly detection. AUC is defined as the area under the ROC curve and the range of values is between 0.5 and 1. The greater the AUC value, the better the detection algorithm effect.

4.3   Comparison in Lower Bound

As for the NT_PAA method, we already prove that our method has tighter lower bound than original PAA, which can be further proved by experiment as shown in Fig. 5. We choose the Euclidean distance as the true distance and make the tightness represent as Eq. (20), where $Dist(P,Q)$ is the approximate distance measure, s represent the reduction ratio, and T is range in $[0,1]$, the closer to 1 the better, 200 time series of length 150 are tested.

$$T(tightness) = \frac{Dist(P,Q)}{ED(P,Q)} \tag{20}$$

From this Fig. 5 we can find that when the reduction ration is 1, the tightness is equal, and as the reduction ratio becomes bigger, the tightness becomes smaller.

4.4   Comparison on Classification

In this experiment, our proposed methods BT_PAA and NT_PAA are compared with three other distance measurements, Cosin [5], Euclidean [7] and PAA, with 24 data sets in UCR are used. The results of classification are shown in Table 2, and the best results are highlighted in bold font.

To measure the improvement that the BT_PAA and NT_PAA classifier provide, the data sets are trained and tested with a varying window size s comparing with original PAA, Cosin and ED. The results in Table 2 show that all methods have different best number of s ratio. Furthermore, our proposed methods

Table 2. The result of 3-NN classification for NT_PAA and BT_PAA. s represents the best number of points in a time series segment. The highest values are highlighted in bold.

Data set	BT_PAA			NT_PAA			PAA			Cosin			ED	
	s	Error	F1	s	Error	F1	s	Error	F1	s	Error	F1	error	F1
1	15	**0.014**	0.821	6	0.015	**0.886**	2	0.018	0.814	3	0.018	0.814	0.023	0.814
2	2	**0.017**	**0.973**	11	0.033	0.944	2	0.067	0.822	3	0.067	0.880	0.133	0.822
3	11	**0.067**	**0.897**	8	0.133	0.780	18	0.083	0.893	18	0.083	0.893	0.158	0.813
4	3	**0.000**	**1.000**	18	0.000	0.982	2	0.018	0.982	2	0.018	0.982	0.018	0.982
5	2	0.396	0.601	9	**0.328**	**0.693**	2	0.406	0.594	4	0.404	0.583	0.410	0.589
6	17	0.215	0.555	18	**0.200**	**0.576**	15	0.226	0.547	15	0.210	0.556	0.265	0.474
7	7	**0.085**	**0.901**	2	0.100	0.880	3	0.090	0.896	3	0.090	0.556	0.090	0.896
8	5	**0.001**	**0.999**	8	0.019	0.973	3	0.002	0.998	3	0.005	0.997	0.009	0.991
9	19	**0.009**	0.947	15	0.027	0.958	19	0.018	0.947	14	0.018	**0.972**	0.027	0.958
10	15	0.080	0.811	2	0.080	**0.825**	2	0.080	0.824	16	0.080	0.825	0.089	0.824
11	4	**0.040**	0.960	4	0.050	**0.965**	7	0.045	0.955	7	0.045	0.955	0.050	0.950
12	13	**0.173**	**0.826**	19	0.248	0.743	9	0.178	0.820	13	0.159	0.816	0.206	0.791
13	6	0.453	0.527	10	**0.336**	**0.611**	15	0.477	0.505	17	0.484	0.505	0.500	0.482
14	19	0.190	**0.789**	13	**0.174**	0.799	17	0.198	0.784	17	0.207	0.784	0.248	0.729
15	8	**0.038**	**0.962**	6	0.046	0.949	8	0.045	0.955	5	0.207	0.951	0.081	0.918
16	2	0.045	0.909	17	**0.041**	**0.901**	2	0.045	0.903	9	0.045	0.903	0.048	0.903
17	17	0.020	0.528	4	**0.019**	**0.541**	17	0.020	0.527	3	0.020	0.534	0.033	0.506
18	19	0.019	0.961	19	**0.014**	**0.970**	14	0.019	0.952	16	0.019	0.960	0.033	0.933
19	2	0.400	0.548	19	0.455	0.560	19	**0.395**	**0.558**	4	0.295	0.547	0.460	0.536
20	19	**0.035**	**0.958**	12	0.055	0.936	10	0.044	0.953	10	0.044	0.953	0.051	0.945
21	14	0.031	**0.856**	18	0.036	0.844	18	**0.030**	0.863	18	0.033	0.863	0.047	0.791
22	8	0.120	0.823	15	**0.108**	**0.836**	9	0.120	0.823	12	0.114	0.823	0.133	0.805
23	15	0.020	0.937	15	0.045	0.991	2	0.020	**1.000**	2	**0.000**	1.000	0.055	1.000
24	16	0.063	0.974	14	0.000	0.924	16	0.000	0.973	4	0.035	**0.980**	0.000	0.921
Average		**0.105**	**0.836**		0.107	**0.836**		0.110	0.829		0.112	0.818	0.132	0.807

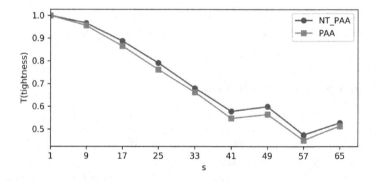

Fig. 5. The comparison of tightness between NT_PAA and PAA

performs better than other three methods in most of the data sets in Table 2, BT_PAA has most of lowest error rate in data sets (11/24) while NT_PAA is less (8/24). On the other hand, our methods perform almost the same in F1 metric. On average (10/24), our proposed methods outperforms than PAA, Cosin and Euclidean under these evaluation metrics.

In additional, we summarize the result between two methods we mentioned above as shown in Fig. 6. If the point (red dot) is in the lower region, the proposed methods are more accurate than PAA or ED, otherwise, the point (blue triangle) are in up region which means they are worsen than original methods. To illustrate the performance, the red dots are the majority apparently in four subfigures, so they works well in classification via different data sets.

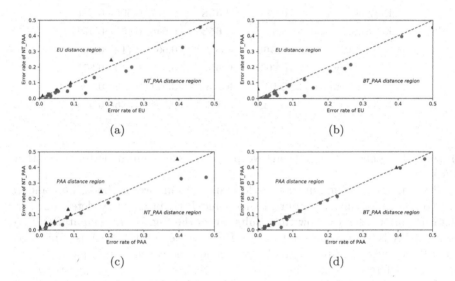

Fig. 6. Comparison of error rate between our proposed methods (NT_PAA and BT_PAA) and other methods (PAA and ED) with 24 data sets. The red dots in below region represent that our method is superior to the existing one, the blue triangles in up region represent that existing methods are better than ours, and the green squares represent the equal error rate. (Color figure online)

4.5 Comparison on Anomaly Detection

In this experiment, we use 12 data sets selected in Table 1, which only have two classes, to conduct the anomaly detection experiment with algorithm of Local Outlier Factor (LOF) [1] to look for relatively anomaly points. We use Area Under Curve (AUC) evaluation metric to measure the performance. The results are shown in Table 3 that our proposed measure BT_PAA with LOF is much greater than other four distance methods, which five out of twelve data sets have a significant increase in AUC, and the other seven have a slight increase. As for NT_PAA, we have eight out of twelve data sets greater than other four

Table 3. The result of anomaly detection. We choose 12 data sets among UCR which contain only two class and the highest values are highlighted in bold.

Data set	AUC				
	BT_PAA	NT_PAA	PAA	Cosin	ED
Coffee	0.719	**0.815**	0.760	0.731	0.672
Computers	0.582	**0.689**	0.581	0.587	0.537
Earthquakes	0.625	**0.673**	0.590	0.665	0.585
ECG200	**0.803**	0.793	0.804	0.849	0.631
Gun_Point	0.639	**0.725**	0.596	0.639	0.538
Ham	**0.645**	**0.645**	0.661	0.645	0.625
Herring	0.623	**0.638**	0.617	0.596	0.581
Lighting2	0.648	**0.653**	0.646	0.657	0.579
ShapeletSim	**0.960**	0.863	0.961	0.712	0.900
Strawberry	0.606	**0.689**	0.629	0.640	0.571
ToeSegmentation2	**0.914**	0.728	0.911	0.772	0.755
Wine	**0.739**	0.681	0.568	0.596	0.540

method. In general, the methods we propose have a much better effect than PAA.

To evaluate the computation performance of our two methods, we compare the computation time with our methods and PAA in anomaly detection. Five data sets are chosen to show the results. From the Fig. 7, the computation time of NT_PAA is approximately twice as PAA, while the BT_PAA is a bit lager than PAA, since all three methods have same time-consuming in piecewise and the only difference is the time to convert time series into binary string and up/below-mean. Therefore, BT_PAA is better than NT_PAA in running time.

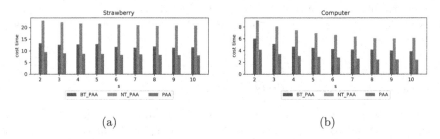

(a)   (b)

Fig. 7. The computation time of different time series with different s ranging from 2 to 10 in anomaly detection.

5   Conclusion

In this paper, we propose two new methods for time series similarity measurement that apply trend information. Our first method use the numerical average in segment which is divided into two parts to represent the trend, and another method use a binary string to record the trend change of a time series. And both the trend distance between two sequence are based on the PAA distance as the final distance to measure the similarity. We have evaluate the proposed methods using the UCR Time Series Archive repository for classification and anomaly detection, and from the view of the accuracy shows that the proposed methods are better than others in both two aspects, despite it costs more time than PAA. In our future work, we are planing to reduce the trend space and improve the run time of trend distance by using hashing.

Acknowledgment. This study is supported by the Shenzhen Research Council (Grant No. JSGG2017-0822160842949, JCYJ20170307151518535).

References

1. Breunig, M.M., Kriegel, H.P., Ng, R.T., Sander, J.: LOF: identifying density-based local outliers. In: ACM SIGMOD International Conference on Management of Data, pp. 93–104 (2000)
2. Cantrell, C.D.: Modern mathematical methods for physicists and engineers. Measur. Sci. Technol. **12**(12), 2211 (2001)
3. Chan, K.P., Fu, W.C.: Efficient time series matching by wavelets. In: 1999 Proceedings of International Conference on Data Engineering, pp. 126–133 (1999)
4. Chen, Y., et al.: The UCR time series classification archive, July 2015. www.cs. ucr.edu/eamonn/time_series_data/
5. Chomboon, K., Chujai, P., Teerarassammee, P., Kerdprasop, K., Kerdprasop, N.: An empirical study of distance metrics for k-nearest neighbor algorithm. In: International Conference on Industrial Application Engineering, pp. 280–285 (2015)
6. Dersch, D.R., Dersch, D.R., Leinsinger, G.L., Hahn, K., Auer, D.: Cluster analysis of biomedical image time-series. Int. J. Comput. Vis. **46**(2), 103–128 (2002)
7. Faloutsos, C., Ranganathan, M., Manolopoulos, Y.: Fast subsequence matching in time-series databases. In: International Conference on Management of Data, vol. 23, no. 2, pp. 419–429 (1994)
8. Guo, C., Li, H., Pan, D.: An improved piecewise aggregate approximation based on statistical features for time series mining. In: Bi, Y., Williams, M.-A. (eds.) KSEM 2010. LNCS (LNAI), vol. 6291, pp. 234–244. Springer, Heidelberg (2010). https:// doi.org/10.1007/978-3-642-15280-1_23
9. Himberg, J., HyvÃrinen, A., Esposito, F.: Validating the independent components of neuroimaging time series via clustering and visualization. Neuroimage **22**(3), 1214–1222 (2004)
10. Hu, L.Y., Huang, M.W., Ke, S.W., Tsai, C.F.: The distance function effect on k-nearest neighbor classification for medical datasets. Springerplus **5**(1), 1304 (2016)
11. Kahveci, T., Singh, A.: Variable length queries for time series data. In: 2001 Proceedings of International Conference on Data Engineering, p. 273 (2002)

12. Keogh, E., Chakrabarti, K., Pazzani, M., Mehrotra, S.: Dimensionality reduction for fast similarity search in large time series databases. Knowl. Inf. Syst. **3**(3), 263–286 (2001)
13. Landesberger, T.V., Brodkorb, F., Roskosch, P.: Mobilitygraphs: visual analysis of mass mobility dynamics via spatia-temporal graphs and clustering. IEEE Trans. Vis. Comput. Graph. **22**(1), 11–20 (2016)
14. Lin, J., Keogh, E., Lonardi, S., Chiu, B.: A symbolic representation of time series, with implications for streaming algorithms. In: ACM SIGMOD Workshop on Research Issues in Data Mining and Knowledge Discovery, pp. 2–11 (2003)
15. Paparrizos, J., Gravano, L.: k-Shape: efficient and accurate clustering of time series. ACM SIGMOD Rec. **45**, 69–76 (2016)
16. Rabiner, L., Juang, B.H.: Fundamentals of Speech Recognition, vol. 1, pp. 353–356. Prentice-Hall, Inc., Upper Saddle River (1993)
17. Rodriguez, A.C., Mozos, M.R.D.L.: Improving network security through traffic log anomaly detection using time series analysis. In: Herrero, Á., Corchado, E., Redondo, C., Alonso, Á. (eds.) Computational Intelligence in Security for Information Systems 2010. Advances in Intelligent and Soft Computing, vol. 85, pp. 125–133. Springer, Heidelberg (2010). https://doi.org/10.1007/978-3-642-16626-6_14
18. Rui, N., Horta, N.: A new SAX-GA methodology applied to investment strategies optimization. In: Conference on Genetic and Evolutionary Computation, pp. 1055–1062 (2012)
19. Shokoohi-Yekta, M., Chen, Y., Campana, B., Hu, B., Zakaria, J., Keogh, E.: Discovery of meaningful rules in time series. In: ACM SIGKDD International Conference on Knowledge Discovery and Data Mining, pp. 1085–1094 (2015)
20. Rhea, S., Wang, E., Wong, E., Atkins E., Storer, N.: Littletable: a time-series database and its uses. In: ACM International Conference on Management of Data, pp. 125–138 (2017)
21. Sun, Y., Li, J., Liu, J., Sun, B., Chow, C.: An improvement of symbolic aggregate approximation distance measure for time series. Neurocomputing **138**(11), 189–198 (2014)
22. Xi, X., Keogh, E., Shelton, C., Wei, L., Ratanamahatana, C.A.: Fast time series classification using numerosity reduction. In: International Conference, pp. 1033–1040 (2006)
23. Yi, B.K., Faloutsos, C.: Fast time sequence indexing for arbitrary LP norms. In: Proceedings of the 26th International Conference on Very Large Data Bases, pp. 385–394 (2000)
24. Yong, Z., Tan, X., Xi, H.: A novel approach to network security situation awareness based on multi-perspective analysis. In: International Conference on Computational Intelligence and Security, pp. 768–772 (2007)
25. Yu, Q., Jibin, L., Jiang, L.: An improved arima-based traffic anomaly detection algorithm for wireless sensor networks. Int. J. Distrib. Sensor Netw. **2016**, 1–9 (2016)
26. Zhang, C., Yin, A., Liu, H., Zhang, J.: Design and application of electrocardiograph diagnosis system based on multifractal theory. In: Sun, G., Liu, S. (eds.) ADHIP 2017. LNICST, vol. 219, pp. 433–447. Springer, Cham (2018). https://doi.org/10.1007/978-3-319-73317-3_50
27. Zhang, C., Yin, A., Deng, Y., Tian, P., Wang, X., Dong, L.: A novel anomaly detection algorithm based on trident tree. In: Luo, M., Zhang, L.-J. (eds.) CLOUD 2018. LNCS, vol. 10967, pp. 295–306. Springer, Cham (2018). https://doi.org/10.1007/978-3-319-94295-7_20

Research on Data Recovery Technology Based on Flash Memory Device

Lele Guan[✉], Jun Zheng[✉], Chenyang Li[✉], and Dianxin Wang

School of Computer Science and Technology, Beijing Institute of Technology,
Beijing 100081, China
734516580@qq.com, zhengjun@bit.edu.cn,
lichenyangbit@yeah.net

Abstract. Due to the significant internal structural difference between flash memory devices and traditional mechanical hard disks, the data recovery technology for traditional mechanical hard disks cannot be directly applied to flash memory devices. Therefore, there is an urgent need to explore a data recovery method specific to flash storage devices. On the premise of obtaining the mirror data structure parameters of the flash memory chip, through analyzing the underlying data from the said chip, determination and analysis can be done to the interleave type of data on the physical structure. And according to the different interleaving granularity, universal formulas can be generalized one by one. Select the data of valid block to be put into the formula which is suitable for interleaving granularity, and then calculate the corresponding logical address. Finally, write the buffers one by one in the order indicated by the logical address to achieve the data recovery. Under the circumstance where the structure parameters cannot be obtained due to mechanical malfunction, to develop a recovery strategy based on an unknown algorithm by constructing a learning disk can be both practical and instructive.

Keywords: Flash memory · Data interleaving · Data recovery

1 Introduction

With the rapid development of science and technology, all kinds of electronic equipment have also become lighter and slimmer. Therefore, the use of flash memory devices such as SSDs and U-disks has also become more and more frequent. Flash memory devices have many excellent features such as non-volatility, high-speed transmission, high shock resistance, low power consumption, compact size and light weight [1]. They are becoming the mainstream storage devices and replacing the traditional disks gradually. However, since there are significant differences such as the physical structure and access methods between disks and flash memory devices, the existing disk-based data recovery technology cannot be directly applied to flash memory devices. The internal of the flash memory device is mainly composed of two chips [2]: One is the main control chip which mainly controls the device to read and write data. The other one is the memory chip which is to receive the control instructions from the main

© Springer Nature Switzerland AG 2018
J. Vaidya and J. Li (Eds.): ICA3PP 2018, LNCS 11335, pp. 263–271, 2018.
https://doi.org/10.1007/978-3-030-05054-2_20

control chip and complete the data storage work [3]. All data will be stored in the memory chip. In addition to reading and writing, the flash memory device also has another basic operation which is erasing [4]. That is, when data are to be updated, they are not directly written in but only after the existing data in the same block are erased first. Reading and writing operate with the page as the minimum unit, but erasing operates with the block as the minimum unit [5].

2 Data Interleaving Type Analysis

Data interleaving refers to flash chips alternately store logically continuous data into two or more different physical spaces in accordance with certain rules [6]. The purposes of using data interleaving are usually served in the following two aspects.

One is due to the rapid speed increasing requirements of flash memory chips for internal data operation, chip manufacturers begin to divide the memory chip into one or more groups. And then combine multiple groups into one storage array [7]. Pages in different groups in the array can be read, written and programmed simultaneously [8]. Take double-grouped flash memory as example, in order to achieve these operations, a set of double-group commands are added to the instruction list in the control chip, including double-group read, double-group programming and double-group erasing instructions [9]. The allocation of address mappings for each group is assigned so that reading, writing, programming and erasing instruction can occur simultaneously within two adjacent groups.

The other one is to increase the chip's addressing space. The same physical address is calculated using the same physical addressing parameters and corresponds to different physical storage spaces in different situations. These physical storage spaces can be within the same group or in different groups [10]. It can expand the groups' space or double the amount of groups which eventually leads to the multiplication of storage space.

Whether the data stored in flash memory devices is interleaving or not is programmed by the device developer according to actual needs and controlled by the internal read-write control program in the main control chip. Here are some common types of data interleaving below. Through analyzing various types of interleaving one by one, the general calculation formula can be summarized with the help of calculating its corresponding LBA (Logical Block Address) which makes it easier to search and compare during date recovery. Firstly by analyzing the data information contained in the metadata area, it is easy to get the ID parameters from physical blocks and pages. Then record the specific physical block ID number and physical page ID number. Assume that one physical page contains 'm' sectors and one physical block contains 'n' sectors. LBA = x (which is from the first sector of any page of any valid block), group number = q. The sum of the valid sectors of all groups before this group is called "Difference". That is, the absolute logical deviation position of the group. The LBA calculation formula with different internal-chip interleaving granularity will be separately analyzed below.

2.1   No Interleaving Within One Group or Between Groups

There is no interleaving in single group or between any two groups, meaning data is stored in the order of physical block number and physical page number. The physical address and logical address of all data are basically in one-to-one correspondence. This is the simplest arrangement.

LBA = Difference + Block ID * n + page ID * m.

However, due to the sequential storage of data, the reliability of the data is not high and it is rarely used in actual situations.

2.2   Page Interleaving in One Group, no Interleaving Among Groups

Since multiple pages cannot be read simultaneously within the same group in order to increase the chip's address space, a commonly used method is to alternately operate between the corresponding pages in adjacent physical blocks. The data which is stored in alternate pattern in the same group under the unit of page according to the rules of odd and even blocks. For example, the data (from Fig. 1.) shown is first stored in the first odd-numbered Page1 in the odd Block1. After the data is filled in Page1, the second data is written in the odd-numbered Page1 of the adjacent even Block2, and the third data is written in the even-numbered Page2 of Block1 and so on until the two data blocks are filled. And then, the writing in the next adjacent data Block3 is started. Data is stored in the interleaved pattern under the unit of page between adjacent parity blocks within the same group. And the pattern will continue alternate among pages until the last page of both blocks are filled. The fact is that two interleaved blocks are logically combined into a larger block that is twice the size of the original block.

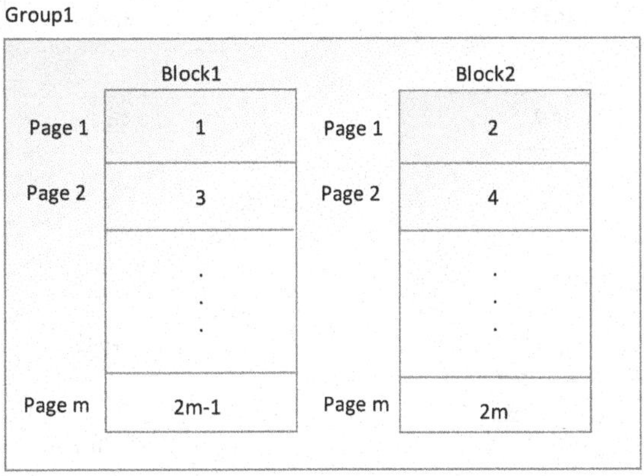

Group1

	Block1		Block2
Page 1	1	Page 1	2
Page 2	3	Page 2	4
	. . .		. . .
Page m	2m-1	Page m	2m

Fig. 1. Data interleaving among groups

If the selected block is an odd block, LBA = Difference + Block ID * n + Page ID * m + m;

If the selected block is an even block, LBA = Difference + Block ID * n + Page ID * m.

2.3 No Interleaving in One Group but Interleaving Among Groups

Inter-group interleaving is to alternately store continuous data among multiple groups in corresponding positions. In inter-group interleaving, data can be interleaved under unit of block or page. In the process of analysis, it is necessary to judge the variation of block ID and page ID and then determine how the data is interleaved among groups. Take the two groups shown below as example (from Fig. 2). Obviously the sector with LBA of '1' in Group0 and the sector with LBA of 'n' in Group1 have the same physical offset address in their respective groups. In Group0, n sectors are consecutively stored starting from the part where the LBA is m. The part where LBA is m + n is stored in the same physical offset address of Group1. Group 1 also stores n sectors consecutively from the position of n, then 2n sectors are stored in the next position of n − 1 in Group0. Interleaving granularity n represents the minimum unit of interleaving among groups.

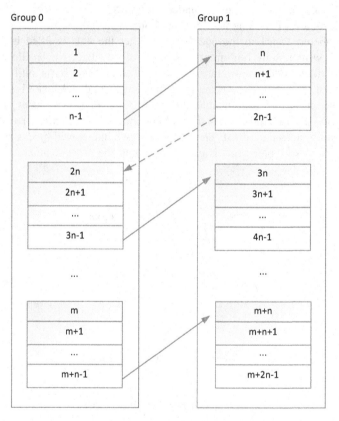

Fig. 2. Data in inter-group interleaving

If 'n' equals the amount of logical sectors contained in a physical page, that means the interleaving rule between these two groups are interleaved with page as the minimum unit, with LBA = Difference + (Block ID * np + Page ID * m) * k + q * m;

If 'n' equals the amount of logical sectors contained in a physical block, that means the interleaving rule between these two groups are interleaved with block as the minimum unit, with LBA = Difference + (Block ID * np) * k + Page ID * m + q * np.

2.4 Page Interleaving in One Group, Interleaving Among Groups

In the case of simultaneous intra-group and inter-group interleaving, usually intra-group interleaving will be done first and considered as a whole part. Then interleaving will be done among groups with blocks or pages as the basic unit. Firstly, execute intra-group interleave on the two adjacent blocks inside the two adjacent groups respectively. Under normal circumstances, the data will be interleaved under the unit of page and the interleaved data in each group will be divided into several parts. Assume that the unit of interleaving granularity is 'k'. That is each part contains k sectors. Between two groups, interleave with 'part' as a unit. The logical sector with LBA of 1 in Group0 has the same physical offset address as the logical sector with LBA of k + 1 in Group1. After the Kth data is stored in the Part1 of Group0, the next data will be stored in the K + 1st data in Group1, which is the second part of the logical data. Then it fills k sectors and goes back to Group0 and continue to store and so on. Determining what rules are used to store data among groups depends on the size of k (Fig. 3).

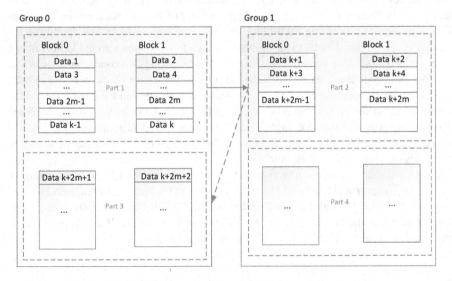

Fig. 3. Data in intra-group interleaving and inter-group interleaving

When k is equal to twice the amount of sectors contained in the physical page, it means intra-group page interleaving and inter-group page interleaving.

LBA = Difference + (Block ID * np + Page ID * m) * 2 k + m.

When k is equal to twice the amount of sectors contained in the physical block, it means intra-group page interleaving and inter-group block interleaving.

LBA = Difference + (Block ID * np) * 2 k + Page ID * m * 2 + m.

3   Data Recovery Technology Process

3.1   Analysis of Structural Parameters

Read the structure of a flash memory device through a hexadecimal programmer to identify the manufacturer and model information. Under normal circumstances, manufacturers will provide a series of basic information, including the chip's block size, page size, internal encryption mode, etc.

Before data recovery gets started, the existence and validity of various parameters in the structure needs to determined firstly. If the structure contains invalid parameters or incomplete parameters, the unknown algorithm recovery strategy shall be adopted; If all parameters exist and are valid, the normal recovery process shall apply.

3.2   Determination of the Validity of Physical Blocks

Since flash memory devices have widely adopted the strategies such as wear leveling and garbage collection, the storage location of logical block is quite chaotic. Some pages of the flash memory chip do not participate in address decoding, but serve as the configuration parameter storage area for the main control chip. In the mean time, due to the read-write feature of Nand Flash, a large number of bad blocks are also generated. Therefore, before processing each block of data, it is necessary to first determine the validity of the physical block to ensure that the data to be written into the logical image is correct and valid. The invalid block includes the following two conditions:One is that the data from the data area to the metadata area in the entire block is all FF. Under normal circumstances, the Nand Flash chip has a continuous full FF block as a hidden storage space in the production process. The other one is bad block produced by Nand Flash during production or use. In the sixth byte of the metadata area of the first page of the bad block, fill in non-0xFF data to mark the block as bad block. Use these tags to distinguish the validity of data blocks.

Use hexadecimal programmer to extract the physical image of Nand Flash and open it read-only. Traverse all physical blocks randomly. XORs the data of the metadata area from one of the pages with the mask of the flag bit. Comparing the results, it is valid if it is the same as the benchmark flag bit, otherwise it is invalid. If any page is determined to be invalid, then the whole block is also invalid.

3.3 Logical Image Generation

Dynamically allocate two buffers in registers. One is called ReadData and is used to store the data read from the source image with the same size of a physical page. The other one is called WriteData and is used to store the data to be written to the logical image, whose size is 512 bytes multiplies the number of sectors contained in a physical page. Due to different internal interleaving granularity of different chips, the corresponding conversion modes between the physical storage location and the logical storage location are also different. During the use of parameters to calculate the logical offset, the corresponding formula needs to be selected according to the internal interleaving granularity parameters of the structure. Then the parameters such as the block ID, page ID and block size which have been analyzed from the metadata area are put into the formula to calculate the logical offset corresponding to the physical page. Move the pointer of the logical image file to the position of the calculated offset and write the data into WriteData buffer.

3.4 Unknown Algorithm Recovery Strategy

Not all flash memory chips contain the parameters for the conversion of physical and logical addresses. Similarly, not all flash memory chips can be manually or automatically analyzed through program to obtain various parameters. For example, the physical sectors of some chips are arranged in logical order or in reverse order. This type of chips does not contain parameters such as block number, page number, etc. For this type of chips, an unknown algorithm recovery strategy shall be adopted. That is to recover the image file of failure flash chip by constructing a learning disk according to the mapping relationship between the physical sector and the logical sector. The so-called learning disk uses the same type of flash memory device. Firstly, connect the flash memory device to the PC. Then write specific data to the logical storage space of entire flash memory using a special program. The specific data written inside a single sector is shown in the Fig. 4 below, including the sector's head and tail flags, sector's LBA and other parameters, which will be used in the analysis of the memory chip's page structure, interleaving type, encryption type and other special fields. After the learning disk is successfully manufactured, remove the flash memory chip from the device. Use hexadecimal programmer to read out the complete physical image of flash. Finally, use the automatic analysis function in the program to get the parameters required for recovery.

Offset	0	1	2	3	4	5	6	7	8	9	10	11	12	13	14	15
00000000	AB	AB	AB	AB	AB	AB	AB	AB	AB	AB	AB	AB	AB	AB	AB	AB
00000016	00	00	00	00	00	00	00	00	FF	FF	FF	FF	FF	FF	FF	FF
00000032	01	23	45	67	89	AB	CD	EF	FE	DC	BA	98	76	54	32	10
00000048	00	C0	06	00	00	00	00	00	00	C0	06	00	00	00	00	00
00000064	00	C0	06	00	00	00	00	00	00	C0	06	00	00	00	00	00
00000080	00	C0	06	00	00	00	00	00	00	C0	06	00	00	00	00	00
00000096	00	C0	06	00	00	00	00	00	00	C0	06	00	00	00	00	00
00000112	00	C0	06	00	00	00	00	00	00	C0	06	00	00	00	00	00
00000128	00	C0	06	00	00	00	00	00	00	C0	06	00	00	00	00	00
00000144	00	C0	06	00	00	00	00	00	00	C0	06	00	00	00	00	00
00000160	00	C0	06	00	00	00	00	00	00	C0	06	00	00	00	00	00
00000176	00	C0	06	00	00	00	00	00	00	C0	06	00	00	00	00	00
00000192	00	C0	06	00	00	00	00	00	00	C0	06	00	00	00	00	00
00000208	00	C0	06	00	00	00	00	00	00	C0	06	00	00	00	00	00
00000224	00	C0	06	00	00	00	00	00	00	C0	06	00	00	00	00	00
00000240	00	C0	06	00	00	00	00	00	00	C0	06	00	00	00	00	00
00000256	00	C0	06	00	00	00	00	00	00	C0	06	00	00	00	00	00
00000272	00	C0	06	00	00	00	00	00	00	C0	06	00	00	00	00	00
00000288	00	C0	06	00	00	00	00	00	00	C0	06	00	00	00	00	00
00000304	00	C0	06	00	00	00	00	00	00	C0	06	00	00	00	00	00
00000320	00	C0	06	00	00	00	00	00	00	C0	06	00	00	00	00	00
00000336	00	C0	06	00	00	00	00	00	00	C0	06	00	00	00	00	00
00000352	00	C0	06	00	00	00	00	00	00	C0	06	00	00	00	00	00
00000368	00	C0	06	00	00	00	00	00	00	C0	06	00	00	00	00	00
00000384	00	C0	06	00	00	00	00	00	00	C0	06	00	00	00	00	00
00000400	00	C0	06	00	00	00	00	00	00	C0	06	00	00	00	00	00
00000416	00	C0	06	00	00	00	00	00	00	C0	06	00	00	00	00	00
00000432	00	C0	06	00	00	00	00	00	00	C0	06	00	00	00	00	00
00000448	00	C0	06	00	00	00	00	00	00	C0	06	00	00	00	00	00
00000464	00	C0	06	00	00	00	00	00	00	C0	06	00	00	00	00	00
00000480	00	C0	06	00	00	00	00	00	00	C0	06	00	00	00	00	00
00000496	DE	DE	DE	DE	DE	DE	DE	DE	DE	DE	DE	DE	DE	DE	DE	DE

Fig. 4. The specific data written inside a single sector

4   Conclusion

This article analyzes and summarizes formulas for calculating logical addresses based on different interleaving granularities of flash memory chips. The formulas play a decisive role in the later data recovery. On the premise of analyzing structural parameters, select valid block data and then put the data into the corresponding formula according to different interleaving granularity to get the corresponding logical address. Finally, recover the logical image file according to the location indicated by the logical address. However, in some cases, structural parameters cannot be easily analyzed. This article conducts an in-depth study on the difficulties of this issue and explores an unknown algorithm recovery strategy using the learning disk to obtain parameter information which has a certain practical and guiding significance.

Acknowledgement. This paper is supported by the Beijing Municipal Natural Science Foundation (No. 4172053).

References

1. Huang, M.: The research on reliability enhancement of MLC Nand flash storage system. Harbin Institute of Technology, Harbin (2015)
2. Yuan, R.: Research of data restructuring on flash chips. Beijing Institute of Technology, Beijing (2011)
3. Lin, C., Wang, X., Yuan, J., et al.: Data recovery technology of Nand-flash-based storage. Inf. Secur. Commun. Priv. **3**, 123–125 (2016)
4. Shang, W.: Design and implementation of data recovery system based on android. Hebei University of Science and Technology, Shijiazhuang (2016)
5. Xie, Y.: On the storage management and data recovery of solid state disks. Hunan University, Chang Sha (2016)
6. Chang, Y.H.: A management strategy for the reliability and performance improvement of MLC-based flash memory storage systems. IEEE Trans. Comput. **60**(3), 305–320 (2011)
7. Chang, L.: The research of data storage technology based on Nand flash array. North University of China, Taiyuan (2011)
8. Sanghyuk, J., Yong, H.S.: Data loss recovery for power failure in flash memory storage systems. J. Syst. Architect. **61**, 12–27 (2015)
9. Tanakanaru, S.: A design strategy of error-prediction low-density parity-check (EP-LDPC) error-correcting code (ECC) and error-recovery schemes for scaled Nand flash memories. IEICE Trans. Electron. **98**, 53–61 (2015)
10. Lan, J.: The research on address mapping and wear leveling algorithms of flash memory based on grouping and biased random walk. Southwest Jiaotong University, Chengdu (2016)

Scheduling DAG Applications for Time Sharing Systems

Shenyuan Ren, Ligang He$^{(\boxtimes)}$, Junyu Li, Chao Chen, Zhuoer Gu, and Zhiyan Chen

Department of Computer Science, University of Warwick, Coventry, UK
`ligang.he@warwick.ac.uk`

Abstract. When computing the makespan of a DAG, it is typically assumed that the tasks scheduled on the same computing node run in sequence. In reality, however, the tasks may be run in the time sharing manner. Our studies show that the discrepancy between the assumption of sequential execution and the reality of time sharing execution may lead to inaccurate calculation of the DAG makespan. In this paper, we first investigate the impact of the time sharing execution on the DAG makespan, and propose the method to model and determine the makespan with the time-sharing execution. Based on this model, we further develop the scheduling strategies for DAG jobs running in time-sharing. Extensive experiments have been conducted to verify the effectiveness of the proposed methods. The experimental results show that by taking time sharing into account, our DAG scheduling strategy can reduce the makespan significantly, comparing with its counterpart in sequential execution.

1 Introduction

DAG is often used to model the precedence constraints of a group of related tasks. Many DAG (Directed Acyclic Graph) scheduling algorithms have been proposed in literature. The makespan of a DAG is an important metric to measure the performance of a DAG scheduling solution. When computing the makespan of a DAG, it is typically assumed that the tasks scheduled on the same computing node run in sequence, i.e., being executed one by one in the computing node (which we call the *sequential execution* in this paper) [3–5]. This assumption is reasonable in the cluster platform, where there is only a central queue in the head node and a new task is sent to a computing node only when the node has completed the execution of the existing task. However, in some situations, such as distributed systems and virtualized environments, there may not be a central queue in the system. In a distributed system, there is no a centralized management mechanism. The tasks in a DAG are often sent to the computing machine as designated in the scheduling solution. After the computing machine receives these tasks, the tasks are run in the time sharing manner by the operating system. In virtualized environments, a VM is often created to run a task.

© Springer Nature Switzerland AG 2018
J. Vaidya and J. Li (Eds.): ICA3PP 2018, LNCS 11335, pp. 272–286, 2018.
https://doi.org/10.1007/978-3-030-05054-2_21

When multiple tasks are scheduled to the same machine, there will be multiple VMs co-running in the physical machine. These VMs will not be executed in sequence, but concurrently (i.e., time sharing) by the schedulers (such as Credit or SEDF) deployed in the Virtual Machine Monitor.

Our studies, the details of which are presented in Sect. 2, show that the discrepancy between the assumption of sequential execution and the reality of time sharing execution may lead to inaccurate calculation for the finish times of individual tasks and further for the execution performance, such as in terms of makespan, of the whole DAG.

In this paper, we first investigate the key difference between the time-sharing execution and the sequential execution, and reveal the impact of the time sharing execution on the DAG makespan. Based on the analysis, we adapt the conventional method of computing the DAG makespan in the sequential execution and present our counterpart makespan model and method in the time-sharing execution. Usually, the makespan in the time sharing execution is worse (longer) than that assumed in the sequential execution. Therefore, we propose the new DAG scheduling strategies (a task migration algorithm and a task allocation algorithm) for time-sharing systems.

The remainder of this paper is organized as follows. In Sect. 2, we give a motivating case study to demonstrate the difference of the time sharing execution from the sequential execution and its impact on the makespan. In Sect. 3, we briefly discuss the current scheduling strategies and the corresponding way of computing the makespan. In Sect. 4, we present the workload and system model and the notations used in this paper. Section 5 presents the makespan models with both sequential and time-sharing executions. Section 6.1 presents the task migration algorithm while Sect. 6.2 presents the DAG allocation algorithm for the time-sharing execution. Experimental results are presented in Sect. 7. Finally, in Sect. 8 the paper is concluded and the future work is planned.

2   A Motivating Example

In this section, we present a case study to illustrate the difference of the time-sharing execution from the sequential execution and its impact on the DAG makespan. This case study considers a DAG job consisting of 7 tasks, whose topology is shown in Fig. 1. The execution times of 7 tasks, t_0 to t_6, are $150, 200, 150, 50, 100, 100, 100$, respectively. There is no communication between tasks. Assume a scheduling decision of such a DAG on a set of two identical PMs (PM_1 and PM_2) is as follows. Tasks t_0, t_1, t_5, t_6 are scheduled to run in PM_1 while t_2, t_3, t_4 are in PM_2. If the tasks allocated to the same PM are run in sequence. Such a schedule leads to the minimal makespan. The corresponding critical path of the DAG is $t_0 \rightarrow t_1 \rightarrow t_5 \rightarrow t_6$.

The left figure in Fig. 2 shows the sequential execution of the tasks in the two PMs. As shown in the figure, t_3 can only start the execution after task t_0 (which is its predecessor of t_3) and t_2 (which is scheduled to run before t_3) in PM_2 have finished. Other tasks have the similar execution precedence. With the sequential

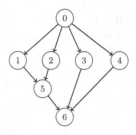

Fig. 1. A motivating example DAG

execution model, it is expected that t_5 starts the execution at the time point 350 ms, and the makespan of the DAG is 550 ms.

As discussed in the first section, when several tasks are allocated to the same PM, they will be run in the time-sharing manner by the OS. The right figure in Fig. 2 shows the times-sharing execution of the tasks. As shown in the figure, t_2, t_3 and t_4 in PM_2 start execution concurrently after their predecessor t_0 finishes. t_2's finish time is then 450 ms, which is later than its finish time under the sequential execution model (300 ms). This difference leads to the delay of t_5's start. In the time-sharing execution, t_5 starts the execution at 450 ms with the delay of 100 ms compared with the sequential execution. Consequently the actual DAG makespan with the time-sharing execution model is 650 ms, which is longer than the one expected with the sequential execution (550 ms). Furthermore, the critical path in the time-sharing execution changes to $t_0 \rightarrow t_2 \rightarrow t_5 \rightarrow t_6$.

In most DAG scheduling algorithm in the literature, the scheduling decision is made based on the tasks' finish times, which are typically calculated by assuming the sequential execution. Although it is fine with the task scheduling in clusters, in which there is a centralized task queue in the head node and a task is sent to a computing node when the existing tasks running in the node have been completed. As discussed in the introduction, however, the tasks are run concurrently in distributed systems or virtualized systems. This may cause the discrepancy between the tasks' actual finish times and the finish times assumed by the task scheduler, as illustrated in this case study.

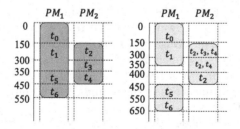

Fig. 2. Non-time-sharing model makespan (left) vs. Time-sharing model makespan (right)

3   Related Work

It is typical to run a DAG application on clusters in order to exploit the inherent parallelism in the DAG topology. Several popular scheduling frameworks have been developed on clusters: YARN [25], Borg [26], Sparrow [24], Apollo [22], Mercury [23], etc. The centralized scheduling frameworks such as YARN and Borg only have the global queues. In order to improve the scheduling performance, it now becomes increasingly popular to employ the distributed scheduling in large-scale data centres, where multiple schedulers make the scheduling decisions for different types of jobs simultaneously and independently. Such distributed scheduling frameworks include Mercury [21], Apollo and our previous work presented in [27], etc. In distributed scheduling frameworks, a PM may receive the tasks dispatched by different schedulers and these tasks are typically run in a time sharing manner in the node.

Scheduling a DAG and minimizing its makespan are proven to be a NP-complete problem when there are more than two PMs [2]. Thus many heuristic and meta-heuristic scheduling approaches are developed to minimize the DAG makespan [6,8–10,12].

Although scientists began to study the scheduling long time ago, it is still a hot topic nowadays to investigate the scheduling strategies for new platforms and scenarios emerging over time, such as virtualized systems [11], multi-sites workflow scheduling [7], soft real-time scheduling in data centres [14], energy-aware scheduling [13], and the scheduling with multiple objectives on IaaS Clouds [13].

However, in these algorithms, the tasks scheduled to the same node are assumed to run in sequence. None of the above work assumes the time-sharing execution when making the scheduling decisions. Our studies show that when the tasks allocated to the same node are run in the time-sharing manner, the finish times of individual tasks may be different from those in the sequential execution and consequently affect the makespan. Therefore, if the existing DAG scheduling algorithms are applied directly in the distributed scheduling, the actual performance of the DAG execution, no matter in terms of makespan or other objectives such as energy consumption, may not be as optimal as these scheduling methods assume. In this paper, we (1) investigate the impact of time-sharing execution on the DAG makespan and further develop a model to calculate the makespan in the time-sharing execution, and (2) develop a scheduling strategy aiming to minimize the DAG makespan when the tasks in DAG are run in the nodes in the time-sharing manner.

4   Workload and Resource Model

This section introduces the main notations used for the workloads and resources in this paper. A DAG-based application T is modelled as a directed acyclic graph (DAG) $G(V, E)$, where each task $t_i \in T$ is represented as a node $v_i \in V$. An edge e_{ij} from v_i to v_j, which is also denoted by (t_i, t_j), represents that there is the precedence constraint between tasks t_i and t_j. The weight of an edge represents the communication time TT_{ij} for sending the data from t_i to t_j. Further, task t_i is called the predecessor of t_j, while t_j is the successor of t_i.

For task $t_i \in T$, its set of predecessors and successors, denoted by $pred(t_i)$ and $succ(t_i)$ respectively, are defined below:

$$pred(t_i) = \{t_j | t_j \in T \wedge (t_j, t_i) \in E\} \qquad (1)$$

$$succ(t_i) = \{t_j | t_j \in T \wedge (t_i, t_j) \in E\} \qquad (2)$$

Tasks without the predecessor or the successor are called the entry task or exit task, respectively.

In a DAG, the distance of a path is the sum of the execution times of all tasks and the weights of the edges (communication times) on the path. The critical path of a DAG is denoted as L. The makespan of a DAG is the distance of the critical path from the entry task to the exit task.

A cluster consists of a set of physical machines (PM), denoted by M, where $M = \{p_1, p_2, \ldots, p_s\}$. c_i denotes the processing capacity of p_i.

A task t_i is modelled by a tuple $t_i = \{st_i, ft_i, s_i, re_i\}$, where st_i is the time when t_i is *ready to start* (a task is ready to start only when all of its predecessors are completed and the relevant data sent by predecessors have been received by t_i); ft_i is the time when t_i is completed, which includes both the task's execution time and its data communication time; s_i is the size of the work (e.g., the number of instructions or the number of CPU cycles) that is to be performed in t_i; re_i is the current remaining work of t_i, which is calculated by the total work minus the finished work so far.

A Schedule is defined by $S = (G, M, Mapping)$, where G is the DAG graph, M is the cluster, and $Mapping$ is the mapping of the tasks in G to M. Figure 2 shows a exemplar schedule for scheduling a graph in Fig. 1 to a cluster of two PMs. In this example, $M = \{p_1, p_2\}$, $Mapping = \{1 : [t_0, t_1, t_5, t_6], 2 : [t_2, t_3, t_4]\}$.

After task t_i finishes the execution, it needs to send the results to its successors. We assume that the communication time can be neglected if the predecessor and the successor are mapped on the same PM. k_i is the number of successors of t_i. The total communication time of task t_i, denoted by TT_i, can be calculated by Eq. 3:

$$TT_i = \sum_1^{k_i} (TT_{ij} * l_{ij}) \qquad (3)$$

$$l_{ij} = \begin{cases} 0 & \text{if } t_i \text{ and } t_j \text{ are on the same PM} \\ 1 & \text{otherwise} \end{cases} \qquad (4)$$

Given the above workload and resource model, our objective is to investigate the impact of the time-sharing execution on the DAG makespan, and further propose the scheduling algorithms to mitigate the impact.

5   The Makespan Model

5.1   The Makespan with the Sequential Execution Model

In non-time-sharing makespan model, tasks are regarded as executing in a one-by-one manner in a PM instance. At least they didn't take the time-sharing executing into consider when calculate finish time of the tasks. Thus, within a PM instance run queue, a ready task (i.e. that has received all results from its predecessors) can not start to execute before its previous task finishes.

Given a Schedule S, the start time st_i for task t_i can be determined by Eq. 6:

$$st_i = max\{lpft_i, prevft_i\} \qquad (5)$$

where $lpft_i$ denotes the latest finish time of all t_i's predecessors, $prevft_i$ denotes the finish time of the task scheduled to run right before t_i.

The finish time ft_i for task t_i executed on PM_r can be derived by Eq. 6:

$$ft_i = st_i + \frac{s_i}{PC_r} + TT_i \qquad (6)$$

where s_i denotes the size of t_i, PC_r denotes the processing capacity of PM_r, TT_i denotes the total transferring time calculated by Eq. 3.

Given the sequential execution, the makespan of a DAG can be calculated by applying Eqs. 5 and 6 iteratively from the entry task to the exit task in the DAG.

5.2   The Makespan with the Time-Sharing Execution Model

In this subsection, we present our method for computing the DAG makespan with the time-sharing execution model.

Given a Schedule S, the start time st_i of task t_i should be derived using Eq. 7.

$$st_i = max\{lpft\} \qquad (7)$$

Comparing Eq. 7 with Eq. 5 used for the sequential execution, the difference lies in the fact that task t_i does not have to wait for the completion of the tasks scheduled ahead of it. t_i can start once it is ready to run, i.e., all of its predecessors have finished.

Given a Schedule S, the finish time of task t_i is influenced by the processing capacity PC_r and the number of tasks that are running concurrently with t_i. When determining t_i's finish time, we divide the entire execution cycle of a task into a number of periods. t_i is regarded as moving into a new execution period when the number of tasks concurrently running with t_i changes.

Assume the number of execution periods of task t_i is m. m_j denotes the j-th period and $Share_j$ denotes the number of tasks that are concurrently running (time-sharing) with t_i. $time_{js}$ and $time_{je}$ denote the start and end time of period m_j, respectively. s_i denotes the size of t_i (e.g., the amount of work in terms of CPU cycles. Then Eq. 8 should hold, in which $(time_{je} - time_{js}) * \frac{PC_r}{Share_j}$ represents the amount of work completed (i.e., the number of CPU cycles dedicated to run t_i) during the period m_j.

$$s_i = \sum_{j=1}^{m} ((time_{je} - time_{js}) * \frac{PC_r}{Share_j}) \tag{8}$$

Given s_i and a scheduling solution, we can determine at any time how many tasks are concurrently running with t_i. Consequently, we can determine m as well as the start and end time of each period (i.e., $time_{je}$ and $time_{js}$). With m, $time_{je}$ and $time_{js}$, we can determine the execution time of t_i, denoted by $time_{je}$ and $time_{js}$, using Eq. 9.

$$et_i = \sum_{j=1}^{m} (time_{je} - time_{js}) \tag{9}$$

The finish time of t_i can then be calculated by 10:

$$ft_i = et_i + TT_i \tag{10}$$

We apply Eqs. 8, 9 and 10 iteratively for all tasks in a DAG from the entry task to the exit task. The finish time of the exit task is the makespan of the DAG. The detailed algorithm for computing the makespan is omitted in this paper due to the limitation of space.

6   DAG Scheduling for Time-Sharing Execution

6.1   Task Migration Algorithm

In this section, we present a Task Migration Algorithm (TMS) to adjust the DAG schedule decided with the assumption of sequential execution, aiming to reduce the actual makespan when the tasks are run in time-sharing in reality.

In our strategy, the makespan of the given DAG schedule S by assuming the sequential execution, which we call makespan in sequential execution, is used as the deadline ddl for our schedule adjustment. We then use the following equation to derive the latest start time lst of every task in order to meet the deadline. Latest Start Time (lst) of a task indicates the urgency of the task.

$$lst_i = \begin{cases} ddl - \frac{s_i}{PC_r} & \text{if } t_i = t_{exit} \\ \min_{t_s \in succ(t_i)} \{lst_s - \frac{s_i}{PC_r}\} & \text{otherwise} \end{cases} \tag{11}$$

Similarly, we can use Eq. 12 to derive the latest finish time lft of every task in the DAG. Every task, t_i should finish by its latest finish time lft_i. Otherwise, the DAG will not meet the deadline.

$$lft_i = \begin{cases} ddl & \text{if } t_i = t_{exit} \\ \min_{t_m \in succ(t_i)} \{lft_m - \frac{s_m}{PC_r}\} & \text{otherwise} \end{cases} \tag{12}$$

lft_i is used to determine the tasks whose allocations need to be adjusted. With Eq. 10, we can calculate the actual finish time ft_i of every task. If ft_i is greater than lft_i calculated by Eq. 12. The allocation of Task t_i needs to be adjusted, which is stored in an *AdjustList* in the increasing order of the task's latest start time (lst_i). For each task t_i in *AdjustList*, we try to migrate it to another *PM* so that ft_i can be no more than lft_i. We deem the adjustment of the Schedule S to be successful only when all tasks in *AdjustList* can find their suitable *PM*s. The task migration algorithm is outlined in Algorithm 1.

6.2 Task Allocation Algorithm

Not all task schedules can be adjusted to meet the deadline. If the task migration algorithm fail to reach a successful adjustment. We develop a Task Allocation Algorithm (TAS) to find a task schedule from scratch for the time-sharing execution. TAS assumes the same number of *PM*s as that in the schedule S generated for sequential execution.

In *TAS*, we still use the makespan in sequential execution as the deadline (target) for finding the schedule solution in time-sharing. *TAS* generates an *Orderlist* in the similar way as we construct the *Ajustlist* in *TMS*. For each task in *Orderlist*, TAS tries to allocate it to a best *PM* based on a metric we propose, which is called Total deadline Miss Time (tmt). tmt is defined as the total of all deadline misses in a PM. The pseudo-code of TAS is shown in Algorithm 2.

7 Evaluation

To facilitate the evaluation of the workflow algorithms, Pegasus has developed a set of synthetic workflow generators. These generators use the information gathered from actual executions of scientific workflows to generate realistic, synthetic workflows resembling those used by real world scientific applications. These workflows come from [19,20] and are widely used in this research field. In this paper, we use these real-world workflows for evaluation. In the experiments, we compare the Makespan in Sequential execution (denoted by makespan-S, which is the makespan by assuming the sequential execution), the Makespan in Time-sharing execution (denoted by makespan-TS, which is the makespan of the DAG when the tasks are run in time-sharing in reality) and the makespan obtained by TAS (denoted by makespan-TAS). Makespan-S and Makespan-TS are computed using the makespan models presented in Sect. 5.

7.1 Performance with Different Number of Tasks

Figure 3 shows the performance of the real-world workflows with different number of tasks in terms of makespan-S, makespan-TS and makespan-TAS.

Algorithm 1. Task Migration Algorithm

Data: DAG G and Schedule $S = (G, PM, Mapping)$, processing capacity PC,
       task size s

Result: Whether S is adjustable (0 or 1), Adjusted S' and its corresponding
       real makespan

1 **for** *All tasks in DAG G* **do**
2   Calculate t_i's real finish time ft_i using time-sharing makespan model;
3   Calculate t_i's latest finish time lft_i using eq. 12 ;
4    $slack_i = lft_i - ft_i$;
5   Calculate t_i's topology level l_i in G;
6    $l\_dict[l_i].append(t_i)$;
7   **if** $slack_i < 0$ **then**
8   Add t_i to $AdjustList$;

9 Sort $AdjustList$ by increasing lst derived from eq. 11;
10 **for** *tasks (marked as t_k) in ordered AdjustList* **do**
11   Mark t_k's current allocated PM as PM_{cur} ;
12   **for** *All PMs (marked as PM_r) except PM_{cur}* **do**
13   Add PM_r to PM_List;
14      $min\_Slack_{l_k}^{PM_r} = 0$;
15   **for** *task $t_a \in PM_r$ and $l_a = l_k$* **do**
16        $min\_Slack_{l_k}^{PM_r} = min\{slack_a\}$;

17   Sort PM_List by decreasing $min\_Slack_l^{PM}$;
18    $PM_{try} = PM\_List[0]$;
19   **while** *PM_List is not empty* **do**
20   Assume t_k changes its allocation to PM_{try};
21   Make $Affec\_list$ of the Affected tasks and calculate their ft';
22   **for** *each task (marked as t_{aff}) in $Affec\_list$* **do**
23        $slack'_{aff} = ft'_{aff} - lft_{aff}$;
24   **if** $slack'_{aff} < 0$ **then**
25   PM_{try} is not a suitable PM to migrate;
26   Remove PM_{try} from PM_List;
27   Break

28   **if** *No more lft missing happens* **then**
29   Migrate t_k to PM_{try};
30   Update all corresponding information;
31   Break;

32   **if** *There is no PM changeable for t_k* **then**
33   Schedule S is non-adjustable;
34   Exit;

35 **if** *Schedule S is adjustable* **then**
36   Update the adjusted Schedule S';
37   Calculate the corresponding real makespan;

Algorithm 2. Task Allocation Algorithm

Data: DAG G and Schedule $S = (G, PM, Mapping)$
Result: A newly Schedule S' and its Makespan
1 Calculate S's non-time-sharing makespan and set to ddl;
2 Calculate the G's topological level $level$;
3 **for** *All tasks in DAG G* **do**
4   Calculate t_i's lst_i and lft_i using eq. 11 and 12, respectively;

5 **for** *level from 0 to the highest topological level* **do**
6   Sort the tasks on the same $level$ by increasing lst and add to the $OrderList$;

7 **for** *From front to back of the OrderList* **do**
8   **for** *all PMs* **do**
9   Calculate ft of all allocated tasks;
10   Calculate the total ddl missing time tmt_s;
11   **if** *total ddl missing time $tmt_s = 0$* **then**
12   Calculate the total ddl slack time tst_s;

13   **if** *there are >1 proposed S' has total $tmt_s = 0$* **then**
14   Allocate t_i to the PM with $max(tst_s)$;

15   **else**
16   Allocate t_i to the PM with $min(tmt_s)$;

17   Update S', all related tasks' ft and child tasks' st;

Montage. Montage has been created by the NASA/IPAC Infrared Science Archive that can be used to generate custom mosaics of the sky using input images in the Flexible Image Transport System (FITS) format [18]. Figure 3a–d shows the gaps among makespan-S, makespan-TS and makespan-TAS. The results indicates that there indeed exits the gap among these makespans. Our TAS algorithm can reduce the realistic makespan by taking the time-sharing execution into account.

Epigenomics. This workflow is being used by the Epigenome Center in the processing of production DNA methylation and histone modification data [16]. It has the largely pipelined tasks and a large degree of parallelism. For example, Epigenomics 997 has 7 entry tasks and a parallel degree of 250. Due to its DAG structure, there is not a big difference between makespan-S and makespan-TS. However, comparing with makespan-S, TAS improves the makespan by 8.88%, 7.9%, 10.7% and 14.3% with 24, 46, 100 and 997 tasks, respectively.

CyberShake. The Cybershake workflow is used by the Southern California Earthquake Center (SCEC) to characterize the earthquake hazards in a region using the Probabilistic Seismic Hazard Analysis (PSHA) technique [15]. Figures 3i–l show a big difference between makespan-S and makespan-TS: 33.1%, 20.4%, 7.4% and 2.52% with 30, 50, 100 and 1,000 tasks, respectively. Given the limited number of *PMs* in the experiments (less than the parallel degree of the workflow), the DAG with the flat structure often cause a big difference between makespan-S and makespan-TS since the time-sharing execution results in the big delay in some tasks' finish time comparing with the sequential execution. *TAS* shows a outstanding optimization ability, improving the makespan by 43.56% and 41.82% with 100 nodes and 1,000 tasks, respectively.

Sipht. The Sipht workflow is used to automate the search for sRNA encoding-genes for all of the bacterial replicons in the National Center for Biotechnology Information (NCBI) database. It is a highly parallel, flat structured DAG application. Figures 3n–p show the gaps of 345.58 s, 696.81 s and 63 s between

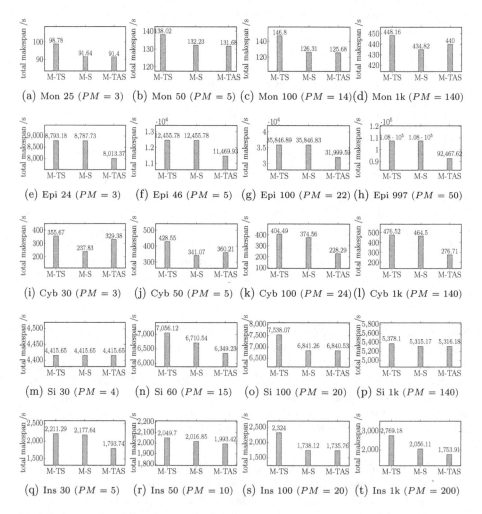

(a) Mon 25 ($PM = 3$) (b) Mon 50 ($PM = 5$) (c) Mon 100 ($PM = 14$)(d) Mon 1k ($PM = 140$)

(e) Epi 24 ($PM = 3$) (f) Epi 46 ($PM = 5$) (g) Epi 100 ($PM = 22$) (h) Epi 997 ($PM = 50$)

(i) Cyb 30 ($PM = 3$) (j) Cyb 50 ($PM = 5$) (k) Cyb 100 ($PM = 24$)(l) Cyb 1k ($PM = 140$)

(m) Si 30 ($PM = 4$) (n) Si 60 ($PM = 15$) (o) Si 100 ($PM = 20$) (p) Si 1k ($PM = 140$)

(q) Ins 30 ($PM = 5$) (r) Ins 50 ($PM = 10$) (s) Ins 100 ($PM = 20$) (t) Ins 1k ($PM = 200$)

Fig. 3. Results for the real-world workflows runtime in different node numbers under $M - TS$, $M - S$ and $M - TAS$

makespan-S and makespan-TS with 60, 100 and 1,000 tasks, respectively. However there is no noticeable difference between two makespans when the number of tasks is less than 30 no matter how many PMs are used.

Inspiral. The LIGO Inspiral Analysis Workflow is used to analyze the data obtained from the coalescing of compact binary systems such as binary neutron stars and black holes [17]. The parallel degree of the DAGs are 7, 12, 23 and 229 with 30, 50, 100 and 1,000 tasks, respectively. There is a gap of 1.87%, 1.61%, 25.2% and 25.7% between makespan-S and makespan-TS with 30, 50, 100 and 1,000 tasks respectively. TAS shows a makespan improvement of 17.6%, 1.18%, 0.01% and 14.7% with 30, 50, 100 and 1,000 tasks, respectively.

7.2   Performance with the Different Number of PMs

Table 1 and Fig. 4 show the makespan of the real-world workflows with 50 and 100 tasks, respectively, when using different number of PMs. As can be seen from Table 1, different number of PMs lead to the different gaps between makespan-S and makespan-TS. The decrease of the makespan is not linear with the increase of the number of PM. When the number of PM reaches the degree of the

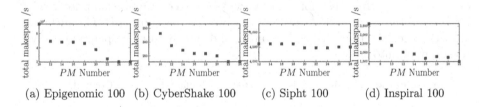

(a) Epigenomic 100   (b) CyberShake 100   (c) Sipht 100   (d) Inspiral 100

Fig. 4. Makespan-TAS with different number of PMs

Table 1. Results of the real-world DAGs makespan

Task	PN	M-TS	M-S	M-TAS	Task	PN	M-TS	M-S	M-TAS
Mon 50	5	138.01	132.23	132.07	Cyb 50	6	585.74	522.03	323.77
Mon 50	8	87.46	87.46	87.28	Cyb 50	10	422.88	416.69	290.62
Mon 50	10	77.12	77.0	76.83	Cyb 50	12	410.19	380.13	262.74
Mon 50	15	66.89	66.43	66.27	Cyb 50	15	313.83	342.87	262.74
Epi 46	4	16584.92	16585.31	13393.97	Si 60	10	7058.11	6712.53	4643.09
Epi 46	5	12455.78	12455.78	11469.93	Si 60	12	4649.64	4640.88	4642.22
Epi 46	7	12226.93	12234.63	10672.41	Si 60	15	7056.12	6710.54	4640.87
Epi 46	10	7744.39	7744.39	7728.24	Si 60	18	4648.72	4640.76	4640.99
Ins 50	5	3354.87	3319.31	2905.17	Ins 50	8	2054.99	2021.44	1939.07
Ins 50	7	2386.88	2372.7	2186.23					
Ins 50	12	1410.8	1410.8	1410.8					

parallelism of the DAG, the gap disappears. In our experiment, the parallel degrees are 15, 10, 23, 50 and 12 for Montage 50, Epigenomics 46, CyberShake 50, Sipht 60 and Inspiral 50 respectively in Table 1; the parallel degrees are 60, 24, 46, 89 and 23 for Montage 100, Epigenomics 100, CyberShake 100, Sipht 100 and Inspiral 100 respectively. For flat and highly parallel DAG such as "Sipht 100", varying the number of PMs (i.e. 12–28) makes almost no difference to the makespan when the number of PM is far less than the parallel degree (i.e. 89 in this case).

8 Conclusions and Future Work

In this paper, we investigate the impact of the time-sharing execution on the DAG makespan. The makespan model in the time-sharing execution is proposed. Based on the makespan model, a Task Migration Algorithm and a Task Allocation algorithm are developed, aiming to reduce the actual makespan of the DAG schedule when the DAG is executed in time-sharing in reality. We conduct the extensive experiments with the real-world workflows. The experimental results show that there exists the gap between the makespan in sequential execution, the makespan in time-sharing execution and the makespan obtained by our DAG scheduling algorithm designed for time-sharing systems. In the future, we will extend our research are two folds: (1) we will set up a energy consumption model for DAG in the time-sharing execution; (2) we will develop the DAG scheduling algorithms for the time-sharing execution and take both makespan and energy consumption into account.

Acknowledgement. This work is supported by China Scholarship Council.

References

1. Zhang, X., Tune, E., Hagmann, R., Jnagal, R., Gokhale, V., Wilkes, J.: CPI2: CPU performance isolation for shared compute clusters, New York, NY, USA, pp. 379–391 (2013)
2. Garey, M.R., Johnson, D.S.: Computers and Intractability. W. H. Freeman, New York (2002)
3. Liao, Q., Jiang, S., Hei, Q., Li, T., Yang, Y.: Scheduling stochastic tasks with precedence constrain on cluster systems with heterogenous communication architecture. In: Wang, G., Zomaya, A., Perez, G.M., Li, K. (eds.) ICA3PP 2015. LNCS, vol. 9532, pp. 85–99. Springer, Cham (2015). https://doi.org/10.1007/978-3-319-27161-3_8
4. Wang, L., et al.: Energy-aware parallel task scheduling in a cluster. Future Gener. Comput. Syst. 29(7), 1661–1670 (2013). https://doi.org/10.1016/j.future.2013.02.010. ISSN: 0167-739X
5. Li, X., Zhao, Y., Li, Y., Ju, L., Jia, Z.: An improved energy-efficient scheduling for precedence constrained tasks in multiprocessor clusters. In: Sun, X., et al. (eds.) ICA3PP 2014. LNCS, vol. 8630, pp. 323–337. Springer, Cham (2014). https://doi.org/10.1007/978-3-319-11197-1_25

6. Liu, L., Zhang, M., Buyya, R., Fan, Q.: Deadline-constrained coevolution-ary genetic algorithm for scientific workflow scheduling in cloud computing. Concurrency Comput. Pract. Exp. **29**(5), e3942 (2017). https://doi.org/10.1002/cpe.3942

7. Maheshwari, K., Jung, E.S., Meng, J., Morozov, V., Vishwanath, V., Kettimuthu, R.: Workflow performance improvement using model-based scheduling over multiple clusters and clouds. Future Gener. Comput. Syst. **54**, 206–218 (2016). https://doi.org/10.1016/j.future.2015.03.017. ISSN: 0167–739X

8. Chen, W., Xie, G., Li, R., Bai, Y., Fan, C., Li, K.: Efficient task scheduling for budget constrained parallel applications on heterogeneous cloud computing systems. Future Gener. Comput. Syst. **74**, 1–11 (2017). https://doi.org/10.1016/j.future.2017.03.008. ISSN: 0167–739X

9. Hu, Y., Liu, C., Li, K., Chen, X., Li, K.: Slack allocation algorithm for energy minimization in cluster systems. Future Gener. Comput. Syst. **74**, 119–131 (2017). https://doi.org/10.1016/j.future.2016.08.022. ISSN: 0167–739X

10. Canon, L.C., Philippe, L.: On the heterogeneity bias of cost matrices for assessing scheduling algorithms. IEEE Trans. Parallel Distrib. Syst. **28**(6), 1675–1688 (2017). https://doi.org/10.1109/TPDS.2016.2629503

11. Wu, H., Hua, X., Li, Z., Ren, S.: Resource and instance hour minimization for deadline constrained DAG applications using computer clouds. IEEE Trans. Parallel Distrib. Syst. **27**(3), 885–899 (2016). https://doi.org/10.1109/TPDS.2015.2411257

12. Xie, G., Xiao, X., Li, R., Li, K.: Schedule length minimization of parallel applications with energy consumption constraints using heuristics on heterogeneous distributed systems. Concurrency Comput. Pract. Exp. **29**, e4024 (2016). https://doi.org/10.1002/cpe.4024

13. Oxley, M.A., et al.: Makespan and energy robust stochastic static resource allocation of a bag-of-tasks to a heterogeneous computing system. IEEE Trans. Parallel Distrib. Syst. **26**(10), 2791–2805 (2015). https://doi.org/10.1109/TPDS.2014.2362921

14. Li, D., Chen, C., Guan, J., Zhang, Y., Zhu, J., Yu, R.: DCloud: deadline-aware resource allocation for cloud computing jobs. IEEE Trans. Parallel Distrib. Syst. **27**(8), 2248–2260 (2016). https://doi.org/10.1109/TPDS.2015.2489646

15. https://confluence.pegasus.isi.edu/display/pegasus/CyberShake

16. https://confluence.pegasus.isi.edu/display/pegasus/Epigenomics

17. https://confluence.pegasus.isi.edu/display/pegasus/LIGO+Inspiral

18. https://confluence.pegasus.isi.edu/display/pegasus/Montage

19. Juve, G., Chervenak, A., Deelman, E., Bharathi, S., Mehta, G., Vahi, K.: Characterizing and profiling scientific workflows. Future Gener. Comput. Syst. **29**(3), 682–692 (2013). https://doi.org/10.1016/j.future.2012.08.015. ISSN: 0167–739X

20. Bharathi, S., Chervenak, A., Deelman, E., et al.: Characterization of scientific workflows. In: Third Workshop on Workflows in Support of Large-Scale Science, WORKS 2008, pp. 1–10. IEEE (2008)

21. Rasley, J., Karanasos, K., Kandula, S., Fonseca, R., Vojnovic, M., Rao, S.: Efficient queue management for cluster scheduling. In: Proceedings of the Eleventh European Conference on Computer Systems (EuroSys 2016), New York, NY, USA, Article 36, 15 p. ACM (2016)

22. Boutin, E., et al.: Apollo: scalable and coordinated scheduling for cloud-scale computing. In: OSDI (2014)

23. Karanasos, K., et al.: Mercury: hybrid centralized and distributed scheduling in large shared clusters. In: USENIX. ATC (2015)

24. Ousterhout, K., Wendell, P., Zaharia, M., Stoica, I.: Sparrow: distributed, low latency scheduling. In: SOSP (2013)
25. Vavilapalli, V.K., et al.: Apache hadoop YARN: yet another resource negotiator. In: SoCC (2013)
26. Verma, A., Pedrosa, L., Korupolu, M., Oppenheimer, D., Tune, E., Wilkes, J.: Large-scale cluster management at Google with Borg. In: EuroSys (2015)
27. Chen, C., He, L., Chen, H., Sun, J., Gao, B., Jarvis, S.A.: Developing communication-aware service placement frameworks in the cloud economy. In: 2013 IEEE International Conference on Cluster Computing (CLUSTER), Indianapolis, IN, pp. 1–8 (2013). https://doi.org/10.1109/CLUSTER.2013.6702668

Job Scheduling with Adaptable Computing Levels for Edge Computing

Huiwen Jiang[(✉)] and Weigang Wu[(✉)]

School of Data and Computer Science, Sun Yat-sen University, Guangzhou, China
jianghw5@mail2.sysu.edu.cn, wuweig@mail.sysu.edu.cn

Abstract. Edge computing is an emerging technology that can help huge number of devices be connected and processed with low latency. However, the performance of edge servers is far less powerful than cloud servers. When dealing with a large number of job requests from user devices, traditional job scheduling methods are not efficient enough. In this paper, we propose a new job scheduling model by considering adaptable jobs that can be executed with different computing levels and accordingly different resource requirements. We design a new job scheduling algorithm based on such an adaptable job model. The algorithm can choose an appropriate level for each job according to resource availability. Compared with existing works, our design can achieve better tradeoff between resource utilization and quality of experience. To the best of our knowledge, this is the first paper that considers adaptable job computing levels.

Keywords: Edge computing · Job scheduling · Quality of experience
Resource utilization · Adaptable computing levels

1 Introduction

According to Cisco's prediction, there will be 50 billion electronic devices connected to the Internet by the year 2020. Various new applications are emerging such as gesture recognition, voice control, recognition assistance, mobile gaming, virtual reality and augmented reality [1]. These kinds of applications are typically computation-intensive and delay-sensitive. Due to the limitation of mobile device performance and battery life, computation offloading has been a popular research topic in the past few years [2]. Offloading mobile workloads to remote data centers or computing clusters, however, incurs long network transmission latency [3], which seriously impairs the mobile application performance. This also implicates the heavy network load, and growing demand of network bandwidth since data have to be transmitted and received to and from mobile devices and cloud data centers. Obviously, the traditional cloud computing paradigm is incapable to meet the new demands brought by the age of Internet of things.

In order to solve the above problems, Edge computing have been proposed [4]. Edge computing refers to the enabling technologies allowing computation

© Springer Nature Switzerland AG 2018
J. Vaidya and J. Li (Eds.): ICA3PP 2018, LNCS 11335, pp. 287–296, 2018.
https://doi.org/10.1007/978-3-030-05054-2_22

to be performed at the edge of the network, on downstream data on behalf of cloud services and upstream data on behalf of IoT services. There are functions in edge servers such as computing offloading, data caching, data processing, request distribution, and service delivery. The aim is to offer users services with high bandwidth and low latency. However, due to the need of large-scale deployment of edge servers to cover users in different places, such edge servers certainly will not have the same powerful performance as traditional centralized cloud servers. Therefore, when facing a large number of computation-intensive application requests, edge servers may be not efficient enough using traditional job scheduling and execution methods. When the edge servers reach a performance bottleneck, the response time of application requests will increase significantly, which degrades the application experience of users.

In this paper, we propose a adaptable job execution model to deal with the above challenges. The traditional job scheduling method is that if servers meet the resource requirements of an arrived job, system will execute it. Otherwise the job will need to wait for the resources to be released after the completion of the running jobs. Instead of 'run-or-wait' strategy, our idea is that for some specific jobs, several computing levels are optional. Different computing levels require different system resources and the higher the computing level a job is executed at, the higher accuracy the job would be done with. These specific jobs are computation-intensive such as virtual reality and augmented reality. We conclude the relationships between the accuracy of jobs and the resource requirements as three models. The first is linearly increasing model; the second is deceleratingly increasing model; and the third is first acceleratingly and then deceleratingly increasing model. Different types of jobs can be set a variety of computing levels according to specification. Through the adaptable job execution model, servers can make the optimal choice for both systems and users according to available resources of the system and the different computing levels of the jobs. To the best of our knowledge, this is the first paper that considers adaptable job computing levels.

Moreover, we also proposed a scheduling algorithm to match our proposed adaptable execution model to improve the utilization of the system resources and improve quality of experience for users. The system may in such a state that one of the resources of the system (such as CPU) is in a state of heavy load while the other resources such as I/O bandwidth is in an idle state. If there is an I/O intensive job arriving, because the CPU is fully occupied, the job is suspended and the idle I/O devices are unable to work. This unbalanced state of resource load should be avoided by the system as much as possible. Our proposed algorithm differentiate jobs between CPU-intensive jobs and I/O-intensive jobs according to [5]. The proposed algorithm uses greedy ideas to prioritize the job's maximum computing level that the current system resources can satisfy to execute. When several jobs arrive simultaneously, we select the jobs that have the same dominant resource as the relatively idle resources of the system so as to achieve load balancing of different system resources and improve resource utilization.

The rest of this paper is organized as follows. Section 2 review the related work. Section 3 describes the details of our proposed models and job scheduling algorithm. Section 4 evaluate our design. Section 5 concludes the paper.

2 Related Work

To address the conflict between locality and fairness, Zaharia et al. [6] propose a simple algorithm called delay scheduling: when the job that should be scheduled next according to fairness cannot launch a local task, it waits for a small amount of time, letting other jobs launch tasks instead. Experiment shows that delay scheduling achieves nearly optimal data locality in a variety of workloads and can increase throughput by up to 2x while preserving fairness. [7] rethink resource allocation and job scheduling on a data analytics system in the cloud to embrace the heterogeneity of the underlying platforms and workloads. To that end, they suggest an architecture to allocate resources to a data analytics cluster in the cloud, and propose a metric of share in a heterogeneous cluster to realize a scheduling scheme that achieves high performance and fairness. Lee et al. [8] propose a adaptable framework and a job scheduling algorithm called adaptable Load Balanced Algorithm (HLBA) for Grid environment. In the algorithm, they use the system load as a parameter in determining a balance threshold. And the scheduler adapts the balance threshold dynamically when the system load changes. Li et al. [9] propose Greedy-Based Algorithm in cloud computing. Compare to other methods, it can decrease the completion time of submitted jobs and improve the quality of experience for users.

However, none of above papers is proposed to deal with the massive requests from users in the time of Internet of thing, especially when jobs are mostly computation-intensive.

3 Design

3.1 Model

We first give a series of definitions as follows:

$$Job = \{J_1, J_2, J_3, \ldots, J_n\} \tag{1}$$

$$J_n = \{ID_n, C_n, M_n, D_n, L_n\} \tag{2}$$

$$Ln = \{level_1, level_2, \ldots, level_m\} \tag{3}$$

$$level_m = \{C\_ratio, D\_ratio, Acc\} \tag{4}$$

ID_n is the identity of a job n, C_n is the number of CPU cycles required for the job, M_n is the amount of running memory, D_n is the size of the job's dataset, and L_n is the computing level that the job can be performed at, which is respectively $level_1, level_2, level_3, \ldots, level_m$. Different jobs have different optional computing levels. C_ratio, D_ratio are the ratios of the max resource usage under the corresponding job computing level with job accuracy Acc. For example, when job x is running on level 2, the actual amount of the job's required CPU cycles is $C_x * L_x.level_2.C\_ratio$.

For the convenience of analysis, we abstract the various system resources into several concrete values, and then superimpose them into a single resource value 'Res' according to a reasonable weight. After that, we conclude the relationships between the accuracy of jobs and the resource requirements as three models that are shown in Fig. 1. The first is linearly increasing model; the second is deceleratingly increasing model; and the third is first acceleratingly and then deceleratingly increasing model. For example, the job type of data compression [10] belongs to the first model. The second fits in speech recognition [11] and the third fits in data mining [12].

Next, we discuss how to divide computing levels of a job according to the above three accuracy-resources models. Our optimization goal is to improve the performance cost of the job, that is, to reduce the system resources occupied by the job as much as possible without excessively reducing the accuracy of the job. We define an accuracy loss function:

$$LF = \frac{Acc_{(max)} - Acc_{(cur)}}{Res_{(max)} - Res_{(cur)}} \tag{5}$$

Acc_{max} means the maximum accuracy of the job, and Acc_{cur} is the accuracy of the job at the current computing level. Res_{max} is the system resource needed by the job at the accuracy Acc_{max} while Res_{cur} is the system resource occupied by the job at the precision Acc_{cur}. Obviously, LF is associated with the certain slope of a function. Our goal is to make the value of the function LF as small as possible, which means we should perform the division of job computing levels via selecting points with small slope in the curve. The analyses of three relationship models are below.

Linear-Increasing Model. The accuracy of a job improves proportionally with the increase of system resources it acquires. In this case, the slope of any point of the curve is the same. LF is constant. Therefore, for example, the computing level division of a job may be performed by selecting three points whose execution accuracy are 100%, 75%, 50% respectively. Levels can be decided according to the specifications of different jobs.

Deceleratingly Increasing Model. The accuracy of the job improves with the increase of the system resources it obtains, but the speed of improvement is getting smaller and smaller. Therefore, in order to obtain a smaller loss function value LF, we can perform the computing level division of a job by selecting points with small slop in the second half of the curve. In this way, the resources occupied by jobs can be greatly reduced without losing the computing accuracy of jobs too much.

First Acceleratingly and Then Deceleratingly Increasing Model. The computing accuracy of the job improves with the increase of the system resources it obtains, but the speed of the increase grow first bigger and then smaller. Similar to the second model, we are also perform the computing level division of a job by selecting points in the flat part of the curve, but the optional range is less. Because if we want to further reduce the system resources needed by the job, there will be a great decrement of the job accuracy, making the loss function LF too large to satisfy quality of experience for users.

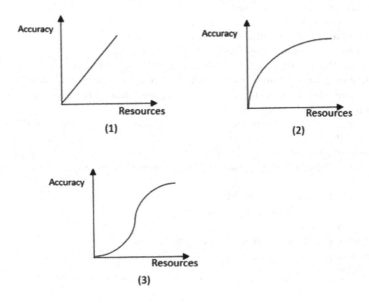

Fig. 1. Three relationship models of job accuracy and resources: (1) is linearly increasing model; (2) is deceleratingly increasing model; (3) is first acceleratingly and then deceleratingly increasing model

3.2 Algorithm

After dividing the execution of a job into several computing levels, the traditional scheduling algorithm will be inappropriate. Therefore, we propose a new job scheduling algorithm. This algorithm is based on greedy ideas, supplemented by load balancing of system resources. If the system resources meet the resource requirements of the arrived job, it will directly execute the job at its highest computing level. Otherwise, system uses the greedy strategy to select the optionally maximum computing level of the job that the available system resources can meet to execute. If multiple jobs arrive simultaneously, our algorithm would choose a certain job to perform preferentially according to the system resource load. According to [5], the types of jobs can be divided into CPU-intensive one and I/O-intensive one. From this perspective, we first judge what type of each job is, and then determine which system resource is relatively idle. For example, job A and job B arrive at the same time. job A is CPU-intensive, and job B is I/O-intensive. The CPU resource of the system is in a relatively idle state which means that job A is prior to be executed. In this way, a better tradeoff between quality of experience and resource utilization is achieved.

Algorithm 1. Job Scheduling Algorithm

1: **while** the job queue is not empty **do**
2:    Get a earliest arrived job from the queue
3:    **if** there are other simultaneously arrived jobs **then**
4:        Judge each type of the simultaneously arrived jobs
5:        Judge the relatively idle resource of the system currently
6:        **if** find a job that matches the complementary resource type **then**
7:            Run the job at the highest computing level that system resources can afford
8:        **else** {not find matched job}
9:            randomly run one of the simultaneously arrived jobs with greedy strategy
10:       **end if**
11:   **else** {no other simultaneous jobs}
12:       Run the job at the highest level that system resources can afford
13:   **end if**
14:   **if** succeed in running a job **then**
15:       Remove the job from the job queue
16:   **else** {fail to run a job}
17:       wait for system resource to be released
18:   **end if**
19: **end while**

The method to judge which one is the relatively idle resource of the system is to calculate the idle ratio of each resource. For example, if CPU idle ratio is larger than I/O idle ratio, CPU is the relatively idle resource while on the contrary, I/O is. The calculation formulas are below.

$$\text{CPU idle ratio} = 1 - \frac{the\ amount\ of\ CPU\ in\ use}{full\ amount\ of\ cpu}$$
$$\text{I/O idle ratio} = 1 - \frac{the\ amount\ of\ I/O\ in\ use}{full\ amount\ of\ I/O}$$

4   Simulation and Analysis

In this section, we conduct simulations over a mixed job stream which includes gradable and non-gradable jobs. Non-gradable jobs can be seen as gradable jobs with only one computing level, so that system can use our proposed algorithm to schedule jobs in two types. We measure the performance of our proposed adaptable job execution model using average job response time, average job accuracy and average system utilization.

4.1   Experiment Setup

We perform our simulations on a computer with i5-4570@3.2Ghz CPU and 16GB RAM. The operating system is Ubuntu 16.04. We use C++ as the programming language and MYSQL5.7 as the database.

In terms of datasets, based on the characteristics of the Internet of Things and edge computing, we mainly emphasize computationally intensive jobs and high-frequency user requests, making the system in a state of heavy load during a certain period of time. And in this case, we evaluate the performance of our adaptable job execution model compared with the traditional scheduling method.

We take scale-invariant feature transform (SIFT) of images as an example to specify the demanded resource of a job. SIFT is an algorithm in computer vision to detect and describe local features in images [13]. We specify its amount of computation needed as the number of CPU cycles. SIFS has a similar computation demand with face recognition application in [14] which needs 1 gigacycles. Other jobs of the job stream for the simulation will be set up with similar resource requirements, but with different computing levels.

Each job is also associated with a data size, which indicates the size of program states being sent to the edge cloud. Each workload size is generated from a probabilistic distribution.

According to the three kinds of relationship model that we present in Sect. 3, we set the proportion of gradable jobs of the proposed relationship models as 1:1:1 in the gradable job request sequence. As for the non-gradable jobs (those with only single computing level), their proportion is changeable. In the whole job request sequence, the proportion of gradable jobs and non-gradable jobs varies from 1:4 to 1:1, so as to analyse the influence of the proportion of these two job types on the performance.

4.2   Result Analysis

First of all, we give an introduction to Apdex. Apdex stands for Application Performance Index [15], which is an industry standard and is used to the evaluation of application performance by the Apdex Alliance. From the perspective of users, the Apdex standard translates the application response time into a user quantifiable satisfaction rating for application performance ranging from 0–1.

Apdex defines the optimal threshold for application response time as T, and defines three different performances based on the application response time:

Satisfied: The application response time is lower than or equal to T (T is determined by the performance appraisers according to the expected performance requirements). For example, if T is 1.5 s, a response result as 1 s can be considered as satisfied.

Tolerating: The application response time is greater than T, but it is less than or equal to 4T. Assuming the application sets a T value of 1s, 4 * 1 = 4 s is an extremely high tolerance for the application response time.

Frustrated: The application response time is greater than 4T.

The apdex formula is:

$$Apdex_t = \frac{SatisfiedCount + \frac{ToleratingCount}{2}}{TotalSamples} \qquad (6)$$

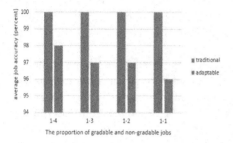 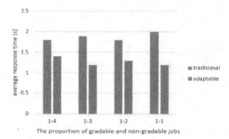

Fig. 2. When all jobs are done, here are the average accuracy of jobs under traditional and adaptable ways with different job proportions

Fig. 3. When all jobs are done, here are the average response time of jobs under traditional and adaptable ways with different job proportions

In the first case, without any limitation, we wait for the system to complete all user requests for a period of time. The results are shown in Figs. 2 and 3. In this case, the average accuracy of the jobs with the traditional scheduling method is 100% surely. Due to the adaptable computing levels, the job accuracy that uses our proposed method has decreased by an average of 3%, but the average response time per job has decreased by 32%. Because the emerging applications are mostly delay-sensitive, the Apdex threshold time T is extremely small. Consequently, according to Apdex formula, users will be more satisfied with the application experience under our scheduling model.

The main motivation of our design is to deal with massive user requests in the era of Internet of things and edge computing. Consequently, in the second case, the system is set to be in a long period of heavy load. Multiple jobs may reach the edge servers simultaneously and subsequent jobs will follow the previous jobs soon. As seen from the Fig. 4, our proposed scheduling method improves the utilization of various resources of the system, respectively, 17% for CPU, 10% for RAM, and 4% for I/O. And we can see that, from Figs. 5 and 6, the job response time was reduced by an average of 28%, and the job accuracy was increased by an average of 24% (the accuracy of the arrived jobs that are still waiting to be run counts 0). With the increment of gradable jobs in the proportion of job stream, compared with the traditional scheduling method, our scheduling method improve the system resource utilization and the average job accuracy much better.

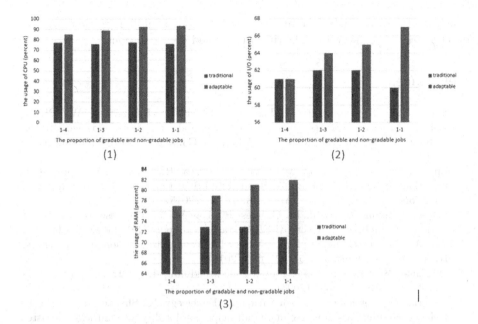

Fig. 4. System resource utilization under heavy load with different job proportions: (1) for CPU, (2) for I/O, (3) for RAM

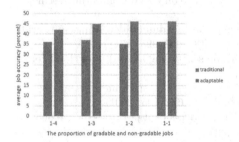

Fig. 5. When the edge servers are in a state of heavy load, here are the average accuracy of jobs under traditional and adaptable ways with different job proportions

Fig. 6. When the edge servers are in a state of heavy load, here are the average response time of jobs under traditional and adaptable ways with different job proportions

5   Conclusion

In this paper, we propose a job execution model with adaptable computing levels for edge servers to process the massive job requests efficiently and improve system resource utilization. The advantage of this adaptable model over traditional job scheduling method is demonstrated through formal analysis. Based on the proposed model, we further develop a job scheduling algorithm to choose which job to run and which computing level the job should be executed at. The effectiveness of the proposed algorithm is verified by simulations.

References

1. Soyata, T., Muraleedharan, R., Funai, C., Kwon, M., Heinzelman, W.: Cloud-vision: real-time face recognition using a mobile cloudlet-cloud acceleration architecture. In: International Symposium on Computers and Communications (2012)
2. Liu, J., Ahmed, E., Shiraz, M., Gani, A., Buyya, R., Qureshi, A.: Application partitioning algorithms in mobile cloud computing: taxonomy, review and future directions. J. Netw. Comput. Appl. **48**, 99–117 (2015)
3. Satyanarayanan, M., Bahl, P., Caceres, R., Davies, N.: The case for VM-based cloudlets in mobile computing. IEEE Pervasive Comput. **8**(4), 14–23 (2011)
4. Shi, W., Cao, J., Zhang, Q., Li, Y., Xu, L.: Edge computing: vision and challenges. IEEE Internet Things J. **3**(5), 637–646 (2016)
5. Wiseman, Y., Feitelson, D.G.: Paired gang scheduling. IEEE Trans. Parallel Distrib. Syst. **14**(6), 581–592 (2003)
6. Zaharia, M., Borthakur, D., Sen Sarma, J., Elmeleegy, K., Shenker, S., Stoica, I.: Delay scheduling: a simple technique for achieving locality and fairness in cluster scheduling. In: European Conference on Computer Systems, pp 265–278 (2010)
7. Lee, G., Chun, B., Katz, H.: Heterogeneity-aware resource allocation and scheduling in the cloud. In: IEEE International Conference on Cloud Computing Technology and Science, p. 4 (2011)
8. Lee, Y.H., Leu, S., Chang, R.S.: Improving job scheduling algorithms in a grid environment. Future Gener. Comput. Syst. **27**(8), 991–998 (2011)
9. Li, J., Feng, L., Fang, S.: An greedy-based job scheduling algorithm in cloud computing. J. Softw. **9**(4), 921–925 (2014)
10. Grgic, S., Grgic, M., Zovko-Cihlar, B.: Performance analysis of image compression using wavelets. IEEE Trans. Ind. Electron. **48**(3), 682–695 (2001)
11. Dahl, G.E., Yu, D., Deng, L., Acero, A.: Context-dependent pre-trained deep neural networks for large-vocabulary speech recognition. IEEE Trans. Audio Speech Lang. Process. **20**(1), 30–42 (2012)
12. Smith: Principles of data mining. Artif. Intell. Med. **26**(1), 175–178 (2002)
13. Lowe, D.: Object recognition from local scale-invariant features. In: International Conference on Computer Vision (1999)
14. Chen, X.: Decentralized computation offloading game for mobile cloud computing. IEEE Trans. Parallel Distrib. Syst. **26**, 974–983 (2014)
15. Application Performance Index. http://www.apdex.org/

A Clustering Algorithm of High-Dimensional Data Based on Sequential Psim Matrix and Differential Truncation

Gongming Wang[1(⊠)], Wenfa Li[2], and Weizhi Xu[3]

[1] Institute of Biophysics, Chinese Academy of Sciences,
No. 15 Datun Road, Beijing, China
gongmingwang@126.com
[2] College of Information Technology, Beijing Union University,
No. 97 Beisihuan East Road, Beijing, China
liwenfa@buu.edu.cn
[3] School of Information Science and Engineering, Shandong Normal University,
No. 88 East Wenhua Road, Jinan, China
xuweizhi@sdnu.edu.cn

Abstract. For high-dimensional data, the failure in distance calculation and the inefficient index tree that are respectively derived from equidistance and redundant attribute, have affected the performance of clustering algorithm seriously. To solve these problems, this paper introduces a clustering algorithm of high-dimensional data based on sequential Psim matrix and differential truncation. Firstly, the similarity of high-dimensional data is calculated with Psim function, which avoids the equidistance. Secondly, the data is organized with sequential Psim matrix, which improves the indexing performance. Thirdly, the initial clusters are produced with differential truncation. Finally, the K-Medoids algorithm is used to refine cluster. This algorithm was compared with K-Medoids and spectral clustering algorithms in two types of datasets. The experiment result indicates that our proposed algorithm reaches high value of Macro-F1 and Micro-F1 at the small number of iterations.

Keywords: High-dimensional data · Clustering · Psim · Differential truncation
Heuristic search · K-Medoids · Spectral clustering

1 Introduction

Clustering has a wide range of applications in biology, statistics, machine learning, and other fields [1]. In recent years, the dimensionality of clustered data has reached dozens, hundreds or even thousands. Generally speaking, the data whose dimensionality is more than 20 belongs to high-dimensional data [2]. The characteristics [3] of equidistance and redundant attribute has affected the clustering performance seriously. Therefore, high-dimensional data clustering is difficult but useful, and was rated as one of the top ten challenging problems in the area of data mining [4].

There are three kinds of clustering algorithms for high-dimensional data: attribute reduction [5], subspace clustering [6], co-clustering [7]. The first method reduces data

© Springer Nature Switzerland AG 2018
J. Vaidya and J. Li (Eds.): ICA3PP 2018, LNCS 11335, pp. 297–307, 2018.
https://doi.org/10.1007/978-3-030-05054-2_23

dimensionality with attribute conversion or reduction, and then carries out clustering. The effect of this method is heavily dependent on the degree of dimension reduction. The second strategy is dividing the original space into several different subspaces, and searching for cluster in subspace. When the dimensionality is high and the accuracy requirement is rigorous, the number of subspaces would increase quickly. Thus, searching cluster in the subspace becomes a bottleneck and may lead to failure [8]. The third one implements clustering iteratively in view of the content and feature. The clustering result is updated according to the semantic relation between the characteristic and theme, in order to realize the balance between attribute and data clustering. This method has two stages, resulting in a high time complexity. In addition to the above three methods, the clustering algorithms of high-dimensional data include parallel clustering [9], hierarchical clustering [10], and knowledge-driven clustering [11], etc. However, these methods have the similar problems.

In essence, the equidistance and redundant attribute are the fundamental factors affecting the clustering performance of high-dimensional data. The equidistance leads to the distance between any two points in a high-dimensional space is approximate equal, causing the failure of clustering algorithm based on distance. The redundant attribute increases the dimensionality of high-dimensional data and the complexity of index structure, whereas decreasing the efficiency of building and retrieving the index structure.

It is reported that some dimensional component of high-dimensional data are non-related noise that hide the real distance, resulting in equidistance. The *Psim* function can determine and eliminate these noise [12], which is very useful for the similarity calculation in the high-dimensional space. In addition, the sequential *Psim* matrix can save the similarity order between the high-dimensional data and not be affected by the dimensionality, which is the better data organization strategy than the common-used index tree. More importantly, the initial cluster can be extracted from our proposed sequential *Psim* matrix with the differential truncation.

To solve the clustering problem derived from equidistance and redundant attribute, an efficient clustering algorithm is proposed by integrating with the *Psim* matrix and differential truncation. In the first, the *Psim* values between all points in the high-dimensional space, and corresponding location numbers are stored into the *Psim* matrix. After that, a sequential *Psim* matrix is generated by sorting the elements in each row of the *Psim* matrix. Then, the initial clusters are produced with the differential truncation. Finally, the initial clusters are iteratively refined with the K-Medoids algorithm until all the cluster medoids are stable.

2 Related Work

2.1 Psim Matrix

The traditional similarity measurement method (e.g., Pearson coefficient [13], Jaccard coefficient [13] and Euclidean distance) failures in the high-dimensional space. To solve this problem, the *Hsim* function [14] was proposed by Fengzhao Yang, but the relative difference and noise distribution were not considered. The proposed *Gsim* function [15] is analyzing the relative difference of properties in different dimensions, but the weight discrepancy is ignored. The *Close* function [16] can reduce the influence from some dimensions with the larger variance. However, the relative difference was not considered and it would be affected by noise. The *Esim* [17] function was designed by improving *Hsim* and *Close* functions and considering the influence of property on similarity. In every dimension, the *Esim* component is positive correlation to the value in this dimension. All the dimensions are divided into two parts: normal dimension and noisy dimension. In the noisy dimension, the noise occupies the main ingredient. When it is similar and larger than the one in the normal dimension, the *Esim* will be invalid. The secondary measurement method [18] was used to calculate similarity by considering the property distribution, space distance, etc. But the noise distribution and weight have not been taken into account. In addition, the formula is complicated and calculation is very slow. In the high-dimensional space, Lihua Yi has found [12] the difference in the noisy dimension was larger, no matter how similar data was. This difference occupied a large portion of similarity calculation, and all the calculation results are similar. Therefore, the proposed *Psim* function [12] is used to diminish the influence of noise in all dimensions. The experimental results indicate that this method is suitable for a variety of data.

When using the *Psim* function to measure similarity, the data component in every dimension must be sorted and the value range is divided into several intervals. The similarity between X and Y in the j-th dimension is added to the *Psim* function, if and only if their data components are in the same interval.

In an n-dimensional space, the *Psim* value between X and Y is as follows.

$$Psim(X, Y) = \sum_{j \in Ds(X,Y)} \left(1 - \frac{|X_j - Y_j|}{l_j - u_j} \right) \cdot \frac{|Ds(X,Y)|}{n} \tag{1}$$

where X_j and Y_j are data components of X and Y in the j-th dimension. $Ds(X, Y)$ is a subscript set of X_j and Y_j that are in the same interval $[u_j, l_j]$, and $|Ds(X, Y)|$ is the number of elements in $Ds(X, Y)$. The above is the outline of the *Psim* function, and the detailed introduction can be found in reference [12].

How to organize data is an important issue of the clustering algorithm. In the traditional method, the data is separated with the index tree and mapped onto the index tree node according to its location. The commonly-used index tree includes R tree [5], cR tree [19], VP tree [20], M tree [21], SA tree [22], etc. In essence, the partition of data space is the foundation of building index tree, but its complexity is increasing with the raise of dimensionality. Thus, it is difficult to build the index tree for high-dimensional data. In addition, the retrieval efficiency of index tree falls sharply with the increase of dimensionality [23]. The retrieval function works effectively when the dimensionality is less than 16. But it weakens quickly when the dimensionality is greater than 16, even downs to the level of the linear search. A sequential *Psim* matrix is used to solve this problem. Firstly, all the *Psim* values between points $S_1, S_2, \cdots, S_M$ are calculated to build the *Psim* matrix *PsimMat*. The size of *PsimMat* is $M \times M$, and *PsimMat*(i, t) is composed of three properties: subscript i, t, and $Psim(S_i, S_t)$. Secondly, the sequential *Psim* matrix *SortPsimMat* is produced by sorting elements in every row of *PsimMat* in the descending order of *Psim* value. The elements in the i-th row of *SortPsimMat* represent the similarities between S_i and other points. It can be seen that the sequential *Psim* matrix is not affected by dimensionality and can represent the similarity distribution of all points.

2.2   Differential Truncation

The elements in every row of *SortPsimMat* are regarded as a sequence A, whose length is M. The sequential *Psim* differential matrix *DeltaPsimMat* is generated with the differential operation the sequence A. The size of *DeltaPsimMat* is $M \times (M - 1)$. The elements in the i-th row of *SortPsimMat* represent the similarities between S_i and other points. From left to right, several points corresponding to the frontier elements in this row would construct the cluster centered with S_i, because the similarity between elements inside the cluster is higher than the one outside. Thus, the similarity difference between elements inside the cluster is less than that of the other one. Assuming the cluster centered with S_i has p_i elements, the left $p_i - 1$ elements in the i-th row of *DeltaPsimMat* are less than the differential threshold ΔA_{max}. Thus, the reasonable ΔA_{max} is set up and all the elements that less than ΔA_{max} in the i-th row of *DeltaPsimMat* are found to construct a cluster centered with S_i.

3   Clustering Algorithm

3.1   Framework of Clustering Algorithm

The proposed clustering algorithm has three steps as shown in Fig. 1. Firstly, the sequential *Psim* matrix is built to represent the similarity levels between points in set S. Secondly, the initial cluster is generated by integrating with differential truncation and heuristic search. Finally, the expected cluster is produced by clustering based on K-Medoids.

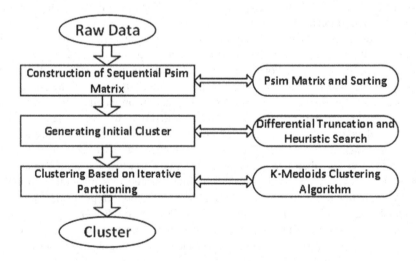

Fig. 1. Framework of proposed clustering algorithm.

3.2   Procedure of Clustering Algorithm

3.2.1   Construction of Sequential Psim Matrix

The *Psim* values between all points in set S are calculated with formula 1, and are saved into the *Psim* matrix *PsimMat*. After that, the elements in every row of *PsimMat* are sorted with quicksort to produce the sequential *Psim* matrix *SortPsimMat*

The point in set S is usually deleted, added or updated, and *SortPsimMat* is changed accordingly as follows.

(1) Adding operation

Assuming S_{M+1} would be added, the operation is as follows.

Step 1: The *Psim* values between S_{M+1} and $S_1, S_2, \cdots, S_M$ are calculated to construct the elements of *SortPsimMat*. Then, they are inserted into the corresponding position of every row.

Step 2: The *Psim* values between S_{M+1} and $S_1, S_2, \cdots, S_{M+1}$ are calculated and sorted in descending order. Then, the corresponding elements of *SortPsimMat* are generated and taken as the $M+1$ th row of this matrix.

(2) Deleting operation

Assuming S_d would be deleted, where $1 \leq d \leq M$, the operation is as follows.

Step 1: The elements in d th row of *SortPsimMat* are deleted.

Step 2: The elements related to S_d in reminder $M - 1$ rows are deleted.

(3) Updating operation

Assuming S_b would be updated, where $1 \leq b \leq M$, the operation is as follows.

Step 1: The *Psim* values between S_b and $S_1, S_2, \cdots, S_M$ are calculated, and the corresponding elements of *SortPsimMat* are replaced.

Step 2: The elements in b th row are sorted in descending order.

Step 3: The positions of elements corresponding to S_b in other $M - 1$ rows are adjusted according to the *Psim* value.

3.2.2   Generating Initial Cluster

Firstly, the Laplacian matrix L is generated by virtue of *PsimMat*, and the distribution of its eigenvalue is used to determine the number of expected clusters [24]. Secondly, the differential threshold $\Delta A_{\max}$ is initialized. Thirdly, let $C_{\max}$ is the maximal time of searching cluster set. The upper bound of $C_{\max}$ is the combinatorial number C_M^K, where K is the number of clusters. It can be seen that searching C_M^K times is time-consuming, because the magnitude of C_M^K is $M!$. In addition, the K expected clusters maybe not found by searching C_M^K times. Thus, the $C_{\max}$ is set as $C_{\max} = M$ and heuristic search is implemented. Finally, the collision list of clusters TBL_C is set as null, and $i = 1$. Then, the initial cluster can be generated with the following steps.

Step 1: The elements in the i th row of *DeltaPsimMat* are visited from left to right until p_i th element is greater than the differential threshold $\Delta A_{\max}$ for the first time.

Step 2: The points corresponding to the left $p_i - 1$ elements in the i th row of *SortPsimMat* are used to construct the cluster C_T^i that is centered with S_i.

Step 3: If $i < M$, then $i = i + 1$ and go to Step 1. Otherwise, then $c = 1$.

Step 4: The K clusters $C_T^{i1}, C_T^{i1}, \cdots, C_T^{iK}$ are selected from M clusters $C_T^1, C_T^2, \cdots,$ C_T^M, make sure that the set composed of K centers of selected cluster are not in TBL_C.

Step 5: If the union of the K clusters is equal to set S, then the set $C_i = \{C_i^0, C_i^1, \cdots, C_i^K\}$ is taken as the initial cluster set, where $C_i^v = C_T^{iv}$. Otherwise, the set C_I is added into TBL_C and go to Step 5.

Step 6: If $c \geq C_{\max}$, then $i = 1$, increase $\Delta A_{\max}$, clear TBL_C and go to Step 1. Otherwise, $c = c + 1$ and go to Step 4.

3.2.3 Clustering Based on Iterative Partitioning

The initial cluster has the basic characteristic of the final result. For further improvement, the clustering based on K-Medoids [25] is implemented as follows.

Step 1: The iterated times is $q = 0$, and the initial cluster set is $C^0 = \{C_1^0, C_2^0, \cdots, C_K^0\}$.

Step 2: The K medoids of clusters in $C^0 = \{C_1^0, C_2^0, \cdots, C_K^0\}$ are calculated to construct the point set $V^0 = \{V_1^0, V_2^0, \cdots, V_K^0\}$.

Step 3: The cluster set after iterating q times is $C^{q+1} = \{C_1^{q+1}, C_2^{q+1}, \cdots, C_K^{q+1}\}$. There is only one element V_w^q in the initial cluster C_w^{q+1}, where $1 \leq w \leq K$.

Step 4: For any element in S, the $Psim$ values between it and all points in $V^q = \{V_1^q, V_2^q, \cdots, V_K^q\}$ are calculated, and it is added into the cluster with highest $Psim$ value in C^{q+1}.

Step 5: The average $Psim$ value between elements in cluster of C^q and corresponding point in V^q is calculated and expressed as E_q.

Step 6: The K medoids of clusters in $C^{q+1} = \{C_1^{q+1}, C_2^{q+1}, \cdots, C_K^{q+1}\}$ are calculated to construct the point set $V^{q+1} = \{V_1^{q+1}, V_2^{q+1}, \cdots, V_K^{q+1}\}$. And the average $Psim$ value between elements in cluster of C^{q+1} and corresponding point in V^{q+1} is calculated and expressed as E_q.

Step 7: If $\left| E_q - E_q^* \right| / M \leq \varepsilon$, then the refinement is stopped. Otherwise, $q = q + 1$, and go to Step 3.

3.3 Convergence Analysis

This proposed clustering algorithm has three steps and the corresponding convergence analysis is as follows.

(1) Construction of Sequential Psim Matrix
   The $Psim$ matrix $PsimMat$ is produced by running formula 1 $M \times M$ times. And the sequential $Psim$ matrix $SortPsimMat$ is generated by sorting elements in every

row of *PsimMat*. The above operation can be finished in the limited time, so this step is converged.

(2) Generating Initial Cluster

Firstly, the number of expected clusters can be determined with spectral clustering in the limited time. Secondly, with the increase of the differential threshold ΔA_{max}, the number of elements in every cluster is increasing. Thus, the union $C_T^{i1} \bigcup C_T^{i1} \bigcup \cdots \bigcup C_T^{iK}$ is close to set S gradually. Thus, this step is converged.

(3) Clustering based on iterative partitioning

This step is worked based on K-Medoids clustering algorithm. From appendix 1, it can be seen that the K-Medoids clustering algorithm is converged. Thus, this step is also converged.

The above statements show the three steps can be finished in the limited time. Thus, the proposed clustering algorithm is converged.

4 Experiment

4.1 Overview

In the following experiment, the hardware includes AMD Athlon(tm) II X2-250 processor and Kingston 4G memory. And the software is WinXP operation system and MicroSoft Visual Studio 2008. Two high-dimensional data sets are downloaded from UCI database, which are CNAE-9 and ISOLET. In order to remove the invalid or missing data, the preprocessing is required.

After that, the number of clusters is determined with spectral clustering algorithm. Then, the two data sets are clustered ten times with our proposed clustering algorithm based on *Psim* matrix and differential truncation (PM-DT clustering algorithm), K-Medoids clustering algorithm [25], and spectral clustering algorithm [24]. In the process of each clustering, the iterations, Macro-F1 and Micro-F1 [26] are calculated. In addition, their average in ten clustering processes must be required. Finally, these algorithms are compared according to the above results.

4.2 Experimental Data

The two main characteristics of tested high-dimensional data are size and classification. A good clustering algorithm should be suitable for the data with the characteristics at different levels. To validate our proposed clustering algorithm fully, the two different data sets are downloaded from UCI database as follows.

1. CNAE-9. This is the frequency of feature words in 1080 documents that are categorized into 9 categories. Each record is the statistical result of one document, which is expressed as a vector whose length is 856. The size, dimension, and classification of this data set are normal, large and normal respectively. In addition, this data set is highly sparse (99.22% of the matrix is filled with zeros).

2. ISOLET. This is the audio data during 150 subjects spoke the name of each letter of the alphabet twice, which has 7797 records and is classified 26 types corresponding

to 26 alphabets. It is divided into training set (6238 records) and test set (1559 records). The training set is used to validate our proposed clustering algorithm. One record includes 617 attributes involved in spectral coefficients, contour features, sonorant features, pre-sonorant features, and so on. The size, dimension, and classification of this data set are all large.

4.3   Stability Analysis

First of all, the method to determine the number of clusters in Sect. 3.2.2 is applied to CNAE-9 and ISOLET. The results are 9 and 26 respectively, which is accord with the reality. After that, the two data sets are clustered ten times with PM-DT clustering algorithm, K-Medoids clustering algorithm [25], and spectral clustering algorithm [24]. The corresponding results are shown in Figs. 2, 3 and 4.

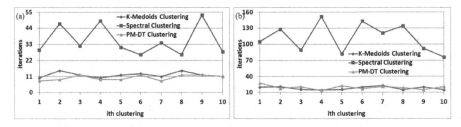

Fig. 2. Iterations of three algorithms running ten times. (a) The result of CNAE-9; (b) The result of ISOLET.

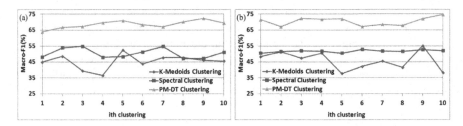

Fig. 3. Macro-F1 of three algorithms running ten times. (a) The result of CNAE-9; (b) The result of ISOLET.

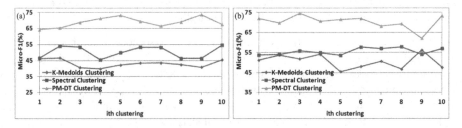

Fig. 4. Micro-F1 of three algorithms running ten times. (a) The result of CNAE-9; (b) The result of ISOLET.

It can be seen that the iterations of PM-DT clustering algorithm is less than the one of K-Medoids clustering algorithm and spectral clustering algorithm, which indicates that our proposed method can get the higher precise initial cluster and is converged more quickly. In most cases, the clustering accuracy (Macro-F1 and Micro-F1) and stability (variations of Macro-F1 and Micro-F1) are both PM-DT clustering algorithm > spectral clustering algorithm > K-Medoids clustering algorithm. In some cases, the clustering accuracies of K-Medoids and spectral clustering algorithms are less than 50%, which indicates clustering failure. But PM-DT clustering algorithm has no similar issue, which shows its validity for high-dimensional data.

4.4   Whole Performance Analysis

The experimental results are averaged and shown in Tables 1, 2 and 3.

Table 1. Average iterations of three algorithms on two data sets.

Data set	K-medoids clustering	Spectral clustering	PM-DT clustering
CNAE-9	12.1	35.5	10.2
ISOLET	18.1	112.2	19.7

Table 2. Average Macro-F1 of three algorithms on two data sets (unit %).

Data set	K-medoids clustering	Spectral clustering	PM-DT clustering
CNAE-9	45.2	50.425	68.645
ISOLET	45.718	51.736	70.508

Table 3. Average Micro-F1 of three algorithms on two data sets (unit %).

Data set	K-medoids clustering	Spectral clustering	PM-DT clustering
CNAE-9	43.127	50.335	68.925
ISOLET	50.561	55.562	70.348

The above results illustrates the better performance of PM-DT clustering algorithm than the one of K-Medoids and Spectral clustering algorithms. On the one hand, its iteration is small and convergence is fast. On the other hand, it has no failure case and Macro-F1/Micro-F1 of CNAE-9 and ISOLET are increased more than 18% and 20%. To sum up the above analysis, the failure in distance calculation, the inefficient index tree, and the overlap of cluster that are derived from the characteristics of high-dimensional data can be corrected with PM-DT clustering algorithm.

5   Conclusion

The high-dimensional data clustering is a challenging but useful issue in data mining. The proposed clustering algorithm based on *Psim* matrix, differential truncation and differential truncation focuses the problems of failure in distance calculation and inefficient index tree. Compared other clustering algorithms, its characteristics are as follows. In high-dimensional space, the sequential *Psim* matrix is used to calculate distance and organize data. The differential truncation are used to obtain the initial cluster. The experimental result indicates the performance of this algorithm is better than the one of K-Medoids and Spectral clustering algorithms. Several heuristic methods used in this algorithm have the potential to be improved. Thus, the future work includes the determination of more effective initial parameters, evaluation function and convergence criteria, in order to improve the accuracy of results.

Acknowledgments. This work is partly supported by the National Nature Science Foundation of China (No. 61502475, 61602285) and the Importation and Development of High-Caliber Talents Project of the Beijing Municipal Institutions (No. CIT & TCD201504039).

References

1. Han, J.W., Kamber, H.L., Pei, J.: Data Mining: Concepts and Techniques, 3rd edn. Morgan Kaufmann, San Francisco (2011)
2. Ericson, K.L., Pallickara, S.D.: On the performance of high dimensional data clustering and classification algorithms. Future Gener. Comput. Syst. **29**(4), 1024–1034 (2013)
3. Keogh, E., Mueen, A.: Curse of dimensionality. In: Encyclopedia of Machine Learning, pp. 257–258. Springer, Berlin (2010)
4. Yang, Q., Wu, X.D.: 10 Challenging problems in data mining research. Int. J. Inf. Technol. Decis. Making **5**(4), 597–604 (2006)
5. Berkhin, P.: A survey of clustering data mining techniques. In: Kogan, J., Nicholas, C., Teboulle, M. (eds.) Grouping Multidimensional Data, pp. 25–71. Springer, Heidelberg (2006). https://doi.org/10.1007/3-540-28349-8_2
6. Parsons, L., Haque, E.S., Liu, H.: Subspace clustering for high dimensional data: a review. ACM SIGKDD Explor. Newsl. **6**(1), 90–105 (2004)
7. Dhillon, I.S.: Co-clustering documents and words using bipartite spectral graph partitioning. In: 7th ACM SIGKDD International Conference on Knowledge Discovery and Data Mining, pp. 269–274. ACM Press, New York (2001)
8. Fu, Q., Li, Z.F.: The research of clustering algorithm based on CLIQUE. J. East China Jiaotong Univ. **23**(5), 79–82 (2006)
9. Feng, Z.H., Zhou, B., Shen, J.Y.: A parallel hierarchical clustering algorithm for PCs cluster system. Neurocomputing **70**, 809–818 (2007)
10. Du, Z., Lin, F.: A novel parallelization approach for hierarchical clustering. Parallel Comput. **31**, 523–527 (2005)
11. Wu, H.Y., Wang, W.T., Wen, J.H., He, G.H.: Research on clustering algorithm of high-dimensional dataset with input knowledge. Comput. Sci. **33**(1), 240–242 (2006)
12. Yi, L.H.: Research on clustering algorithm for high dimensional data. Master's thesis, Yan Shan University, Qinhuangdao Hebei, China (2011)
13. Tan, P.N., Steinbach, M., Kumar, V.: Introduction to Data Mining. Addison-Wesley Publishing Company, Boston (2005)
14. Yang, F.Z., Zhu, Y.Y.: An efficient method for similarity search on quantitative transaction data. J. Comput. Res. Dev. **41**(2), 361–368 (2004)

15. Huang, S.D., Chen, Q.M.: On clustering algorithm of high dimensional data based on similarity measurement. Comput. Appl. Softw. **26**(9), 102–105 (2009)
16. Shao, C.S., Lou, W., Yan, L.M.: Optimization of algorithm of similarity measurement in high-dimensional data. Comput. Technol. Dev. **21**(2), 1–4 (2011)
17. Wang, X.Y., Zhang, H.Y., Shen, L.Z., Chi, W.L.: Research on high dimensional clustering algorithm based on similarity measurement. Comput. Technol. Dev. **23**(5), 30–33 (2013)
18. Jia, X.Y.: A high dimensional data clustering algorithm based on twice similarity. J. Comput. Appl. **25**(B12), 176–177 (2005)
19. Brakatsoulas, S., Pfoser, D., Theodoridis, Y.: Revisiting R-tree construction principles. In: Manolopoulos, Y., Návrat, P. (eds.) ADBIS 2002. LNCS, vol. 2435, pp. 149–162. Springer, Heidelberg (2002). https://doi.org/10.1007/3-540-45710-0_13
20. Nielsen, F., Piro, P., Barlaud, M.: Bregman vantage point trees for efficient nearest Neighbor Queries. In: 10th IEEE International Conference on Multimedia and Expo, pp. 878–881. IEEE Computer Society, Birmingham (2009)
21. Kunze, M., Weske, M.: Metric trees for efficient similarity search in large process model repositories. Lect. Notes Bus. Inf. Process. **66**, 535–546 (2011)
22. Navarro, G.Z.: Searching in metric spaces by spatial approximation. VLDB J. **11**(1), 28–46 (2002)
23. Chen, J.B.: The Research and Application of Key Technologies in Knowledge Discovery of High-Dimensional Clustering. Publishing House of Electronics Industry, Beijing (2011)
24. Andrew, Y.N., Jordan, M.I., Weiss, Y.: On spectral clustering: analysis and algorithm. In: Advances in Neural Information Processing Systems, pp. 121–526. MIT Press, Cambridge (2002)
25. Raymond, T.N., Han, J.W.: Efficient and effective clustering methods for spatial data mining. In: 20th International Conference on Very Large Data Bases, pp. 144–155. IEEE Computer Society, Birmingham (1994)
26. Chen, L.F., Ye, Y.F., Jiang, Q.S.: A new centroid-based classifier for text categorization. In: 22nd IEEE International Conference on Advanced Information Networking and Applications, pp. 1217–1222. IEEE Computer Society, Birmingham (2008)

Enhanced Differential Evolution with Self-organizing Map for Numerical Optimization

Duanwei Wu, Yiqiao Cai$^{(\boxtimes)}$, Jing Li, and Wei Luo

College of Computer Science and Technology,
Huaqiao University, Xiamen, China
yiqiao00@163.com

Abstract. In Differential evolution (DE), the valuable information from the data generated during the evolutionary process has not yet fully exploited to guide the search. As a clustering algorithm based on neural network structure, Self-organizing map (SOM) method can effectively preserve the topological structure of the data in the high dimensional input space. By taking the advantage of SOM, this paper presents a SOM-based DE variant (DE-SOM) to utilize the neighborhood information extracted by the SOM method. In DE-SOM, the neighborhood relationships among the individuals are firstly extracted by the SOM method. Then, with the obtained neighborhood relationships, a self-adaptive neighborhood mechanism (SNM) is introduced to dynamically adjust the neighborhood size for selecting parents involved in the mutation process. The performance of DE-SOM has been evaluated on the benchmark functions from CEC2013, and the results show its effectiveness when compared with the original DE algorithms.

Keywords: Differential evolution · Self-organizing map
Self-adaptive neighborhood mechanism · Numerical optimization

1 Introduction

Differential evolution (DE), proposed by Storn and Price, is an efficient and simple evolutionary algorithm (EA) for global optimization, which is widely applied in science and engineering fields [1]. Compared with other EAs, DE has the advantages of simple structure, easy to use, fast convergence and strong robustness. However, in the original DE algorithms, most of the data generated during the evolutionary process are knocked out through the greedy selection operator. Thus, the information contained in these data will be neglected to guide the search, especially for the computationally expensive problems. As the previous research shows, fully mining and utilizing these history data can effectively enhance the performance of algorithm [2]. Therefore, how to effectively utilize the information generated in the evolutionary process is a promising direction to improve the performance of DE.

Clustering algorithm is an unsupervised learning method for grouping data to achieve higher similarity between data of the same group and lower similarity between data of different groups [3]. Due to the good feature in data mining and analysis,

J. Vaidya and J. Li (Eds.): ICA3PP 2018, LNCS 11335, pp. 308–318, 2018.
https://doi.org/10.1007/978-3-030-05054-2_24

clustering algorithm is suitable for extracting the population information from the data generated during the iteration process. Self-organizing map (SOM), developed by Kohonen, is a sheet-like artificial neural network [4]. As an unsupervised learning method, SOM firstly determines the best matching neurons and regulates the weights of neighboring neurons and ultimately constructs the weight network with data characteristics through continues iterative learning. By using SOM, the data from a high dimensional input space can be represented in a low dimensional space. Further, SOM can effectively preserve the topological structure of the data in the original input space [4].

By taking the above advantages of SOM, a SOM-based DE variant (DE-SOM) is proposed by introducing SOM into DE. The primary purpose of SOM in the proposed algorithm is to extract the neighborhood information to guide the search of DE. First, with SOM, the neighborhood relationships among the individuals are extracted. Then, a self-adaptive neighborhood mechanism (SNM) is designed to dynamically adjust the neighborhood size. After that, the vectors are selected from the neighbors of target individual that are defined by SOM for the mutation process.

To evaluate the effectiveness of the proposed method, the experimental study has been carried out on a suite of benchmark functions from the CEC2013 special session on real-parameter optimization [5]. Experimental results show the promising performance of DE-SOM.

The rest of this paper is organized as follows. Section 2 describes the background of DE and SOM. Section 3 describes the proposed DE-SOM in detail. In Sect. 4, the experimental results are shown and discussed. Finally, the final conclusions are drawn in Sect. 5.

2 Background

2.1 Differential Evolution (DE)

DE is a population-based stochastic searching algorithm for global numerical optimization problem [1]. In DE, the candidate solutions are expressed as a population composed of NP individuals. Each individual is denoted as $Xi, G = \left(x_{i,G}^1, x_{i,G}^2, \ldots, x_{i,G}^D \right)$, where i = 1, 2, ..., NP, NP is the population size, D is the dimension of the problem, and G is the number of the current generation. For Xi,G, the jth parameters can be initialized as follows: $x_{i,G}^j = L_j + \text{rand}(0, 1) \times (U_j - L_j)$, where rand(0,1) represents a uniformly distributed random number within the range [0, 1], and L_j and U_j represent the lower and upper bounds of the jth variable. After that, DE enters the evolutionary loop with three operators: mutation, crossover, and selection.

- Mutation: DE uses the mutation strategy to generate a mutant vector $V_{i,G}$ for each target individual $X_{i,G}$. Two commonly used mutation strategies are as follows:

$$\text{DE/rand/1:} \qquad V_{i,G} = X_{r1,G} + F \times (X_{r2,G} - X_{r3,G}) \qquad (1)$$

$$\text{DE/best/1:} \qquad V_{i,G} = X_{best,G} + F \times (X_{r1,G} - X_{r2,G}) \qquad (2)$$

where F is called the mutation scaling factor. The indices $r1$, $r2$, $r3$, $r4$, $r5$ represent the integers randomly selected from the range $[1, NP]$ and are not equal to index i. $X_{best,G}$ is the is the best-so-far individual at the Gth generation.

- Crossover: After mutation, the crossover operator is applied to pair of mutant vector and target vector to generate a trial vector $U_{i,G}$. The classical binomial crossover is defined as follows:

$$u_{i,G}^j = \begin{cases} v_{i,G}^j & \text{if } rand(0,1) \leq CR \text{ or } j = j_{rand} \\ v_{i,G}^j & \text{otherwise} \end{cases} \qquad (3)$$

where $CR \in [0,1]$ is called crossover rate, j_{rand} is a randomly chosen integer in the range $[1, D]$.

- Selection: Selection operator is used to select better individual from $U_{i,G}$ and $X_{i,G}$ entering the next generation based on their fitness values, which can be outlined as follows:

$$X_{i,G+1} = \begin{cases} U_{i,G} & \text{if } f(U_{i,G}) \leq f(X_{i,G}) \\ X_{i,G} & \text{otherwise} \end{cases} \qquad (4)$$

2.2   Self-organizing Map (SOM)

SOM is a typical clustering algorithm based on neural network. There are main two operations in SOM: selection of the best-matching cell and adaptation (updating) of the weight vectors [4].

The two-dimensional network structure of SOM is shown in Fig. 1. Suppose that S is a set of training points in the n-dimensional input space and the latent space is $(m-1)$-dimensional. That is, There are $D = D_1 \times \dots \times D_{m-1}$ neurons in the latent space. A coordinate $Z^u = (z_1^u, \dots, z_{m-1}^u)^T$, $z_i^u \in \{1, \dots, D_i\}$, $i = 1, \dots, m-1$ is pre-set for each neuron u ($u = 1, \dots, D$). In the input space, each neuron u has a weight vector $W^u = (w_1^u, \dots, w_n^u)^T$.

The purpose of SOM is to find the weight vector W^u of each neuron through the training data to recognize their features [4]. The training process of SOM is carried out as follows. At the beginning of training, each neuron in the latent space is assigned a random data point selected from S as the initial weight vector. The closest training data points to these weights are used for iteratively updating them. After updating the weight vector, SOM maps the input data to the neurons in the latent space according to

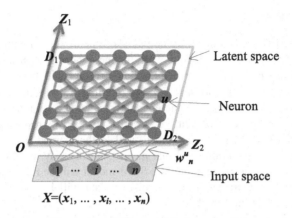

$$X=(x_1, \ldots , x_i, \ldots , x_n)$$

Fig. 1. An illustration of SOM with 2-dimensional latent space.

the similarity between the data and the neuron's weight vector. That is, similar data points are mapped to adjacent neurons. In this way, the topology of the input data is preserved in the neural network of latent space and thus the input data are clustered based on this structure.

3 DE-SOM

In DE-SOM, the SOM method is used to extract the neighborhood relationships among the individuals. With the neighborhood relationships, DE-SOM employs a self-adaptive neighborhood mechanism (SNM) to construct the mating pool for each individual to guide the mutation process.

3.1 Motivations

In the literature of DE, the clustering technology has been used in many variants to improve its performance. In these works, the role of clustering technology can be roughly classified into the following categories: dividing population to maintain diversity (e.g., [6, 7]), partitioning population to assign different mutation strategies (e.g., [8, 9]), and extracting population information for crossover (e.g., [10–12]). However, in most of these variants, the clustering technology is only used for population division based on the Euclidean distance metric. By this way, the local topological properties of the individuals cannot be preserved in the high dimensional search space during the evolutionary process. On the other hand, the neighborhood information of individuals in the current population cannot be effectively and fully extracted to guide the search. Based on these considerations, SOM, as an unsupervised learning method, is introduced into DE to extract the neighborhood information of individuals.

3.2 SOM in DE-SOM

In DE-SOM, SOM is used to map the individuals to neurons in the network and then extract the neighborhood information with the neighboring neurons. That is, the individuals that are mapped to the neighboring neurons will be recognized as the neighbors. Different from the original SOM algorithm, the training data in the SOM used in the proposed algorithm are incrementally generated during the evolutionary process. Further, when the new data are included, instead of restarting the learning process, DE-SOM will directly use them to update the learned neighborhood information in the previous generation, as that in [16]. In this way, on the one hand, the computational cost caused by retaining the SOM model will be reduced. On the other hand, the information extracted from the history data will be reused with the new generated data to guide the search.

3.3 Self-adaptive Neighborhood Mechanism (SNM)

In DE-SOM, a self-adaptive neighborhood mechanism (SNM) is proposed to dynamically adjust the neighborhood size. Different evolutionary stages require different sizes of neighborhood. Based on the learned weight vectors with SOM, SNM can adaptively choose appropriate neighborhood sizes during the evolutionary process to construct different neighborhood for each individual. In this paper, we use two types of neighborhood sizes, large neighborhood (r_{max}) and small neighborhood (r_{min}). Then, the probability of selection (φ) is introduced to decide which neighborhood size is used. If the value randomly generated is smaller than φ, the small neighborhood size will be used to define the neighborhood size (r) of population. Otherwise, the large neighborhood is used. After that, the neuron linked with each individual Xi in the input space will locate the r closest neighboring neurons in the SOM structure. After that, the r individuals linked with the r neighboring neurons are identified as the neighbors of Xi. Further, if the trial vector is better than the target vector, the selection probability of the corresponding type of neighborhood size will be raised by Δ. Otherwise, it will be reduced by Δ.

3.4 The Framework of DE-SOM

The framework of DE-SOM is shown in Algorithm 1, where G is the maximum number of iterations, rand(0, 1) is a random decimal selected from 0 to 1, φ is the rate of choosing a neighborhood size, Δ is used to adjust φ, r_{min} is the small neighborhood size and r_{max} is the large one. From Algorithm 1, the neighbors of each individual are defined based on the learned structure from the SOM method. Further, the neighborhood size is adaptively adjusted during the evolutionary process with SNM, which can effectively reflect the neighborhood relationship between individuals at different stages.

Algorithm 1. SOM-based DE with DE/rand/1 (DE-SOM/rand/1)

1: Random initialization population $P= \{x^1, ..., x^N\}$. Initialize the training set $S=$ $\{T^1,..., T^N\}=P$, and the neuron weight vectors $\{w^1, ... , w^N\}=P$. Setting the initial value of the φ, Δ, r_{min} and r_{max}.

2: **For** t=1, ..., G **do**

3:     **For each** $T^i \in S$, $i=1$, ..., $|S|$ **do** /**The training process of SOM**/

4:         Update training parameters:

5:         $$\sigma = \sigma_0 \times \left(1 - \frac{(t-1)N+s}{GN}\right), \tau = \tau_0 \times \left(1 - \frac{(t-1)N+s}{GN}\right).$$

6:         Find the nearest neuron to T^i:

7:         $$u' = \arg\min_{1 \le u \le N} \left\| T^i - W^u \right\|_2$$

8:         Decide the neurons in the neighborhood of u':

9:         $$U = \left\{ u \mid 1 \le u \le N \wedge \left\| z^u - z^{u'} \right\|_2 < \sigma \right\}$$

10:        Update the weight vectors of all the neighboring neurons:

11:        $$w^u = w^u + \tau \times \exp\left(- \left\| z^u - z^{u'} \right\|_2 \right)\left(x - w^u\right) \quad u \in \mu.$$

12:     **End For**

13:     **If** $S \ne \emptyset$ **then**

14:         Empty training set S

15:     **End If**

16:     **For each** individual $X^i \in P$ **do**

17:         Map the neuron u to X^i, where u has not yet mapped to any individuals and $u = \arg\min_{1 \le u \le N} \left\| X^i - W^u \right\|_2$

18:     **End For**

19:     **If** $rand(0,1) < \varphi$ **then**/**Self-adaptive neighborhood mechanism (SNM)**/

20:         $r=r_{min}$

21:     **Else**

            $r=r_{max}$

22:     **End if**

23:     **For each** individual $X^i \in P$ **do**

24:         Locate the r closest neurons in the latent space to the neuron linked with X_i

25:         Set the r individuals linked with the r neurons as the neighborhood of X_i

26:         Select Xr_1, Xr_2, Xr_3 from the neighborhood of X_i

27:         Use Equation (1) to generate a mutant vector V_i

28:         Use Equation (3) to generate a trail vector U_i

29:         **If** U_i is better than X_i **then**

30:             Replace X_i with U_i

31:             Add U_i into the training set S

32:         **End if**

33:     **End For**

34:     **If** $S = \emptyset$ **then**

35:         **If** $r=r_{min}$ and $\varphi \ge \Delta$ **then**

36:        $\varphi = \varphi - \Delta$
37:    **Else**
38:        **If** $\varphi < 1$ **then**
39:            $\varphi = \varphi + \Delta$
40:        **End if**
41:    **End if**
42: **Else**
43:    **If** $r = r_{min}$ **and** $\varphi < 1$ **then**
44:        $\varphi = \varphi + \Delta$
45:    **Else**
46:        **If** $\varphi \geq \Delta$ **then**
47:            $\varphi = \varphi - \Delta$
48:        **End if**
49:    **End if**
50: **End if**
51: **End For**

4 Empirical Studies

To evaluate the performance of DE-SOM, the experimental study is carried out on a suite of benchmark functions from the CEC2013 special session on real-parameter optimization [5]. The CEC13 benchmark functions set consists of 28 test functions, which includes the unimodal function F1 to F5, the basic multimodal function F6 to F20, and the composition function F21 to F28. More details of them can be found in [5]. For a fair comparison, the same random initial population is used to evaluate the performance of different algorithms. The parameters of the DE algorithms studied in this paper are set as Table 1 unless a change is mentioned.

Table 1. Parameters setting for DE and SOM.

Parameters	Values
Dimension of each functions (D)	30 and 50
External archive size	100
Independent number of runs	30
Maximum number of evaluations	$10^4 \times D$
The structure of SOM	2-dimensional structure with 10×10
Initial learning rate (τ)	0.9
The small neighborhood size (r_{min})	5
The large neighborhood size (r_{max})	100
Initial neighborhood choosing rate (φ)	0.5
Adjustment value of the choosing rate (Δ)	0.25

To show the significant differences among the competitors, the non-parametric statistical tests are carried out by the KEEL software [13]. The results of the single-problem analysis by the Wilcoxon test at $\alpha = 0.05$ are shown in the tables as "+/=/–", which means that DE-SOM wins, ties and loses on the number of functions when compared with its corresponding competitor [14, 15]. The R+ and R– in the multiple-problem analysis by the Wilcoxon test mean the sum of ranks that DE-SOM performs significantly better than and worse than its competitor overall, respectively.

4.1   Effect on the Original DE Algorithms

To test its effectiveness of DE-SOM on the original DE algorithm, the proposed algorithm is applied to six mutation strategies, i.e., DE/rand/1, DE/rand/2, DE/best/1, DE/best/2, DE/current-to-best/1 and DE/rand-to-best/1. The comparison results for the CEC2013 functions at 30D and 50D are shown in Tables 2 and 3.

Table 2. Results of the single- and multi-problem Wilcoxon's test for DE-SOM versus the original DE algorithms for the CEC2013 functions at 30D.

DE-SOM vs	+/=/–	R+	R–	p-value	$\alpha = 0.05$	$\alpha = 0.1$
DE/rand/1	10/18/0	283.0	95.0	0.023	Yes	Yes
DE/rand/2	20/8/0	355.0	230.0	0.000	yes	Yes
DE/best/1	14/12/2	328.0	78.0	0.004	Yes	Yes
DE/best/2	10/17/1	307.5	98.5	0.016	Yes	Yes
DE/current-to-best/1	7/21/0	270.0	136.0	0.123	No	No
DE/rand-to-best/1	9/19/0	388.0	18.0	0.000	Yes	Yes

Table 3. Results of the single- and multi-problem Wilcoxon's test for DE-SOM versus the original DE algorithms for the CEC2013 functions at 50D.

DE-SOM vs	+/=/–	R+	R–	p-value	$\alpha = 0.05$	$\alpha = 0.1$
DE/rand/1	10/18/0	360.0	46.0	0.000	Yes	Yes
DE/rand/2	20/8/0	351.5	26.5	0.000	Yes	Yes
DE/best/1	14/13/1	325.0	53.0	0.001	Yes	Yes
DE/best/2	14/13/1	333.5	72.5	0.002	Yes	Yes
DE/current-to-best/1	9/18/1	370.0	36.0	0.000	Yes	Yes
DE/rand-to-best/1	8/20/0	342.0	36.0	0.000	Yes	Yes

From Tables 2 and 3, DE-SOM can obtain significantly better results than most of the original DE algorithms overall. Specifically, DE-SOM is significantly better than the corresponding DE on 10, 20, 14, 10, 7 and 9 functions at 30D, respectively, and on 10, 20, 14, 14, 9 and 8 functions at 50D, respectively. Further, according to the results of the multi-problem Wilcoxon signed-rank tests, DE-SOM can obtain the higher R + values than R− values in the most cases, and the p values in most cases are less than 0.05. These results indicate that DE-SOM can improve the performance of the original DE algorithms on the test functions.

4.2 Effectiveness of the Self-adaptive Neighborhood Mechanism (SNM)

To investigate the influence of neighborhood size on the performance of DE-SOM, different neighborhood sizes, i.e., $r = 20$, $r = 40$, $r = 70$, and $r = 90$ are used to replace SNM. The comparisons between DE-SOM with SNM and single neighborhood size are made, and the results are shown in Table 4.

Table 4. Results of the single- and multi-problem Wilcoxon's test for DE-SOM/rand/1 with SNM versus that with single neighborhood size for the CEC2013 functions at 30D and 50D.

DE-SOM/rand/1 with SNM vs	+/=/−	R+	R−	p-value	$\alpha = 0.05$	$\alpha = 0.1$
DE-SOM/rand/1($r = 20$) at 30D	12/15/1	301.0	77.0	0.007	Yes	Yes
DE-SOM/rand/1($r = 40$) at 30D	15/13/0	296.5	109.5	0.030	Yes	Yes
DE-SOM/rand/1($r = 70$) at 30D	12/16/0	294.0	84.0	0.011	Yes	Yes
DE-SOM/rand/1($r = 90$) at 30D	12/16/0	303.0	75.0	0.006	Yes	Yes
DE-SOM/rand/1($r = 20$) at 50D	14/12/2	312.0	94.0	0.012	Yes	Yes
DE-SOM/rand/1($r = 40$) at 50D	12/15/1	354.0	52.0	0.001	Yes	Yes
DE-SOM/rand/1($r = 70$) at 50D	13/14/1	319.5	58.5	0.002	Yes	Yes
DE-SOM/rand/1($r = 90$) at 50D	10/18/0	337.0	41.0	0.000	Yes	Yes

According to the results in Tables 4, the effectiveness of SNM for DE-SOM is demonstrated when compared with the variants with single neighborhood size. Based on the multi-problem Wilcoxon signed-rank tests, DE-SOM with SNM obtain the higher R+ values than R− values in all the cases. In addition, the p values in all the cases are less than 0.05. These results show that SNM can obtain the significantly better results than single neighborhood size for DE-SOM. Further, the advantages of using SNM with multiple different neighborhood sizes for different evolutionary stages are also exhibited.

5   Conclusion

In this study, a Self-organizing map (SOM) based DE algorithm, DE-SOM, is proposed to extract the neighborhood information to guide the search of DE. With the advantages of SOM that preserves the topological structure of the data in the original input space, DE-SOM constructs the neighborhood relationships among the individuals. In addition, a self-adaptive neighborhood mechanism (SNM) is used to dynamically adjust the neighborhood size during the process of evolution. To evaluate the performance of the proposed algorithm, DE-SOM is applied to six original DE algorithms. The experimental results on the CEC2013 benchmark functions clearly show that DE-SOM can significantly improve the performance of the corresponding DE algorithm overall. Moreover, the effectiveness of SNM is demonstrated through the comparisons between DE-SOM with SNM and that with single neighborhood size. In the future, more comparisons with the advanced DE variants will be carried out to evaluate the effectiveness of DE-SOM. On the other hand, different SNMs for adjusting the neighborhood size will be investigated to further enhance the search ability of DE-SOM.

Acknowledgement. This work was supported in part by the Natural Science Foundation of Fujian Province of China (2018J01091, 2015J01258), the Postgraduate Scientific Research Innovation Ability Training Plan Funding Projects of Huaqiao University (17013083021) and the Opening Project of Guangdong Province Key Laboratory of Computational Science at the Sun Yat-sen University.

References

1. Storn, R., Price, K.: Differential evolution–a simple and efficient heuristic for global optimization over continuous spaces. J. Global Optim. **11**, 341–359 (1997)
2. Chow, C.K., Yuen, S.Y.: An evolutionary algorithm that makes decision based on the entire previous search history. IEEE Trans. Evol. Comput. **15**(6), 741–769 (2011)
3. Xu, R., Wunsch, D.: Clustering. Wiley, Hokoben (2008)
4. Kohonen, T.: The self-organizing map. Neurocomputing **21**(1), 1–6 (1998)
5. Liang, J., Qu, B., Suganthan, P., Hernández-Díaz, A.: Problem definitions and evaluation criteria for the CEC 2013 special session on real-parameter optimization. Computational Intelligence Laboratory, Zhengzhou University, Zhengzhou, China and Nanyang Technological University, Singapore, Technical report, vol. 201212 (2013)
6. Gao, W., Yen, G.G., Liu, S.: A cluster-based differential evolution with self-adaptive strategy for multimodal optimization. IEEE Trans. Cybern. **44**(8), 1314–1327 (2014)
7. Wang, Y., Zhang, J., Zhang, G.: A dynamic clustering based differential evolution algorithm of Global Optimization. Eur. J. Oper. Res. **183**(1), 56–73 (2007)
8. Ali, M.Z., Awad, N.H., Duwairi, R., Albadarneh, J., Reynolds, R.G., Suganthan, P.N.: Cluster-based differential evolution with heterogeneous influence for numerical optimization. In: IEEE Congress on Evolutionary Computation, pp. 393–400 (2015)
9. Kundu, D., Suresh, K., Ghosh, S., Das, S., Abraham, A., Badr, Y.: Automatic clustering using a synergy of genetic algorithm and multi-objective differential evolution. In: Corchado, E., Wu, X., Oja, E., Herrero, Á., Baruque, B. (eds.) HAIS 2009. LNCS (LNAI), vol. 5572, pp. 177–186. Springer, Heidelberg (2009). https://doi.org/10.1007/978-3-642-02319-4_21
10. Cai, Z., Gong, W., Ling, C.X., Zhang, H.: A clustering-based differential evolution for global optimization. Appl. Soft Comput. **11**, 1363–1379 (2011)
11. Liu, G., Li, Y., Nie, X., Zheng, H.: A novel clustering-based differential evolution with 2 multi-parent crossovers for global optimization. Appl. Soft Comput. **12**, 663–681 (2012)
12. Tran, D.H., Cheng, M.Y., Pham, A.D.: Using fuzzy clustering chaotic-based differential evolution to solve multiple resources leveling in the multiple projects scheduling problem. Alexandria Eng. J. **55**(2), 1541–1552 (2016)
13. Jesus, M.J.D., Ventura, S., Garrell, J.M., Otero, J., Romero, C., Bacardit, J., et al.: Keel: a software tool to assess evolutionary algorithms for data mining problems. Soft. Comput. **13**(3), 307–318 (2009)

14. García, S., Fernández, A., Luengo, J., Herrera, F.: A study of statistical techniques and performance measures for genetics-based machine learning: accuracy and interpretability. Soft. Comput. **13**(10), 959–977 (2009)
15. Derrac, J., García, S., Molina, D., Herrera, F.: A practical tutorial on the use of nonparametric statistical tests as a methodology for comparing evolutionary and swarm intelligence algorithms. Swarm Evol. Comput. **1**(1), 3–18 (2011)
16. Zhang, H., Zhou, A., Song, S., Zhang, Q., Gao, X., Zhang, J.: A self-organizing multiobjective evolutionary algorithm. IEEE Trans. Evol. Comput. **20**(5), 792–806 (2016)

Similarity Measure for Patients
via A Siamese CNN Network

Fangyuan Zhao[1,2], Jianliang Xu[1(✉)], and Yong Lin[3]

[1] College of Information Science and Engineering Ocean University of China,
Qingdao, China
XJL9898@OUC.EDU.CN
[2] Weifang Public Security Bureau, Weifang, China
[3] Weifang Power Supply Company, Weifang, China

Abstract. In the medical health field, assessing the similarities between patients is a basic task. A suitable patient similarity measurement has a very wide range of applications. For example, patient group identification, comparative study of treatment methods, etc. The electronic health records (EHRs) contain rich personal information of patient, which is hierarchical, longitudinal, and sparse. Although there have been some studies aimed at learning the similarities of patients from EHRs to solve real medical problems, there still exist some problems. Many works lack of effective patient representation. In addition, most of the research works are limited to one or more specific diseases. However, in fact, many diseases accompany with other diseases. In this case, the similarity of patients with multiple diseases are ignored. In this paper, we designed a siamese CNN network structure to learn patient expression while effectively measure the similarity between patient pairs. The experimental results show the effectiveness of this method.

1 Introduction

Electronic health records refer to the storage, management, transmission and reproduction of medical records, including structured data and unstructured data. Structured data is represented by tables and images. Unstructured data mainly include discharge summary, pathography, doctor-patient communication record, current medical history and other personalized information. In recent years, the scale of electronic health records has been increasing sharply, and the EHRs has become a valuable resource for medical tasks such as disease prediction, disease analysis and auxiliary diagnosis. The information mining from EHRs data gradually attracts a large number of researchers. However, due to the existence of noise data, irregular data and longitudinal data, mining information from EHRs data faces more challenges than the regular data mining task.

It is an important task in the research of clinical decision support and patient population identification that how to give a clinically meaningful measure of patient similarity through the patient's EHRs. Case query based on patient similarity can be a technical supplement for doctors. Based on this technology,

© Springer Nature Switzerland AG 2018
J. Vaidya and J. Li (Eds.): ICA3PP 2018, LNCS 11335, pp. 319–328, 2018.
https://doi.org/10.1007/978-3-030-05054-2_25

doctors can perform initial diagnosis of patients. Patient similarity can also be used in patient identification and patient risk classification.

How to obtain the appropriate patient similarity has become a key problem in the patient similarity measurement system. The earlier patient similarity measurement system uses the known metric formula to directly measure the similarity of the patient vector, for example, using Euclidean distance [1], and other methods to directly operate on the vector.

At current, widely used method is the patient similarity measurement system based on metric learning. In order to rationally use the feedback information of medical experts, the system transforms the patient similarity problem into a supervised distance metric learning problem. However, many methods for measuring the similarity of patients only consider the case of patient similarity under one specific disease. It is not practical that only one disease is considered in many researches. Therefore, we are committed to solving similar problems in patients with multiple diseases. This paper designs a patient similarity label generation method for patients with multiple diseases, and converts the patient similarity measurement method into a multi-label classification problem.

In conclusion, the contribution of this paper is as follows:

- In this paper, a patient similarity label generation method is designed for patients with multiple diseases, and the patient similarity measurement method is transformed into a multi-label classification problem.
- In this paper, a deep siamese CNN structure is designed, which measures the similarity between patient pairs while learning the representation of patients.
- In this paper, a number of experiments are designed to evaluate the performance of the model. The experimental results confirm the effectiveness of the method.

2   Related Work

In the field of measuring similar patients, there have been a lot of research works. Our research work has been done on the basis of these works.

SimSVM algorithm [2] is proposed for patients similarity measure. The algorithm uses 14 similarity measure indicators as input and the output predicts corresponding category (survival time is longer than 12 months or not) and similar degree. The used data set has a total of 30 patients and consists of 300 and 135 patient pairs for training and testing. The experimental results obtains an accuracy of 66.7%. However, the size of this data set is relatively small, so this result is not particularly convincing. A Local Spline Regression(LSR) based similarity measurement was used to design a collaborative disease prediction strategy [3]. The algorithm also integrates expert feedback information into the framework to improve the accuracy of predictions.

Many studies have clustered patients to find similar patients. For example, work [4] uses diagnose data to form different clusters, and then calculates the distance between clusters instead of directly calculating the distance between patients. Sewitch, et al. [5] use the K-Means algorithm based on their responses to the Patient- Physician Discordance Scales (PPDS) to divided the different patients into subgroups. Eventually, they identified five different groups of patients.

In addition, there are also a number of patients measure methods based on deep learning. For example, work [6] uses a similarity measure method to find similar patients based on CNN, and then based on similar patients performed personalized disease prediction. The method only considers diagnosis concept and treatment concept in EHRs as the patient's characteristics to represent the patient, and it integrates each patient's visiting data together to form a patient matrix representation with time characteristics. Finally, a matching matrix is used to calculate the distance between each patient pair. There is another similar work [7] that uses patient's diagnostic concepts and visits information to represent a patient. With their method, each patient is represented as a matrix with time characteristics. The above two methods all take into account the time of different medical concepts and patient visits in the EHRs. However, their methods are limited to patients with single disease, and the patients with a variety of diseases have been discarded directly.

3   Methodology

In this section, we first obtain each patient's matrix representation by learning the context representation of each medical concept. And then design a patient label representation method that takes into account of multiple label similarities. In next step, we design a siamese CNN neural network to measure the similarity between patient pairs and describes the optimization process of this neural network. The frame diagram of our method is shown in Fig. 1.

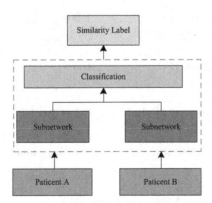

Fig. 1. The frame diagram of our patient similarity measurement method

3.1   Patient Representation

First, we obtain the context embedding of each medical concept from each patient's EHR, which provides more semantic information than one-hot representation. For each patient, we get a detailed representation of the patient by concatenating the embedding of all medical concepts orderly that appear in the EHR. The patient representation contains the patient's symptom information, treatment information, disease and diagnostic information, and body part information. Through skip-gram neural network [8], each medical concept is mapped to a low-dimensional dense vector representation. Then concatenate all medical concepts of a patient into a matrix, which is the patient's matrix representation.

3.2   Patient Pair Label Similarity Representation

We use patient's disease and diagnostic information as the patient's label, and the similarity between patient pairs is measured by whether or not the labels are similar. In addition, we consider that a patient may suffer multiple diseases and the disease label between two patients may be partially similar. We use one-hot encoding method to draw with each patient's label. First, we get 197 diseases and diagnoses of all patients in the data set. Each patient's disease label is then represented as a vector of 197 dimensions. The value of each position in the vector is 1 or 0. A value of 0 indicates that the patient does not suffer from a certain disease, and a value of 1 indicates that the patient has a certain disease. We perform the XOR logical operation on the labels of each patient pair in a bit-by-bit manner. That is, if the labels are the same, the corresponding value is 1. Otherwise, the corresponding value is 0. The label similarity of each patient pair is obtained and the schematic diagram is shown in Fig. 2.

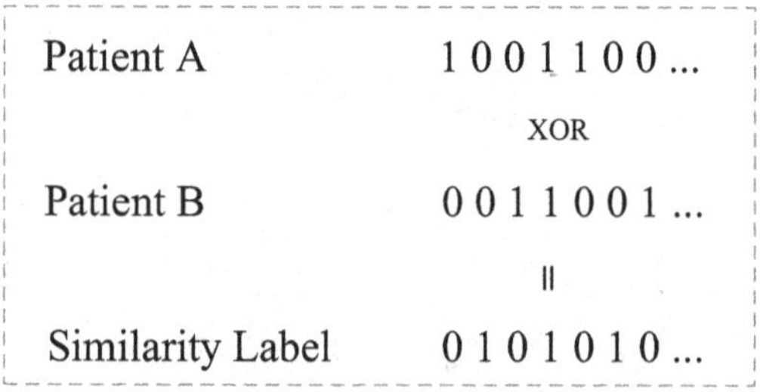

Patient A	1 0 0 1 1 0 0 ...
	XOR
Patient B	0 0 1 1 0 0 1 ...
	‖
Similarity Label	0 1 0 1 0 1 0 ...

Fig. 2. The schematic diagram of similarity label generation

3.3   Patient Similarity Measure Method

We propose a deep learning model to assess the similarities between patient pairs. The siamese network is used to evaluate the similarity of two input samples. It has two branches with exactly the same structure, and these two branches share weights. They receive two inputs x1 and x2 respectively, and then learn the characteristics of the subnetworks. Calculate the similarity of two output vectors by some distance measure. However, we don't want to calculate the distance between two samples, so we have turned this similarity into a multi-label classification problem, so the last part of our model is the fully connected layer and the classification layer. In our structure, we use Convolutional Neural Network (CNN) to process patient data. The transformed siamese network is shown in Fig. 3.

Our deep learning parameters are set as follows: the width of the convolution filter is 3, and the number of convolution filters takes on 32, 64, 64, 64 respectively. A max-pooling is added after each convolution operation. We use the stochastic gradient descent algorithm to train the parameters of the model. Each time using 100 examples as the shuffled min-batch to train the model, and the model is trained a total of 1000 times. Considering the over-fitting problem, we added a dropout normalization with dropout rate setting 0.5 after the fully connected layer of the subnetwork. In each subnetwork, the last two layers are two full connected layers, where the neurons number of per layer is 128.

After the subnetwork, the first step is concatenating two vectors from two subnetworks, After that, a fully connected layer is followed, which has 128 neurons. The last layer is a classification layer, and the number of neurons is the total number of labels. At the same time, the last layer is activated with sigmoid function. The following paragraphs describe the details of each kind of operation.

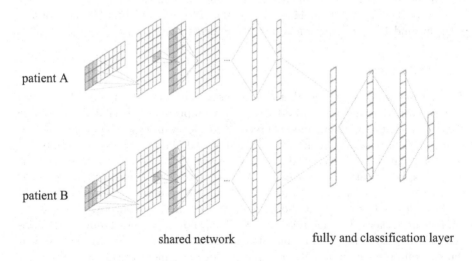

Fig. 3. The schematic diagram of siamese CNN neural network

3.4   Optimization

For different tasks, we need to use different loss function to train model. Taking the classification problem as an example, the most commonly used loss function is the cross entropy loss function. In our task, we turned the patient-pair similarity problem into a multi-label classification problem. So we use the sigmoid to get the probability value for each output of label, and then use the binary cross entropy as the loss function. The binary cross entropy loss function has the following formula:

$$loss(y, \tilde{y}) = - \sum_i [y_i * log\tilde{y}_i + (1 - y_i) * log(1 - \tilde{y}_i))] \tag{1}$$

where y indicates target label and the $\tilde{y}$ represents the output of siamese network. The y_i indicates the ith label in the multiple labels and similarly the $\tilde{y}_i$ represents the ith output probability that the patients pairs share the ith disease.

All parameters of the model, including word embedding, CNN convolution filters, full connectivity layers and other parameters are all trained by a stochastic gradient descent algorithm. Specifically, we use the RMSprop [9,10] on all parameters during the training phase.

4   Evaluation

In this section, we use a real medical EHRs data set to evaluate our framework. At first, we introduce the data set used, and then give a detailed description on experimental settings. In addition, we also show the result and have a discussion on our model. All the experiments are conducted on a machining of Windows 7 with Intel (R) Core(TM) i5-4460 with 3.20 GHZ CPU and 16.0 GB memory. It takes around 15 h to train and validate the detection model.

4.1   Data Set

The dataset we used is a competition dataset that comes from the China Conference on Knowledge Graph and Semantic Computing(CCKS)2017 [11]. There are a total of 300 electronic medical records in the training set. The medical concept in this dataset has been manually annotated. There are 5 types of medical concepts, which are disease and diagnosis, inspection and inspection, symptoms and signs, body part and treatment. We counted the total number of each type of medical concept in the data set. The statistical results are shown in Table 1.

From Table 1, we can get the number of each medical concept, of which the number of diseases and diagnoses is 197. This shows that our model is a multi-label classification model, in which the number of label is 197. In fact, patient representation is the different combinations of these medical concept. Since our model is to classify the patient pairs similarities, we need to combine these 300 EHRs data in pairs. Eventually 44,850 patient pair records were obtained. We randomly split 80% of data as a training set and the remaining data as a test set. All evaluation results are obtained on the test set.

Table 1. Summary of EHRs dataset for different medical concepts

Medical concept	Number
Disease and diagnosis	197
Inspection and inspection	343
Symptoms and signs	86
Body part	885
Treatment	89

4.2 Experimental Settings

Medical Concept Embedding: We use word embedding to represent each medical concept in EHRs as a vector. In order to learn the embedding of each medical concept, we use bag of words with window size 5 and the word frequency is not less than 2. The Embedding vector dimensions are setted to 20, 40, 60, 80, 100,120,140,160,180 and 200. We train the model under different vector dimensions, and based on the results on test set, we finally select 60 as the dimension of each medical concept. Figure 4 shows the performance of the model under different dimensions. From this figure, we can see that the embedding size have a slight influence on model's performance on test set. Comparing the experimental results, the model has the best performance when the embedding size is 60.

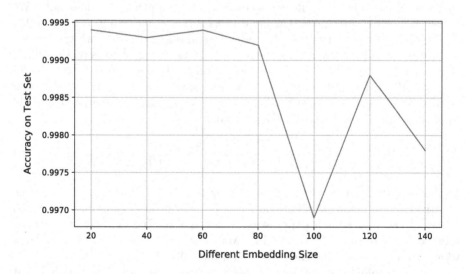

Fig. 4. Model's accuracy on different embedding size

Similarity Threshold for Each Label: For multi-label classification task, we use sigmoid active function to process the output of the last layer. However, we need to choose a threshold for each label. When the label's output value is

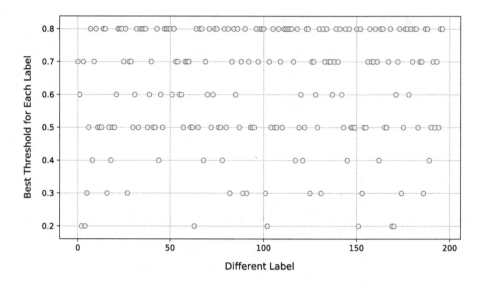

Fig. 5. The best threshold for each label

greater than the threshold, it means that the patient pair is consistent with the disease (either has same disease or have no disease). When the output of the label value is less than the threshold, it indicates that the patient pair is inconsistent with the disease (ie, one suffers the disease and the other one does not). We pre-set 9 possible thresholds that are 0.1, 0.2, 0.3, 0.4, 0.5, 0.6, 0.7, 0.8 and 0.9. As for every label, we try these 9 thresholds, and select the one with the highest matthews correlation coefficient (MCC) [12,13] for binary classes as the label's threshold. The MCC is in essence a correlation coefficient value between -1 and +1. A coefficient of +1 represents a perfect prediction, 0 an average random prediction and -1 an inverse prediction. The MCC can be calculated directly from the confusion matrix using the formula:

$$MCC = \frac{TP \times TN - FP \times FN}{\sqrt{(TP + FP)(TP + FN)(TN + FP)(TN + FN)}} \qquad (2)$$

In this equation, TP is the number of true positives, TN the number of true negatives, FP the number of false positives and FN the number of false negatives. If any of the four sums in the denominator is zero, the denominator can be arbitrarily set to one; this results in a Matthews correlation coefficient of zero, which can be shown to be the correct limiting value.

The threshold for each label is shown in Fig. 5. It can be concluded that different labels have different thresholds. Most labels have a threshold above 0.5 and only a few labels have a threshold below 0.5.

4.3   Result and Discussion

In the multi-classification problem, the overall classification accuracy is very important, but the classification accuracy of single labels is also a problem that we need to care about. Therefore, for each label, we calculate the accuracy of the label on the test set as shown in Fig. 6. We can see that most of the labels have a classification accuracy over 95%. A small part of labels' accuracy is between 90% and 95%. This shows that our model can effectively classify most of the labels, the best label classification can even reach 100%.

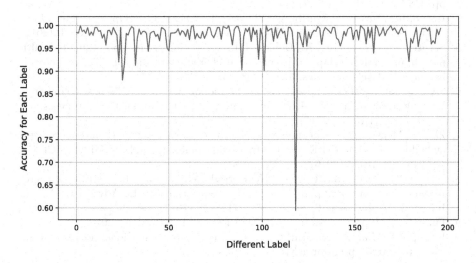

Fig. 6. The final classification accuracy for each label

5   Conclusion

Patient similarity measurement is a fundamental issue in the field of disease health. It has a wide range of applications, such as disease prediction, disease evolution, and selection of treatment methods. However, due to the complexity of the patient's condition and medical data, extracting effective features from the EHRs faces a great challenge. Most of the patients measure method ignores timeliness or neglects the patient's complicated conditions of multiple diseases. Therefore, a deep learning network structure based on siamese CNN is designed to automatically learn the patient's vectorized representation. Based on this representation, the patients similarity degree was effectively classified. We evaluate the impact parameters of multiple sets of experimental evaluation models and showed the accuracy of the classification for each label. Experimental results show that the accuracy of most label is more than 95% and prove this method is effective.

References

1. Wang, L., Zhang, Y., Feng, J.: On the Euclidean Distance of Images. IEEE Computer Society, Washington (2005)
2. Chan, L., Chan, T., Cheng, L., Mak, W.: Machine learning of patient similarity: a case study on predicting survival in cancer patient after locoregional chemotherapy. In: 2010 IEEE International Conference on Bioinformatics and Biomedicine Workshops (BIBMW), pp. 467–470. IEEE (2010)
3. Wang, F., Hu, J., Sun, J.: Medical prognosis based on patient similarity and expert feedback. In: 2012 21st International Conference on Pattern Recognition (ICPR), pp. 1799–1802. IEEE (2012)
4. Henao, R., Murray, J., Ginsburg, G., Carin, L., Lucas, J.E.: Supplementary Material to Patient Clustering With Uncoded Text in Electronic Medical Records (2012)
5. Sewitch, M.J., Leffondre, K., Dobkin, P.L.: Clustering patients according to health perceptions: relationships to psychosocial characteristics and medication nonadherence. J. Psychosom. Res. **56**(3), 323–332 (2004)
6. Suo, Q., et al.: Personalized disease prediction using a CNN-based similarity learning method. In: 2017 IEEE International Conference on Bioinformatics and Biomedicine (BIBM) (2017)
7. Zhu, Z.: Measuring patient similarities via a deep architecture with medical concept embedding. In: 2016 IEEE 16th International Conference on Data Mining (ICDM), pp. 749–758. IEEE (2016)
8. Mikolov, T., Sutskever, I., Chen, K., Corrado, G.S., Dean, J.: Distributed representations of words and phrases and their compositionality. In: Advances in Neural Information Processing Systems, pp. 3111–3119 (2013)
9. Funk, S.: RMSprop Loses to SMORMS3-Beware The Epsilon! (2015)
10. Khan, M.E., Liu, Z., Tangkaratt, V., Gal, Y.: Vprop: Variational inference using RMSprop, arXiv preprint arXiv:1712.01038 (2017)
11. China conference on knowledge graph and semantic computing. http://www.ccks2017.com/?page_id=51
12. Matthews correlation coefficient accuracy. https://en.wikipedia.org/wiki/Matthews_correlation_coefficient
13. Baldi, P., Brunak, S., Chauvin, Y., Andersen, C.A., Nielsen, H.: Assessing the accuracy of prediction algorithms for classification: an overview. Bioinformatics **16**(5), 412–424 (2000)

A New Artificial Bee Colony Algorithm
for Solving Large-Scale Optimization Problems

Hui Wang[1,2(⊠)], Wenjun Wang[3], and Zhihua Cui[4]

[1] Jiangxi Province Key Laboratory of Water Information Cooperative Sensing and Intelligent Processing, Nanchang Institute of Technology, Nanchang 330099, China
huiwang@whu.edu.cn
[2] School of Information Engineering, Nanchang Institute of Technology, Nanchang 330099, China
[3] School of Business Administration, Nanchang Institute of Technology, Nanchang 330099, China
wangwenjun881@126.com
[4] Complex System and Computational Intelligence Laboratory, Taiyuan University of Science and Technology, Taiyuan 030024, China
zhihuacui@gmail.com

Abstract. Artificial bee colony (ABC) is an efficient global optimizer, which has bee successfully used to solve various optimization problems. However, most of these problems are low dimensional. In this paper, we propose a new multi-population ABC (MPABC) algorithm to challenge large-scale global optimization problems. In MPABC, the population is divided into three subpopulations, and each subpopulation uses different search strategies. During the search, all subpopulations exchange there best search experiences to help accelerate the search. Experimental study is conducted on ten global optimization functions with dimensions 50, 100, and 200. Results show that MPABC is better than three other ABC variants on all dimensions.

Keywords: Artificial bee colony · Swarm intelligence · Multi-population
Global optimization · Large-scale optimization

1 Introduction

Many real world problems can be formulated to optimization problems over continuous or discrete search space. Compared to traditional mathematical optimization techniques, bio-inspired optimization methods do not consider whether the optimization problems are continuous or differentiable. So, they can be easily used to solve complex optimization problems.

In the past decades, many bio-inspired optimization method have been proposed, such as genetic algorithms (GAs) [1], simulated annealing (SA) [2], particle swarm optimization (PSO) [3], ant colony optimization (ACO) [4], artificial bee colony (ABC) [5], and others [6, 7]. Although these algorithms have been achieved success on many low-dimensional optimization problems, they suffer from the curse of

© Springer Nature Switzerland AG 2018
J. Vaidya and J. Li (Eds.): ICA3PP 2018, LNCS 11335, pp. 329–337, 2018.
https://doi.org/10.1007/978-3-030-05054-2_26

dimensionality. It means that their optimization performance deteriorates quickly with increasing of dimensions. To tackle this issue, some good algorithms were proposed in the literature [8–15].

ABC is one of the most popular optimization algorithm, which is inspired by the social behaviors of bees [16]. Since the introduction of ABC, it has been used to solve various optimization problems, but most of these problems are low-dimensional. To challenge large-scale global optimization problems, this paper proposes a new multi-population ABC (MPABC). Compared to the original ABC, MPABC employs three subpopulations, and each one use different search strategies. Ten benchmark optimization problems with dimensions 50, 100, and 200 are utilized in the experiments. Computational results show that MPABC is superior to three other ABC algorithms.

The rest of the paper is organized as follows. In Sect. 2, the original ABC is briefly described. Our approach MPABC is proposed in Sect. 3. Benchmark functions, results and discussions are presented in Sect. 4. Finally, this work is concluded in Sect. 5.

2   Artificial Bee Colony

In ABC, three are three different kinds of bees, employed, onlooker and scout. The number of employed bees is equal to the onlooker bees. The search of ABC is completed by different types of bees. Firstly, the employed bees search the neighborhood of each food source (solution) and find new better solutions. Secondly, the onlooker bees select some good solutions and search their neighborhoods to find better solutions. The scout bees randomly generate new solutions to replace the trapped ones.

For each solution X_i, an employed bee searches its neighborhood and find a new solution V_i [16].

$$v_{ij}(t) = x_{ij}(t) + \phi_{ij}\big(x_{ij}(t) - x_{kj}(t)\big), \tag{1}$$

where j is a random integer between 1 and D; X_k is randomly selected from the population $(i \neq j)$; t is the iteration index; ϕ_{ij} is a random value uniformly distributed with the range $[-1, 1]$. If V_i is better than its parent X_i, then replace X_i with V_i; otherwise keep X_i unchangeable.

When all employed bees complete the search, the selection probability p_i for each food source X_i is calculated by [16]:

$$p_i = \frac{fit_i}{\sum_{i=1}^{N} fit_i}, \tag{2}$$

where fit_i is the fitness value of X_i. When a solution X_i is selected, an onlooker bee searches the neighborhood of X_i and obtain a new food source V_i according to Eq. (1). Like the employed bees, the onlooker bees also use the same method to compare V_i with X_i. If V_i is better than its parent X_i, then replace X_i with V_i; otherwise keep X_i unchangeable.

If a solution X_i cannot be improved by employed or onlooker bees in *limit* iterations, it seems that X_i may be trapped into local minima. Then, a scout bee randomly generates a solution to replace X_i.

3 Proposed Approach

3.1 Multi-population Technique

In our previous study [17], we presented a multi-strategy ensemble ABC (MEABC), in which each food source is assigned a search strategy selected from a strategy pool. Results proved that ABC with two or more search strategies are better than that with a single strategy. Inspired by MEABC, we propose a new multi-population ABC (MPABC), which consists of three subpopulations, Subpop1, Subpop2, and Subpop3. Each subpopulation uses different search strategies to find new candidate solutions. In MPABC, Subpop1, Subpop2, and Subpop3 employ the original ABC, *gbest*-guided ABC (GABC) [18], and modified ABC (MABC) [19], respectively. Figure 1 shows the multi-population technique used in MPABC. As seen, all subpopulations share their best search experiences during the search.

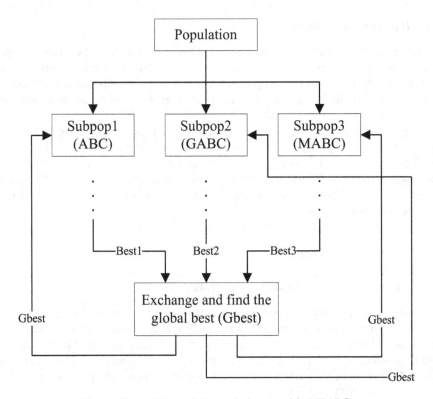

Fig. 1. The multi-population technique used in MPABC.

In the first subpopulation (Subpop1), MPABC uses the original ABC to execute the iteration and try to find new solutions. In the second subpopulation (Subpop2), MPABC employs GABC to execute the iteration and generate offspring. GABC and ABC are very similar, and they use the same framework and different search strategies. In GABC, a new search strategy incorporated with the best search experience is defined as follows.

$$v_{ij} = x_{ij} + \phi_{ij}(x_{ij} - x_{kj}) + \varphi_{ij}(gbest_j - x_{ij}), \tag{3}$$

where φ_{ij} is a random number within $[0, C]$, and C is a constant value. $C = 1.5$ is suggested in [18].

In the third subpopulation (Subpop3), MPABC uses the MABC to execute the iteration and find new solutions. MABC is inspired by the differential evolution (DE) mutation, and it is defined by [19]:

$$v_{ij} = gbest_j + \phi_{ij}(x_{aj} - x_{bj}), \tag{4}$$

where X_a and X_b are two randomly selected solutions ($a \neq b \neq i$), and $gbest$ is the global best solution in the Subpop3.

3.2   Information Exchange

For multi-population technique, information exchange is an important operation, which can greatly affect the performance of algorithm. In MPABC, we use a new information exchange method. Assume that the population size is N. Each subpopulation consists of n food sources (solutions), and $n = N/3$. Every m fitness evaluations, all subpopulations exchange their best search experiences.

First, assume that the best solutions of Subpop1, Subpop2, and Subpop3 are Best1, Best2, and Best3, respectively. The best one Gbest is selected from Best1, Best2, and Best3 (please see Fig. 1). Then, we use Gbest to replace the 20%*n solutions in each subpopulation. For Subpop1, we randomly selected 20%*n solutions, and Gbest is assigned to these solutions. It is hopeful that Gbest can accelerate the search on large-scale optimization problems.

4   Experimental Study

4.1   Large-Scale Global Optimization Problems

There are ten large-scale global optimization problems used in the experiments. Problems F1-F6 were chosen from the CEC 2008 Special Session on large scale global optimization [20], and the rest problems F7-F10 were taken from the Special Issue of Soft Computing on large scale continuous optimization problems [21]. Table 1 present a brief description of the ten test problems. In the experiments, the problem dimension (D) is set to 50, 100, and 200.

Table 1. Ten large-scale global optimization problems used in the experiments.

Problems	Search range	Global optimum
Shifted Sphere Problem (F1)	[−100, 100]	−450
Shifted Schwefel's Problem 2.21 (F2)	[−100, 100]	−450
Shifted Rosenbrock's Function (F3)	[−100, 100]	390
Shifted Rastrigin's Function (F4)	[−5, 5]	−330
Shifted Griewank's Function (F5)	[−600, 600]	−180
Shifted Ackley's Function (F6)	[−32, 32]	−140
Shifted Schwefel's Problem 2.22 (F7)	[−10, 10]	0
Shifted Schwefel's Problem 1.2 (F8)	[−65.536, 65.536]	0
Shifted Extended f_{10} (F9)	[−100, 100]	0
Shifted Bohachevsky (F10)	[−15, 15]	0

4.2   Parameter Settings

This paper aims to use an improved ABC to challenge large-scale global optimization problems. Although several good bio-inspired optimization algorithms have been proposed to solve large-scale optimization problems, we only compare our approach MPABC with some ABC variants on the test suite. The compared algorithms are listed as follows.

- ABC;
- GABC [18];
- MABC [19];
- Our approach MPABC.

For all algorithms, the same parameter settings are used for common parameters. In ABC, GABC, MABC, and MPABC, the maximum number of fitness evaluations (*MaxFEs*) and population size (N), and *limit* are set to 5000*D, 60, and 100, respectively. In GABC and MPABC, the parameter C is equal to 1.5 [18]. In MABC and MPABC, the parameter p is set to 0.7 [19]. The parameters m used in MPABC is set to 500 based on our empirical study. Because the population size N is 60, the size (n) of each subpopulation in MPABC is 20.

Each run stops when the maximum number of fitness evaluations is achieved. Throughout the experiments, the mean errors of the best solution found in the 25 runs are reported (For a solution X, the error value is calculated by F(X)-F(X^o), where X^o is the global optimum of the problem).

4.3   Computational Results

Tables 2 presents the computational results of MAPBC, ABC, GABC, and MACB on problems with $D = 50$, where "Mean Error" indicates the mean error values between the best solution found so far and the global optimum. Compared to ABC, MPABC achieves better solutions on 8 problems. For the rest of 2 problems, both of them can converge to the global optimum. MPABC significantly improve the performance of

ABC on F4, F6, F7, and F9. GABC and MPABC find the same solutions on two problems F4 and F5. For the rest of 8 problems, MPABC is better than GABC. MABC and MPABC can find the global optimum on 4 problems F1, F4, F5, and F7, while MPABC outperforms MABC on the rest of 6 problems.

Table 2. Computation results for $D = 50$.

Problems	ABC	GABC	MABC	MPABC
	Mean error	Mean error	Mean error	Mean error
F1	**0.00E+00**	3.34E−25	**0.00E+00**	**0.00E+00**
F2	1.02E+02	6.77E+01	2.30E+01	**3.21E+00**
F3	4.50E+00	3.50E+00	5.35E+00	**2.02E+00**
F4	1.22E+00	**0.00E+00**	**0.00E+00**	**0.00E+00**
F5	5.73E−13	**0.00E+00**	**0.00E+00**	**0.00E+00**
F6	2.46E−06	1.17E−12	6.74E−14	**5.86E−14**
F7	7.01E−09	1.04E−13	**0.00E+00**	**0.00E+00**
F8	1.52E+04	1.34E+04	1.45E+04	**8.08E+03**
F9	2.77E+00	5.39E−02	8.48E−04	**5.13E−05**
F10	**0.00E+00**	3.31E−26	1.81E−36	**0.00E+00**

Table 3 gives the comparison results of MAPBC, ABC, GABC, and MACB on problems with $D = 100$. When the dimension increases to 100, ABC cannot converge to F1 and F10, and MPABC outperforms ABC on all problems. Especially for problems F1, F4, F5, F6, F7, F9, and F10, MPABC is much better than ABC. GABC performs better than MPABC on F3, but MPABC outperforms GABC on the rest of 9 problems. GABC falls into local minima on F1, F4, F5, F7 and F10, while our approach can find the global optimum. MABC is better than ABC and GABC. Both MABC and MPABC achieve the same results on F4 and F5. For the rest of 8 problems, MPABC outperforms MABC.

Table 4 presents the computational results of MAPBC, ABC, GABC, and MACB on problems with $D = 200$. As the dimension increases to 200, MPABC still converges to the global optimum on 4 problems F1, F4, F7, and F10. MABC can find the global optimum on only one problem F4. For ABC and GABC, they fall into local minima on all problems. MABC is slightly better than MPABC on F5 and F6, while MPABC outperforms MABC on 7 problems. MPABC achieves much better solutions than ABC and GABC on all problems.

In order to identify the significant differences between two algorithms, Wilcoxon test is conducted [22]. Tables 5, 6, and 7 present the p-values of applying Wilcoxon test among MPABC and other three ABC variants for $D = 50$, 100, and 200, respectively. The p-values below 0.05 (the significant level) are shown in bold. As shown, MPABC is significantly better than ABC, GABC, and MABC for $D = 50$ and 100. For $D = 200$, MPABC is only significantly better than ABC and GABC.

Table 3. Computation results for $D = 100$.

Problems	ABC	GABC	MABC	MPABC
	Mean error	Mean error	Mean error	Mean error
F1	5.20E−15	6.66E−24	4.77E−30	**0.00E+00**
F2	1.34E+02	1.20E+02	5.66E+01	**1.35E+01**
F3	1.47E+01	**1.04E+01**	4.05E+01	1.43E+01
F4	4.54E+00	1.03E−13	**0.00E+00**	**0.00E+00**
F5	2.54E−13	7.33E−16	**0.00E+00**	**0.00E+00**
F6	6.04E−06	3.64E−12	1.82E−13	**1.37E−13**
F7	2.07E−08	7.52E−13	6.96E−17	**0.00E+00**
F8	5.10E+04	5.88E+04	5.68E+04	**3.14E+04**
F9	7.46E+00	2.33E−01	7.65E−03	**5.24E−05**
F10	2.57E−14	8.88E−25	1.94E−30	**0.00E+00**

Table 4. Computation results for $D = 200$.

Problems	ABC	GABC	MABC	MPABC
	Mean error	Mean error	Mean error	Mean error
F1	8.93E−14	7.27E−23	5.76E−28	**0.00E+00**
F2	1.54E+02	1.51E+02	8.90E+01	**3.58E+01**
F3	1.57E+01	4.35E+01	2.97E+01	**1.50E+01**
F4	9.86E+00	2.86E−12	**0.00E+00**	**0.00E+00**
F5	7.67E−13	2.40E−15	**1.11E−16**	1.48E−16
F6	9.87E−06	1.08E−11	**4.19E−13**	5.43E−13
F7	8.65E−08	3.35E−12	3.75E−15	**0.00E+00**
F8	1.90E+05	2.13E+05	2.01E+05	**1.14E+05**
F9	1.75E+01	6.76E−01	3.86E−02	**4.08E−04**
F10	3.02E−13	1.29E−23	5.33E−29	**0.00E+00**

Table 5. Wilcoxon test between MPABC and the other three ABC variants for $D = 50$.

MPABC vs.	p-values
ABC	**1.17E−02**
GABC	**1.17E−02**
MABC	**2.77E−02**

Table 6. Wilcoxon test between MPABC and the other three ABC variants for $D = 100$.

MPABC vs.	p-values
ABC	**5.06E−03**
GABC	**4.69E−02**
MABC	**1.17E−02**

Table 7. Wilcoxon test between MPABC and the other three ABC variants for $D = 200$.

MPABC vs.	p-values
ABC	**5.06E−03**
GABC	**5.06E−03**
MABC	8.58E−02

5 Conclusions

In the past decade, many different ABC algorithms have been proposed to various optimization problems. However, most of these problem are low-dimensional. To challenge large-scale optimization problems, this paper presents an improved ABC variant (called MPABC), which employs a new multi-population. MPABC consists of three subpopulations, and they use ABC, GABC, and MABC to execute iterations and generate new solutions, respectively. During the search, each subpopulation exchange their best search experiences with others. To validate the performance of MPABC, ten large-scale global optimization problems with dimensions 50, 100, and 200 are utilized in the experiments.

Computational results show that MPABC is superior to ABC, GABC, and MABC on most test problems. As the dimension increases, the performance of ABC, GABC, and MABC is seriously affected, while MPABC still can achieve good solutions. It demonstrates that the proposed multi-population technique can effectively combine the advantages of ABC, GABC, and MABC during the search.

In this paper, we only test MPABC on $D = 50$, 100, and 200. For problems with larger scale (such as $D = 500$, 100, and 2000), we did not investigate the effectiveness of MPABC. Moreover, MPABC introduces two new parameters m and n. The first parameter determine the exchange gap. Different m may affect the convergence speed. The second parameter is the size of subpopulation. In MPABC, we assume that all subpopulations have the same size. For different sizes of subpopulations, we have not studied its effects. The above issues will be our research directions in the future work.

Acknowledgement. This work was supported by the Science and Technology Plan Project of Jiangxi Provincial Education Department (No. GJJ170994), the National Natural Science Foundation of China (No. 61663028), the Distinguished Young Talents Plan of Jiangxi Province (No. 20171BCB23075), the Natural Science Foundation of Jiangxi Province (No. 20171BAB-202035), and the Open Research Fund of Jiangxi Province Key Laboratory of Water Information Cooperative Sensing and Intelligent Processing (No. 2016WICSIP015).

References

1. Schmitt, L.M.: Theory of genetic algorithms. Theor. Comput. Sci. **259**(1–2), 1–61 (2001)
2. Kirkpatrick, S., Gelatt, C.D., Vecchi, M.P.: Optimization by simulated annealing. Science **220**(4598), 671–680 (1983)
3. Kennedy, J., Eberhart, R.C.: Particle swarm optimization. In: Proceedings of IEEE International Conference on Neural Networks, pp. 1942–1948 (1995)

4. Dorigo, M., Maniezzo, V., Colorni, A.: The ant system: optimization by a colony of cooperating agents. IEEE Trans. Syst. Man Cybern. Part B Cybern. **26**, 29–41 (1996)
5. Karaboga, D.: An idea based on honey bee swarm for numerical optimization. Technical report-TR06, Erciyes University, engineering Faculty, Computer Engineering Department (2005)
6. Wang, H., et al.: Firefly algorithm with neighborhood attraction. Inf. Sci. **382–383**, 374–387 (2017)
7. Cui, Z., Sun, B., Wang, G., Xue, Y., Chen, J.: A novel oriented cuckoo search algorithm to improve DV-Hop performance for cyber-physical systems. J. Parallel Distrib. Comput. **103**, 42–52 (2017)
8. Wang, H., Wu, Z., Rahnamayan, S.: Enhanced opposition-based differential evolution for solving high-dimensional continuous optimization problems. Soft Comput. **15**(11), 2127–2140 (2011)
9. Brest, J., Maučec, M.S.: Self-adaptive differential evolution algorithm using population size reduction and three strategies. Soft Comput. **15**(11), 2157–2174 (2011)
10. Long, W., Jiao, J., Liang, X., Tang, M.: Inspired grey wolf optimizer for solving large-scale function optimization problems. Appl. Math. Model. **60**, 112–126 (2018)
11. LaTorre, A., Muelas, S., Peña, J.M.: A comprehensive comparison of large scale global optimizers. Inf. Sci. **316**, 517–549 (2015)
12. Mahdavi, S., Shiri, M.E., Rahnamayan, S.: Metaheuristics in large-scale global continues optimization: a survey. Inf. Sci. **295**, 407–428 (2015)
13. Mohapatra, P., Das, K.N., Roy, S.: A modified competitive swarm optimizer for large scale optimization problems. Appl. Soft Comput. **59**, 340–362 (2017)
14. Ali, A.F., Tawhid, M.A.: A hybrid particle swarm optimization and genetic algorithm with population partitioning for large scale optimization problems. Ain Shams Eng. J. **8**(2), 191–206 (2017)
15. Hu, X.M., He, F.L., Chen, W.N., Zhang, J.: Cooperation coevolution with fast interdependency identification for large scale optimization. Inf. Sci. **381**, 142–160 (2017)
16. Akay, B., Karaboga, D.: A modified Artificial bee colony algorithm for real-parameter optimization. Inf. Sci. **192**, 120–142 (2012)
17. Wang, H., Wu, Z.J., Rahnamayan, S., Sun, H., Liu, Y., Pan, J.S.: Multi-strategy ensemble artificial bee colony algorithm. Inf. Sci. **279**, 587–603 (2014)
18. Zhu, G., Kwong, S.: Gbest-guided artificial bee colony algorithm for numerical function optimization. Appl. Math. Comput. **217**, 3166–3173 (2010)
19. Gao, W., Liu, S.: A modified artificial bee colony algorithm. Comput. Oper. Res. **39**, 687–697 (2012)
20. Tang, K., et al.: Benchmark functions for the CEC'2008 special session and competition on large scale global optimization. Nature Inspired Computation and Applications Laboratory, USTC, China (2007)
21. Herrera, F., Lozano, M., Molina, D.: Test suite for the special issue of Soft Computing on scalability of evolutionary algorithms and other metaheuristics for large scale continuous optimization problems. Technical report, University of Granada, Spain (2010)
22. Wang, H., Rahnamayan, S., Sun, H., Omran, M.G.: Gaussian bare-bones differential evolution. IEEE Trans. Cybern. **43**(2), 634–647 (2013)

Implementation and Optimization
of Multi-dimensional Real FFT
on ARMv8 Platform

Xiao Wang[1,2], Haipeng Jia[1(✉)], Zhihao Li[1,2], and Yunquan Zhang[1]

[1] State Key Laboratory of Computer Architecture,
Institute of Computing Technology, Chinese Academy of Sciences, Beijing, China
{wangxiao17s,jiahaipeng,lizhihao,zhangyunquan}@ict.ac.cn
[2] School of Computer and Control Engineering, University of Chinese
Academy of Sciences, Beijing, China

Abstract. Fourier Transform is one of the most critical algorithms, and is applied in a wide range of fields like signal processing and data compression. In real world applications, such as image compression (JPEG), Fourier Transform is concentrated in processing real number input. These transforms are called real DFT (real discrete fourier transform) in this paper. Thus it is critical to optimize real DFT for specific platforms. In this paper, we implement 1D and 2D real DFT on ARMv8 platform which is the flagship architecture of ARM. Real DFT kinds implemented and optimized include R2HC, HC2R, DHT, DCTI-IV, DSTI-IV and are especially optimized when input size is $2^q 3^n 5^m$. In order to achieve high performance, optimization is carried out in following aspects: (1) Reduction of the computation complexity of real DFT. (2) Implementation of high performance 1D complex DFT algorithm to support real DFT. (3) For the 2D real DFT, we propose a cache-aware blocking approach to improve cache performance. Experimental results show that: Compared with FFTw 3.3.7, 1D-Float DFT gains 1.52x speedup in average across all real DFT kinds, maximum speedup reaches 1.79x; 1D-Double DFT gains 1.34x speedup in average across all real DFT kinds, maximum speedup reaches 1.61x; 2D-Float DFT gains 1.41x speedup in average across all real DFT kinds, maximum speedup reaches 1.70x; 2D-Double DFT gains 1.10x speedup across all real DFT kinds, maximum speedup reaches 1.25x.

Keywords: Real Fast Fourier Transform · Program optimization
ARMv8

1 Introduction

Fourier transform has been applied widely across various fields including signal processing and data compression [1,2]. On one hand, input of most real world applications is of real number format, such as pixel value or super parameters

© Springer Nature Switzerland AG 2018
J. Vaidya and J. Li (Eds.): ICA3PP 2018, LNCS 11335, pp. 338–353, 2018.
https://doi.org/10.1007/978-3-030-05054-2_27

of neural network [5–7], On the other hand, with thriving of ARM ecosystem, ARMv8 platform is being promoted to server market, computation efficiency is becoming critical in ARM platforms. Therefore, a high performance real number discrete fourier transform library on ARMv8 platform is of paramount importance.

In this paper, we implement and optimize a high performance 1D and 2D real DFT library using Cooley-Tukey FFT algorithm on ARMv8 platform. Implemented real DFT kinds include R2HC, HC2R, DHT, DCTI-IV, DSTI-IV. $2^q 3^n 5^m$ computation size is especially optimized. In order to achieve high performance, challenges need to be coped: (1) Diversity of real DFT brings difficulties. Different definitions of real DFT bring challenges to the choice of optimization approaches. (2) Real DFT depends on complex DFT. So the first step of developing real DFT is to develop complex DFT with high performance. Although there are various algorithms have been proposed for FFT, developing a high performance FFT library on new hardware still is a challenging work. (3) Architecture exploration of ARMv8 platform. Although there are already some libraries have been developed on ARM architecture, few optimization techniques for FFT on ARMv8 platform is recorded. This work explores utilization of SIMD instructions and registers besides methods for tuning cache performance.

As a summary, our contributions are focused on addressing following challenges: (1) We first summarize and abstract real DFT optimization algorithms into an unified two reduction form. With benefits of this, optimizations on real DFT are of an unified form. Meanwhile, we reduce original real DFT to less computational intensive transforms by taking advantage of symmetry of real DFT. (2) We implement and optimize 1D Cooley-Tukey complex FFT algorithm with high performance on ARMv8 platform through re-constructing butterfly network, simplifying butterfly calculations and using SIMD assembly instructions. (3) For 2D real DFT, we propose a cache-aware algorithm for ARMv8 platform to improve cache performance. After adopting these optimization techniques, high performance is obtained.

Because there is only few libraries support ARMv8 platform, and FFTw's excellent performance across all platforms, FFTw 3.3.7 is selected as our comparison baseline. Although ARM Performance Library implements complex DFT on ARMv8 CPUs, real DFT is still not supported yet. Experimental results show that: Compared with FFTw 3.3.7, 1D-Float DFT achieves around 1.52x speedup in average across all real DFT kinds, maximum speedup reaches 1.79x; 1D-Double DFT gains speedup 1.34x in average across all real DFT kinds, maximum speedup reaches 1.61x; 2D-Float DFT achieves 1.41x speedup in average across all real DFT kinds, maximum speedup reaches 1.70x; 2D-Double achieves 1.10x speedup across all real DFT kinds, maximum speedup reaches 1.25x.

The rest of this paper is organized as following: Sect. 2 summarizes related works; Sect. 3 introduces details of optimization of real DFT; Sect. 4 presents details of implementation and optimization of 1D complex DFT; Sect. 5 introduces 2D cache-aware algorithm; Sect. 6 analyzes experimental results; summary and future work considerations are presented in Sect. 7.

2   Related Work

There are a lot researches on efficient real DFT algorithms. Two approaches mentioned in [3] are complex DFT based approaches and approach of customizing real DFT computation within every FFT stage. For the sake of diversity of real DFT and code size, a stage level customized optimization is not practical besides poor extensibility for newly added real DFT kind.

Therefore, in this paper, we implement real DFT based on complex DFT, and unify these transforms into an unified form. Transforms with random input such as R2HC (real to Half complex transform), HC2R (Half complex to real) and DHT (discrete hartley transform) are optimized as a halved complex transform; Transforms with symmetrical input such as DCT/DST I-IV are optimized case by case: For DCT/DST I, method that reduces the original transform into a real DFT with half size is mentioned in [13]. But the loss of accuracy is unacceptable. Therefore, we solve DCT/DST I directly as DHT and R2HC, HC2R cases. For DCT II and III, a concise computation approach has been proposed in [12]. Original problem is solved with a halved real DFT, meanwhile, [14] points out DST II and III is equivalent to corresponding DCTs inherently. For consideration of flexibility, method in [12,14] is adopted, as more conditions are handled compared with methods mentioned in [8]. In the end, DCT/DST IV are solved based on DCT/DST II/III with method mentioned in [15] to integrate all real DFT kinds together.

There are already several FFT computation libraries, such as FFTW [10], PFFT [4], MPFFT [11], PKUFFT [9] and ARM Performance Library [16], but only FFTw and Arm Performance Library have implemented and optimized FFT on ARMv8 platform. Further, real DFT kinds are still not supported by ARM Performance Library. Therefore, FFTw3.3.7 is chosen as our comparison baseline.

3   Optimization of Algorithm for 1D Real DFT

3.1   Introduction to DFT

Given a sequence of sampled complex number: $x_0, x_1, ..., x_{n-1}, x_n$. DFT transform this sequence into frequency domain by Eq. 1:

$$X_k = \sum_{n=0}^{N-1} x_n W_N^{nk} \tag{1}$$

Here W_N^{nk} is also called twiddle factors which is defined as $e^{\frac{-2nkj\pi}{N}}$ essentially, DFT can be expressed as a matrix multiplication between input vector and a pre-defined DFT matrix, take five points for example:

$$X = \begin{bmatrix} 1 & 1 & 1 & 1 & 1 \\ 1 & W_N^1 & W_N^2 & W_N^3 & W_N^4 \\ 1 & W_N^2 & W_N^4 & W_N^6 & W_N^8 \\ 1 & W_N^3 & W_N^6 & W_N^9 & W_N^{12} \\ 1 & W_N^4 & W_N^8 & W_N^{12} & W_N^{16} \end{bmatrix} \times x, \tag{2}$$

real DFT is a special DFT with input sequence is real number. The rest of this section classify these real DFT kinds based on property of their input vector and clarify proposed two reduction approaches: (1) Reduction from real DFT to halved complex DFT; (2) Reduction from real DFT to halved real DFT. Reductions above are called real reduction and complex reduction in Table 1 respectively. Two reduction approaches are both used for decreasement of computation of real DFT. For clarity, Table 1 shows each implemented real DFT's adopted reduction approach. As Table 1 shows, complex reduction is adopted by all real DFT kinds. In fact, complex reduction is adopted to reduce the output of real DFT if real reduction is adopted. Rest of this section presents details of implementation of two reduction approaches.

Table 1. Relation between all real DFT kinds and reduction approach

Real DFT kind	R2HC	HC2R	DHT	DCT I	DCT II	DCT III	DCT IV	DST I	DST II	DST III	DST IV
Real reduction	No	No	No	No	Yes	Yes	Yes	No	Yes	Yes	Yes
Complex reduction	Yes	Yes	Yes	Yes	Yes	Yes	Yes	Yes	Yes	Yes	Yes

3.2 Reduction from Real DFT to Halved Complex DFT

To solve a transform with input is pure real number sequence, a naive method is to regard real DFT as complex DFT with each input elements' imaginary part is zero. However, it brings unnecessary calculations and extra storage space. Therefore, this paper reduce real DFT into complex transform with half size and split result from complex transform's output. Given Eq. 1, its right part can be splited as sum of F_r, G_r:

$$F_r = \sum_{l=0}^{\frac{N}{2}-1} f_l W_{\frac{N}{2}}^{rl} \quad G_r = \sum_{l=0}^{\frac{N}{2}-1} g_l W_{\frac{N}{2}}^{rl} \tag{3}$$

Basic motivation of following steps is to extract F_r and G_r from result of a complex transform of only half size.

As $f_l = x_{2l}$, $g_l = x_{2l+1}$, we regard the adjacent two number f_l and g_l as a complex number $f_l + g_l j$. Based on Eq. (1), we achieve a transform of only half size:

$$Y_r = \sum_{l=0}^{\frac{N}{2}-1} (f_l + jg_l) W_{\frac{N}{2}}^{rl} = F_r + jG_r \tag{4}$$

Next step, we split F_r and G_r from Y_r based on Eq. 5:

$$F_r = \frac{1}{2}(Y_r + \overline{Y}_{\frac{N}{2}-r}) \quad G_r = \frac{j}{2}(\overline{Y}_{\frac{N}{2}-r} - Y_r) \tag{5}$$

Therefore, we reduce a real DFT into a halved complex transform. The distinct part of different real DFT kinds is relied on the way of organizing imaginary parts and real parts. Take DHT (Discrete Hartley Transform) for example:

$$X_k = \sum_{n=0}^{N-1} x_n [cos(\frac{2\pi njk}{N}) + sin(\frac{2\pi njk}{N})] \tag{6}$$

Result is achieved directly as sum of imaginary part and real part once we retrieve X_k's imaginary part and real part from F_r and G_r. As a summary, general reduction algorithm is given as Algorithm 1. Computation steps of line 1–8 is the common part. After we retrieve real and imaginary parts, re-construction steps are carried out according to specified transform's definition.

Algorithm 1. ComplexReduction(Input x, Output X, Direction dir, kind k)

1: Complex DFT(x,Y, Direction)
2: Compute X[N/2], X[0];
3: **for** each $i \in [1, N/4]$ **do**
4:     $Y_r \leftarrow Y[i]$
5:     $Y_{nr} \leftarrow \overline{Y[\frac{N}{2}]}$
6:     $Fr \leftarrow Y_r + Y_{nr}$
7:     $gr \leftarrow j*(Y_{nr} - Y_r)$
8:     $Gr \leftarrow gr * W_N^r$
9:     Retrive real part and imginary part from Fr Gr
10:    $X[r] \leftarrow$ Reconstruct real part and imaginary part based on real DFT type(k).
11: **end for**
12: return;

3.3   Reduction from Real DFT to Halved Real DFT

Different from transforms above, DCT/DST possess special symmetry property within input. So generally input vectors of these transforms are often given only half of input. Based on choice of symmetry position, we implement the four most common kinds of DCT and DST respectively.

In this part, we give definition of these transforms and introduce specific considerations brought by symmetry: DCT/DST I are solved by Algorithm 1 due to accuracy consideration mentioned in [10]. Thus there is no extra introduction. DCT/DST III is reduced to another real DFT with half size. DCT/DST IV are divided into sub-transform of DCT/DST III [15]. Given DCT II/III:

$$DCTII : X_k = x_0 + (-1)^k x_{N-1} + 2 \sum_{n=1}^{N-2} x_n cos(\frac{\pi nk}{N-1}) \tag{7}$$

$$DCTIII : X_k = x_0 + (-1)^k x_{N-1} + 2 \sum_{n=1}^{N-2} x_n cos(\frac{\pi nk}{N-1}) \tag{8}$$

Based on Fast DCT algorithm from [12], DCT II is re-expressed as Eq. 9:

$$X_k = 2RealPart[W_{2N}^k \sum_{n=0}^{N/2-1} v_n W_{N/2}^{nk})] \tag{9}$$

$$v_k = \frac{2}{N} \sum_{n=0}^{\frac{N}{2}-1} V_n W_{N/2}^{-nk} \tag{10}$$

$$DCTIV : X_k = 2 \sum_{n=0}^{N-1} x_n cos(\frac{\pi(n+1/2)(k+1/2)}{N}) \tag{11}$$

For DCT II, based on Eq. 9, original transform is reduced into a real DFT of v_k with $N/2$ size. v_n is constructed by interleaving even indexed and odd indexed elements from x_n. For DCT III, based on Eq. 10, original transform is reduced

---

Algorithm 2. DCT/DST(Input x, Output X, Direction dir, Kind k)

1: N here is input size of DCT/DST, which is near half of logical transform size.
2: **if** k equals DSTIV/DCTIVs **then**
3:     $dct - input/dst - input \leftarrow x$.
4:     Algorithm 2(dct-input, X_1, backward, dctIII);
5:     Algorithm 2(dst-input, X_2, backward, dstIII);
6:     **for** each $i \in [0, N/2]$ **do**
7:         $X[i] \leftarrow X_1[i] * sptws[i].r + X_2[i] * sptw[i].i$
8:         $X[i + N/2] \leftarrow X_1[N/2 - 1 - i] * sptw[N/2 - 1 - i].i + X_2[N/2 - 1 - i] * sptw[N/2 - 1 - i].r$
9:     **end for**
10:     return;
11: **end if**
12: **if** k equals DST II **then**
13:     $xm[i] \leftarrow x[i] * (-1)^{i \bmod 2}$ i from 0 to N
14:     Algorithm2 (xm, X, forward, dctII);
15: **end if**
16: **if** k equals DST III **then**
17:     $xm[i] \leftarrow x[N - 1 - i]$
18:     Algorithm2 (xm, X, forward, dctIII);
19: **end if**
20: **if** k equals DCT II **then**
21:     **for** each $i \in [0, N/2 - 1]$ **do**
22:         $xm_i \leftarrow x[2i]$
23:         $xm_{N-i} \leftarrow x[2i + 1]$
24:     **end for**
25: **end if**
26: **if** k equals DCT III **then**
27:     $xm[i] \leftarrow x[N - 1 - i]$
28: **end if**
29: Algorithm1 (xm, X, dir, kind);

---

into a real DFT of V_n. V_n is defined as: $V_k = \frac{1}{2}W_{2N}^{-k}[X_k - jX_{N-k}]$. Then we need to split x_k from v_k. To avoid repeated memory visit cost, split operation for v_k is finished by re-mapping result and output vector's index. For DST II/III, they can be derived from DCT II/III by flopping sign of input vector or reversing sequence order. DCT IV is given as Eq. 11. Based on matrix factorization method, we can factorize a DCT IV transform into a DCT III and a DST III sub-transforms with N/2 input size, meanwhile, DST IV is solved based on DCT IV through flipping operations. As a summary, DCT II/III is the core transforms as other transforms are derived from DCT II/III with split operations. Algorithm 2 gives the summary of integration of DCT I-IV. In description of Algorithm 2, for clarity, we pack operations needed for v_n and V_n into Algorithm 1.

4   Implementation and Optimization of 1D Complex DFT

From discussion above, although we have cut off much redundant computations by transform reduction, final computational steps are still relied on 1D complex DFT. Therefore, in this paper, we implement and optimize a high performance 1D complex DFT library using cooley-Tukey FFT algorithm to support real transforms. Optimization considerations include designing a SIMD friendly FFT butterfly network without data copying, reducing computational complexity of butterfly, optimizing butterfly with SIMD techniques.

4.1   Butterfly Network Optimization

In solving FFT, Cooley-Tukey algorithm is one of the most famous FFT algorithms, In this algorithm, DFT is solved stage by stage, with butterfly kernel computation processed repeatedly in each stage. So the way butterfly network is organized affects optimization as a whole. Generally, there are two approaches in implementing this algorithm: (1) Decimation-in-time, DIT (2) Decimation-in-frequency, DIF. Take network of DIT of eight points and radix is 2 for example in Fig. 1.

When using DIT, input vector is of bit-reversed order, output vector is of nature order. For DIF, this condition is reversed. However, bit-reversed order not only brings extra memory cost, but also increases difficulties for blending mix

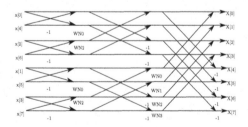

Fig. 1. DIT radix-2 butterfly network with 8 points

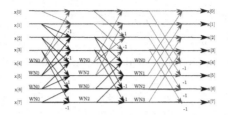

Fig. 2. Unified network with 8 points. (Color figure online)

radixes into an unified framework. Thus, this paper adopts an unified butterfly network structure shown in Fig. 2.

This network has three advantages compared with the network described above: (1) No need to be bit-reversed. Both DIT and DIF need bit-reverse operation to calibrate input or output elements' order. Thus this extra memory accessing cost is saved by our network structure. (2) Simd-friendly. To efficiently wield SIMD, data to be loaded from and stored into memory should be consecutive. Within structure of this network, input and output of consecutive butterflies is located consecutively. Besides that, section in every stage is an independent computational unit. It is convenient to arrange our SIMD parallelization within the same section. In Fig. 2, one red color part represents one section in each stage. (3) Mix-radix friendly, different radix algorithm is solved coherently in an unified approach. Because order of input and output of every stage is of natural order, it is convenient to concatenate stages of different radixes together. Computation is processed stage by stage naturally. To gain a better performance, we split the first stage out of the general computation network. There are two reasons: (1) As twiddles used in first stage is constant 1, it is unnecessary to read twiddles from memory and compute with them. So, this method reduces unnecessary memory access and computation cost. (2) The layout of first stage output is different from other stags, Thus zip instructions must be applied to rearrange result. Separating the first stage from other stags is convenient for us to do special SIMD optimization for this stage without affecting other stags.

4.2 Bufferfly Computation Optimization

In computational process, butterfly computation is invoked repeatedly, naturally, attention needs to be paid on this process to gain better performance. This paper takes radix-5 computation for example to illustrate the way of optimizing a kernel computation. This method can be generalized to other radix. given x_0, x_1, x_2, x_3, x_4 as kernel input, X_0, X_1, X_2, X_3, X_4 as kernel output. The original computation steps are given as:

$$X_0 = x_0 + x_1 + x_2 + x_3 + x_4$$

$$X_1 = x_0 + W_5^1 x_1 + W^2 x_2 + W^{-2} x_3 + W_5^{-1} x_4$$

$$X_2 = x_0 + W_5^2 x_1 + W_5^{-1} x_2 + W_5^1 x_3 + W_5^{-2} x_4$$

$$X_3 = x_0 + W_5^{-2}x_1 + W_5^1 x_2 + W_5^{-1}x_3 + W_5^2 x_4$$
$$X_4 = x_0 + W_5^{-1}x_1 + W_5^{-2}x_2 + W_5^2 x_3 + W_5^1 x_4$$

Because W_N^k and W_N^{-k} is symmetrical with the x-axis. we can merge the same terms:

$$X_0 = x_0 + (x_1 + x_4) + (x_2 + x_3)$$
$$X_1 = x_0 + (A - B) \quad X_2 = x_0 + (C + D)$$
$$X_3 = x_0 + (C - D) \quad X_4 = x_0 + (A + B)$$
$$A = (x_1 + x_4) * W_5^1.r + (x_2 + x3) * W_5^2.r$$
$$B = [(x_1 - x_4) * W_5^1.i + (x_2 - x3) * W_5^2.i] * (-j)$$
$$C = (x_1 + x_4) * W_5^2.r + (x_2 + x3) * W_5^1.r$$
$$D = [(x_1 - x_4) * W_5^2.i - (x_2 - x3) * W_5^1.i] * j$$

the repeated term here are: $x_1 + x_4$, $x_1 - x_4$, $x_2 - x_3$, $x_2 + x_3$ and A, B, C, D. through combination of same term, extra float computation can be saved compared with direct computation. This method can be extended to radix-3, radix-7 and other radix cases. So we can implement various radixes with the most streamlined computational complexity.

4.3 Butterfly SIMD Optimization

ARMv8 is the most up-to-date architecture of ARM cooperation. Both 32-bit execution status and 64-bit status are supported. Besides 31 64-bit general purpose registers (X0-X30), this architecture also provides 32 128-bit vector/scalar registers (V0-V31/Q0-Q31). These vector registers could store 4 floats or 2 doubles number, therefore, 4 float or 2 double operations are finished in parallel.

(1) **Inter-Butterfly Parallelization:** With benefits from the structure of butterfly-network described above, input and output data of continuous butterflies are arranged consecutively, with good locality. Therefore, it's very suitable to use SIMD technology to process multiple butterflies in the same time. For clarity, we take radix-5 for example.

In Fig. 3, four colors stand for four different butterflies, thus, input of four butterflies can be loaded into a 128-bit vector register and processed in the same time. For example, input from x_0[0] to x_4[0] is loaded into a vector register which is the first input across four butterflies.

(2) **Assembly Instruction Selection:** We improve performance of core computational part by using assembly instructions. Through tuning the execution order of instructions, we avoid pipeline bubbles. Through optimizing the usage of vector register, on-chip memory is efficiently used. Meanwhile, we also adopted extra optimizations to improve performance further: (1) Through zip1 instruction to rearrange output elements' order within the first stage. (2) Use ld2, faddq, st2 and other instructions to efficiently do complex number arithmetic operation. (3) Apply fmla/fmls properly to gain better computational performance.

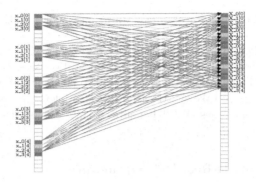

Fig. 3. Parallelization of 4 butterfly computations when radix is 5 (Color figure online)

(3) Reuse of Vector Register: To cope with shortage of vector register when solving very large radix computation, register reuse is applied. Through defining register using table and reusing rules, vector register is reused efficiently: Registers are enough when radix is 3, 4, 5, so we split register into four groups: input register groups input; output register group; intermediate result register group; twiddles register group. When radix is so large that it is necessary to reuse register. We define register groups' reuse attribution, combined with computational condition to decide if to reuse register group.

(4) Optimization for Small Scale: When input scale is small enough (3, 5, 7, etc.), special implementations and optimizations are taken to achieve high performance. Optimization techniques include: (1) Twiddle factors are pre-computed and prepared in micro format to save relevant computations and memory accessing costs. (2) Loop-unrolling is properly applied. (3) Manage to pack as many as possible computations into the same function to avoid function invocation cost.

5 Implement and Optimization of 2D Real DFT

2D DFT is essentially based on 1D real DFT. The critical issue of 2D transform is non-consecutive memory visit when transform column data. Thus the essential part of 2D optimization is to improve cache performance.

5.1 Consideration of 2D Real DFT Optimization

Based on this consideration, we propose following techniques to improve cache performance:

(1) Cache block method: To avoid non-consecutive memory visit in visiting column data, we need to transpose output every time we have finished row computation. However, this behavior has poor cache performance. To decrease cache miss rate, in plan stage, an extra buffer is prepared whose size is fit with L2 cache size. Every time before dense computation is carried out, data is read

into this buffer. This behavior assures data using in computation step is on the cache.

(2) Memory alignment: Although cache performance is improved through cache blocking, due to the uncertainty of computation size. It is quit possible that input matrix is not aligned which bates the efficiency of cache line usage. To handle this issue, we take ARM cache line size into consideration and align row of buffer with 64 bytes. With benefits of this, cache miss rate is reduced further.

5.2   Procedure of 2D Real DFT Optimization

Figure 4 shows procedures of cache blocking approach: Scan input matrix with an aligned row buffer which is fit with L2 cache size. Every time we fill row buffer with block of data, dense computation is carried out with output is transposed into another buffered matrix.

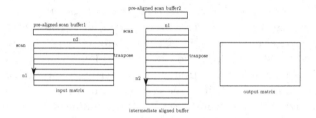

Fig. 4. General procedure of 2D transform

6   Experimental Results and Analysis

6.1   Test Platform and Comparison Baseline

Our experiment is carried out with (1) Hardware: CPU in this paper is ARM Cortex A57, 2.1 GHZ. (2) Software: Operation system is Ubuntu 15.04 with main memory size is 64 GB. FFTw 3.3.7 is chosen as comparison baseline. (3) Performance metric: Gflops = Floats Operations/Wall time. Float Operations are calculated as sum of logarithmic each dimension size multiplicated by whole computation. It is defined as $Float\ Operations = (\prod_{i=1}^{max-dim} Ni) * (\sum_{j=1}^{max-dim} logNj)$.

6.2   Experimental Results and Evaluations

In these figures, cold-coloured full line is used to stand for our transforms called OpenFFT, light-coloured dotted line is used to stand for FFTw 3.3.7's transforms. Figures 5, 6, 7, 8, 9, 10, 11, 12, 13, 14, 15, 16, 17, 18, 19, 20 and 21 show our experimental results compared with FFTw3.3.7. Figures 5, 6, 7 and 8 show that our 1D float transforms outperform FFTw3.3.7 significantly with even greater advantage when input size is becoming larger. Speedup is from 1.22x to

1.79x across all real DFT kinds. Figures 9, 10, 11 and 12 show that our 1D double transforms also outperform FFTw3.3.7 a lot, except for DCT/DST IV when input size is small, the cause will be analyzed in rest of this section. Speedup is from 1.04x to 1.61x across all real DFT kinds.

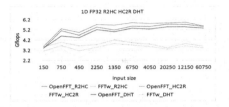

Fig. 5. 1DFP32 R2HC/HC2R/DHT (Color figure online)

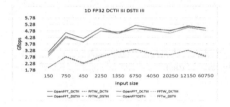

Fig. 6. 1DFP32 DCT/DST I (Color figure online)

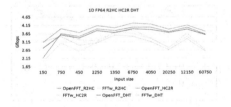

Fig. 7. 1DFP32 DCT/DST II/III (Color figure online)

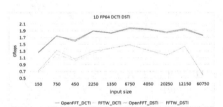

Fig. 8. 1DFP32 DCT/DST IV (Color figure online)

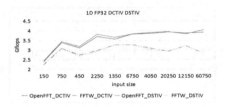

Fig. 9. 1DFP64 R2HC/HC2R/DHT (Color figure online)

Fig. 10. 1DFP64 DCT/DST I (Color figure online)

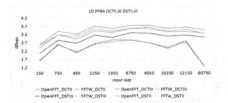

Fig. 11. 1DFP64 DCT/DST II/III (Color figure online)

Fig. 12. 1DFP64 DCT/DST IV (Color figure online)

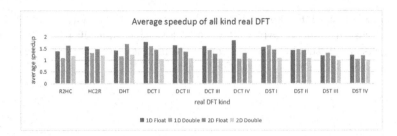

Fig. 13. Speedup across all transform kinds and types (Color figure online)

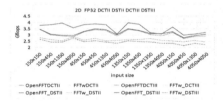

Fig. 14. 2DFP32 R2HC/HC2R/DHT (Color figure online)

Fig. 15. 2DFP32 DCT/DST I (Color figure online)

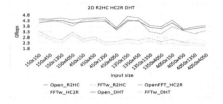

Fig. 16. 2DFP32 DCT/DST II/III (Color figure online)

Fig. 17. 2DFP32 DCT/DST IV (Color figure online)

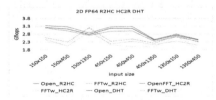

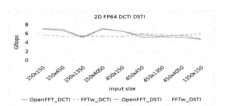

Fig. 18. 2DFP64 R2HC/HC2R/DHT (Color figure online)

Fig. 19. 2DFP64 DCT/DST I (Color figure online)

Due to alignment and double data type, memory size of our test machine is limited for 2D transforms. Thus the test size of 2D transforms is tuned smaller. Figures 14, 15, 16 and 17 show our 2D float transforms outperform FFTw3.3.7

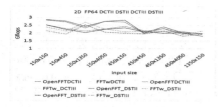

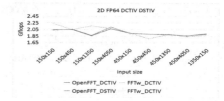

Fig. 20. 2DFP64 DCT/DST II/III (Color figure online)

Fig. 21. 2DFP64 DCT/DST IV (Color figure online)

a lot, and speedup is from 1.20x to 1.70x. The abnormal peak point in Fig. 17 is analyzed in the rest of this section. Figures 18, 19, 20 and 21 show 2D double transforms' speedup across all kind is from 0.99x to 1.25x. Performance degeneration in DCT/DST I/IV 2D is analyzed in next section.

6.3 Performance Analysis

This section summarizes and analyzes performance comparison between ours and FFTw3.3.7's: As a whole, our transforms outperform FFTw3.37's a lot except for some transform cases. Moreover, speedup of double data type is not as significant as float as shown in Fig. 13. Causes are presented:

(1) 1D Double DCT/DST IV: To obtain transform result, operations applied to combine two sub-transform's results are not optimized well on double data type. costs brought by these operations are significant when input size is relatively small.

(2) General Analysis of Performance Degeneration Between 2D and 1D Transforms: Performance degeneration is caused by pre-process of input. For example sign flip operations of DCT/DST II/III and extension operations of DCT/DST I. And the degree of it is related to the complexity of these operations. Further overheads are accumulated with increased transform dimensions.

(3) Analysis of Performance of 2D DCT/DST I/IV: As DCT/DST I are solved based on Algorithm 1, Extension operations of intermediate result of row transforms are inevitable before solving column transforms. Cache misses brought by data copying of extension operation bring non-ignorable overhead. Except for general pre-process of input, DCT/DST IV need extra combining operations to achieve final results, which are not optimized enough for multi-dimensional condition.

(4) Abnormal Performance Peak Point of Fig. 17: Order of radix derived from prime factorization affects performance as a whole. As our implementation does not support optimization on radix generation, the radix order is not optimal when size is 1350.

(5) Influence of Double Data Type: Type of data has influence on performance as a whole. For the limitation of vector length, the parallelized double operations are inherently limited than float. Therefore more cares of optimization need to be taken into double cases, and effect of optimization is inevitably abated.

7   Conclusion and Future Work

In this paper, we implement and optimize 11 1D/2D real DFT kinds on ARMv8 platform. Experiments show that we outperform FFTw3.3.7 in most cases. In the future, we plan to further optimize double DCT/DST IV, moreover, a strategy to optimize radix order needs to be designed. In the end, optimization for 2^n input size needs to be researched in the future.

Acknowledgments. This work is supported by the National Key Research and Development Program of China under Grant No.2017YFB0202105 and No.2016YFE0100300; The National Natural Science Foundation of China under Grant No.61432018, No.61521092 and No.61502405; Key Technology Research and Development Programs of Guangdong Province under Grant No.2015B010108006.

References

1. Oran Brigham, E.: The Fast Fourier Transform and Its Applications, vol. 1. Prentice Hall, Englewood Cliffs (1988)
2. Reddy, B.S., Chatterji, B.N.: An FFT-based technique for translation, rotation, and scale-invariant image registration. IEEE Trans. Image Process. **5**(8), 1266–1271 (1996)
3. Sorensen, H.V., Jones, D., Heideman, M., Burrus, C.: Real-valued Fast Fourier Transform algorithms. IEEE Trans. Acoust. Speech Signal Process. **35**(6), 849–863 (1987)
4. Pippig, M.: PFFT: an extension of FFTW to massively parallel architectures. SIAM J. Sci. Comput. **35**(3), C213–C236 (2013)
5. Abtahi, T., Kulkarni, A., Mohsenin, T.: Accelerating convolutional neural network with FFT on tiny cores. In: IEEE International Symposium on Circuits and Systems (ISCAS), pp. 1–4. IEEE (2017)
6. Cecotti, H., Graeser, A.: Convolutional neural network with embedded Fourier Transform for EEG classification. In: 19th International Conference on Pattern Recognition, ICPR 2008, pp. 1–4. IEEE (2008)
7. Lavin, A., Gray, S.: Fast algorithms for convolutional neural networks, pp. 4013–4021 (2016)
8. Lee, B.: FCT-a fact cosine transform. In: IEEE International Conference on Acoustics, Speech, and Signal Processing, ICASSP 1984, vol. 9, pp. 477–480. IEEE (1984)
9. Chen, Y., Cui, X., Mei, H.: Large-scale FFT on GPU clusters, pp. 315–324 (2010)
10. Frigo, M., Johnson, S.G.: FFTW: an adaptive software architecture for the FFT, vol. 3, pp. 1381–1384. IEEE (1998)
11. Li, Y., Zhang, Y.-Q., Liu, Y.-Q., Long, G.-P., Jia, H.-P.: MPFFT: an auto-tuning FFT library for OpenCL GPUs. J. Comput. Sci. Technol. **28**(1), 90–105 (2013)
12. Makhoul, J.: A fast cosine transform in one and two dimensions. IEEE Trans. Acoust. Speech Signal Process. **28**(1), 27–34 (1980)
13. Press, W.H.: Numerical Recipes: The Art of Scientific Computing, 3rd edn. Cambridge University Press, New York (2007)

14. Shao, X., Johnson, S.G.: Type-II/III DCT/DST algorithms with reduced number of arithmetic operations. Signal Process. **88**(6), 1553–1564 (2008)
15. Wang, Z.: On computing the discrete fourier and cosine transforms. IEEE Trans. Acoust. Speech Signal Process. **33**(5), 1341–1344 (1985)
16. ARM Performance Library. https://developer.arm.com/products/software-development-tools/hpc/arm-performance-libraries

SPMP: A JavaScript Support for Shared Persistent Memory on Node.js

Qipeng Zhang[1], Tianyou Li[2], Pan Deng[2], Yuting Chen[1], Linpeng Huang[1(✉)],
and Andy Rudoff[3]

[1] Shanghai Jiao Tong University, Shanghai, China
{zqp19941019,chenyt,lphuang}@sjtu.edu.cn
[2] Intel Asia Pacific R&D Co. LTD, Shanghai, China
{tianyou.li,pan.deng}@intel.com
[3] Intel Corporation, Santa Clara, CA, USA
andy.rudoff@intel.com

Abstract. JavaScript is widely used for scripting on client side. Node.js is a JavaScript runtime environment, allowing Javascript to be used for building scalable network applications on server side. However, Node.js does not support parallel programming, making it difficult to enhance applications' performance. Meanwhile, persistent memory (PM) shows optimistic prospects of being used in server-side applications, while few researches do exist in allowing script languages to support PM-based parallel programming. In this paper, we introduce SPMP, a JavaScript support for shared persistent memory on Node.js. With SPMP, each process needs to hold `PersistentArrayBuffer`, an object that is responsible for allocating, managing, and accessing persistent memory. Multiple processes can then share persistent memory and communicate each other by their `PersistentArrayBuffer` objects. Furthermore, SPMP supports dynamic load-balancing strategies and ensures data coherency, and also supports data persistence in a secondary storage. We have evaluated SPMP against Extended Memory Semantics (EMS, a state-of-the-art model for parallel programming on Node.js) on two data-intensive tasks. The results show that SPMP is $100 \sim 300\times$ faster than EMS on five basic operations, and $2\times$ faster on complicated parallel computing tasks such as counting words, due to its particular way on memory allocation and mapping.

Keywords: Node.js · Parallel programming
Shared persistent memory

1 Introduction

Persistent memory (PM) is a novel technique for improving the performance of data-intensive software applications and guaranteeing their fault-tolerance. It removes the boundary between the memory and the storage when storing data structures: Memory can still be accessed by the *load* and *store* instructions, while

J. Vaidya and J. Li (Eds.): ICA3PP 2018, LNCS 11335, pp. 354–366, 2018.
https://doi.org/10.1007/978-3-030-05054-2_28

the data in the memory is persistent (i.e., the data needs to be retained at the time of power loss or application crashes and can be recovered when needed). Many persistent memory products, such as RamDisk [1], Phase Change Memory (PCM) [2] and STT-RAM [3], have been developed. They do provide several exciting features, including DRAM-like access speed, high data persistence and endurance, retention and byte-addressability.

Persistent memory can be shared among processes. Shared memory [4] is a programming paradigm for parallel computing: Memory may be simultaneously accessed by multiple processes, and thus processes can communicate directly without data replication or transfer. **Shared persistent memory** (Shared PM) brings the ideas of shared memory and persistent memory together – several processes can access the persistent memory in parallel, and the data in the memory needs to be persistent. Many efforts have been spent on supporting shared PM [5,6]. They mainly tackle two challenges: (1) how to support multiple processes/threads on persistent memory, and (2) how to keep data coherency.

This paper presents **SPMP**, a JavaScript support for shared PM on Node.js. JavaScript is a popular scripting language for creating web applications on client side [7]. It can be interpreted and JIT'ed by JavaScript engines, such as Google's V8 in Chrome [8], SpiderMonkey in Firefox [9] and FLT in Safari [10]. **Node.js**, a JavaScript runtime environment, was further developed on V8 engine, allowing JavaScript code to run on server-side [11]. SPMP is designed for supporting parallel programming on Node.js, and as well leveraging persistent memory to keep data persistence.

The objective of this paper is to

1. **Support Shared Memory on Node.js**
   Node.js does not allow applications to be run in parallel. Despite many efforts in introducing parallel computing into Node.js, the performance of the server-side applications can still be low due to many constraints. For example, Web-Workers [12] is a parallel programming model for Node.js applications based on share-nothing parallel workers: data needs to be explicitly partitioned and distributed [13]; workers exchange data via asynchronous messages, which may be frequent and incur high overhead. Shared memory, which alleviates the overhead of data copying/transfer, can thus become an alternative to parallel computing on Node.js.

2. **Utilize PM to Enhance Performance and Keep Memory Persistent**
   Shared persistent memory enhances the performance of Node.js applications on the server side, because data copying and transfer among processes are waived. Comparatively, performance of applications can be enhanced by shared PM because memory and disks can be taken as a whole, providing with DRAM-like access speed. Memory persistence can also be held when PM is employed.

As Fig. 1 shows, SPMP provides a JavaScript support such that each Node.js process can manage and access persistent memory through Google's V8 and some other libraries. SPMP also provides multiple processes with facilities (including some objects and load-balancing strategies) in allocating and sharing persistent memory and communicating each other.

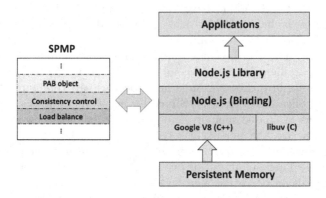

Fig. 1. An overview of SPMP.

This paper makes the following contributions:

1. **A JavaScript Support for Shared PM on Node.js.** SPMP is a JavaScript support that allows multi-processes to share persistent memory on Node.js. It provides facilities for managing processes and simplifying many challenging issues in parallel programming such as data coherency, synchronization and dynamic load balance. It also supports data persistence on PM and on a secondary storage.
2. **A Persistent Memory Object.** We have implemented a JavaScript object, `PersistentArrayBuffer`. It represents a persistent, fixed-length buffer. Each process needs to hold such an object for allocating, managing, and accessing persistent memory. Multiple processes can then share persistent memory and communicate each other by their `PersistentArrayBuffer` objects.
3. **Evaluation and Results.** We have implemented SPMP for parallel programming on Node.js. We have evaluated SPMP against Extended Memory Semantics (EMS, a state-of-the-art model for parallel programming on Node.js) on two data-intensive tasks. The results show that SPMP is 100–300× faster than EMS on five basic operations, and 2× faster than EMS on complicated parallel computing tasks such as counting words, due to its particular way on memory allocation and mapping.

The remainder of this paper is structured as follows. In Sect. 2, we introduce the design details of SPMP. Section 3 evaluates SPMP. Section 4 presents related work, and Sect. 5 concludes.

2   Design and Implementation

Shared memory is a memory region that can be simultaneously accessed by multiple processes. SPMP provides a JavaScript support for shared persistent memory on Node.js.

2.1   Background

SPMP is built on the base of Chrome V8 [8]. It also employs the Intel's PMDK [14] to access and share the persistent memory.

Chrome V8 [8] is an open-source JavaScript engine developed in C++ by Google. It performs ahead-of-time compilation of JavaScript code to native machine code, and re-optimizes the compiled code dynamically at runtime. We design a persistent array buffer object on V8 and expose it as a Node.js object for managing the persistent memory. Thus SPMP benefits from native high performance of V8.

The Persistent Memory Development Kit (PMDK), developed by Intel, is a growing collection of libraries and tools for persistent memory [14]. The kit allows persistent memory to be accessed via memory mapping files in a PM-aware file system. With PMDK, a C programmer can manage persistent memory much more efficiently. Binding supports have also been developed for other programming languages (e.g., C++, python) such that the programmers can use PMDK in their software development.

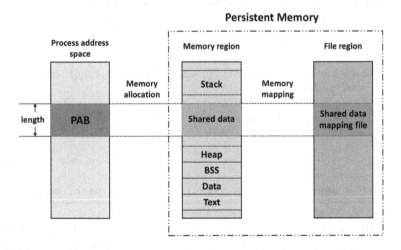

Fig. 2. Memory allocation and mapping with PAB on process.

2.2   Shared Persistent Memory

In SPMP, processes on Node.js can manage and share persistent memory using their `PersistentArrayBuffer` (PAB) objects. As Fig. 2 shows, each process holds a PAB object that points to a memory region, which is further mapped to a memory mapping file to ensure data persistence. Let two or more PAB objects point to the same memory region where the shared data is stored, shared persistent memory can then be realized.

Creating a PAB Object. PAB objects are designed to manage and share persistent memory. Next shows a code snippet for creating a PAB object. PAB object is created using function `new PersistentArrayBuffer(length, path, mode)`, where `length` and `path` correspond to the size of allocated memory and the memory-mapping file, respectively; `mode` is a mode denoting whether the created PAB object needs to create a mapping file or open an existing one. Note that contents of PAB cannot be manipulated directly but with a typed array object. A TypedArray object describes an array-like view of PAB and underlying elements can then be referenced with array index.

```
1    function PersistentArrayBuffer(length, path, mode){
2        this.length = length;
3        this.path = path;
4        this.mode = mode;
5        this.buffer = this.prototype.newbuffer(length, path,
             mode)
6        this.msync = function(offset, length){
7            //sync memory to mapped file
8            call_msync(this.buffer, offset, length);
9        }
10   }
11   PersistentArrayBuffer.prototype.newbuffer = function(length,
         path, mode){
12       //create or open a buffer
13       call_newbuffer(length, path, mode);
14   }
15
16   //Next creates a PAB object. It also creates/opens
17   // a memory mapped file for memory persistence.
18   var pab = new PersistentArrayBuffer(length, path, mode);
```

Memory Allocation and Mapping. A PAB object employs the PMDK libraries, rather than `malloc()`, to allocate, manage and release memory. One main reason is that `malloc()` is anonymous. Instead, PMDK can record the path of the allocated memory, making PM manageable. Furthermore, PAB uses `pmem_mmap()`, rather than `mmap()`, in memory mapping. It supports an alignment mechanism for speeding up memory reading and writing.

Keeping Memory Persistence. SPMP guarantees memory persistence using memory-mapping files. A memory mapping file can be stored in PM or in a disk, and thus can be taken as a backup of the memory. With memory mapping files, PAB objects can also provide persistence support for RAMs.

2.3   Process Spawning

A Node.js module, child_process, is responsible for spawning child processes. In particular, a function child_process.fork() needs to be invoked to fork processes. In SPMP, this function is wrapped to fork child processes. Each child process is independent from its parent process except that a communication channel (between a process and its child) is established. Tasks are assigned to the function as a parameter, and need to be further partitioned by each process.

SPMP also creates a new memory region and maps it into a file called "shared configuration file". The file saves configurations listed in Table 1. It can be accessed by the PAB objects of processes. Any change to these configurations needs to be broadcasted.

Table 1. Shared configurations.

Configuration	Meaning
NPROC	Number of processes
BAR	Processes that are not at barrier
FLAG	Barrier state
START	Starting index of a task
END	Ending index of a task
SIZE	Designated chunk size
MINSIZE	Minimum chunk size
STRATEGY	Strategy taken for task decomposition

As Fig. 3 shows, SPMP spawns processes for parallel computing as follows. First, the main process creates a PAB object and a shared mapping file. The main process holds a memory region mapped to the file. Second, child processes are spawned from the main process. Each child process shares the task module and configurations with the main process. Each child process also creates a PAB object for opening the shared data mapping file, whose length and path are same as the main process. Thus, all of the processes have their PAB objects that can access the same memory region corresponding to a shared file.

2.4   Load Balance

In order to complete a large task, child processes need to be spawned from the main process. Strategies are designed for partitioning a task and balancing workloads of the spawned processes.

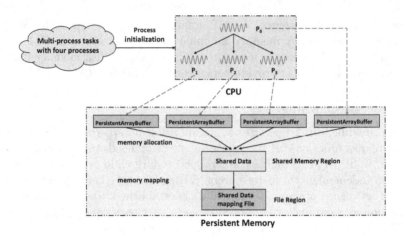

Fig. 3. Sharing PM among spawned processes.

SPMP supports three strategies for keeping load balance among processes.

1. A *static* strategy that requires each task to be evenly partitioned for all processes.
2. A *preemptive* strategy. Each task is divided into $4 \times NPROC$ subtasks evenly. Processes compete for acquiring subtasks: When a process is free, it raises requests to occupy a subtask.
3. A *guided* strategy. It requires a subtask's size to be dynamically assigned, usually according to the total size of the uncompleted tasks. Processes preemptively occupy these subtasks. Here the size of a subtask is calculated using

$$SIZE = max((END - START)/(2 \times NPROC), MINSIZE) \quad (1)$$

Both of the *preemptive* and the *guided* strategies allow processes to preempt subtasks. Once success, shared configurations needed to be update so that processes can preemptively occupy the remaining subtasks.

2.5 Consistency Control

Consistency control aims to coordinate processes to access the shared memory and shared mapping files that otherwise race conditions can occur frequently. For instance, let two processes (say $Proc_1$ and $Proc_2$) preempt a subtask whose indexes range from $START$ to $START + SIZE$. If $Proc_1$ occupies, it needs to modify the value of $START$ to $START + SIZE$. Without consistency control, $Proc_2$ may fetch the same configurations and work on the same subtask. SPMP supports consistency control on Node.js in two respects: (1) enabling native consistency control functions, and (2) enabling a barrier mechanism.

Native functions for controlling consistencies can be invoked in an N-API function. Here N-API is a Node.js API for building native addons, which are dynamically-linked shared objects providing glue to C/C++ libraries. Many lower level operations, such as `__sync_fetch_and_add()`, `__sync_fetch_and_and()`, support consistency control. These functions can be exposed to JavaScript using N-API.

For example, the native function `type __sync_fetch_and_add(type *ptr, type value)` can be exposed to JavaScript as follows. First, since JavaScript has no pointer and variable type, this function is wrapped as `var fetch_and_add(Array, offset, value)`, where the pointer `*ptr` used in the native function is replaced by an array and an offset. Next, the wrapped function is compiled and files in Node.js are binded. It creates a binary node module that can be imported, using the function `require()`, into JavaScript. Thus the function `var fetch_and_add(Array, offset, value)` wrapped in the addon can be invoked in JavaScript.

3   Evaluation

We have implemented SPMP and evaluated it against EMS (Extended Memory Semantics, a state-of-the-art model for parallel programming on Node.js). Our evaluation is designed to answer the following questions:

1. *Parallelism.* How does SPMP support parallel programming on Node.js?
2. *Strategy.* Which strategy needs to be chosen for load balance?
3. *SPMP vs. EMS.* What are the advantages of SPMP, compared with EMS?

3.1   Preparation

Tasks and Metrics. Our evaluation is mainly performed on two parallel computing tasks:

- *STREAMS.* It processes a test file containing five basic operations: (1) *read*, (2) *write*, (3) *copy*, (4) $c = a * b$, and (5) $c+ = a * b$. Each operation is performed 20M times in an experiment. A metric, *AOS* (Atomic Operations per Second), is measured. In the evaluation we performed STREAMS 10 times, and computed the average results for operations.
- *WordCount.* WordCount counts words in a directory of 18,510 text files, with 1.7G+ words and 7G+ bytes in total. WordCount counts the total number and size of words. Two metrics, *WS* (words per second) and *MS* (Megabytes per second), are calculated for every 100 text files.

Model for Comparison. Extended Memory Semantics (EMS) is a model for parallel programming on Node.js. It supports shared objects, synchronization, persistence and load balance. To the best of our knowledge, EMS is the only model that is comparable to SPMP. Both of SPMP and EMS can be equipped with our strategies for load balance. Correspondingly, we have SPMP_{static}, $\text{SPMP}_{preemptive}$, SPMP_{guided}, EMS_{static}, and EMS_{guided}.

Configuration. The evaluation was performed on a server (CPU: Intel(R) Xeon E5-2643 v3 @ 3.40 GHz, RAM: 64 GB, OS: Ubuntu 14.04). In order to check supportability of PM, we emulated a PM device with RAM and mounted it using DAX in order to set up a PM-aware environment.

3.2 Evaluation on Parallelism

We employed $SPMP_{static}$, with different number of processes to complete the STREAMS task. $SPMP_{static}$ requires each task to be equivalently partitioned to all processes. As Fig. 4(a) shows, SPMP spends less time to finish the STREAMS tasks when the number of processes increases. More accurately, a linear correlation exists between the time and number of processes. It clearly indicates that (1) all of the processes have been involved in the computing task, and (2) a small subtask usually requires less cost than a large one.

We calculated AOS for the five atomic operations. It decreases in an order of read, write, copy, $c = a * b$ and $c+ = a * b$. The main reason is that the later three operations are in fact combinations of read and write operations. Thus the time consumed is much relevant to the number of read/write operations involved.

From the above analysis, we draw out our first observation:

> **Observation 1:** SPMP supports parallelism, making use of computing resources; the efficiency can get increased when the number of processes increases.

3.3 Evaluation on Strategies

We compared the strategies taken by SPMP. Figure 4(a), (b) and (c) show the results for $SPMP_{static}$, $SPMP_{guided}$ and $SPMP_{preemptive}$ on STREAMS, respectively. It is clear that the linear correlation between number of processes and time spent exist for all strategies. $SPMP_{guided}$ performs better than $SPMP_{preemptive}$ on STREAMS. The main reason is, compared with $SPMP_{preemptive}$, $SPMP_{guided}$ partitions each task into more but smaller subtasks, and thus achieves higher parallelism. As for $SPMP_{preemptive}$, processes need to wait for each other until they complete their subtasks. Thereafter, we believe that $SPMP_{guided}$ is more well-balanced than $SPMP_{preemptive}$.

Both of $SPMP_{guided}$ and $SPMP_{preemptive}$ perform worse than $SPMP_{static}$, as they need more inter-process communications. Nevertheless, $SPMP_{static}$ requires the programmers to explicitly partition the tasks, but the other two do not. It is believed that a programmer needs to choose the specific strategy on the basis of the scenario in practice.

Thus we draw out our second observation:

> **Observation 2:** All of the three strategies help balance workloads; the strategies are applicable for different scenarios.

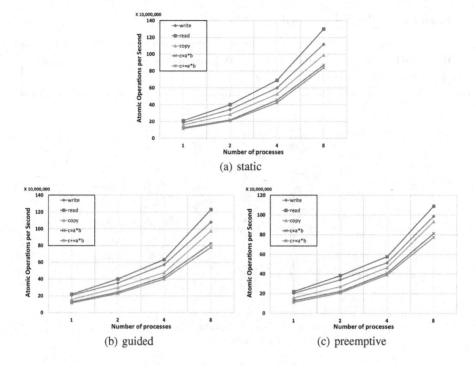

Fig. 4. Evaluating SPMP on STREAMS.

3.4   SPMP vs. EMS

We compared SPMP and EMS on the two computing tasks.

STREAMS. SPMP and EMS with different strategies were compared on STREAMS. Each algorithm (SPMP$_{static}$, SPMP$_{preemptive}$, SPMP$_{guided}$, EMS$_{static}$, or EMS$_{guided}$) manages four processes. Figure 5 shows the results for comparing SPMP with EMS on STREAMS, where the x-axis denotes five different operations, and the y-axis is $\log_{10} AOS$. For all of the five operations, SPMP is $100 \sim 300\times$ faster than EMS.

WordCount. We compared EMS$_{guided}$ strategy and SPMP$_{guided}$ on WordCount. Figure 6 show the processing rates of words and bytes. The both rates are linearly related to the number of processes.

Furthermore, SPMP is $2\times$ faster than EMS. Here both of SPMP and EMS implement parallelism with shared memory, but SPMP outperforms EMS due to its way of memory management. EMS allocates and maps its memory with JavaScript functions, which are exposed from C functions using C/C++ addons (nan). Thus it takes time in transferring objects and translating functions between C and JavaScript. On the contrary, SPMP takes use of PAB implemented on V8 engine. It manages and shares memory by following a much more native style, and thus becomes efficient.

From the results, we draw out our third observation:

> **Observation 3:** SPMP outperforms EMS because of its native way of memory allocation and mapping.

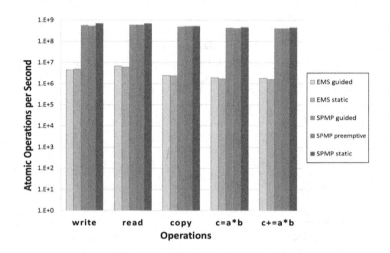

Fig. 5. Comparing SPMP with EMS on STREAMS.

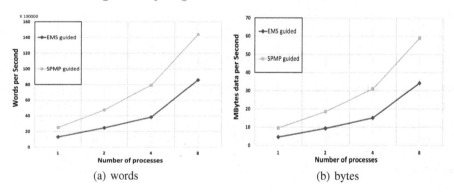

Fig. 6. Comparing SPMP with EMS on WordCount.

4   Related Work

We discuss two strands of related work: shared memory programming models and JavaScript parallelism.

Shared Memory Programming Models. Shared memory is well supported in many programming languages. One typical effort is hyperobjects in Cilk++ [15]. It implements programming abstractions that provide shared memory between threads, and thus allows C++ to enable dynamic, multi-threaded programming. As for Node.js, GEMs [16] is a shared-memory parallel programming abstraction. It combines message passing with shared memory to generate and share messages among workers. Comparatively, SPMP provides a much more efficient solution to shared memory and memory mapping such that parallelism on persistent memory is supported.

JavaScript Parallelism. Some researches, including WebWorkers [12], Cluster and RiverTrail [17], have been conducted to enable parallelism in JavaScript. These efforts are mainly designed as the sharing nothing parallelism that requires the workers to transfer copies of data to each other via message passing when needed. Comparatively, SPMP supports parallelism and communications through shared memory, rather than passing messages.

Extended Memory Semantics (EMS) [5] supports parallelism on Node.js and persistent memory. EMS implements a shared address space with a rich set of primitives for accessing data structures in parallel. However, EMS is based on nan – a Node.js addon. With nan, any JavaScript operation should at first be translated into an addon function, and then into a C/C++ operation. It can significantly reduce the efficiency of Node.js applications at runtime. SPMP can achieve higher performance than EMS because it makes use of native interfaces.

5   Conclusion

SPMP is a JavaScript support for shared persistent memory on Node.js. Persistent memory is leveraged to maintain data persistence and as well enhance performance of applications by eliminating data transfers between RAM and disks. `PersistentArrayBuffer` is designed to manage the shared persistent memory and coordinate processes. Our evaluations have clearly shown that SPMP can enhance the performance of applications significantly by taking use of persistent memory. Besides continuing our own development efforts, we plan to make SPMP be integrated into the PMDK libraries for aiding JavaScript developers in their routine development.

Acknowledgements. We thank the anonymous reviewers for their feedbacks and suggestions. This work is supported by the National Key Research and Development Program of China (No. 2018YFB10033002) and the National Natural Science Foundation of China (No. 61472241, 61572312). This work was also partially supported by Shanghai Municipal Commission of Economy and Informatization (No. 201701052).

References

1. Diehl, S.T.: System and method for persistent ram disk. US Patent 7,594,068, 22 September 2009
2. Burr, G.W., et al.: Recent progress in phase-change memory technology. IEEE J. Emerg. Sel. Top. Circuits Syst. **6**(2), 146–162 (2016)
3. Kültürsay, E., Kandemir, M., Sivasubramaniam, A., Mutlu, O.: Evaluating STT-RAM as an energy-efficient main memory alternative. In: 2013 IEEE International Symposium on Performance Analysis of Systems and Software (ISPASS), pp. 256–267. IEEE (2013)
4. Gharachorloo, K., Lenoski, D., Laudon, J., Gibbons, P., Gupta, A., Hennessy, J.: Memory consistency and event ordering in scalable shared-memory multiprocessors, vol. 18. ACM (1990)
5. Mogill, J.A.: Extended memory semantics (2017). http://syntheticsemantics.com/EMS.js
6. Shan, Y., Tsai, S.Y., Zhang, Y.: Distributed shared persistent memory. In: Proceedings of the 2017 Symposium on Cloud Computing, pp. 323–337. ACM (2017)
7. Selakovic, M., Pradel, M.: Performance issues and optimizations in Javascript: an empirical study. In: Proceedings of the 38th International Conference on Software Engineering, pp. 61–72. ACM (2016)
8. GoogleDevelopers: V8 engine (2018). https://developers.google.com/v8/
9. Mozilla: Spidermonkey engine (2018). https://developer.mozilla.org/en-US/docs/Mozilla/Projects/SpiderMonkey
10. Webkit: FTL JIT (2014). https://webkit.org/blog/3362/introducing-the-webkit-ftl-jit/
11. Tilkov, S., Vinoski, S.: Node. js: using javascript to build high-performance network programs. IEEE Internet Comput. **14**(6), 80–83 (2010)
12. Verdu, J., Pajuelo, A.: Performance scalability analysis of javascript applications with web workers. IEEE Comput. Archit. Lett. **15**(2), 105–108 (2016)
13. Lester, B.P.: The art of parallel programming. In: A Logical Calculus of the Ideas Immanent in Nervous Activity (1993)
14. Intel: The persistent memory development kit (2018). http://pmem.io/
15. Frigo, M., Halpern, P., Leiserson, C.E., Lewin-Berlin, S.: Reducers and other cilk++ hyperobjects. In: SPAA 2009: Proceedings of the ACM Symposium on Parallelism in Algorithms and Architectures, Calgary, Alberta, Canada, August, pp. 79–90 (2009)
16. Bonetta, D., Salucci, L., Marr, S., Binder, W.: Gems: shared-memory parallel programming for Node.js. In: Proceedings of the 2016 ACM SIGPLAN International Conference on Object-Oriented Programming, Systems, Languages, and Applications, pp. 531–547. ACM (2016)
17. Herhut, S., Hudson, R.L., Shpeisman, T., Sreeram, J.: Parallel programming for the web. In: USENIX Conference on Hot Topics in Parallelism, p. 1 (2012)

Dynamic Obstacle Avoidance Planning Algorithm for UAV Based on Dubins Path

Na Wang[1], Fei Dai[1(✉)], Fangxin Liu[2], and Guomin Zhang[1]

[1] Army Engineering University of PLA, Nanjing 210007, China
daifei08@163.com
[2] Shanghai Branch, Coordination Center of China,
National Computer Network Emergency Response Technical Team,
Shanghai 201315, China

Abstract. By considering the influence of turning radius on UAV movement, the Dubins path can use geometric methods to plan the shortest curve between the initial state and the end state of UAV. But, the important prerequisite for this path planning is that the location and size of obstacles should be known and it is assumed that the obstacles are round. However, in actual tasks, UAV often cannot know the position, shape, and size of obstacles in advance during the movement. Therefore, it is difficult to efficiently implement obstacle avoidance planning in an unknown dynamic environment. In view of the dynamic mission environment and low-cost UAV system, this paper proposed a UAV dynamic obstacle avoidance planning algorithm based on Dubins path, which make use of real time detection and estimation and can be used to optimize the real-time obstacle avoidance path of UAV under the premise of unknown obstacle's position, shape and size. Simulation results show that the algorithm is correct and can improve the efficiency of low-cost UAVs performing tasks in a dynamic environment.

Keywords: UAV · Dynamic obstacle avoidance planning · Dubins path

1 Introduction

As the technology of unmanned aerial vehicle (UAV) becomes more and more mature, UAVs are gradually used to solve problems that many traditional methods cannot effectively solve, such as target monitoring and tracking, airspace situational awareness interaction, unmanned aerial vehicle automatic collision avoidance, and empty sea-land cooperation. It has played a vital role in the emergency assistance and urban emergency [1]. UAVs have the advantages of flexibility, low cost, small size, low environmental requirements, and high flying height, and can adapt to more complex and dynamic uncertain environments [2]. UAV's low-altitude autonomous flight is a research hot-spot, and the core technology in the path planning for autonomous flight are the automatic obstacle avoidance technology during flight. Traditional UAV obstacle avoidance planning algorithms include gradient method, spline interpolation method, nonlinear programming method, optimal control method, A* algorithm, neural network method, simulated annealing method, genetic algorithm, ant colony algorithm, dynamic

© Springer Nature Switzerland AG 2018
J. Vaidya and J. Li (Eds.): ICA3PP 2018, LNCS 11335, pp. 367–377, 2018.
https://doi.org/10.1007/978-3-030-05054-2_29

programming algorithm, etc. [3–9], but the above methods treat the UAV as a particle, without considering its own flight performance and the influence of the minimum turning radius on the establishment of the obstacle avoidance model. Dubins [10] considered the influence of the turning radius on the UAV motion and first discussed the shortest curve problem between the initial state and the end state of the motion using the geometric method. The concept of the Dubins path was first proposed. Based on the Dubins path, the researchers discussed how to choose the optimal path from many Dubins paths on the premise of multiple obstacles, and designed a large number of intelligent algorithms to solve. However, most of the traditional Dubins path-based methods do not consider the dynamic task environment, especially where the obstacle position, shape, and size are unknown. Although some real-time path planning algorithms can also respond well to the dynamic environment with uncertain obstacles, they usually require stronger, higher-cost sensors as auxiliary support. For low-cost UAVs, how to achieve dynamic obstacle avoidance during autonomous flight is an important issue that needs urgent solution.

This paper makes full use of Dubins path planning method and uses a simple forward detection sensor to implement a UAV dynamic obstacle avoidance planning algorithm based on the Dubins path through obstacle estimation and the real-time iterative planning. The remainder of the paper is organized as follows: Sect. 2 describes the related works. Section 3 briefly reviews the basic process of Dubins path planning. Section 4 conducts problem modeling and dynamic obstacle avoidance planning algorithm design. Section 5 presents a simulation experiment to discuss the advantages and disadvantages of different obstacle avoidance schemes. Section 6 summarizes the full text.

2 Related Works

At present, the research on the obstacle avoidance methods of UAVs mainly focuses on three aspects.

(1) Based on image recognition. Such methods generally install cameras and vision processors on UAVs. The position of the obstacle is calculated from the image acquired by the camera. The reactive collision-avoidance algorithm based on the closest point of approach (CPA) using a single vision sensor for UAVs is proposed [11]. It can avoid a collision with an intruder while overcoming the loss-of-depth problem of the single vision sensor. However, when the shape of the obstacle is irregular, the calculation of the algorithm is more complicated. The method for design a controller of autonomous collision avoidance based on EKF-OSA was proposed [12]. However, this method only applies to static obstacle scenes. In [13], it introduces an efficient approach for sky segmentation in a cluttered environment that is considered as a vital step for UAV autonomous obstacle avoidance. In order to ensure the safety of UAVs flying at low altitude, the grayscale is adjusted according to the captured image to achieve segmentation of the sky, so that obstacles are identified. Through this method, the accuracy of obstacle recognition can be improved.

(2) Based on searching. The A* algorithm performs route planning by constructing the cost function. In theory, the UAVs can achieve the shortest path by using A*. It is verified that the planned track satisfies all kinds of flight requirements for hypersonic vehicles and can avoid various threats. For two-dimensional obstacles, obstacle regions is wrapped using elliptical geometry. For three-dimensional obstacles, obstacle regions is wrapped using ellipsoids [14]. However, at present, this method is only aimed at static obstacles. A method of obstacle avoidance for UAV based on Dubins path planning is proposed [15]. This method takes into account the factors of the minimum turning radius of the drone. The path planning is solved by using genetic algorithms under the condition that the obstacle has prior knowledge. In [16], Dubins paths were applied for both static and moving ground obstacle avoidance by using a variation of the Rapidly-exploding Random Tree (RRT) planner. In [17], Search-and-avoid algorithms for Dubins paths can be developed by using several different techniques.

(3) Based on potential field. The artificial potential field method is used to plan the targets and obstacles for UAVs. The gravitational function of artificial potential field method is improved, and a sufficient smooth flight path is obtained by several iterations and curvature checking [18]. It is a static path planning method. The geometric constraints of the artificial potential field are added to the kinematics equation, and the collision detection angle is calculated to determine the shortest avoidance path for UAVs [19, 20]. The method can be used to solve the collision avoidance problem during the UAV flight from the initial position to the destination point in a static and dynamic environment. Based on the traditional artificial potential field method, the velocity vectors of the target and the obstacle are respectively introduced into the functions of the gravitational field and the repulsive field in the relative position. The method can meet the safety, real-time and reachability of the path planning of drones under dynamic change of targets and obstacles, and improve the speed of tracking and obstacle avoidance of drones in dynamic environment.

3   Overview of Dubins Path Planning

Assume that the UAV's initial coordinate is $<x_s, y_s>$, the initial velocity is v_s, the endpoint coordinate is $<x_f, y_f>$, and the endpoint velocity v_f. As shown in Fig. 1, two directed starting circles and two directed target circles are generated with the minimum turning radius of the UAV. There must be a directed common tangent between any starting circle and the target circle so that the UAV reaches the target position and state from the initial position and state through a starting circular arc, a common tangent line, and a target circular arc (specifically, the common tangent between the two circles with the same orientation is the tangent of the grandfather, and the common tangent between the two circles with the opposite directions is the tangent of the male tangent). This path from the initial position and status to the target position and status is called the Dubins path. Obviously, there are four such combinations. That is, there must be four Dubins paths. The shortest Dubins path is the shortest path from the starting position and state to the target position and state.

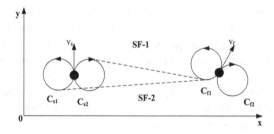

Fig. 1. Dubins path between the start position and final position.

When there is an obstacle in the path, the shortest Dubins path is found between the start circle, the obstacle circle, and the target circle. As shown in Fig. 2, there are two Dubins paths <SO-1, OF-1> and <SO-2, OF-2> between the start circle, the obstacle circle, and the target circle. Different start circles and target circles exist. There are also different Dubins paths. The shortest of all Dubins paths is the shortest path from the start position and state to the target position and state. In particular, when there are more obstacles, the more Dubins paths are available, the more complex the algorithm for choosing the shortest Dubins path from them.

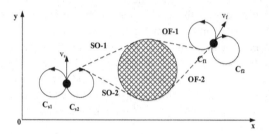

Fig. 2. Dubins path when obstacle exists.

4   Problem Description and Algorithm Design

4.1   Problem Description and Conditional Assumptions

Taking Fig. 3 as an example, assume that the UAV's initial coordinate is $<x_s, y_s>$, the initial velocity is v_s, the endpoint coordinate is $<x_f, y_f>$, and the endpoint velocity v_f. A clockwise starting circle generated with the UAV minimum turning radius is the counterclockwise target circle generated with the UAV minimum turning radius. When the obstacle is not considered, the shortest path between the UAV from the starting position to the target position is the Dubins path. Assume that UAVs perform tasks in unknown areas, only knowing the position and status of the initial point and target point. There are obstacles with uncertain quantities, shapes, and sizes randomly in the task area. The problem to be solved at this time is how to minimize the UAV. The distance from the starting position to the target position.

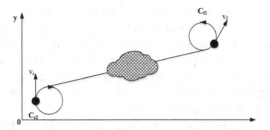

Fig. 3. Figure of problem description.

Other assumptions are as follows:

Assumption 1: UAV's flight altitude and flight speed remain the same;

Assumption 2: UAV flight process always meets the constraints of the minimum turning radius;

Assumption 3: The UAV only carries sensors that are detected in front of the flight, and can sense the distance from the UAV to the obstacle in the front; the maximum detection distance is D_{sens};

Assumption 4: The safety distance between the UAV and the obstacle in front is D_{safe}. If the distance between the UAV and the obstacle in front of the UAV is larger than D_{safe}, the UAV may not make any adjustment. When the distance between the UAV and the obstacle in front of the obstacle is less than or equal to D_{safe}, the UAV must bypass.

4.2 Dynamic Estimation of Obstacle Circle

Since only low-cost detection sensors can be used, the UAV constantly sends detection signals forward during flight and takes corresponding measures based on the distance from the obstacle in front. The Dubins path planning method must know the size and position of obstacles, and the obstacles must be circular. Therefore, when faced with unknown obstacles, it is necessary to first solve the problem of obstacle circle estimation.

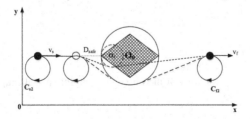

Fig. 4. Estimation of the obstacle circle.

As shown in Fig. 4, UAV first calculates the shortest Dubins path based on the initial position $<x_s, y_s>$, initial speed v_s, and end point $<x_f, y_f>$. If it is detected that there is an obstacle entering the safety distance D_{safe} during the flight, it is estimated based on the detected obstacle point. A circle of obstacles and re-plan Dubins path. From Fig. 4, we can see that the accuracy of the obstacle circle estimation directly determines the length of the Dubins path and the number of replanning. When the obstruction circle is estimated to be too small (O1 in the figure), frequent replanning is prone to occur; and when the obstruction circle is estimated to be too large (O0 in the figure), although the number of replanning is reduced, it may bypass farther distance. Therefore, the first problem to be solved is the estimation of the size of the obstacle circle.

In order to reduce the number of plans and the distance of detours as much as possible, this paper designs a dynamic estimation method of obstacle circle, as follows:

(1) Considering that obstacles are mostly continuous spatial geometries, a relatively small radius R1 is first used as the radius of the obstruction circle, and the obstruction circle is used for Dubins path planning.

(2) Starting from the previous route planning, if there is an obstacle within the safe distance ahead of UAV Flight T, the obstacle is the same obstacle as the last estimated obstacle. At this time, combining the positions of the obstacles detected twice, the Dubins path planning is performed again using the radius R2 as a new obstacle circle (R2 > R1);

(3) If no obstacle was detected during UAV flight T from the previous route planning, clear the historical information, and deal with new obstacles when obstacles are re-detected, as in step 1).

In particular, when the obstacle itself is a circle, according to the principle that a circle is determined by three points, the UAV can only achieve a short obstacle avoidance flight by only requiring dynamic programming three times during the flight. As shown in Fig. 5, when the obstacle itself is a circle, the third estimated obstacle circle is the shape of the obstacle itself.

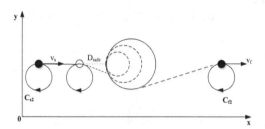

Fig. 5. Estimation of the obstacle circle for special shape.

4.3   Dynamic Obstacle Avoidance Planning Algorithm

Algorithm 1: Dynamic Obstacle Avoidance Planning
Input: $loc_s=<x_s,y_s>$, $loc_f=<x_f,y_f>$, v_s, v_f

1:	$path$ = Dubins($loc_s, loc_f, Null, 0$)
2:	t_0=0, list=Null
3:	**while** $path \neq Null$
4:	flying($path$)
5:	**if** $d_{obstacle} \leq D_{safe}$ **then**
6:	t = time_now()
7:	**if** $t-t_0 > T$ **then**
8:	clear_list$(list)$
9:	add_list$(list, loc_o)$
10:	$R=R_1$
11:	**else**
12:	add_list$(list, loc_o)$
13:	$R=R \times 1.5$
14:	**end**
15:	$t_0=t$
16:	$loc_{ocircle}$ = obstacle($list$)
17:	$path$ = Dubins($loc_{now}, loc_f, v_{now}, v_f, loc_{ocircle}, R$)
18:	**end**
19:	**end**

Obviously, it is impossible to find the shortest Dubins path when the obstructions in the environment are completely unknown. Therefore, the goal of this algorithm is to find a Dubins path that can bypass the unknown obstacles from the starting point to the end point, and the Dubins path should be as short as possible. According to the dynamic estimation method of obstacle circle in Sect. 4.2, Dubins path planning method, the dynamic obstacle avoidance planning algorithm designed in this paper is as above.

Among them, the initial Dubins path is determined by the position and status of the starting point and the target point (line 1). If the UAV encounters an obstacle during the flight, it first determines whether the obstacle has connections with the previous obstacle (line 5–7). If it is unrelated, it directly estimates the obstacle circle based on the current obstacle point, and if it is relevant, the estimation of the obstacle circle based on historical information (line 8–16) will be conducted. Finally, a new Dubins path (line 17) is generated based on the estimated obstacle circle.

5 Simulation Results and Analysis

In order to verify the effectiveness of the proposed algorithm named UAV dynamic obstacle avoidance planning algorithm, experiments are carried out for different types of obstacles. In experiment, the location and state of UAV's initial point and target point are known, and the location, shape and size of the obstacles are unknown, then set the speed of UAV to 2 m/s, the minimum turning radius to r, the safe distance to Ds.

Experiment 1: Three experiments were carried out for non-circular obstacles, as shown in Figs. 6 and 7.

Under the condition that the safe distance is set to 15 m, the obstacle avoidance path of UAV under different turning radius is shown in Fig. 6(a). It can be seen that with the increase of the minimum turning radius, the detour distance increases when UAV meets obstacles. The reason for this phenomenon is that the smaller the turning radius of UAV is, the more flexible its motion is, and it can use the shorter route to bypass obstacles. Figure 6(b) shows the obstacle avoidance path of UAV at different safe distances under the condition that the minimum turning radius of UAV is set to 5 m. It can be found that with the increase of safety distance, the smaller the distance traveled by UAV when obstacles are encountered, the less likely it is to collide with obstacles. Because the greater the safety distance, UAV can detect obstacles ahead, and advance obstacle avoidance planning in advance. In particular, when the safety distance is too small, UAV may collide with obstacles due to failure to detect obstacles in time. Figure 7 shows the obstacles avoidance path of UAV when it encounters a number of obstacles. Moreover, it can be seen from the figure that when facing obstacles, UAV can provide a real-time path planning with the help of dynamic algorithm to avoid obstacles.

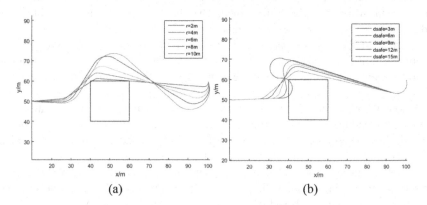

(a)   (b)

Fig. 6. (a) Path under different turning radius, (b) Path under different safe distances.

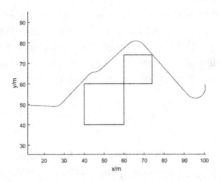

Fig. 7. Path under multi obstacles.

Experiment 2: Comparison experiment between the proposed algorithm and the basic Dubins path planning algorithm.

Since the basic Dubins path planning method is mainly aimed at known circular obstacles, the circular obstacle is experimentally contrasted in this paper. When a plurality of circular obstacles exist, the path comparison between the dynamic obstacle avoidance planning algorithm and the basic Dubins planning algorithm is presented in Fig. 8(a). We can conclude from the Fig. 8(a) that the path generated by the two algorithms can successfully bypass the obstacles. Compared to the UAV optimal path as a red curve representation in Fig. 8(a) generated by the basic Dubins programming algorithm, the real-time path as a blue curve representation in Fig. 8(a) generated by the dynamic obstacle avoidance planning algorithm is slightly longer than the optimal path. However, the dynamic obstacle avoidance planning algorithm is carried out under the condition that the location, shape and size of obstacles are completely unknown, which is more consistent with the actual UAV task environment.

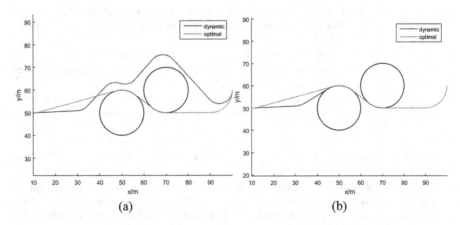

Fig. 8. (a) Comparison between Dynamic and Basic Dubins planning with round obstacle, (b) Path when the shape of obstacles are known. (Color figure online)

Figure 8(b) shows the path of the dynamic algorithm in the case of the shape of circle obstacles is known, location and size are unknown. We can conclude from Fig. 8(b) that comparing with the situation of obstacles completely unknown, the path generated by dynamic algorithm for planning path to avoid obstacles is relatively close to the optimal path, as the shape of obstacles is known to us.

6 Conclusion

In most of the task scenarios, it is difficult to obtain the specific location, shape and size of an obstacle. This paper proposes a dynamic obstacle avoidance planning algorithm based on Dubins path planning. The UAV constantly transmits detection signals in the forward direction during flight, estimates the shape of the obstacles, and detects the distance from obstacles, ensuring that obstacle avoidance is achieved under the minimum turning radius. UAV can plan a better obstacle avoidance path in real time without knowing the shape, location and size of obstacles. Simulation results show that the algorithm is correct and can improve the efficiency of low-cost UAVs performing tasks in a dynamic environment.

References

1. Wang, L., Zhou, W., Zhao, S.: Application of Mini-UAV in emergency rescue of major accidents of hazardous chemicals. In: The International Conference on Remote Sensing, pp. 152–155 (2013)
2. Bogatov, S., Mazny, N., Pugachev, A., et al.: Emergency radiation survey device onboard the UAV. ISPRS – Int. Arch. Photogramm. Remote Sens. Spatial Inf. Sci. 1, 51–53 (2013)
3. Ducard, G., Kulling, K.C., Geering, H.P.: A simple and adaptive online path planning system for a UAV. In: Proceedings of 2007 Mediterranean Conference on Control and Automation, Athens, Greece, pp. 1–6 (2007)
4. Ju, H.S., Tsai, C.C.: Design of intelligent flight control law following the optical payload. In: Proceedings of the 2004 IEEE International Conference on Networking, Sensing & Control, Taibei, pp. 761–766 (2004)
5. Lee, J., Huang, R., Vaughn, A., et al.: Strategies of path planning for a UAV to track a ground vehicle. In: Proceedings of IEEE Conference on Autonomous Intelligent Networked Systems, Menlo Park, USA, pp. 602–607 (2003)
6. Wang, T., Wei, X., Sun, Q., et al.: GSA-based jammer localization in multi-hop wireless network. In: IEEE International Conference on Computational Science and Engineering, pp. 410–415. IEEE (2017)
7. Enomoto, K., Yamasaki, T., Takano, H., et al.: Automatic following for UAVs using dynamic inversion. In: Proceedings of SICE Annual Conference, SICE 2007, pp. 2240–2246 (2007)
8. Cao, C., Hovakimyan, N., Kaminer, I., et al.: Stabilization of cascaded systems via L1 adaptive controller with application to a UAV path following problem and flight test results. In: Proceedings of the 2007 American Control Conference, New York, pp. 1787–1792 (2007)

9. Wei, X., Hu, F., Sun, Q., et al.: Association graph based jamming detection in multi-hop wireless networks. In: IEEE International Conference on Computational Science and Engineering, pp. 397–402. IEEE (2017)
10. Dubins, L.E.: On plane curves with curvature. Pacif. J. Math. **11**(2), 471–481 (1961)
11. Choi, H., Kim, Y., Hwang, I.: Reactive collision avoidance of unmanned aerial vehicles using a single vision sensor. J. Guidance Control Dyn. **36**(36), 1234–1240 (2015)
12. Zhang, L.P., Guan, X.N.: Design of autonomous collision avoidance controller for UAVs. Electron. Opt. Control **22**(4), 13–18 (2015)
13. Mashaly, A.S., Wang, Y., Liu, Q.: Efficient sky segmentation approach for small UAV autonomous obstacles avoidance in cluttered environment. In: Geoscience and Remote Sensing Symposium, pp. 6710–6713. IEEE (2016)
14. Meng, Z.J., Huang, P.F., Yan, J.: Exploring trajectory planning for hypersonic vehicle using improved sparse A* algorithm. J. Northwest. Polytechnical Univ. **28**(2), 182–186 (2010)
15. Guan, Z.Y., Yang, D.X., Li, J., et al.: Obstacle avoidance planning algorithm for UAV based on Dubins path. Trans. Beijing Inst. Technol. **34**(6), 570–575 (2014)
16. Aguilar, W., Casaliglla, V., Pólit, J.: Obstacle avoidance based-visual navigation for micro aerial vehicles. Electronics **6**, 10 (2017)
17. Kikutis, R., Stankūnas, J., Rudinskas, D., et al.: Adaptation of Dubins paths for UAV ground obstacle avoidance when using a low cost on-board GNSS sensor. Sensors **17**(10), 2223 (2017)
18. Ding, J.R., Deng, C.P., et al.: Path planning algorithm for unmanned aerial vehicles based on improved artificial potential field. J. Comput. Appl. **36**(1), 287–290 (2016)
19. Zhao, Y., Jiao, L., Zhou, R., et al.: UAV formation control with obstacle avoidance using improved artificial potential fields. In: Chinese Control Conference, pp. 6219–6224 (2017)
20. Tian, Y.Z., Zhang, Y.J.: UAV path planning based on improved artificial potential field in dynamic environment. J. Wuhan Univ. Sci. Technol. **40**(6), 451–456 (2017)

An Energy Efficient and Lifetime Aware Routing Protocol in Ad Hoc Networks

Wuyungerile Li, Bing Jia[✉], Qinan Li, and Junxiu Wang

Inner Mongolia University, Hohhot 010021, Inner Mongolia, China
jiabing@imu.edu.cn

Abstract. In recent years, with the rapid development of Internet technology and wireless communication technology, wireless Ad hoc network has been received more attention. Due to the limited transmission range and energy of nodes in Ad hoc networks, it is important to establish a reliable and energy-saving transmission path in Ad hoc networks. In this paper we proposed an energy efficient routing algorithm EAODV. The algorithm is based on the AODV routing protocol mainly in the following two aspects of improvement: (1) In the route discovery process, when a node selects a routing node, it dynamically selects one of the minimum power consumption routes and the energy balanced route designed in this paper based on a marker bit representing the remaining energy, then establishes a transmission path; (2) Based on (1), a route interruption update strategy was proposed to make the RERR message to restart the route discovery process to find new routes when node energy was used excessively. Simulation results show that compared with AODV and other existing routing protocols, EAODV can reduce network energy consumption and improve network performances.

Keywords: Ad hoc network · Energy efficient · AODV · TrueTime

1 Introduction

With the rapid development of Internet, wireless network technology has become one of the most popular research areas. The conventional wireless communication is generally centralized or decentralized, and it needs infrastructure of the network to operate normally [1, 3, 10]. However, in some special application scenarios such as environment monitoring and disaster relief, there are always have no pre-deployed infrastructures, and these applications require the network can be set up quickly and transmit data as soon as possible. So as this, wireless Ad hoc network is widely concerned. Wireless Ad hoc network is divided into high mobility network and low mobility network according to whether or not the node moves. In low mobility (or static) Ad hoc network, nodes' moving frequency is low, and network topology changes rarely. In addition, the communication range of nodes in Ad hoc network is limited. When a node wants to communicate with a long distance node, it needs to establish a routing path. Some intermediate nodes act as relay nodes and undertake more data forwarding tasks. Hence there occurs a problem that unfairness of energy consumption among nodes [11, 12]. Therefore it is important to study routing protocols

© Springer Nature Switzerland AG 2018
J. Vaidya and J. Li (Eds.): ICA3PP 2018, LNCS 11335, pp. 378–387, 2018.
https://doi.org/10.1007/978-3-030-05054-2_30

that consider the fairness of energy consumption among nodes. In recent years, researchers have made a great deal of research and improvement on the routing protocols applicable to Ad hoc networks. AODV is a typical Ad hoc network routing protocol that formed by the broadcast route discovery mechanism of the DSR routing protocol [2]. AODV routing protocol has become a hot-spot in the research of Ad hoc network routing protocol because of its own characteristics and good adaptability.

An ESAR (Energy Saving Ad hoc Routing) algorithm is proposed in [4]. In ESAR data are transmitted via the selected path until the node in the path reaches a given energy threshold, and another alternative path is used for transmission. ESAR increases the network lifetime by applying the concept of thresholds. However ESAR requires the establishment of many alternative paths, so that the energy consumption of the network is high. Another energy-efficient algorithm is proposed in [5], which uses node lifetime as a cost measure. Literature [6, 7] proposed routing algorithm where they took the residual energy as a cost metric. In [6], an MMBCR (Min-Max Battery Cost Routing) algorithm is proposed and in which it focuses on the remaining energy of the bottleneck node on the path, then selects a bottleneck node that has the largest remaining energy value as the next hop node. Although it delays the occurrence time of the first death node in the network, but the overall network lifetime has not been greatly improved. The ALMEL-AODV (Alternate Link Maximum Energy Level) algorithm proposed in [7] takes residual energy of node as a cost metric and focuses on the remaining energy of nodes on the path. The standard for selecting routes is that if the sum of the remaining energy of the nodes on the path is the largest, then select it as the route and transmit data through the path. Although ALMEL-AODV has improved the node energy consumption to a certain extent, it pays attention to the residual energy in the entire path and does not consider the residual energy of a single node.

The work presented in [8, 9] combines the energy consumption and residual energy in the transmission process as a cost measure for routing. Literature [8] proposed an EEPR (Energy efficient Path Routing) algorithm to realize the fairness of saving energy consumption and energy consumption, thus improving the network lifetime. In [9], the AODV routing protocol is improved for low-speed Ad hoc networks. A new path cost measurement function is proposed based on the energy consumption and the ratio of the remaining energy to the battery capacity. It has a good performance in Ad hoc networks with low speed. However, this algorithm only considers the path selection at the source node and lacks real-time performance. By analyzing the research status of Ad hoc networks and combining with the shortcomings of AODV routing protocols and other routing protocols [4–6], this paper proposes a new energy-efficient routing protocol to deeply study how to better integrate the path energy consumption and node residual energy. These cost metrics were improved on the basis of AODV routing protocols to achieve fairness in the energy consumption of nodes in the network, thus improving network lifetime and other network performances.

The paper is organized as follows: Firstly, we present our proposed energy efficient routing protocol in Sect. 2. Then the Simulation results are shown in the Sect. 3. At last the conclusion is presented.

2   Design of Energy Efficient and Network Lifetime Aware Routing Protocol

2.1   The Main Idea of Proposed Routing Protocol

The AODV routing protocol is an on-demand routing protocol. There are three kinds of control messages: route request (RREQ), route response (RREP), route error (RERR). The AODV routing protocol is bi-directional. The source node sends RREQ message to initiate route discovery, establishes the reverse path. The routing response message RREP transfers the back source node through the reverse path to establish the forward path. The AODV routing protocol is used to establish routes on an as-needed basis. It does not need to maintain the topology of the entire network, thereby reducing the amount of route broadcasting and reducing energy consumption.

The energy-efficient and network lifetime aware routing protocol is proposed for low mobility Ad hoc networks and is named as EAODV. Considering the limited energy of the nodes, and for extending the network lifetime, we have two improvements to AODV protocol:

Firstly, when route is established, the EAODV protocol no longer adopts the "shortest path" selection strategy. It proposes a dynamic routing algorithm, which defines a rule that if the energy of nodes are overused or not and represents them with a mark of 0 and 1. When a neighbor node receives a message with a tagged message, it reads the information of the mark, and selects a suitable route selection algorithm from the proposed minimum energy consumption routing algorithm and the energy balanced routing algorithm according to the mark bit, and establishes the route.

Secondly, the EAODV protocol improves the routing interrupt update strategy of the original AODV protocol. The routing interrupt update policy adopted in the original AODV protocol, only when the node moves out of the communication range or the node dies, the interrupt update policy is enabled. The EAODV routing protocol proposes a passive interrupt update strategy, which uses the residual energy of a node and the remaining energy of its neighbor nodes to trigger the routing interruption update algorithm. When there is too much data transmitted on a path, the energy consumption of some nodes is too fast. Through the passive interrupt update strategy, it can switch to more energy path in time. With this kind of routing interruption update policy, the energy consumption between nodes in the network can be more equitable, thus prolonging the network lifetime.

2.2   Network Model

In the network model, the nodes are distributed within the monitoring area. This work assumes the network model as follows:

(1) The location information of each node in the network is known, the node IDs are incremented in order from 0 and are globally unique IDs.
(2) The initial energy of all nodes is limited, and the greater the amount of data transmitted, the faster the energy consumption.

(3) All nodes receive the same sensitivity and run the same routing protocol.
(4) All nodes have the same data processing capabilities and radio communication capabilities.

2.3   Dynamic Route Selection Algorithm of EAODV Routing Protocol

The EAODV routing protocol proposed in this paper consists of two dynamic route selecting algorithms, namely, the minimum energy consumption route selecting algorithm (MER) and the energy balanced route selecting algorithm (EBR). When a node needs to send data, each node in the path dynamically selects one of the routing algorithms to establish a path.

(1) The Design of MER
The minimum energy consumption route selecting algorithm (MER), that is, this policy selects the path with the smallest total energy consumption among the numerous available paths from the source node to the destination node. MER uses the path selection algorithm of the AODV routing protocol. When the path is established, the source node broadcasts the RREQ firstly, and the intermediate node only accepts and processes the same first arrival RREQ message of the source node, thus creating a route. This is the "shortest path", which is the central idea of the AODV routing protocol. However, the improved routing protocol in this paper will calculate a reasonable transmitting energy based on the distance between two points in the path. If the established route is the "shortest path" in the network, then the total transmitting energy of this path is the smallest. Because the amount of data transmitted by the source node is certain, the sensor models of the nodes in the network are the same, that is, the bandwidth of each node is the same, then, the transmission time when each node transmits data will be the same.

(2) The Design of EBR
Energy balanced route selecting algorithm (EBR), that is, when forward and reverse routes are established, among the numerous available routes, select the route with node's smallest residual energy is the biggest among the routes.

$$R = \max\{\min\{E_{left}^{i,t}\}\}$$

Here i is the node that passes through the path from the source node to the destination node. $E_{left}^{i,t}$ is the residual energy of node i at time t.

In the network, if the above-mentioned minimum energy consumption routing is always used, it may lead to premature exhaustion of some nodes on the path. For this reason, energy balanced routing is proposed. During the establishment of the route, the node selects the minimum energy consumption route or the energy balanced route according to the Mark field value in the RREQ message and the RREP message to establish the reverse path and the forward route.

(3) Format Design of RREQ, RREP and Routing Table

According to the design idea of energy efficient algorithm, it is necessary to modify the RREQ and RREP packets based on the AODV protocol, and an example is shown in Table 1.

Table 1. Message format of RREQ

Type	Reserved	Hop Count
RREQ ID		
Destination IP Address		
Destination Sequence Number		
Originator IP Address		
Originator Sequence Number		
Mark		
Minimum remaining energy		

Here, the Mark bit value is 0 or 1. The proposed routing protocol works according to the value of the mark bit in the RREQ or RREP transmitted from the previous hop. If the value is 0, the MER is used to establish the route. If the value is 1, the EBR is used to establish the route. The minimum remaining energy of the nodes in the path, which represents the minimum remaining energy of all nodes that have passed during the route establishment. The same with RREQ, we add "Mark" and "Minimum remaining energy" items into the message format of RREP and routing table. The converting strategy between EBR and MER is presented in the following section.

2.4 Passive Interrupt Update Strategy

Based on the remaining energy of the node, this paper proposes a passive interruption update policy based on the original update strategy of AODV. It is divided into two methods to trigger the route interruption update strategy: At first, with the node sending and receiving data packet, node energy is continuously consumed. When the ratio of the real-time residual energy and the battery capacity of the node is less than a threshold α (0.4 in this paper), the interrupt update strategy starts. Secondly, while nodes in the network transmit data according to the established route, as long as the node satisfies the overuse rule, it initiates an interrupt update strategy.

The overuse rule of node is as follows:

$$E_{left}^{j,t} * \frac{1}{\beta} < E_{neig\_aver}^{j,t}$$

That is, if the residual energy of node j is multiplied by the parameter $1/\beta$ (4 in this paper) is less than the average value of the remaining energy of the neighbor node, it is determined that the node is overused.

When the node initiates an interrupt update policy, the node queries the routing table, sends a RERR packet to the next node in the routing table whose next hop is this node, and sets the state field of all routing entries of this node to "invalid." After receiving the RERR data packet, the upstream node first looks for a route whose next hop is to send the RERR data packet in the local node, and sets the state field of the route entry to "invalid" and continues to send the RERR data packet to the upstream node.

3   Simulation

We use the Simulink/Truetime toolbox in Matlab to evaluate the performance of the algorithm. The proposed EAODV routing protocol is verified with a typical AODV routing protocol, and compared with the ALMEL-AODV routing protocol proposed in [5] and the LMAODV routing protocol presented in [7]. This experiment selects Win7 operating system and uses Matlab's TrueTime tool as the simulation platform to perform experiments.

3.1   Simulation Setting

Simulation parameters are shown in Table 2.

Table 2. Simulation parameters.

Parameter type	Parameter value
MAC layer protocol type	802.15.4 (ZigBee)
Node communication range	250 m
Packet transmission rate	2 packet/s
Data packet size	4 bytes
Bandwidth	0.125 Mb/s
Node position	Static
Simulation time	20 s
Initial energy of node	0.05 J
Initial transmit power	37 dBm
Receiver signal threshold	−48 dBm

The results of the experiment in this paper are to compare the average of the 50 experiments. 36 nodes are randomly distributed in a region of 800 * 800 m^2.

3.2   Simulation Results

For examining the impact of α and β on network lifetime, we set the range of α as 0.1, 0.2.....0.9, and β as 1, 2,... 9. In 800 s simulation time, the result of Fig. 1 shows that network lifetime is generally longer when the α value is 0.3 to 0.5 and the β value is 4 to 6. Therefore, in the following experiment we set α as 0.4, β as 4.

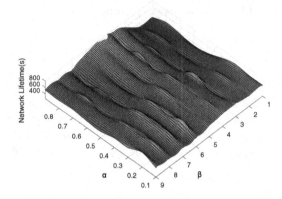

Fig. 1. The relationship between α, β and network lifetime

This experiment verifies the effectiveness of the MPR and EBR, and evaluates the EAODV routing protocol on the network lifetime in Fig. 2. The EAODV-1 in Fig. 2 is the MER, and EAODV-2 is EBR. The combination of these two routing algorithms is EAODV routing protocol that proposed in this paper. It can be clearly seen from the figure that the use of an energy-balanced routing protocol alone can achieve the balance of energy consumption in the network, but the node's death time is too early. Using the minimum power routing protocol alone, after the number of dead nodes reaches 6, the node's dead time is later than the EAODV routing protocol. Therefore, the EAODV routing protocol combines the two routing protocols. Using EBR in the network, the lifetime of nodes in the network is improved, so that all the nodes in the network can have a longer network lifetime, and there is no premature death of the relay nodes.

Figure 3 shows the energy consumption of successfully transmitting a single packet when the four routing protocols transmit data at different numbers of nodes. It can be intuitively found that the energy consumption of the EAODV routing protocol and LMAODV transmission unit data packets is low. The ALMEL-AODV routing protocol performs slightly better than the AODV routing protocol. From the figure, it can be concluded that the EAODV routing protocol and the LMAODV routing protocol are lower in energy consumption of a single packet.

Table 3 shows the performance comparison of the four routing protocols under the simulation of a static model. The EAODV routing protocol proposed in this paper has a slight difference in average delays compared with AODV routing protocol, ALMEL-AODV routing protocol, and LMAODV routing protocol because EAODV routing

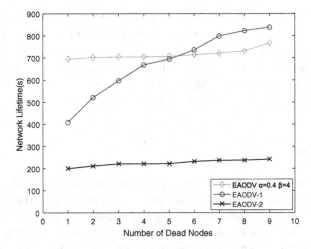

Fig. 2. Relationship between the number of dead nodes and network lifetime

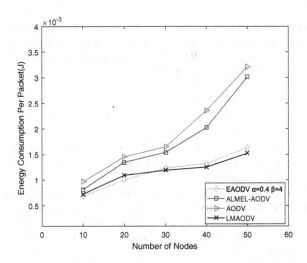

Fig. 3. Energy consumption of single packet of nodes

protocol selects one of the two routing algorithms to establish a route, and the gap is negligible. However, EAODV performs better on delivery rate and throughput performance indicators. The increase in delivery rate and throughput is attributed to the path selection algorithm. It selects energy-rich lines to establish routes and improves network lifetime. The energy consumption per unit packet of the EAODV routing protocol and the total energy consumption during the simulation time are lower than those of the AODV and ALMEL-AODV routing protocols.

Table 3. Performances of network when the node is stationary and the initial energy is sufficient

	EAODV	LMAODV	ALMEL-AODV	AODV
Average throughput	7.96 bytes	7.81 bytes	7.79 bytes	7.79 bytes
Average end-to-end delay	0.00218 s	0.00205 s	0.001903 s	0.00201 s
Total energy consumption	0.586 J	0.567 J	0.92 J	0.93 J
Packet delivery ratio	99.749	97.134	98.517	97.417

4 Conclusion

In this paper, an energy-efficient routing protocol EAODV that based on traditional AODV is proposed for low speed Ad hoc networks. In EAODV routing protocol there are two path selection algorithms. Through the comparison and analysis of the experiment, the design of EAODV routing protocol is proved to improve the packet delivery rate and throughput, reduce the total energy consumption of the network and the energy consumption per unit packet, so that improves the performance of network lifetime.

Acknowledgement. Thanks to the National Natural Science Foundation of China (Grants No. 61761035, 41761086, 61461037, 61661041) and "Scientific and Technological Innovation Project of Inner Mongolia Autonomous Region System Development and Product Application of Urban Flood Disaster Monitoring and Early-warning Management".

References

1. Perkins, C.E., Royer, E.M.: Ad-hoc on-demand distance vector routing. In: 1999 2nd IEEE Workshop on Mobile Computing Systems and Applications (WMCSA 1999), New Orleans, pp. 90–100. IEEE Press (1999)
2. Utkarsh, M.M., Chinara, S.: ESAR: an energy saving ad hoc routing algorithm for MANET. In: IEEE Fourth International Conference on Advanced Computing, pp. 13–15 (2012)
3. Shivashankar, G.V., Narayanagowda, S.H.: Implementing a new power aware routing algorithm based on existing dynamic source routing protocol for mobile ad hoc networks. IET Netw. **3**, 137–142 (2014)
4. Cao, L., Sharif, K., Wang, Y., et al.: Adaptive multiple metrics routing protocols for heterogeneous multi-hop wireless networks. In: Consumer Communications and NETWORKING Conference, CCNC 2008, pp. 13–17. IEEE (2008)
5. Tai, H.T., Tan, C.E., Lau, S.P.: Alternate link maximum energy level ad hoc distance vector scheme for energy efficient ad hoc networks routing. In: International Conference on Computer and Communication Engineering, pp. 423–428. IEEE (2010)
6. Khanna, N., Krishna Naik, K.: Design and implementation of an energy efficient routing approach based on existing AODV protocol in mobile adhoc networks for military. In: International Conference on Emerging Trends in Electrical Electronics & Sustainable Energy Systems (ICETEESES). IEEE (2016). 7581388
7. Chen, J., Chen, J., Li, Z.: Energy-efficient AODV for low mobility ad hoc networks. In: International Conference on Wireless Communications, NETWORKING and Mobile Computing, pp. 1512–1515. IEEE (2007)

8. Das, C.R., Dhara, S., Jeng, Y.R., et al.: An efficient routing protocol for wireless networks. Mob. Netw. Appl. **1**(2), 183–197 (1996)
9. Roth, U.: Highly dynamic destination-sequenced distance-vector routing. In: Proceedings of ACM SIGCOMM 1994, pp. 234–244, August 1994
10. Perkins, C.E., Royer, E.M.: Ad-hoc on-demand distance vector routing. In: The Workshop on Mobile Computing Systems & Applications, pp. 94–95. IEEE (2002)
11. Liu, Z., Luo, D., Li, J., Chen, X., Jia, C.: N-Mobishare: new privacy-preserving location-sharing system for mobile online social networks. Int. J. Comput. Math. **93**(2), 384–400 (2016)
12. Liu, Z., Li, T., Li, P., Jia, C., Li, J.: Verifiable searchable encryption with aggregate keys for data sharing system. Future Gener. Comput. Syst. **78**, 778–788 (2018)

On Optimization of Energy Consumption in a Volunteer Cloud

Strategy of Placement and Migration of Dynamic Services

Omar Ben Maaouia[1,2(✉)], Hazem Fkaier[2], Christophe Cerin[3],
Mohamed Jemni[2], and Yanik Ngoko[3]

[1] University of Tunis El Manar, FST, Tunis, Tunisia
omarbenmaaouia@gmail.com
[2] LATICE, ENSIT, University of Tunis, Tunis, Tunisia
omarbenmaaouia@gmail.com, hazem.fkaier@gmail.com,
mohamed.jemni@gmail.com
[3] LIPN/UMR 7030, CNRS/Université Paris 13, Villetaneuse, France
{christophe.cerin,yanik.ngoko}@lipn.univ-paris13.fr

Abstract. Traditional Cloud computing has emerged as a new paradigm for providing computing resources on demand and outsourcing software and hardware infrastructures. Cloud computing is rapidly changing the way IT services are made available and managed. These services can be requested by several Cloud providers, hence the need for networking between IT service components distributed in geographically diverse locations. Like the traditional Cloud computing, the volunteer computing paradigm has become increasingly important. For this paradigm, the resources on each personal machine are shared, thanks to the will of their owners. Cloud and volunteer paradigms have been recently seen as complementary technologies to better exploit the use of local resources. Besides execution time and cost, energy consumption is also becoming more important in the Cloud computing environments. Thus, it has become a major concern for the widespread deployment of Cloud data centers. Among methods that can overcome this problem, we are interested in planning services that improve the use of data center resources in a dynamic environment. In this context, we propose throughout this paper a heuristic that predicts the allocation of dynamic and independent services to reduce the total energy consumption. Our proposal respects various constraints: availability, capacity of machines and the number of applications duplications. A series of experiments illustrates and validates the potential of our approach.

Keywords: Volunteer cloud · Energy consumption
Minimization of energy consumption · Scheduling

© Springer Nature Switzerland AG 2018
J. Vaidya and J. Li (Eds.): ICA3PP 2018, LNCS 11335, pp. 388–398, 2018.
https://doi.org/10.1007/978-3-030-05054-2_31

1 Introduction

Cloud providers offer to their customers computing resources, as virtual machines, and enable the networking between the virtual resources. Thus, customer's needs have evolved beyond having a simple virtual machine to acquiring complex, flexible, resilient and intelligent virtual resources and services.

Cloud computing enables customers to access to an infinite (virtual) pool of resources. This leads to a huge number of physical machines and data centers in order to fulfil all the continuously increasing needs. The rise of the number of active physical machine number affects the rise of the energy consumption. Therefore, minimization of energy consumption has become one of the major challenges of Cloud computing. Consequently, any Cloud system needs an efficient algorithm for task scheduling [1]. The scheduling problem is related to resources distribution and utilization within a limited environment. It may be divided into two kinds: static scheduling and dynamic scheduling. In the static case, the set of jobs are known a-priori, while the dynamic one performs scheduling at job arrival so that it depends not only on the tasks and environment but also on the current system state in order to produce a scheduling plan [2].

In particular, jobs' arrival rate and the status of some nodes (offline or online) may change without any a-priori knowledge. In this case, the dynamic scheduling method is privileged.

In this paper, we propose two algorithms, one for creating an application graph and the other one for assigning applications to the least loaded machines. The trick is based on computing the shortest path in the graph to plan the execution of independent applications while respecting several constraints of availability and capacity of the machines as well as the constraint of applications duplication. In short, our purpose is to reduce the energy consumption by using low-consumption machines and decreasing the number of migrations, as much as possible.

The remainder of the paper involves six sections organized as follows: In Sect. 2, we present a background related to the energy consumption evolution in the Cloud environment; then we define the volunteer Cloud concept. In Sect. 3, we present the state of the art of the most known methods for optimizing energy consumption in both the traditional and the volunteer Cloud concepts. Section 4 is devoted to the description of our proposed approach namely our SPS heuristics to minimize the overall energy consumption relying on dynamic job placement. In Sect. 5, we detail an experimental study on a platform that allows our theoretical contribution validation and evaluation. We finally conclude and present our perspectives in Sect. 6.

2 Backgrounds

2.1 Energy Consumption

There are several recent studies interested in the energy consumption of data centers. On one side, a 12.7% growth has been observed since 2011. On the other side, Cloud computing revenue has been forecasted to jump from US \$163 billion in 2011 to

US \$240 billion in 2016 [3]. Therefore, reducing energy consumption in data centers has become a critical dilemma for industry and academia.

2.2   Volunteer Cloud

Unlike the infrastructure of the traditional Clouds, in the volunteer Cloud (VC), customers and data centers can process multiple requests. Indeed, the volunteer nodes are useful for the elasticity of Cloud. However, they cannot always be available. From an energy point of view, VC may lead to two new costs for the application placement. The first one is related to the applications migration when a volunteer node is no longer available. The second one is related to the use of replicas to avoid the unavailability of nodes [4].

Therefore, we will focus on the recent well-known works on energy optimization in the volunteer Cloud, i.e. the efficient distribution of energy for applications across the volunteer Cloud and the forecast of long-term availability for volunteer resources.

3   Related Work

There are diverse studies in the literature aiming to minimize the energy consumption of a Cloud computing infrastructure. From an industrial point of view, the EECLOUD project[1] aims to offer services for energy monitoring of physical and virtual resources, energy usage exposing for users and Clouds managers and energy monitoring streams for upper layers software. This is an example embracing more general problems than our current problem but it illustrates the challenging placement problem, which takes into account both, the user and data center objectives: maximize performance and minimize the energy consumption.

As said previously, we are interested in works aiming at minimizing the energy consumption of a Cloud computing. In [5], Ghribi et al. proposed an assembly of two algorithms; the first one is used for task allocation and the second one aims at optimizing the migration of virtual machines. Hsu et al. developed an energy-aware approach for virtual clusters by consolidating tasks [6]. Unfortunately, these approaches do not consider the impact of startup time of 'down' hosts on the timing requirements of real-time tasks, inevitably violating deadlines of some real-time tasks. These studies involved the optimization of the energy consumption on a traditional Cloud where there are as many resources available, unlike to the volunteer Cloud. Hussain et al. [7] proposed a static task scheduling strategy, which supports the execution of modules on a set of interconnected processors. They depicted a job in the form of a direct acyclic graph (DAG). They calculated the overall energy consumption and they allocated tasks to processors, in such a way that the scenario consumes less power regarding a reference scenario. Beloglazov et al. [8] were interested in dynamic consolidation of virtual machines. In [9], the authors presented two algorithms for scheduling tasks in a private Cloud environment, where the main purpose is to obtain a

---

[1] http://www.ens-lyon.fr/LIP/RESO/eecloud/.

minimum completion time. The main contributions of [10] are twofold. First, the scheduling algorithm balances the system load with an adaptive threshold and second, it minimizes the makespan (completion time) of jobs. In [11], the goal of the research is to select a subset of jobs that constitutes a feasible solution to the shortest path problem, and to execute the selected jobs on the flow shop machines to minimize the makespan. In [12], authors proposed a new modeling and scheduling approaches for offline jobs. They proposed an optimal algorithm for offline scheduling considering Map and Reduce stages by adapting to classical Johnson's model. Yanik et al. proposed an approach to reduce energy consumption for running applications where volunteer nodes are used to build a Cloud [4, 13]. The heuristic proposed in [13], can minimize the energy consumption in a volunteer Cloud only in short-term point of view. On the other hand, our proposal, described in the following section, will study this problem also in a long-term point of view.

Most conventional researches were interested only in makespan. However, we propose a cost efficient and energy effective placement, which optimizes cost while mapping tasks to hosts.

4 Proposed Approach

In this section, we explain and motivate again our problem and we describe the general principle of our proposal through an illustrative example that highlights the interest of our contribution. Our main allocation strategy is called SPS (Shortest Path Strategy).

Such a strategy can fit in both classes:

(a) Bin-Packing problems, from the point of view of allocation of jobs to the least consuming available machine.
(b) Stochastic Integer Programming problems category, from the point of view of the prediction of job allocation to minimize the energy consumption [14].

4.1 Abbreviations and Acronyms

According to previous works especially those of [15, 16], we present our notation and hypothesis as follows. We consider $N = \{1...n\}$ as a set of applications to be executed on $M = \{1...m\}$ which is a set of machines belonging to a Cloud. Note that the word 'application' in our context may actually stand either for a simple application or for the container containing it, or even the virtual machine running it.

Our purpose is to build a strategy, which assigns the multiple applications to the different machines during a predefined time interval. Therefore, the time interval is composed of a set of phases that we note $P = \{0 ...p - 1\}$. This latter contains phase intervals with predefined duration. We suppose that the machines may be part of a data center, or of a volunteer Cloud. In this context, the unavailability phenomenon should be taken in consideration. Thus, we take as input a matrix D, whose generic element D $[p, i]$ states if the selected machine i (in M) is available at the phase p or not. The applications to be deployed exists in one or multiple copies. For an application $j \in N$, we let k_j be the number of copies of j that should be deployed. We associate a maximal capacity q_i for each machine $i \in M$. This capacity denotes the number of applications copies that could be unfolded in order to minimize as much as possible the excessive load. The principle goal here is to prevent excessive load. An application can be migrated from a machine to another one because of unavailability. Given two machines $i, i' \in M$. Let $C_{jii'}$ be the required energetic cost for migrating a copy of application of j from i to i', knowing that $C_{jii'} = 0 \; \forall \; j, i$. We suppose that the main characteristics of energy consumption E_{ji} and $C_{jii'}$ are not time-dependent. Therefore, we aim at deploying the application copies on the machines during the phase interval, e.g. reducing the energy consumption due to the migrations and the different runs on the machines. Moreover, this deployment is followed by some constraints, for each phase $p \in T$. The first one ensures that each application copy can only be deployed on an available machine (C1).

The second one supposes that all the copies of an application should be assigned to distinct machines (C2), and the third one specifies that the number of applications assigned to a given machine is capped by qi for any machine i (C3). The overall energy generated by applications deployed on a machine (EGM) must be less than the maximum threshold (C4). Note that the environment is heterogeneous. Therefore, we assume that each application has diverse energy consumptions on the different machines and that these machines consume diverse amounts of energy. Besides, we suppose that the power increases linearly regarding the percentage of CPU. Table 1 describes the numerous adopted notations.

Table 1. Summary of input data of the outlined problems

Symbol	Description
P	Number of execution phases
$n, j \in N = \{1..N\}$	Number, index and set of applications
$m, i \in M = \{1..M\}$	Number, index and set of machines
$K = (kj)\| \; j \in N$	Vector of number of required instances of each application
$q = (qj)\| \; i \in M$	Machine capacity vector
D	Machine availability matrix
E	Energy consumption matrix
C	Transfer Energy matrix
S	Maximum threshold of machine availability
PA	Phase of job arrival
PE	Phase of job end

4.2 Assignment Based on the Shortest Path Strategy (SPS)

In the past, we have proposed a static approach to allocate the applications on the servers of a Volunteer Cloud in [19, 20] where the arrival and finished dates of every jobs are known a priori. Based on our previous works we propose a dynamic approach where jobs arrive and end at any moment. In others words, our contribution consists in modeling our problem through a graph in order to reduce the energy consumption.

Then, we compute the shortest path of the generated graph. We assume that the consumption of an application relies not only on the machine that executes it, but also on the migration from one machine to another one. Indeed, we aim to deploy several copies of applications on machines during a time interval in order to decrease the energy consumption. This latter can be induced due to the migration and the multiple machine operations. Moreover, the deployment must respect the four above-mentioned constraints *C1, C2, C3* and *C4*. Thus, in order to schedule *N* independent jobs on *M* heterogeneous machines interconnected during a determined phase interval and after the assignments of the different applications among this interval, we minimize, through our proposed approach, the sum of the induced consumptions. One can see the time interval in the data center as an alternation of execution phases where all applications are being executed on different machines, and migration phases where (some/all) applications are being migrated from one machine to another. We can formulate our approach in the form of a directed acyclic graph *(DAG) G = (V, E)*, where *V* is set of *v* nodes and *E* is a set of E directed edges. An edge corresponds either to the execution of an application on a given machine (execution phase) or the migration of that application from one machine to another one (migration phase). In both cases, the edge has a cost that depicts the energy consumption of that operation (execution or migration). A vertex stands for starting an application on machine i or starting a migration from that machine.

General Principle

Our approach composed of two stages as follows:

Stage 1:

For each application *a*, we:

- Verify the phases of both job arrival and the job end. Note that the jobs may arrive to at the machines at different phases and may end at diverse phases.
- Create a graph that consists of p computation phases separated by p-1 migration phases and contains all possible assignments on all available machines during all these phases (see Stage 2).
- Compute the shortest path by adapting the Dijkstra algorithm and bringing out its trajectory) during its execution i.e. select the adequate machine (SM) for running that application.
- Assign the current application to the least energy-consuming machine when all the constraints (C1, C2, C3 and C4) are verified.
- Minimize the capacity of the selected machine (SM).
- Add the energy generated by the running application on the selected machine (EGM).
- Compute the number of migrations from one machine to another.

Note that each time any machine changes its availability; there is an opportunity to adjust assignment through migrations.

In this stage, we perform the rescheduling of the jobs on the machines during each phase in order to update the machines states when the jobs finish at any unexpected time, and when new jobs arrived.

Stage 2:

For each phase:

For each machine: if all the constraints (*C1, C2, C3* and *C4*) are verified, we process either execution phase or migration phase:

- *Execution phase*: we place the application on all possible available machines, which verify the mentioned constraints.
- *Migration phase*: if there is a migration, then the corresponding arc will take as value the cost of the application migration from the source machine to the destination one. Otherwise, the arc takes the value 0. An application keeps jumping from one machine to another so that its power consumption stays minimal.

5 Experimental Results and Discussion

5.1 Simulation Setup

We use C++ to develop our simulator using the lemon library[2]. In this section, we introduce a series of experiments to illustrate our approach and compare it to the three basic following strategies: *(i)* the **random** heuristic **"RAND"** which assigns an application (ranked at the top of the list of applications) in a random way to an available machine during the current phase; *(ii)* the **"FIRST-Fit"** heuristic which permits to assign the application existing at the top of the applications list to the first available machine, and *(iii)* the **"BEST-fit"** heuristic which allows the application made at the top of the applications list to be assigned to the best available machine (according to the least energy consuming) during the current execution phase.

5.2 Instances

We describe in Table 2 the multiple studied instances [16] that allow performing our theoretical and experimental evaluation works. Next, we analyze the different outputs.

To summarize, we adopt the instances from the framework of Ngoko et al. [4]. Each instance is identified by: a number of applications, a number of machines, the number of execution phases, the capacities of those machines and the bounds on application copies. The energy expected for the move of the application and the energy consumed in migrations is defined in [4]. The start and end time are recovered from the Google cluster traces [17]. We consider the 12 instances (i.e. configurations) shown in Table 2.

---

[2] http://lemon.cs.elte.hu/trac/lemon.

Table 2. Description of configurations

Configuration	N	M	P	k_{min}	k_{max}	q_{min}	q_{max}
1	30	50	10	3	6	2	5
2	30	60	10	3	6	2	4
3	40	80	10	3	7	2	6
4	50	100	10	3	7	2	5
5	30	50	12	3	7	2	5
6	30	60	12	3	7	2	5
7	60	100	12	3	7	1	4
8	40	80	12	3	7	1	4
9	30	60	16	3	7	1	4
10	40	80	16	3	7	1	4
11	50	100	16	3	7	1	4
12	80	100	16	3	7	1	4

5.3   Results Analysis

Given that arrival dates and end dates of jobs are dynamic but known a priori, we may experimentally investigate the two following scenarios:

- Scenario 1: We consider the offline box in which all jobs are available at time 0.
- Scenario 2: Jobs arrival and end dates are dynamic but are not known a priori.

Scenario 1
We study the migration and energy consumption of multiple applications for the SPS method (respectively Best-fit, First-fit and Random), and for the different twelve instances. A series of experiments and comparisons of the applications migration and the energy consumption was carried out for the random assignment (respectively for the First Fit, Best Fit and SPS methods).

There are some excerpts of our performed tests that are illustrated in Table 3 and Fig. 1.

Through Table 4, we can note the number of migrations of the different applications from a machine to another for the studied instances. We notice that for SPS, it is possible to avoid migrations. Therefore, the overheads will also decrease. This observation is inherited through a series of experiments (See Table 3 and Fig. 1).

Scenario 2
During the 'formal' comparison between the static scheduling and the dynamic one, we noticed that when all the tasks are known in advance, so that the corresponding applications are statically assigned, the migrations number as well as the energy consumption significantly decrease. Let us denote the comparative reducing ratio as follows:

Table 3. Energy consumption (MW)

	RAND	FIRST_fit	BEST_fit	SPS
IN1	0.606	0.582	0.453	0.081
IN2	0.811	0.898	0.692	0.078
IN3	1.043	1.275	0.966	0.098
IN4	1.211	1.258	0.915	0.115
IN5	0.658	0.633	0.596	0.083
IN6	0.866	0.711	0.591	0.065
IN7	1.180	1.097	0.976	0.101
IN8	1.171	1.151	0.839	0.106
IN9	1.037	0.666	0.592	0.121
IN10	1.949	1.145	1.087	0.174
IN11	2.238	1.649	1.769	0.190
IN12	1.877	1.395	1.253	0.150

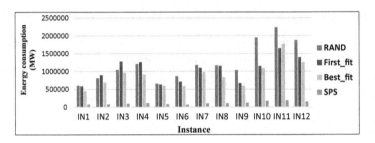

Fig. 1. Energy consumption

Table 4. Number of applications migration

	RAND	FIRST_fit	BEST_fit	SPS
IN1	141	155	135	1
IN2	214	237	180	2
IN3	233	313	235	0
IN4	313	340	263	0
IN5	184	180	190	0
IN6	197	148	151	1
IN7	273	250	271	0
IN8	310	279	236	0
IN9	298	175	199	10
IN10	387	241	296	11
IN11	464	396	504	1
IN12	464	343	224	2

$$R2(\text{heuristic}) = EC(\text{Static\_SPS})/EC(\text{Dynamic\_SPS})$$

Table 5 reinforces this remark.

Table 5. Comparison of static and dynamic SPS (MW)

Instances	Static_SPS	Dynamic_SPS	R2
IN1	0.081	0.265	3.26
IN2	0.078	0.237	3.05
IN3	0.098	0.229	2.35
IN4	0.115	0.266	2.31
IN5	0.083	0.243	2.94
IN6	0.065	0.198	3.06
IN7	0.101	0.236	2.33
IN8	0.106	0.217	2.05
IN9	0.121	0.327	2.71
IN10	0.174	0.478	2.74
IN11	0.190	0.458	2.42
IN12	0.150	0.418	2.78

In short, all the results proved that our "SPS" proposal are better than the other strategies. In fact, SPS allows an energy consumption reduction, thanks to the reduction of the number of inter-machines applications migration.

6   Conclusion and Perspectives

Volunteer Cloud is an upcoming technology which includes motivating problems for the researcher e.g. energy consumption. Maintaining the efficiency of energy consumption has become a major problem with increased usage of devices consuming more energy. In this paper, we are interested in the optimization of energy consumption in a volunteer Cloud setting. We proposed a shortest path inspired algorithm to predict the long-term allocation of dynamic independent services to reduce the total energy consumption of the volunteer Cloud. Our proposed solution considers several constraints of the application such as availability, capacity of the machines and the replication factor of applications. We have conducted extensive simulation experiments to analyze the benefits of our algorithms. These latter show good improvements through diverse simulations. From the results, the SPS (shortest path strategy) algorithm is the most efficient in terms of energy consumption compared to the other classical methods. The benefits of SPS derive from the fact that, the number of inter-machine application migrations are greatly reduced. Note that in our approach, dynamic job arrival and end time are also considered, which means that jobs are not always ready at the beginning of the scheduling horizon. Therefore, the jobs may arrive at a certain time and end at diverse phases. A series of experimentations validated our approach and exemplified its practical interest. However, several interesting points remain unexplored, particularly: (i) the extension of our approach to the case of the addition or the omission of a volunteer node, where the number of nodes will be dynamic from one phase to another. (ii) The study of our contribution when the machines availability will also be dynamic.

References

1. Fox, A., et al.: Above the clouds: a Berkeley view of cloud computing, University of California at Berkley, USA, Technical report UCB/EECS-2009-28
2. Thakur, P., Manish, M.: Different scheduling algorithm in cloud computing: a survey. Int. J. Mod. Comput. Sci. (2017)
3. G. Group, Forecast: Data centers, worldwide, 2010–2015
4. Ngoko, Y., Gianessi, P., Cérin, C.: Energy-aware service provisioning in volunteers clouds. Int. J. Big Data Intell. **2**(4), 262–284 (2015)
5. Ghribi, C., Hadji, M., Zeghlache, D.: Energy efficient VM scheduling for cloud data centers: exact allocation and migration algorithms. In: IEEE CCGrid 2013 (2013)
6. Hsu, C.H., Slagter, K.D., Chen, S.C., Chung, Y.C.: Optimizing energy consumption with task consolidation in clouds. Inf. Sci. **258**, 452–462 (2014)
7. Hussain, S., Raza, Z.: An energy aware resource allocation model for cloud computing. In: International Conference on Science and Technology and Management, India (2016)
8. Beloglazov, A., Buyya, R.: Optimal online deterministic algorithms and adaptive heuristics for energy and performance efficient dynamic consolidation of virtual machines in cloud data centers. Concurr. Comput. Pract. Exp. **24**(13), 1397–1420 (2012)
9. Sindhu, S., Mukherjee, S.: Efficient task scheduling algorithms for cloud computing environment. In: Mantri, A., Nandi, S., Kumar, G., Kumar, S. (eds.) HPAGC 2011. CCIS, vol. 169, pp. 79–83. Springer, Heidelberg (2011). https://doi.org/10.1007/978-3-642-22577-2_11
10. Lee, Y.H., Leu, S., Chang, R.S.: Improving job scheduling algorithms in a grid environment. Future Gener. Comput. Syst. **27**(8), 991–998 (2011)
11. Nip, K., Wang, Z., Nobibon, F., Fabrice, T., et al.: A combination of flow shop scheduling and the shortest path problem. J. Comb. Optim. **29**(1), 36–52 (2015)
12. Gaujal, B., Navet, N., Walsh, C.: Shortest-path algorithms for real-time scheduling of FIFO tasks with minimal energy use. TECS **4**(4), 907–933 (2005)
13. Jiang, C., Wan, J., Cérin, C., Gianessi, P., Ngoko, Y.: Towards energy efficient allocation for applications in volunteer cloud. In: IPDPSW, pp. 1516–1525 (2014)
14. Usmani, Z., Singh, S.: A survey of virtual machine placement techniques in a cloud data center. Procedia Comput. Sci. **78**, 491–498 (2016)
15. Maaouia, O.B., Jemni, M., Fhaier, H., Cerin, C.: Towards optimizing energy consumption in cloud. In: 2017 International Conference on Engineering & MIS (ICEMIS). IEEE (2017)
16. Maaouia, O.B., Jemni, M., Fhaier, H., Cerin, C.: A novel optimization technique for mastering energy consumption in cloud data center. In: 2017 IEEE International Symposium on Parallel and Distributed Processing with Applications, pp. 475–480 (2017)
17. Reiss, C., Wilkes, J., Hellerstein, J.L.: Google cluster-usage traces: format+ schema. Google Inc., White Paper (2011)

Big Data and Information Processing

More Effective Distributed Deep Learning Using Staleness Based Parameter Updating

Yan Ye[1,2(✉)], Mengqiang Chen[1,3], Zijie Yan[1,2],
Weigang Wu[1,3], and Nong Xiao[1,2]

[1] School of Data and Computer Science, Sun Yet-Sen University,
Guangzhou, China
yeyan5@mail2.sysu.edu.cn,
{wuweig,xiaon6}@mail.sysu.edu.cn
[2] Guangdong Province Key Laboratory of Big Data Analysis and Processing,
Guangzhou, China
[3] MoE Key Laboratory of Machine Intelligence and Advanced Computing,
Guangzhou, China

Abstract. Deep learning technology has been widely applied for various purposes, especially big data analysis. However, computation required for deep learning is getting more complex and larger. In order to accelerate the training of large-scale deep networks, various distributed parallel training protocols have been proposed. In this paper, we design a novel asynchronous training protocol, Weighted Asynchronous Parallel (WASP), to update neural network parameters in a more effective way. The core of WASP is "gradient staleness", a parameter version number based metric to weight gradients and reduce the influence of the stale parameters. Moreover, by periodic forced synchronization of parameters, WASP combines the advantages of synchronous and asynchronous training models and can speed up training with a rapid convergence rate. We conduct experiments using two classical convolutional neural networks, LeNet-5 and ResNet-101, at the Tianhe-2 supercomputing system, and the results show that, WASP can achieve much higher acceleration than existing asynchronous parallel training protocols.

Keywords: Distributed deep learning · Parallel computing · Parameter server
Asynchronous parallel · Supercomputing system

1 Introduction

Deep learning is attracting more and more attention in recent years, due to outstanding results in a wide range of applications like image classification, object detection, self-driving cars, computer vision, and natural language processing [1]. Convolutional Neural

This research is partially supported by The National Key Research and Development Program of China (No. 2016YFB0200404, 2018YFB0203803), National Natural Science Foundation of China (U1711263), MOE-CMCC Joint Research Fund of China (No. MCM20160104), and Program of Science and Technology of Guangdong (No. 2015B010111001).

© Springer Nature Switzerland AG 2018
J. Vaidya and J. Li (Eds.): ICA3PP 2018, LNCS 11335, pp. 401–416, 2018.
https://doi.org/10.1007/978-3-030-05054-2_32

Network (CNN) is the typical architecture of deep learning, and large multi-layer neural networks are trained without pre-conceived models to learn complex features from raw input data, such as the pixels of labeled images. In addition to CNN, people also propose many other types of deep neural networks, e.g., Recurrent Neural Networks (RNNs), Deep Boltzmann Machine (DBM) and Time-delay Neural Networks (TDNN) et al. [2], and they are suitable for different application scenarios.

To minimize the prediction error, a deep neural network usually uses an iterative-convergent algorithm, such as stochastic gradient descent (SGD) [3], to get a set of optimal parameters from the training data. However, with the increasing of the scale of data set and the depth of neural networks, the training cost, including time and memory, also increases significantly. It may take days or even weeks to train a deep neural network to converge. The long time cost has become a bottleneck for deep learning. To cope with such a challenge, distributed and parallel computing has been considered for deep neural network training.

Multiple training workers (threads or processes) can be deployed at a distributed system of computer cluster. The training data set is divided and assigned to the workers, and each worker is in charge of processing a data-subset. During the training process, the workers need to exchange parameters so as to update the neural network via aggregated training results across all the nodes. Such a parallel data processing approach can speed up the training procedure while satisfactory accuracy can be achieved.

There are two different paradigms for parameter exchanging. In synchronous training, the parameters are synchronized at the end of each iteration, and next iteration is blocked until all the workers receive the updated parameters. Through such a barrier synchronization, the workers will perform gradient computation using the identical set of neural network parameters so as to guarantee the convergence of the training.

The above synchronization is usually realized by message passing or data sharing among workers. Since the slowest worker determines the speed of training in each synchronous batch, synchronous training usually suffers from long waiting time and low scalability. To circumvent this problem, researchers have restored to asynchronous approaches which emphasize speed by using potentially stale information for computation [4]. In asynchronous training, workers calculate the gradients separately, and can turn into next iteration without waiting for other workers. Although some of the workers compute gradients using parameters that may be several gradient steps behind the most updated set of the network parameters, it eliminates the synchronization barriers caused by the slowest worker, improving the data throughput of the distributed system.

Asynchronous training is generally realized based on the parameter server architecture [3]. All state shared among workers (i.e., the network parameters being learned) is kept as a specialized key-value store in parameter servers. Workers pull the up-to-date parameters from the parameter servers and compute gradients of the loss with respect to these parameters. Then, parameter servers collect gradients from workers and update the network using these gradients.

Asynchronous training has proven to be faster than synchronous training. However, due to the use of stale gradients, asynchronous training often has a convergent phenomenon of oscillation in the later phase of training. It is hardly as stable as the synchronous training and often results in poorer convergence. Therefore, there have been many works to deal with this problem. Ho et al. [5], presented a parameter server based distributed learning system where the staleness in parameter updates is bounded by forcing faster workers to wait for the slower ones. Gupta et al. [6] introduced a new learning rate modulation strategy to counter the effect of stale gradients, improving the convergence rate in asynchronous training.

In this paper, we attempt to combine the advantages of synchronous training and asynchronous training. Compared with the general asynchronous training, we propose a new definition of gradient staleness, and uses it to weight the stale gradient to reduce the damage of delayed updates during the asynchronous training. Based on the new gradient staleness metric, we design new parameter update mechanism for parameter servers. Therefore, we can not only guarantee the speed of training, but also solve the convergence of the oscillation phenomenon due to the stale gradients. Furthermore, in order to ensure the stability of convergence, forced synchronization is also used. Unlike the usual synchronized training, we make all computing nodes shift from asynchronous to synchronous in a periodic way, according to the number of updates at parameter servers. Combining the gradient staleness weighting based asynchronous training and parameter server based synchronization, we design the new distributed training protocol, WASP (Weighted Asynchronous Parallel).

We prove a theoretical-convergence upper bound for our proposed protocol and conduct experiments at a large scale cluster of the Tianhe-2 supercomputer. Compared with existing asynchronous training protocols in distributed deep learning, such as N-Soft, WASP can achieve the same accuracy with much less time. Moreover, WASP can converge in a more stable way than existing asynchronous training protocols.

The remainder of this paper is organized as follows. Section 2 summarizes and discusses existing works on distributed deep learning, including the parameter server architecture and different parameter update protocols. The design and implementation of our design is described in Sect. 3. The upper bound of convergence is also presented in this section. Section 4 presents experiment results and finally, Sect. 5 concludes the paper with future directions.

2 Related Work

2.1 Parameter Server Architecture

Before popularizing the parameter server architecture in deep learning, many traditional distributed systems have been applied in machine learning. However, these systems are usually constrained by the synchronous iterative communication pattern and cannot scale well. The concept of parameter came from the parallel LDA (Latent Dirichlet Allocation) framework [7], which uses distributed cache storage to synchronize parameters between different workers. YahoolDA [8] adds dedicated servers to store parameters, and provides user-defined update primitives and basic load balancing algorithms to improve the performance. The more abstract and general parameter server architecture was proposed by Li et al. [3, 9], which is easy to scale, efficient, and reliable. Following this architecture, many variants and extensions have been proposed, such as DistBelief [4], Petuum [5], Poseidom [10] and Tensorflow [11]. Parameter server architecture can be easily used to build and scale distributed deep learning across CPU clusters or GPU based heterogeneous clusters [4, 8, 12].

An illustration of the basic parameter server architecture [3] is shown in Fig. 1. There is one or more parameter servers, which are responsible for storing and updating the global shared parameters. Workers are in charge of training the neural network of deep learning based on input data set. Workers exchange parameter values with parameter servers.

As introduced in [3], each worker trains its own network, respectively. At the end of each iteration, a worker sends the gradients newly calculated to the parameter servers. Then, it pulls the up-to-date neural network parameters from the parameter server and update its local copy. The new parameters will be used for the next training iteration. A parameter server collects gradients from workers and aggregate them and calculates new parameters based on distributed training protocols (described in the next sub-section). Consistency of parameters across workers is usually guaranteed by mechanisms at parameter servers.

Since both workers and parameter servers execute in a concurrent way, the training procedure and parameter calculating procedure is decoupled. Then, different workers may proceed with different speeds, and they may execute asynchronously so as to increase distributed training speed.

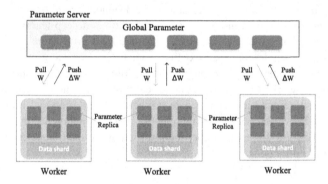

Fig. 1. An illustration of parameter server

2.2 Distributed Training Protocol

In distributed deep learning, the training protocol mainly describes how the parameter servers process the gradients and complete the global parameters update. There are three frequently-used protocols: BSP (Bulk Synchronous Parallel) [13, 14], ASP (Asynchronous Parallel) [4, 8] and SSP (Stale Synchronous Parallel) [5].

In BSP, each worker l compute a gradient ΔW_l using a mini-batch size of data and send it to the parameter server. The parameter server averages the gradients over λ workers and updates the parameters according to Eq. 1, where α is the learning rate. The workers are forced to wait for pulling the updated parameters until the parameter server has received the gradient contribution from all the workers and finished the update operation. This means that the faster workers must wait for the slowest worker to complete the training and the computation proceeds at the rate of the slowest worker in each iteration. The average running time is greatly increased [15]. Usually, we call the slowest worker straggler. Although suffering from high overheads because of the synchronization barriers separating iterations, BSP protocol guarantees that each worker computes gradients on the exactly the same set of parameters. It provides the best accuracy baseline, when fixing the number of training epochs. Jian et al. [16] proposed a synchronous optimization with backup workers under the BSP protocol that runs independent instances on several machines more than the training actually requires. It avoids stragglers by not forcing updates to wait for the slowest worker.

$$W_{i+1} = W_i - \alpha \frac{1}{\lambda} \sum_{l=1}^{\lambda} \Delta W_l \tag{1}$$

ASP is an improvement based of BSP. The parameter server updates global parameters as soon as it receives a gradient, without waiting for all gradient aggregations to average. As shown in Eq. 2. Although this protocol show faster convergence than BSP protocol, it does not enjoy the assurance of formal convergence guarantees [10]. The main reason is that when a worker computes gradients of parameters and sends back to the parameter servers, the global parameters may have been updated more than once by other workers. For the global parameters at this point, these gradients are already obsolete values. We refer to these as stale gradients, and its staleness as the number of updates that have occurred between its corresponding read and update operations.

An alternative solution, N-Soft, is presented in Zhang et al. [6], which proposed batching gradients from multiple machines before performing an asynchronous SGD update, thereby reducing the effective staleness of gradients. In particular, the N can vary from 1 to λ and the algorithm has different performances by setting different N.

$$W_{i+1} = W_i - \alpha \Delta W_i \tag{2}$$

SSP is a flexible protocol which allows computations to use stale parameters with the purpose of reducing synchronization overheads. It permits the workers to perform asynchronously, but the fastest worker cannot exceed the slowest one more than a predefined staleness S. The users can vary the value of S to control the constraints degree, and even get the BSP and ASP protocols flexibly. Although it is not strictly synchronous, it controls the gradient delay of the whole neural network to a certain extent. In the case of adjusting the training algorithm's hyper-parameters (such as learning rate, mini-batch size), it can balance the training efficiency and the convergence of the neural network well. And the theory proves that when staleness is not equal to infinity, the SSP protocol can achieve stable convergence after several iterations [5]. Jiang et al. [17] introduces a heterogeneity-aware distributed SGD algorithm under the SSP protocol. It use a sophisticated learning rate schedule that takes into consideration the delay information of each update before adding them to the global parameters, and achieve the improvement of the convergence robustness.

3   Weighted Asynchronous Parallel Protocol

In this paper, we design a novel distributed training protocol, WASP, which combines the advantage of synchronous and asynchronous training.

3.1   Basic Idea of WASP

In WASP, each worker conducts training asynchronously and computes the gradients based on a mini-batch of examples randomly selected from the training data. When a parameter server gets new gradients and parameter version number from some workers, there are two ways to handle the gradients. If the parameters used by the worker in training process are consistent with those at the parameter server, the gradients will be used to calculate the new global parameters as it is processed in ASP normally. Otherwise, these gradients are computed from delayed parameters. We define the staleness of the gradients as the difference between the parameter version number of the worker and the parameter server and weighted the gradients by their staleness before they are used to compute the new global parameters. Therefore, the protocol can maintain the asynchronous training speed and at the same time reduce the damage of delayed updates. However, the gradient weighting operation has lost some of the updated information, which may result in a poorly learned model. In order to solve this problem, we propose the forced synchronization interval.

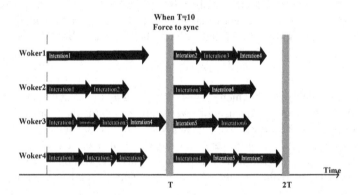

Fig. 2. The WASP protocol

The parameter version number of parameter servers increases gradually after the whole training has been performed asynchronously several times. When the parameter server's version reaches the threshold of forced synchronization interval, all workers are forced to update its parameters to the newest version. This operation ensures that the overall training for the next iteration will start with the same version of the parameters. By forcing synchronization, the impact caused by the loss of partial gradients can be weakened, and the training convergence rate is improved. The execution procedure WASP is illustrated in Fig. 2.

3.2   Operations of WASP

We describe the detailed operations of WASP below. We use the following notations:

- λ: number of workers
- α: learning rate
- T: forced synchronization interval
- θ_l: parameter version number of worker l. The range of l is from 1 to λ.
- θ_0: parameter version number of the parameter server
- $\sigma_{i,l}$: staleness of the gradient from worker l at the iteration i. A worker l pushes its gradient with parameter version θ_l to the parameter server of parameter version θ_0, where $\theta_0 \geq \theta_l$. We calculate the staleness $\sigma_{i,l}$ of this gradient as $\theta_0 - \theta_l$.

For each worker l, first of all, it randomly initializes the neural network's layer parameters according to the structure and sets the current parameter version number θ_l to 0. Second, the worker reads a mini-batch of data from memory for training. Thirdly, the worker uses the samples and labels to perform forward propagation and gets the output value. In this process, each worker is calculating independently and doesn't communicate with each other. Then, the worker use the *Loss* function to calculate the error between the network's output value and the sample's label, carries on the back propagation, and calculates the gradient ΔW_l of the parameter by layers. Finally, the worker sends the gradients ΔW_l and the parameter version number θ_l to the parameter server, waiting for the parameters to be updated. Then, the worker pulls the latest parameters and version number from the parameter server and use them to replace the local parameters status: $\theta_l = \theta_0$. Next, the worker repeats the second step and goes to the next iteration.

Algorithm. 1. WASP worker l, where $l = 1, ..., \lambda$

Input: Dataset Y
Input: Mini-batch size M
Input: Iteration I
1.   if i = 0 :

         // The worker in the first iteration

2.   Set parameters version $\theta_l = 0$

3.   Initialize the global variable

4.   else:

5.   Pull global parameter W_i and parameter version
       θ_0 from Parameter Servers

6.   Set parameters version $\theta_l = \theta_j$

7.   for i in range(I):

8.   Load a mini-batch of training data {images, lables}
       from Y

9.   for Sample X in range(M):

10.   Logits = inference(X_{images})

11.   Loss = loss(Logits, X_{labels})

12.   Grads = Compute Gradient(Loss)

13.   Send Grads and θ_l to Parameter Servers

For a parameter server, firstly, it initializes the global parameter version number as $\theta_0 = 0$ when the parameters of each worker are initialized, and initializes the forced synchronization interval value T to a constant value based on the definition of the user. Second, once the parameter server receives a gradient ΔW_1 from a worker, it increases the parameter version number by 1 and judges it. If the $\theta_0 \% T$ is not equal to 0, the parameter is updated using a gradient weighting method, with the following Eq. 3 to define the staleness of the gradient from this worker.

$$\sigma_{i,l} = \theta_l - \theta_0 \qquad (3)$$

Then the parameter server use Eq. 4 to update the global parameters:

$$W_{i+1} = W_i - \alpha \frac{\Delta W_l}{\sigma_{i,l}} \qquad (4)$$

If the $\theta_0\%T$ is equal to 0, indicating that all workers have made a total of T-time asynchronous update operations, requiring a forced synchronization. The parameters need to be updated by aggregating and averaging the all gradients according to the Eq. 5.

$$W_{i+1} = W_i - \alpha \frac{1}{\lambda} \sum_{l=1}^{\lambda} \Delta W_l \tag{5}$$

Finally, the parameter server repeats the second step and goes to the next parameter version. Our method is presented in Algorithms 1 and 2.

Algorithm. 2. WASP parameter server j

Input: Predefined forced synchronization interval T
Input: Learning rate α

1. Initialize the Parameters version $\theta_j = 0$ and $T = t$

2. Receive Grads and θ_l from worker l
3. Set $\theta_j = \theta_j + 1$

4. if $\theta_j \% t == 0$:
5. $\mid$ Grads $\leftarrow$ Grads - α * Grads * $\frac{1}{\theta_j - \theta_l}$
6. else:
7. $\mid$ Aggregate the Grads from all workers
8. $\mid$ Grads $\leftarrow \frac{1}{\lambda} \sum_{l=1}^{\lambda}$ Grads
9. $\mid$ Grads $\leftarrow$ Grads - α * Grads

3.3   Correctness Analysis

Here we analyze the correctness of WASP by discussing its convergence. We will consider the convergence of WASP using a bounded stale parameters with forced synchronization interval. In essence, we are solving the following generic optimization problem:

$$min_x \ F(x) := \sum_{t=1}^{T} f_t(x) \tag{6}$$

Theorem 1 (adapted from [18]). SGD under stale parameters convergence in probability:

Let it be a convex function, where f_t is also convex. We search for a minimizer x^* via stochastic gradient descent on each component ∇f_t under stale parameters, with P workers and the forced synchronization interval s. Let $u_t := -\eta_t \nabla \widetilde{f_t(x_t)}$ with $\eta_t = \frac{\eta}{\sqrt{t}}$. Under suitable conditions (f_t are L-Lipschitz and bounded divergence $D(x\|x') \leq F^2$), we have:

$$P\left[\frac{R[X]}{T} - \frac{1}{\sqrt{T}}\left(\eta L^2 + \frac{F^2}{\eta} + 2\eta L^2 \mu_r\right) \geq \tau\right] \leq exp\left\{\frac{-T\tau^2}{2\bar{\eta}T\sigma_r + 2/3\eta L^2(2s+1)P\tau}\right\}$$

where $R[X] := \sum_{t=1}^{T} f_t(\widetilde{x_t}) - f(x^*)$, and $\bar{\eta}T = \frac{\eta^2 L^4(\ln T + 1)}{T} = o(1)$ as $T \to \infty$.

This means that $\frac{R[X]}{T}$ converges to $O(T^{-1/2})$ in probability with an exponential tail-bound; convergence is faster when the observed staleness average μ_r and variance σ_r are smaller. Therefore, when we give a smaller μ_r, σ_r in WASP, the training will eventually converge with a finite number of iterations.

3.4   Implementation of WASP

The implementation of WASP protocol is based on TensorFlow [11], a deep learning framework that supports distributed training and allows computing using CPU and GPU cluster nodes. We define two types of jobs in TensorFlow: Parameter server (PS) and Worker, which communicate with each other through GRPC. TensorFlow initiates (N+M) processes, including N PS processes and M Workers processes, which are on different computing nodes respectively. Here PS process is mainly responsible for communicating and updating the new parameters. Worker process chiefly computes the gradients.

During the training process, a worker pulls parameters from the parameter server, starts training when the parameters arrive, and then calculates gradients. Finally, it pushes the gradients back to the parameter server before it can pull the parameters again. We do not "accrue" gradients at the workers so that each gradient pushed to the parameter server is always calculated out of one mini-batch size as accruing gradients generally lead to a worse model. Note that the computation in parameter servers and workers are concurrent (except for the worker that is communicating with the server, if any).

Since memory is abundant on each computing node, our implementation does not split the neural network across multiple nodes. In particular, we pack one worker on each computing node.

4   Performance Evaluation

To evaluate the performance of the proposed protocol, we conduct experiments at the "Tianhe-2" supercomputer system[1], which is currently ranked No. 2 in Top500.

Besides ASP and BSP, we also consider N-Soft [6], an improvement of ASP, for comparison purpose.

---

[1] http://nscc-gz.cn/

4.1   Experiments Setup

The Cluster of Computing Nodes. Experiments are conducted at the partition of CPU pool of Tianhe-2. Each node of this partition contains two 12-core Intel Xeon E5-2692v2 processors with a clock frequency of 2.2 GHz. A single CPU has a theoretical double-precision floating point peak performance of 211.2Gflop/s, and the computing node peak performance up to 3.432Tflop/s. The memory capacity of each node is 64 GB and nodes are connected through Intel's Ivy Bridge micro-architecture built-in PCI-E 2.0, with a single lane bandwidth of 10 Gbps, providing a powerful speed support for cross-node data communications.

Data Sets and Models. We present results on two data sets: MNIST and CIFAR-10 and all experiments in this paper are using the TensorFlow system. The MNIST database [19] of handwritten digits contains 28 × 28 images in 10 classes, with 7000 images per class. It has a training set of 60,000 examples, and a test set of 10,000 examples. For this data set, we use the LeNet-5 [20], a deep convolutional neural network with 2 convolutional layers, each followed by a pooling layer, and 3 fully-connected layers. The last layer outputs the probability distribution over the 10 classes. The second data set used is CIFAR-10 [21]. It comprises of a total of 60,000 RGB images of size 32 × 32 pixels partitioned into the training set (50,000 images) and the test set (10,000 images). Each image belongs to one of the 10 classes, with 6000 images per class. For this database, we use the ResNet-101 [22], a convolutional neural network with three levels of residual learning units, which has a depth of 101 layers.

Training Algorithm Setup. The LeNet-5 is trained for 11 epochs, using momentum-accelerated mini-batch SGD with a batch size of 64 and momentum is set to 0.9. We fix learning rate to be 0.01, the frequently used value.

For ResNet-101, the neural network's mini-batch size is set to 128 and the neural network is trained for 30 epochs using SGD optimizer. The base learning rate is set to 0.1 and decays by 0.04 every 10,000 iterations. In order to eliminate the interference caused by artificially selected parameters during the training process, the above parameters are selected referencing to the model zoo of TensorFlow. In this parameter configuration, the neural network can achieve the best training results.

4.2   Performance Metrics

We use three major metrics are used to measure performance of distributed deep learning protocols:

- Average backward time: the average backward time of each worker during training, including calculating gradients and applying gradients. This shows the time cost of processing gradients.
- Training error: the misclassification error rate on the test dataset of the neural network trained using a distributed training protocol. This metric is measured by periodically testing during the training process. The lower the training error, the more stable convergence and better training performance.

- Speedup: the ratio of training time to convergence against BSP. We use BSP as the baseline protocol and calculate the speedup for each other protocol, including WASP.

4.3   Experiments Results

We conduct experiments using varying number of workers and set the forced synchronization interval T to 500. We fix the N in the N-Soft protocol to 4, so parameters are updated as soon as the parameter servers receive four gradients from any four workers. In order to make the comparison more obvious, we make each computing node has only one task for PS or Worker.

Average Backward Time. Since we add a weighted gradients operation and forced synchronization in WASP, the training inevitably incurs extra time cost. Figure 3 plots the average backward time using different training protocols. For the LeNet-5 on the MINST data set, the average backward time of WASP is much lower than that of BSP and N-Soft and is slightly more than that of ASP. When the number of workers is small ($\lambda. = 4$), the time cost is not significant compared to the ASP. When the number of workers is comparatively large ($\lambda. = 16$), the average backward time increases by 0.018 s, which is a relatively minor increase.

As for the ResNet-101 on the CIFAR-10 data set, the calculation of gradients accounts for a large proportion of backward time. Therefore, our additional processing operations in the gradients applying phase have little effect on the overall backward time. As shown in the Fig. 3, the time gap between these four training protocols is imperceptible. The WASP protocol is only 0.175 s longer than the ASP protocol and increases the time cost by 0.02%.

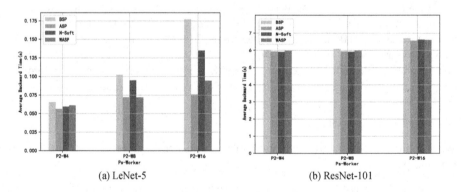

(a) LeNet-5   (b) ResNet-101

Fig. 3. Average backward time

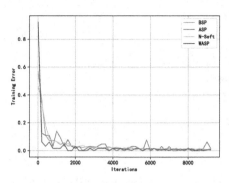

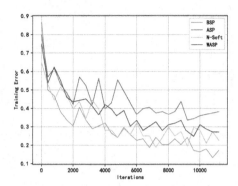

Fig. 4. The training error of LeNet-5   **Fig. 5.** The training error of ResNet-101

Training Error. We use the iteration number as the horizontal coordinate, in which the time of each iteration varies according to the protocols. For LeNet-5, as a representative result, Fig. 4 shows the training error obtained for different training protocols when using λ. = 16 workers. We can observer that the WASP's training error drops faster than the rest of protocols at the beginning. When iterations is about 500, the training error of WASP is nearly 0, exceeding all the other training protocols and keeping. Although the convergence of WASP has a slight oscillation, it is more stable than ASP. With a limited number of iterations, the WASP can get the same convergence as the BSP protocol at last.

In Fig. 5, we demonstrate the training error of the ResNet-101 using 16 workers. The corresponding curves for training error for different protocols are virtually distinguishable.

During the training process, the training error of WASP is basically between 28% and 40%. However, the training error of ASP is about $2\times$ larger than that of WASP, meaning that the convergence is endured with drastic oscillation. After 12,000 iterations, the BSP protocol achieve the best performance as a baseline and its training error is about 17%, followed by N-Soft, about 23%. The training error of the WASP can reach about 27%, which is much lower than ASP' training error of 38%, showing that WASP is effective in reducing the damages of delayed updates to obtain more stable convergence and achieves better training performance than ASP.

Speedup. Figures 6 and 7 plot the convergence time on LeNet-5 and ResNet-101 models. As the number of workers increases, the time to convergence required for each protocol decreases significantly, but the WASP keeps the fastest convergence rate on both models. Most obviously, it only needs 5243 s to convergence to the accuracy threshold using 16 workers on LeNet-5 model, while BSP needs 27335 s.

Table 1 shows the speedup of the LeNet-5 under different numbers of workers. In order to achieve comparable speedup as the single-worker in BSP, all the hyper-parameters are kept unchanged from the single-worker case. As shown in Table 1, the WASP protocol has a $6.85\times$ acceleration effect to achieve an accuracy of 0.98, representing a more efficient performance than other protocols.

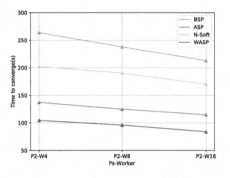

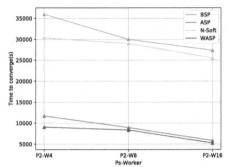

Fig. 6. Time to converge of LeNet-5   **Fig. 7.** Time to converge of ResNet-101

The speedup of ResNet-101 model is shown in Table 2. Since the training time of ResNet-101 is very long, the acceleration effect is remarkable. When the accuracy threshold is achieved using 16 worker, the WASP accomplishes a 16 times-fold acceleration effect. Furthermore, due to the unstable convergence, the accuracy of the ASP protocol cannot be maintained at about 0.68. So our protocol is more than 1.7× faster than ASP.

Table 1. The speedup of LeNet-5

Distributed training protocols	PS/Worker	Speedup	Accuracy
BSP	2/4	2.18	0.987
	2/16	2.69	0.988
N-Soft	2/4	2.84	0.983
	2/16	3.38	0.985
ASP	2/4	4.18	0.986
	2/16	5.01	0.983
WASP	2/4	5.5	0.985
	2/16	6.85	0.984

Table 2. The speedup of ResNet-101

Distributed training protocols	PS/Worker	Speedup	Accuracy
BSP	2/4	2.43	0.693
	2/16	3.2	0.698
N-Soft	2/4	2.88	0.684
	2/16	3.44	0.689
ASP	2/4	7.48	0.682
	2/16	15.04	0.679
WASP	2/4	9.68	0.687
	2/16	16.7	0.688

Overall, the WASP protocol which we proposed achieves stable convergence, significant acceleration, and low time cost, in comparison with the conventional training protocols and the N-Soft protocol.

5 Conclusions

Distributed training protocols for deep learning architectures will become more important as the size of data sets increases. However, both synchronous and asynchronous training suffer from their respective weaknesses of stragglers and staleness. This leads us to propose a Weighted Asynchronous Parallel (WASP) protocol, which combines the advantages of both synchronous and asynchronous training. We define the staleness of gradients by parameter version number and use it to alleviate the unstable convergence. To further improve the convergence rate, we convert the parameter update method from asynchronous to synchronous in a periodic way. Besides, we prove the valid convergence of our approach in theory.

We conduct the experiments at a large scale cluster of the Tianhe-2 supercomputer and demonstrate the effectiveness of WASP on standard benchmarks (MNIST and CIFAR-10). The experimental results show that our protocol achieves significantly stable convergence and a rapid convergence rate on the neural network of LeNet-5 and ResNet-101.

References

1. Lecun, Y., Bengio, Y., Hinton, G.: Deep learning. Nature **521**(7553), 436–444 (2015)
2. Li, X., Zhang, G., Huang, H., et al.: Performance analysis of GPU-based convolutional neural networks. In: International Conference on Parallel Processing, Philadelphia, USA, pp. 67–76. IEEE (2016)
3. Li, M., Andersen, D., Park, J., et al.: Scaling distributed machine learning with the parameter server. In: International Conference on Big Data Science and Computing, Beijing, China, pp. 583–598. ACM (2014)
4. Dean, J., Corrado, G., Monga, R., et al.: Large scale distributed deep networks. In: International Conference on Neural Information Processing Systems, Lake Tahoe, Nevada, USA, pp. 1223–1231. Curran Associates Inc. (2012)
5. Ho, Q., Cipar, J., Cui, H., et al.: More effective distributed ML via a stale synchronous parallel parameter server. In: International Conference on Neural Information Processing Systems, Daegu, South Korea, pp. 1223–1231. Curran Associates Inc. (2013)
6. Zhang, W., Gupta, S., Lian, X., et al.: Staleness-aware async-SGD for distributed deep learning. In: International Joint Conference on Artificial Intelligence, vol. 1511(05950), pp. 2350–2356 (2016)
7. Smola, A., Narayanamurthy, S.: An architecture for parallel topic models. Very Large Data Bases **3**(1–2), 703–710 (2010)
8. Ahmed, A., Aly, M., Gonzalez, J., et al.: Scalable inference in latent variable models. In: ACM International Conference on Web Search and Data Mining, Seattle Washington, USA, pp. 123–132. ACM (2012)
9. Li, M., Zhou, L., Yang, Z., et al.: Parameter server for distributed machine learning. In: Big Learning NIPS Workshop, Lake Tahoe, Nevada, USA, pp. 1–10. ACM (2013)

10. Zhang, H., Hu, Z., Wei, J., et al.: Poseidon: A system architecture for efficient GPU-based deep learning on multiple machines. Comput. Sci. **1512**(06216), 10–21 (2015)
11. Abadi, M., Barham, P., Chen, J., et al.: TensorFlow: a system for large-scale machine learning. In: OSDI 2016 Proceedings of the 12th USENIX conference on Operating Systems Design and Implementation, Savannah, USA, pp. 265–283. USENIX Association (2016)
12. Wang, M., Xiao, T., Li, J., Zhang, J., Hong, C., et al.: Minerva: a scalable and highly efficient training platform for deep learning. In: NIPS 2014 Workshop of Distributed Matrix Computations, Montreal, Canada, pp. 1–9. ACM (2014)
13. Valiant, L.: A bridging model for parallel computation. Commun. ACM **33**(8), 103–111 (1990)
14. McColl, W.: Bulk Synchronous Parallel Computing. Oxford University Press, Oxford (1995)
15. Cui, H., Cipar, J., Ho, Q., et al.: Exploiting bounded staleness to speed up big data analytics. In: Usenix Conference on Usenix Technical Conference, Philadelphia, USA, pp. 37–48. USENIX Association (2014)
16. Jiang, C., Xing, P., Rajat, M., et al.: Revisiting distributed synchronous SGD. In: International Conference on Learning Representations, vol. 1604(00981), pp. 1–10 (2017)
17. Jiang, J., Cui, B., Zhang, C., et al.: Heterogeneity-aware distributed parameter servers. In: ACM International Conference, Glasgow, Scotland, pp. 463–478. ACM (2017)
18. Dai, W., Kumar, A., Ho, Q., et al.: High-performance distributed ML at scale through parameter server consistency models. In: Twenty-Ninth AAAI Conference on Artificial Intelligence, Austin, Texas, pp. 79–87. AAAI Press (2015)
19. Lecun, Y., Cortes, C.: The MNIST database of handwritten digits. Courant Inst. Math. Sci. **3**(7), 1–10 (2010)
20. Lecun, Y., Bottou, L., Bengio, Y., et al.: Gradient-based learning applied to document recognition. Proc. IEEE **86**(11), 2278–2324 (1998)
21. Krizhevsky, A., Hinton, G.: Learning multiple layers of features from tiny images. Comput. Sci. Dept. **1**(4), 1–60 (2009)
22. He, K., Zhang, X., Ren, S., et al.: Deep residual learning for image recognition. Comput. Vis. Pattern Recogn. **1512**(03385), 770–778 (2016)

A Game Theoretic D2D Local Caching System under Heterogeneous Video Preferences and Social Reciprocity

Kaichuan Zhao[1]($\boxtimes$), Yuezhi Zhou[1], Wenjuan Tang[2], Shuang Li[1],
and Yaoxue Zhang[1]

[1] Beijing National Research Center for Information Science and Technology,
Department of Computer Science and Technology,
Tsinghua University, Beijing, China
{zhaokc13,lishuang13}@mails.tsinghua.edu.cn, {zhouyz,zyx}@tsinghua.edu.cn
[2] Department of Information Science and Engineering,
Central South University, Changsha, China
wenjuantang@csu.edu.cn

Abstract. To accommodate the increasing rich multimedia mobile traffics, especially the mobile video traffics, local caching becomes an effective approach to improve the quality of content delivering services in the cellular networks. Mobile devices with large storage capacities and high speed device-to-device (D2D) links become important elements of the local caching system. In this paper, we propose a D2D local caching system under heterogeneous preferences of mobile subscribers (MS), and investigate the utility maximization problem using Stackelberg game solution. In particular, the MSs form different groups, according to their social relationships, and determine the price policies to maximize their utilities, while the video provider (VP) aims to maximize his profits by deciding the rent policies and the budget plan. We investigate the equilibrium of the Stackelberg game in details and propose a water-filling based iterative algorithm to obtain the Stackelberg equilibrium. Extensive results demonstrate efficient performance of the D2D local caching system.

Keywords: Local caching · Device-to-device communication
Social relationships · Stackelberg game

1 Introduction

The advent of mobile devices (e.g., large-screen phones and tablet computers) immensely enriches mobile users experience by providing a proliferation of multimedia services for their mobile domain. This, in turn, has driven a dramatically growth of the mobile data traffic, especially, mobile video data accounts for the major part of the total mobile data traffic [5]. When the same video is requested from mobile subscribers (MS), numerous repetitive downloads and duplicate

© Springer Nature Switzerland AG 2018
J. Vaidya and J. Li (Eds.): ICA3PP 2018, LNCS 11335, pp. 417–431, 2018.
https://doi.org/10.1007/978-3-030-05054-2_33

transmissions occur. To deal with this problem, assisting the content dissemination through local caching [23] has recently been proposed as an promising approach. It trades off the limited backhaul resource with the storage capacity of end devices (e.g. mobile phones), the deployment cost of which is getting lower. Popular videos, which usually account for a small fraction of the whole library, can be prefetched at the end devices during off-peak time, while during peak hours, the videos can be delivered locally to the MSs through the high speed links (e.g. device-to-device (D2D) communications). By this means, local caching provides a way to bring the videos closer to users, which can mitigate the congestion in the core networks and reduce the average video access delay [6].

As an effective method to accommodate the mobile data traffic surge, numerous recent works have utilized local caching to improve the system performance of the wireless networks. Authors in [10] and [11] study the cooperative content distribution with local caching. By caching videos in the mobile devices, and by utilizing the short range transmissions, large amount of data can be effectively offloaded through the cooperative local sharing [17]. Although the MSs can make contributions to the local caching system as helpers, it also incurs extra costs to them (e.g., caching storage cost and D2D transmissions cost). The performance of D2D caching networks are greatly dependent on the sharing willingness of the MSs. Due to the selfishness of the MSs, it is essential to design an incentive mechanism to encourage MSs and the video provider (VP) to participate in the video local sharing.

Designing incentive mechanism in the caching system faces critical challenges. The VP aims to maximize the video local sharing among MSs with a small budget, thus reducing the transmission cost and improving the service quality. Whereas, MSs will make profits from the rewards of participating in the local caching system. Both the VP and MSs want to obtain optimal profits. Due to the limited budget of the VP, MSs need to compete with others to get more rewards, which raises a non-cooperative game between them. In addition, from the work on the incentive mechanism design in the literature [16,26], prior works pay little attention to the social attribute of MSs and assume they have the same interests and share willingness. More practically, the MSs usually have the similar interests of videos in the same social group. What's more, the MSs prefer to share their cached videos to the neighbors with close social relationship, which will be considered in our system [20].

In this paper, we will design a D2D local caching system, which consists of one VP and multiple MSs, based on a Stackelberg game framework. In addition, we design an incentive mechanism to promote participation of the VP and MSs. Specifically, the MSs are divided into different disjoined groups according to their social relationships, and the videos can be shared locally in the same social group. We consider the MSs' group to be the leaders, which decides the charge price for leasing one fraction of MSs, while the VP as the follower responds with a fraction of the seed MSs to rent from each MSs' group. We also formulate the interaction among different MSs' group as a non-cooperative sub-game, where each group competes for the limited rewards budget. For the sake of analysis, we model the MSs in the system as a Homogeneous Poisson Point Process (HPPP), following the theory of stochastic geometry [4]. Under this model, we investigate the equilibrium of our Stackelberg game. Numerical results are finally given to quantify the performance of the D2D local caching system.

The remainder of the paper is organized as follows. Section 2 gives a brief review of the related works. In Sect. 3, we introduce the system model. Section 4 defines the utility functions of the VP and MSs' groups, and presents a two-stage Stackelberg game for the system. The game analysis is conducted in Sect. 5. In Sect. 6, extensive experimental results are provided. Finally, we conclude this paper in Sect. 7.

2   Related Works

Recently, the use of local caching to improve the system performance of the wireless networks has received much interest. According to the location of storage medium, the literature can be classified into two lines of works: caching in the base stations (BS) [1,9,23] and caching in the end devices [8,13,22,25]. By caching videos in the BSs, the videos, which has been downloaded frequently or predicted to be popular in near future, are selected by the VPs and cached in the cache-enabled BSs. Then BSs cooperatively utilize local caching and transmission resource to serve MSs in the cellular networks. The authors in [2] and [23] have proposed FemtoCaching systems with helper stations for video on-demand streaming. In [14], authors developed a commercial video caching prototype using cache-enabled small base stations. In [21], authors proposed a mobile data offloading framework with cache-enabled small base stations, which can effectively reduce the mobile network operators' cost.

Apart from base stations acting as helpers, the MSs equipped with storage capacities can also contribute to the cooperative local caching system [11,19]. By caching popular videos on the mobile devices, they can act as seed nodes to share the videos to their neighbors by short range communications (e.g., Bluetooth and WiFi) during peak time, which can reduce the repetitive transmissions [22]. In [18], the caching strategy based on the distribution of users request was proposed to maximize the probability of content hit ratio. In [8,24], the designs of the D2D caching system were investigated. [25] investigates the impact of user mobility on D2D caching, and proposes a mobility-aware caching strategy to improve the data offloading performance.

While the existing works above mainly focus on the optimization of cache placement aiming to reduce the transmission cost and delay, the authors in [16,27] consider comprehensive systems from a financial perspective. In [16], the contract theory is used to address the resource-trading problems in a commercial small-cell caching system. [27] proposes an incentive cache mechanism to stimulate the small base stations and multiple content providers in a caching system.

In this work, mobile devices are used as storage medium to cache popular videos and share them locally. From the commercial perspective, we investigate

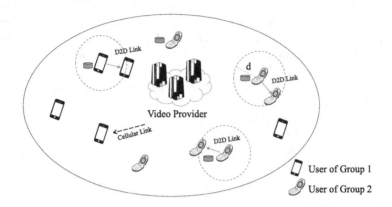

Fig. 1. An illustration of the D2D local caching system

the resource allocation problem of local caching using Stackelberg game theory. Unlike the works above, the share willingness, especially in a social reciprocity aspect, are utilized to design an incentive mechanism in this D2D local caching system. Besides, in this work, heterogeneous video preferences information of MSs are used for caching placement instead of the global preference information.

3   System Model

We consider a D2D local caching system in a cellular network, consisting of one VP and a large number of MSs. The MSs are served by the base stations, and they can also share cached videos with others by leveraging D2D connections. For simplicity, in this D2D local caching system, we focus on how to transmit a certain video among MSs[1]. Let $\mathcal{L}$ denote the VP, which has a reference popular video to disseminate. Figure 1 shows a scenario of the D2D local caching system. In this system, the VP first stimulates and selects some MS as seed MSs to push the video into their local memories during off-peak time. During peak times, if there are seed MSs in proximity, the requesting MSs can fetch the video directly through D2D Links. Otherwise, they will download the video via cellular links with longer service delay. With effective mechanisms to allocate wireless resources, we assume that there is no interference among MSs [12]. Table 1 lists the notations used in the rest of the paper.

Share willingness of MSs is an important factor in the D2D local caching system. If MSs did not prefer to share their resource, this system would not achieve any performance improvement by utilizing local sharing. As each MS has different social communities, we divide these MSs into K disjoined groups according to their social relationships. Without loss of generality, we assume that MSs have full willingness to share the cached video with partners in the same group, and refuse any transmissions with foreigners (i.e., MSs in different

---

[1] The results can be easily extended to the scenarios with multiple videos.

Table 1. Key Notations

$\mathcal{L}$	VP
$\mathcal{K} = \{1, 2, ..., K\}$	Set of MS groups
λ_k	Density of MS in the group $\mathcal{G}_k$
d	D2D transmission distance
p_k	Average popularity of the reference video in group $\mathcal{G}_k$
π_k	charge prices of the group $\mathcal{G}_k$
ϕ_k	Renting fraction of group $\mathcal{G}_k$
c_k	Maintaining cost of group $\mathcal{G}_k$
q	Unit profit obtained by the VP
β	Average number of requests by each MS

groups). Let $\mathcal{K} = \{1, 2, ..., K\}$ denote the set of MS groups. The group $k \in \mathcal{K}$ is denoted by $\mathcal{G}_k$. As illustrated in Fig. 1, the MSs are divided into two social groups, i.e., $\mathcal{G}_1$ and $\mathcal{G}_2$. For each group, we assume that the locations of the MSs in $\mathcal{G}_k, k \in \mathcal{K}$ follow a HPPP ψ_k, which is independent of the other groups. Let λ_k denote the density of MS in the group $\mathcal{G}_k$, which represents the average number of MSs in one unit area. For a certain MS in each group, he can download the video from seed MSs within the D2D transmission distance, as denoted by the radius d in Fig. 1. Under the assumption of HPPP model, the average number of seed MSs of group $\mathcal{G}_k$ in the range of d is denoted by $\pi d^2 \lambda_k$. In reality, MSs with close social relationships will probably have the similar interests [15]. Thus, p_k is defined as the average popularity of the reference video in group $\mathcal{G}_k$, where $0 \leq p_k \leq 1, k \in \mathcal{K}$. Then, the interested density of group $\mathcal{G}_k$ is denoted by $p_k \lambda_k$, which means the average video request number of MSs in group $\mathcal{G}_k$ in one unit area.

In this local caching system, there are two important phases: the caching phase and sharing phase: (1) In the caching phase, the VP will provide a budget plan M to stimulate the MSs to participate in this local caching system. Each MSs group announces the price of seed MSs. Let the set of $\mathbf{\Pi} = \{\pi_1, \pi_2, ..., \pi_K\}$ denote the charge prices of these social groups, and π_k denote the price of the group $\mathcal{G}_k$. Given the price profile $\mathbf{\Pi}$, the VP decides on renting a fraction of the seed MSs, denoted by $\mathbf{\Phi} = \{\phi_1, \phi_2, ..., \phi_K\}$. Let ϕ_k denote the renting fraction of group $\mathcal{G}_k$. (2) In the sharing phase, for an requesting MS in group $\mathcal{G}_k$, the video download protocol is defined as follows:

- *Self caching*: If the video is already cached in the memory of this MS, he will obtain this video directly.
- *Local sharing*: If the video is not found in his cache, he will request the video from the seeds of his social group within the transmission range d, and obtain the video directly though D2D links. If multiple seeds response this request, he will select one seed randomly.

- *Cellular downloading*: If the MS can not get the video from either his own cache or seeds' cache, he will obtain it from the VP via the cellular links.

It is assumed that the seed MSs are selected randomly in each group. The density of seed MSs for group $\mathcal{G}_k$ is denoted by θ_k. According to the HPPP model, θ_k is given as:

$$\theta_k = \phi_k \lambda_k, \ \forall k \in \mathcal{K}. \tag{1}$$

When a MS is interested in the reference video, he will connect to the nearest seed MSs in his group or the VP to get the video. Let $\mathbb{P}_k$ denote the video offloading probability of the group $\mathcal{G}_k$. Under the HPPP model, the probability that there are n seed MSs of the group $\mathcal{G}_k$ within the transmission range d can be calculated as:

$$P_k(n, \pi d^2) = \frac{(\pi d^2 \theta_k)^n}{n!} e^{-\pi d^2 \theta_k}, \ \forall k \in \mathcal{K}. \tag{2}$$

According to Eq.(2), the video offloading probability of the group $\mathcal{G}_k$ is calculated as:

$$\mathbb{P}_k = 1 - P_k(0, \pi d^2) = 1 - e^{-\pi d^2 \theta_k}, \ \forall k \in \mathcal{K}, \tag{3}$$

where $P_k(0, \pi d^2)$ means that no seed MSs of the group $\mathcal{G}_k$ is within the transmission range d.

4   Problem Formulation

In the D2D local caching system, both the VP and each group try to maximize their own profits. The VP intends to rent a fraction of MSs from each group $\mathcal{G}_k, k \in \mathcal{K}$, as seed MSs for caching the popular video and local sharing. This can make profits for the VP by providing faster service of video delivery and reducing the transmission cost. For each group, they can also obtain profits for the VP by renting their cache storage of seed MSs. In this section, we first model the utilities of the VP and the groups respectively. Then, we present a two-stage Stackelberg game for the D2D local caching system in detail.

4.1   Utility Modeling

For each MSs' group, the income is the rent charge from the VP for leasing the fraction of MSs as seeds. Meanwhile, it needs to pay for certain cost (e.g., the local transmission cost and caching energy cost) to maintain the local caching system, which is linear with the fraction of leased seed MSs [21]. Let c_k denote as such cost on each group $\mathcal{G}_k, k \in \mathcal{K}$, during a unit period. Then the utility of a group $\mathcal{G}_k$ is expressed as:

$$U_k = (\pi_k - c_k)\phi_k \lambda_k, \ \forall k \in \mathcal{K}. \tag{4}$$

According to all the charge prices $\mathbf{\Pi}$ set by the groups, the VP will decide the fraction of seed MSs to rent from each group. For the VP, the utility is the difference between revenue and cost. The revenue of the VP is gained from the shorter service delay and mitigating the congestion of its central servers, with the help of the video offloading. Let q denote the profit obtained by the VP when a video clip is requested by a MS from the local caching system, and β denote the average number of the reference video requests from each MS within an unit period. Then the overall revenue is given as:

$$R_{\mathcal{L}} = \sum_{k=1}^{K} p_k \lambda_k \mathbb{P}_k q \beta = \sum_{k=1}^{K} p_k \lambda_k (1 - e^{-\pi d^2 \theta_k}) q \beta. \tag{5}$$

To provide the local caching service, the VP needs to pay for renting a fraction of MSs. Therefore, the cost of the VP is calculated as:

$$C_{\mathcal{L}} = \sum_{k=1}^{K} \pi_k \phi_k \lambda_k. \tag{6}$$

Then, the utility function of the VP is expressed as:

$$\begin{aligned} U_{\mathcal{L}} &= R_{\mathcal{L}} - C_{\mathcal{L}} \\ &= \sum_{k=1}^{K} p_k \lambda_k \mathbb{P}_k q \beta - \sum_{k=1}^{K} \pi_k \phi_k \lambda_k. \end{aligned} \tag{7}$$

4.2   Stackelberg Game Formulation

For the D2D local caching system, we design an incentive mechanism to stimulate the MSs groups to share their cache storage and transmission resource. The mechanism can increase the probability of the video offloading and hence enhance the quality of video delivery service on the VP. The MSs can get rewards from serving other MSs. For the limited budget of the VP, the MSs' groups also need to compete with each other for more rewards. Both the VP and MSs aim to maximize their own benefits. This raise a competition problem between them. Therefore, we model the interaction between the VP and MSs as a two-stage Stackelberg game $\mathbb{G}_{\mathcal{L}}$. Stackelberg Game is an extension of non-cooperative game, which consists of leaders and followers. The leaders (MSs' groups) first announce the charge price for leasing one unit fraction of MSs as seeds. Then the follower (the VP) responses the fraction of MSs ϕ_k that it tends to rent from the group $\mathcal{G}_k$.

We formally define the following two-stage game $\mathbb{G}_{\mathcal{L}}$:

- *Players*: The set of MSs' groups $\mathcal{K}$ and the VP $\mathcal{L}$ are the players of the game, especially the MSs' groups act as leaders and the VP is the follower.
- *Strategies*: The strategy of each leader (i.e., a MSs' group $\mathcal{G}_k, k \in \mathcal{K}$) is the charge price π_k for leasing one unit fraction of MSs as seeds. Accordingly, the set of leaders' strategies is denoted by $\Pi = \{\pi_1, \pi_2, ..., \pi_K\}$. For the follower (i.e., the VP $\mathcal{L}$), the strategy is the fraction vector of the seed MSs to rent as $\Phi = \{\phi_1, \phi_2, ..., \phi_K\}$.

- *Payoff*: (i) for the VP, the utility $U_{\mathcal{L}}$, (ii) for each group $\mathcal{G}_k, k \in \mathcal{K}$, the utility U_k.

In Stage I, each MSs' group $k \in \mathcal{K}$ determines the charge price, aiming at the highest utilities:

$$\pi_k^* = \arg\max_{\pi_k} \left\{ (\pi_k - c_k)\phi_k\lambda_k \right\}, \ \forall k \in \mathcal{K}. \tag{8}$$

In Stage II, given the charge price vector of all MSs' group, the VP decides the faction ϕ_k of the seed MSs to rent from each MSs' group $k \in \mathcal{K}$, with the goal to maximize its utility:

$$\mathbf{\Phi}^* = \arg\max_{\mathbf{\Phi}} \left\{ \sum_{k=1}^{K} p_k\lambda_k\mathbb{P}_k q\beta - \sum_{k=1}^{K} \pi_k\phi_k\lambda_k \right\}. \tag{9}$$

For this Stackelberg game, we define the Stackelberg Equilibrium as follows.

Definition 1. (Stackelberg Equilibrium): *A strategy profile* $(\mathbf{\Pi}^*, \mathbf{\Phi}^*)$, *including the optimal charge strategies of MSs' groups* $\mathbf{\Pi}^* \triangleq \{\pi_1^*, \pi_2^*, ..., \pi_K^*\}$ *and the optimal rent fraction vector* $\mathbf{\Phi}^* \triangleq \{\phi_1^*, \phi_2^*, ..., \phi_K^*\}$, *is a Stackelberg equilibrium of this game* $\mathbb{G}_{\mathcal{L}}$, *if the following conditions are satisfied,*

$$U_k(\pi_k^*, \mathbf{\Pi}_{-k}^*, \mathbf{\Phi}^*) \geq U_k(\pi_k, \mathbf{\Pi}_{-k}^*, \mathbf{\Phi}^*), \ \forall k, \tag{10}$$
$$U_{\mathcal{L}}(\mathbf{\Pi}^*, \mathbf{\Phi}^*) \geq U_{\mathcal{L}}(\mathbf{\Pi}^*, \mathbf{\Phi}).$$

where $\mathbf{\Pi}_{-k}^* = \{\pi_1^*, ..., \pi_{k-1}^*, \pi_{k+1}^*, ..., \pi_K^*\}$.

In the next section, we will investigate on the Stackelberg game $\mathbb{G}_{\mathcal{L}}$ optimization in details.

5   Stackelberg Game Analysis

The two-stage game $\mathbb{G}_{\mathcal{L}}$ is a complete information dynamic game. We use the method of backward induction [7] to analyse its equilibrium. We will begin with Stage II and analyse the strategy of the VP, given the profiles of the charge price chosen by the MSs' groups. Then we will investigate Stage I and analyse the MSs' groups' optimal decisions based on the anticipated strategy of the VP and the VP's budget plan $\sum_{k=1}^{K} \pi_k\phi_k\lambda_k \leq M$.

Stage II: VP Problem. In the Stackelberg formulation, the VP finds the optimal rent strategy based on the charge price announced by all the MSs' groups, by solving the following problem:

$$\mathcal{P}1: \max_{\mathbf{\Phi}} \ U_{\mathcal{L}}(\mathbf{\Phi}), \tag{11a}$$

$$\text{s.t.} \ \sum_{k=1}^{K} \pi_k\phi_k\lambda_k \leq M, \ k \in \mathcal{K}, \tag{11b}$$

$$0 \leq \phi_k \leq 1, \ k \in \mathcal{K}, \tag{11c}$$

where the vector $\boldsymbol{\Phi} = \{\phi_1, \phi_2, ..., \phi_K\}$ represents the rent strategy of the VP. The constraint (11b) ensures that the total payment is under the VP's budget plan. (11c) ensures that $\phi_k, \forall k \in \mathcal{K}$ is a valid fraction.

Lemma 1. *The VP problem $\mathcal{P}1$ in Stage II is convex.*

Proof. Here we prove that $\mathcal{P}1$ is a convex problem. The second-order partial derivations of $U_{\mathcal{L}}$ is given as,

$$\frac{\partial^2 U_{\mathcal{L}}}{\partial \phi_k^2} = -p_k \lambda_k q\beta (\pi d^2 \lambda_k)^2 e^{-\pi d^2 \lambda_k \phi_k} < 0, \quad \frac{\partial^2 U_{\mathcal{L}}}{\partial \phi_k \partial \phi_j} = 0. \quad (12)$$

It is easy to prove that $\mathcal{P}1$ is a convex problem, for the reason that the second-order derivation of $U_{\mathcal{L}}(\boldsymbol{\Phi})$ is less than zero, i.e., $\partial^2 U_{\mathcal{L}}/\partial \phi_k^2 < 0$.

It is easy to prove that $\mathcal{P}1$ is a convex problem, for the reason that the second-order derivation of $U_{\mathcal{L}}(\boldsymbol{\Phi})$ is less than zero, i.e., $\partial^2 U_{\mathcal{L}}/\partial \phi_k^2 < 0$. To obtain the optimal decision of the VP, we propose a modified water-filling algorithm with the budget constrain. As $\mathcal{P}1$ is a convex problem, the solution is analysed using the Lagrange Function [3],

$$L(\boldsymbol{\Phi}, \xi, \boldsymbol{\mu}, \boldsymbol{\nu}) = -\left(\sum_{k=1}^{K} p_k \lambda_k \mathbb{P}_k q\beta - \sum_{k=1}^{K} \pi_k \phi_k \lambda_k \right) + \xi \left(\sum_{k=1}^{K} \pi_k \phi_k \lambda_k - M \right)$$
$$+ \sum_{k=1}^{K} \nu_k (\phi_k - 1) - \sum_{k=1}^{K} \mu_k \phi_k. \quad (13)$$

Here, ξ, $\boldsymbol{\mu} \triangleq \{\mu_1, \mu_2, ..., \mu_K\}$ and $\boldsymbol{\nu} \triangleq \{\nu_1, \nu_2, ..., \nu_K\}$ are the Lagrange multipliers. For a convex optimization problem, if points $<\boldsymbol{\Phi}, \xi, \boldsymbol{\mu}, \boldsymbol{\nu}>$ satisfy the Karush-Kuhn-Tucher(KKT) conditions, they will suffice to be the optimal solutions. Then we obtain the KKT conditions as follows,

$$\frac{\partial L(\boldsymbol{\Phi}, \xi, \boldsymbol{\mu}, \boldsymbol{\nu})}{\partial \phi_k} = 0, \quad (14a)$$

$$\mu_k^* \phi_k^* = 0, \quad (14b)$$

$$\nu_k^* (\phi_k^* - 1) = 0, \quad (14c)$$

$$\mu_k^* \geq 0, \quad (14d)$$

$$\nu_k^* \geq 0, \ \forall k \in \mathcal{K}. \quad (14e)$$

With (14a), we obtain that

$$\phi_k = \frac{1}{B\lambda_k} \ln \left(\frac{p_k \lambda_k Bq\beta}{(1+\xi)\pi_k} + \nu_k - \mu_k \right), \quad (15)$$

where $B = \pi d^2$. At the global optimum, if $0 \leq \phi_k^* \leq 1$, then $\nu_k = 0$ and $\mu_k = 0$. Then we arrive at

$$\phi_k^* = \frac{1}{B\lambda_k} \ln \left(\frac{p_k \lambda_k Bq\beta}{(1+\xi)\pi_k} \right). \quad (16)$$

Algorithm 1. Water-filling Algorithm for Computing the equilibrium in Stage II

Require: precision threshold δ_ξ;
Ensure: $\mathbf{\Phi}^*$;
1: **Initialize:** $\xi^{(l)} := 0$, $\xi^{(h)} := \infty$, **bool** Convergence = **false**;
2: **while** Convergence is **false do**
3:     $\xi := \frac{1}{2}(\xi^{(l)} + \xi^{(h)})$;
4:     **for** $k \in \mathcal{K}$ **do**
5:         $\phi_k(\pi_k) = \left[\frac{1}{B\lambda_k} \ln\left(\frac{p_k \lambda_k Bq\beta}{(1+\xi)\pi_k}\right)\right]^{\pm}$;
6:     **end for**
7:     **if** $\sum_{k=1}^{K} \pi_k \phi_k \lambda_k < M$ **then** set $\xi^{(h)} := \xi$;
8:     **else** set $\xi^{(l)} := \xi$;
9:     **if** $|\xi^{(l)} - \xi^{(h)}| \leq \delta_\xi$ **then** Convergence is **true**;
10: **end while**

Therefore, given the charge price vector $\mathbf{\Pi} = \{\pi_1, \pi_2, ..., \pi_K\}$ set by the MSs' groups, the optimal decision of the VP with the consideration of the budget plan M, can be derived as:

$$\phi_k(\pi_k) = \left[\frac{1}{B\lambda_k} \ln\left(\frac{p_k \lambda_k Bq\beta}{(1+\xi^*)\pi_k}\right)\right]^{\pm}, \forall k \in \mathcal{K}, \tag{17}$$

where $(\omega)^{\pm}$ represents $\omega \in [0,1]$, and ξ^* is the optimal dual variable of constraint (11b), which satisfies $\sum_{k=1}^{K} \pi_k \phi_k \lambda_k = M$.

Based on the optimal solution above, we propose Algorithm 1 for obtaining the optimal rent strategy of the VP based on bi-section.

Stage I: MSs' Groups Problem. In the above analysis, optimal response from the VP $\mathbf{\Phi}^*(\mathbf{\Pi}^t)$ is obtained. Then, the optimal charge price strategies of the MSs' groups in Stage I will be analysed according to the response of the VP. Knowing the optimal response from the VP, each of the MSs' groups can calculate the optimal charge price π_k by solving problem (8). Substituting Eq. (17) to Eq. (8), we obtain the following problem to determine the optimal price strategies in Stage I:

$$\mathcal{P}2: \max_{\pi_k} \quad U_k = (\pi_k - c_k)\lambda_k \phi_k^*(\mathbf{\Pi}), \ \forall k \in \mathcal{K}. \tag{18}$$

Note that, due to the insufficient payment of the VP, the optimal price strategy of each group $\mathcal{G}_k$ depends on other groups' strategies, causing a non-cooperative game between them.

The optimal charge price can be obtained by taking the derivation of U_k with respect to π_k and equating it to zero,

$$\frac{\partial U_k}{\partial \pi_k} = (\pi_k - c_k)\lambda_k \frac{\partial \phi_k^*(\mathbf{\Pi})}{\partial \pi_k} + \lambda_k \phi_k^*(\mathbf{\Pi}) = 0, \ \forall k \in \mathcal{K}. \tag{19}$$

Since each group's optimal price is dependent on other price, no closed-form for π_k^* can be found. Due to the insufficient budget plan, one MSs' group will

---

Algorithm 2. The best price strategies in Stage I

Require: precision threshold δ_π;
Ensure: $\mathbf{\Phi}^*$, $\mathbf{\Pi}^*$;
  1: **Initialize:** $\pi_k^{(0)} = c_k$;
  2: **repeat**
  3:     Update $\mathbf{\Phi}^{(t)}$ by Algorithm 1;
  4:     Each MSs' group updates $\pi_\mathbf{k}^{(t+1)}$ by solving (20);
  5:     $t \leftarrow t + 1$;
  6: **until** $\pi_k^{(t+1)} - \pi_k^{(t)} < \delta_\pi$.

---

update its strategy when other groups change their price. Hance we use an iterative optimization process to solve the MSs' groups strategies problem.

In each iteration $t = 1, 2, ...$, for the MSs' groups problem, the formula that gives the update price of the group $\mathcal{G}_k$ is:

$$\pi_k^{(t+1)} = c_k - \frac{\phi_k^*(\mathbf{\Pi}^{(t)})}{\partial \phi_k^*(\mathbf{\Pi}^{(t)})/\partial \pi_k^{(t)}}, \forall k \in \mathcal{K}. \qquad (20)$$

Based on the analysis above, we propose Algorithm 2 to get the optimal price strategies of the MSs' groups. Once the iterative optimization process converges, we can get the optimal solution $\mathbf{\Pi}^*$, together with the solution of $\mathbf{\Phi}^*$.

6 Simulation Results

In this section, we investigate the performance of the proposed D2D local caching system versus some key parameters. Although there are many factors in this system, the budget plan M constrain, the density of MSs and popularity of the reference video among MSs are three important ones. It is observed that the proposed system can be easily extended to multiple videos, so in this simulation, only one reference video is adopted.

To illustrate the impact of these key parameters on the D2D local caching system, we consider the system setting as follows. The range of D2D communications is set to be $d = 5m$. We set the average number of the reference video requests as $\beta = 5$. If a video clip is requested, the VP can get a profit as $q = 0.2$.

We first evaluate the impact of the budget plan in a homogeneous MSs' groups scenario with two MSs' group. In this homogeneous scenario, the MS densities of both groups are set as $\lambda_1 = \lambda_2 = 0.1\ user/m^2$. The reference video's popularity among the MSs is set to be $p_1 = p_2 = 0.6$. Figure 2 shows the utilities of the VP and each MSs' group under different budget plans. It shows that the utility of the VP does not always increase with the budget plan increasing. When the budget plan $M = 80$, the VP can get the optimal utility from the D2D local caching system. Additionally, the utility of each MSs' group is almost linear with the budget plan M, until that there is no competition between the groups. Therefore, a proper budget plan can help the VP to get an optimal profit.

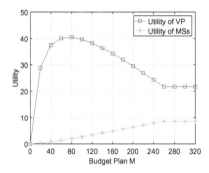

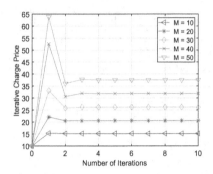

Fig. 2. Utilities of the VP and each MSs' group with different budget plan M.

Fig. 3. The updating charge price of each MSs' group vs. the number of iterations.

Figure 3 shows the iterative charge price of one MSs' group with different budget plan. As the budget plan increases, the MSs' groups will decide higher price for leasing one unit fraction of MSs. For a large budget, the iterative process is shown to converge slowly.

Then, we investigate the impacts of the density of MSs and popularity of the reference video among MSs. Figure 4 demonstrates the optimal fraction chosen by the VP with respect to the density of MSs. As the density increases, the VP will choose a little fraction to rent from the MSs' groups. It is because, the MSs can get the reference video via D2D transmission more easily in a larger MSs' density scenario. Besides that, the optimal fraction is impacted with the budget plan. The VP will rent a large fraction for local caching with a enough budget plan. Figure 5 shows the impact of the interest probability of MSs on the utility of the VP. As the interest increases, the VP can get a larger utility, for the reason that the MSs have the trend to get the reference video.

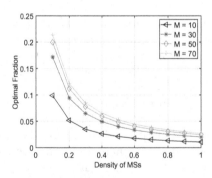

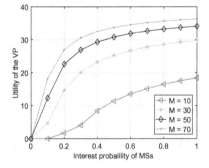

Fig. 4. Density of MSs vs. optimal fraction.

Fig. 5. Utility of the VP vs. interest probability of MSs

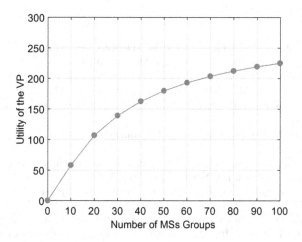

Fig. 6. Impact of number of MSs groups on the VP's utility

Figure 6 shows how the number of different MSs' groups affects the utility of the VP, under the budget plan $M = 60$. It can be seen that, as the number of MSs' groups increases, the utility of the VP increases as well. This is because, as the number of groups increases, many MSs may choose to be the seeds, which leads to the increase of the probability of the video offloading.

7   Conclusions

In this paper, we have proposed a D2D local caching system to provide better services of video downloading in a social-aware environment. The MSs, forming different groups, lease their storage capacity to the VP for getting profits, while the VP can gaining more profits through the local sharing. We have formulated the competitions between the VP and MSs as a two-stage Stackelberg game by viewing the MSs as a type of resource. The Stackelberg equilibrium has been investigated by solving a series of optimization problems. In order to promote both the VP's and MSs' participation, an incentive mechanism has been designed for the system. Extensive simulation results have demonstrated the efficiency in both charging and MSs allocation. In the future, the impact of the update frequency of the popular videos will be investigated, which is an important issue in the real caching system.

Acknowledgement. This work is supported by the Tsinghua University Initiative Scientific Research Program (Grant No. 20161080066).

References

1. Baştuğ, E., Bennis, M., Kountouris, M., Debbah, M.: Cache-enabled small cell networks: modeling and tradeoffs. EURASIP J. Wirel. Commun. Netw. **2015**(1), 1–11 (2015)
2. Baştuğ, E., Bennis, M., Kountouris, M., Debbah, M.: Cache-enabled small cell networks: Modeling and tradeoffs. EURASIP J. Wirel. Commun. Netw. **2015**(1), 41–41 (2015)
3. Boyd, S., Vandenberghe, L.: Convex Optimization. Cambridge University Press, New York (2004)
4. Chiu, S.N., Stoyan, D., Kendall, W.S., Mecke, J.: Stochastic Geometry and its Applications. John Wiley & Sons, New York (2013)
5. Cisco, C.V.N.I.: Global mobile data traffic forecast update. 2016–2021 (white paper) (2017)
6. Dehghan, M., et al.: On the complexity of optimal routing and content caching in heterogeneous networks. In: 2015 IEEE Conference on Computer Communications (INFOCOM 2015), pp. 936–944. IEEE, Hong Kong (2015)
7. Fudenberg, D., Tirole, J.: Game Theory, p. 86. MIT press, Cambridge (1991)
8. Golrezaei, N., Dimakis, A.G., Molisch, A.F.: Scaling behavior for device-to-device communications with distributed caching. IEEE Trans. Inf. Theor. **60**(7), 4286–4298 (2014)
9. Golrezaei, N., Shanmugam, K., Dimakis, A.G., Molisch, A.F., Caire, G.: Wireless video content delivery through coded distributed caching. In: 2012 IEEE International Conference on Communications (ICC 2012), pp. 2467–2472. IEEE, Ottawa (2012)
10. Guo, Y., Duan, L., Zhang, R.: Cooperative local caching and file sharing under heterogeneous file preferences. In: 2016 IEEE International Conference on Communications (ICC 2016), pp. 1–6. IEEE, Kuala Lumpur (2016)
11. Guo, Y., Duan, L., Zhang, R.: Cooperative local caching under heterogeneous file preferences. IEEE Trans. Commun. **65**(1), 444–457 (2017)
12. Janis, P., Koivunen, V., Ribeiro, C., Korhonen, J., Doppler, K., Hugl, K.: Interference-aware resource allocation for device-to-device radio underlaying cellular networks. In: VTC Spring 2009 - IEEE 69th Vehicular Technology Conference, pp. 1–5. IEEE, Barcelona (2009)
13. Ji, M., Caire, G., Molisch, A.F.: The throughput-outage tradeoff of wireless one-hop caching networks. IEEE Trans. Inf. Theor. **61**(12), 6833–6859 (2015)
14. Li, J., Sun, J., Qian, Y., Shu, F., Xiao, M., Xiang, W.: A commercial video-caching system for small-cell cellular networks using game theory. IEEE Access **4**, 7519–7531 (2016)
15. Li, Y., Su, G., Wu, D.O., Jin, D., Su, L., Zeng, L.: The impact of node selfishness on multicasting in delay tolerant networks. IEEE Trans. Veh. Technol. **60**(5), 2224–2238 (2011)
16. Liu, T., Li, J., Shu, F., Tao, M., Chen, W., Han, Z.: Design of contract-based trading mechanism for a small-cell caching system. IEEE Trans. Wireless Commun. **16**(10), 6602–6617 (2017)
17. Malak, D., AI-Shalash, M.: Optimal caching for device-to-device content distribution in 5G networks. In: 2014 IEEE Globecom Workshops (GC Wkshps), pp. 863–868. IEEE, Austin (2014)
18. Malak, D., Al-Shalash, M., Andrews, J.G.: Optimizing content caching to maximize the density of successful receptions in device-to-device networking. IEEE Trans. Commun. **64**(10), 4365–4380 (2016)

19. Pan, Y., Pan, C., Zhu, H., Ahmed, Q.Z., Chen, M., Wang, J.: Content offloading via D2D communications based on user interests and sharing willingness. In: 2017 IEEE International Conference on Communications (ICC 2017), pp. 1–6. IEEE, Paris (2017)
20. Pan, Y., Pan, C., Zhu, H., Ahmed, Q.Z., Chen, M., Wang, J.: On consideration of content preference and sharing willingness in D2D assisted offloading. IEEE J. Sel. Areas Commun. **35**(4), 978–993 (2017)
21. Poularakis, K., Iosifidis, G., Tassiulas, L.: A framework for mobile data offloading to leased cache-endowed small cell networks. In: 2014 IEEE 11th International Conference on Mobile Ad Hoc and Sensor Systems (MASS 2014), pp. 327–335. IEEE, Philadelphia (2014)
22. Sciancalepore, V., Giustiniano, D., Banchs, A., Hossmann-Picu, A.: Offloading cellular traffic through opportunistic communications: analysis and optimization. IEEE J. Sel. Areas Commun. **34**(1), 122–137 (2016)
23. Shanmugam, K., Golrezaei, N., Dimakis, A.G., Molisch, A.F., Caire, G.: Femtocaching: wireless content delivery through distributed caching helpers. IEEE Trans. Inf. Theor. **59**(12), 8402–8413 (2013)
24. Wang, K., Yu, F.R., Li, H.: Information-centric virtualized cellular networks with device-to-device communications. IEEE Trans. Veh. Technol. **65**(11), 9319–9329 (2016)
25. Wang, R., Zhang, J., Song, S.H., Letaief, K.B.: Mobility-aware caching in D2D networks. IEEE Trans. Wireless Commun. **16**(8), 5001–5015 (2017)
26. Zhang, N., Cheng, N., Lu, N., Zhang, X., Mark, J.W., Shen, X.: Partner selection and incentive mechanism for physical layer security. IEEE Trans. Wireless Commun. **14**(8), 4265–4276 (2015)
27. Zhao, K., Zhang, S., Zhang, N., Zhou, Y., Zhang, Y., Shen, X.: Incentive mechanism for cached-enabled small cell sharing: a stackelberg game approach. In: 2017 IEEE Global Communications Conference (GLOBECOM 2017), pp. 1–6. IEEE, Singapore (2017)

SMIM: Superpixel Mutual Information Measurement for Image Quality Assessment

Jiaming Wang, Tao Lu$^{(\boxtimes)}$ ⓘ, and Yanduo Zhang

Hubei Key Laboratory of Intelligent Robot, School of Computer Science and Engineering, Wuhan Institute of Technology, Wuhan 430205, China
lutxyl@gmail.com

Abstract. The image quality assessment (IQA) is a fundamental problem in signal processing that aims to measure the objective quality of an image by designing a mathematical model. Most full-reference (FR) IQA methods use fixed sliding windows to obtain structure information but ignore the variable spatial configuration information. In this paper, we propose a novel full-reference IQA method, named "superpixel normalized mutual information (SMIM)" based on the perspective of variable receptive field and information entropy. First, we find that consistence relationship exists between the information fidelity and human visual of individuals. Thus, we reproduce the human visual system (HVS) to semantically divide the image into multiple patches via superpixel segmentation. Then the weights of each image patches are adaptively calculated via its information volume. We verified the effectiveness of SMIM by applying it to data from the TID2008 database and data generated using some real application scenarios. Experiments show that SMIM outperforms some state-of-the-art FR IQA algorithms, including visual information fidelity (VIF).

Keywords: Image quality assessment · Mutual information
Superpixel segmentation

1 Introduction

With the rapid development of digital communication, images play an increasingly important role in modern society. However, the process of image acquisition, compression, storage, and transmission, can be naturally degraded into low quality. Image quality assessment (IQA) is a basic problem in the image

This work is supported by the National Natural Science Foundation of China (61502354, 61671332, 61771353), Central Support Local Projects (2018ZYYD059), the Natural Science Foundation of Hubei Province of China (2012FFA099, 2012FFA134, 2013CF125, 2014CFA130, 2015CFB451), Scientific Research Foundation of Wuhan Institute of Technology (K201713), Graduate student scientific research innovation projects (CX2017069, CX2017070).

ⓒ Springer Nature Switzerland AG 2018
J. Vaidya and J. Li (Eds.): ICA3PP 2018, LNCS 11335, pp. 432–444, 2018.
https://doi.org/10.1007/978-3-030-05054-2_34

processing research fields. Determining image quality using only human-in-the-loop based qualitative measures is not only time-consuming and labor-intensive, but it cannot be applied to real-time or autonomous systems. Depending on the availability of a reference image, objective IQA metrics can be divided into full-reference (FR), no-reference (NR) and reduced-reference (RR) method [16]. The IQA metrics process is a task-driven problem in computer vision task, so this paper only focuses on FR methods.

We divide the FR-based IQA metrics into two classes: error-statistic and human visual system (HVS) based. Error-statistic methods measure the distance between the distorted image and the reference image from the pixel level. The peak signal-to-noise ratio (PSNR) and the mean-squared error (MSE) are the most widely used image quality assessment methods. Those methods are compared at the pixel level, thus, they are less relevant to HVS.

HVS-based methods use visual quantifiable features such as brightness, contrast, and frequency content of the image to construct a visual model. These factors, are important when simulating human perception of image distortion [2,3,10]. A process called the noise quality measure (NQM) [3] uses these factors to find an image quality measure. Wavelet-based visual signal-to-noise ratio (VSNR) [2] compares the low-level HVS property of the perceived contrast and the mid-level HVS property of global precedence. The structural similarity (SSIM) index [15] suggests that the human eye is more sensitive to structural information depending on the field-of-view, and quantifies the degree of distortion by comparing brightness, contrast, and mechanism similarities. Wang et al. [14] combines the multi-scale SSIM (MS-SSIM) of the wavelet domain and obtained better performance. From the perspective of information theory, Sheikh et al. [11] proposed the information fidelity criterion (IFC) to quantify the mutual information of reference images and distorted images. In [10], IFC was expanded to contain visual information fidelity (VIF). The feature similarity (FSIM) index [17] determines the visual difference of images in the feature domain by comparing the gradient and phase consistency. Li et al. [7] demonstrated the effectiveness of regional mutual information for IQA.

Recent studies conducted in [12,17] show that VIF and FSIM have better accuracy than other IQA metrics. This research is still has a far way to go to provide an excellent IQA criterion for real applications. HVS attention mechanism always play an important role in human vision. For example, at a normal sight distance, people naturally pay attention to a certain area of the image, also known as the receptive field. Therefore, finding image quality assessment metrics often uses fixed sliding windows to simulate human visual system like the receptive field. SSIM and its extensions are effectively verifying this fact [17]. However, they ignore the fact that the content and distribution of the images are irregular and inhomogeneous. Using a fixed sliding window with a single scale, the IQA metrics cannot accurately evaluate the flexible structure information in images. Moreover, the attention mechanisms of HVS reveals that a weighting method can truly reflect the differences in image content. Thus, the shape and weighting of receptive field should play a more important role in IQA. Compared with the existing IQA metrics, we propose a novel superpixel mutual information measurement (SMIM) to emphasize the shape and weight of a receptive field, which can better simulate HVS. First, we divide the reference image into irregular image patches based on spatial semantic information. In this step, we use the same regional label to split the distorted image to guarantee the same semantic content will have an equivalent weight with HVS. Thus, HVS is a method that can be used to assess if human vision is sensitive to structural information, gradient information, and contrast in the image. For images, they mean the amount of information in the image. Therefore, we automatically generate weights based on the information entropy in the reference image patch. Finally, the SMIM index is calculated by calculating the mutual information weight between the distorted image patch and the corresponding reference image patch. Overall, the contributions of this paper are highlighted as following:

1. We propose an IQA metric, that first semantically divides the image into multiple flexible patches via superpixel segmentation. This is done to simulate the variable shape of the receptive field. Here, superpixel segmentation of images provides spatial content clustering information.
2. We propose an weighting scheme which judges the importance of an image patch via its the information volume. This weighting method reveals the attention-seeking mechanism of HVS, which favors visual features i.e., brightness, contrast, and frequency content.
3. SMIM evaluates the objective quality of images from the perspective of information fidelity, so it can be used to full-reference but also in real-world applications which are difficult to obtain reference images.

2   Related Work

2.1   Image Quality Assessment

There is a nonlinear relationship between the objective qualities of an image and the subjective qualities. To compare the evaluation consistency between objective and subjective quality, we use a multi-parameter nonlinear equation [12] to define the objective quality and the mean opinion score (MOS) fitting. This curve can help us to determine the accuracy of our IQA metrics.

The function is defined as follows:

$$q(x_i) = \beta_1 \left(\frac{1}{2} - \frac{1}{1 + e^{\beta_2(x_i - \beta_3)}} \right) + \beta_4 x_i + \beta_5, \tag{1}$$

where β_1 to β_5 are parameters to be fitted and x_i is the objective score of the i-th image. $q(x_i)$ is the objective quality assessment result of the i-th image after nonlinear transformation.

2.2   Information Entropy

Image entropy is a statistical feature that reflects the amount of the average information in an image. Therefore, this metric can be used effectively in no-reference scenarios. The one-dimensional entropy of the image indicates the amount of information contained in the aggregation characteristics of the gray distributed in the image, as follow:

$$H(I) = -\sum_{i \in I} p(i) \lg p(i), \tag{2}$$

where $p(i)$ represents the proportion of pixels in the image I with gray value i. The information entropy is an unreferenced measure. The greater the information entropy of an image, the greater the amount of information contained in the image aggregation feature.

3   Superpixel Mutual Information Measurement(SMIM)

The illustration of the SMIM is shown in Fig. 1. Mutual information (MI) can measure the degree of image distortion by quantifying the information dependence between the reference image Y and the distorted image $\hat{Y}$ [8]. The joint entropy $H(\hat{Y}, Y)$ of an mage $\hat{Y}$ and the image Y is as follow (Fig. 2):

$$H(\hat{Y}, Y) = \sum_{s \in \hat{Y}} \sum_{t \in Y} p(s, t) \log p(s, t). \tag{3}$$

Thus, MI is as follow:

$$I(\hat{Y}, Y) = H(\hat{Y}) + H(Y) - H(\hat{Y}, Y) = \sum_{s \in \hat{Y}} \sum_{t \in Y} p(s, t) \log \frac{p(s, t)}{p(s)p(t)}, \tag{4}$$

where $H(\hat{Y})$ and $H(Y)$ are conditional entropies.

The relationship between MI and entropy is provided via a Venn diagram, as shown in Fig. 2. The greater MI between images, the greater the similarity information between images. However, MI does not make use of the visual perception characteristics of the HVS, ignoring visual perception effects such as

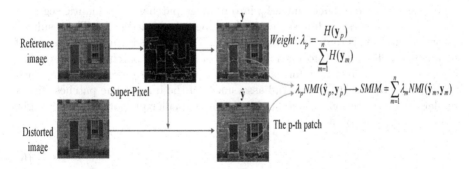

Fig. 1. Illustration of the SMIM. Superpixel segmentation provides clustering information of spatial pixels which contains flexible image semantic information.

image patch weighting and contrast sensitivity. For a more intuitive comparison, we normalize the MI [4] as follows:

$$NMI(\hat{Y}, Y) = \frac{2I(\hat{Y}, Y)}{H(\hat{Y}) + H(Y)}. \tag{5}$$

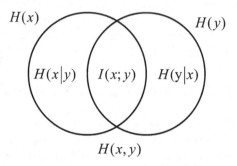

Fig. 2. The Venn diagram represents the relationship between information entropy, conditional entropy and joint entropy.

Information entropy can reflect the information volume in an image, but the interference caused by distorted images will increase the information volume in that image; this additional information will have a negative impact. Therefore, the mutual information is not robust to the interference in the image, resulting in inaccurate evaluation of the image quality of the distorted image.

Various semantic image patches are significant to the overall image. Various semantic objectives in the image have different levels of importance to the image. For objects with small variation, the amount of information, such as the sky and sea, distortion has little effect on the subjective quality of the image. For larger patches of information, such as airplanes and ships, each image section contains a lot of gradient and structural information, as shown in Fig. 3. Thus the human eye is very sensitive to their distortion.

We divide the reference image Y_p into n image patches via semantic segmentation [1]. The corresponding segmentation label is recorded as l_Y. The resulting distorted image $\hat{Y}$ is divided by the label l_Y. Then, we determine the weight of the image patch via the information entropy of the image patch. We believe that the larger the amount of information in the image, the more important each information object is to the overall assessment of the image. The patches with a smaller amount of information should occupy a smaller proportion. The weight of p-th patch is as follows:

$$\lambda_p = \frac{H(Y_p)}{\sum\limits_{m=1}^{n} H(Y_m)}, \tag{6}$$

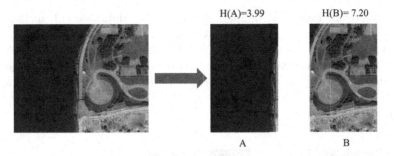

Fig. 3. We divide the image into two parts of the same size. The information of the image with abundant edge information and obvious contrast is more abundant.

where n represents the total number of segmented image patches and Y_p denotes the p-th image patch. Superpixel mutual information measurement (SMIM) is defined as follows:

$$SMIM = \sum_{m=1}^{n} \lambda_m NMI(\hat{Y}_m, Y_m) \tag{7}$$

Our proposed SMIM is described in Algorithm 1.

Algorithm 1. SMIM index for IQA

Input: Reference images Y, distorted images $\hat{Y}$, number of image patches n.
Superpixel:
 1: Superpixel segmentation is performed on the reference image Y. The corresponding segmentation label is recorded as l_Y. The divided image patches are labelled $\{Y_i\}_{i=1}^n$.
 2: According to the label l_Y, the distorted image $\hat{Y}$ is divided into $\left\{\hat{Y}_i\right\}_{i=1}^n$.
SMIM:
for each patch: $i=1$ to n.
 3: Compute weighted λ_i by using (6).
 4: Compute the mutual Information $NMI(\hat{Y}_i, Y_i)$ by using (5).
end.
 5: Compute SMIM by using (7).

---

4 Experiments

4.1 Databases

The TID2008 dataset [9] is a commonly used public database in the IQA community. The data set contains 25 reference images and 1700 distorted images. Each reference image corresponds to 68 different distorted images and includes 17 different types of distortion. The Mean Opinion Score (MOS) of the image was scored by 838 observers. The IQA is task-driven, so we use data from the actual algorithm task as a sample. The FEI faces database [13] includes 400 images of 200 people (100 men and 100 women). Each person has two frontally aligned face images. One with frontal facial image and the other with a smiling image. The size of the image is 260×360 pixels. All images are RGB images, but for fairness, all image quality assessment algorithms are used in single-channel images. We converted the image pixels to YCbCr color space, using only the Y channel for testing.

(a)   (b)   (c)

(d)   (e)   (f)

Fig. 4. Six reference images used for the parameter tuning process.

4.2   Parameter Settings

The number of image patches is an important parameter in SMIM. To save time, we select the first 6 images from the TID2008 reference image and the corresponding 408 distorted images for testing. The six reference images from the TID2008 database [9], used in the parameter tuning process, are shown in Fig. 4. We set n at 0, 5, 20, 50, and perform the SMIM evaluation. The curve fitting processing results are shown in Fig. 5. When n is 0 and 5, the patch is not accurate enough. SMIM cannot accurately evaluate all images with high MOS. As n increases, performance does not always improve. When MOS is 50, the image patch is more, which leads to the low recognition degree of SMIM for MOS greater than 5 and the higher time complexity. Thus, we set n to 20.

4.3   Performance Comparisions to State-of-the-Arts

We compare the evaluation results with some representative IQA indicators, including some state-of-art algorithms: MS-SSIM [14], SSIM (One of the most widely used methods for image quality assessment) [15], FSIM (The best performance image quality assessment method based on structural information) [17], VSNR [2], IFC [11], NQM [3], PSNR (One of the most widely used methods for

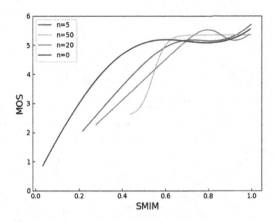

Fig. 5. The fitting curve of the number n of different image patches. When n takes values to 20 and 50, SMIM has better performance.

IQA), VIF (The best image quality assessment method based on information theory) [10]. Here, we use the wavelet domain version of VIF. Except fot FSIM, other comparison algorithm results are provided by the TID2008 [9] datasets. For FSIM, we directly use the open source code provided by the author and the parameters of the paper.

The curve fit to the MOS process and image objective scoring is shown in Fig. 6. A variety of IQA metrics apply to different scenarios (scene of interest). Compared with the optimal algorithm, FSIM has poor performance in the low MOS image, which is dense in the high MOS subregion, and the hiding is not accurate. VIF has good performance in low MOS subregion, but it is less than FSIM in high MOS sub-region. The SMIM distribution is even more uniform. SMIM can describe the degree of dependence of information between a reference image and a distorted image.

4.4 The Application of the Algorithmic Scenario

The IQA metric is task-driven. Therefore in next sections, we discuss the application of SMIM in practice. The distorted image is obtained by adding random Gaussian noise to the FEI dataset images. We convert the image to the Ycbcr color space, adding noise only to the Y channel.

A common practice in image normalization is to divide all the pixels by the value 255 in the image. SRResnet[1] is an algorithm that uses a different normalization. In this case, the pixel is divided by the image's maximum value. As shown in Fig. 7, VDSR [5] and SRResnet [6] are obtained via an algorithm test. The standard deviation σ of the noise added to the images ranges in value from 5 to 20. We use the most widely-used SSIM and PSNR in the image field to score images. SRResnet's subjective quality is higher than VDSR and distorted

---

[1] https://github.com/brade31919/SRGAN-tensorflow.

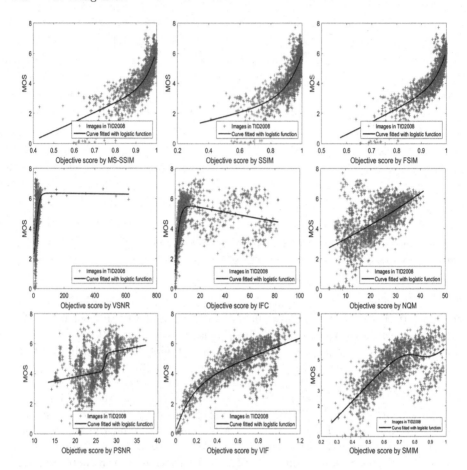

Fig. 6. Scatter plots of subjective MOS versus scores obtained by model prediction on the TID2008 database.

images, but its objective score is not as good as them. This also proves the inapplicability of PSNR and SSIM in the case of such image distortion.

We use SMIM, FSIM and VIF to re-evaluate the objective quality of images. The score data is shown in Table 1. The scores of SMIM, FSIM and VIF are in line with our subjective assessment. The last column of Table 1 has a small difference in FSIM scores. When the similarity between the distorted image and the original image is high, the FSIM has a small degree of discrimination.

4.5   The Application of the Real World

In the field of remote sensing satellites, due to the particularity of the shooting equipment, it is impossible to obtain a distorted image and corresponding reference image in the same time and the same place. Therefore entropy is a commonly used indicator.

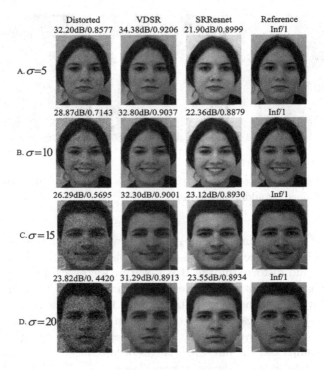

Fig. 7. The comparison of algorithm results.

Table 1. The average of SMIM/FSIM/VIF values with different noise levels.

Noise Level	Eval. Mat	Distorted	VDSR	SRResnet	Reference
$\sigma = 5$	SMIM	0.3518	0.4450	0.4451	1
	FSIM	0.9121	0.9354	0.9370	1
	VIF	0.3864	0.4752	0.5243	1
$\sigma = 10$	SMIM	0.2957	0.3827	0.4174	1
	FSIM	0.8273	0.9186	0.9277	1
	VIF	0.2563	0.3863	0.4759	1
$\sigma = 15$	SMIM	0.2558	0.3728	0.4001	1
	FSIM	0.7427	0.9054	0.9273	1
	VIF	0.1864	0.3388	0.4507	1
$\sigma = 20$	SMIM	0.2248	0.3501	0.3910	1
	FSIM	0.6702	0.8948	0.9261	1
	VIF	0.1429	0.3020	0.4389	1

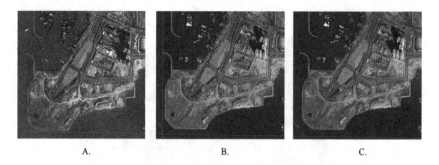

A.   B.   C.

Fig. 8. The image A and the image B are Victoria Harbour at different times. The image C is obtained by adding noise to B.

We collect satellite images (Google Earth) with a resolution of 1066×942 pixels. In Fig. 8, reference image A is taken in the Victoria Harbour on November 23, 2000, and distorted image B is taken in Victoria Harbor on December 31, 2000. Information entropy is often used to evaluate B. We add a Gaussian random noise with a standard deviation $\sigma = 10$ in B, denoted as C. Due to the large temporal differences of photo-takings, the objective of the measurement image changes greatly over time. A few samples of these changes include the movement of ships and the physical changes of buildings.

The subjective scores of the images are shown in Table 2. After adding image noise, the subjective effect of the image deteriorates, but $H(B) = 6.62$ is less than $H(C) = 7.22$. Information entropy can only evaluate the amount of information in an image. Because noise is also an extra piece of information, information entropy is not robust to noise. Thus, the score cannot be normalized to 0 to 1, which is not intuitive. SMIM performs image evaluation via the information dependence between images, so image A can be used as a reference image to evaluate image B. Between images A and B, there is a large difference between the signal level and the structure level, this difference is not caused by distortion. Therefore, the SSIM and PSNR scores cannot accurately evaluate the image.

Table 2. Subjective scores for the image B and the image C

Image	PSNR(dB)	SSIM	VIF	MI	SMIM
B	17.36	0.3831	0.0166	6.62	0.3605
C	17.04	0.2070	0.0085	7.22	0.3451

5   Conclusion

In this paper, we propose a novel superpixel mutual information measurement (SMIM) for image quality assessment. We replace the traditional sliding window-based segmentation method by a superpixel segmentation method that is more in line with human vision and perception. HVS is sensitive to the features of an image and uses it to perceive the image. We consider that the importance of different semantic content to the image can change. SMIM uses information entropy to determine the richness of features in the image. This information entropy is also used to determine the appropriate weighting of image patches. SMIM has performed well when used with data from the benchmark database and in practical applications, demonstrating that it is a robust IQA metric.

References

1. Achanta, R., Shaji, A., Smith, K., Lucchi, A., Fua, P., Süsstrunk, S.: Slic superpixels compared to state-of-the-art superpixel methods. IEEE Trans. Pattern Anal. Mach. Intell. **34**(11), 2274–2282 (2012)
2. Chandler, D.M., Hemami, S.S.: VSNR: a wavelet-based visual signal-to-noise ratio for natural images. IEEE Trans. Image Process. **16**(9), 2284–2298 (2007)
3. Damera-Venkata, N., Kite, T.D., Geisler, W.S., Evans, B.L., Bovik, A.C.: Image quality assessment based on a degradation model. IEEE Trans. Image Process. **9**(4), 636–650 (2000)
4. Flannery, B.P., Flannery, B.P., Teukolsky, S.A., Vetterling, W.T.: Numerical Recipes: The Art of Scientific Computing. Cambridge University Press, New York (1986)
5. Kim, J., Lee, J.K., Lee, K.M.: Accurate image super-resolution using very deep convolutional networks. In: The IEEE Conference on Computer Vision and Pattern Recognition (CVPR Oral), June 2016
6. Ledig, C., et al.: Photo-realistic single image super-resolution using a generative adversarial network. In: 2017 IEEE Conference on Computer Vision and Pattern Recognition (CVPR), pp. 105–114, July 2017. https://doi.org/10.1109/CVPR.2017.19
7. Li, J., Zhang, X., Ding, M.: Image quality assessment based on regional mutual information. AEUE - Int. J. Electron. C. **66**(9), 784–787 (2012)
8. Maes, F., Collignon, A., Vandermeulen, D., Marchal, G., Suetens, P.: Multimodality image registration by maximization of mutual information. IEEE Trans. Med. Imaging **16**(2), 187–198 (1997)
9. Ponomarenko, N., Lukin, V., Zelensky, A., Egiazarian, K., Carli, M., Battisti, F.: TID 2008 - a database for evaluation of full-reference visual quality assessment metrics. Adv. Modern Radioelectron. **10**, 30–45 (2004)
10. Sheikh, H.R., Bovik, A.C.: Image information and visual quality. IEEE Trans. Image Process. **15**(2), 430–444 (2006). A Publication of the IEEE Signal Processing Society
11. Sheikh, H.R., Bovik, A.C., Veciana, G.D.: An information fidelity criterion for image quality assessment using natural scene statistics. IEEE Trans. Image Process. **14**(12), 2117–2128 (2005)
12. Sheikh, H.R., Sabir, M.F., Bovik, A.C.: A statistical evaluation of recent full reference image quality assessment algorithms. IEEE Trans. Image Process. **15**(11), 3440–3451 (2006)
13. Thomaz, C.E., Giraldi, G.A.: A new ranking method for principal components analysis and its application to face image analysis. Image Vis. Comput. **28**(6), 902–913 (2010). https://doi.org/10.1016/j.imavis.2009.11.005

14. Wang, Z., Simoncelli, E.P., Bovik, A.C.: Multiscale structural similarity for image quality assessment. In: Conference Record of the Thirty-Seventh Asilomar Conference on Signals, Systems and Computers 2004, vol. 2, pp. 1398–1402 (2004)
15. Wang, Z., Bovik, A.C., Sheikh, H.R., Simoncelli, E.P.: Image quality assessment: from error visibility to structural similarity. IEEE Trans. Image Process. **13**(4), 600–612 (2004)
16. Wang, Z., Sheikh, H.R., Bovik, A.C., et al.: Objective video quality assessment. Handb. Video Databases Des. Appl. **41**, 1041–1078 (2003)
17. Zhang, L., Zhang, L., Mou, X., Zhang, D.: Fsim: A feature similarity index for image quality assessment. IEEE Trans. Image Process. **20**(8), 2378–2386 (2011)

DARM: A Deduplication-Aware Redundancy Management Approach for Reliable-Enhanced Storage Systems

Yukun Zhou, Dan Feng$^{(\boxtimes)}$, Wen Xia, Min Fu, and Yu Xiao

Wuhan National Laboratory for Optoelectronics (WNLO),
Key Laboratory of Information Storage System, Ministry of Education of China
School of Computer, Huazhong University of Science and Technology, Wuhan, China
{ykzhou,dfeng,xia,fumin,yuxiao}@hust.edu.cn

Abstract. Chunk-based deduplication has been widely used in storage systems to save storage space. However, deduplication impairs data reliability due to the inter-file chunk sharing. The loss of shared chunks will make these referenced files inaccessible. Meanwhile, we find that inter-file and highly-referenced chunks are important that need higher reliability assurance, but occupy a small fraction of physical storage. Traditional deduplication systems utilize erasure coding or replication techniques to ensure data reliability. With the growth of shared chunks, promoting the reliability of erasure-coded systems incurs large I/O cost because of the weakness of coding scalability. Although replication is easy to scale, it incurs larger storage overhead. In this paper, we present DARM, a Deduplication-Aware Redundancy Management approach via exploiting deduplication semantics (e.g., inter-/intra-file duplicates, chunk size and reference count) to improve data reliability with low overhead. DARM leverages erasure coding for storing unique and low-referenced chunks to improve both storage reliability and space efficiency, and employs Selective and Dynamic Chunk-based Replication (SDCR) for maintaining inter-file and highly-referenced chunks to enhance storage reliability. Experimental results based on real-world datasets show that DARM reduces storage overhead by up to 43.4% and achieves at most 12.7% reliability improvements over the state-of-the-art schemes.

1 Introduction

With the explosive growth of digital data [2], data deduplication has been widely adopted as a system-level compression technology to improve storage efficiency. Deduplication eliminates redundant data by storing only one physical instance and other duplicate data just refer to it. The instance can be a file, or a more fine-grained chunk, which chunk-level deduplication is more efficient [23]. Deduplication has been deployed in the backup systems [7,28], primary systems [20], visual machines [15], and cloud storage [21].

Although deduplication can reduce storage cost, it inevitably impairs the data reliability compared to storage systems without deduplication [8]. First,

© Springer Nature Switzerland AG 2018
J. Vaidya and J. Li (Eds.): ICA3PP 2018, LNCS 11335, pp. 445–461, 2018.
https://doi.org/10.1007/978-3-030-05054-2_35

one single chunk may be shared by different files after deduplication. The loss of the shared chunks will cause a disproportional large amount of data loss for the unavailability of multiple referenced files. Second, chunks of individual files are scattered across storage devices rather than sequentially stored. The reliability of a file depends on the reliability of multiple devices, which makes the file more vulnerable. To improve data reliability, adding redundancy in the storage back-end is a practical method for fault tolerance. Erasure coding and replication are the commonly used reliability-enhanced schemes in storage systems. In general, erasure coding is space-efficient that transforms data into multiple objects. Obtaining sufficient subset of the objects can rebuild the data. While replication strategy is easy-to-use that additionally stores replicas for identical data. Recent studies have applied erasure coding [11,12] or replication [4,8] for post-deduplication data to mitigate the degree of damage of the system failures.

However, there are still some challenges on guaranteeing data reliability in deduplication-based storage systems. **First**, some deduplication systems (e.g., CodePlugin [24], DAC [22]) adopt Fix-Sized Chunking (FSC) algorithm because it is easy for data placement and erasure coding. However, FSC algorithm suffers from a "boundary-shift" problem [26], thus sacrifices compression effect of deduplication. **Second**, erasure coding stores all chunks with the same redundancy level. While the loss of inter-file and highly-referenced chunks will increase the severity of file loss. These chunks should be guaranteed with a higher level of data reliability. With the growth of reference counts, erasure-coded systems need to load the original chunks for coding scalability with heavy I/O overhead. For instance, R-ADMAD [12] packs some variable-length chunks into fix-sized objects and performs erasure coding on multiple objects. To ensure higher reliability, R-ADMAD has to recode a large number of chunks, which is inefficient. **Third**, replication scales well, but reduces the efficiency of deduplication. For example, Deep Store [4] remains at least two copies of each duplicated chunks and more copies for higher referenced chunks. How to ensure high reliability in deduplication systems becomes a critical problem.

To overcome these shortcomings, we analyze the deduplication semantics (e.g., inter-/intra-file duplicates, chunk size, and reference count) of workloads. Then we obtain the key observations: inter-file and highly-referenced chunks only occupy a small fraction of total chunks. They are mostly of small size and occupy a little storage capacity. In this paper, we propose a Deduplication-Aware Redundancy Management (DARM) approach that improves the reliability with the growth of reference counts. The design goal of DARM is to make a tradeoff between system reliability and storage cost. DARM employs content-defined chunking algorithm (e.g., AE [26]) to achieve better redundancy elimination. Then DARM effectively combines erasure coding and Selective and Dynamic Chunk-based Replication (SDCR) via exploiting deduplication semantics. With the growth of reference counts, SDCR will dynamically add replicas for inter-file and highly-referenced chunks. This paper makes the following contributions.

- We obtain key observations based on trace-driven experiments. We find that inter-file and highly-referenced chunks occupy a small fraction of physical space, but they heavily impair the reliability of deduplication systems.
- DARM proposes a hybrid redundancy scheme. In particular, DARM employs erasure coding for low-referenced chunks with large space occupation to reduce space cost. And DARM applies SDCR on inter-file and highly-referenced chunks with small storage space to improve data reliability.
- We design and implement DARM prototype which combines erasure coding and SDCR. Experimental results based on real-world datasets show that DARM saves 43.4% storage space with comparable reliability as Deep Store. In addition, DARM achieves at most 12.7% reliability improvements and only incurs little storage overhead compared with R-ADMAD.

In the rest of the paper, we introduce background and related work in Sect. 2. Section 3 elaborates observations and motivation of DARM. Section 4 presents the design and implementation of DARM. Section 5 evaluates the experimental results of DARM and compares it with existing schemes. Finally, Sect. 6 concludes the paper and describes the future work.

2   Background and Related Work

2.1   Basics

Data Deduplication. In a deduplication-based system, data streams will be divided into chunks and each chunk will be identified by a hash digest (i.e., SHA1), called fingerprint. Two chunks with the same fingerprint will be regarded as duplicated chunks. The probability of a hash collision is too small that can be negligible [17]. Existing chunking algorithms contain: Fix-Sized Chunking (FSC) and Content-Defined Chunking (CDC). FSC is time-efficient, but it suffers from a boundary-shift problem [26]. While CDC defines the boundary based on data content that avoids the boundary-shift problem. Second, deduplication utilizes a *fingerprint index* for duplicate detection. The *fingerprint index* is a key-value structure that stores the mapping between chunks and their addresses.

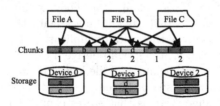

Fig. 1. The dependencies between files and scattering storage of chunks.

After duplicate detection, unique chunks that need to be written are aggregated into containers to preserve the locality of the data stream. The data chunks of the file will be dispersed into different containers [7]. The logical layout and physical layout of the files are inconsistent. As illustrated in Fig. 1, chunks in different files depend on a single instance. Thus, the loss of this instance will lead to more severe secondary loss across underlying storage. Thus, improving the reliability of a deduplication system is a serious challenge.

Table 1. Comparison between replication and erasure coding strategies.

Strategies	Storage cost	Scalability	Degraded read performance	Recovery
Erasure coding	Low	Poor	Low	Hard
Replication	High for large size	Good	High	Easy

Erasure coding vs Replication. Two common redundancy methods used in storage systems to achieve high reliability are erasure coding and replication [14]. They both have their own advantages and disadvantages as summarized in Table 1. **First**, erasure coding divides data into k objects and transforms them into $k + m$ objects. The original data can be recovered from any k objects. As described in Table 1, erasure coding is more space-efficient than replication. With the increasing of shared chunks, the system needs to add redundancy and reconfigure the parameters of (k, m) to improve data reliability. However, erasure coding needs to read large amount of data to recode data for coding scalability, which will incur large I/O and computational cost. **Second**, replication adds a number of copies to achieve high reliability. Replication is easy for scaling and can improve the degraded read performance [10]. It nevertheless incurs extra storage overhead, especially for large volume of datasets. While the storage overhead can be acceptable for datasets with small size.

2.2   Related Work

Traditional storage systems maintain certain redundancy policies for reliability assurance. While deduplication reduces the fault incidence, it increases the impact of faults. A quantitative modeling of reliability consequences of deduplication is proposed by Rozier et al. [18]. They combine data deduplication model with a hardware reliability model, investigate the reliability impact of data deduplication, and prove that data deduplication harms reliability. Similar results are explored by Fu et al. [8], who derive a close to real disk model and analyze the data loss in both chunk and file levels due to various disk errors.

Erasure coding is a more space-efficient strategy. HYDRAstor [5] is a deduplicated secondary storage systems that stores chunks with different resilience class of different level of reliability. Xu et al. [25] deploy erasure coding in a distributed deduplication system and propose a even data placement (EDP) algorithm to achieve a nice balance between read performance and storage overhead. R-ADMAD [12] first packs variable-length chunks into a fix-sized object. The object is encoded and distributed over multiple storage nodes. However, the resilience class of each chunk is determined by user and have no relationship to the shared chunks. Wu et al. [22] leverage deduplication in cloud-of-clouds and improves the reliability by erasure coding and a fixed number of replication. But they use the fix-sized chunking algorithm due to the configuration of cloud-of-clouds, which will increase storage overhead. They also do not consider the features of deduplication semantics, such as inter-/intra-file duplicates. They do not support dynamic replication strategy with the increasing of reference counts.

Replication is a redundancy scheme with little computational overhead. To ensure the overall reliability of deduplication system, Bhagwat el at. [4] suggest to keep at least two copies for deduplicated chunks which may greatly increase the storage overhead. Fu et al. [8] propose a delicate copy technique (DCT) to carefully place and first repair highly- referenced chunks and improves reliability to a certain extent. However, with the increasing of reference counts, the number of replicas should be configured in a dynamic way.

3 Observation and Motivation

In this section, we will exploit the deduplication semantics based on the real-world datasets. We obtain eight snapshots of FSL (i.e., Usr11-Usr26, also used by Fu et al. [8]). *Backup* contains ten versions snapshots collected from Mac OS X server [1]. Then we present the motivation to construct our design of DARM.

Table 2. The analysis of deduplication semantics on realistic datasets.

Sets	Size (GB)	# Files	# Chunks	Dedup (%)	References per Chunk			
					Max.	<2 (%)	>3 (%)	>7 (%)
Usr11	289.86	2.45M	33.73M	36.0	50,976	80.78	3.49	**1.29**
Usr12	251.01	0.04M	26.41M	64.6	660	78.02	5.45	**0.75**
Usr14	161.19	1.34M	16.71M	61.1	34,300	66.26	8.15	**3.46**
Usr15	257.76	0.83M	30.98M	39.1	4,129	86.08	2.12	**0.19**
Usr20	592.73	0.84M	47.88M	79.8	2,621	84.51	2.21	**0.35**
Usr21	140.50	0.06M	14.29M	56.7	7,148	71.54	2.53	**0.15**
Usr24	168.70	0.21M	20.66M	24.4	3,296	86.76	1.48	**0.03**
Usr26	154.24	0.09M	16.44M	33.3	385	87.82	0.81	**0.06**
Backup	1634.27	27.07M	214.91M	93.94	Max.	<11 (%)	>20 (%)	>50 (%)
					59,440	71.68	9.93	**1.13**

Table 2 summarizes the statistical analysis of each dataset, including data size, number of files/chunks, deduplication ratio, and the fraction of chunks on some reference counts. First, only a small fraction of data chunks are highly referenced after deduplication. For example, the fraction of chunks with references more than 3 are less than 5% (i.e., Usr11-Usr26). Chunks with inter-file reference more than 50 account for 1.13% (i.e., backup). Second, inter-file reference count of some chunks is extremely high. For example, one chunk is shared by 34, 300 files in Usr14. Third, highly-referenced chunks account for a small fraction of storage overheads. In Usr20, duplicated chunks only occupy 16.49% fraction of chunks, but refers to 79.8% original data. The first observation follows.

> *Observation (1): Highly-referenced chunks eliminate the majority of data redundancy, but occupy only a small fraction of data chunks.*

To explore the trend of chunk size along with reference counts, we classify duplicated chunks into four redundancy levels: Low(L), Middle(M), High(H) and Extre-High(EH). For Usr11-Usr26, the levels are the reference count with 2, $3 - 4$, $5 - 6$, and more than 6 respectively. For backup dataset, the levels are the reference count with 11, $12 - 20$, $20 - 50$ and more than 50 respectively. In Fig. 2, we observe that the chunk size is getting smaller with the growth of reference counts. In Table 2 and Fig. 2, the second observation is described.

> *Observation (2): Highly-referenced chunks are the large probability of small chunk size, and incur a small fraction of physical storage.*

What's more, inter-file duplicated chunks are critical to the robustness of files. The loss of one inter-file duplicated chunk may cause a disproportional large amount of the loss of multiple files. Bhagwat et al. [4] and Fu et al. [8] also have the same findings. Data deduplication decreases the incidence of faults by reducing the devices, but the impact on improving reliability is much smaller than the damage brought by deduplication [18].

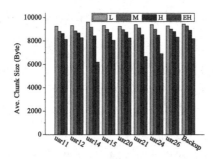

Fig. 2. The variation trend of chunk size along with the reference counts.

Previous work [4, 12, 18] are either lack of analysis of deduplication semantics, or sacrificing much storage overhead to ensure reliability. Based on observations, we present DARM in storage systems to make a tradeoff between data reliability and storage efficiency. Specifically, DARM firstly performs erasure coding on unique and low-referenced chunks to ensure high reliability with low storage overhead. With the growth of reference counts, we find that only inter-file and highly-referenced chunks are required to add redundancy for reliability improvements. Meanwhile, these chunks are of small chunk size and occupy a small fraction of physical storage. Compared with the scalability of erasure coding, replication is easy to improve data reliability and the storage cost is acceptable. DARM proposes a dynamic replication method for highly-referenced chunks.

4 Design and Implementation

4.1 Architecture Overview

Figure 3 shows the system architecture overview of DARM. The system is a client-server mode architecture. The client side is responsible for data chunking, fingerprint generation, metadata collection and data transferring. The metadata contains file information, sequence of chunk fingerprints and chunk size etc. The DARM resides on the server side and interacts with the client. DARM supports duplicate detection, redundancy management and data storage.

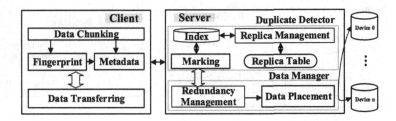

Fig. 3. The architecture of DARM.

DARM consists of two main modules: duplicate detector and data manager. The *duplicate detector* module consists of an index, a marking module and a replica management with a replica table. The index is responsible for checking the chunk whether or not duplicated. Then DARM detects the status of chunks aided by the file metadata and reference count in the marking module. Yet replica management evaluates chunks for dynamic replicas reservation. The metadata of replicas (e.g., device id, address and offset etc.) is stored in the replica table. The *data manager* module consists of redundancy management and data place-ment. The redundancy management performs different redundancy methods on different status of chunks according to the results of marking. Finally DARM reliably distributes data chunks to suitable devices by data placement.

4.2 The Design of DARM

DARM aims to achieve the following goals: (1) Improving data reliability with the growth of reference counts. (2) Ensuring the storage efficiency. We highlight the design phases: the process of data writing and data reading.

Data Writing. In Fig. 4, DARM consists of three stages: data deduplication, chunk marking and data distribution. DARM identifies and marks the different status of chunks via exploiting deduplication semantics. The status of chunks consist of unique chunk, duplicates to be reserved and duplicates to be removed. Different status of chunks has various degrees of effect on data reliability. Thus we should utilize different reliability guarantee mechanisms.

Data Deduplication: Given an input file, the client firstly uses a content-defined chunking algorithm (e.g., AE [26]) to divide files into variable-length chunks. Then the client uses a hash function (e.g., SHA-1) to compute a fingerprint for each chunk. The client sends the sequence of fingerprints to the server. The server establishes a fingerprint index and performs duplicate detection. If the fingerprint exists in the index, the chunk is duplicated. Otherwise, it is a non-duplicate chunk. The file metadata is also stored in the server.

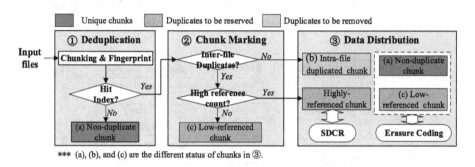

*** (a), (b), and (c) are the different status of chunks in ③.

Fig. 4. The procedure of data writing and redundancy management in DARM.

Chunk Marking: Chunk marking is an important stage in DARM. It classifies chunks into different status by exploiting deduplication semantics (e.g., intra-/inter-file duplicates, and reference count). Specifically, (1) DARM identifies unique chunks and duplicated chunks by duplicate detection. (2) Through checking the metadata of file information, DARM can distinguish intra-file duplicates and inter-file duplicates. To recognize inter-file duplicates that severely affect data reliability, DARM preserves an entry in fingerprint index especially in order to record the information of referenced files for each chunk. (3) By comparison of reference count for inter-file duplicates, chunks are initially grouped into two categories: highly-referenced and low-referenced chunks. In DARM, *duplicate detector* marks the above chunks with consecutive flags as the status. There are three status in DARM. First, a non-duplicate chunk is labeled with a unique chunk. Second, intra-file duplicated chunks are tagged as duplicates to be removed. By reducing storage overhead, intra-file redundancy will benefit reliability rather than harm reliability [8]. Third, inter-file duplicated chunks are marked with duplicates to be reserved. Whereas the loss of highly-referenced chunks has greater impact on data reliability compared with low-referenced chunks.

Data Distribution: Data distribution realizes redundancy management, which can improve data reliability and balance storage overhead. Specifically, after chunk marking, client transfers the data chunks to the server, including unique chunks and duplicates to be reserved. For unique chunks and low-referenced chunks, DARM will write them into containers, and encode data into multiple objects. Finally the objects will be stored in the corresponding devices. (Details in Subsect. 4.3). For chunks that are duplicates to be reserved, *replica management* evaluates the inter-file duplicates with selective and dynamic chunk-based replication (SDCR) (Details in Subsect. 4.3). Data manager assigns the most suitable devices to store replicas based on its previously stored places.

Data Reading. The client sends a reading request of file F to the server. The server will get the file metadata of F and the objects information of each chunk of F. For a chunk c_i, the server gets the objects from k devices and reconstructs the chunk $c_i (0 \leq i < n)$. Then the server sends all chunks to the client in sequence according to the file metadata. The client creates a new file F locally and writes all chunks to the file. If some devices fail, DARM firstly recovers data from other devices by performing erasure coding. If a chunk c_i is still unreadable, DARM will check the *replica table* whether or not in other devices via SDCR. If yes, DARM will get the address of c_i and rebuild it in the failed device.

4.3 Deduplication-Aware Redundancy Management

In this subsection, we will describe the design of DARM. It utilizes erasure coding for unique and low-referenced chunks, while performs SDCR on inter-file and highly-referenced chunks. We will present the procedure of the redundancy methods of erasure coding and SDCR in DARM as follows.

Erasure Coding: For unique chunks, and low-referenced chunks, DARM only keeps one single instance. As the majority of chunks are low-referenced and unique chunks after deduplication, DARM stores these chunks of large storage occupation with erasure coding (i.e., Reed Solomon (RS) Codes [24]). Specifically, all chunks that need to be preserved will be written to a container in sequence. The container is a fix-sized and self-organizing data structure. When the container is full, DARM will divide the container into k blocks and encode them into $k + m$ objects (i.e., m parity objects). The $k + m$ objects are packed into a strip and will be distributed to $k + m$ devices. The configuration of k and m in erasure coding is related to the reference count (See Sect. 5.2). The metadata of each strip will be written into a metadata file. If some devices fail, DARM will get the metadata file to obtain the objects of corrupted data. Then DARM reads sufficient objects and decodes them to reconstruct data.

Selective and Dynamic Chunk-based Replication (SDCR): We measure the importance (or weight) of a chunk based on deduplication semantics (e.g., inter-/intra-file duplicates, and reference count). SDCR is a dynamic method to improve data reliability for inter-file and highly-referenced chunks. In particular, SDCR firstly uses the parameter *level* (i.e., boundary of reference count) to distinguish highly-referenced chunks with low-referenced chunks. If the reference count is lower than the *level*, DARM keeps only one copy. Otherwise, SDCR

Algorithm 1. SDCR: Selective and Dynamic Chunk-based Replication

---

Input: An incoming chunk c;

Output: T: Reference count of a chunk; T_r: Reference count of the rth replicas; **r**:
   Number of replicas; **mcp**: Maximum number of replicas.
 1: Predefined values: $a, and\ b$ for the function to add a replica;
 2: **if** chunk c is unique **then**
 3:     $T \leftarrow 1, r \leftarrow 1, T_r \leftarrow 1$
 4:     Store chunk c as a new chunk
 5: **else if** c is an inter-file duplicate **then**
 6:     $T \leftarrow T + 1$
 7:     **if** $r < mcp$ **then**
 8:         **if** $(T = level)$ or $(T > level\ and\ T - T_r = a * r + b)$ **then**
 9:             $r \leftarrow r + 1$
10:             $T_r \leftarrow T$
11:             Store chunk c as the rth replica
12:         **end if**
13:     **else**
14:         c is a duplicated chunk that need to be removed.
15:     **end if**
16: **end if**

---

will add multiple replicas for highly-referenced chunks. Second, SDCR uses a heuristic function to calculate the number of replicas for a chunk. Specifically, SDCR utilizes a typical liner polynomials (e.g., $T - T_r = a * r + b$) Algorithm 1 to simulate the interval between inter-file reference counts and the number of replicas. In addition, SDCR sets the maximum number of replicas (i.e., mcp) to limit the extra storage overhead. Thus, SDCR tremendously decreases the data loss severity and increases data reliability.

Algorithm 1 presents the procedure of SDCR. We denote r to be the number of replicas. Concretely speaking, for an incoming chunk c, SDCR will check it whether or not an inter-file duplicate. If no, c is a unique chunk. SDCR will store c as a new chunk. Otherwise, the reference count T will be $T \leftarrow T + 1$. Next, SDCR will check if the number of replicas r exceeds the maximum number of replicas of mcp. If so, SDCR will remove the chunk c. Because even if the number of replicas exceeds mcp, the effect on improving data reliability is diminished [4,18]. Otherwise, SDCR will increase the number of replicas only in two cases. First, the reference count T is equal to $level$, then the chunk c will be an inter-file and highly-referenced chunk. Second, if $T > level$, we choose a function, $T - T_r = a * r + b$, which is inspired by Bhagwat et al. [4]. We leverages it to calculate the relationship between reference count and the number of replicas. Here, a and b are constants that are limited by storage utilization and data reliability. With the increasing of T, SDCR needs to add a new replica to improve data reliability for the selective chunk c. If the above conditions are met, SDCR will preserve c as a replica and update T_r. Thus, SDCR can dynamically improve data reliability for the selective chunks.

4.4 Prototype Implementation

Deduplication. DARM uses AE algorithm [26] to divide a file into chunks. The average chunk size can be configured to 2 KB, 4 KB and 8 KB. While the default average chunk size is 8 KB. DARM uses a linked list to record the file metadata, called recipe [7], including file information, sequence of chunk fingerprints etc. DARM utilizes a hash table as the index to map chunk fingerprints with their physical address. We also keep an entry in the fingerprint index to update the reference count. Items in the index are written into disks for persistent storage.

Data Layout. We use a log-structured unit (i.e., container) to store chunks [7]. Unique chunks are sequentially appended to the end of the last write position, and the container size can be configured as 4 MB or 8 MB. We try to store chunks belong to one file on the same device and the replicas of chunks on different devices. First, we reserve a small fraction of storage on each device and use a hash table to preserve the mapping of copies of inter-file and highly-referenced chunks. And DARM writes them to the file metadata for data backup. Second, DARM applies Reed-Solomon (RS) code [24] to transform data in containers into multiple objects. If the container is not full, DARM will fill in some '0' bytes. Each object will be consequently written to the corresponding devices.

5 Performance Evaluation

5.1 Experiment Setup

Simulation Assumptions: (1) Storage systems are susceptible to both uncorrectable disk failures (UDFs) [16,19] and latent sector errors (LSEs) [3]. In this paper, we only consider UDFs to evaluate the effect of data deduplication, similar with Fu et al. [8]. (2) Due to the lack of field data, our analysis assumes constant failure rates, constant repair rates and the independent failures [13]. We focus on the reliability and storage efficiency of our method compared with other strategies under the same environment configurations.

Platform: We conduct experiments to evaluate the performance of DARM. The hardware configuration of the machine is equipped with an Intel(R) Core(TM) i7-4770@3.40GHZ 8-core CPU, 16 GB memory and 2 TB hard disk. The machines are installed with an Ubuntu 14.04 LTS 64-bit operation system.

Methodology: We test the storage overhead, and data availability on different datasets, which is similar to Bhagwat et al. [4] and Fu et al. [8]. Dedup ratio is the ratio of duplicated data size and total data size. And we utilize the fraction of data available to evaluate the reliability of different methods. The metric is defined as the percentage of recoverable data while a certain percentage of devices suffering whole disk failures, which is derived from the popular used reliability metric called Normalized Magnitude of Data Loss (NOMDL) [9]. The traditional metric, Mean Time to Data Loss (MTTDL), is inadequate for the analysis of reliability because of its simplistic failure modeling of real world storage [6,9].

Table 3. The Statistics of three datasets.

Datasets	FSL	Backup	Linux
# Chunks	66M	42M	10.41M
# Files	3.14M	2.64M	258
Total space (GB)	597.78	458.91	111.32
Dedup ratio	49.93%	96.74%	41.43%

Datasets: Three datasets are listed in Table 3. *FSL* dataset is composed of snapshots from part of eight users' home directories (also used in [27]), which is collected by the File system and Storage Lab (FSL) at Stony Brook [1]. *Backup* dataset consists of part of snapshots from a randomly selected user's home directory. *Linux* dataset contains 258 versions of tar files of Linux source codes from Linux-2.6.X to Linux-3.9.X.

Setting: (1) To simulate large-scale storage systems, we use artificial defined small devices to store data [4]. We set the device size for each dataset to 2 GB, 128 MB and 256 MB for FSL, Backup, and Linux respectively. All the data are stored evenly on each device. By randomly selecting a small fraction of disk failure, we simulate the low disk failure rate in storage systems. Then we calculate data availability at a low level of disk failure and simulate the effect of temporary whole disk failure. (2) We firstly give a sensitivity study of DARM with various parameters. To test the effectiveness of DARM, we compare our performance evaluation with deduplication without redundancy strategy, selective replication strategy [4] and distributed erasure codes strategy [12]. For simplicity, we use Dedup, DeepStore and R-ADMAD to donate these strategies respectively.

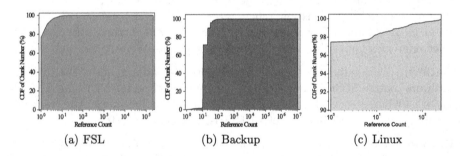

(a) FSL   (b) Backup   (c) Linux

Fig. 5. Cumulative probability density function of the number of references to each deduplicated chunk for FSL, Backup and Linux respectively.

5.2 A Sensitivity Study of DARM

Experiment 1 (Impact of Reference Count): In Fig. 5, we analyze the distribution of chunk references of each dataset. The fraction of chunks which are referenced by files more than 20 times is 3.28%, 8.76%, and 1.31%, for FSL, Backup, and Linux, respectively. The characteristics they have in common is that highly-referenced chunks always account for the minority among the chunks after deduplication (See Sect. 3).

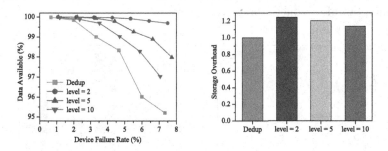

Fig. 6. The impact of parameter *level* of DARM on FSL dataset.

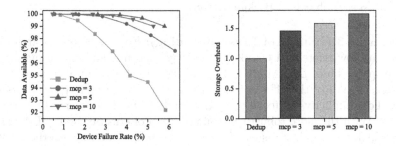

Fig. 7. The impact of parameter *mcp* of DARM on Backup dataset.

Experiment 2 (Impact of Parameters in SDCR): To study the effect of each parameter on balancing the tradeoff, we vary the parameter *level*, and *mcp*. We normalize the storage overhead for DRAM on varying different parameters with the storage occupation after data deduplication.

To choose an appropriate *level* is important, since it determines the fraction of chunks from which to start for replicas preservation. The smaller *level*, the more duplicated chunks should be preserved. Figure 6 describes the evaluation of the parameter *level*. With the increasing of *level*, the data reliability gradually decreases, while the storage overhead increases. The configuration of *level* is related to the reference count. For example, it is more scientific to set the *level* to be more than 1 and less than 10 for *FSL* dataset. Because most chunks are unique chunks, while only 23.2% chunks are referenced by two more files for FSL. As for Backup, we had better to set the *level* to be more than 10. Most of chunks are shared by more than ten files, only minority chunks (e.g. account for 1.8%) have less reference counts.

Figure 7 describes the impact of *mcp* on DARM performance, and experiments are conducted with level = 11, a = 5, b = 0, k = 10, m = 1, on Backup dataset. With the increasing of *mcp*, DARM improves data reliability through reducing chunk loss severity by preserving more replicas for highly-referenced chunks. However, excessive replicas are not only overmuch for improving data reliability, but also reduce storage efficiency.

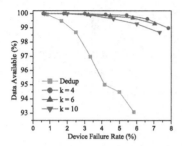
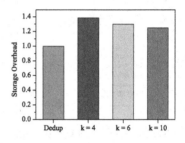

Fig. 8. The impact of erasure coding configuration. Experiments are conducted with level = 11, a = 10, b = 5 on Backup dataset.

Experiment 3 (Impact of Erasure Coding): Erasure coding is applied for unique and low-referenced chunks that always account for a large majority of storage space. Thus, DARM not only provides robustness but also more storage efficiency. To study the effect of erasure coding, we vary the parameters of k and m. For simplicity, we fix m to 1, and conduct the experiments by varying k in Fig. 8. With the more robustness configuration of erasure coding, DARM can provide higher reliability assurance, but incurs higher storage overhead. With the increasing of k, DARM will require more restore time for data loss events.

5.3 Overall Performance of DRAM

We conduct the performance comparison of DARM with Dedup, DeepStore, and R-ADMAD on FSL and Linux datasets. We aim to evaluate the effectiveness of

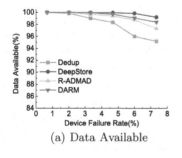
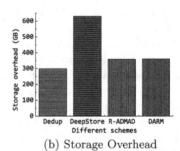

(a) Data Available   (b) Storage Overhead

Fig. 9. Effectiveness of DARM. Experiments are conducted with level = 2, mcp = 5, a = 10, b = 5, k = 10, m = 1 on FSL dataset.

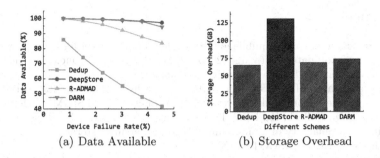

(a) Data Available   (b) Storage Overhead

Fig. 10. Effectiveness of DARM. Experiments are conducted with level = 2, mcp = 10, a = 5, b = 0, k = 10, m = 1 on Linux dataset.

DARM on the tradeoff between data reliability and space overhead. In Fig. 9, the parameters a and b of DeepStore and DARM are the same, and mcp is configured with 5. Compared with DeepStore, DARM reduces 42.6% storage cost and sacrifices 0.25%–0.82% assurance of data reliability.

In Fig. 10, the parameters of erasure coding in DARM and R-ADMAD are the same with $k = 10$ and $m = 1$. DARM can achieve good reliability guarantee with lower storage capacity by choosing the appropriate parameters. Compared with R-ADMAD, DARM achieves 1.5%–12.7% improvements on data reliability, and only incurs little space overhead. Compared with DeepStore, DARM saves 43.4% storage space and brings a 0.07%–2.9% reduction of data reliability. Thus, DARM achieves a good balance between data reliability and storage cost.

6 Conclusion and Future Work

In this paper, we present DARM, a deduplication-aware redundancy management approach for storage systems. DARM smartly combines erasure coding with selective and dynamic chunk-based replication (SDCR) based on the deduplication semantics (e.g., inter-file duplicates, chunk size and reference count). DARM utilizes erasure coding for low-referenced chunks and employs SDCR for inter-file and highly-referenced chunks. Experimental results show that, DARM not only reduces the storage cost, but also guarantees high reliability.

In the future, we will improve the read performance via the combination of DARM with rewriting algorithms [7]. Second, we will improve the security of DARM to simultaneously ensure security, reliability and cost-efficiency [27,28].

Acknowledgment. The authors are grateful to the anonymous reviewers. The work was partly supported by the National Natural Science Foundation of China No. U1705261, No. 61772222 and 61502190; Shenzhen Research Funding of Science and Technology - Fundamental Research (Free exploration) JCYJ20170307172447622. This work was also supported by Engineering Research Center of data storage systems and Technology, Ministry of Education, China.

References

1. Fsl traces and snapshots public archive (2014). http://tracer.filesystems.org
2. The future of data: Data age 2025 (2017). http://www.emc.com/leadership/digital-universe/2014iview/executive-summary.htm
3. Bairavasundaram, L.N., Goodson, G.R., Pasupathy, S., Schindler, J.: An analysis of latent sector errors in disk drives. In: Proceedings of ACM SIGMETRICS (2007)
4. Bhagwat, D., Pollack, K., Long, D.D., Schwarz, T., Miller, E.L., Pâris, J.F.: Providing high reliability in a minimum redundancy archival storage system. In: Proceedings of IEEE MASCOTS (2006)
5. Dubnicki, C., et al.: HYDRAstor: a scalable secondary storage. In: Proceedings of USENIX FAST, pp. 197–210 (2009)
6. Elerath, J.G., Schindler, J.: Beyond MTTDL: a closed-form raid 6 reliability equation. ACM Trans. Storage (TOS) **10**(2), 7 (2014)
7. Fu, M., et al.: Accelerating restore and garbage collection in deduplication-based backup systems via exploiting historical information. In: Proceedings of USENIX ATC (2014)
8. Fu, M., Lee, P.P., Feng, D., Chen, Z., Xiao, Y.: A simulation analysis of reliability in primary storage deduplication. In: Proceedings of IEEE IISWC, pp. 199–208 (2016)
9. Greenan, K.M., Plank, J.S., Wylie, J.J.: Mean time to meaningless: MTTDL, Markov models, and storage system reliability. In: Proceedings of USENIX HotStorage (2010)
10. Li, R., Lee, P.P., Hu, Y.: Degraded-first scheduling for MapReduce in erasure-coded storage clusters. In: Proceedings of IEEE/IFIP DSN (2014)
11. Li, X., Lillibridge, M., Uysal, M.: Reliability analysis of deduplicated and erasure-coded storage. ACM SIGMETRICS Perform. Eval. Rev. **38**(3), 4–9 (2011)
12. Liu, C., Gu, Y., Sun, L., Yan, B., Wang, D.: R-ADMAD: high reliability provision for large-scale de-duplication archival storage systems. In: Proceedings of ACM ICS (2009)
13. Ma, A., et al.: RAIDShield: characterizing, monitoring, and proactively protecting against disk failures. ACM TOS **11**(4), 17 (2015)
14. Mao, B., Wu, S., Jiang, H.: Improving storage availability in cloud-of-clouds with hybrid redundant data distribution. In: Proceedings of IEEE IPDPS, pp. 633–642 (2015)
15. Ng, C.-H., Ma, M., Wong, T.-Y., Lee, P.P.C., Lui, J.C.S.: Live deduplication storage of virtual machine images in an open-source cloud. In: Kon, F., Kermarrec, A.-M. (eds.) Middleware 2011. LNCS, vol. 7049, pp. 81–100. Springer, Heidelberg (2011). https://doi.org/10.1007/978-3-642-25821-3_5
16. Pinheiro, E., Weber, W.D., Barroso, L.A.: Failure trends in a large disk drive population. In: Proceedings of USENIX FAST, pp. 17–29 (2007)
17. Quinlan, S., Dorward, S.: Venti: a new approach to archival storage. In: Proceedings of USENIX FAST (2002)
18. Rozier, E.W., Sanders, W.H., Zhou, P., Mandagere, N., Uttamchandani, S.M., Yakushev, M.L.: Modeling the fault tolerance consequences of deduplication. In: Proceedings of IEEE SRDS (2011)
19. Schroeder, B., Gibson, G.A.: Disk failures in the real world: what does an MTTF of 1,000,000 hours mean to you? In: Proceedings of USENIX FAST, pp. 1–16 (2007)
20. Srinivasan, K., Bisson, T., Goodson, G., Voruganti, K.: iDedup: latency-aware, inline data deduplication for primary storage. In: Proceedings of USENIX FAST (2012)

21. Vrable, M., Savage, S., Voelker, G.M.: Cumulus: filesystem backup to the cloud. ACM Trans. Storage (TOS) **5**(4), 14 (2009)
22. Wu, S., Li, K.C., Mao, B., Liao, M.: DAC: improving storage availability with deduplication-assisted cloud-of-clouds. FGCS **74**, 190–198 (2017)
23. Xia, W., et al.: A comprehensive study of the past, present, and future of data deduplication. Proc. IEEE **104**(9), 1681–1710 (2016)
24. Xiao, M., Hassan, M.A., Xiao, W., Wei, Q., Chen, S.: CodePlugin: plugging deduplication into erasure coding for cloud storage. In: Proceedings of the USENIX Workshop HotCloud, pp. 1–6 (2015)
25. Xu, M., Zhu, Y., Lee, P.P.C., Xu, Y.: Even data placement for load balance in reliable distributed deduplication storage systems. In: Proceedings of IEEE/ACM IWQoS, pp. 349–358 (2015)
26. Zhang, Y., et al.: AE: an asymmetric extremum content defined chunking algorithm for fast and bandwidth-efficient data deduplication. In: Proceedings of IEEE INFOCOM, pp. 1337–1345 (2015)
27. Zhou, Y., et al.: A similarity-aware encrypted deduplication scheme with flexible access control in the cloud. Future Gener. Comput. Syst. (FGCS) **84**, 177–189 (2017)
28. Zhou, Y., et al.: SecDep: a user-aware efficient fine-grained secure deduplication scheme with multi-level key management. In: Proceedings of IEEE MSST, pp. 1–14 (2015)

K-Anonymity Algorithm Based on Improved Clustering

Wantong Zheng[1], Zhongyue Wang[1], Tongtong Lv[1], Yong Ma[2], and Chunfu Jia[1(✉)]

[1] College of Cyberspace Security, Nankai University, Tianjin 300350, China
cfjia@nankai.edu.cn
[2] Civil Aviation University of China, Tianjin, China

Abstract. K-anonymity is the most widely used technology in the field of privacy preservation. It has a good performance particularly in protecting data privacy in the scenarios of data publication, location-based service and social network. In this paper, we propose a new algorithm to achieve k-anonymity in a better way through improved clustering, and we optimize the clustering process by considering the overall distribution of quasi-identifier groups in a multidimensional space. With the local optimal clustering, we try our best to guarantee minimized intra-cluster distances and maximized inter-cluster distances. Therefore, the quality of anonymized data can be greatly improved. Compared with some popular algorithms like k-member, Mondrian, and one-time k-means, the experimental results show our algorithm can effectively reduce the information loss while generating equivalence classes. The total information loss of the anonymized dataset decreases by about 20% on average than that of other algorithms. It also performs well in dealing with both numerical attributes and categorical attributes.

Keywords: Information loss · Privacy preservation · K-anonymity
Clustering

1 Introduction

Minimizing the risk of privacy leaks and maximizing data availability are both the goals of privacy protection in data publishing scenario. In order to protect personal privacy, some organizations usually delete or encrypt explicit identifiers which can clearly identify users from the published data tables, such as name and social insurance code, etc. However, this approach cannot effectively prevent attackers from linking other information in the published data with data obtained from other sources (i.e., linking attacks) [3]. Moreover, privacy can be

This project is partly supported the National Natural Science Foundation of China (No. 61772291), the Natural Science Foundation of Tianjin (No. 17JCZDJC30500), the Open Project Foundation of Information Security Evaluation Center of Civil Aviation, Civil Aviation University of China (No. CAAC-ISECCA-201702).

J. Vaidya and J. Li (Eds.): ICA3PP 2018, LNCS 11335, pp. 462–476, 2018.
https://doi.org/10.1007/978-3-030-05054-2_36

violated through three types of attack, including linking attack, homogeneity attack and background knowledge attack.

In order to solve the privacy leakage problem caused by linking attacks, Sweeney et al. [12–14] proposed the k-anonymity privacy protection model. This model requires that the value of each quasi-identifier sequence in the published anonymous dataset appear at least k $(k > 1)$ times, that is, at least k records have to use the same quasi-identifier attribute value. However, the research in [9] shows that it is an NP-hard problem to implement optimal data anonymization. The popular k-anonymity techniques usually generalize and suppress the quasi-identifier attributes that may leak information. As shown in Fig. 1, the basic idea of generalization is that the quasi-identifier attributes in the same equivalence class should be replaced by the same generalized values. The generalization process reduces the accuracy of the data, but it preserves the original semantics of the data. However, excessive generalization can also cause unnecessary information loss and then reduce the effectiveness of data. Suppression techniques can be regarded as a special form of generalization, where all values are replaced by "*". Although suppression can hide users' information effectively, it causes a larger information loss than generalization at the same time. To sum up, it is challenging to keep the quality of published data and protect their privacy at the same time. Data privacy preservation, especially privacy-preserving data publishing, must take the tradeoff between data quality and data security into account.

Research shows that most of the typical k-anonymity methods are based on generalization and suppression techniques. All of them suffer from significant information loss because they rely heavily on the ordering relations from pre-defined generalization layers on the attribute domains. Hence, the anonymization results often produce high information loss and further result in poor availability. Moreover, the existing anonymization algorithms mainly focus on the protection of private information but ignore the actual utility of anonymized data. As a result, the availability of anonymized data is low in actual scenes.

In this paper, we propose an improved k-anonymity privacy protection algorithm based on clustering. We devote in optimizing the clustering process and making it more suitable for data anonymity scenarios. Experimental results show that the scheme we propose has significantly improved data availability compared with other algorithms including k-member clustering, Mondrian multidimensional and one-time k-means.

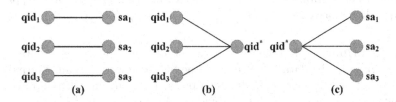

Fig. 1. The process of generating an equivalence class

The remainder of this paper is organized as follows. In Sect. 2, we review the existing techniques of k-anonymity and introduce some basic concepts of the k-anonymity model. And in Sect. 3, we propose an improved k-anonymity algorithm based on clustering. Then we conduct some experiments, illustrate the experimental data, and conduct a theoretical analysis of the experimental results in Sect. 4. Finally, we conclude the paper in Sect. 5.

2   Related Work

Data privacy preserving has been applied in data publishing as well as location-based service during the past few decades [7]. A number of heuristic data anonymization methods have been proposed to improve the degree of privacy protection of published data and reduce the information loss during data anonymization. Wang et al. [15] proposed an anonymous method of bottom-up progressive generalization. While Fung et al. [4] proposed a top-down specialization method. Aggarwal et al. [1] first proposed an efficient method for anonymizing data through clustering techniques. The data sets are divided into clusters using clustering algorithms, and they used cluster centroids to replace data points in the clusters along with the cluster characteristics at the same time. LeFever et al. [6] proposed a greedy top-down algorithm to find the smallest k-anonymity in the multidimensional generalization model.

Also, many researchers proposed respective anonymization methods for different types of data. Ozalp et al. [10] proposed anonymization techniques for privacy-preserving publishing of hierarchical data. Terrovitis [5] proposed the $k^{(m,n)}$-anonymity definition for tree-structured data. In their work, attackers' background knowledge is limited to m vertex labels and n structural relations between vertices (i.e., ancestor/descendant relationships). But this algorithm has no distinction between quasi-identifier and sensitive attribute. As for graph-based data, Palanisamy [11] presented an anonymization framework for publishing large association graph datasets with the goal of supporting multilevel access-controlled query.

2.1   Basic Conceptions of K-Anonymity

Identifier. An attribute or a set of attributes that can identify a unique individual, such as ID card number, name, etc. Before publishing the microdata, these identifier attributes are usually deleted, masked, or encrypted to protect the individual's privacy.

Quasi-Identifier. Quasi-identifier is a set of non-sensitive attributes (e.g., $q_1, q_2, \ldots, q_m$) in the data table that can be SQL-connected to an external data table so that at least one individual can be identified again, wherein any single attribute cannot identify a unique individual. A set of attributes like this is called quasi-identifier (QI) or semi-identifier. Linking a set of quasi-identifiers together can potentially identify the individual's attributes. For example, suppose that there is a set of quasi-identifiers including *age*, *gender*, and *zipcode* in medical privacy preservation scenario, each of the attributes is stored in different tables, and *patient's disease* is regarded as the sensitive identifier. Attackers can connect these tables to a medical record table through the quasi-identifiers above, and then they can infer the patient's disease information easily.

Sensitive Identifier. Sensitive identifiers are fields that need to be protected at the highest level, such as disease information in medical data, employee salaries, ID card numbers, cell phone numbers, etc.

Equivalent Class. In k-anonymity, each equivalent class contains at least k records. Quasi-identifier groups of all records should have the same value in one equivalent class. The raw data table will produce m equivalent classes after k-anonymous, where $m = \left\lfloor \frac{n}{k} \right\rfloor$, and n is the number of records in the data table.

2.2   Distance and Information Loss Metric

In the process of clustering, the definition of distance is a critical factor of clustering results. A good choice of distance metric for a particular scene can make the clustering method achieve more optimal results. For numerical attributes, although they can be calculated directly using classical algorithms such as Euclidean distance and Manhattan distance, these distances are incapable of handling categorical attributes (such as *occupation*, *native countries*).

An important factor for evaluating k-anonymity in data anonymization is the loss of data information. Data anonymization methods will inevitably cause information loss to the data set, however, information loss can measure data availability and anonymization effect accurately and intuitively. These exactly satisfy the conditions of k-anonymity. We define a set of algorithms to calculate the distance between records as well as between records and clusters. It can not only take the difference between numerical attributes and categorical attributes into account but also use the numerical values to describe the similarities between records and clusters.

We use the definition of Normalized Certainty Penalty (NCP) [16] as the standard for measuring the loss of information. NCP is a kind of algorithm to measure the degree of loss, which is efficient and easy to use.

Distance Between Numerical Data. For numerical attributes, we define D as the domain of one numerical attribute, and T as the table with quasi-identifier $(q_1, \ldots, q_n)$ for any two values $v_i, v_j \in D$, and then the distance between them is defined as (1)

$$\delta_N(v_i, v_j) = \frac{|v_i - v_j|}{|D|} \tag{1}$$

Categorical attributes are a type of data attributes with multiple discrete values. The values do not have a complete ordering relation, so the distance definition of numerical attribute could not be applied to categorical attributes. However, there is some semantic correlation between most of the categorical attributes. So it's reasonable to use the correlation between data semantics to define the distance between categorical data. In general, the semantic relevance of data can be represented by a classification tree. Assume that a balanced classification tree is used to represent the relationship on an attribute domain whose leaf nodes represent all the different attribute values in the attribute domain. A numeric generalized tree is shown in Fig. 2 as an example.

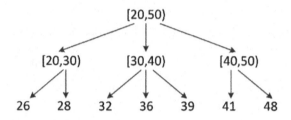

Fig. 2. Numeric generalized tree

Distance Between Categorial Data. We define T_D as a generalized tree for one categorical attribute. For any two values $v_i, v_j \in D$, the distance between them is defined as

$$\delta_C(v_i, v_j) = \begin{cases} 0, & v_i = v_j \\ \frac{|Common(v_i, v_j)|}{|T_D|}, & v_i \neq v_j \end{cases} \tag{2}$$

$|T_D|$ denotes the number of all leaf nodes in the generalized tree of the attribute D, and $|Common(v_i, v_j)|$ is the number of leaf nodes in the lowest common tree of v_i and v_j. If the values of v_i and v_j are the same, then their generalized values are equal to v_i and v_j respectively, and the information loss is zero. A categorical generalized tree is shown in Fig. 3.

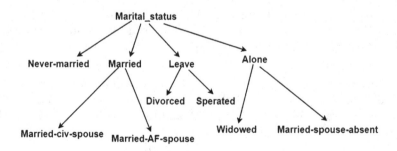

Fig. 3. Categorial generalized tree

Distance Between Records. The distance between two records is the sum of the distances between the corresponding continuous and categorical quasi-identifiers in the two records. Let $QI = \{N_1, \ldots, N_m, C_1, \ldots, C_n\}$ be the quasi-identifier of dataset T, where N_i $(i = 1, \ldots, m)$ is continuous numeric attribute, and C_j $(j = 1, \ldots, n)$ is categorical attribute. Then the distance between records r_i and r_j is defined as

$$\Delta(r_i, r_j) = \sum_{i=1}^{m} w_i \delta_N(r_1[N_i], r_2[N_i]) + \sum_{j=1}^{n} w_j \delta_C(r_1[C_j], r_2[C_j]) \qquad (3)$$

In the equation, $r[N]$ represents the value of quasi-identifier N in record r, and w_i represents the weight of quasi-identifier i.

In our algorithm, we use the above definition of distance in our improved clustering. The distance between the record and the cluster centroid also represents the generalization degree of the record, which means the size of the information loss. And we calculate the information loss of all records as the information loss of the whole cluster.

3 Our Scheme

Anonymization algorithms need the information loss to be as low as possible so that the premise of the k-anonymity requirements could be met. We could then obtain a better data quality to the anonymized dataset.

The results of clustering-based anonymous algorithms depend on the concrete design of clustering. We propose an improved clustering-based k-anonymity algorithm which is more accurate and reasonable in cluster position selection.

3.1 Clustering and Anonymity

Information loss can reflect the similarity degree between records in a data set, but it also causes some problems. To calculate the distance between two records, we must generalize the values first. However, as for clustering, the distance definition and centroids selection are two significant factors that must be preferentially considered. The centroid of each cluster is the average value of each numerical attribute value. As for categorical attributes, there is no average value or any similar definition to describe the centroid. The centroid can only be a generalized record value. And the generalization of categorical attributes is accomplished by setting up a generalized tree. So it is a one-way process, from bottom to top and from concrete to abstract.

When the k-means clustering algorithm copes with numerical attributes, it will perform multiple iterations until the cluster allocation result of all records no longer changes, so that the centroid value of the numerical attributes will become stable. However, while dealing with categorical attributes, the process of clustering is a continuous generalization since the generalization tree should be traversed only from bottom to top. While clustering, the k-means algorithm can only change the value of the centroid to a higher level of the generalization tree. If it iterates to convergence, then we are likely to get the root node's value as it's generalized value. The one-time k-means algorithm solves the problem which k-means is incapable of while dealing with categorical attributes. This algorithm conducts the clustering process only once. However, since the initial centroid of k-means is randomly selected, it greatly influences the final clustering result, resulting in a large information loss.

Without iterating many times, the k-member algorithm [2] performs well in generalizing categorical attributes and can acquire a better data quality. However, there is still a problem. While generating a new cluster, k-member only takes the last cluster into consideration regardless of the clusters generated earlier. This may result in some bad cluster distributions. As shown in Fig. 4, cluster C_1 is the latest generated cluster, and cluster C_2 is the cluster generated before C_1. Point p_1 and point p_2 are the centroid candidates. According to k-member, p_2 is the farthest point from C_1. But if we choose p_2 as the next centroid, the new cluster will be too close to C_2. The record p_2 may be very similar to records in C_2 and the following $k - 1$ records added into the new cluster will not be in their optimal clusters. The principle of inter-cluster distances maximum will be broken. Therefore, our algorithm takes the previous clusters into consideration, p_1 has the farthest average distance from other clusters. Choosing p_1 as the next centroid will make the distribution of the clusters homogeneous. Obviously, the choice of p_1 is much better than that of p_2. With the maximum non-similarity between clusters, the information loss will be greatly reduced.

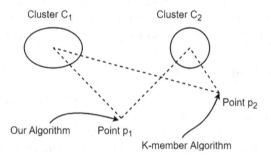

Fig. 4. Selection of new cluster centroid

In order to avoid the shortcoming of k-means and obtain better performance when dealing with both numeric attributes and categorical attributes, we propose an improved clustering algorithm for data anonymization. Through one-time clustering, we optimize the selection of centroids, and the clustering results are significantly improved. We redefine the distance calculation method in clustering, as a result, the information loss is reduced.

3.2   Algorithm Description

Our anonymity clustering algorithm follows the steps outlined below: Given a set S with n records, we first randomly pick a record r_i and let it be the centroid of the first cluster c_1. Then we choose $k-1$ records closest to r_i $(i = 1,\ldots,k-1)$ from S. This step means the information loss $c_1 \cup \{r_i\}$ is minimal. Now the first cluster meets the requirements of k-anonymity. Next, for each of the rest

$$m = \left\lfloor \frac{n}{k} \right\rfloor - 1 \text{ centroids } m_i,$$ we consider the effect of the positional relationship of

the previous $i-1$ cluster on its choice. Here, for each remaining record in the data set S, we calculate the total distance between itself and all the existed centroids m_j $(j = 1,\ldots,i-1)$, and we choose the record with largest mean distance as the ith centroid. This clustering process takes the distribution of global data points into account. Then we repeat the clustering process until every cluster contains k records. At this moment, we iterate the remaining records and insert each record into a cluster with respect to which the increment of the information loss is minimal.

The algorithm is described as follows

Algorithm 1. Improved K-Anonymity Algorithm based on Clustering.

Input:
    The initial data set S;
    Generalization parameter K;
Output:
    Anonymized table AT with K;
1: Let clusters=$\varnothing$, record = the index of record picked randomly from S;
2: **while** len(S) $>= k$ **do**
3:    **if** len(clusters) < 1 **then**
4:        nextrecord = the furthest record to record;
5:    **else**
6:        New_centroid_choice_function()
7:    **end if**
8:    **while** len(clusters) $< k$ **do**
9:        Choose the best record and insert into the cluster
10:    **end while**
11:    **while** len(S) > 0 **do**
12:        Get a record and choose the best cluster and insert into it
13:    **end while**
14: **end while**

And we improve the process of centroid selection in the clustering, as in Algorithm 2:

Algorithm 2. New_centroid_choice_function().

Input:
    The initial data set S;
    The existed cluster group *clusters*;
Output:
    The final clusters;
1: sum_distance $= 0$
2: max_cluster_dis $= 0$ and max_cluster_dis_index $= 0$
3: **for** each record in range(len(S)) **do**
4:    **for** each cluster in *clusters* **do**
5:        Calculate the distance between cluster and record
6:    **end for**
7:    Store the biggest distance between cluster and record
8: **end for**
9: Choose the record be the centroid of the next cluster

After completing the clustering process, each cluster satisfies the number of records required for k-anonymity. The next step is to generalize each cluster. The quasi-identifier of every cluster need to be set as the same attribute value. For each quasi-identifier attribute of each cluster, its generalized value is set as the value of the centroid of its cluster, while the centroid of each cluster is the average of all records in the cluster.

Our ideas are inspired by the k-nearest neighbor algorithm which is well-known in Machine Learning as a classification algorithm. As we discussed before, the effect of k-means while dealing with data anonymity is severely influenced by the choice of original centroids and the iteration times. Our algorithm minimizes the impact of random selection of the initial centroids on the final clustering results by selecting new centroids gradually during clustering. In this way, we can avoid the terrible cluster distribution at the beginning. So our algorithm finds a pretty balance between time and data quality, and it has a great improvement in reducing information loss.

Moreover, our algorithm considers the impact of positions of existed clusters on the selection of new centroids. The position of each generated cluster is used as a reference point to select new centroids. This discriminates the newest cluster from previous clusters to the greatest degree and merges the record to its cluster with better effectiveness. In other words, the distribution of clusters avoids the situation where the new clusters are very similar to the old ones in the process of clustering. This can lead to bad clustering results due to improper selection of new cluster centroids (such as k-member). Our algorithm also adopts the idea of one-time clustering, this can not only avoid the unnecessary and irreversible information loss due to multiple iterations while generalizing categorical attributes but also allocate the data to more suitable clusters.

4   Experiments and Analysis

In this section, we conduct a series of experiments with the real-world typical data set, and we compare our algorithm with other three popular k-anonymity algorithms. As for the quality of the anonymized data, we measure the performance of these algorithms by information loss.

4.1   The Data Set

Our experiment uses the Adult dataset from the UCI machine learning database to test the performance of the proposed algorithms. The dataset includes part of the US population census data. It has been widely used in the study of anonymized privacy protection and has become the de facto standard in this field. In our data preprocessing, we remove records with missing values. We choose 8 attributes as quasi-identifier which includes *age, workclass, education, marital_status, race, sex, occupation* and *native_country*, and *income* is chosen as the sensitive attribute.

4.2   Experimental Environment

We implement the algorithms in Python and run these experiments on a desktop PC with Intel(R) Core(TM) i7-6700 CPU @ 3.40 GHz 3.41 GHz and 16.0 GB of RAM under Windows 10.

In this paper, our improved algorithm is compared with the k-member clustering algorithm [2], Mondrian multidimensional k-anonymity algorithm [6] and one-time k-means anonymity algorithm [8]. We observe the information loss of data by changing the value of parameter k and the value of data size n.

4.3   Data Quality

In order to unify the evaluation criteria and measure the data quality better, we use NCP as the assessment of data quality. As we mentioned before, NCP is defined from a perspective of attributes, and it is consistent with the definition of distance in clustering that we mentioned above. Here we need to measure the information loss of generalized records and of the whole dataset, so we normalize NCP for records and dataset as follows:

$$NCP(record) = \frac{\sum_{i=1}^{d} NCP(attribute_i)}{d} \tag{4}$$

$$NCP(dataset) = \frac{\sum_{i=1}^{n} NCP(record_i)}{n} \tag{5}$$

In Eq. (4), i represents the number of the attributes in a record, in (5), the value n means the number of the records in the dataset. As we can see, the NCP of records and datasets is averaged. This contributes to the normalized measure of the data quality, and it is also direct in comparison with different algorithms.

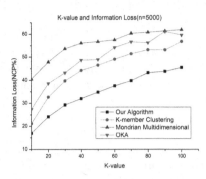

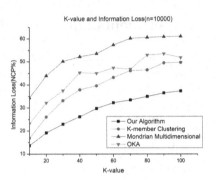

Fig. 5. Information loss metric (a)   **Fig. 6.** Information loss metric (b)

First, we fix the record number n in the data set and change the value of anonymous algorithm k for experimentation.

As shown in Fig. 5, when $n = 5000$, our algorithm obviously outperforms k-member and Mondrian in data loss metrics, and it has a higher data quality. Also, as the value of k increases, the more records are contained in the equivalent class, the higher information loss of the three algorithms have after anonymization. When the data size n is set as 10000 (shown in Fig. 6), the clustering result is better due to the increase of records, so the data points in the equivalent class are more compact and the data loss degree is significantly reduced.

We also conduct a test with a larger size of dataset, this time we handle almost the whole Adult dataset. Considering the influence of k on the experimental results, we try some bigger values of k. The result is satisfying (shown in Fig. 7). Compared with other algorithms, even when k is 500, the information loss of our algorithm is within 50%, about 10% lower than that of the others. And the smooth curve shows the stable performance. There are no random floats which are caused by the random choice of initial centroids just like one-time k-means.

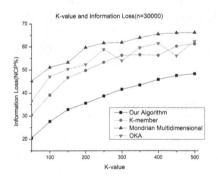

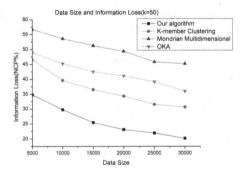

Fig. 7. Information loss with bigger k and dataset   **Fig. 8.** Information loss metric (c)

Then we consider the impact of the size of the data on the clustering result. We fixed the k-anonymous parameter k to 50, and adjust the data size n. The experimental results are shown in Fig. 8.

As we can see, with the increase of data volume, the information loss gradually decreases. When the data volume is 30,000, the information loss of our algorithm is about 20%, while the k-member clustering algorithm reaches about 30%, and the Mondrian algorithm even reaches 50%.

4.4   Analysis and Discussion

Time Complexity Analysis. K-anonymity is applied in the area of privacy data publishing, which is not sensitive to the execution time of data masking. So the clustering algorithms can come in handy though they have a little bit high time complexity. In other words, k-anonymity techniques are usually used in an offline environment. So the quality of anonymized data is a matter that should be taken into account first. From the experimental data above, we can see that our algorithm greatly reduces the information loss when the generalized dataset meets the k-anonymity standard, and it can provide better data for subsequent data mining and data analysis. Generally speaking, while the execution time in the offline environment is within an acceptable range, it's far more important to guarantee data quality than to reduce the running time. It is noted that a low information loss after k-anonymity is the basic support to a higher level of anonymization operation such as l-diversity.

In our experiment, we found that the execution time is influenced by both k and n. With the increase of k, the number of clusters will decrease accordingly. This will influence the times of calculating distance between records and existed clusters. The execution time will decrease while k increases.

In our algorithms, the vast majority of time complexity is caused by selecting records from the initial dataset S. At the same time, locating the latest centroid also holds a definite proportion. Because every new centroid is chosen according to the generated clusters. As the clustering goes on, the count of existing clusters increases at the same time. So the times of compare will go up from $1 * (n - k)$ to $(n - mk) \lfloor \frac{n}{k} \rfloor$. As (6) shows below, we can easily calculate that the time complexity of locating the latest centroid is $O(n^2)$. As for the record selecting, every cluster needs to add records until the number of members in the cluster reach k, the selecting process needs to find the closest record to the centroid. It is done by a traversal, and every time to find the best record means a traversal. Of course, the total number of traversal decreases as the residual dataset becomes smaller and smaller. This is where this part of time complexity comes from. We can also get the time complexity $O(n^2)$ as well from the following formula (7). So the total execution time is in $O(n^2)$.

$$T(clustering) = (n - k) * 1 + (n - 2k) * 2 + \cdots + (n - mk) \left\lfloor \frac{n}{k} \right\rfloor \qquad (6)$$

$$T(selectrecord) = (n - 1) + (n - 2) + \cdots + k \qquad (7)$$

Isolated Point in Anonymity Situation. Our algorithm takes the existence of isolated points in the data set into account. Some of the previous algorithms simply delete the isolated points, resulting in a large information loss in published data. While selecting the centroid of the next cluster, the positions of the previous clusters play an auxiliary role. Our clustering process has better fault tolerance. Isolated points in many data analysis scenarios have a certain influence on the clustering effect, so they are usually filtered out artificially. However, in data-oriented data anonymization scenarios, any discard of records will have some impact on the overall statistical characteristics of the data set. Though we cannot totally ensure data integrity, we should still try our best. Conversely, the existence of isolated points also guarantees the difference of data in the cluster in our opinion, making the anonymized data set more secure.

Moreover, it's better to handle the isolated points problem at an early stage. In this way, we can locate the closest record to the isolated points in advance, and minimize the inevitable information loss while generalizing. Locating isolated points first also ensure the long inter-cluster distances and uniform distribution of clusters. While looking for new centroids, we can first calculate distances between the candidate point and a few points around it so as to identify whether it is an isolated point. If the candidate point is an isolated point, then we put it in the residual dataset which is waiting to be processed after m clusters having been constructed. And the point near it will become a new candidate.

$$NCP(record) = \frac{1}{d} \left(NCP(attr_1) + NCP(attr_2) + \cdots + NCP(attr_d) \right) \qquad (8)$$

$$Manhattandis = \frac{1}{d} \left(diff_1 + diff_2 + \cdots + diff_d \right) \qquad (9)$$

It is mentioned in the previous chapters that we use the maximum average value of the total distance from new record to each generated centroid as the metric for the new centroid. As (8) and (9) shown above, this metric is very similar to the definition of the Manhattan distance. The Manhattan distance is the average value of distances in each dimension, which avoids the squared calculation in Euclidean distance and reduces the influence of a strict isolated points identifying strategy. A more important reason we choose the Manhattan distance is that the Manhattan distance fits with the definition of NCP well. Our thought is to distinguish the points which are too far from the normal data groups, and not to involve some "innocent" data. So the limit of the isolated distance could influence the results to some extent. To avoid some incorrect involvement, we could set the limit as 50% or even higher.

5   Conclusion

In this paper, we propose a new k-anonymity algorithm based on clustering for privacy preserving in data publishing. Compared with the classical k-anonymity algorithms, this algorithm can efficiently reduce the information loss, improve the accuracy of the quasi-identifier group in the published dataset, and provide better data for subsequent data mining. The experiment result shows that our algorithm could reduce the information loss generated by anonymization by about 20%. It also performs well with different values of k and n. We also propose some analysis according to our algorithm in the scenario of data anonymization.

References

1. Aggarwal, G., Kenthapadi, K., Khuller, S., Panigrahy, R., Thomas, D., Zhu, A.: Achieving anonymity via clustering. In: ACM SIGMOD-SIGACT-SIGART Symposium on Principles of Database Systems, pp. 153–162 (2006)
2. Byun, J.-W., Kamra, A., Bertino, E., Li, N.: Efficient k-anonymization using clustering techniques. In: Kotagiri, R., Krishna, P.R., Mohania, M., Nantajeewarawat, E. (eds.) DASFAA 2007. LNCS, vol. 4443, pp. 188–200. Springer, Heidelberg (2007). https://doi.org/10.1007/978-3-540-71703-4_18
3. Fung, B.C.M., Wang, K., Chen, R., Yu, P.S.: Privacy-preserving data publishing: a survey of recent developments. ACM Comput. Surv. **42**(4), 14 (2010)
4. Fung, B.C.M., Wang, K., Yu, P.S.: Top-down specialization for information and privacy preservation. In: International Conference on Data Engineering, pp. 205–216 (2005)
5. Gkountouna, O., Terrovitis, M.: Anonymizing collections of tree-structured data. IEEE Trans. Knowl. Data Eng. **27**(8), 2034–2048 (2015)
6. Lefevre, K., Dewitt, D.J., Ramakrishnan, R.: Mondrian multidimensional k-anonymity. In: International Conference on Data Engineering, p. 25 (2006)
7. Li, H., Zhu, H., Du, S., Liang, X., Shen, X.: Privacy leakage of location sharing in mobile social networks: attacks and defense. IEEE Trans. Dependable Sec. Comput. **PP**(99), 1 (2016)
8. Lin, J.L., Wei, M.C.: An efficient clustering method for k-anonymization. In: International Workshop on Privacy and Anonymity in Information Society, pp. 46–50. ACM (2008)
9. Meyerson, A., Williams, R.: On the complexity of optimal k-anonymity. In: Proceedings of the ACM Symposium on Principles of Database Systems, PODS 2004, pp. 223–228. ACM (2004)
10. Ozalp, I., Gursoy, M.E., Nergiz, M.E., Saygin, Y.: Privacy-preserving publishing of hierarchical data. ACM Trans. Priv. Secur. **19**(3), 7 (2016)
11. Palanisamy, B., Liu, L., Zhou, Y., Wang, Q.: Privacy-preserving publishing of multilevel utility-controlled graph datasets. ACM Trans. Internet Technol. **18**(2), 24 (2018)
12. Samarati, P., Sweeney, L.: Generalizing data to provide anonymity when disclosing information. In: The ACM SIGACT-SIGMOD-SIGART Symposium on Principles of Database Systems, vol. 98, p. 188. Citeseer (1998)
13. Samarati, P., Sweeney, L.: Protecting privacy when disclosing information: k-anonymity and its enforcement through generalization and suppression. Technical report, SRI International (1998)

14. Sweeney, L.: k-anonymity: a model for protecting privacy. Int. J. Uncertainty Fuzziness Knowl.-Based Syst. **10**(05), 557–570 (2002)
15. Wang, K., Yu, P.S., Chakraborty, S.: Bottom-up generalization: a data mining solution to privacy protection, pp. 249–256. IEEE (2004)
16. Xu, J., Wang, W., Pei, J., Wang, X., Shi, B., Fu, A.W.C.: Utility-based anonymization for privacy preservation with less information loss. ACM SIGKDD Explorations Newsl. **8**(2), 21–30 (2006)

Adaptive DAG Tasks Scheduling
with Deep Reinforcement Learning

Qing Wu[1], Zhiwei Wu[1], Yuehui Zhuang[2], and Yuxia Cheng[1(✉)]

[1] Hangzhou Dianzi University, Hangzhou, China
yxcheng@hdu.edu.cn
[2] Zhejiang Fangzheng Media Technology Research Institute, Hangzhou, China

Abstract. Efficient task scheduling is critical for improving system performance in the distributed heterogeneous computing environment. The DAG (Directed Acyclic Graph) tasks scheduling problem is NP-complete and it is hard to find an optimal schedule. Due to its key importance, the DAG tasks scheduling problem has been extensively studied in the literature. Many previously proposed heuristic algorithms are usually based on greedy methods, which still exists large optimization space to be explored. In this paper, we proposed an adaptive DAG tasks scheduling (ADTS) algorithm using deep reinforcement learning. The scheduling problem is properly defined with the reinforcement learning process. Efficient scheduling state space, action space and reward function are designed to train the policy gradient-based REINFORCE agent. Leveraging the algorithm's capability of exploring long term reward, the ADTS algorithm could achieve good scheduling policies. Experimental results showed the effectiveness of the proposed ADTS algorithm compared with the classic HEFT/CPOP algorithms.

Keywords: DAG scheduling · Heterogeneous
Deep reinforcement learning

1 Introduction

In distributed heterogeneous computing systems, a variety of computing resources are interconnected with high speed networks to support compute-intensive parallel and distributed applications. In these systems, efficient task scheduling is critical for improving system performance. Especially, as the modern hardware technology evolves rapidly, diverse sets of computing hardware unit, such as CPU, GPU, FPGA, TPU, and other accelerators, constitute more and more complex heterogeneous computing system. Modern high performance compute applications typically use the DAG (Directed Acyclic Graph) based compute model to represent an application's parallel compute tasks and their dependencies. How to schedule DAG tasks in the distributed heterogeneous computing system is an open research question.

© Springer Nature Switzerland AG 2018
J. Vaidya and J. Li (Eds.): ICA3PP 2018, LNCS 11335, pp. 477–490, 2018.
https://doi.org/10.1007/978-3-030-05054-2_37

Most parallel applications, including HPC applications, machine learning applications [1] etc., use the DAG tasks model in which nodes represent application tasks and edges represent inter-task data dependencies. Each node holds the computation cost of the task and each edge holds inter-task communication cost. To improve system efficiency, the goal of DAG tasks scheduling is to map tasks onto heterogeneous computing units and determine their execution order so that the tasks' dependencies are satisfied and the application's overall completion time is minimized.

Previous research [18] has shown that the general tasks scheduling problem is NP-complete and is hard to find an optimal schedule. Researchers [10] theoretically proved that the DAG tasks scheduling problem is also NP-complete and is more complex in practical scheduling system. Due to its key importance, the DAG tasks scheduling problem has been extensively studied in the literature.

Many heuristic algorithms have been proposed, such as list scheduling algorithms [17], genetic and evolutionary based random search algorithms [19], task duplication-based algorithms [2], etc. These algorithms are mostly heuristic in restricted application scenarios, and lack generality in the adaptation of various heterogeneous hardware and rapid changing application demand [11]. Machine learning based method is a reasonable way of adapting to the ever-changing hardware and software environment by learning from past scheduling policies.

Reinforcement learning [22] could be used for learning smart scheduling policies from past experiences. Recent researches have proposed task scheduling and device placement algorithms based on reinforcement learning. However, existing approaches either greatly simplify the scheduling model [9,14] that are unpractical or need a great amount of computing resources [6,11] to train the scheduling policies that are inefficient for most application scenarios.

In this paper, we proposed an Adaptive DAG Tasks Scheduling (ADTS) algorithm using deep reinforcement learning. The scheduling problem are properly defined with the reinforcement learning process. Efficient scheduling state space, action space and reward function are designed to train the policy gradient-based REINFORCE agent. Leveraging the algorithm's capability of exploring long term reward, we could achieve better scheduling efficiency. Experimental results showed the effectiveness of the proposed ADTS algorithm compared with the classic HEFT/CPOP algorithms. The main contributions of this paper include:

(1) We proposed an accurate and practical DAG tasks scheduling model based on reinforcement learning. To the best of our knowledge, this is the first work of addressing the static DAG tasks scheduling problem with the reinforcement learning process. Previous research have proposed similar model [14], but over simplifies the problem with assumptions of restricted machine performance, cluster status, and task classification.

(2) We designed efficient representations of state space, action space and reward function. Too large state space and action space without careful design will make the algorithm training time-consuming or even unable to convergence. The reward function design also plays an important role in the reinforcement learning process.

(3) We conduct extensive experiments to compare ADTS algorithm with the classic HEFT/CPOP algorithms under various types of DAG tasks and different configurations of heterogeneous systems.

The rest of this paper is organised as follows: Sect. 2 describes the related work. Section 3 presents the Adaptive DAG Tasks Scheduling (ADTS) algorithm design. Section 4 shows the experimental results. Finally, Sect. 5 concludes this paper and discusses future work.

2   Related Work

DAG tasks scheduling in the distributed heterogeneous computing environment has been extensively studied. The DAG tasks scheduling algorithms could be typically divided into static and dynamic scheduling. In static scheduling [8], the tasks' runtime and data dependencies are known in advance, and the scheduling policy is determined off-line. In dynamic scheduling [3], the tasks are assigned to processors at their arrival time and the schedule policy is determined on-line. Most DAG tasks scheduling algorithms belong to static scheduling.

Traditional static DAG tasks scheduling algorithms mainly include: (1) List scheduling algorithms [4,17]. The key idea of list scheduling algorithm is to order the scheduling tasks priority list and select a proper processor for each task. (2) Clustering based algorithms [7,15]. The key idea of clustering based algorithm is to map DAG tasks to a number of clusters. Tasks assigned to the same cluster will be executed on the same processor. (3) Genetic and evolutionary based random search algorithms [19,21]. The key idea of this group of algorithms is to use random policies to guide the scheduler through the problem space. The algorithms combine the results gained from previous search with some randomizing features to generate new results. (4) Task duplication based algorithms [2,20]. The key idea of these algorithms is to duplicate some of the tasks in different processors, which reduces the communication overhead in data-intensive applications.

These DAG tasks scheduling algorithms are heuristic and mainly designed by experts, which are carefully adapted to different application scenarios. However, with the rapid development of heterogeneous hardware and ever changing applications, traditional DAG tasks scheduling algorithms can not fully exploit system performance [6,11]. To design adaptive algorithms, researchers proposed machine learning based algorithms.

Zhang et al. [22] first proposed using classic reinforcement learning to address job-shop scheduling problem. However, the job-shop scheduling is different from the DAG tasks scheduling problem, where DAG tasks have more complex dependencies and data communication cost. Mao et al. [9] proposed using deep reinforcement learning to solve a simplified task s scheduling problem. The policy gradient based REINFORCE algorithm is used to train a fully connected policy network with 20 neurons. However, the scheduling problem is over simplified that treats the compute cluster as a single collection of resources, which is unpractical in real systems. Orhean et al. [14] proposed reinforcement learning based scheduling approach for heterogeneous distributed systems. This approach has additional assumptions such as machine performance, cluster status, and tasks types, which can not be easily applied in real DAG tasks scheduling. Mirhoseini et al. [6,11] proposed using reinforcement learning method to optimize device placement for TensorFlow computational graphs. These methods require a large amount of hardware to train policy network. The state space and action space definitions cannot accurately reveal the DAG and hardware topologies, which results in many invalid placement trials. Though previous researches have these shortcomings, the reinforcement learning based approach have demonstrated its benefits in terms of adaptiveness and better scheduling quality.

Unlike previous researches, we proposed a new reinforcement learning based scheduling algorithm that defines more accurate scheduling model using DAG graph structures and efficient state/action space representations. The proposed ADTS algorithm can be used in practice as the same way as traditional static DAG tasks scheduling algorithms.

3   Adaptive DAG Tasks Scheduling Algorithm Design

In this section, we present the ADTS algorithm design. First, the DAG tasks scheduling problem is defined. Second, we formulate the reinforcement learning process and present the design of three key elements of RL, the state space, the action space, and the reward function. Finally, we show the policy gradient based training algorithm and the policy network architecture design.

3.1   Problem Definition

We leverage the definition of DAG tasks graph in distributed heterogeneous system [17]. The scheduling model consists of three parts:

(i) **An application represented by a DAG tasks graph**, $G = (V, E)$, where V is a set of v tasks in the application, and E is the set of e edges between tasks.

- edge $(i, j) \in E$ denotes the precedence constraint such that task n_j must wait until task n_i finishes its execution.
- $data_{i,j}$ denotes the amount of data to be sent from task n_i to task n_j.

(ii) **A distributed heterogeneous computing system**, which consists of a set Q of q heterogeneous processors with a fully connected topology.

- W is a $v \times q$ computation cost matrix, and $w_{i,j}$ denotes the execution time of task n_i on processor p_j.
- B is a $q \times q$ matrix of the data communication bandwidth between processors, and $B_{m,n}$ denotes the communication bandwidth between processor p_m and processor p_n.
- L is a q-dimensional vector that denotes the communication initialization costs of processors, and L_m denotes the initialization costs of processor p_m.

- $c_{i,j} = L_m + \frac{data_{i,j}}{B_{m,n}}$ denotes the communication cost of edge (i, j), which is for the cost of sending data from task n_i (running on p_m) to task n_j (running on p_n).

(iii) **Performance criterion for scheduling.** Before presenting the final scheduling objective function, we first define the EST (Earliest Start Time), EFT (Earliest Finish Time), AST (Actual Start Time), and AFT (Actual Finish Time) attributes.

- $EST(n_i, p_j) = max \left\{ avail\,[j], \max_{n_m \in pred(n_i)} (AFT(n_m) + c_{m,i}) \right\}$ denotes the earliest start time of task n_i on processor p_j, where $avail\,[j]$ is the earliest time at which processor p_j is available for execution, and $pred(n_i)$ is the set of immediate predecessor tasks of task ni. The inner max block returns the time when all data required by task n_i has arrived at processor p_j.
- $EFT(n_i, p_j) = w_{i,j} + EST(n_i, p_j)$ denotes the earliest finish time of task n_i on processor p_j.
- $AST(n_m)$ denotes the actual start time of task n_m when it is scheduled on a processor p_j to execute.
- $AFT(n_m)$ denotes the actual finish time of task n_m after it is scheduled on a processor p_j and finishes execution.

The EST and EFT values can be computed recursively from the entry task n_{entry}, where $EST(n_{entry}, p_j) = 0$. After all tasks in a graph are finished execution, the AFT of the exit task n_{exit} is named the schedule length (also named $makespan$), which is defined as:

$$makespan = max\,\{AFT(n_{exit})\} \tag{1}$$

The objective function of the DAG tasks scheduling is to determine the assignment policies of an application's tasks to heterogeneous processors so that the schedule length is minimized.

3.2   Reinforcement Learning Formulation

Once the scheduling problem is defined, we propose to address the scheduling problem with the reinforcement learning method [16]. Figure 1 shows a brief diagram of the reinforcement learning based scheduling model. At time t, the scheduler observes the environment and receives an observation O_t. Depending on O_t, the scheduler determines an scheduling action A_t. After A_t is executed, the scheduler receives a reward R_t. The scheduler continues this process $(..., O_t, A_t, R_t, O_{t+1}, A_{t+1}, R_{t+1}, ...)$ until the end of schedule (task n_{exit} is scheduled). The observation O_t typically could be denoted as an state S_t.

We use the policy gradient method to optimize the scheduling actions so that the expected total reward could be maximized. The optimization objective function is defined as:

$$J(\theta) = E_{A \sim \pi(A|G;\theta)}[R(A)|G] \tag{2}$$

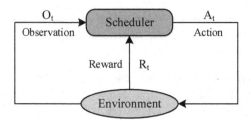

Fig. 1. Reinforcement learning based scheduling model

where θ denotes parameters of the policy network; A denotes the scheduling policy (a sequence of actions); $\pi(A|G; \theta)$ denotes the probabilities of scheduling policy A produced by policy network (defined by parameters θ) given the DAG tasks graph and heterogeneous system G; $R(A)$ denotes the total reward under the scheduling policy A; $J(\theta)$ denotes the expected reward of the scheduling policy A.

In the reinforcement learning, the design of the state space and action space representations as well as the design of reward function are important for the algorithm's overall performance. We describe the three key elements as follows.

State Space. The state space of the scheduling problem could be very large, which would include the state of the DAG tasks graph and the state of the distributed heterogeneous computing system. We design an efficient and compact representations of the state space, which is defined as:

$$S_t = [n, EST(n_i, p_1), ..., EST(n_i, p_q), w_{i,1}, ..., w_{i,q}] \qquad (3)$$

where S_t is the state (observation) at time t. n denotes the number of tasks that are not scheduled so far (listed in a waiting queue). $EST(n_i, p_j)$ is the earliest start time of task n_i on processor p_j, task n_i is the current task to be scheduled. We use the task's EST on all processors (from processor 1 to processor q) to represent the state of current system. The EST as described in Sect. 3.1 contains both the information of processor's load and the communication cost. Based on the Markov property, the current task's ESTs can be used as the state to summarize the previous situations before task n_i. $w_{i,j}$ is the computation cost of task n_i on processor p_j. To preserve the tasks precedence relationship in DAG, we adopt the upward rank [17] to list tasks in the waiting queue so that tasks with higher rank values are scheduled before tasks with lower rank value. Note that other task list methods are possible provided that the task precedence constraints must be satisfied.

Action Space. Once the state space is defined, the action space of the scheduling problem is straightforward. The action space is defined as:

$$A_t = \{p_i | p_1, ..., p_q\} \qquad (4)$$

where A_t is the scheduling action at time t. p_i denotes that the scheduler assigns processor p_i for the current task in the head of the waiting queue. The possible action at each time step is to assign one of the processors (range from processor p_1 to processor p_q) for the task to be scheduled.

Reward Function. The design of reward function could impact the scheduling policies, which is critical for the policy training. The reward at each time step should help guide the actual scheduling actions, and the accumulative long term reward should also reflect the final scheduling objective. Based on the above understanding, the reward function is defined as:

$$R_t = max\{EST(n_{i+1}, p_j)|_{j=1..q}\} - max\{EST(n_i, p_j)|_{j=1..q}\} \qquad (5)$$

where R_t is the immediate reward at time t. Task n_{i+1} is the task in the head of waiting queue after task n_i is scheduled with action A_t at time t. The reward R_t is obtained by calculating the increment of current schedule length after task n_i is scheduled. The current schedule length is represent by $max\{EST(n_i, p_j)|_{j=1..q}\}$.

3.3   Training Algorithm

We train an adaptive DAG tasks scheduling agent with the REINFORCE algorithm. The training algorithm is based on the policy gradient methods with many Monte-Carlo trials. The algorithm input consists of a differentiable parameterization $\pi(a|s, \theta)$ and the training step size α. Initially, the policy parameters θ are set to random numbers. During the training process, we generate N number of episodes to train the policy network. Each episode represents a complete schedule of DAG tasks, which starts from the entry task state S_0, action A_0, and the corresponding reward R_1, to the end of the exit task state S_{T-1}, action A_{T-1}, and the final reward R_T. For each step of an episode, the algorithm calculates the long term reward G with an discounted factor γ. The policy parameter θ is updated in every step with $\nabla ln\pi(A_t|S_t, \theta)$, which equals the fractional vector $\frac{\nabla \pi(A_t|S_t, \theta)}{\pi(A_t|S_t, \theta)}$ named the *eligibility vector*.

Algorithm 1. REINFORCE: Monte-Carlo Policy-Gradient Control for π_*.

Input:
    A differentiable policy parameterization $\pi(a|s, \theta)$;
    Algorithm parameter: step size $\alpha > 0$;
1: Initialize random policy parameter $\theta \in R$;
2: Loop for N episodes:
3:    Generate an episode $S_0, A_0, R_1, ..., S_{T-1}, A_{T-1}, R_T$, following $\pi(*|*, \theta)$;
4:    Loop for each step of the episode $t = 0, 1, ..., T - 1$:
5:       $G \leftarrow \sum_{k=t+1}^{T} \gamma^{k-t-1} R_k$
6:       $\theta \leftarrow \theta + \alpha\gamma^t G\nabla ln\pi(A_t|S_t, \theta)$

---

4   Experiments

In this section, we evaluate the proposed ADTS algorithm comparing with the classic baseline algorithms. The DAG tasks graphs are generated using the graph generator [17] to represent the real world applications. First, we present the experiment settings and the performance evaluation metrics. Then, the comparative experimental results are described in the following subsection.

4.1   Methodology

The experiment hardware platform is configured with two Intel Xeon E5-2600V3 processors, four NVIDIA TITAN Xp GPUs, 64 GB DDR4 memory, and 4 TB hard disk. The server is connected with S5150X-16S-EI high speed switch. The software platform is configured with ubuntu 16.04, Tensorflow 1.5, python 2.7, cuda9.1 and cudnn7.7. We generate a total of 1000 DAG tasks graphs using the graph generator [17], and simulate the DAG tasks scheduling process with a in-house simulator. The distributed heterogeneous system is configured with 3–7 heterogeneous processors with fully connected communication networks.

In the ADTS algorithm, the parameters used in the reinforcement learning are described as follows. The policy network architecture is configured with 3–5 layers of sequence-to-sequence neural networks with each layer having 10–50 neurons. The scale of policy networks depend on the problem space of DAG graphs and the heterogeneous hardware configuration. The learning rate step size α is 0.0005 and the discounted factor γ is 0.99. The number of Monte-Carlo training episodes N is configured with 2500.

In the comparative evaluation, we use the following three performance metrics.

- **Schedule Length Ratio (SLR).** The key performance metric of a scheduling algorithm is the schedule length (makespan) of its schedule policy. As the sizes of DAG graphs are different among applications, we normalize the schedule length to a lower bound, which is named SLR. The SLR value is defined as
$$SLR = \frac{makespan}{\sum_{n_i \in CP_{MIN}} min_{p_j \in Q} \{w_{i,j}\}} \tag{6}$$
  where the CP_{MIN} denotes that the critical path of a DAG graph is based on the minimum computation costs.
- **Speedup.** The value of speedup for a given graph is the ratio of the sequential execution time to the makespan. The speedup is defined as
$$Speedup = \frac{min_{p_j \in Q} \left\{ \sum_{n_i \in V} w_{i,j} \right\}}{makespan} \tag{7}$$

  where the sequential execution time is obtained by scheduling all DAG tasks to a single processor that minimizes the overall computation costs (denoted as $min_{p_j \in Q} \left\{ \sum_{n_i \in V} w_{i,j} \right\}$).

– **Running time of the Algorithms.** An scheduling algorithm's running time is its execution time of producing the output schedule policy for a given DAG tasks graph. This metric represents the cost of the scheduling algorithm.

The DAG tasks graph generator uses the following parameters to quantify the characteristics of the generated DAG graphs, which is similar to [17].

$^*SET_V = \{20,40,60,80,100\}$
$^*SET_{CCR} = \{0.1,0.5,1.0,5.0,10.0\}$
$^*SET_\alpha = \{0.5,1.0,2.0\}$
$^*SET_{out\_degree} = \{1,2,3,4,5,v\}$
$^*SET_\beta = \{0.1,0.25,0.5,0.75,1.0\}$

where SET_V denotes the number of tasks in the graph, SET_{CCR} denotes the set of parameter values of the Communication to Computation Ratio (CCR), SET_α denotes the set of parameter values of the graph shape parameter α. SET_{out_degree} denotes the set of values of out degree of a task. SET_β denotes the set of parameter values of the range percentage of computation costs on processors (β) that quantifies the heterogeneity of the processors.

4.2 Performance Comparison

In this subsection, we show the performance comparisons of three DAG tasks scheduling algorithms, the proposed ADTS algorithm, the classic HEFT algorithm and CPOP algorithm [17]. The HEFT (Heterogeneous Earliest Finish Time) algorithm selects the task with the highest upward rank value at each scheduling step and assigns the selected task to the processor that minimizes its earliest finish time. The CPOP (Critical-Path-on-a-Processor) algorithm uses the summation of the upward rank and downward rank to denote a task's priority and the selected tasks with the highest priority is assigned to the critical-path processor; otherwise, it is assigned to a processor that minimizes the earliest finish time.

The ADTS algorithm is non-deterministic, we show the average value of ten individual runs in the experiment. The DAG tasks graphs are generated using the parameters listed in Sect. 4.1. As modern big data and machine learning based applications are mostly data-intensive, the DAG graphs are generated with a higher portion of CCR value.

Figure 2 shows the comparison of the average schedule length ratio between the ADTS, HEFT, and CPOP algorithms. The SLR metric represents the schedule quality of each algorithm (lower is better). The closer the SLR value to one, the better the scheduling policy. As the normalization uses the theoretical minimum computation costs, the SLR cannot be less than one.

As can be seen from Fig. 2, the ADTS algorithm outperforms both the HEFT and CPOP algorithms. In the 20 tasks DAG graph, the average SLR of ADTS algorithm is 3.391 and the average SLR of HEFT and CPOP are 4.262 and 4.323 respectively, which has 25% reduction of the average SLR. Similarly, in the

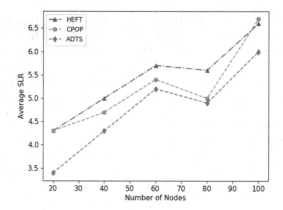

Fig. 2. Comparison of the Schedule Length Ratio (SLR).

40, 60,80 and 100 tasks of DAG graph scheduling experiments, the SLR of ADTS is consistently lower than both HEFT and CPOP algorithms. The lower SLR achieved by the ADTS algorithm demonstrates that the reinforcement learning could better explore the long term reward, which leads to the better scheduling policies than the heuristic algorithms.

Figure 3 shows the comparison of the average speedup between the ADTS, HEFT, and CPOP algorithms. The average speedup represents the algorithm's ability of scheduling tasks to explore parallel performance (higher is better). Note that the speedup value is calculated via dividing the sequential execution time by the makespan. The sequential execution time is represented by assigning all tasks to a single processor that minimizes the cumulative computation costs. If selecting the processor that maximizes the cumulative computation costs, the value of speedup will be higher. As can be seen from Fig. 3, the ADTS algorithm

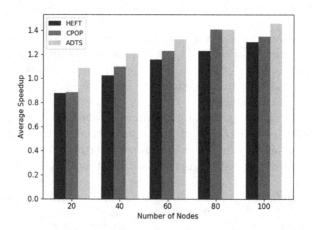

Fig. 3. Comparison of the average speedup.

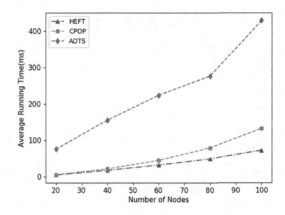

Fig. 4. Comparison of the average running time.

achieves better speedup than HEFT and CPOP algorithms. In the 20 tasks DAG graph experiment, the speedup of ADTS algorithm is 1.087, while the speedup of HEFT and CPOP algorithms are 0.879 and 0.886 respectively. The ADTS algorithm could achieve more than 20% speedup improvement compared with HEFT and CPOP algorithms.

Figure 4 shows the comparison of the average running time of the ADTS, HEFT, and CPOP algorithms. The average running time of an scheduling algorithm represents the average computation costs of execution the algorithm. As can be seen from Fig. 4, the ADTS algorithm has higher running time compared with the HEFT and CPOP algorithms. This is because the HEFT algorithm involves the deep neural network reference computations to produce the scheduling policy, which has higher overhead compared with the HEFT and CPOP algorithm. The CPOP algorithm has higher running time compared with the HEFT algorithm. The time complexity of both the CPOP algorithm and the HEFT algorithm is $O(e \times q)$, where e is the number of edges in the graph and q the number of processors. The time complexity of the ADTS algorithm depends on the policy network architecture. If the neural network reference computation cost is defined as c, then the time complexity of the ADTS algorithm is $O(c \times v)$, where v is the number of tasks.

4.3 Discussion

From the above comparative performance evaluation, we observe that the reinforcement learning algorithm could achieve better scheduling policies than the classic HEFT and CPOP algorithms. However, as the deep reinforcement learning involves neural network parameters training and inference computation overhead, the running time of the ADTS algorithm is somewhat higher than the heuristic greedy-based algorithms. Fortunately, the ADTS algorithm is designed for static DAG scheduling, which is acceptable of the relatively high running time considering its better schedule quality. What's more, the ADTS algorithm

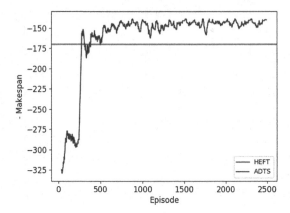

Fig. 5. The learning curve of the ADTS training algorithm.

is non-deterministic. In some cases, the training process could not successfully converge to obtain the good policy network model. The reinforcement learning parameters tuning and the network architecture design need some trials to obtain a robust algorithm.

Figure 5 shows an learning curve of the ADTS training algorithm under the 20 tasks DAG scheduling environment. As can be seen from the learning curve, the algorithm learns very fast within 400 episodes and gradually exceeds the classic HEFT algorithm after 500 episodes training. In our experiments, some of the DAG graphs can not be successfully trained to surpass the classic algorithms. We infer that this problem is due to the unsuitable parameters and the neural network architecture configurations. This unstable training problem needs further investigation and remains the future work.

5   Conclusion

In this paper, we proposed an adaptive DAG tasks scheduling (ADTS) algorithm using deep reinforcement learning. The efficient scheduling state space, action space, and reward function were designed to train the policy gradient-based REINFORCE agent. Using the Monte-Carlo method, a large amount of training episodes were generated in a scheduling simulator and the policy network parameters were updated using the simulated episodes. Experimental results showed the effectiveness of the proposed ADTS algorithm compared with the competitive HEFT and CPOP algorithms.

In the future work, we plan to integrate more advanced algorithms, such as DQN [13], A3C [12], Monte-Carlo Tree Search [5], as well as new network architectures into the reinforcement learning process and study their performance in addressing the DAG tasks scheduling problem.

References

1. Abadi, M., et al.: TensorFlow: a system for large-scale machine learning. OSDI **16**, 265–283 (2016)
2. Ahmad, I., Kwok, Y.K.: On exploiting task duplication in parallel program scheduling. IEEE Trans. Parallel Distrib. Syst. **9**(9), 872–892 (1998)
3. Amalarethinam, D., Josphin, A.M.: Dynamic task scheduling methods in heterogeneous systems: a survey. Int. J. Comput. Appl. **110**(6), 12–18 (2015)
4. Arabnejad, H., Barbosa, J.G.: List scheduling algorithm for heterogeneous systems by an optimistic cost table. IEEE Trans. Parallel Distrib. Syst. **25**(3), 682–694 (2014)
5. Browne, C.B., et al.: A survey of monte carlo tree search methods. IEEE Trans. Comput. Intell. AI Games **4**(1), 1–43 (2012)
6. Goldie, A., Mirhoseini, A., Steiner, B., Pham, H., Dean, J., Le, Q.V.: Hierarchical planning for device placement. In: Proceedings of ICLR, pp. 1–11 (2018)
7. Kanemitsu, H., Hanada, M., Nakazato, H.: Clustering-based task scheduling in a large number of heterogeneous processors. IEEE Trans. Parallel Distrib. Syst. **27**(11), 3144–3157 (2016)
8. Kwok, Y.K., Ahmad, I.: Static scheduling algorithms for allocating directed task graphs to multiprocessors. ACM Comput. Surv. **31**(4), 406–471 (1999)
9. Mao, H., Alizadeh, M., Menache, I., Kandula, S.: Resource management with deep reinforcement learning. In: Proceedings of the 15th ACM Workshop on Hot Topics in Networks, pp. 50–56. ACM (2016)
10. Mayer, R., Mayer, C., Laich, L.: The TensorFlow partitioning and scheduling problem: it's the critical path! In: Proceedings of the 1st Workshop on Distributed Infrastructures for Deep Learning, pp. 1–6. ACM (2017)
11. Mirhoseini, A., et al.: Device placement optimization with reinforcement learning. In: Proceedings of ICML, pp. 2430–2439 (2017)
12. Mnih, V., et al.: Asynchronous methods for deep reinforcement learning. In: International Conference on Machine Learning, pp. 1928–1937 (2016)
13. Mnih, V., et al.: Human-level control through deep reinforcement learning. Nature **518**(7540), 529 (2015)
14. Orhean, A.I., Pop, F., Raicu, I.: New scheduling approach using reinforcement learning for heterogeneous distributed systems. J. Parallel Distrib. Comput. (2017)
15. Palis, M.A., Liou, J.C., Wei, D.S.L.: Task clustering and scheduling for distributed memory parallel architectures. IEEE Trans. Parallel Distrib. Syst. **7**(1), 46–55 (1996)
16. Sutton, R.S., Barto, A.G.: Reinforcement Learning: An Introduction. MIT Press, Cambridge (2011)
17. Topcuoglu, H., Hariri, S., Wu, M.Y.: Performance-effective and low-complexity task scheduling for heterogeneous computing. IEEE Trans. Parallel Distrib. Syst. **13**(3), 260–274 (2002)
18. Ullman, J.D.: NP-complete scheduling problems. J. Comput. Syst. Sci. **10**(3), 384–393 (1975)
19. Wu, A.S., Yu, H., Jin, S., Lin, K.C., Schiavone, G.: An incremental genetic algorithm approach to multiprocessor scheduling. IEEE Trans. Parallel Distrib. Syst. **15**(9), 824–834 (2004)
20. Xian-Fu, M., Wei-Wei, L.: A DAG scheduling algorithm based on selected duplication of precedent tasks. J. Comput.-Aided Des. Comput. Graph. **6**, 023 (2010)

21. Xu, Y., Li, K., Hu, J., Li, K.: A genetic algorithm for task scheduling on hetero-geneous computing systems using multiple priority queues. Inf. Sci. **270**, 255–287 (2014)
22. Zhang, W., Dietterich, T.G.: A reinforcement learning approach to job-shop scheduling. IJCAI **95**, 1114–1120 (1995)

RFGRU: A Novel Approach for Mobile Application Traffic Identification

Yu Zhang[1(✉)], Yufei Jin[1], Jianzhong Zhang[1], Huan Wu[1], and Xueqiang Zou[2,3]

[1] College of Cyberspace Security, Nankai University, Tianjin 300350, China
{zhangyu1981,zhangjz}@nankai.edu.cn, {jinyufei,wuhuan}@mail.nankai.edu.cn
[2] National Computer Network Emergency Response Technical Team/Coordination Center of China, Beijing, China
zouxueqiang@iie.ac.cn
[3] School of Cyber Security, University of Chinese Academy of Scienses, Beijing, China

Abstract. Billions of users access the Internet through their mobile devices to get services. Mobile traffic classification has become a hot topic in recent years due to its large volume of traffic data. Many of the studies that have been done show that the key point of mobile traffic identification is to extract signatures. However, the process of signature extraction is usually too complex to perform. In this paper, we propose a novel method RFGRU which is based on the Random Forest and gated recurrent unit, to address the mobile traffic classification problem. Several experiments are performed to verify the effectiveness of RFGRU. The results show that RFGRU delivers a good recognition rate and can accurately identify the traffic of the mobile applications.

Keywords: Mobile traffic classification · Random Forest
Gated recurrent unit

1 Introduction

Traffic classification is crucial to classic network management tasks, such as service quality assurance, bandwidth provisioning, billing, and abnormal behavior detection and so on [1].

Nowadays mobile devices such as smart phones and tablets PC have become more and more popular. Mobile traffic from these mobile devices has grown rapidly in recent years and is expected to reach 49 exabytes per month by 2021 [2]. Therefore, it is important to analyze mobile application flows.

Most mobile applications run over the HTTP or HTTPS protocol [3,4]. This means the traditional port-based classification techniques or machine learning classification techniques [5–8] cannot be applied effectively for the mobile traffic classification. Most of the recent studies aim at HTTP packet classification. Some studies make use of the unique strings that exist on HTTP packet load [3,4,9], others rely on setting up a profile for each mobile application [10–12], or the

© Springer Nature Switzerland AG 2018
J. Vaidya and J. Li (Eds.): ICA3PP 2018, LNCS 11335, pp. 491–506, 2018.
https://doi.org/10.1007/978-3-030-05054-2_38

reverse engineering [13–15]. However, all these previous methods pay attention to find the fixed characters of the payload, and ignore the important information implied by the word order. We propose RFGRU which concentrates on the order information of words in the payload and uses the sequence prediction model for classification.

LSTM model is a well-known sequence prediction model which overcomes the long distance dependence of traditional recurrent neural network (RNN), and is often used in event prediction, sentiment classification and handwritten word recognition [16–18]. However, this model is very complex which results in the problem of long training and predicting time. Therefore, we adopt the much simpler variant gated recurrent unit (GRU) [19], however it is still time-consuming.

Random Forest constructs a collection of trees [20], wherein each tree is grown by random independent data sampling and feature splitting. Each tree's training and forecasting process is independent and fast. It is easy to parallelize, and can handle high dimensional data. It is a widely used classifier, and its effect has been proved effective in many situations [21]. But it is prone to over-fitting problem, resulting in lower accuracy of classification.

Thus, we propose RFGRU, which absorbs the advantages of the fast speed of Random Forest and the high accuracy of GRU. RFGRU uses Random Forest model to filter out easily categorized samples, and the rest is left to GRU model. RFGRU mainly consists of two stages: the training phase and the identification phase. In training phase, we use labeled training data to establish RFGRU model and divide the payload into word sequence and extract simple text features as classification features of Random Forest model. There is no need to extract features when training GRU model, and the last word of the word sequence will be used as the predicted category. As a result, the mobile application classification problem is transformed into the word sequence prediction problem. In the identification phase, we need to extract the same features as the training phase and use RFGRU model for classification.

The major contributions of our work are summarized as follows.

- To the best of our knowledge, this is the first work to use GRU model in mobile application traffic classification;
- The proposed RFGRU method absorbs the advantages of the Random Forest model and GRU model, and eliminates the complex feature extraction process;
- The parameters of RFGRU are simulated through experiments and the validity of the method is proved.

The rest of this paper is organized as follows. Section 2 presents a critical review of traffic classification. In Sect. 3, we propose the architecture of mobile traffic classification. For performance evaluation, experiments and results are reported on Sect. 4. Finally, Sect. 5 concludes this paper.

2   Releated Work

Traffic classification methods fall into three categories: port-based methods [22], machine learning based methods [5–8] and payload-based methods [23].

Most mobile applications use the HTTP protocol for data transmission. In this case, not only the ports are fixed, but also the traffic features are similar, as a result the first two methods are no longer suitable for mobile traffic classification. We mainly introduce the payload-based methods.

The payload-based methods are also known as deep packet inspection (DPI), which can be classified into two subcategories: application signature-based methods and protocol parsing-based methods.

The main idea of the first subcategory (application signature-based methods) is to extract fixed strings from the application traffic, or to establish the profile of an application. Erman [3] used the User-Agent filed of HTTP header to identify mobile traffic. This method is effective for applications of iOS. However, for android apps, since the android developers generally put some generic strings in the User-Agent field, this method cannot recognize the traffic well, and the application coverage is very low. Tongaonkar [4] used Manifest.xml file to extract unique identifiers embedded by third parties for classification, which not only relies on human experience, but also delivers limited application coverage. FLOWER system extracted the HTTP header field as the app feature [9], and new app signatures can be inferred by observing the co-occurrence of app features. But this approach still requires an initial set of features at the beginning.

In the AMPLES framework, the problem of mobile application identification was regarded as information retrieval [10]. Each application was represented as a document, and the document content represented the characteristics of the application. The process of identifying the application traffic is equivalent to searching the most similar document in the document library. The SAMPLES framework used a small collection of samples to extract identifiers and lexical context associated with identifier strings, both of which were used to construct the conjunctive rules [11]. However, complex sequence alignment and regular extraction process are required to construct the conjunction rules. The literature [12] collected traffic of all possible operations in the android application, and generated the application's network profiles. When unknown network flow arrives, find the state machine with the highest matching rate, and the corresponding application is the label of network flow. However, this method needs to collect the traffic of the target android application for various operations in advance, and the computational complexity is high when calculating the matching degree of state machines.

The main idea of the second subcategory (protocol parsing-based methods) is to extract the format of the application protocol through reverse engineering. The authors of [13] proposed a semantic approach to identify traffic. Payload data is represented as n-gram and the LDA method is used to extract the keywords which are used for classification. The main drawback is that this method has high computational complexity and slow recognition speed. ProHack extracted the protocol keywords from traffic based on the Bayesian statistical model, and used the extracted keywords to identify network protocol traffic by semi-supervised learning method [14]. Based on the improved voting system algorithm, the authors of [15] divided the payload into words which were ranked according to the length, frequency and position. The words with high score are used as keywords to identify the traffic. However, this method might filter out some low-frequency keywords, which leads to the reduction of classification effect.

In summary, the previous studies mainly focus on the extraction of characteristic characters, but RFGRU do not pay much effort for it. Instead, it concentrates on the implicit information between word sequences.

3   Architecture

This section will give a detailed description of RFGRU. Firstly, the overall framework of RFGRU will be explained. Then we will introduce each component of the framework.

3.1   System Framework

In RFGRU, we need to calculate the probability that a sample belongs to each category. If the difference between probabilities is very small, the sample is likely to be misclassified, otherwise we tend to think that the samples is classified correctly. In terms of using a binary classifier, consider the following two cases: the probability that a sample belongs to the first category is 0.4, the probability that it belongs to the second category is 0.6, and the final classification result is the second category; the probability that a sample belongs to the first category is 0.1, and the probability that it belongs to the second category is 0.9, the final classification result is the second category too. We believe that the second case is more credible. For the first case, we need a more powerful classifier in order to get more accurate result.

In this paper, traffic is classified into two categories: traffic of target applications and non-target applications. The first classifier of RFGRU uses Random Forest. For each category, predict the probability that each sample belongs to it. If the difference between the two probabilities is less than the threshold, then GRU model is required to reclassify the sample. There are two reasons for using cascades of classifiers. Firstly, the classification accuracy of Random Forest is not very high. Secondly, if only using GRU for classification, we will get a much higher accuracy, and a much longer predicting time. With the combination of these two classifiers, we can not only save time, but also get a higher accuracy.

Figure 1 presents the details of the proposed framework. Our framework involves two major phases: (I) Training phase; (II) Identifying phase.

We work on labeled samples to build a classification model for each target application. The Training phase includes (1) Preprocessing stage, (2) Random Forest modeling stage, and (3) GRU modeling stage. In the Preprocessing stage,

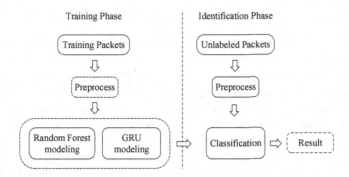

Fig. 1. The system framework

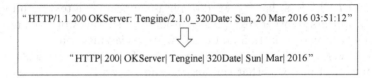

Fig. 2. An example of word segmentation

HTTP payload will be extracted and preprocessed. In the stage of Random Forest modeling, each payload obtained in the previous stage will be regarded as a text. This text is used to establish Vector Space Model (VSM) and Random Forest classifier. Since the GRU is a deep learning model, it does not need to extract features manually. The original payload data can be imported into GRU model for training.

The Identifying phase consists of two stages, including: (1) Preprocessing stage; (2) Classification. In this phase, RFGRU will combine the Random Forest classifier and the GRU classifier to predict unlabeled samples.

Each stage is described in detail below.

3.2 Preprocess Phase

In this stage, the HTTP payload will be processed and the contents before ''\r\n\r\n'' will be intercepted. The contents contain the HTTP request line and request message, which provides rich information. Meanwhile, all the invisible characters are filtered to reduce the training time, that is to say, we only keep ASCII characters between 32 and 126.

After that, we need to conduct word segmentation on each payload. Since most loads are in English, we can simply use spaces, slashes, etc. to split. Then we exclude the words that are too short, since those words are more likely to be meaningless. In this work, we delete words with length less than 2. An example of participle is shown in Fig. 2.

3.3   Random Forest Classification Modeling Phase

The input to this stage is the preprocessed payload, and the output is the Random Forest model.

We regard the payload as text data. Since the Random Forest can only accept mathematical input, we need to transform texts into vectors, that is, to establish VSM. The main idea of VSM is to map each text to a point in the vector space. The biggest advantage is that text can be represented as a vector, which makes all kinds of mathematical processing possible.

In Preprocessing stage, we can get all words that have appeared, denoted by $W = \{w_1, w_2, ..., w_n\}$, which is called "bag of words". Calculate $TFIDF$ (term frequency–inverse document frequency) value of all words in W, where TF denotes Term Frequency, IDF denotes Inverse Document Frequency. The basic idea of $TFIDF$ is that if a word or phrase appears in a text with high TF and rarely appears in other texts, it is considered that this word or phrase has a good ability of categorization and is suitable for classification.

Given a corpus D, let $tf_{i,j}$ be the frequency of word w_i in payload j, let df be the number of payloads that contain w_i, and let $|D|$ be the total number of packet payloads. The $TFIDF$ value of w_i in payload j is defined as follows.

$$TFIDF(w_i) = log(tf_{i,j}) \times log(\frac{|D|}{df}) \tag{1}$$

Each word can be represented by a $TFIDF$ value. A $TFIDF$ vector can represent a payload. However, if all words are used, the computation is large and the result contains noise. We sort $TFIDF$ values of all words and select the top $Ratio \times |D|$ words in the rankings, as the word bag for VSM.

So far, we have converted payload to $TFIDF$ vector and set up VSM. Then, $TFIDF$ vector is used as classification feature to establish the Random Forest model.

3.4   GRU Classification Modeling Stage

GRU Model Design. We regard the traffic classification of mobile application as a sequence prediction problem, so we can regard the load as a word sequence, and the predicted category as the last word of the word sequence. The GRU model extracts the hidden information of word sequences and reclassifies samples that cannot be accurately classified by random forest.

We use a single layer GRU network for traffic classification, and the network structure is shown in Fig. 3. The preprocessed text is used as the input of the input layer. In our approach, the input layer converts the load to a word sequence of the specified length, which is denoted as *sequence_length* and is set to 20,000. The words exceeding *sequence_length* are ignored, and insufficient parts are padded with 0. Embedding layer is added between the input layer and the GRU layer, which is used to create word vectors for incoming words. The output of the embedding layer will be entered into the GRU layer. The weights of the embedding layer are initialized with third-party word embeddings, word2vec, which can translate words into vectors in vector space, including two training models: CBOW and Skip-Gram. In this paper, we select CBOW model and set *embedding_dim* to 300.

A payload is processed through the embedding layer and is represented as *sequence_length* × *embedding_dim* tensor. This tensor is the input of GRU layer and is used to calculate GRU cell. We also insert the dropout layer to discard hidden layer neurons with a certain probability to prevent over-fitting. Finally, the class distribution vector is obtained through the softmax layer.

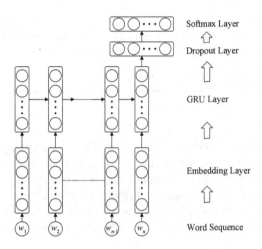

Fig. 3. Overview of the GRU model

Function Details. The equations for calculating GRU cell is shown below:

$$r_t = \sigma(W_r \cdot [h_{t-1}, x_t]) \tag{2}$$

$$z_t = \sigma(W_z \cdot [h_{t-1}, x_t]) \tag{3}$$

$$h_t = (1 - z_t) * h_{t-1} + z_t * \widetilde{h}_t \tag{4}$$

$$\widetilde{h}_t = \tanh(W_{\widetilde{h}} \cdot [r_t * h_{t-1}, x_t]) \tag{5}$$

x_t is the input data at t th time step, which represents the $1 \times embedding\_dim$ vector of the t th word. The reset gate r_t is computed by Eq. 2, where σ is the sigmoid function and h_{t-1} is the previous state. Symbol $[h_{t-1}, x_t]$ represents a hidden state h_{t-1} is connected to an input vector x_t. z_t denotes update gate, which controls how much information is memorized to current hidden state, its formula is Eq. 3. The activation value of hidden node h_t is computed by Eq. 4, where $\widetilde{h}_t$ is computed by Eq. 5.

The initial value of W_r, W_z and $W_{\widetilde{h}}$ are randomly generated and their values are constantly updated during GRU training. When the maximum number of iterations is reached, GRU model training is completed.

Algorithm 1. Mobile traffic identification

Input: T_l: test set;

        Threshold: if lower than *Threshold* need *GRU* to reclassify;

        RF: Random Forest classify model;

        GRU: GRU classify model;

Output: *Classtype*: the classification results

1: **for all** $x \in T_l$ **do**

2:    *class_prob* = $RF(x)$

3:    **if** $|class\_prob[target] - class\_prob[non - target]| \leq Threshold$ **then**

4:        *Classtype* $\leftarrow GRU(x)$

5:    **else**

6:        *Classtype* $\leftarrow$ label corresponding to the maximum probability in *class_prob*

7:    **end if**

8: **end for**

9: **return** *Classtype*

3.5   Identification

The identification phase consists three parts: (1) Preprocessing stage, performs the same operation as the training phase; (2) Random Forest classification stage, calculates the probability that a sample belongs to two categories. If the difference of these two probabilities exceeds *Threshold*, the category with the higher probability can be directly outputted as the predict label. Otherwise, the sample needs to be reclassified by GRU classifier; (3) GRU classification stage, outputs the final results.

Algorithm 1 describes the Identification phase.

4   Experimental Evaluation

In order to verify the effectiveness of the proposed method, we select 15 applications that are popular in China for testing. These applications cover most software categories, including social networking, shopping, instant messaging, and so on. The input of the framework is mobile application traffic, and the output is the estimated classification result. In this section, we first introduce our dataset used in the experiment. Then the process of tuning parameters is introduced. Finally, the experimental results are shown and compared with other methods.

4.1   Data Set

We collect traffic for 15 applications, including Taobao, Youku, BaiduSearch, etc., and then download and install these applications to Android phones. When capturing traffic, only the target application runs, other applications are closed to ensure the purity of captured traffic. We use the monkey tool [24] to launch the application and simulate various operations. And then we mix the target application traffic and non-target application traffic, randomly select 90% as the training set, 10% as the test set. The data description is shown in Table 1.

Table 1. Dataset description

Size	Packets	HTTP packets
11.1G	11,223,324	550,581

Table 2. Parameter description

Parameter	Description
Ratio	Proportion of keywords in Random Forest modeling stage
Epochs	Epochs in GRU modeling stage
Outdim	Output size of GRU layer
Batchsize	Used in Adam to optimize the loss function
Thresold	Bound of reclassified

4.2 Parameter Tuning

The parameters used in this paper are shown in Table 2.

We first discuss how to select a suitable value for *Ratio*, and then study the value of *Thresold*. Finally, present results for different values of *Epochs*, *Outdim* and *Batchsize*.

Ratio affects the accuracy and time consumption of Random Forest classifier. If *Ratio* is too small, the accuracy of Random Forest is low, and the number of samples that need to be reclassified increases. If *Ratio* is set too large, Random Forest classification will not only increase the prediction time, but also may contain noise and reduce accuracy. Therefore it is very important to choose a suitable *Ratio* value.

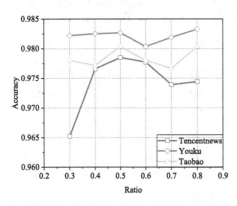

Fig. 4. Relationship of *Ratio* and *Accuracy*

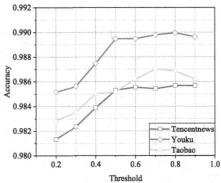

Fig. 5. Accuracy of different *Thresold*

For this purpose, we take different values of *Ratio* to observe the classification accuracies of Tencentnews, Taobao and Youku. We carry out experiments for $Ratio = \{0.3, ..., 0.7, 0.8\}$. Figure 4 shows the accuracy of different *Ratio*.

As we can see from the Fig. 4, when $Ratio < 0.5$, the accuracy of Youku does not change much, and the curves of Tencentnews and Taobao show a general upward trend. The accuracy is the highest when $Ratio = 0.5$, and then begins to decline. Therefore, we choose $Ratio = 0.5$ for the accuracy test of the final application recognition.

We then carry out experiments for $Threshold = \{0.2, 0.3, ..., 0.8, 0.9\}$. It can be seen from the Fig. 5, the higher the *Threshold*, the better the classifying performance will be. This is because the accuracy of the GRU classifier is originally higher than the Random Forest classifier. The high *Threshold* allows the GRU model to classify more traffic, and thus the accuracy of the model increases. The drawback is that it will take much longer training and predicting time. For the tradeoff between the time and performance, we set $Threshold = 0.7$.

We introduce how to use the GRU model for mobile traffic classification in Sect. 3.4. We use the loss value of the training set as a measure of model classification. The training model classifier needs to iterate continuously until the loss converges to the minimum. Therefore, it is very important to select the appropriate number of iterations (*Epochs*). In addition, we use the Adam optimization strategy. Adam is an optimization algorithm that can replace the traditional stochastic gradient descent process. It was first proposed in the 2015 ICLR paper, and obtained better experimental results than SGD [25]. As a result, we present the loss value of the training set for varying values of *Epochs*, *Outdim* and *Batchsize*.

For this purpose, we set $Epochs = \{2, 4, 8, 16, 32, 48\}$, $Outdim = \{64, 128, 256\}$, $Batchsize = \{256, 512, 1024\}$, and observe the quality of the trained classifier.

Figures 6, 7 and 8 shows the impact of different *Epochs*, *Outdim* and *Batchsize* on the model when training HTTP packets of Tencentnews, Youku and Taobao.

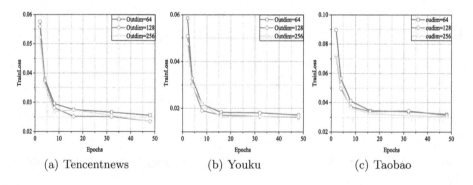

(a) Tencentnews   (b) Youku   (c) Taobao

Fig. 6. Parameter selection for $Batchsize = 256$

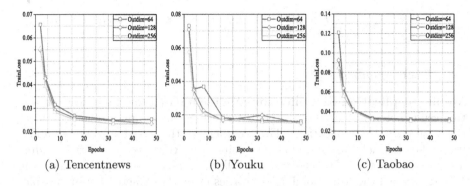

Fig. 7. Parameter selection for $Batchsize = 512$

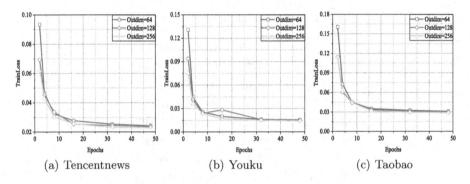

Fig. 8. Parameter selection for $Batchsize = 1024$

We observed that when $Epochs$ is less than 10, the training loss decreases monotonically. After 10 iterations, the training loss tends to be stable.

The higher the value of $Batchsize$, the higher the initial loss value, and the more iterations. Take Tencentnews as an example, when $Batchsize = 256$, the training loss converges after 20 iterations, but when $Batchsize = 512$ and $Batchsize = 1024$, the training loss still decreases after 20 iterations. In addition, we find that the training loss decreases with the increase of $Outdim$.

Meanwhile, we calculate the time used by different $Outdim$ for an iteration and record in Table 3. As can be seen from Table 3, the iteration time increases with the increase of $Outdim$.

Table 3. Time consumption of different $Outdim$

Mobile app	$Outdim = 64$	$Outdim = 128$	$Outdim = 256$
Tencentnews	110 s	135 s	165 s
Youku	97 s	118 s	136 s
Taobao	58 s	109 s	130 s

In this work, we set $Epochs = 32$, $Outdim = 128$, and $Batchsize = 512$ for the final application recognition.

4.3   Experiment Results

Mobile Application Identification. We use RFGRU to classify test set, and the result is shown in Table 4. RFGRU has achieved good performance in identification of the 15 applications. The accuracies of the tested apps are all above 97%. The accuracies of 11 applications using RFGRU exceed the corresponding accuracies using the GRU classifier alone. The accuracies of all applications using RFGRU exceed the corresponding accuracies using the Random Forest classifier alone. The average accuracy is increased from 97.46% to 98.43%.

Table 4. Accuracies of different applications

Mobile app	RFGRU	GRU	RF
Amap	97.73%	97.64%	96.19%
BaiduSearch	98.16%	98.12%	96.58%
JD	98.36%	98.33%	97.81%
Kuwo music	98.12%	98.13%	97.24%
Meituan	98.83%	98.78%	98.14%
QQ music	97.42%	97.38%	96.76%
Taobao	98.70%	98.60%	98.04%
Tencent news	98.54%	98.57%	97.85%
Youku	98.98%	98.95%	98.27%
Yuedongquan	98.68%	98.67%	98.18%
WeChat	98.76%	98.28%	98.58%
TouTiao	99.00%	98.94%	98.32%
UCBrowser	98.00%	98.11%	96.55%
Weibo	98.22%	98.26%	97.30%
Zhihu	98.97%	98.87%	96.07%
Average	98.43%	98.38%	97.46%

Time Consumption. We test the time consumption in identifying applications. The results are displayed in Table 5. In this table, we can see that RFGRU is obviously much more time-efficient, which requires only about 1/7 time as compared to that of GRU.

Table 5. Used time of different applications

Mobile app	RFGRU	GRU	RF
Amap	98.75 s	464.25 s	0.13 s
BaiduSearch	78.16 s	639.53 s	0.28 s
JD	75.55 s	613.88 s	0.27 s
Kuwo music	57.21 s	598.93 s	0.14 s
Meituan	55.89 s	661.06 s	0.18 s
QQ music	61.85 s	374.19 s	0.08 s
Taobao	75.30 s	449.49 s	0.10 s
Tencent news	79.31 s	560.47 s	0.16 s
Youku	44.99 s	467.06 s	0.15 s
Yuedongquan	116.69 s	689.26 s	0.14 s
WeChat	14.62 s	110.71 s	0.04 s
TouTiao	54.42 s	377.76 s	0.08 s
UCBrowser	71.50 s	375.45 s	0.09 s
Weibo	37.80 s	350.83 s	0.11 s
Zhihu	39.90 s	312.31 s	0.06 s
Average	64.13 s	469.68 s	0.13 s

4.4   Compared with Other Approach

In this section, we compare RFGRU with two state-of-the-art approaches –
LSTM and RNN, in terms of accuracy and time consumption. Both methods
are widely used in natural language processing, sequence prediction and other
fields. In the following experiments, all methods perform the same preprocessing
operations before classification.

Figure 9 shows the accuracies of three traffic classification methods. LSTM is
slightly better than RFGRU in identifying Tencentnews. But in the identification of Youku and Taobao, RFGRU outperforms LSTM and RNN. The average
accuracy of LSTM and RNN are 98.68% and 97.91% respectively. The average
accuracy obtained by RFGRU is 98.74%, which is higher than that of LSTM
and RNN. In a word, the accuracy of RFGRU is close to or higher than that
obtained by using LSTM and RNN.

The results of time consumption are shown in Fig. 10. The average time
consumed by RFGRU is 66.53 s, the LSTM is 530.34 s, and RNN is 230.69 s.
RFGRU consumes far less time than the other two methods. This is due to the
fact that most samples are easy to classify. Random Forest can filter out most
samples and leave the remaining to the GRU model. In short, RFGRU is much
superior to LSTM and RNN in terms of time.

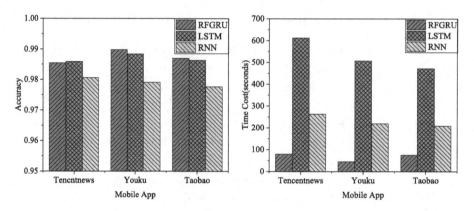

Fig. 9. Accuracies of different methods   **Fig. 10.** Time cost of different methods

5   Conclusion

In this paper, we propose a novel mobile traffic identification method RFGRU, which absorbs the advantages of Random Forest and GRU neural network. RFGRU does not require extracting complex characteristics. As far as we know, this is the first work to apply the GRU model to solve the mobile traffic classification problem. Meanwhile, by combining with the Random Forest, we can effectively reduce the number of samples that need to be classified by GRU model, and reduce the classification time. We capture the traffic of several popular mobile applications in China, and use the RFGRU model to identify the apps. Experimental results show that RFGRU saves more time as compared to using GRU model alone, moreover the application recognition accuracy of RFGRU can be even higher.

Acknowledgment. This work was supported by the National Natural Science Foundation of China (No. 61702288), the Natural Science Foundation of Tianjin in China (No. 16JCQNJC00700), the National Information Security Research Plan of China, and the Fundamental Research Funds for the Central Universities.

References

1. Gowsalya, R., Amali, S.M.J.: Naive Bayes based network traffic classification using correlation information. Int. J. Adv. Res. Comput. Sci. Softw. Eng. **4**(3) (2014)
2. Cisco visual networking index: Global mobile data traffic forecast update 2014–2019. http://goo.gl/Zu8f2r
3. Xu, Q., Erman, J., Gerber, A., Mao, Z., Pang, J., Venkataraman, S.: Identifying diverse usage behaviors of smartphone apps. In: Proceedings of the 2011 ACM SIGCOMM Conference on Internet Measurement Conference, pp. 329–344. ACM (2011)

4. Tongaonkar, A., Dai, S., Nucci, A., Song, D.: Understanding mobile app usage patterns using in-app advertisements. In: Roughan, M., Chang, R. (eds.) PAM 2013. LNCS, vol. 7799, pp. 63–72. Springer, Heidelberg (2013). https://doi.org/10.1007/978-3-642-36516-4_7

5. Moore, A.W., Zuev, D.: Internet traffic classification using Bayesian analysis techniques. In: ACM SIGMETRICS Performance Evaluation Review, vol. 33, pp. 50–60. ACM (2005)

6. Auld, T., Moore, A.W., Gull, S.F.: Bayesian neural networks for internet traffic classification. IEEE Trans. Neural Netw. **18**(1), 223–239 (2007)

7. Este, A., Gringoli, F., Salgarelli, L.: Support vector machines for TCP traffic classification. Comput. Netw. **53**(14), 2476–2490 (2009)

8. Lin, P., Xun-yi, Y., Liu, F., Zhen-ming, L.E.I.: A network traffic classification algorithm based on flow statistical characteristics. J. Beijing Univ. Posts Telecommun. **31**(2), 15–19 (2008)

9. Xu, Q., et al.: Automatic generation of mobile app signatures from traffic observations. In: 2015 IEEE Conference on Computer Communications (INFOCOM), pp. 1481–1489. IEEE (2015)

10. Ranjan, G., Tongaonkar, A., Torres, R.: Approximate matching of persistent lexicon using search-engines for classifying mobile app traffic. In: IEEE INFOCOM 2016-The 35th Annual IEEE International Conference on Computer Communications, pp. 1–9. IEEE (2016)

11. Yao, H., Ranjan, G., Tongaonkar, A., Liao, Y., Mao, Z.M.: Samples: self adaptive mining of persistent lexical snippets for classifying mobile application traffic. In: Proceedings of the 21st Annual International Conference on Mobile Computing and Networking, pp. 439–451. ACM (2015)

12. Dai, S., Tongaonkar, A., Wang, X., Nucci, A., Song, D.: Networkprofiler: towards automatic fingerprinting of android apps. In: INFOCOM 2013, Proceedings IEEE, pp. 809–817. IEEE (2013)

13. Yun, X., Wang, Y., Zhang, Y., Zhou, Y.: A semantics-aware approach to the automated network protocol identification. IEEE/ACM Trans. Netw. (TON) **24**(1), 583–595 (2016)

14. Wang, Y., Yun, X., Zhang, Y.: Rethinking robust and accurate application protocol identification: a nonparametric approach. In: 2015 IEEE 23rd International Conference on Network Protocols (ICNP), pp. 134–144. IEEE (2015)

15. Zhang, Z., Zhang, Z., Lee, P.P., Liu, Y., Xie, G.: Proword: an unsupervised approach to protocol feature word extraction. In: INFOCOM, 2014 Proceedings IEEE, pp. 1393–1401. IEEE (2014)

16. Hu, L., Li, J., Nie, L., Li, X.L., Shao, C.: What happens next? Future subevent prediction using contextual hierarchical LSTM. In: AAAI, pp. 3450–3456 (2017)

17. Yang, M., Tu, W., Wang, J., Xu, F., Chen, X.: Attention based LSTM for target dependent sentiment classification. In: AAAI, pp. 5013–5014 (2017)

18. Stuner, B., Chatelain, C., Paquet, T.: Cascading BLSTM networks for handwritten word recognition. In: 2016 23rd International Conference on Pattern Recognition (ICPR), pp. 3416–3421. IEEE (2016)

19. Cho, K., et al.: Learning phrase representations using RNN encoder-decoder for statistical machine translation. arXiv preprint arXiv:1406.1078 (2014)

20. Breiman, L.: Random forests. Mach. Learn. **45**(1), 5–32 (2001)

21. Montillo, A., Shotton, J., Winn, J., Iglesias, J.E., Metaxas, D., Criminisi, A.: Entangled decision forests and their application for semantic segmentation of CT images. In: Székely, G., Hahn, H.K. (eds.) IPMI 2011. LNCS, vol. 6801, pp. 184–196. Springer, Heidelberg (2011). https://doi.org/10.1007/978-3-642-22092-0_16

22. Karagiannis, T., Papagiannaki, K., Faloutsos, M.: BLINC: multilevel traffic classification in the dark. In: ACM SIGCOMM Computer Communication Review, vol. 35, pp. 229–240. ACM (2005)
23. Nguyen, T.T.T., Armitage, G.: A survey of techniques for internet traffic classification using machine learning. IEEE Commun. Surv. Tutor. **10**(4), 56–76 (2008)
24. Android monkey tool. http://developer.android.com/tools/help/monkey.html
25. Kingma, D., Ba, J.: Adam: a method for stochastic optimization. arXiv preprint arXiv:1412.6980 (2014)

Energy-Efficient Data Temporal Consistency Maintenance for IoT Systems

Guohui Li[1], Chunyang Zhou[1(✉)], Jianjun Li[1], and Bing Guo[2]

[1] School of Computer Science and Technology,
Huazhong University of Science and Technology, Wuhan, China
{guohuili,zhouchunyang,jianjunli}@hust.edu.cn
[2] School of Computer Science, Sichuan University, Chengdu, China
guobing@scu.edu.cn

Abstract. In many Internet of Things systems, it is required to process a good supply of real-time data from the physical world. An important goal when designing such systems is to maintain data temporal consistency while consuming less power. In this paper, we propose, to our knowledge, the first solution to the energy-efficient temporal consistency maintenance problem on Dynamic Voltage and Frequency Scaling (DVFS)-capable multicore platforms. We consider the problem of how to minimize the overall total power consumption on multicore, while the temporal consistency of real-time data objects can be maintained. To end this, firstly, we propose an efficient per-CPU DVFS solution, under which the transaction set can be scheduled to meet the temporal consistency requirement while resulting in significant energy savings. Next, by adopting the proposed unicore DVFS techniques on each core, we further propose new energy-efficient mapping techniques to explore energy savings for multicore platforms. Finally, extensive simulation experiments are conducted and the results demonstrate the proposed solutions outperforms existing methods in terms of energy consumption (up to 55%).

Keywords: Internet of Things · Real-time data service
Energy efficient · Multicore platform · Algorithms

1 Introduction

Internet of Things (IoT) has become one of the current wave of computing, examples of IoT include health monitoring [14], road traffic control [22] and industrial automation [21]. In these applications, the system receives and processes a good supply of real-time data from the physical space through wireless sensors, so as to

The work was partially supported by the State Key Program of National Natural Science of China under Grant No. 61332001, National Natural Science Foundation of China under Grant Nos. 61572215, 61672252, Wuhan Youth Science and Technology Plan under Grant No. 2017050304010287, and the Fundamental Research Funds for the Central Universities, HUST-2016YXMS076.

© Springer Nature Switzerland AG 2018
J. Vaidya and J. Li (Eds.): ICA3PP 2018, LNCS 11335, pp. 507–523, 2018.
https://doi.org/10.1007/978-3-030-05054-2_39

sense, monitor, and respond to the external environmental changes in a timely fashion. Therefore, there is the need for using Real-Time DataBase Systems (RTDBSs) which enables "Things" to be stored and analyzed in cyber-space.

In RTDBs, a real-time data object models the current status of a physical world entity, such as the temperature of the engine, the position of aircraft, etc. The state of the real-time object in RTDBSs is only valid for a given period of time, which is known as temporal validity interval [20]. It is important to refresh a sampled real-time data before it becomes invalid, i.e., before the old value expires. In addition, due to the fact that the battery capacity is limited in devices with communication and networking capabilities, an important issue when designing such IOT systems is to schedule transactions so that the temporal consistency of real-time data objects can be maintained, while reducing the energy consumption to prolong the battery life.

Dynamic Voltage and Frequency Scaling (DVFS) [3] is one of the major techniques for power saving in embedded real-time applications. DVFS uses a never-idle scheme to save energy. That is, when a processor is not fully utilized, it can reduce the overall energy consumption by decreasing the voltage and frequency of the processor. More recently, there has been an increasing trend towards design embedded systems on multi-core platforms, since multi-core platforms offer greater computational capacity with less size, weight and power (SWaP) compared to a single-core platform.

In this paper, we address the problem of energy-efficient transaction scheduling problem through DVFS on a DVFS-capable multicore system. In this work, for unicore solution, we propose per-CPU DVFS solution(assigns a constant frequency for each processor) due to its practicality. Next, we extend it to multi-core systems by designing energy-efficient task-to-processor mapping solution. The main contribution of this paper can be summarized as follows:

- We first propose a per-CPU DVFS solution, called ML-CS (More-Less with Constant Slowdown), to achieve energy saving. We also develop deadline and period assignment strategy for ML-CS, called EML (Energy-efficient More-Less), which ensures the whole update transaction set DM-schedulable.
- To address the energy minimization multicore problem globally, we propose energy-efficient transaction-to-processor mapping techniques called TCBM(Temporal Consistency Balanced Mapping), which assigns the total density factor evenly among all the cores, and then apply our unicore DVFS techniques on each core.
- We evaluate and comment on the performance of the proposed methods. Compared to previous solutions, the experimental results show that our methods exhibit significant improvement(up to 55%) in terms of energy saving.

The remainder of this paper is organized as follows. Section 2 describes the system, power model and problem definition, along with some assumptions we make. In Sect. 3, we present our energy efficient solutions on unicore. In Sect. 4, by using our single core solutions, we present an energy-efficient task mapping technique for multi-core platform. Section 5 presents and discusses the

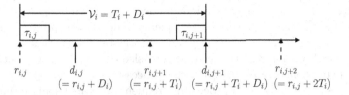

Fig. 1. Illustration of more-less scheme.

experimental results. Section 6 reviews related work. We conclude the paper with some remarks in Sect. 7.

2 Background, Assumptions and Problem Definition

In this section, we first review the definition of temporal validity for data freshness, and then introduce the power model, some notations and important assumptions made throughout the paper. Finally, we define the problem to be addressed.

2.1 Temporal Validity for Data Freshness

The correctness of a real-time data object x_i is defined below.

Definition 1. *A real-time data object (x_i) at time t is temporally valid (or absolutely consistent) if its jth sampling time ($r_{i,j}$) plus the validity interval ($\mathcal{V}_i$) of the data object is not less than t, i.e., $r_{i,j} + \mathcal{V}_i \geq t$.*

According to Definition 1, a data object value of x_i sampled at time t will be valid from t to $t + \mathcal{V}_i$. To satisfy the validity constraint, the update transaction τ_i should update x_i at least twice during $\mathcal{V}_i$. For periodic transaction model, both Half-Half [9] and More-Less [24] are available for maintaining temporally valid. The periods and deadlines of all the transactions are set to half of their corresponding validity interval lengths in Half-Half scheme, while More-Less scheme assigns shorter deadline (longer period) to each transaction to further reduce the update workload. Figure 1 gives an illustration of the More-Less scheme. As can be seen, there is $\mathcal{V}_i = T_i + D_i$, where T_i and D_i represent the period and deadline of τ_i, respectively.

2.2 Power Model

Our power model is based on the one in [27], which focuses on frequency-dependent and frequency-independent power. The power consumption is P_{idle} when the system is idle, and the power consumption is $P_{idle} + P_d(f)$ when the system is executing a task at frequency f. In particular,

$$P_d(f) = P_{ind} + P_{dep}(f) \tag{1}$$

where P_{ind} denotes the frequency-independent power and $P_{dep}(f)$ represents the frequency-dependent power. The frequency-independent power mainly consists of the components of memory and processor power that can be efficiently removed by putting the system into sleep state. On the contrary, the frequency-dependent power includes the processor's dynamic power and any power that depends on system processing frequency f, which can be represented as $P_{dep}(f) = C_{eff}f^{\alpha}$, where C_{eff} and α denote the effective switch capacitance and the dynamic power exponent, respectively. In general, $2 \leq \alpha \leq 3$ is a common assumption [7,27]. It is clear that lower frequency result in less frequency-dependent active energy consumption.

In this paper, we focus on reducing the CPU energy consumption by utilizing DVFS since it is the main energy cost parts for modern computer systems, i.e., up to 80% of total system power consumption. For convenience, we define a *slowdown factor* η as the ratio of the current operating frequency to the maximum frequency. In addition, if all the transactions are assigned the same slowdown factor, it is called a *constant slowdown*. Note that speed change can only occur at context switch. Therefore, we assume that the speed change overhead, similar to the context switch overhead, is constant and can be incorporated into the worst case execution time of a transaction.

2.3 Notations

In this paper, we consider a real-time system $\mathcal{T}$ which consists of a set of user transactions $\mathcal{T}^c = \{\tau_i^c\}_{i=1}^{n'}$ and a set of update transactions $\mathcal{T}^u = \{\tau_i^u\}_{i=1}^n$. Our objective is to consider the energy-efficient scheduling of $\mathcal{T}$ on a set of m identical multicores $\mathcal{M} = \{M_i\}_{i=1}^m$.

For update transactions, each update transaction τ_i^u is characterized by the following 2-tuple: $\{C_i^u, \mathcal{V}_i\}$, where C_i^u is the worst-case execution time, and $\mathcal{V}_i$ is the validity interval length of the data object it updates. The deadline and period of τ_i^u are denoted by D_i^u and T_i^u respectively, and need to be determined. To satisfy the temporal validity constrains, there is $D_i^u + T_i^u = \mathcal{V}_i (1 \leq i \leq n)$. U_i^u and λ_i^u is used to denote the utilization and density factor of τ_i^u, respectively, i.e., $U_i^u = C_i^u + T_i^u$ and $\lambda_i^u = \frac{C_i^u}{\mathcal{V}_i}$. We use $\mathcal{T}_k^u$ to denote the update transaction set assigned to one core M_k, the utilization and density factor of $\mathcal{T}_k^u$ on core M_k is defined as $\mathcal{U}_{sum}^k = \sum_{i=1}^n \frac{C_i^u}{T_i^u}$ and $\lambda_{sum}^k = \sum_{i=1}^n \frac{C_i^u}{\mathcal{V}_i}$, respectively. For the whole update transactions $\mathcal{T}^u$ scheduled on m multicore platform, the total utilization and total density factor of $\mathcal{T}^u$ is defined as $\mathcal{U}_{tot}^u = \sum_{i=1}^m \frac{C_i^u}{T_i^u}$ and $\lambda_{tot}^u = \sum_{i=1}^m \frac{C_i^u}{\mathcal{V}_i}$, respectively.

For user transactions, each user transaction τ_i^c follows traditional sporadic task model and can be characterized by a 3-tuples: $\{C_i^c, D_i^c, T_i^c\}$, where C_i is the worst-case execution time, D_i^c is the relative deadline and T_i^c is the period. We consider *constrained deadline* user transactions, i.e., $D_i^c \leq T_i^c$. The total utilization of $\mathcal{T}^c$ is defined as $\mathcal{U}_{tot}^c = \sum_{i=1}^m \frac{C_i^c}{T_i^c}$.

Based on our power model, we use E_s^i and λ_{sum}^i to denote the energy consumption on core M_i and the total density factor on core M_i, respectively.

Similar to previous work such as [26], the energy consumption is measured within a large enough interval L. The overall power consumption can be calculated as $E_t = \sum_{i=1}^{m} E_s^i$, and the energy consumption of all k tasks allocated to one processor m_i is $E_s = \sum_{i=1}^{k} \frac{L}{T_i} \frac{C_i}{\eta} P_d(\eta)$.

2.4   Problem Statement

In this research, our aim is to address the following problem.

Energy-Efficient Multi-Core Scheduling Problem (EEMCS): Given a set of transactions $T = \{\tau_i\}_{i=1}^{n}$ to be scheduled on a multi-core platform with m identical cores, we should determine a transaction to processor mapping strategy, so that the transactions assigned to each processor can be scheduled in a feasible manner, while minimizing the overall total power consumption E_t for the assigned cores.

It is easy to find that **EEMCS** is also NP-Hard in the strong sense, since Energy-optimal scheduling of periodic tasks on multi-cores is NP-hard in the strong sense [1]. The reduction is as follows: For each update transaction τ_i, we set the deadline and period to be half of the validity interval length of the data object it updates, that is, $T_i = D_i = V_i/2$. Therefore, we transform our model to normal implicit deadline task system. Since checking the feasibility of a set of real-time tasks on a multiprocessor platform even with the full speed is NP-Hard in the strong sense, and thus **EEMCS** is also NP-Hard in the strong sense.

Due to the inherent intractability of the problem, we will divide and tackle **EEMCS** by solving the following two subproblems:

1. Unicore DVFS problem: **Energy-Efficient UniCore Scheduling problem (EEUCS):** Given a set of update transactions $T^u = \{\tau_i\}_{i=1}^{n}$ with C_i^u and V_i specified for each τ_i^u to be scheduled on a DVFS-capable unicore, determine D_i^u and T_i^u and a slowdown factor η_i for τ_i, such that, the validity constraint of each update transaction τ_i^u must be maintained, while the energy consumption E_s is minimized.
2. Multicore mapping problem: **Energy-Efficient Multi-Core Mapping problem (EEMCM):** Given a set of transactions consist of $T^c = \{\tau_i\}_{i=1}^{n'}$ and $T^u = \{\tau_i\}_{i=1}^{n}$, and a multi-core platform with m identical processors, finding a transaction to processor mapping, such that the total energy consumption E_t is minimized.

3   Solutions for EEUCS

In this subsection, we propose our solution, More-Less with Constant Slowdown (ML-CS), to the **EEUCS** problem. As mentioned before, the deadlines and periods of update transactions are unknown initially. Hence, to address this problem, we should develop a hybrid method, which considers both slowdown factor selection and deadlines/periods assignment strategy systematically, to solve the problem.

In the following, we design a solution for the **EEUCS** problem, namely More-Less with Constant Slowdown (ML-CS). We propose to solve the problem by first determining one constant slowdown factor, and then computing deadlines and periods for update transactions. Firstly, ML-CS tries to select one slowdown factor η for the whole transaction set to reduce energy consumption. To improve the execution efficiency, we adopt the bisection method to search the proper constant slowdown factor. After determining a constant slowdown factor η, the next question is how to compute deadline and period for each update transaction, so that the temporal consistency of the transaction set can be guaranteed. As mentioned earlier, in this work, we use the ML scheme to compute transaction deadlines. Specifically, we first compute deadline for τ_k $(1 \leq k \leq n)$ by finding the minimum solution of the following recursive equation:

$$\sum_{i=1}^{k} \left\lceil \frac{D_k^u}{T_i^u} \right\rceil \frac{C_i^u}{\eta} = D_k^u \tag{2}$$

and then assign a period to τ_k^u by $T_k^u = \mathcal{V}_k - D_k^u$. ML-CS reports success only when both η is determined and deadlines/periods for each update transaction is assigned.

Algorithm 1 presents the pseudo-code of ML-CS. We first define the upper and lower bounds of the slowdown factor, and we use a threshold number θ which is a user defined parameter to bound the number of loops (line 3). Next, a binary search is performed in the range of $[\eta_{lb}, \eta_{ub}]$ to find the final slowdown factor (line 4). At each iteration, we first set $R_{i,0} = C_i^u/\eta$ as a initial deadline solution (line 6), and then we solve Eq. 2 at line 7–12. If all the transaction deadlines can be derived to be no larger than half of their corresponding validity interval lengths (line 13), and the given transaction set with η is DM-schedulable (line 17), then we update the upper bound of the slowdown factor to be $\eta_{ub} = \eta$ and go to the next iteration (line 18). Otherwise, we update the lower bound of the slowdown factor to be $\eta_{lb} = \eta$ and proceed to the next iteration (line 21). It is not difficult to see that the time complexity of ML-CS mainly comes from that the deadline and period assignment process needs to be executed for several times. Since solving the Eq. 2 has a pseudo-polynomial time complexity, ML-CS also runs in pseudo-polynomial. The following theorem shows the correctness of ML-CS.

Theorem 1. *Given an update transaction set $T^u = \{\tau_i\}_{i=1}^{n}$ and a constant slowdown factor η, if ML-CS can derive deadlines and periods to each transaction, then T is guaranteed to be temporal consistency schedulable under DM.*

Proof. To prove the correctness of ML-CS, we need to prove that all the constraints of the **EEUCS** problem can be satisfied when using ML-CS to derive a solution. Firstly, if there is a constant slowdown factor η makes T schedulable,

---

Algorithm 1. ML-CS

---

    input : A real time update transaction set $\mathcal{T}^u = \{\tau_i^u\}_{i=1}^n$ sorted in
           non-decreasing order of $\mathcal{V}_i$, and $\eta_{ub} = 1$ and η_{lb} is set to be
           $\max\{\eta_{min}, \min_{i=1}^n\{\frac{C_i^u}{\mathcal{V}_i}\}\}$.

   output: Slowdown factor η, deadlines $\{D_i^u\}_{i=1}^n$ and periods $\{T_i^u\}_{i=1}^n$.

1 **begin**
2     $Flag = false$;
3   **while** $(\eta_{ub} - \eta_{lb} > \theta)$ **do**
4        $\eta = (\eta_{lb} + \eta_{ub})/2$;
5   **for** $i = 0; i \le n; i++$ **do**
6           $R_{i,0} = C_i^u/\eta$;
7   **repeat**
8               $D_i^u = R_{i,0}$;
9               $R_{i,0} = C_i^u/\eta$;
10   **for** $j = 0; j \le i; j++$ **do**
11                  $R_{i,0} = R_{i,0} + \left\lceil \frac{D_i^u}{T_j^u} \right\rceil \times \frac{C_j^u}{\eta}$;
12   **until** $R_{i,0} == D_i^u$ or $R_{i,0} > \frac{\mathcal{V}_i}{2}$;
13   **if** $R_{i,0} \le \frac{\mathcal{V}_i}{2}$ **then**
14               $T_i^u = \mathcal{V}_i - D_i^u$;
15   **else**
16   **return** Abort;

17   **if** $\mathcal{T}$ *is DM-schedulable with* η **then**
18           $\eta_{ub} = \eta$ {update upperbound};
19           $Flag = true$;

20   **else**
21           $\eta_{lb} = \eta$ {update lowerbound} ;

22   **if** *!Flag* **then**
23   **return** Abort;
24   **return** Success;

ML-CS will be able to find this η because it utilizes bisection method to search in the whole range. Then, it is known that a transaction set is schedulable by DM if the first instance of each task after a *critical instant*, i.e., when all the first jobs of transactions are released simultaneously, meets its deadline. Recall that ML-CS calculates deadlines by using Eq. 2 and terminals when $R_{i,0} == D_i^u$ or $R_{i,0} > \frac{\mathcal{V}_i}{2}$, it is obvious that $\sum_{i=1}^{k-1} \left\lceil \frac{D_k^u}{T_i^u} \right\rceil \cdot \frac{C_i^u}{\eta} + \frac{C_k^u}{\eta} = D_k^u \le T_k^u \le \frac{\mathcal{V}_k}{2}(1 \le k \le n)$, which means $\mathcal{T}^u$ is schedulable under DM. Finally, once the deadline of each update transaction satisfies $D_i^u \le \frac{\mathcal{V}_i}{2}$, the period is computed as $T_k^u = \mathcal{V}_k - D_k^u$, we know that the temporal consistency can also be guaranteed. Hence, the set of transactions is deemed to be temporal consistency schedulable under DM.

4   Solutions for EEMCS

In this section, we try to address the **EEMCS** problem globally. To avoid the interference between user transactions and update transactions, we adopt partitioned scheduling on multi-core platforms, and assign two different types of transactions to separate identical cores. Note that user transactions are traditional periodic tasks, and many existing sophisticated DVFS or DPM algorithms [3], can be utilized. Therefore, we can focus on handling update transactions. We first focus on exploring energy-efficient transaction to processor mapping techniques to solve the **EEMCM** subproblem, and then apply our unicore DVFS techniques on each core.

Generally, for partitioned scheduling on multi-core platforms, four traditional bin-packing heuristics have been well explored based on system utilization, that is Next Fit (NF), First-Fit (FF), Best-Fit (BF) and Worst-Fit (WF). In particular, the Worst-Fit Decreasing (WFD) has been proved to be effective by previous work [5,18]. In this paper, to facilitate distinction, we use Temporal Consistency Fit, abbreviated TCNF (TCFF, TCBF and TCWF, resp.), to denote the corresponding heuristics which are adopted to solve our problem. As far as we know, the study in [15] is the only work that address the partitioned multiprocessor scheduling problem for maintaining temporal consistency. However, the proposed methods, called TCP and DBF, are designed to enhance system schedulability rather than energy efficiency. In this paper, our goal is to derive energy minimization partitioned scheduling strategy. We first present a useful lemma based on our previous work [15], which states a sufficient condition for any transaction sets to be partitioned successfully on multi-core.

Lemma 1 [15]. *Given an update transaction set T^u, if the density factor of T^u is not larger than 0.5, i.e., $\lambda_{sum} \leq 0.5$, then T^u is deemed to be temporal consistency schedulable under DM on a uniprocessor system.*

According to Lemma 1, we can obtain a constant slowdown factor on each core immediately, as given in the following theorem.

Theorem 2. *Given an update transaction set T^u, if T^u's density factor $\lambda_{sum} \leq 0.5$, then it is temporal consistency schedulable under DM on a uniprocessor system with a constant slowdown factor of $\eta = \max\{\eta_{min}, 2\lambda_{sum}\}$.*

Proof. Given a constant slowdown factor η, we know that, $\lambda_{sum} = \sum\limits_{i=1}^{n} \frac{C^u}{\eta \cdot V}$. From Lemma 1, it it clear that T^u is DM-schedulable with $\eta \geq 2\lambda_{sum}$. Hence, the minimum constant slowdown factor is $\eta = \max\{\eta_{min}, 2\lambda_{sum}\}$. The theorem thus follows.

Then, the next question is what is the best mapping strategy which minimize the total energy consumption. To address this problem, we have several important observations, which is briefly described as follows.

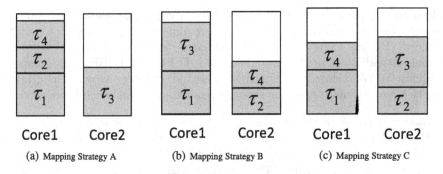

Fig. 2. Different transaction mapping strategies.

- Observation 1. TCWF partitioning should be adopted to save energy. TCWF always selects the core with the minimal total density, so that the occupied capacities of all cores will be increased in turn.
- Observation 2. Given a transaction set $\mathcal{T}$, the transaction to processor mapping strategy which divides the total density factor λ_{tot}^u evenly among all the cores, will minimize the total energy consumption.
- Observation 3. To achieve a more density factor balanced partition, update transactions τ_i^u with $\lambda_i^u > \frac{\lambda_{tot}^u}{m}$ must be assigned to a separate processor exclusively.

We only show these results here and omit the detailed proofs due to space limited. As an alternative, we give an intuitive example to illustrate these results.

Example 1.
Consider a transaction set comprised of four transactions with execution times and validity interval lengths $\mathcal{T} = \{\tau_1 = (1,5), \tau_2^u = (1,10), \tau_3^u = (4,15), \tau_4^u = (3,20)\}$ to be executed on 2 identical processors. The formalized energy consumption is calculated by $E_t = \sum_{i=1}^{m} E_s^i = \sum_{i=1}^{m} \sum_{i=1}^{n} \frac{L}{T_i} C_i \eta_i^2$. We compare the energy consumptions of the following three different transaction mapping strategies, as shown in Fig. 2.

- **Mapping Strategy A** - The first three transactions are allocated to one core, and τ_4^u is allocated to the other core. The slowdown speed on the two cores is 0.9 and 0.4, respectively. The resulted energy consumption is 55799.
- **Mapping Strategy B** - τ_1 and τ_3 are allocated to one core, while τ_2 and τ_4 are allocated to the other core. The slowdown speed on the two cores is 0.8 and 0.4, respectively. The resulted energy consumption is 48383.
- **Mapping Strategy C** - τ_1 and τ_4 are allocated to one core, while τ_2 and τ_3 are allocated to the other core. The slowdown speed on the two cores is 0.7 and 0.6, respectively. The resulted energy consumption is 43919.

The above example reveals us some useful information. It can be seen that all the three strategies can make the transaction set DM-schedulable. When only judged by the feasibility criterion, all three strategies are equally acceptable. However, the energy consumption of them are quite different. Strategy C results in about 21% less energy consumption than the mapping strategy A. In fact, strategy A and B are produced by heuristics TCFF and TCBF, while strategy C adopts TCWF. Moreover, as can be observed, Strategy C which is a more density factor balanced mapping strategy tends to consume much lower energy.

Based on the above discussion, we propose our heuristic, Temporal Consistency Balanced Mapping (TCBM), as follows: Given a set of transactions $\mathcal{T} = \{\tau_i\}_{i=1}^n$ to be scheduled on a multi-core platform with m identical cores $\{M_1, M_2, ..., M_m\}$, Algorithm TCBM first assigns user transactions to k separate processors using WF in the order of decreasing utilization, with cumulative utilization on each core upper bounded by Liu & Laylands bound (RM-schedulable) or 1.0 (EDF-schedulable). Then, for each update transaction τ_i^u, TCBM first checks whether it is a heavy density loaded transactions or not, i.e., $\lambda_i^u > \frac{\lambda_{tot}^u}{m}$. If yes, TCBM assigns τ_i^u to a separate processor $M_s(k+1 \leq s \leq m)$ with the minimal total density, and then assigns τ_i^u to processor M_s that satisfies inequality $\lambda_i^u + \lambda_{sum}^s \leq 0.5$. Otherwise, TCBM tries to find the core M_j with the minimal total density, and assigns τ_i^u to processor M_j that satisfies inequality $\lambda_i^u + \lambda_{sum}^j \leq 0.5$ by using TCWF. If no such M_j exists, TCBM declares failure. TCBM repeats the above steps until all the transactions are mapped to cores. Detail of TCBM is shown in Algorithm 2.

Complexity of TCBM: It can be observed that TCBM essentially checks whether τ_i^u is a heavy density loaded transaction, and evaluates the cumulative density factor on each of the m cores. Since these values can be computed in constant time, it is clear that the run-time of the algorithm in allocating all n transactions is no more than $O(nm)$.

5   Experimental Evaluation

In this section, we first introduce the experimental setup in Sect. 5.1, then discuss the results on unicore in Sect. 5.2, and the results on multicore in Sect. 5.3.

5.1   Experimental Setup

The default settings and parameters for the simulations are summarized in Table 1. To enable easy comparison and continuity with previous studies, we adopt the same baseline values for the parameters as given in [16, 25], which are originally from air traffic control applications [17].

In all experiments, all the algorithms are evaluated on actual Intel XScale processor model, which has five speeds available (0.15, 0.4, 0.6, 0.8, 1.0) GHz with corresponding power consumptions $(80, 170, 400, 900, 1600)mWatt$ on each core. The power consumption function can be modeled approximately as $P(s) = 0.08 + 1.52s^3$ by treating 1 GHz as the reference speed unit. It should be noted that there exists a critical speed [27], i.e., $\eta_{ee} = \sqrt[\alpha]{\frac{P_{ind}}{C_{ef}(\alpha-1)}}$, in which executing

---

Algorithm 2. TCBM($\mathcal{T}$)

---

input : a transaction set $\mathcal{T}$, which consists of a set of user transactions $\mathcal{T}^c = \{\tau_i^c\}_{i=1}^{n'}$ sorted in a non-decreasing order of T_i and a set of update transactions $\mathcal{T}^u = \{\tau_i^u\}_{i=1}^{n}$ sorted in a non-decreasing order of $\mathcal{V}_i$.

output: a transaction to processor mapping.

1 **begin**
2   Assign user transactions to the first k cores $\{M_0, M_1, ..., M_k\}$ using WFD ;
3   **for** $i = 0; i \leq n; i++$ **do**
4   **if** $\lambda_i^u > \frac{\lambda_{tot}^u}{m}$ **then**
5   Find a separate core $M_s(k+1 \leq s \leq m)$ with the minimal total density ;
6   **if** τ_i^u *satisfies* $\lambda_i^u + \lambda_{sum}^s \leq 0.5$ *on core* M_s **then**
7   Assign τ_i^u to core M_s ;
8   break;
9   **for** $j = k+1; j \leq m; j++$ **do**
10   Find the core M_j with the minimal total density ;
11   **if** τ_i^u *satisfies* $\lambda_i^u + \lambda_{sum}^j \leq 0.5$ *on core* M_j **then**
12   Assign τ_i^u to core M_j;
13   break;
14   **else**
15   **return** Failure;
16   **return** Success;

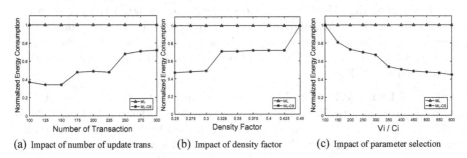

(a) Impact of number of update trans.   (b) Impact of density factor   (c) Impact of parameter selection

Fig. 3. Performance comparison on unicore

task at slowdown factor less than the critical speed would only consume more energy. In our Intel XScale processor model, the effective switching capacitance $C_{ef} = 1.52$ and the dynamic power exponent $m = 3$. Thus the critical speed for Intel XScale is about 0.3 (0.297 GHz). All the algorithms to be evaluated are implemented in Java. In each simulation set, we randomly generate 1000 qualified update transaction sets and take the average value as the reported results.

Table 1. Experiment settings

Platform	Para. class	Parameters	Meaning	Value
Unicore	System	N_{cpu}	No. of CPU	$\{1\}$
	Update trans	N_T	No. of data objects	[100, 300]
	Update trans	$V_i(ms)$	Validity interval of x_i	[4000, 8000]
	Update trans	$C_i^u(ms)$	Time for updating x_i	[5, 15]
	Update trans	Trans. length	No. of data to update	1
Multicore	System	N_{cpu}	No. of CPU	$\{4, 6, 8, 10, 12\}$
	User trans	N_C	No. of user trans	[10, 60]
	User trans	T_i^c	Periods	[100, 500]
	User trans	C_i^c	Time for execution	[10, 20]
	Update trans	N_T	No. of data objects	[100, 300]
	Update trans	$V_i(ms)$	Validity interval of x_i	[4000, 8000]
	Update trans	$C_i^u(ms)$	Time for updating x_i	[5–15, 15–50, 50–150]
	Update trans	Trans. length	No. of data to update	1

5.2   Experiment Results on Unicore

Impact of the Number of Update Transactions. In this set of experiments, the total number of update transactions (denoted as N_T) is varied from 100 to 300. Figure 3(a) shows the energy performance of the tested algorithms. To facilitate comparison, the energy consumed by ML is used as the baseline. It can be observed that ML-CS saves more energy (about 60%) compared to the traditional non-DVFS ML approach. As N_T grows, the normalized energy consumption of all the tested algorithms increase gradually, due to that the system workload increases with the increase of N_T, which results in less idle time that can be used for DVFS.

Impact of Density Factor. In this set of experiments, we fix the number of update transactions to $N_T = 200$ and vary the density factor (λ) from 0.25 to 0.475. The increase of the density factor is achieved by fixing the computation time C_i and decreasing the valid interval length V_i. Figure 3(b) shows the energy consumption performance. ML-CS outperforms the ML method consistently. As λ_{sum} increases, the energy consumption of ML-CS basically presents ladder form rise. This is mainly due to that the available speeds in Intel Xscale model is discrete and ML-CS relies on a density-based sufficient feasibility test or the DM scheduling itself to calculate the slowdown factors.

Impact of Parameter Selection. In this set of experiments, we change the V_i/C_i ratio of transactions. We randomly choose 20% transactions out of $N_T = 200$, and varied their V_i/C_i ratio from 100 to 600 to show its impact on performance. Figure 3(b) shows the comparison of the resulting normalized energy consumption. The achieved normalized energy consumption of all approaches decreases along with the increase of the V_i/C_i ratio. ML-CS can greatly reduce energy consumption especially when the V_i/C_i ratio is high, for instance, when

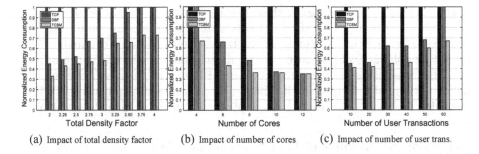

(a) Impact of total density factor   (b) Impact of number of cores   (c) Impact of number of user trans.

Fig. 4. Normalized energy consumption on multicore.

$V_i/C_i = 600$, the performance gap between ML-CS and ML reaches about 52%. This is expected, because a larger ratio of V_i/C_i can result in leaving more free time slices for DVFS to reduce energy cost.

In summary, the experimental results show that the per-CPU DVFS based ML-CS outperforms ML in terms of energy consumption on unicore.

5.3   Experiment Results on Multicore

For evaluating energy consumption performance on multicore, we compare three different approaches: two state of the art mapping techniques (TCP and DBF [15]), and TCBM proposed in this paper. For a fair comparison with other methods, we run different task mapping techniques on the random generated transaction sets. Then, we sum up the energy consumption on each core(applying our unicore method, i.e., ML-CS, to minimize energy on all cores) to calculate the overall energy consumption.

Impact of Density Factor. In this set of experiments, we obtain our results by performing experiments on 8 cores, and vary the total density factor (λ_{tot}) from 2 to 4 to show its impact on total energy consumption. The results are shown in Fig. 4(a), respectively. As can be seen, TCBM obtain considerable energy saving compared to other mapping techniques, such as, 55% more saving than TCP and 18% more than DBF method when the total density factor is 3.0. The energy consumption of DBF is the same as TCP when the total density factor reaches 4.0, while the energy consumption of TCBM with ML-CS is still no more than 65%. The reason why TCBM has a better energy performance lies in that, both TCP and DBF use First-Fit to enhance system schedulability which may lead to unbalanced partition and decrease the chance to slowdown on active cores to save energy, while TCBM can make better use of multiple cores to save energy by adopting Worst-Fit strategy.

Impact of the Number of Cores. In this set of experiments, we fix the number of total density of update transactions to $\lambda_{tot} = 2.0$, and the number of cores is selected from $\{4, 6, 8, 10, 12\}$. Figure 4(b) shows the energy performances of tested mapping algorithms. With increasing number of cores, the energy consumption for DBF and TCBM tends to decrease. This is because more cores can be used to balance the assignment of the transactions, and thus can make more room for applying DVFS to save energy on each core. The energy consumption of TCBM is significantly lower than that of DBF and TCP, especially when the number of available cores is small. The largest performance gap between TCBM and DBF is about 33% with ML-CS applied on each core when the number of cores is 4.

Impact of the Number of User Transactions. In this set of experiments, we fix the number of total density of update transactions to $\lambda_{tot} = 2.0$, and the number of cores is fixed at $m = 8$. The number of user transaction is varied from 10 to 60. The results are shown in Fig. 4(c). It can be viewed that, the energy consumption increase with the increases of the number of user transactions, but the energy consumption of TCBM increases much smoother than that of DBF. It is also clear to see that TCBM still outperforms TCP and DBF considerably, and the performance gap becomes larger with the increase of the number of user transactions.

In summary, compared to TCP and DBF, the proposed TCBM mapping techniques can distribute the density factor evenly among the available cores, thus lead to considerable (up to 55%) lower energy consumption.

6   Related Work

In this section, we briefly review some work on energy-aware real-time scheduling with DVFS and temporal consistency maintenance in RTDBS.

Energy-Aware Real-Time Scheduling with DVFS. DVFS is a widely used technique for saving processor energy consumption. For example, hybrid DVFS strategies [19] and slack reclamation for DVFS [2]. A recent survey on energy-efficient scheduling in real-time systems can be found in [3]. Multi-core scheduling approaches can be divided into three groups: *global* [4], *partitioned* [6], *semi-partitioned* [12]. Specially, partitioned scheduling allocates each task to one processor permanently (task migrations are not allowed). In addition, for DVFS applied in multi-core, most of the existing work can be divided into two branches: *per-CPU DVFS* [1] and *per-task DVFS* [5]. Per-CPU DVFS method assigns a constant frequency for each processor, while per-task DVFS assigns one execution frequency for each task and the frequency of each processor is depending on the running task. However, all the work mentioned above assumes the deadlines and periods of real-time tasks are given, hence gives no answer to the problem studied in this work.

Temporal Consistency Maintenance in RTDBS. There has been a lot of work on RTDBS for maintaining real-time data freshness. The Half-Half scheme [13] is proposed to reduce workload by skipping the execution of task instances. The More-Less scheme was proposed in [24] with deadline monotonic scheduling. The deferrable scheduling algorithm for fixed priority transactions

(DS-FP) proposed in [23] follows an aperiodic task model. For dynamic priority scheduling, Xiong *et al.* [25] proposed solutions maintaining data freshness under EDF, and later an improved solution was given in [16]. Recently, Han *et al.* [8] studied the problem of how to maintain the temporal validity of real-time data objects in the presence of mode changes in cyber-physical systems. Li *et al.* [15] studied the temporal consistency maintenance problem upon multiprocessor platforms. Most of the work mentioned above did not take the issue of energy consumption into consideration.

Power-Aware Technologies in RTDBS. Research on power management in RTDBS is relatively new. In [10], Kang proposed a real-time query aggregation approach which combines with DPM to reduce both the deadline miss ratio and power consumption in RTDBS. Recently, these methods have been extended to multicore plantform in [11]. Unfortunately, simply postponing the execution of task to create CPU idle time may not applicable in certain applications, e.g., during the rush hours in transportation management. Hence, we believe that DVFS approach should be considered as well to maximize energy saving. Nevertheless, our work could still benefit more from these researches.

7   Conclusions and Future Work

Energy management is one of the key issues in the design of modern embedded real-time systems. In this paper, we study the energy-aware transaction scheduling problem for maintaining temporal consistency of real-time data objects in RTDBS. As far as we know, this work serves as the first attempt to solve the given problem. We propose effective per-CPU DVFS technique, called ML-CS, for maintaining data freshness by applying DVFS on multicore systems. We further propose energy-efficient mapping techniques to explore energy savings for multicores. The experimental evaluation demonstrates that the proposed methods are superior to the traditional scheduling method (up to 55%) from the perspective of energy consumption. For future work, we plan to extend our research to heterogeneous multicore platforms.

References

1. Aydin, H., Yang, Q.: Energy-aware partitioning for multiprocessor real-time systems. In: Proceedings of IPDPS, pp. 9–pp (2003)
2. Aydin, H., Melhem, R., Mossé, D., Mejía-Alvarez, P.: Power-aware scheduling for periodic real-time tasks. IEEE Trans. Comput. **53**(5), 584–600 (2004)
3. Bambagini, M., Marinoni, M., Aydin, H., Buttazzo, G.: Energy-aware scheduling for real-time systems: a survey. ACM Trans. Embed. Comput. Syst. (TECS) **15**(1), 7 (2016)
4. Baruah, S.: Techniques for multiprocessor global schedulability analysis. In: Proceedings of RTSS, pp. 119–128 (2007)
5. Chen, G., Huang, K., Knoll, A.: Energy optimization for real-time multiprocessor system-on-chip with optimal DVFS and DPM combination. ACM Trans. Embed. Comput. Syst. (TECS) **13**(3), 111 (2014)

6. Chen, J.J., Chakraborty, S.: Partitioned packing and scheduling for sporadic real-time tasks in identical multiprocessor systems. In: Proceedings of ECRTS, pp. 24–33 (2012)
7. Chen, J.J., Kuo, C.F.: Energy-efficient scheduling for real-time systems on dynamic voltage scaling (DVS) platforms. In: Proceedings of RTCSA, pp. 28–38. IEEE (2007)
8. Han, S., et al.: Online mode switch algorithms for maintaining data freshness in dynamic cyber-physical systems. IEEE Trans. Knowl. Data Eng. **28**(3), 756–769 (2016)
9. Ho, S.J., Kuo, T.W., Mok, A.K.: Similarity-based load adjustment for real-time data-intensive applications. In: Proceedings of RTSS, pp. 144–153 (1997)
10. Kang, K.D.: Reducing deadline misses and power consumption in real-time databases. In: Proceedings of RTSS, pp. 257–268 (2016)
11. Kang, K.D.: Enhancing timeliness and saving power in real-time databases. Real-Time Syst. **30**(1), 1–30 (2018)
12. Kato, S., Yamasaki, N.: Semi-partitioned fixed-priority scheduling on multiprocessors. In: Proceedings of RTAS, pp. 23–32 (2009)
13. Kuo, T.W., Ho, S.J.: Similarity-based load adjustment for static real-time transaction systems. IEEE Trans. Comput. **49**(2), 112–126 (2000)
14. Lam, K.Y., Tsang, N.W.H., Han, S., Zhang, W., Ng, J.K.Y., Nath, A.: Activity tracking and monitoring of patients with alzheimer disease. Multimedia Tools Appl. **76**(1), 489–521 (2017)
15. Li, J., Chen, J.J., Xiong, M., Li, G., Wei, W.: Temporal consistency maintenance upon partitioned multiprocessor platforms. IEEE Trans. Comput. **65**(5), 1632–1645 (2016)
16. Li, J., Xiong, M., Lee, V., Shu, L., Li, G.: Workload-efficient deadline and period assignment for maintaining temporal consistency under EDF. IEEE Trans. Comput. **62**(6), 1255–1268 (2013)
17. Locke, D.: Real-time databases: real-world requirements. In: Bestavros, A., Lin, K.J., Son, S.H. (eds.) Real-Time Database Systems, pp. 83–91. Springer, Boston (1997). https://doi.org/10.1007/978-1-4615-6161-3_5
18. Narayana, S., Huang, P., Giannopoulou, G., Thiele, L., Prasad, R.V.: Exploring energy saving for mixed-criticality systems on multi-cores. In: Proceedings of RTAS, pp. 1–12 (2016)
19. Quan, G., Niu, L., Hu, X.S., Mochocki, B.: Fixed priority scheduling for reducing overall energy on variable voltage processors. In: Proceedings of RTSS, pp. 309–318 (2004)
20. Ramamritham, K.: Real-time databases. Distrib. Parallel Databases **1**(2), 199–226 (1993)
21. Saifullah, A., Xu, Y., Lu, C., Chen, Y.: End-to-end delay analysis for fixed priority scheduling in WirelessHART networks. In: Proceedings of RTAS, pp. 13–22 (2011)
22. Wu, W., Zhang, J., Luo, A., Cao, J.: Distributed mutual exclusion algorithms for intersection traffic control. IEEE Trans. Parallel Distrib. Syst. **26**(1), 65–74 (2015)
23. Xiong, M., Han, S., Lam, K.Y., Chen, D.: Deferrable scheduling for maintaining real-time data freshness: algorithms, analysis, and results. IEEE Trans. Comput. **57**(7), 952–964 (2008)
24. Xiong, M., Ramamritham, K.: Deriving deadlines and periods for real-time update transactions. IEEE Trans. Comput. **53**(5), 567–583 (2004)
25. Xiong, M., Wang, Q., Ramamritham, K.: On earliest deadline first scheduling for temporal consistency maintenance. Real-Time Syst. **40**(2), 208–237 (2008)

26. Zhang, F., Chanson, S.T.: Processor voltage scheduling for real-time tasks with non-preemptible sections. In: Proceedings of RTSS, pp. 235–245 (2002)
27. Zhu, D., Aydin, H.: Reliability-aware energy management for periodic real-time tasks. IEEE Trans. Comput. **58**(10), 1382–1397 (2009)

GpDL: A Spatially Aggregated Data Layout for Long-Term Astronomical Observation Archive

Zhen Li[1], Ce Yu[1(✉)], Chao Sun[1], Shanjiang Tang[1(✉)], Jie Yan[1],
Xiangfei Meng[2], and Yang Zhao[2]

[1] School of Computer Science and Technology, Tianjin University,
Tianjin 300350, China
{lizhencs,yuce,sch,tashj,jerryan}@tju.edu.cn
[2] National Supercomputer Center in Tianjin, Tianjin 300457, China
{mengxf,zhaoyang}@nscc-tj.gov.cn

Abstract. A great number of excellent astronomical academic achievements are built on historical observation data. So long-term astronomical observation archive has great significance for astronomical research. At the observation site, data from different sky areas shot in a consecutive time period are stored in one disk. So original data layout is temporally aggregated and spatially scattered. After an observation cycle, data are backuped into long-term astronomical observation archive. Astronomers request data from archive. But original data layout does not match requests' spatial locality, i.e., one request focuses on specific sky area during a time period. In this situation, archive adopting original data layout consumes lots of energy and shortens disk life. Therefore, a reorganized spatially aggregated data layout is indispensable for archive. But how to aggregate observation data from nearby sky areas into one disk while keeping high disk capacity utilization is challenging. In this paper, we propose a spatially aggregated data layout based on HEALPix and graph partition for long-term astronomical observation archive, named GpDL. GpDL is generated based on distribution-known original data layout before observation data are backuped into archive. GpDL saves a lot of resources for archive while keeping up to 91% disk capacity utilization. In simulation experiments, compared with TaDL (original temporally aggregated data layout) and AmrDL (another spatially aggregated data layout based on thought of Adaptive Mesh Refinement), GpDL effectively reduces open disks number and energy cost for the same requests.

Keywords: Spatially aggregated · Data layout
Astronomical observation · Long-term archive · Energy cost

1 Introduction

Astronomy has been at the forefront of the development of the techniques and methodologies of data intensive science for over a decade with large sky surveys and distributed efforts such as the Virtual Observatory [4]. In recent years,

© Springer Nature Switzerland AG 2018
J. Vaidya and J. Li (Eds.): ICA3PP 2018, LNCS 11335, pp. 524–537, 2018.
https://doi.org/10.1007/978-3-030-05054-2_40

various astronomical observation infrastructures have been established, such as Automated Planet Finder (APF) [15] in California, Antarctic Schmidt Telescopes (AST3) [1] at Dome A and Five hundred meters Aperture Spherical Radio Telescope (FAST) [11] in Guizhou China. A great number of excellent academic achievements are built on historical observation data shot by these infrastructures. So long-term astronomical observation archive is indispensable. However, data obtained by astronomical observation show an explosive growth in recent years, which has brought challenges for efficiency and resources consumption to long-term astronomical observation archive. And different data layouts have a significant impact on the resources consumption of archive. So archive needs a data layout adapting to astronomers' specific requests characteristics.

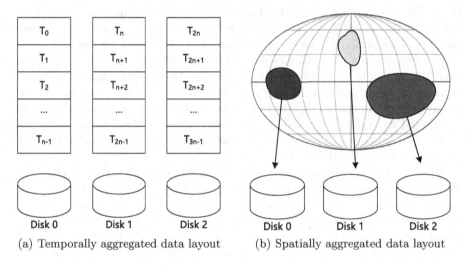

(a) Temporally aggregated data layout   (b) Spatially aggregated data layout

Fig. 1. Two types of data layouts

At the observation site, data from different sky areas shot in a consecutive time period are stored in one disk. So original data layout is temporally aggregated and spatially scattered (see Fig. 1(a)). The storage of telescopes at the observation site is not permanent. After an observation cycle, data are transmitted to data center and backuped into long-term astronomical observation archive. Archive belongs to cold storage, write only once, most data rarely read, so most of disks are in low-power state at ordinary times for saving energy. Astronomers request data from long-term archive. However, the original temporally aggregated data layout in chronological order does not match requests' spatial locality, i.e., one request focuses on specific sky area during a time period to research the change of celestial objects. If still use the original temporally aggregated data layout in long-term archive, it needs to open all disks consisting of the requests' sky area, resulting that much energy is consumed and frequent opening and closing may shorten disk life or even damage disk. Hong [6] proposes an efficient method to speed up the requests, but he doesn't consider data layout optimization. For the requests' spatial locality and resources-saving, spatially aggregated data layout is more suitable for long-term archive. That is to say, neighboring sky areas should be aggregated into one disk (see Fig. 1(b), the celestial sphere surface is shown in mollweide projection and centralized region with the same color is stored in one disk). Compared with temporally aggregated data layout, archive adopting spatially aggregated data layout opens fewer disks for the same requests. After data are transmitted to data center, the data distribution on celestial sphere surface is known. So we can convert original temporally aggregated data layout into spatially aggregated. But how to aggregate observation data from nearby sky areas into one disk while keeping high disk capacity utilization is challenging.

In this paper, we propose a spatially aggregated data layout based on HEALPix and graph partition for long-term astronomical observation archive, named GpDL. After data are transmitted to data center, GpDL is generated based on distribution-known original temporally aggregated data layout before observation records are backuped into archive. GpDL saves a lot of resources while keeping up to 91% disk capacity utilization. In our simulation experiments, we compare three data layouts for the same requests. The three data layouts are TaDL (original temporally aggregated data layout), AmrDL (another spatially aggregated data layout based on thought of Adaptive Mesh Refinement) and GpDL. GpDL effectively reduces open disks number and energy cost in comparison to TaDL and AmrDL.

The structure of this paper is as follows. Section 1 introduces the background of our work. Section 2 shows related work on data layout in storage system. Section 3 focuses on GpDL, defines the GpDL optimizing model of long-term astronomical observation archive and explains the methods to obtain GpDL. Simulation experiments and results analysis are presented in Sect. 4. The last section concludes our work and puts forward further research opportunities.

2   Related Work

There has existed research on data layout optimization for high performance and low energy cost in storage system. Some researchers attempt to copy data blocks into free space on disks to shorten the disk response time [9,13,16]. But long-term astronomical observation archive needs to keep high disk capacity utilization, there being no free space to copy data blocks. Huang [8] proposes an almost latency-free and hard-disk-dominated storage system. His system changes data layout in a hybrid storage hierarchy using low-latency SSD and high-latency HDD. Rubin [12] proposes a parameterizable framework for data-layout optimization of general-purpose applications. However, their research is based on universal data, not referring to scientific data archive.

Astronomical observation data has spatial and temporal attributes. Gong [2] proposes a parallel query-processing engine for spatio-temporal data, optimizing query processing on scientific data. But the data must be isabela-compressed. Nevertheless, given the response time, the observation data shouldn't be compressed in archive. He [5] optimizes the data layout of the large-scale video storage server based on parallel disk array, which is not suitable for astronomical observation archive because of the different read-write characteristics and encoding formats. Hoque's disk layout techniques leverage community structure in a social graph to optimize read latency [7], which uses graph-partition-driven community detection to confirm the social network data layout. However, the method he used can't be applied to long-term astronomical observation archive directly.

Research mentioned above doesn't take specificity of astronomical observation archive into account. [14] introduces the designing and mining multi-terabyte astronomy of SDSS (Sloan Digital Sky Survey), which optimizes the spatial data structures of observation storage. But the density of observation records on the celestial sphere surface doesn't be considered in his research. Yan [17] optimizes data layout for AST3's spatio-temporal observation data. Although he takes density into account, not a little disk capacity is wasted in his method. Furthermore, his layout works on production environment when AST3 is running, not designed for astronomical observation archive.

In conclusion, there hasn't been a suitable data layout for long-term astronomical observation archive.

3   GpDL Design

This section introduces GpDL Design. As mentioned in the Sect. 1, every record has temporal and spatial attributes. The original data layout are temporally aggregated and spatially scattered. The task of our data layout is to choose which disk to store for every observation record. For the requests' spatial locality and resources-saving, we need to aggregate observation data from nearby sky areas into one disk and keep high disk capacity utilization based on distribution-known original temporally aggregated data layout. So the requirement is that records fill every disk as far as possible. In this situation, the numbers of records stored in different disks are approximately equal. The goal is that the distribution of records stored in each disk is aggregated on celestial sphere surface.

This section consists of three subsections. Subsection 3.1 introduces a spatially aggregated data layout called AmrDL based on thought of AMR. Subsection 3.2 puts forward the optimizing model of GpDL. Subsection 3.3 introduces the method to obtain GpDL. AmrDL and GpDL are both built on HEALPix[1].

---

[1] HEALPix is an acronym for Hierarchical Equal Area isoLatitude Pixelation of a sphere. HEALPix divides a sphere surface into many blocks with equal surface area and each block has a unique *BlockID*. The sphere is divided into curvilinear quadrangles hierarchically [3]. Resolution increases by division of each block into four small equal-area ones. Different resolutions correspond to different *NSIDE*s. (see Fig. 2. The lowest resolution is $NSIDE = 1$. When $NSIDE = 1, 2, 4, 8$, clockwise from upper-left to bottom-left, the sphere surface is divided into 12, 48, 192, and 768 blocks.)

3.1   AmrDL Introduction

AmrDL is a simple spatially aggregated data layout easy to think about. AmrDL uses the thought of AMR (Adaptive Mesh Refinement) to design data layout based on HEALPix. Figure 3 shows sketch of our AMR strategy. AmrDL divides the celestial sphere surface into 12 blocks when $NSIDE = 1$ initially. Then blocks whose records can't be stored in one disk are divided into four smaller equal blocks. Repeat this step until every block's records can be stored in one disk. Finally each block corresponds to one disk.

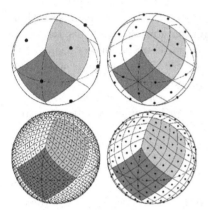 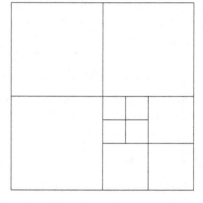

Fig. 2. HEALPix [3]   **Fig. 3.** Sketch of our AMR strategy

3.2   GpDL Optimizing Model

AmrDL aggregates records from nearby sky areas into one disk using thought of AMR. However, there is a serious issue in AmrDL: because four smaller blocks divided from a big block may differ a lot in corresponding records number, some disks may only store few records resulting low disk capacity utilization and imbalance between disks. Our designed GpDL solves this issue using graph partition. Above all, GpDL optimizing model is built in this subsection. Notations used in GpDL optimizing model are listed in Table 1.

Problem Description. Given set of astronomical observation records denoted by RS, the model outputs the set of required disks denoted by DS and the map from RS to $DS(f : RS \rightarrow DS)$.

RS is defined as follows:

$$RS = \left\{ R_1, R_2, ..., R_i, ..., R_{|RS|} \right\} \tag{1}$$

The size of RS is $|RS|$. Any two records have equal file size, denoted by RC. The definition of R_i, the ith observation record, is as follows:

$$R_i = (R_{i_t}, R_{i_s}) \tag{2}$$

Table 1. Notations used in GpDL optimizing model

Notation	Description
RS	Set of observation records
DS	Set of required disks
RC	File size of one record
DC	Storage capacity of one disk
RN	The value is $\frac{DC}{RC}$, maximum records number one disk can store
Ω_i	Set of records stored in the ith disk

where R_{i_t} is the temporal attribute of R_i. R_{i_s} is the spatial attribute of R_i, defined by

$$R_{i_s} = (R_{i_{ra}}, R_{i_{dec}}) \tag{3}$$

where $R_{i_{ra}}, R_{i_{dec}}$ are right ascension and declination of record R_i, representing a point on celestial sphere surface. Their ranges are as follows:

$$R_{i_{ra}} \in [0°, 360°) \tag{4}$$

$$R_{i_{dec}} \in [-90°, +90°] \tag{5}$$

The required disks set DS is defined by:

$$DS = \{D_1, D_2, ..., D_i, ..., D_{|DS|}\} \tag{6}$$

Size of DS is $|DS|$. Any two disks in set DS are exactly the same except for disk id, i.e., any two disks have the same brand, capacity, performance, and so on. The disk capacity is denoted by DC.

A disk can store a number of records. The task is to choose which disk to store for every record. According to the requirement and goal, GpDL optimizing model has following objective and constraint.

Objective. The output includes map from RS to DS. From the map, every disk has a corresponding set of records stored in it denoted by Ω_i. There exist $\bigcup_{i=1}^{|DS|} \Omega_i = RS$ and $\Omega_i \bigcap_{i \neq j} \Omega_j = \emptyset$. Every Ω_i constitutes a region on the celestial sphere surface. The goal is to make the distribution of records in every Ω_i is aggregated on the celestial sphere surface. So the objective of GpDL optimizing model is as follows:

$$max \left(\sum_{R_a \in \Omega_i} \sum_{R_b \in \Omega_j, i \neq j} \|R_{a_s} - R_{b_s}\|_2 \right) \tag{7}$$

where $\|R_{a_s} - R_{b_s}\|_2$ is the angular distance between point R_{a_s} and R_{b_s} on sphere surface. A higher value means that records stored in different disks are more far away. That is to say, the distribution of records stored in each disk is more aggregated. The objective maximizes the spatial aggregation of GpDL.

Constraint. Long-term astronomical observation archive needs a large number of disks, a significant expense can't be ignored. So fewer disks mean higher disk capacity utilization. Every disk needs to store as more records as possible. Based on this, GpDL optimizing model has following constraint:

$$\forall_{i=1}^{|DS|} \frac{RC \times |\Omega_i|}{DC} > r \tag{8}$$

where r is a coefficient, meaning that every disk uses at least r of disk capacity.

This is a typical partition problem. Unfortunately, most partition problems are NP-hard [10]. There exists no polynomial time algorithm to get the perfect solution of this model. So we can only find approximate solutions of this problem. The GpDL solution method based on HEALPix and graph partition is introduced in the next subsection.

3.3   GpDL Solution Based on Graph Partition

Outwardly, the model is looking for the map from RS to DS. After long-term observation, different celestial sphere surface regions have been shot at different frequency. So we are looking for a celestial sphere surface partition actually. The surface is parted into several subregions, every subregion corresponding to one disk unit. Each subregion has approximately equal number of records which can almost fill one disk. On the celestial sphere surface, single subregion is concentrated, and different subregions are far away. Now the celestial sphere surface partition problem is similar to graph partition problem. The introduction to graph partition problem is presented in Definition 1.

Definition 1 (Introduction to Graph Partition). *Given an undirected weighted graph $G = (V, E)$, where V is set of vertices and E is set of edges, weight of vertex i is denoted by M_i, weight of edge between the vertex i and j is denoted by N_{ij}, and number of partitions k. Output vertices partition $V = V_1 \bigcup V_2 \bigcup V_3 \bigcup ... \bigcup V_k$, satisfying following three items:*

(1) $\{V_i\}$ are disjoint, $V_i \bigcap V_j = \emptyset$, $i \neq j$.
(2) $\{V_i\}$ are roughly balanced, $\sum_{a \in V_i} M_a \approx \sum_{b \in V_j} M_b$, $i \neq j$.
(3) The   edge-cut   between   different   parts   is   minimized, $min \sum_{u \in V_i} \sum_{v \in V_j, i \neq j} N_{uv}$.

An example of graph partition is shown in Fig. 4. This is an undirected weighted graph with 7 vertices and 11 edges. The graph is divided into three subgraphs, while keeping roughly balanced vertices wight and minimized edge-cut.

When $k = |DS|$, the implications of the item (2)/(3) and formula (8)/(7) are essentially the same, V_i corresponding to Ω_i. So it is possible to convert GpDL optimizing model to graph partition problem. The key point is to generate an undirected weighted graph from RS. Although the graph partition problem is NP-complete [10], there are many approximation algorithms can be used to get a high-quality solution in an acceptable time. We use following four steps to convert GpDL optimizing model to graph partition problem based on HEALPix, apply graph partition methods and obtain the map from RS to DS.

Step 1: Divide the celestial sphere surface into equal-area small blocks using HEALPix and count the number of observation records for each block. Given an appropriate $NSIDE$, divide the celestial sphere surface into equal-area blocks. Different records during long-term observation may locate on the same block. Count the number of records for each $BlockID$. The $BlockID$ and corresponding records number are denoted by $BlkRNo[BlockID] = RNo$, where RNo is the number of records located on block numbered $BlockID$.

Step 2: Preprocess blocks having singular records number. According to the shoot feature of observation, the celestial sphere surface consists of cold regions and hot regions. Specially, the observation records located on the hottest region may occupy a large part of the entire records, which needs not only one disk but also a group of disks to store. Let $RN = \frac{DC}{RC}$ be the number of records one disk can store. Preprocess $BlkRNo$ using $BlkRNo[BlockID] = BlkRNo[BlockID] \bmod RN$, which means $\lfloor BlkRNo[BlockID]/RN \rfloor$ disks have been used to store records located on block numbered $BlockID$.

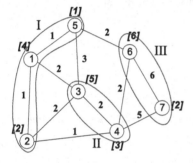

Fig. 4. A sample of graph partition ($k = 3$)

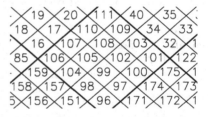

Fig. 5. Part of cylindrical projection of the HEALPix division of sphere surface ($NSIDE = 4$) [3]

Step 3: Generate an undirected weighted graph G based on preprocessed blocks. Let blocks still consisting of records after preprocessed be the vertices of G. For each vertex v let its corresponding $BlkRNo[BlockID]$ be v's weight. Because the goal is to gather nearby blocks into one disk, we can set the weight of edges through the angular distance between blocks. Longer distance between two blocks is, smaller weight is set for the corresponding edge. But if any two vertices have an edge, G is a complete graph. Graph partition on a complete graph wouldn't get a satisfactory result. So simplifications on edges are necessary. The neighboring blocks of one block can be found using HEALPix's function $get\_all\_neighbours$. The distance between any two blocks can be confirmed through function $get\_all\_neighbours$ and BFS (Breadth First

Search)[2]. Any two blocks whose distance smaller than L have an edge weighted $(L - distance) * (L - distance)$, and any two blocks whose distance bigger or equal than L have no edge (the weight is 0). Now undirected weighted graph G has been generated.

Algorithm 1. GpDL for long-term astronomical observation archive

---

Input: RS: set of observation records. RN: the maximum number of records one disk can store. $NSIDE$: the resolution of HEALPix. L: threshold value of distance.

Output: DS: set of required disks, map from RS to DS.

1: Divide sphere surface into N equal-area blocks using HEALPix with resolution $NSIDE$.
2: $BlkRNo[N] \leftarrow \{0\}$ // Initialize $BlkNo$ to $\{0\}$.
3: **for all** $R_i \in RS$ **do**
4:     Compute $BlockID$ of block R_i is located.
5:     $BlkRNo[BlockID] \leftarrow BlkRNo[BlockID] + 1$
6: **end for**
7: **for** $BlockID = 0$ **to** $N - 1$ **do**
8:     $BlkRNo[BlockID] \leftarrow BlkRNo[BlockID] \bmod RN$
9: **end for**
10: $V \leftarrow \{\}, E \leftarrow \{\}$ // Initialize vertices and edges to empty set.
11: **for** $BlockID = 0$ **to** $N - 1$ **do**
12:     **if** $BlkRNo[BlockID] > 0$ **then**
13:         Add Block numbered $BlockID$ into V.
14:     **end if**
15: **end for**
16: **for all** $i \in V$ **do**
17:     **for all** $j > i \in V$ **do**
18:         Compute the distance between i and j using HEALPix's *get_all_neighbours* and BFS, and set this distance to *dis*.
19:         **if** $dis < L$ **then**
20:             Add edge (i, j) into E, and the weight of edge (i, j) is $(L - dis) * (L - dis)$.
21:         **end if**
22:     **end for**
23: **end for**
24: $G \leftarrow (V, E)$ // Generated undirected weighted graph
25: Apply graph partition methods to G to get k subparts of G, corresponding to set of k disks DS. Subsequently infer map from RS to DS.

Step 4: Apply graph partition methods to G and get the map from records to disks. Our method is based on the multilevel graph partitioning paradigm [10], which has been shown to quickly produce high-quality partitions.

---

[2] see Fig. 5. Take block 102 as an example. The distance to neighboring blocks from 102 is set to 1, e.g., the distance of (102, 99), (102, 97)... is set to 1. The distance to neighboring of neighboring blocks from 102 is set to 2, e.g., the distance of (102, 32), (102, 34)... is set to 2. The distance to neighboring of neighboring of neighboring blocks from 102 is set to 3, and so on.

It consists of three phases: graph coarsening, initial partitioning, and uncoarsening. In the graph coarsening phase, graph is coarsened into a small number of vertices. In the initial partitioning phase, the coarsened small graph is computed using simple approaches. Finally, in the uncoarsening phase, the partitioning of the coarsened small graph is projected to larger graph with refining using various heuristic methods. When all three phases end, G is parted into k parts, meaning that the HEALPix blocks has been gathered to k parts corresponding to k disks. Because the map from observation records to HEALPix blocks is known, we can easily obtain the map from records RS to k disks DS.

Step 1–4 are formally described in Algorithm 1. Now GpDL is solved using graph partition methods. Implementation details can be found in the next section.

4   Implementation and Experimental Results

4.1   Implementation

The Choice of Parameters. $NSIDE$, resolution of HEALPix, is set to 64. In this situation, the sphere surface is divided into 49152 blocks. Each block's size is about $1° * 1°$, sufficient precision for requests. The sphere surface is divided into 196608 blocks when NSIDE is 128, which makes the final graph too complicated to execute graph partition in a short time. k, namely the number of required disks, is set by

$$k = \frac{|RS|}{0.9 * RN} \tag{9}$$

which means the disk capacity utilization is about 90%. Because the result of graph partition is approximately equal subgraphs, not exactly equal, add a factor 0.9 to ensure that each subdivision can be stored in one disk. L, the threshold value of distance, is set to 10, which is a suitable number tested in simulation experiments.

Simulation Environment. The disk model used in simulation experiments is Seagate ST1000DM003. Some parameters of ST1000DM003 are shown in Table 2. All parameters are fetched from Seagate official documents (https://www.seagate.com/files/www-content/product-content/desktop-hdd-fam/en-us/docs/100768625g.pdf).

Data Set. The data set we used is the observation records of AST3 during 2016. It consists of 71536 records. We expanded it to 298080 records according to its observation features. The 298080 records make up the set RS. One record's file size $RC = 200$ MB. So $RN = \frac{DC}{RC} = \frac{1000GB}{200MB} = 5000$.

Experiments Procedure. The graph partition method uses the METIS library (http://glaros.dtc.umn.edu/gkhome/metis/metis/overview). Three data layouts TaDL, AmrDL, GpDL are compared in our experiments. Before simulation experiments start, the three data layouts (three maps from records to disks) have been stored in three tables of MySQL database. We first visualized GpDL

Table 2. Parameters of ST1000DM003

Value (Unit)	Description
1000 (GB)	Disk capacity DC
10 (s)	Time from power-on to ready for read/write
300 (J)	Energy cost from power-on to ready for read/write
10 (s)	Time from running to power-off
54 (J)	Energy cost from running to power-off
156 (MB/s)	Average data read/write rate
6.19 (W)	Disk power when running

in orthographic projection. Then analyzed the disk capacity utilizations of three data layouts. Finally, for each layout, we produced 35000 requests in seven scales (scale $= 1°, 2°, 3°, 4°, 5°, 10°, 20°$), each scale 5000 requests. These requests are all independent considering that requests of archive are not frequent. For each request, given time period denoted by T, a sphere surface point (ra, dec) and scale representing a region (region's right ascension is from ra - scale to ra + scale, region's declination is from dec - scale to dec + scale), find disks storing records inside this region during the time period T according to data layout tables, then open these disks, fetch required records and close disks. In this process, we analyzed the open disks number and energy cost.

4.2 Experimental Results

Experimental results consist of four parts: data layout visualization, disk capacity utilization, open disks number and overhead energy cost.

Data Layout Visualization. GpDL is visualized in Fig. 6. There are 66 different colors in this figure. Because AST3 is located on Antarctica, only view from the south pole is shown. One color corresponds to one disk. Adjacent area has the same color, meaning that neighboring records are stored in one disk and GpDL is spatially aggregated.

Disk Capacity Utilization. We compared three data layouts' disk capacity utilizations. Because records are stored in chronological order in TaDL, the disk capacity utilization is 100%. The disk capacity utilizations of AmrDL and GpDL are shown in Fig. 7. The horizontal axis X is disk ID and the vertical axis Y is disk capacity utilization. In AmrDL, 131 disks are used. The average disk capacity utilization is 46%. In GpDL, 66 disks are used. The average disk capacity utilization is 91%. GpDL saves almost half of disks compared with AmrDL. The distribution of data among disks in GpDL is more uniform than AmrDL. So GpDL has a big advantage over AmrDL in disk capacity utilization. And the GpDL's 91% utilization doesn't drop much compared with TaDL. The reason for AmrDL's low capacity utilization is that there may be a big difference in numbers of records among four smaller blocks divided from a big block.

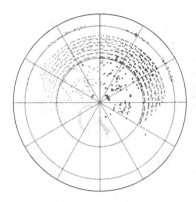

Fig. 6. GpDL visualization in orthographic projection

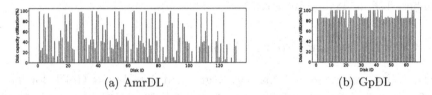

(a) AmrDL   (b) GpDL

Fig. 7. Disk capacity utilizations of AmrDL and GpDL

Open Disks Number. Disks are closed at ordinary times in our designed long-term archive. When a request arrives, open required disks to fetch records. The opening and closing have a negative impact on disk. Frequent opening and closing shortens disk life, or even damage disk. So a well-behaved data layout will open fewer disks for the same request. The open disks number during 35000 requests in seven scales for each data layout are shown in Fig. 8. AmrDL and GpDL observably reduces the open disks number in comparison to TaDL. This is due to the spatially aggregated layout's advantage over temporally aggregated. With the scale increasing, GpDL's advantage over AmrDL becomes more and more obvious. This is because the disks used in AmrDL is much more than GpDL. When scale $= 20°$, open disks number of GpDL is 45% of TaDL, 76% of AmrDL.

Overhead Energy Cost. Figure 9 shows the overhead energy cost of three layouts in seven scales. As the number of fetched records is fixed for one request, the read energy cost is equal in three layouts. The overhead energy cost is overall energy cost not including read energy cost. So the overhead energy cost is in approximate proportion to open disks number. That's why Fig. 9 is similar to Fig. 8 in trend. The overhead energy cost in AmrDL and GpDL decreases by more than half of TaDL. With the scale increasing, the advantage over TaDL becomes smaller and smaller, but still much better. And bigger the scale is, more energy GpDL saves than AmrDL. On the average, overhead energy cost of GpDL is 27% of TaDL, 85% of AmrDL.

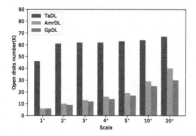

Fig. 8. Open disks number

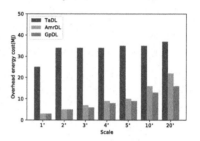

Fig. 9. Overhead energy cost

In conclusion, GpDL is a spatially aggregated data layout which gathers nearby records into one disk and saves a lot of resources including required disks number, disk life and energy cost.

5   Conclusion and Future Work

In this paper, we propose a spatially aggregated data layout GpDL for long-term astronomical observation archive, which is based on HEALPix and graph partition. After original data are transmitted to data center, GpDL is generated based on distribution-known original temporally aggregated data layout before observation records are backuped into archive. GpDL saves a great number of resources in comparison with TaDL and AmrDL while keeping up to 91% disk capacity utilization. In simulation experiments, GpDL effectively reduces the number of open disks, which helps to extend disk life. Furthermore, the overhead energy cost is reduced to 27% of TaDL and 85% of AmrDL on the average.

R-tree is a tree data structure used for indexing multi-dimensional information such as geographical coordinates. There may be any possibility to use R-tree to solve this layout problem. One request of astronomers focuses on a region. Archive must open multiple disks if the region covers the border of partitions. How to solve the border problem is also worthy to research.

Acknowledgments. This work is supported by the Joint Research Fund in Astronomy (U1531111, U1731423, U1731125) under cooperative agreement between the National Natural Science Foundation of China (NSFC) and Chinese Academy of Sciences (CAS), the National Natural Science Foundation of China (11573019, 61602336).

References

1. Cui, X., Yuan, X., Gong, X.: Antarctic schmidt telescopes (AST3) for dome A. In: Ground-Based and Airborne Telescopes II, vol. 7012, p. 70122D. International Society for Optics and Photonics (2008)
2. Gong, Z., et al.: Multi-level layout optimization for efficient spatio-temporal queries on ISABELA-compressed data. In: 2012 IEEE 26th International Parallel and Distributed Processing Symposium (IPDPS), pp. 873–884. IEEE (2012)

3. Gorski, K.M., et al.: HEALPix: a framework for high-resolution discretization and fast analysis of data distributed on the sphere. Astrophys. J. **622**(2), 759 (2005)
4. Graham, M.J., Djorgovski, S.G., Mahabal, A., Donalek, C., Drake, A., Longo, G.: Data challenges of time domain astronomy. Distrib. Parallel Databases **30**(5–6), 371–384 (2012)
5. He, Y.Q., Sun, S.X.: A data layout and access control strategies of the video storage server based disk array. In: 2008 International Conference on Intelligent Information Hiding and Multimedia Signal Processing, IIHMSP 2008, pp. 433–437. IEEE (2008)
6. Hong, Z., et al.: AQUAdex: a highly efficient indexing and retrieving method for astronomical big data of time series images. In: Wang, G., Zomaya, A., Perez, G.M., Li, K. (eds.) ICA3PP 2015. LNCS, vol. 9529, pp. 92–105. Springer, Cham (2015). https://doi.org/10.1007/978-3-319-27122-4_7
7. Hoque, I., Gupta, I.: Disk layout techniques for online social network data. IEEE Internet Comput. **16**(3), 24–36 (2012)
8. Huang, D., Zhang, X., Shi, W., Zheng, M., Jiang, S., Qin, F.: LiU: hiding disk access latency for HPC applications with a new SSD-enabled data layout. In: 2013 IEEE 21st International Symposium on Modeling, Analysis and Simulation of Computer and Telecommunication Systems (MASCOTS), pp. 111–120. IEEE (2013)
9. Huang, H., Hung, W., Shin, K.G.: FS2: dynamic data replication in free disk space for improving disk performance and energy consumption. In: ACM SIGOPS Operating Systems Review, vol. 39, pp. 263–276. ACM (2005)
10. Karypis, G., Kumar, V.: Multilevelk-way partitioning scheme for irregular graphs. J. Parallel Distrib. Comput. **48**(1), 96–129 (1998)
11. Nan, R.: Five hundred meter aperture spherical radio telescope (FAST). Sci. China Ser. G **49**(2), 129–148 (2006)
12. Rubin, S., Bodík, R., Chilimbi, T.: An efficient profile-analysis framework for data-layout optimizations. In: ACM SIGPLAN Notices, vol. 37, pp. 140–153. ACM (2002)
13. Son, S.W., Chen, G., Kandemir, M.: Disk layout optimization for reducing energy consumption. In: Proceedings of the 19th Annual International Conference on Supercomputing, pp. 274–283. ACM (2005)
14. Szalay, A.S., Kunszt, P.Z., Thakar, A., Gray, J., Slutz, D., Brunner, R.J.: Designing and mining multi-terabyte astronomy archives: the Sloan digital sky survey. ACM SIGMOD Rec. **29**(2), 451–462 (2000)
15. Vogt, S.S., et al.: APF-the lick observatory automated planet finder. Publ. Astron. Soc. Pac. **126**(938), 359 (2014)
16. Xiao, L., Yu-An, T.: TPL: a data layout method for reducing rotational latency of modern hard disk drive. In: 2009 WRI World Congress on Computer Science and Information Engineering, vol. 7, pp. 336–340. IEEE (2009)
17. Yan, J., et al.: Optimized data layout for spatio-temporal data in time domain astronomy. In: Ibrahim, S., Choo, K.-K.R., Yan, Z., Pedrycz, W. (eds.) ICA3PP 2017. LNCS, vol. 10393, pp. 431–440. Springer, Cham (2017). https://doi.org/10.1007/978-3-319-65482-9_30

A Virtual Machine Dynamic Adjustment Strategy Based on Load Forecasting

Junjie Peng[1(✉)] ⓘ, Yingtao Wang[1], Gan Chen[1], Lujin You[2], Feng Cheng[3], and Weiqiang Lv[1]

[1] Shanghai University, Shanghai 200444, China
jjie.peng@shu.edu.cn
[2] Tongji University, Shanghai 200433, China
[3] Hasso Plattner Institute, 14482 Potsdam, Germany

Abstract. Uneven assignment of tasks may cause virtual machine (VM) overload or underload in cloud computing environment. No matter overload or underload, the efficiency of cloud resources will be much affected. Especially underload, a lot of resources are not utilized which causes much waste. To solve this problem, a VM dynamic adjustment strategy based on load forecasting is proposed. Through load forecast, the strategy predicts the bottleneck of the key resources that affect the performance of the system. Utilizing the prediction results the resources are dynamically and effectviely adjusted. Extensive experiments show the strategy is correct and efficient. It can much improve the utilization efficiency of resources and lay a foundation for further study of VM adjustment strategy.

Keywords: Cloud computing · Load forecasting
Dynamic adjustment · Virtual machine

1 Introduction

Compared with traditional IT services, cloud computing has many advantages as it enables users access the resources in cloud data center such as networks, servers, storage and so on conveniently, on-demand without needing to grasp any details about the infrastructure. Because of the advantages of cloud computing, many studies have set focuses on it and many applications and services have moved onto the cloud [1–6]. This causes the amount and the scale of cloud data centers that provide cloud services become larger and larger and energy consumption of cloud data centers has become a widely concerned problem. Studies shows that the utilization rate of current data centers is generally between 5% and 20% [7–9]. It is estimated that a data center (DC) with 50,000 computing nodes will consume 100 million kwh of electricity each year with cost $9,300,000 [10]. Various data shows that cloud DCs are increasingly consuming tremendous energy

Granted by National Natural Science Foundation of China (61572305, 61103054, and 61540054)

J. Vaidya and J. Li (Eds.): ICA3PP 2018, LNCS 11335, pp. 538–550, 2018.
https://doi.org/10.1007/978-3-030-05054-2_41

worldwide. However the utilization and efficiency of resources are relatively low in DCs which wastes a lot of power energy.

How to reduce energy consumption of DC and improve the utilization of resources has become an urgent problem to be solved. To reduce energy consumption and improve the utilization of resources, a feasible method is appropriately allocating the resources according to the demand of applications. However, it is impossible to reasonably allocate resources at the beginning due to the complexity and variability of cloud environment which causes waste of resources. For a VM with fixed resource configuration, if its load is too low, many resources are not used. In this case, it will result in the low utilization rate of resources. On the contrary, if the load of a VM is too heavy, it will cause shortage of resources. At this case, the execution efficiency of the applications will be affected due to resource shortage which results in the increase of application execution time and the decrease of the quality of service (QoS).

This paper analyses the above problems and proposes a VM dynamic adjustment strategy based on load forecasting. It tries to find the key resource which affects the performance of the system by load forecasting, and adjust the appropriate scale of the key resource. That is the key resources are dyanmically adjusted based on prediction which ensures the utilization of resources as well as QoS. Meanwhile, it can save energy.

2 Related work

For given resources and different kinds of applications, many scholars have done a lot of studies on how to efficiently schedule the resources in cloud [1, 11–14]. However, as different types of applications have different resource preferences, the classification of applications and efficient allocation of cloud resources are very complex.

To increase the utilization of cloud resources, Taylor et al. made a research on the short-term prediction models which include autoregressive integrated moving average model (ARIMA), autoregressive model(AR) and Holt winters exponential smoothing [15]. Sorjanmaa et al. provided both short-term and long-term prediction by using fractional autoregressive integrated moving average model (FARIMA), and proposed a global method for long-term prediction [16]. Hu et al. [17] proposed a load balancing algorithm of virtual resources based on genetic algorithm. According to thestudy, the algorithm calculates the resource configuration of VMs in advance with mapping tasks by genetic algorithm based on historical data and real-time state of the cloud system.

In addition to the traditional model, there are some other models. For example, Chen et al. proposed a model for periodic load mode [18]. Peng et al. extracted the characteristics of the application according to the characteristics of CPU intensive application, based on which they put forward a scheduling strategy for CPU intensive applications [19]. Shen et al. put forward a cloudscale system [20] which can adaptively allocate cloud resources by using online resource prediction in cloud environment. Padala et al. proposed a virtual resource control system called AutoControl [21]. In the system of AutoControl, model estimator was designed to gain the application performance goals in the future by analysing the resource allocation information and performance information in the past. Using the information collected and analysed, the required resources and the optimizer were allocated. Meng et al. [22] proposed a feedback load balancing strategy with a dual monitor mechanism. It quantified the usage of multiple types of resources in cloud DC and defined different load balancing types based on resource granularity with which appropriate load balancing type under different conditions was selected.

Based on cloud computing platform, the consumptions of resources are monitored which can be utilized to characterize the load of VM, and timely predict the state of VM (for example, low load, overload, normal state). Based on the prediction and resource utilization of VM, cloud resources can be efficiently used with high QoS.

3   Dynamic adjustment strategy of virtual machine

In cloud environment, when applications running on a VM in a fixed configuration, it may cause the VM low load or overload due to the variability and complexity of the applications. When VM is in low load, it has the best performance. However at this case, it will cause serious waste of resources or a lot of resources such as CPU, memory, network and IO resources etc. be in idle state. Besides, low utilization of resoures causes waste of energy. On the other hand, when a VM is in overload, it leads to low performance of VM and inefficient use of resources. As if the load is too high, it will exceed the processing capability of the VM. A lot of extra cost will occur in frequent switching or scheduling the resources. This causes VM behaves in extremely low performance and results in inefficient utilization of cloud resources and lowering the QoS of applications. Therefore, dynamic adjustment of the load on VM to reasonable range is very important. That is, when the load on a VM is in low state, part of the resources are appropriately reclaimed on the premise that the QoS and the performance of VM are not much affected. This ensures the resources can be more reasonable utilized and energy consumption can be reduced. On the other hand, when a VM is in an overload state, the bottleneck of the key resources is determined through analysis and prediction of the utilization of resources. By increasing the key resources with the dynamic adjustment stragegy, the performance of VM can be improved and QoS be guaranteed.

3.1   Status and load analysis of virtual machine

Resources of VM are mainly CPU, memory, network (sending and receiving through network) and IO resources (disk read and write). When the load of a VM is very heavy, the utilization of the resources is very high. On the contrary, when the load of a VM is very light, the utilization of the resources is relatively less.

Therefore, the utilization of the resources can be used to characterize the load of VM to some extent. It is considered that the load of VM can be judged according to the application service response time of the system. The load can be determined through predicting the service response time at the next moment of the system. In order to get the application service response time and system resource utilization at the next time, some historical data is utilized with the LPC method which benefits the analysis of key resources.

According to the response time of the system service, the state of VM is governed by formula (1).

$$C = \begin{cases} 1 & R_{pt} < T_{lownormalMin} \\ 2 & T_{lownormalMin} \leq R_{pt} < T_{normalMax} \\ 3 & R_{pt} > T_{normalMax} \end{cases} \tag{1}$$

Among them as well as the following sections of the paper, the meaning of each variable is as follows:

Cpu: the resource utilization of cpu

Read: speed of disk reading data

Write: speed of disk writing data

Mem: memory usage

Recv: speed of network receiving data

Send: speed of network sending data

R_{pt}: the response time of application service

$T\_lownormalMin$: The minimum value of the application service response time in normal state.

$T\_normalMax$: The maximum value of the application service response time in normal state.

C is the parameter that indicates the state of VM. When $C = 1$, it means VM is in low load. In this state the performance of VM is optimal. However, the utilization of resources is too low. It will result in serious waste of resources. $C = 2$ means VM is in normal state or the load of VM is in reasonable range. In this state, resources are high efficiently utilized, and the application service response time as well as QoS are in acceptable range. It is the right state in which VM should keep. $C = 3$ means the resources are over utilized, or the load is beyond the bearing range of VM. In this state, the response time of the application service will be far more prolonged compared with that in normal state, and QoS decreases dramatically or be unacceptable. It is also a state in which VM should avoid working.

3.2   Dynamic adjustment of resources

When prediction of the R_{tp}R in the next moment, VMs are classified according to the formula (1), and the categories of the VMs in the next moment are obtained. If a VM belongs to category 2, it means it is in the normal state and does not need to be processed with any operations. However, if the VM is in class 1 or 3, it means it is in the state of low load or overload. Correspondingly, the resources of the VM should be reclaimed or expanded following the appropriate rules. At this time, the CPU, Read, Write, Mem, Recv, Send value and the classification of the VM at the next moment should be predicted, which are used to analyze the key resources that may affect the performance of the VM.

When the VM at the next moment is in state 1, or in low load, it should meet the conditions (2) and (3) according to Bias classification formula.

$$P(C_1 \mid X) > P(C_2 \mid X) \tag{2}$$

$$P(C_1 \mid X) > P(C_3 \mid X) \tag{3}$$

Note: $X = (x_{cpu}, x_{read}, x_{write}, x_{mem}, x_{recv}, x_{send})$ are the eigenvectors at some specific time, characterized the state of the VM. C_1, C_2 and C_3 represents $C = 1$, $C = 2$, and $C = 3$ respectively.

According to formula (2), assume the variables $x_{cpu}, x_{read}, x_{write}, x_{mem}, x_{recv}, x_{send}$ are independent mutually, formula (4) can be obtained:

$$\frac{P(C_1) \times \sum_{k=1}^{n} P(x_k \mid C_1)}{P(X)} > \frac{P(C_2) \times \sum_{k=1}^{n} P(x_k \mid C_2)}{P(X)} \tag{4}$$

Note: Here $n = 6$, $(x_1, x_2, x_3, x_4, x_5, x_6)$ means $x_{cpu}, x_{read}, x_{write}, x_{mem}, x_{recv}, x_{send}$ respectively.

For $P(X) > 0$, rewrite formula (4) and get:

$$\frac{P(C_1) \times \sum_{k=1}^{n} P(x_k \mid C_1)}{P(C_2) \times \sum_{k=1}^{n} P(x_k \mid C_2)} > 1 \tag{5}$$

Do logarithms calculations to the both sides of formula (5), formula (6) is obtained.

$$\log_{10} \frac{P(C_1)}{P(C_2)} + \sum_{k=1}^{n} \log_{10} \frac{P(x_k \mid C_1)}{P(x_k \mid C_2)} > 0 \tag{6}$$

Since $(x_1, x_2, x_3, x_4, x_5, x_6)$ represents $x_{cpu}, x_{read}, x_{write}, x_{mem}, x_{recv}, x_{send}$, formula (7) can be obtained.

$$\begin{aligned}
\log_{10} \frac{P(C_1)}{P(C_2)} &+ \log_{10} \frac{P(x_{cpu} \mid C_1)}{P(x_{cpu} \mid C_2)} + \log_{10} \frac{P(x_{read} \mid C_1)}{P(x_{read} \mid C_2)} \\
&+ \log_{10} \frac{P(x_{write} \mid C_1)}{P(x_{write} \mid C_2)} + \log_{10} \frac{P(x_{mem} \mid C_1)}{P(x_{mem} \mid C_2)} \\
&+ \log_{10} \frac{P(x_{recv} \mid C_1)}{P(x_{recv} \mid C_2)} + \log_{10} \frac{P(x_{send} \mid C_1)}{P(x_{send} \mid C_2)} > 0
\end{aligned} \tag{7}$$

Through the formula (7), it is easy to find if a VM is in the state $C = 1$, the sum of each items should be greater than 0. To some specific VM, $\log_{10} \frac{P(C_1)}{P(C_2)}$ is constant. Therefore among the other items, the one which has the maximum value is the largest contribution factor that makes the VM in state $C = 1$. This means when $C = 1$ the VM is in low load or the resource is too surplus for the current applications. So the resource corresponding to this factor can be reclaimed. Based on the analysis mentioned above, the key resource factor is defined as formula (8) shows.

$$key_{i,j,m} = \log_{10} \frac{P(x_m \mid C_i)}{P(x_m \mid C_j)} \tag{8}$$

Note: i, j can be taken as 1, 2, 3, and m can be regarded as $cpu, read, write, mem, recv, send$. Combine formula(7) and formula(8), formula (9) is obtained.

$$\log_{10} \frac{P(C_1)}{P(C_2)} + key_{1,2,cpu} + key_{1,2,read} + key_{1,2,write}$$
$$+ key_{1,2,mem} + key_{1,2,recv} + key_{1,2,send} > 0 \tag{9}$$

Now, all the key factors are as follows.
$P(C_1 \mid X) > P(C_2 \mid X)$: $key_{1,2,cpu}, key_{1,2,read}, key_{1,2,write}, key_{1,2,mem}, key_{1,2,recv}, key_{1,2,send}$.

Similarly, according to formula (3), it also can obtain formula (10).

$$\log_{10} \frac{P(C_1)}{P(C_2)} + key_{1,3,cpu} + key_{1,3,read} + key_{1,3,write}$$
$$+ key_{1,3,mem} + key_{1,3,recv} + key_{1,3,send} > 0 \tag{10}$$

For the same reason, all the possible key factors that make $P(C_1 \mid X) > P(C_3 \mid X)$ are $key_{1,3,cpu}, key_{1,3,read}, key_{1,3,write}, key_{1,3,mem}, key_{1,3,recv}$ and $key_{1,3,send}$. According to formula (2) and (3), all the possible factors that make are $key_{1,2,cpu}, key_{1,2,read}, key_{1,2,write}, key_{1,2,mem}, key_{1,2,recv}, key_{1,2,send}$ and $key_{1,3,cpu}, key_{1,3,read}, key_{1,3,write}, key_{1,3,mem}, key_{1,3,recv}, key_{1,3,send}$. Therefore, among all of these factors, the one of largest value is the most critical resource factor.

$$KeyResource = m, \quad \max_{j,m}\{key_{1,j,m}\} \tag{11}$$

Note: j can be taken as 2, 3; m can be taken as cpu, read, write, mem, recv, send. That is, resource KeyResource is the factor that contributes most to have the VM in state $C = 1$ that the resource is surplus and can be reclaimed in order to reduce the idle resources and avoid waste.

Similarly, when the VM is predicted in state 3 or overload state at the following moment, it meets the condition (12) and (13) according to Bias classification formula.

$$P(C_3 \mid X) > P(C_1 \mid X) \tag{12}$$
$$P(C_3 \mid X) > P(C_2 \mid X) \tag{13}$$

Derive from the formula (12), formula (14) can be obtained.

$$\log_{10} \frac{P(C_3)}{P(C_1)} + key_{3,1,cpu} + key_{3,1,read} + key_{3,1,write}$$
$$+ key_{3,1,mem} + key_{3,1,recv} + key_{3,1,send} > 0 \tag{14}$$

All possible key factors that make $P(C_3 \mid X) > P(C_1 \mid X)$ are $key_{3,1,cpu}$, $key_{3,1,read}$, $key_{3,1,write}$, $key_{3,1,mem}$, $key_{3,1,recv}$ and $key_{3,1,send}$.

Derive from the formula (13), formula (15) is obtained.

$$\log_{10} \frac{P(C_3)}{P(C_2)} + key_{3,2,cpu} + key_{3,2,read} + key_{3,2,write}$$
$$+ key_{3,2,mem} + key_{3,2,recv} + key_{3,2,send} > 0 \tag{15}$$

Similarly all possible key factors that make $P(C_3 \mid X) > P(C_2 \mid X)$ include $key_{3,2,cpu}$, $key_{3,2,read}$, $key_{3,2,write}$, $key_{3,2,mem}$, $key_{3,2,recv}$ and $key_{3,2,send}$.

According to formula(12) and (13), all possible key factors that make VM in overload state are $key_{3,1,cpu}$, $key_{3,1,read}$, $key_{3,1,write}$, $key_{3,1,mem}$, $key_{3,1,recv}$, $key_{3,1,send}$ and $key_{3,2,cpu}$, $key_{3,2,read}$, $key_{3,2,write}$, $key_{3,2,mem}$, $key_{3,2,recv}$ and $key_{3,2,send}$. Among all of these factors, the largest one is the most critical resource factor.

$$KeyResource = m, \quad \max_{j,m}\{key_{3,j,m}\} \tag{16}$$

Note: j can be taken as 1,2, and m can be one of the factor in cpu, read, write, mem, recv and send.

Resource KeyResource is the factor that contributes most to have the VM in state $C = 3$ or the overload state. In other words, the resource is the bottleneck of the VM which should be increased to improve the performance of the system and ensure the quality of service. After getting the key resources, the method that is used to dynamically scale the resource is discussed as follows.

(1) Judge the state of the VM according to the prediction of the application service response time. If the VM is in normal state, no special operation is needed and go to step 4. If the VM is in low load, go to step 2. Otherwise, when the VM is overload, go to step 3.
(2) Calculate the main idle resources of the VM according to formula (11). And reclaim part of the idle resources to reduce wasting the resources. Go to step 4.
(3) Calculate the key bottleneck resource of the VM according to formula (16). And increase the key resource dynamically to ensure the performance of the system as well as the quality of user service. Go to step 4.
(4) Exit the resource adjustment operation.

4   Experiment and results

Extensive experiments have been done to verify the Load forecasting method and dynamic scheduling strategy.

4.1   Experimental environment

The experimental environment was based on cloudstack cloud computing platform version 5.0. We built a private cloud computing platform, which includes a management node, two host nodes and a storage node. The operating system of the host node is redhat server 6.4. CPU is Intel I5 3470@3.60 GHz. Memory is DDR3 8 GB. The volume of hard disk is 1 TB. The operating system of VM in host is Ubuntu 15.04, CPU is 1 GHz*2, memory is 1 GB, the network bandwidth is 150 Mbps, and the disk rotational speed is 7200 r/min (Table 1).

Table 1. Hardware parameters of experiment environment

Node	CPU (GHz)	Memory (GB)	Disk volume (GB)	Disk speed (r/min)
Management	3.4	4.0	1000	5400
Storage	3.6	8.0	1000	5400
Host1	3.6	8.0	1000	7200
Host2	3.2	4.0	500	7200

4.2   Results and analysis

In order to verify the load prediction method and virtual machine dynamic scheduling method, httping tool is used to send requests to the system. And Linux monitoring tool dstat is used to monitor the resource usage in the process of system running with which the service response time of the system is obtained. Through comparing the response time using and not using the strategy proposed, the effectiveness of the strategy is verified.

The application running on the VM is to compute the prime numbers less than 20000 with sysbench. Figures from Figs. 1, 2, 3, 4, 5 and 6 are the experimental results of the utilization of different resources when four applications running simultaneously on the VM. From Figs. 1, 2, 3, 4, 5 and 6. It is easy to find out, the predictive values and actual observation ones are very close or almost the same with regard to system resources such as CPU, disk reading and writing, memory, network receiving and sending. It indicates that the prediction method is effective.

Figure 7 represents the response time with and without using the proposed strategy when the load on VM increases from the beginning with low load till to that with over load. According to the figure, at the beginning, due to the low system load, the corresponding response time of the two methods are basically the same. However, with the increasing number of the requests, that is to say, with the increasing of system load, the corresponding response time of the method increases sharply without using our strategy, which seriously lowers the quality of service. However, the response time approximately keeps stable using the proposed strategy. Moreover, it is easy to find that using the propsed strategy, the response time is much lower than that without using the proposed strategy. It can ensures the quality of service.

Figure 8 presents the response time with and without using the proposed strategy when the system is in low load. According to the figure, the response

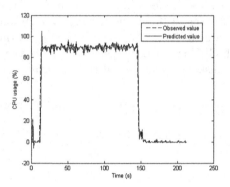

Fig. 1. The prediction value of CPU usage

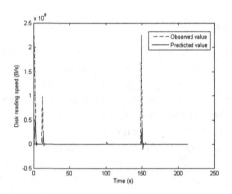

Fig. 2. The prediction value of disk reading speed

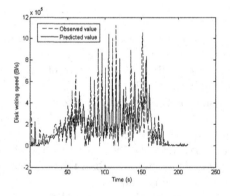

Fig. 3. The prediction value of disk writing speed

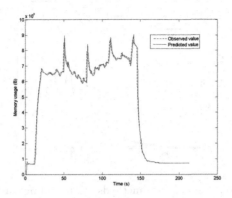

Fig. 4. The prediction value of memory usage

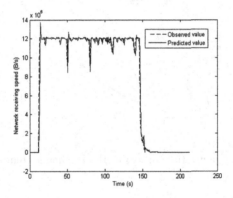

Fig. 5. The prediction of network receiving speed

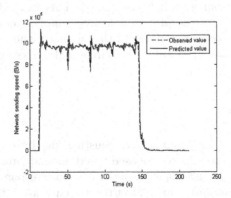

Fig. 6. The prediction of network sending speed

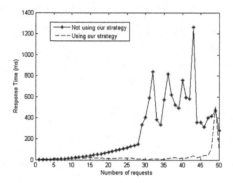

Fig. 7. The response time of two methods when load increases till overload

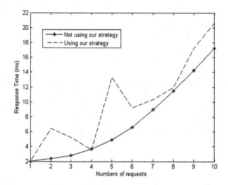

Fig. 8. The response time of two methods when system in low load

time of the proposed strategy is slightly larger than that without using the proposed strategy even though the values for both methods are approximately the same, both within the acceptable range. This is because with the proposed stategy, some surplus resources will be reclaimed. This will slightly lead to some extra cost. However with the proposed strategy applications will be processed with much less resources compared with that without using the proposed strategy. This can avoid wasting the cloud resources and reduce energy consumption.

5   Conclusions

To solve the problem of dynamically adjusting the resources of VM, a VM dynamic adjustment strategy is proposed based on load forecasting. By predicting the system resources usage and application service response time the strategy tries to find the key resource which affect the system state with which the bottleneck of the VM is drawn out. Baed on the bottleneck, a method dynamically and appropriately scaling the key resources is presented. With the scaling method, the surplus resources are reclaimed if the VM is in low load which can reduce the waste of resources. Meanwhile the key resources which is the bottleneck affecting the performance of the system are increased when the VM is overload. This can much improve the performance of the system and ensure the QoS of the system. Extensive experiments show the strategy is correct and efficient, and it lays a foundation for reasonably using cloud resources.

References

1. Foster, I., Zhao, Y., Raicu, I., Lu, S.: Cloud Computing and Grid Computing 360-Degree Compared. In: 2008 Grid Computing Environments Workshop Proceedings, pp. 1–10. IEEE, Austin (2008)
2. Nicolae, B.: High throughput data-compression for cloud storage. In: Hameurlain, A., Morvan, F., Tjoa, A.M. (eds.) Globe 2010. LNCS, vol. 6265, pp. 1–12. Springer, Heidelberg (2010). https://doi.org/10.1007/978-3-642-15108-8_1
3. Fang, Y., Wang, F., Ge, J.: A task scheduling algorithm based on load balancing in cloud computing. In: Wang, F.L., Gong, Z., Luo, X., Lei, J. (eds.) WISM 2010. LNCS, vol. 6318, pp. 271–277. Springer, Heidelberg (2010). https://doi.org/10.1007/978-3-642-16515-3_34
4. Aluvalu, R., Vardhaman, J.M.A., Kantaria, J.: Performance evaluation of clustering algorithms for dynamic VM allocation in cloud computing. In: Proceedings of 2017 International Conference On Smart Technologies For Smart Nation (SmartTechCon), pp. 1560–1563. IEEE (2017)
5. Basu, S., et al.: Cloud computing security challenges & solutions-a survey. In: Proceedings of 2018 IEEE 8th Annual Computing and Communication Workshop and Conference (CCWC), pp. 347–356. IEEE (2018)
6. Kapil, D., Tyagi, P., Kumar, S., Tamta, V.P.: Cloud computing: overview and research issues. In: Proceedings of 2017 International Conference on Green Informatics (ICGI), pp. 71–76. IEEE (2017)
7. Pastaki Rad, M., Sajedi Badashian, A., Meydanipour, G., Ashurzad Delcheh, M., Alipour, M., Afzali, H.: A survey of cloud platforms and their future. In: Gervasi, O., Taniar, D., Murgante, B., Laganà, A., Mun, Y., Gavrilova, M.L. (eds.) ICCSA 2009. LNCS, vol. 5592, pp. 788–796. Springer, Heidelberg (2009). https://doi.org/10.1007/978-3-642-02454-2_61
8. Zhang, Q., Cheng, L., Boutaba, R.: Cloud computing: state-of-the-art and research challenges. J. Internet Serv. Appl. 1, 7–18 (2010)
9. Yara, P., Ramachandran, R., Balasubramanian, G., Muthuswamy, K., Chandrasekar, D.: Global software development with cloud platforms. In: Gotel, O., Joseph, M., Meyer, B. (eds.) SEAFOOD 2009. LNBIP, vol. 35, pp. 81–95. Springer, Heidelberg (2009). https://doi.org/10.1007/978-3-642-02987-5_10
10. Greenberg, A., Hamilton, J., Maltz, D.A.: The cost of a cloud: research problems in data center networks. ACM SIGCOMM Comput. Commun. Rev. 39(1), 68–73 (2008)
11. Schopf, J.M., Berman, F.: Stochastic scheduling. In: Proceedings of ACM/IEEE 1999 Conference on Supercomputing, pp. 235-258. IEEE (2000)
12. Yang, Y., Casanova, H.: RUMR: robust Scheduling for Divisible Workloads. In: Proceedings of IEEE International Symposium on High PERFORMANCE Distributed Computing, pp. 114–123. IEEE (2003)

13. Padmavathi, S., Soniha, P.K., Soundarya, N., Srimathi, S.: Dynamic resource provisioning and monitoring for cloud computing. In: Proceedings of 2017 IEEE International Conference on Intelligent Techniques in Control, Optimization and Signal Processing (INCOS), pp. 1–6. IEEE (2017)
14. Zhao, L., Du, M., Chen, L.: A new multi-resource allocation mechanism: a tradeoff between fairness and efficiency in cloud computing. China Commun. **15**(3), 57–77 (2018)
15. Taylor, J.W., Menezes, L.M.D., Mcsharry, P.E.: A comparison of univariate methods for forecasting electricity demand up to a day ahead. Int. J. Forecast. **22**(1), 1–16 (2006)
16. Sorjanmaa, A., Hao, J., Reyhani, N., et al.: Methodology for long-term prediction of time series. Neurocomputing **70**(16–18), 2861–2869 (2007)
17. Hu, J., Gu, J., Sun, G., Zhao, T.: A scheduling strategy on load balancing of virtual machine resources in cloud computing environment. In: Proceedings of Third International Symposium on Parallel Architectures, Algorithms and Programming, pp. 89–96. IEEE (2010)
18. Chen, G., He, W., Liu, J., et al.: Energy-aware server provisioning and load dispatching for connection-intensive internet services. In: Proceedings of Usenix Symposium on Networked Systems Design and Implementation, NSDI 2008, pp. 337–350. Usenix (2008)
19. Peng, J., Dai, Y., Rao, Y., Chen, J., Zhi, X.: Research on processing strategy for CPU-intensive application. J. Syst. Archit. **70**, 39–47 (2016)
20. Shen, Z., Subbiah, S., Gu, X., et al.: CloudScale: elastic resource scaling for multitenant cloud systems. In: Proceedings of ACM Symposium on Cloud Computing, pp. 1-14. ACM (2011)
21. Padala, P., Hou, K.Y., Kang, G.S., et al.: Automated control of multiple virtualized resources. In: Proceedings of 2009 ACM European Conference on Computer Systems, pp. 13-26. ACM (2009)
22. Meng, F., Zhang, H., Chu.: Cloud computing resource load balancing study based on ant colony optimization algorithm. J. Huazhong Univ. Sci. Technol. **41**(s2), 57–62 (2013)

A Data-Aware Energy-Saving Storage Management Strategy for On-Site Astronomical Observation at Dome A

Xiaoxiao Lu[1], Chao Sun[1(✉)], Ce Yu[1(✉)], Jizhou Sun[1], Ming Che[1], Zijun Xia[2], Zhaohui Shang[3], and Yi Hu[3]

[1] School of Computer Science and Technology, Tianjin University,
Tianjin 300350, China
{luxiaoxiao,sch,yuce,jzsun,cheming}@tju.edu.cn
[2] National Supercomputer Center in Tianjin, Tianjin 300457, China
xiazj@nscc-tj.gov.cn
[3] National Astronomical Observatories, Chinese Academy of Sciences, Beijing
100000, China
zshang@gmail.com, huyi.naoc@gmail.com

Abstract. The high energy consumption of storage system has always been a thorny issue especially when power supply is limited, e.g. the case of astronomical observation at Dome A in the Antarctic. Many general-purpose energy-efficient strategies are designed to be applied in common data centers, which is still quite different from disk array at Dome A where extreme restrictions would influence the effect of solutions. Besides, maintaining the reliability is as important as saving energy because most of the time, nobody is there to solve the disk failure problem. In this paper we propose a data-aware energy-saving storage management strategy, named DAES, for astronomical observation whose purpose is to reduce the energy consumed while mitigating the loss of the reliability of disks. A metric named hit index is designed for each disk from the perspective of astronomy to manage the power state of disks more accurately. A customized file scheduler is also drafted to improve data layout dynamically. Simulation experiments show that it reduces energy consumption by up to 56.6% and cuts down the switches of power state by up to 66.8% compared with common energy-saving strategies.

Keywords: Astronomical observation data · Disk array
Disk reliability · Energy efficient · Storage system

1 Introduction

Astronomy has been at the forefront of the development of techniques and methodologies of data intensive science for over a decade with large sky surveys and distributed efforts [6]. China is building its astronomical observatory in Antarctic Dome A and a series of telescopes, AST3, have been conducted. The

© Springer Nature Switzerland AG 2018
J. Vaidya and J. Li (Eds.): ICA3PP 2018, LNCS 11335, pp. 551–566, 2018.
https://doi.org/10.1007/978-3-030-05054-2_42

AST3 project consists of three large field of view survey telescopes with 680 mm primary mirror, mainly for observations of supernovas and extrasolar planets searching from Antarctic Dome A which is likely to be the best astronomical site on earth for astronomical observation [20]. The first set of AST3 telescope system was mounted at Dome A in Jan. 2012 and the second one was installed in Feb. 2015. Each telescope of AST3 theoretically produces a 200 MB image every 2.4 min, thus 360 GB per day.

The growing massive observation data need to be analyzed in time otherwise the discovery of some astronomical phenomenon would be delayed for a long time. The telescope assesses to the Internet via Iridium satellite constellation whose expensive and narrow bandwidth makes it unrealistic to transfer all the raw data back. So it is necessary to establish a data center to provide local data processing service for astronomers.

The energy consumption of the storage system accounts for a significant proportion of the total energy consumption of the data center while maintaining rapid growth [17]. Due to the harsh environment of Dome A, however, the power supply is extremely limited. Considering that raw and processed data may reach PB level in the near future, more disks would be used, making the energy consumption of the storage system hardly affordable. Therefore, the storage system must be strictly energy-efficient to not affect other devices of the whole system like the master computer and telescopes.

Various energy-efficient strategies has been proposed, including improved architectures, methods about caching and data migration, etc. However, they are mainly designed for general purposes and not suitable for the case of antarctic astronomical observation where power supply is extremely limited so that only a small part of disks could work at the same time. All the equipments, including telescopes, industrial computer, data center, etc., share a same jet fuel generators whose maximum power is about 1kW. The fuel is replenished by the Antarctic expedition team annually. Furthermore, stability is also of urgent requirement, which means that the common way of powering off disks to save energy is limited because excessive power state switches would shorten the life of disks.

To achieve this goal, the idle disk, or the disk with no I/O tasks at present, need to be powered off or switched into low power state. However, spinning up a disk again also consumes much energy and too many switches between states shorten the life cycle of disks, thereby degrading the reliability [14]. Therefore, it is significant to recognize the I/O scheme of the disks and switch the disk state according to it. In other words, switch disks into lower power state prudently to save energy and make the most of every switch.

The access to astronomical data usually follows a spatio-temporal pattern. For example, when a user need to research the changes of a target celestial body within a certain period, all the files that covers this object with eligible generate time need to be picked out. Since the observation data rarely move once written to a disk, the probability of a certain disk to be hit in the near future could be quantified according to the past requests.

In this paper, a new data-aware energy-efficient storage management strategy named DAES is designed for on-site astronomical observation at Dome A. It does not care much about the structure of the whole storage system, whether it is a multi-level caching or a hybrid storage system, as long as it is possible to switch the states of hard disk drives. DAES figures out a correlated files list for each file from historical file access log from the perspective of astronomy. Then it develops a metric called hit index for each disk to judge the probability for it to be hit from its data and historical requests. With the help of hit index, power state is arranged more smartly by reducing unreasonable switches and idle spinning of disks. To make full use of a disk while it is working, a smart file scheduler is utilized to adopt customized caching, prefetching and replication strategies. Therefore, data layout is optimized dynamically to get less disks involved while handling a request.

Specially, this paper makes the following contributions:

(1) We propose an innovative data-aware storage management strategy for on-site astronomical observation at Dome A that not only saves energy but also preserves the reliability of disks under limited power supply.
(2) We design a specific metric named hit index for each disk to manage its power state from the perspective of astronomy. A lazy file scheduler is also customized to improve the original data layout dynamically with a little cost.
(3) We evaluate the proposed method with dataset of AST3 in 2016. The results show that our approach outperforms its alternative in all experiments.

The remainder of this paper is organized as follows. Section 2 presents the related work. Section 3 discusses the challenges of the storage server at Dome A. Section 4 elaborates on details of DAES, including hit index calculation and file scheduling. Section 5 evaluates the performance of DAES with related discussion. Finally, we conclude this paper and discuss future work in Sect. 6.

2   Related Work

Numerous studies have been conducted about energy conservation of disk storage and various energy-saving methods have been proposed, mainly including caching, prefetching and data migration. Most of them intend to extend the idle time of disks so that they can be turned into low power state to save energy.

2.1   Caching, Prefetching and Replication Strategy

The main centerpiece of caching is to use extra cache disks to store popular and prefetched data in order to concentrate workload. MAID (Massive Arrays of Idle Disks) is typical representative of this kind of energy-saving technology [5]. A small part of disks serves as cache disks which always keep rotating while others serve as data disks which stop rotating after a certain period of idle time.

Some strategies utilize energy-aware storage media such as SSD as cache disks, such as E-HASH [7].

Prefetching is another way to save energy. It raises the hit rate of cache by prefetching the potential required data into cache devices. Therefore data disks could have more idle time if they are hit as predicted. Powerful prefetching strategy should prefetch as many useful data as possible while eliminate as few useless data as possible, such as PRE-BUD [10–13] and Eco-storage [2].

Replication strategies distribute copies of popular data into different storage devices. Therefore requested data could be accessed from working disks rather than powered-off ones if it has replicas in both disks. Proper data replication could save energy and minimize bandwidth usage in cloud computing data centers [3]. It should also take both load balance and power proportionality into consideration [9]. Replicas could be put into data disks such as HDD, or cache disks such as SSD. From this perspective, caching and prefetching are generalizations of replication.

2.2 Data Migration Strategy

PDC (Popular Data Concentration) [16] migrates frequently accessed data to a subset of the disks. The goal is to skew the workload towards a few of the disks, so that others can be transitioned to low-power modes. PDC is suitable for the application with part of its data being of high access frequency. PDC-NH [8] extends PDC by adding NAND flash based Solid State Drive (SSD). It places large and sequential read files on HDD and small and random read files on SSD to achieve better performance and energy savings. FDTM [22] works on block-level data and aims to get a trade-off between storage QoS and migration costs. EDM [15] is an endurance-aware data migration scheme with careful data placement and movement to minimize the data migrated, so as to limit the worn-out of SSDs while improving the performance. There are some other improved algorithms, such as EESDC [4] and LAM [21].

2.3 Summary of Related Work

These related researches have a common goal to maximize the idle interval of disks and put them into low-power modes in time to save energy. However, they cannot be adopted directly for astronomical observation data. Firstly, this kind of data has its own format and usage mode. Thus the caching and prefetching strategy need to be adjusted accordingly. Secondly, all disks may still be working simultaneously in the worst case, which is not allowed in case of the Antarctic. Thirdly, the astronomical observation data mainly consists of FITS files whose size is often several hundred MB. Correspondingly, the cost of caching and migration would be enlarged, making common strategies inefficient especially when operating a file inappropriately.

3   Challenges

Due to the limited power supply in the Antarctic or just the goal of green data center, the storage system must be energy-efficient. Normally, an energy-aware storage server turns idle disks into low-power state to save energy. In common practice, an idle time threshold is set for disks and a disk is powered off if it reaches this point. The main problem is that how to set a proper value for the threshold. A small one may reduce the working time of disks and therefore cut down the energy consumed. On the other hand, however, it causes more disk state switches which consume additional energy and impair the reliability of disks. It is hard to predict the workload of disks and change disk states accordingly.

Each telescope continues producing observation data, making it essential to have a data center around it. The storage system of the data center stores raw observation data and preliminary processed data such as FITS or catalogue. As shown in Fig. 1, a typical time domain astronomical research that an astronomer needs to do is to research changes of a certain celestial body in a period of time, which defines the typical workflow of the storage server. Users give the coordinate of target celestial body (e.g. RA and DEC) and target time period. RA (right ascension) and DEC (declination) are to the sky what longitude and latitude are to the surface of the Earth. Note that the target celestial body, as well as the changes, is captured within an area on the photograph rather than a single point, making target point become target sky zone. The storage server then returns back to users the correlated FITS files that cover whole or part area of the target sky zone and meet the time requirements.

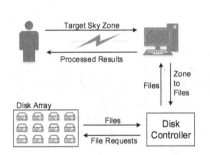

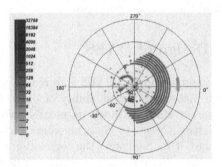

Fig. 1. Workflow of typical time domain astronomical research

Fig. 2. Footprint of astronomical data by AST3 in 2016

This work, however, is not easy for the storage server. Firstly, it is difficult to determine the correlated files set. An efficient index is needed to reduce the workload of checking the astronomical attributes of all files.

Secondly, the correlated files need to be selected by their fitness degrees with the request, which needs quite a lot calculation. Telescopes may work in different modes, e.g. sky survey or fixed point, making the footprint of its data unbalanced.

Consequently, the correlated files sets of different requests may differ a lot in quantity. Figure 2 shows the footprint of astronomical data of AST3 in 2016. Some areas were covered evenly while other areas were extremely unbalanced. Therefore, some requests may match numerous files covering the whole target area while some may match few files covering only a small part of target area. If too many files are matched, only the most correlated files were selected due to the fact that these files already contain enough information. Figure 3 illustrates this case. The grey area is the target sky zone a user requests. For this request, file 0 is better than file 1 and file 1 is better than file 2. Instead of using the recommended files, some advanced users may even choose target files themselves.

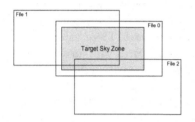

Fig. 3. Different fitness for a request

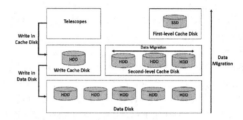

Fig. 4. Architecture of MCS-B [18]

The complex workflow, together with the irregular footprint and placement of astronomical data, makes it hard to predict which disks a request would hit, in which case it is difficult to employ energy-aware strategies. That's maybe the reason that rule-based approaches fail and statistical methods work.

4   Design of DAES

The main purpose of DAES is to reduce the energy consumed by storage system while preserving the reliability of disks. In other words, switch idle disks into low-power state as much as possible while reducing the number of switches. Obviously, these two goals are contradictory and a balance is necessary. DAES manages it by analyzing the correlation of files from historical file access mode.

In fact, the data layout among disks has a remarkable effect on the performance of energy saving. An optional optimized placement concentrates files with similar sky zone into the same disk then a single request would have only a few disks involved. However, this placement is hard to manage because the telescope continues producing new data and the cost of reaching it may not be offset by its benefit over a long time [19]. How the data is placed is beyond the scope of this paper. DAES cares little about it because DAES focuses more on power management of underlying disks and manages an optimized layout dynamically.

As shown in Fig. 4, our previous work proposed a new energy-efficient architecture named MCS-B for the same application scenario [18]. It focuses more on the upper layer of the storage system while this paper focuses more on the power management. What this work focuses on is all the hard disks of a storage system, no matter whether it is a data disk or a cache disk. DAES manages to calculate a hit index for each disk and then decide its power state.

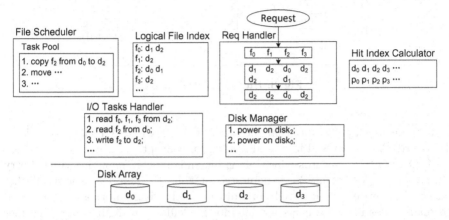

Fig. 5. Structure of DAES

The structure of DAES is shown in Fig. 5. **Logical file index** indexes all logical files and the disk information of their instances. A telescope generates one file at a time. It can be identified as a triple $\langle ra, dec, observe\_time\rangle$, which makes up a logical file. It has more meanings in logic rather than in file system. If we replicate a file into another disk, they are two files in view of file system, but one file in logic which shares a same entry in logical file index. Remember that astronomical file is usually several hundred MB, which means that a storage system cannot hold too many files. Supposing that each astronomical file is about 500 MB, then a 2TB disk could only hold about four thousand files, making it possible to index all files in this data center in the memory. That is to say, updating and querying operations are of high efficiency.

Request handler translates requests to files and then to disks. It chooses the least amount of disks to serve a request. It performs a great effect if related files has duplications. **File scheduler** deals with file replications. It analyses the historical log to find closely related files on different disks and then concentrates them into the same disk at convenience. It is further discussed in Subsect. 4.2. **Hit index calculator** calculates a hit index for each disk indicating its probability of being hit in the short future. It is elaborated in Subsect. 4.1. **I/O tasks handler** sends I/O requests to disk array. **Disk manager** decides the power state of each disk according to its I/O tasks and hit index.

4.1 Hit Index Calculator

Figure 6 gives an example of how hit index of each disk is calculated. Overall, it contains four parts: I/O event log, sorted correlated files lists, logical file index

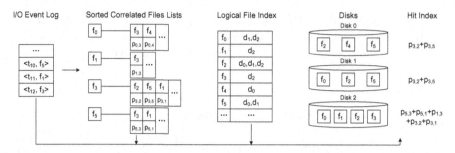

Fig. 6. Hit index calculation

and the hit index part. Note that the logical file index is also displayed in Fig. 5. The word "file" discussed here is also a logical concept.

I/O event log records which file is hit and the corresponding time. Entry $\langle t_i, f_j \rangle$ means logical file f_j is requested at time t_i. This log is a simple list into which entries are inserted chronologically. It gives information to sorted correlated files lists and helps the hit index calculator to figure out which files have been recently requested.

Sorted correlated files lists are the main part of the whole correlation analysis. Overall, it is a key-value map. The key part is just logical files while the value part is a list of correlated files to the key file along with related probabilities that these files would be requested after the key file is requested. For example in Fig. 6, the probability of file f_3 to be requested within a certain period after file f_0 is requested is $p_{0,3}$ from a historical point of view. That of f_4 is $p_{0,4}$. In order to accelerate search service, the key part is stored in a red-black tree. For ease of use later, each list in the value part is sorted in descending order of $p_{i,j}$. Let T_{cor_itv} be the max time interval between two correlated files and t_{now} to be the current time. Every time a new entry, marked as $\langle t_{now}, f_{now} \rangle$, is inserted into I/O event log, these lists are updated as follows:

1. Find the oldest entry within the time period $[t_{now} - T_{cor\_itv}, t_{now}]$ from I/O event log;
2. Mark the file of this entry as f_i. If the sky zone of f_i partially overlaps with file f_{now}, update $p_{i,now}$ in the sorted correlated files list. If $p_{i,now}$ does not exist, create it first.
3. Check the next entry in I/O event log as step 2 until it comes to entry $\langle t_{now}, f_{now} \rangle$.

In order to update $p_{i,now}$, we also need to record how many times f_i is requested and how many times f_{now} is requested within a period of T_{cor_itv} after f_i is requested, which is not displayed in Fig. 6.

Organized as a binary search tree, **logical file index** supplies quick search and update for the metadata of all files. The metadata part stores not only the information about which disks its instances are stored in, but also some statistical data.

Each disk has a **hit index**. It is calculated at regular intervals as follows:

1. Set the hit index of every disk to 0;
2. Find the oldest entry within the time period $[t_{now} - T_{cor\_itv}, t_{now}]$ from I/O event log;
3. Mark the file of this entry as f_i. Find the correlated files list of f_i. For each file f_j in this list, find which disks its instances are stored in from logical file index and then add $p_{i,j}$ respectively to the hit index of these disks;
4. Check the next entry in I/O event log as step 3 until the last entry in the log is processed.

A classical power management strategy sets the disk into standby state when the idle interval is larger than the break-even time T_{be} which means the minimum idle time required to compensate the cost of entering low power state [14]. This makes sense, but it could be smarter. Idle state is a waste of energy no matter how short it lasts. With the help of hit index, we could decide which power state a disk should be at more accurately. If the hit index is too low, we switch the disk state into low power mode in advance for that it is unlikely that the following requests would hit this disk again, in which case, we shorten the useless spinning of disks. On the other hand, if the hit index is still high, we may not switch the disk state into low power mode because it is quite likely that the following requests would hit this disk again, in which case we reduce useless state switches and delay the aging of hard disks.

It is because the number of astronomical files is limited by their large size that the hit index method does not require much calculation. Furthermore, the item with an absolutely small probability in the correlated files list would be removed at regular intervals to keep this system running in a light way.

4.2   File Scheduler

In order to achieve better energy saving effect and reduce the number of disks a request involves, a file scheduler is built to improve data layout dynamically by combining various means, including caching, prefetching and replication strategies.

Due to the large size of a single astronomical file, it costs much to copy or move a file, which undermines the effect of caching, prefetching and replication strategies to some degree. Thus, it is a wisdom to take a prudent attitude towards these strategies.

Caching is to copy requested files into cache disks or memory; prefetching is to cache related files of requested files in advance; replication is to copy files to another place, usually in other data disks of the same level. The first two strategies could be treated as the third one to some degree. They all copy files and only differ in the place to put them. We need to track these files. The logical file index shown in Fig. 5 exists for this purpose. It records the places where a file and its copies are stored. Actually, there is no such view that the original file and its copies should be treated differently. They are the same for that they share the same entry. This setting gives us more freedom to replicate files and optimize as much as possible without the limitation that original files cannot be moved.

Furthermore, this system weakens the role of cache disks. Any hard drive disk could be used as a cache disk if it is busy most of the time. If the workload is skewed to other disks, the new disks could be treated as cache disks to store some temporarily popular files.

Table 1 gives power management specifications of four WD Blue^{TM} PC hard drive models [1]. There is no significant difference in energy consumption whether the disk has I/O tasks or not as long as it is spinning. It inspires us that we should make full use of a disk while it is idle. A copy/move to/from a disk in idle state could obtain benefit of this schedule with only a little cost. This is the main spirit of replication strategy in this system.

Table 1. Power management specifications of WD Blue^{TM} hard drives [1]

Model	WD10EZEX	WD10EZRZ	WD20EZRZ	WD40EZRZ
Capacity	1 TB	1 TB	2 TB	4 TB
12VDC ±10% (A, peak)	2.5	1.2	1.73	1.75
Average power requirements (W)				
Read/Write	6.8	3.3	4.1	5.3
Idle	6.1	2.5	3.0	3.4
Standby/Sleep	1.2	0.4	0.4	0.4

All the file scheduling tasks are put into a task pool, including caching, prefetching and replication tasks. A task is an order to move/copy a file from one place to another with a priority. The source disk could be several disks if the file has several instances. A task in the pool is processed when its source disk and destination disk are both idle. A task in process occupies the two disks until the file transmission is completed. If a task conflicts with another, the one with higher priority is processed first.

The scheduler tries to concentrate correlated files into the same disk like PDC. It periodically search the sorted correlated files lists to check whether there are some highly correlated files with a high probability close to 1. If found, check whether there is an instance of the key file and an instance of the correlated file stored in the same disk. If not found, add a task into the pool to copy or move one file to a disk where another file is stored.

The scheduler also attempts to prefetch the most likely hit files. When a file is requested, the scheduler searches its correlated files list to check whether it has some highly correlated files. If so, the scheduler puts this task into the pool with a high priority. This kind of tasks would be canceled if they are not handled within a short period. In which case, it expires even this prediction is right.

Replication strategies is very effective to reduce I/O time and enhance data security because we can choose the least busy disk to handle this task. However, astronomical files are large in size, which makes the cost of replication not ignored. Therefore, it should focus more on those most visited files. The more times a file is hit, the more replicas it should have. Replication tasks are also handled by the pool with a low priority.

5   Experimental Evaluation

It is necessary to carry out effective simulation experiments of the storage system before it is applied to a real one. This section introduces the simulation experiment of DAES, including simulator architecture, data set and the comparison between DAES and common strategy.

5.1   Simulator Architecture

The disk array in the Antarctic is customized, which means that each disk could be powered on or off separately. Together with the unique workflow of the storage server, it makes common disk system simulators unsuitable. We build a light and effective simulator for it.

As shown in Fig. 7, the disk simulator consists of six parts. The storage devices is used to simulate the behaviors of true disks, mainly including the state switches and I/O operations. The data generator parses the data set and stores them into storage devices. The request generator provides requests with target sky zone and period following a pattern of astronomical research. The resource scheduling controller transforms the requests to files and sends the I/O commands to storage devices. Besides, it is also in charge of the power management of disks. The hit index calculator updates the hit index for each disk every a certain period. Finally, the trace and statistics module tracks the entire life cycle of each request and records disk status and work duration for further analysis.

This simulator is also highly-configurable due to its modular design. Most functions of it can be configured via parameters, including but not limited to the way to generate requests, the number of disks and detailed

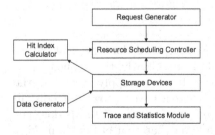

Fig. 7. Architecture of simulator

Table 2. Key parameters of the simulator

Parameter name	Default value
Capacity of each disk (MB)	1000000
Idle time threshold (s)	$10, 20, \cdots, 120$
Max files a request mapped to	10
Number of users	1000
Range of requests' RA	$0 \sim 360$
Range of requests' DEC	$-90 \sim -30$
$T_{cor\_itv}(s)$	60

behavior of power management. Key parameters are shown in Table 2. Source code of the simulator and original experimental data are available at *github.com/mldssr/DiskArraySim*.

5.2 Data Set

We choose the astronomical data of AST3 in 2016. From Mar.14 to Aug.14, 2016, it contains 71536 FITS files in total. These files are of many observation modes, including Survey, Focus, ImageTest, Nontracking, etc. The footprint is shown in Fig. 2. The long regular band with the declination ranging from $-60°$ to $-40°$ is related to files of Survey mode. Other points in that figure correspond to other modes.

These files are stored into the disk array from the first disk chronologically in the order of their observe time. As a layout currently in use, it is the most energy-efficient way when the footprint and the popularity of each file are unknown. To enlarge the scale of this experiment, we expand the data set according to its scheme, making the final data set stored in 70 HDDs.

In the requests part, we simulate 1000 users and each user makes a request of their own at a random time. For those requests with too many related files, the controller returns the best 10 files. Since each file is several hundred MB, a 10-file transmission still costs a lot of time.

5.3 Experimental Results

In common practice, a disk is powered off when it reaches a fixed idle time threshold (FixTh). It is clear that this threshold determines the basic level of energy consumption and spin-up times. It is also one of determining factors when DAES judges the power state of disks. Therefore, we made comparative experiments in different idle time thresholds from 10 to 120 step by 10 in seconds. In case of each threshold, we compare FixTh and DAES when all the requests are handled over.

Energy and Power. As shown in Fig. 8, DAES consumes only a half of the energy in FixTh under any threshold. It saves energy by 56.6% at threshold being 10 and by 41.4% at threshold being 120. Figure 9 gives a comparison in terms of average power of the disk array. Since the total time is very similar, the result is almost the same as Fig. 8. We also record the average top 100 peak power of the disk array, which is shown in Fig. 10. Note that the peak power in FixTh is close to 700 watts when threshold is 10. Clearly, the frequent spin-up and spin-down consumes much more power. If power supply is limited, the storage system would face a difficult situation where it have to power off a disk in order to power on another one, which may cause performance jitter. It does not bother DAES for that its peak power is much lower than that of FixTh, making it hard to reach the limitation. As the threshold grows, the impact of spin-up and spin-down shrinks, causing the peak power slowly decreasing in FixTh.

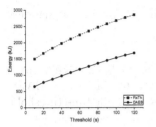
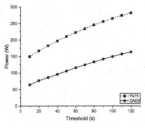
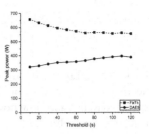

Fig. 8. Total energy of the disk array

Fig. 9. Average power of the disk array

Fig. 10. Average top 100 peak power of the disk array

As to DAES, less spin-up and spin-down make this part of power negligible compared with operating power of disks. As the threshold grows, more power are used to support the operating disks, causing the peak power slowly increasing.

Spin-up Times. The average spin-up times of all disks as idle time threshold changes is shown in Fig. 11. DAES reduces spin-up times by 66.8% at threshold being 10 and by 46.3% at threshold being 120. As the threshold increases, the spin-up times significantly decreases in case of FixTh while decreasing slowly in case of DAES. Threshold has less effect on DAES, which means DAES has more relative advantage when threshold is small. In short, DAES effectively decreases the average spin up times of all disks. Therefore, the reliability of the disk array of DAES is better than that of FixTh with a great probability.

Served Files Per Spin-up. Figure 12 explains why DAES significantly decreases spin-up times of each disk under the same request trace. As expected, DAES makes the most of each spin-up for that a disk serves more files once spun up. For one thing, DAES will not turn a disk into low power state if it still has a high hit index even if it has reached the threshold, which reduces the times of spinning it up again right after it is powered off. For another, the file scheduler

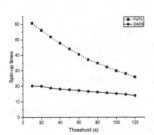
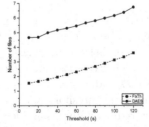
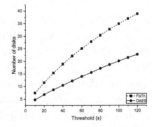

Fig. 11. Average spin-up times of each disk

Fig. 12. Average number of served files per disk's spin-up

Fig. 13. Average number of disks operating simultaneously

concentrates correlated files into same disks, which makes the request handler spins up less disks to fetch the same target files.

Operating Disks at the Same Time. As shown in Fig. 13, DAES significantly decreases the number of disks operating simultaneously. On one hand, DAES switches a disk into low power state before it reaches the fixed idle time threshold if it has a low hit index. On the other hand, the file scheduler duplicates and rearranges files at convenience, making some requests involve less disks to spin up. The latter reason is detailed below.

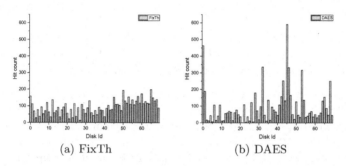

(a) FixTh   (b) DAES

Fig. 14. Hit distribution of FixTh and DAES with threshold being 60

Hit Distribution. To demonstrate the effect of file scheduler, we record the hit distribution of total 70 disks, which is shown in Fig. 14(a) and (b). The total hit count of FixTh is the same as DAES for that they process the same trace of requests. However, the workload skews to part of disks in case of DAES. This is mainly because DAES duplicates and rearranges files dynamically so that the storage system may spin up less disks to serve a request. In this way, both the total energy and spin-up times are reduced.

6   Conclusion and Future Work

In this paper, a new data-aware energy-saving storage management strategy is designed for on-site astronomical observation at Dome A, aiming at saving energy while maintaining the reliability of disks. It analyzes logical file correlations from I/O event log according to the characteristic of astronomical data. Then a hit index is calculated for each disk indicating the probability for it to be hit in the near future. Based on idle time threshold and hit index, their power states are managed more smartly by reducing unreasonable switches and idle spinning. In addition, considering that a disk in idle state still consumes much power as in read/write state, we adopt customized caching, prefetching and replication strategies to make full use of a disk while it is working. They submit tasks into a task pool where tasks are processed at convenience. Therefore, data layout is optimized dynamically at a little cost to get less disks involved while handling requests. Comparative experiments in different idle time thresholds prove that DAES saves 41.4% to 56.6% of energy consumption and reduces 46.3% to 66.8% of power state switches compared with FixTh which is a commonly used energy-saving strategy.

For future work, data storage with fault-tolerant might bring new interesting challenges to DAES. Furthermore, cache of disk drive should be explored to offer a low level optimization.

Acknowledgments. This work is supported by the National Natural Science Foundation of China (11573019, 61602336), the Joint Research Fund in Astronomy (U1531111) under cooperative agreement between the National Natural Science Foundation of China (NSFC) and Chinese Academy of Sciences (CAS).

References

1. WD blue PC hard drives specifications data sheet (2015). https://www.wdc.com/content/dam/wdc/website/downloadable_assets/eng/spec_data_sheet/2879-771436.pdf. Accessed 31 July 2018
2. Al Assaf, M.M., Jiang, X., Abid, M.R., Qin, X.: Eco-storage: a hybrid storage system with energy-efficient informed prefetching. J. Signal Process. Syst. **72**(3), 165–180 (2013)
3. Boru, D., Kliazovich, D., Granelli, F., Bouvry, P., Zomaya, A.Y.: Energy-efficient data replication in cloud computing datacenters. Clust. Comput. **18**(1), 385–402 (2015)
4. Chai, Y., Du, Z., Bader, D.A., Qin, X.: Efficient data migration to conserve energy in streaming media storage systems. IEEE Trans. Parallel Distrib. Syst. **23**(11), 2081–2093 (2012)
5. Colarelli, D., Grunwald, D.: Massive arrays of idle disks for storage archives, pp. 1–11. IEEE Computer Society Press (2002)
6. Graham, M.J., Djorgovski, S.G., Mahabal, A., Donalek, C., Drake, A., Longo, G.: Data challenges of time domain astronomy. Distrib. Parallel Databases **30**(5–6), 371–384 (2012)
7. Jensen, R., Cornelis, C.: Fuzzy-rough nearest neighbour classification. In: Peters, J.F., Skowron, A., Chan, C.-C., Grzymala-Busse, J.W., Ziarko, W.P. (eds.) Transactions on Rough Sets XIII. LNCS, vol. 6499, pp. 56–72. Springer, Heidelberg (2011). https://doi.org/10.1007/978-3-642-18302-7_4
8. Lee, D.K., Koh, K.: PDC-NH: popular data concentration on NAND flash and hard disk drive. In: 2009 10th IEEE/ACM International Conference on Grid Computing, pp. 196–200. IEEE (2009)
9. Luo, X., Xin, G., Wang, Y., Zhang, Z., Wang, H.: Superset: a non-uniform replica placement strategy towards perfect load balance and fine-grained power proportionality. Clust. Comput. **18**(3), 1127–1140 (2015)
10. Manzanares, A., Bellam, K., Qin, X.: A prefetching scheme for energy conservation in parallel disk systems. In: IEEE International Symposium on Parallel and Distributed Processing, IPDPS 2008, pp. 1–5. IEEE (2008)
11. Manzanares, A., Qin, X., Ruan, X., Yin, S.: PRE-BUD: prefetching for energy-efficient parallel I/O systems with buffer disks. ACM Trans. Storage (TOS) **7**(1), 3 (2011)

12. Manzanares, A., et al.: Energy efficient prefetching with buffer disks for cluster file systems. In: 2010 39th International Conference on Parallel Processing (ICPP), pp. 404–413. IEEE (2010)

13. Manzanres, A., Ruan, X., Yin, S., Nijim, M., Luo, W., Qin, X.: Energy-aware prefetching for parallel disk systems: algorithms, models, and evaluation. In: Eighth IEEE International Symposium on Network Computing and Applications, NCA 2009, pp. 90–97. IEEE (2009)

14. Nijim, M., Qin, X., Yin, S., Ruan, X., Manzanres, A., Luo, W.: Energy-aware prefetching for parallel disk systems: algorithms, models, and evaluation. In: 2009 Eighth IEEE International Symposium on Network Computing and Applications, pp. 90–97 (2009)

15. Ou, J., Shu, J., Lu, Y., Yi, L., Wang, W.: EDM: an endurance-aware data migration scheme for load balancing in SSD storage clusters. In: 2014 IEEE 28th International Parallel and Distributed Processing Symposium, pp. 787–796. IEEE (2014)

16. Pinheiro, E., Bianchini, R.: Energy conservation techniques for disk array-based servers, pp. 369–379. ACM (2014)

17. Shehabi, A., et al.: United states data center energy usage report (2016)

18. Sun, C., et al.: MCS-B: an energy efficient storage system for astronomical observation data based on logical block replacement strategy. In: 2017 IEEE International Symposium on Parallel and Distributed Processing with Applications and 2017 IEEE International Conference on Ubiquitous Computing and Communications (ISPA/IUCC), pp. 198–205. IEEE (2017)

19. Yan, J., Yu, C., Sun, C., Shang, Z., Hu, Y., Feng, J., Sun, J., Xiao, J.: Optimized data layout for spatio-temporal data in time domain astronomy. In: Ibrahim, S., Choo, K.-K.R., Yan, Z., Pedrycz, W. (eds.) ICA3PP 2017. LNCS, vol. 10393, pp. 431–440. Springer, Cham (2017). https://doi.org/10.1007/978-3-319-65482-9_30

20. Yuan, X., et al.: The AST3 project: Antarctic survey telescopes for Dome A. In: Ground-based and Airborne Telescopes V, vol. 9145, p. 91450F. International Society for Optics and Photonics (2014)

21. Zhang, G., Chiu, L., Dickey, C., Liu, L., Muench, P., Seshadri, S.: Automated lookahead data migration in SSD-enabled multi-tiered storage systems. In: 2010 IEEE 26th Symposium on Mass Storage Systems and Technologies (MSST), pp. 1–6. IEEE (2010)

22. Zhao, X., Li, Z., Zeng, L.: FDTM: block level data migration policy in tiered storage system. In: Ding, C., Shao, Z., Zheng, R. (eds.) NPC 2010. LNCS, vol. 6289, pp. 76–90. Springer, Heidelberg (2010). https://doi.org/10.1007/978-3-642-15672-4_8

Distancer: A Host-Based Distributed Adaptive Load Balancer for Datacenter Traffic

Songyun Wang[1], Xin Li[1,2(✉)], Zhuzhong Qian[2], and Jiabin Yuan[1]

[1] College of Computer Science and Technology,
Nanjing University of Aeronautics and Astronautics, Nanjing 211106, China
lics@nuaa.edu.cn
[2] State Key Laboratory for Novel Software Technology,
Nanjing University, Nanjing 210023, China

Abstract. Contemporary datacenter networks are typically organized with multi-rooted tree topologies. To fully utilize the multiple end-to-end paths, effective mechanisms are required to balance traffic across them. However, existing load balancers for datacenters either operate at a coarse granularity, or support little for network failures, or necessitate customized hardware. We propose *Distancer*, a host-based distributed adaptive load balancer for datacenter traffic, which requires no coordination and modification of switches. Based on a deep investigation of TCP feedback mechanism, we firstly design Congestion Detector (C-Detector), which exploits ACKs to effectively handle network hot-spots and path anomalies in real time; Then we develop Load-Balancer (L-Balancer) to select best paths for both data packets and ACKs. According to our extensive evaluations, *Distancer* can achieve up to 40% and 20% better average flow completion times (AFCTs) than ECMP and CONGA respectively. Under the presence of path failures, *Distancer* improves the AFCT up to 400% and 30% over ECMP and CONGA.

Keywords: Data center networking · Flow scheduling · Load balance

1 Introduction

High demand for dynamic scaling and benefits from economies of scale have spurred the deployment of large-scale datacenters. Recent proposed data centers primarily use cheap commodity switches to construct multi-rooted tree topologies [3,13,15]. By creating redundant paths between host pairs, these architectures significantly increase the bisection bandwidth of datacenters. While multi-paths provide flexibility and agility, the transmission performance may decrease if flows are poorly routed and collide on the same path. To address this issue, modern datacenters often run ECMP [16] to balance traffic load. However, ECMP is a typically load-agnostic strategy, which uses flow identifiers as keys

© Springer Nature Switzerland AG 2018
J. Vaidya and J. Li (Eds.): ICA3PP 2018, LNCS 11335, pp. 567–581, 2018.
https://doi.org/10.1007/978-3-030-05054-2_43

and randomly hashes flows to different paths. Consequently, it cannot avoid traffic collision effectively and may lead to network hot spots frequently [5, 24, 26].

To overcome the weakness of ECMP, multiple adaptive load balancers have been proposed for datacenters. While these solutions expose their attractive properties, they have some limitations. Flow-based centralized approaches (e.g., Hedera [4], MicroTE [7], DFFR [10]) are simple to implement but a misfit for volatile datacenter traffic. Switch-local protocols (e.g., Localflow [25], DRB [8]) operate in a distributed manner and scale better. Yet, they may cause severe performance dip when network failures appear. Typical host-based methods like MPTCP [24, 28] require no specialized hardware support and facilitate the deployment. However, they are always reactive and respond to congestion slowly. Recently proposed in-network solutions (e.g., CONGA [5]) have more visibility of active flows and work well in asymmetric networks. But they introduce extra challenges to deploy due to their requirement of modifying switch fabrics to support new protocols.

In this paper, we propose *Distancer*, a novel distributed load balancer for datacenter traffic. We devise it as a purely host-based protocol to facilitate deployment, while simultaneously enable it to handle traffic congestion proactively. With a deep investigation of TCP feedback mechanism, we skillfully leverage ACKs to monitor network status and we also design *reverse load balancing* for ACKs that can remarkably improve the performance. More specifically, *Distancer* is built below TCP layer at the host network stacks. It adaptively balances traffic through the interaction of two components, which are called congestion detector (C-Detector) and load-balancer (L-Balancer) respectively.

The key insight of C-Detector is that we leverage the flexibility of end-hosts to measure the path states in real time. It innovatively exploits ACK arrival times and the incremental acknowledged data to estimate the available capacities of different paths. It also utilizes the feedback such as TCP retransmissions and timeouts to detect non-local path failures. As the functionalities of C-Detector are embedded into the normal process of packet reception/transmission, *Distancer* has the ability to perceive traffic congestion at fast timescales.

Based on the path-wise metrics from C-Detector, L-Balancer shifts traffic from the overburdened paths to under-utilized paths proactively. With deep investigation and bandwidth experiments, we argue that congested ACKs will significantly reduce transmission throughput. Thus, we design *reverse load balancing* in L-Balancer to carefully select back paths for reverse ACKs as well as data packets. L-Balancer also skillfully uses *fliers* as basic scheduling units and adaptively allocates paths for them to further improve network performance. *Distancer* does not require switches to record flow statistics and path states which are necessary for previous distributed solutions (e.g., DARD [29], CONGA [5], LetFlow [27]). Thus, *Distancer* is purely host-based that requires no modification of switches and highly facilitates the deployment in large-scale datacenters.

In summary, the main highlights of *Distancer* can be concluded as follows:

1. *Distancer* is an end-host solution that is fully compatible with current commodity switches.
2. *Distancer* can react to network hot spots proactively and handles path failures rapidly.
3. *Distancer* achieves load balance for ACKs as well as data packets, which remarkably improve datacenter performance.

We conduct extensive evaluations to validate *Distancer*. Our results show that in normal datacenter networks *Distancer* can achieve up to 40% and 20% better average flow completion times (AFCTs) than ECMP and CONGA respectively. Under the presence of multiple path failures, *Distancer* can improve the AFCT up to 400% and 30% over ECMP and CONGA respectively.

The remainder of this paper is organized as follows. In Sect. 2, we briefly overview the existing work. We present the system framework of *Distancer* in Sect. 3. Sections 4 and 5 are dedicated to the two important components of *Distancer* respectively. We evaluate *Distancer* and compare it with other approaches in Sect. 6. Finally we conclude our work in Sect. 7.

2 Related Work

The latest large-scale datacenters are often built with multi-rooted topologies such as Fat-tree [3] and Clos [13], which rely on multiple end-to-end paths to meet high-bandwidth requirement. To fully use these paths, a great number of load balancers have been proposed for datacenter traffic. These approaches exhibit their attractive properties, but they cannot meet all the requirements for practical load balancing in datacenters. The requirements include *rapidly responsive*, *fine-grained*, *highly robust* and *readily deployable*.

For the first two properties, *rapidly responsive* and *fine-grained* are the basic requirements for an effective load balancer. As previous literature suggests [6,19], datacenter traffic are extremely volatile. To handle the highly dynamic traffic, load balancers must respond to hot spots and make routing adjustment rapidly. Among existing solutions, ECMP [16], Hedera [4] and FlowBender [17] schedule traffic at flow-level. They either randomly hash flows onto different paths or periodically reallocate paths based on network states. Thus, they cannot meet the requirement of *fine-grained*. In contrast, PacketScatter [11] and MPTCP [24,28] which operate at packet-level or subflow-level provide higher granularity alternatives. Yet, PacketScatter is typically load-oblivious and MPTCP always handles congestion reactively. So they neither are competent to cope with traffic bursts at fast timescale.

The last two properties impose key requirements for practical deployment. *Highly robust* requires the solutions amenable to network anormalies. In fact, network failures are quite common in large-scale datacenters [12]. If the underlying load balancer is insensible to failures, they may misguide traffic onto the abnormal paths and aggravate the performance dip. Another demand, *readily deployable*, requires the protocols to be readily implementable without modifying any network hardware. This property ensures the convenient and costless deployment. Switch-local solutions like Localflow [25], DRB [8] only can guarantee their efficiency in normal networks. They are unable to perceive remote network failures so that they cannot satisfy the requirement of *highly robust*. The recently proposed strategies like DARD [29], CONGA [5] can perform well under the presence of failures. However, deployers must modify switch fabrics to support their protocols, which violates the requirement of *readily deployable*.

We ensure *Distancer* to meet all the requirements when designing it. *Distancer* monitors path states in real-time so that it can react to congestion rapidly. Unlike previous coarse-grained solutions, *Distancer* employs *flier-switching* and *reverse load balancing* techniques to attain high-granularity scheduling. Compared with switch-local methods, we enhance *Distancer* to detect network anomalies and remedy performance degradation caused by network failures. Finally, the protocol of *Distancer* is quite simple, which does not necessitate any customized hardware.

3   Distancer in a Nutshell

As an end-host solution, *Distancer* is implemented as a lightweight layer at the host network stacks. It logically resides below TCP layer and performs real-time load balancing for TCP traffic. Before a TCP agent sends out load units, *Distancer* is invoked to make routing decisions based on current network states. Upon the arrivals of ACKs, *Distancer* derives the necessary information from the packets, estimates current path states and caches the results into the memory. To handle the non-local path failures, *Distancer* leverages the essential feedback from TCP to perceive link anomalies. There are two significant features of *Distancer*: (1) All interactions for load balancing take place between the *Distancer* layer and TCP layer. They are entirely transparent to the upper applications. (2) The mechanism does not require any coordination with switches. It can be easily deployed by directly update the network stacks.

From a functional standpoint, *Distancer* mainly comprises two components: congestion detector (C-Detector) and load-balancer (L-Balancer). C-Detector is responsible to evaluate path states and detect path failures while L-Balancer acts as the routing logic to enforce fine-grained traffic scheduling. C-Detector and L-Balancer interact through the congestion table, which records the real-time path states and is maintained by the host. Once C-Detector obtains newer path states, it will immediately update the congestion table. Before making balancing decisions, L-Balancer will refer to the table and use the congestion information to conduct adaptive routing. In next two sections, we will further explicate how they incorporate to achieve fine-grained and effective load balancing.

4   Host-Based Congestion Detector

This section presents the details of C-Detector. We begin with the introduction of our *flier switching* technique which provides a better granularity for load balancing. Then we elaborate on the details of utilizing feedback from TCP to estimate network states rapidly. The estimated path metrics of C-Detector will be utilized by L-Balancer to make scheduling decisions.

4.1 Flier-Based Switching

To make *Distancer* effective, we must choose a proper scheduling granularity for it. Broadly speaking, prior approaches mostly balance traffic at the flow-level, the packet-level or the subflow-level respectively. Flow-based solutions [4,16] group packets into different flows and dynamically allocate paths for them. Thus they fail to handle the sporadic congestion caused by packet bursts. Packet-based methods [11] select path for every packet to balance link utilizations. They are more fine-grained, yet introducing the risk of packet reordering. Subflow-based protocols like MPTCP [24] open up multiple subflows to fully utilize the redundant paths. However, they have the potential to exacerbate the network competition and traffic Incast [5,24].

Recent mechanisms [5,18,25] also propose to employ flowlet switching for load balancing. Flowlets are sequences of packets from one flow which are separated by predetermined time gaps. These methods use flowlets as the basic scheduling units and adaptively allocate paths for them. However, flowlet-based solutions have to face the difficulty of determining a proper time interval to split flowlets. As indicated in [5], the actual time gaps between two adjacent flowlets in datacenters are highly variable and unpredictable. We can hardly choose a reasonable time gap to split flows in datacenter networks.

To step aside the problem associated with flowlet-switching, we skillfully introduce *flier-switching* technique. A *flier* is defined as a congestion window of a TCP agent. *Distancer* utilizes fliers as basic scheduling units and dynamically distributes them to different paths. Since TCP sources always send out a whole congestion window at once[1], it is more natural and convenient to detect fliers at host stacks than split flowlets at switches. In addition, authors in [18] have proved that a flowlet is typically a congestion window or a portion of it. So we believe that our flier switching technique is a reasonable alternative. By employing *flier-switching*, we do not need to decide a rational time gap for fliers and modify switches to add more functionalities, thus avoiding the extra overhead and costs introduced by flowlet detection.

4.2 Estimating Congestion Levels of Different Paths

One of *Distancer*'s innovations is to directly estimate path states at host stacks. To achieve this goal, we introduce the key idea of TCP westwood (TCPW) [22]. In TCPW, senders rely on ACK packets to calculate available path capacities. *Distancer* employs the similar idea to acquire the network-wide path status.

---

[1] In the TCP implementation of Linux kernel, the function *tcp_output* always sends out a whole congestion window at once.

Algorithm 1. Estimating Path States

1: **while** receive a new ACK **do**
2:    $ackno_{cur} \leftarrow ACK.ackno$;
3:    $t_{cur} \leftarrow now.time()$;
4:    $pid_{cur} \leftarrow getPidFromTuples(ackno_{cur})$;
5:    **if** $pid_{cur} = pid_{last}$ **then**
6:       $CL(pid) \leftarrow \frac{t_{cur} - t_{last}}{(ackno_{cur} - ackno_{last}) * 8}$;
7:       Insert $CL(pid)$ into the congestion table;
8:    $t_{last} \leftarrow t_{cur}$;
9:    $ackno_{last} \leftarrow ackno_{cur}$;
10:   $pid_{last} \leftarrow pid_{cur}$;

The algorithm for congestion estimation in C-Detector is presented in Algorithm 1. For a flier transmitted through path p, the sender will receive several ACKs to acknowledge it. *Distancer* uses two kinds of information: (1) the arrival times of these ACKs and (2) the incremental acknowledged data to calculate the available bandwidth. We denote the acknowledge number of the ACK packet arriving at time t_i as $ackno_i$. Then $(ackno_{i+1} - ackno_i)$ denotes the data bytes which have been recently received by destination. $(t_{i+1} - t_i)$ records the elapsed time to transmit these data. Then the current available bandwidth of path p can be calculated as:

$$ABW(p) = \frac{(ackno_{i+1} - ackno_i) * 8}{t_{i+1} - t_i}$$

Naturally, current congestion level (CL) of path p can be defined as the reciprocal of $ABW(p)$, which is:

$$CL(p) = \frac{1}{ABW(p)}$$

In this way, we attach a lower CL to the path which has higher available bandwidth.

The next question is to determine which flier the received ACKs are acknowledging so that we can use them to estimate path states. Before we send out a flier, we record its first byte number, its last byte number and its path id as a tuple (seq_b, seq_e, pid). Once an ACK arrives, its $ackno$ can be used to determine which flier it is acknowledging. For example, a tuple $(32, 5872, 2)$ means we have sent a flier which contains data bytes from sequence 32 to sequence 5872 via path 2. Assuming that the sender later receives several acks with $acknos$ 1492, 2952, 4412, 5872 respectively. It can quickly find that these $acknos$ fall into the sequence section of tuple $(32, 5872, 2)$ and they are acknowledging data travelling via path 2 (*getPidFromTuples* on line 4). Then the sender can immediately calculate the CL of path 2. Note that we only store tuples for fliers which have not be completely acknowledged. Once a flier has been totally acknowledged, its tuple will be deleted. Therefore, the memory space used for storing tuples can almost be ignored.

In addition, every host in *Distancer* manages a congestion table to stash the real-time CLs of different paths. C-Detector continually updates the table

---

Algorithm 2. Detecting Path Anomalies

1: **while** detect a RTO timeout or fast retransmission **do**
2:    get the highest ack number $ackno_h$;
3:    $pid \leftarrow getPidFromTuples(ackno_h)$;
4:    set $CL(pid)$ to a large number;
5:    insert $CL(pid)$ into the congestion table;

---

by inserting newer CLs into it. Note that TCP agents on the same host are allowed to invoke C-Detector to update the table entry simultaneously. In this way, TCP agents on the same host can exchange their path information through the shared congestion table. Once an agent refreshes the metrics, the others can immediately get aware and make use of them to adjust traffic routing.

4.3 Detecting Path Anomalies

As introduced above, returned ACKs play a crucial role in the congestion estimation. However, once link failures or severe congestion occurs, ACKs may get lost halfway so that senders in *Distancer* cannot receive ACKs timely. To address the problem caused by path anomalies, *Distancer* takes advantages of other feedback such as RTO timeouts and retransmissions to update congestion tables.

Algorithm 2 describes what a TCP sender will do when RTO timeouts or fast retransmissions appear in *Distancer*. Firstly, the sender will check current highest ACK number $ackno_h$ it has received. To recognize the abnormal path, it invokes function $getPidFromTuples$. Remember that we have cached a tuple for every flier sent out. If $ackno_h$ falls into the sequence section of tuple (seq_b, seq_e, pid), the function will return pid which means some packets transmitted through path pid are dropped or delayed. In this way, the sender will realize that path pid is aberrant and assigns a large number to $CL(pid)$. By inserting $CL(pid)$ into the congestion table, other agents on this host will be informed to bypass the abnormal path.

Since *Distancer* does not probe paths proactively, an aging mechanism for the congestion table must be introduced. We adopt a simple aging strategy for *Distancer*. If the table entry has not been updated for a while, it will gradually decay to zero (which represents the most healthy path). This mechanism ensures that the severely congested path can become available again after a proper period.

5 Two-Way Load Balancer

In this section, we explicate the core routing logic of *Distancer* called Two-way Load Balancer (L-Balancer). We first explain how *Distancer* employs source routing technique to schedule traffic distributedly. Then we present two main functionalities: (1) adaptively selecting paths for fliers to avoid path oscillation; (2) conducting reverse load balancing for ACK packets.

5.1   Hierarchical Addressing Based Source Routing

According to our design principles, hosts in *Distancer* should be able to determine routing paths by themselves. To this end, *Distancer* introduces the source routing technique which has been successfully applied in current datacenters [14,29]. Unlike the Internet or enterprise network, datacenter networks often have stable hierarchical topology. So it's natural and convenient to deploy source routing in datacenters.

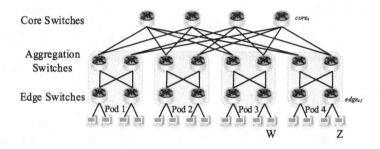

Fig. 1. A fat tree topology with 16 hosts

To simplify switch functionalities, *Distancer* leverages hierarchical addressing technique [29] to implement source routing. Hierarchical addressing allocates IP addresses to servers based on their locations. For example, we respectively numerate the core switches, the pods, the aggregation switches and edge switches in Fig. 1 from left to right. We use $aggr_{mn}$ ($egde_{mn}$) to denote the nth aggregate switch (edge switch) in the mth pod. Then we can assign server Z an address $core_4.aggr_{42}.edge_{42}.z$, which means server Z can be reached from $core_4$ downto switch $aggr_{42}$ and switch $edge_{42}$.

With hierarchical addressing, every server in the network will receive multiple IP addresses, which can be configured via IP alias. Each address of a host represents a unique path to that host. For instance, server Z in Fig. 1 can also have the address $core_3.aggr_{42}.edge_{42}.z$, which determines another path ($core_3 \rightarrow aggr_{42} \rightarrow edge_{42} \rightarrow z$) to reach it. In this way, source servers can encode different addresses into the packet headers to control their routing. Note that we need to correctly configure the routing table in switches to ensure right forwarding. However, this can not be a problem in datacenter environment. As datacenters are always under the centralized administration and have highly regular topologies, servers can easily know network topology in advance. Thus we can directly initialize forwarding tables of switches at once and enables them to support the routing for hierarchical addressing.

5.2   Routing Logic for Fliers

One of L-Balancer's responsibilities is to adaptively schedule fliers. By querying the congestion table, it seems better for agents to always pick the least congested path for their fliers. However, previous literature [20,29] suggests that load-sensitive routing may result in path oscillations and instability, which in turn harms the network performance. *Distancer* is no exception.

To overcome the instability brought by load-sensitive mechanism, we employ *the power of d-choice* [21,23] which is widely applied into load balancing. At the beginning of every routing decision, the sender first randomly sample half of the paths into path set $\mathcal{P}$ and then select the best one as the final routing path. Since *Distancer* updates the path states quite rapidly, such a technique can avoid too many fliers to crowd into the same path by introducing randomness. In addition, we also practically verify that this simple *random-then-best* strategy can effectively prevent path oscillation in *Distancer*.

5.3   Reverse Load Balancing

TCP receivers in *Distancer* also carefully select back paths for reverse ACKs[1], which we call as *reverse load balancing*. The reverse load balancing guarantees that ACKs won't be congested and simultaneously ensures the ACK arrival times obtained in C-Detector are accurate.

We present the core steps of L-Balancer in Algorithm 3. Different from the way to handle data packets, receivers always send out ACKs through the best path since ACK packets won't bring about path oscillation. However, if the receiver also acts as a sender, it's still required to exploit *random-then-best* strategy to avoid path oscillation.

Algorithm 3. Load Balancing Logic

1: **while** send packets **do**
2:     **if** send a flier **then**
3:         randomly select half of the paths into set $\mathcal{P}$
4:         select the path with the least CL from $\mathcal{P}$ as p;
5:         send out the flier through path p;
6:         cache the tuple $(seq_{beg}, seq_{end}, p)$ for the flier;
7:     **else if** send an ACK **then**
8:         select the path with the least CL as p;
9:         route the ACK packet through path p

So far, we have presented all the details and characteristics of *Distancer*. In next section, we extensively evaluate *Distancer*, compare it with several typical solutions and validate its effectiveness.

---

[1] Here we mean pure ACKs. The piggybacking ACKs are viewed as data packets by *Distancer*.

6 Evaluation

We evaluate the performance of *Distancer* with ns2 network simulator [2]. We mainly compare *Distancer* with four typical load balancing techniques, which respectively exploit four different granularities for datacenter load balancing:

- **ECMP (flow-level):** Randomly hashing flows onto different paths based on their flow identifiers.
- **PacketScatter (packet-level):** Uniformly spraying packets through all the output ports.
- **MPTCP[1] (subflow-level):** Establishing subflows to fully utilize the multiple paths.
- **CONGA (flowlet-level):** The newly proposed in-network load balancer that is failure-robust.

It should be reminded that the first two methods are load-agnostic and the latter two solutions are load-sensitive.

To elaborately validate the effectiveness of *Distancer*, we build a 250-host fat-tree topology to evaluate the efficiency of above load balancers in normal datacenter environment, and set up a 16-host network with multiple failed paths to evaluate *Distancer*'s ability in handling path failures.

In all experiments, we set the link capacities to 1 Gbps, the link propagation delay to $100\,\mu s$ and the queue size to 100 packets which are similar to [25]. Flows in our simulations arrive according to a Poisson process and their sizes are draw from a Pareto distribution with a mean of $5M$ bytes. Unless specially specified, we set the *minRTO* of TCP to 200 ms and the default packet size to 1500 bytes.

6.1 Load Balancing Efficiency

We generate three types of traffic patterns similar to [9,29] for this evaluation: (1) *Random pattern*, where an end host communicates with any other host with 0.5 probability. This pattern helps to evaluate *Distancer* at relatively light workload. (2) *Stride Pattern*, where a host initializes TCP flows to other hosts that reside in different racks. This pattern can highly stress out the links in the core of the network. (3) *Permutation pattern*, where a host establishes connections with all other hosts. This traffic pattern is utilized to saturate the whole network. The evaluation results are as follows:

Average Flow Completion Times. Figure 2 shows the average flow completion times (AFCTs) of different strategies under different traffic patterns. From Fig. 2(a) and (b), we can see that under random and stride patterns *Distancer* achieves 28%–40% and 18%–25% better AFCT than ECMP and PacketScatter respectively. Actually, ECMP and PacketScatter are totally load-oblivious,

---

[1] We moderately modify the MPTCP implementation on ns2 [1] to support our evaluation. We establish four subflows for every MPTCP connection in our experiments.

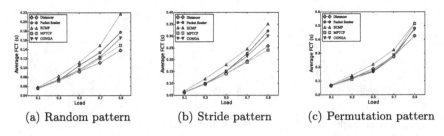

| (a) Random pattern | (b) Stride pattern | (c) Permutation pattern |

Fig. 2. AFCTs for different traffic patterns. The results are the average of 5 runs

they will either cause flow collisions or bring about packet reordering, so their transmission performance is highly affected. In contrast, *Distancer* makes balancing adjustment based on network states. It monitors path qualities in real time and avoids traffic congestion before-the-fact. This enables it to behave better than ECMP and PacketScatter. Figure 2(c) shows their performance under permutation pattern. *Distancer* only achieves 16% and 10% better AFCT than ECMP and PacketScatter respectively. This happens because the network is highly saturated by the permutation pattern and *Distancer* can only remedy the performance degradation moderately.

In addition, *Distancer* achieves very similar performance with MPTCP under the stride pattern and random pattern. Actually, these patterns generates interpod flows which stretch across the core switches. It provides path diversity for MPTCP to exploit so that it operates quite well. However, Fig. 2(c) shows that *Distancer* can achieve up to 25% better AFCT than MPTCP under permutation pattern at 90% workload. This happens due to the large number of rack-local flows. Under permutation pattern, MPTCP cannot help much with the intra-pod traffic and its subflows will exacerbate the competition at the access links. Compared with CONGA, *Distancer* also improves AFCT up to 20% under different patterns. This happens because CONGA is designed for spine-leaf[2] networks on purpose. It only controls the load balancing decisions on edge switches and spine switches in CONGA employ ECMP. Thus CONGA can not operate optimally in 3-tier networks so that its performance cannot catch up to *Distancer*.

Average Retransmission Times. Figure 3 shows that *Distancer* can reduce up to 100% and 200% average retransmission times (ARTs) over PacketScatter and ECMP respectively. This happens due to their improper utilizing of granularities for load balancing. Flow-based ECMP may result in frequent path collisions and continual packet drops. So its retransmission times are out of control. Packet-based solutions like PacketScatter have the potential to be affected by packet reordering. Its retransmission times reasonably go between *ECMP* and *Distancer*. Unlike the former two solutions, *Distancer* employs flier-switching technique to provide precise load balancing while simultaneously avoiding too

---

[2] A multi-rooted tree topology that only comprises the edge switch layer and core switch layer.

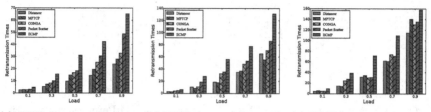

(a) RTX times under random pattern (b) RTX times under stride pattern (c) RTX times under permutation pattern

Fig. 3. Retransmission times for different traffic patterns. The results are the average of 5 runs

many retransmissions. We should also note that CONGA effectively avoids a large number of retransmissions. Yet, since aggregate switches in CONGA have to leverage ECMP to make routing decisions, its retransmissions are slightly higher than *Distancer*. Moreover, *Distancer* is less likely to drop packets than MPTCP at most times. This happens because that *Distancer* detects path failures more quickly and prevents network hot spots proactively while MPTCP reacts to congestion until it happens. The proactive response helps *Distancer* outperform MPTCP.

6.2 Handling Path Failures

To prove that *Distancer* can overcome the path failures well, we set up a 16-host fat-tree network with one of the core links cut off (shown as the dotted line in Fig. 1). The failed core link will cause several abnormal paths which can bring severe side effects for traffic load balancers. We repeat the former three traffic patterns on the asymmetric network and use the same metrics to evaluate these mechanisms. According to our evaluations, ECMP performs very poorly under stride and permutation traffic patterns. It even cannot terminate all flows after a sufficient long period. We believe that the stride and permutation patterns may exert high load pressure which is beyond the capability of ECMP. Thus we only show the evaluation results under random pattern.

AFCTs and ARTs. Figure 4(a) shows the AFCT of different methods. It can be observed that *Distancer* achieves almost 4× and 1× better AFCT than ECMP and PacketScatter respectively. When compared with CONGA and MPTCP, *Distancer* also improves the AFCT up to 30% and 40% respectively. Actually, ECMP and PacketScatter have no ability to address path failures so that they fail to work well in asymmetric networks. While CONGA is designed as a failure-robust mechanism for 2-tier networks, it cannot cope well with the 3-tier link failure since it randomly selects the uphill paths at aggregate switches. *Distancer* outperforms MPTCP due to its proactive reactions. Different from MPTCP which handles packet drops reactively, *Distancer* perceives path failures quickly and shifts traffic to normal paths at RTT timescale. Thus it can

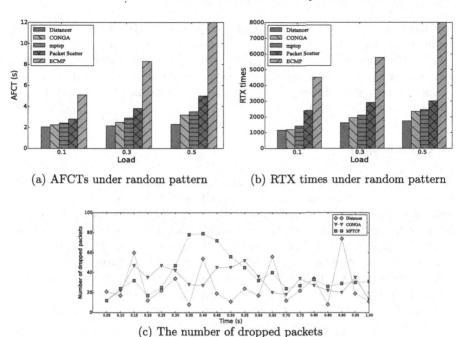

(a) AFCTs under random pattern   (b) RTX times under random pattern

(c) The number of dropped packets

Fig. 4. Evaluation results under path failures. The results are the average of 5 runs

improve the transmission performance more effectively. In fact, if we compare the performance of *Distancer* from a horizontal view, we can see its AFCT is only slightly lengthened when we increase traffic load from 10% to 50%. This suggests that *Distancer* is rather robust to network failures. In addition, We also depict their retransmission times in Fig. 4(b), it also helps to demonstrate *Distancer*'s advantages in addressing path anomalies.

The Rate of Dropping Packets. To further explain why *Distancer* addresses path failures better, we track the number of dropped packets at the aberrant link every 50 ms. Figure 4(c) illustrates our results in detail. Note that for simplicity we only depict the results for the three load-sensitive approaches. From Fig. 4(c), we see that MPTCP may drop a large number of packets at the failed link at once (0.35–0.50 s). And then its drop rate will decrease to a normal level. This happens because MPTCP adjusts the congestion windows of different subflows a little slowly. It gradually shifts traffic from failed links to normal paths after congestion happens. In contrast, CONGA behaves better than MPTCP. CONGA tries to avoid routing via failed path through the load balancing logic at edge switches. However, it still cannot prevent packet drops at the 3-tier failed link since it cannot control the routing path at the third tier. *Distancer* exhibits better overall performance than its two counterparts. Even its dropped packets surpasses others occasionally, it effectively avoids packet losses at most time.

This happens due to the failure-avoiding capability of *Distancer*. As we have highlighted before, once an agent detects severe congestion or link failures, all other TCP connections can quickly realize it and keep away from them. However, after several aging periods, congestion metric of the failed path will gradually decays. So the path will be probed again and packets may be discarded there again (0.40 s, 0.65 s, 0.90 s).

7 Conclusion

We propose *Distancer*, a distributed adaptive load balancing strategy for datacenters. Based on our investigation of TCP feedback mechanism, *Distancer* employs C-Detector to estimate path states at host stacks and relies on L-Balancer to perform fine-grained two-way load balancing, so that it can handle traffic congestion and link failures proactively. As an end-host mechanism, *Distancer* is compatible with commodity switches and introduces little overhead to the network. We evaluate *Distancer* on the network simulator ns2. The final results show that *Distancer* can achieve higher performance than current typical load balancing strategies in both normal and asymmetric datacenter networks.

References

1. Multipath TCP on NS-2. https://code.google.com/p/multipath-tcp/
2. The NS-2 network simulator. http://www.isi.edu/nsnam/ns
3. Al-Fares, M., Loukissas, A., et al.: A scalable, commodity data center network architecture. In: ACM SIGCOMM CCR, vol. 38, pp. 63–74 (2008)
4. Al-Fares, M., Radhakrishnan, S., et al.: Hedera: dynamic flow scheduling for data center networks. In: Proceedings of NSDI, vol. 10, p. 19 (2010)
5. Alizadeh, M., Edsall, T., et al.: CONGA: distributed congestion-aware load balancing for datacenters. In: Proceedings of ACM SIGCOMM, pp. 503–514 (2014)
6. Benson, T., Akella, A., et al.: Network traffic characteristics of data centers in the wild. In: Proceedings of ACM IMC, pp. 267–280 (2010)
7. Benson, T., Anand, A., et al.: MicroTE: fine grained traffic engineering for data centers. In: Proceedings of ACM CoNEXT, p. 8 (2011)
8. Cao, J., Xia, R., et al.: Per-packet load-balanced, low-latency routing for clos-based data center networks. In: Proceedings of ACM CoNEXT, pp. 49–60 (2013)
9. Cao, Y., Xu, M., et al.: Explicit multipath congestion control for data center networks. In: Proceedings of ACM CoNEXT, pp. 73–84 (2013)
10. Cheung, C.M., Leung, K.C.: DFFR: a flow-based approach for distributed load balancing in data center networks. Comput. Commun. **116**, 1–8 (2018)
11. Dixit, A., Prakash, P., et al.: On the impact of packet spraying in data center networks. In: Proceedings of IEEE INFOCOM, pp. 2130–2138 (2013)
12. Gill, P., Jain, N., et al.: Understanding network failures in data centers: measurement, analysis, and implications. In: ACM SIGCOMM CCR, vol. 41, pp. 350–361 (2011)
13. Greenberg, A., Hamilton, J.R., et al.: Vl2: a scalable and flexible data center network. In: ACM SIGCOMM CCR, vol. 39, pp. 51–62 (2009)

14. Guo, C., Lu, G., et al.: SecondNet: a data center network virtualization architecture with bandwidth guarantees. In: Proceedings of ACM CoNEXT, pp. 15–26 (2010)
15. Guo, C., Wu, H., et al.: DCell: a scalable and fault-tolerant network structure for data centers. ACM SIGCOMM CCR **38**(4), 75–86 (2008)
16. Hopps, C.E.: Analysis of an equal-cost multi-path algorithm (2000)
17. Kabbani, A., Vamanan, B., et al.: FlowBender: flow-level adaptive routing for improved latency and throughput in datacenter networks. In: Proceedings of the 10th ACM International on Conference on emerging Networking Experiments and Technologies, pp. 149–160. ACM (2014)
18. Kandula, S., Katabi, D., et al.: Dynamic load balancing without packet reordering. ACM SIGCOMM CCR **37**(2), 51–62 (2007)
19. Kandula, S., Sengupta, S., et al.: The nature of data center traffic: measurements & analysis. In: Proceedings of ACM IMC, pp. 202–208 (2009)
20. Khanna, A., Zinky, J.: The revised arpanet routing metric. In: ACM SIGCOMM CCR, vol. 19, pp. 45–56 (1989)
21. Luczak, M.J., McDiarmid, C., et al.: On the power of two choices: balls and bins in continuous time. Ann. Appl. Probab. **15**(3), 1733–1764 (2005)
22. Mascolo, S., Casetti, C., et al.: TCP westwood: bandwidth estimation for enhanced transport over wireless links. In: Proceedings of ACM MobiCom, pp. 287–297 (2001)
23. Mitzenmacher, M.: The power of two choices in randomized load balancing. IEEE Trans. Parallel Distrib. Syst. **12**(10), 1094–1104 (2001)
24. Raiciu, C., Barre, S., et al.: Improving datacenter performance and robustness with multipath TCP. In: ACM SIGCOMM CCR, vol. 41, pp. 266–277 (2011)
25. Sen, S., Shue, D., et al.: Scalable, optimal flow routing in datacenters via local link balancing. In: Proceedings of ACM CoNEXT, pp. 151–162 (2013)
26. Shafiee, M., Ghaderi, J.: A simple congestion-aware algorithm for load balancing in datacenter networks. IEEE/ACM Trans. Netw. **25**(6), 3670–3682 (2017)
27. Vanini, E., Pan, R., Alizadeh, M., Taheri, P., Edsall, T.: Let it flow: resilient asymmetric load balancing with flowlet switching. In: Proceedings of NSDI. USENIX (2017)
28. Wischik, D., Raiciu, C., et al.: Design, implementation and evaluation of congestion control for multipath TCP. In: Proceedings of NSDI, vol. 11, p. 8 (2011)
29. Wu, X., Yang, X.: DARD: distributed adaptive routing for datacenter networks. In: Proceedings of IEEE ICDCS, pp. 32–41 (2012)

MoSa: A Modeling and Sentiment Analysis System for Mobile Application Big Data

Yaocheng Zhang[1,2,6], Wei Ren[1,2,3,6](✉), Tianqing Zhu[4], and Wei Bi[5]

[1] School of Computer Science, China University of Geoscience,
Wuhan 430074, People's Republic of China
[2] Guizhou Provincial Key Laboratory of Public Big Data, GuiZhou University,
Guiyang 550025, Guizhou, People's Republic of China
[3] Hubei Key Laboratory of Intelligent Geo-Information Processing,
China University of Geosciences (Wuhan), Wuhan 430074, People's Republic of China
weirencs@cug.edu.cn
[4] School of Software, University of Technology Sydney, Ultimo, NSW 2007, Australia
[5] SeeleTech Corporation, San Francisco 94107, USA
[6] School of Computer Science, China University of Geosciences,
Wuhan 430074, People's Republic of China

Abstract. A large amount of data about ending users are generated in the interaction over mobile applications, which becomes a valuable data source for sensing human behaviors and public sentiment trends on some topics. Existing works concentrate on traditional feedback data from web sites, which usually come from desktops instead of from mobile terminals. Few studies have been conducted on interactive data from mobile applications such as news aggregation and recommendation applications. In this paper, we propose a system that can model feedback behaviors of mobile users, and can analyze sentiment trends in mobile feedbacks. The testing data are authentic and are dumped from the most frequently used mobile application in China called Toutiao. We propose several analysis methods on sentiment of comments, and modeling algorithms on feedback behaviors. We build a system called MoSa and by using the system, we discover several implicit behavior models and hidden sentiment trends as follows: During news spreading stage, the number of comments grow linearly per month with slope of 3 in 3 months; The dynamics of replying comments are positively correlated with personal daily routines in 24 h; Replying comment behaviors are much more rare than clicking agreement behaviors in mobile applications; The standard deviation of sentiment values in comments are highly influenced by timing stages. Our system and modeling methods provide empirical results for guiding interaction design in mobile Internet, social networks, and blockchain-based crowdsourcing.

Keywords: Mobile big data · Sentiment analysis
Behavior modeling · Mobile applications

© Springer Nature Switzerland AG 2018
J. Vaidya and J. Li (Eds.): ICA3PP 2018, LNCS 11335, pp. 582–595, 2018.
https://doi.org/10.1007/978-3-030-05054-2_44

1   Introduction

With the development of mobile Internet, Android has become the world's largest operating system since 2017 according to the data proposed by the Internet counting web site - Statcounter. According to the data proposed by Ministry of Industry and Information Technology in China, the number of 4G users have reached to 1.03 billion since February 2018. By analyzing those data we find that the number of personal mobile computing devices are increasing rapidly. Meanwhile, the average time that is spent by persons in ages of 18 to 45 is about 4 h per day.

Because much time are spent in using mobile Apps, there will be more data such as feedback are being generated by users who use those Apps (called endogenous data). By analyzing those data, we can optimize the recommendation systems, monitor suspicious entities in the network, and collect online large-scale public opinion events early. Therefore, feedback data from mobile Apps will become a valuable data source for sensing public opinion trends after sufficient data are accumulated and captured.

To analyze opinion implications and public trends from those mobile application big data, we always need to use sentiment analysis. Traditional sentiment analysis may perform well for long texts. However, comments, especially comments from mobile applications, which is always shorter, are more difficult to analyze. Because the comment from mobile applications are always be changeful in format, and in most time it is too short to get some meaningful information about with sentiment by using traditional methods. It imposes much more difficulties to reveal the implications in short comments comparing with other text sources from network such as forums and blogs. In this paper, we explore a new kind of big data from mobile Internet - feedback data, which mainly come from mobile applications such as news application, in which consists of replying comments and the number of clicking agreement. Moreover, we also explore the feedback model of users in mobile applications on mobile devices. The contribution of the paper is as follows:

1. We propose a new method to analysis comment's sentiment trend from mobile applications.
2. We propose a new model to quantifying user's feedback behaviors in mobile news applications, which can facilitate to understand feedback utilities.

The rest of the paper is organized as follows: Previous works are reviewed in Sect. 2. We present basic setting on sentiment analysis methods in Sect. 3. We propose a method to compute sentiment scores of special texts such as short comments in Sect. 4. The evaluation of our proposed system is conducted in Sect. 5. The paper is concluded in Sect. 6.

2   Related Work

In general, the research works for text sentiment analysis including machine learning based method and semantic dictionary based method. In the machine-based sentiment analysis method, Yang et al. [4] use SVM-based classification methods to conduct sentiment classification of four kinds of granularity. According to the results analysis, it performs well in COAE2009's evaluation task. In addition, Fan et al. [5] proposed K-neighborhood scheme. They firstly determine the local sentiment tendencies of texts, then use KNN algorithm to calculate the sentiment tendencies of full texts. This algorithm still needs to mark some text sentiment values artificially. It has certain advantages compare with traditional machine learning methods in judgment accuracy, but the result is mainly influenced by subjective. In the study of Liu et al. [14], they use three different machine learning programs including SVM scheme, Naive Bayes scheme, and N-meta-language model. Their scheme selects three different features include IG [3], CHI statistics, and TF (document frequency) as well as three different calculation schemes about feature's weight: Boolean feature weight, word frequency characteristic weight, and TF-IDF [8], to classify the data from micro-blog through sentiment analysis. Their result shows that SVM, IG and TF-IDF are the best combination to get good results in classification. But, their program can only resolve specific area data. For different area's analysis, a different model need to be established. Popescu et al. [6] firstly calculate the PMI value and then using Bayes classifier to process the data.

For semantic dictionary-based research programs, most works are based on existing sentiment dictionaries. For example, Zhou et al. [11] use HowNet and SentiWordNet to decompose a number of words into sense words, and then calculate the sentiment value of words, lastly use SVM method to calculate a text's sentiment values. Delan et al. [1] use the algorithm on word similarity degree, the algorithm on semantic similarity degree, and the algorithm on grammatical similarity degree to calculate sentence complacency degree. The result shows that their scheme is similar to manual judgment. Dong et al. [2] introduce the related knowledge about HowNet, and the description of ever sense words in the HowNet by details. Wang et al. [13] use HowNet and PMI to calculate the sentiment polarity of a word. Their schemes improve the accuracy up 5% compared with general scheme.

As the number of texts in the network are huge, Yang et al. [9] adapt the concept of comment cluster to replace of a class of comments, and use the comment cluster's sentiment tendencies to instead of all comments sentiment tendency in the cluster. Their method can improve the efficiency of sentiment mining algorithm with adding 58% accuracy of checking network public opinion.

To analyzing comments from mobile applications, we use the method based on sentiment dictionary. However different with old methods only with sentiment dictionary, we also propose some new dictionaries to strengthen the effect of our work, such as negative word dictionary and similarity sentiment dictionary. Also, we propose a new method in below to get the comment's sentiment score. By using those new methods and tools we complete our work in this paper.

3   Sentiment Analysis Method

Sentiment analysis is a subjective text mining and analysis technology to get useful knowledge and information [7,10,12] from texts. Its main objective is to determine the sentiment tendencies of the subjective text. In this paper, we use the method based on sentiment dictionary from HowNet and degree adverb dictionary with some new dictionaries as negative word dictionary and similarity sentiment dictionary constructed by us.

Our sentiment analysis method consists of three steps: (1) text preprocessing, (2) sentiment information extraction, and (3) sentiment classification. Specific descriptions of each step are shown as follows:

(1) Text preprocessing.

To analyzing a text's sentiment tendency, pretreatment is required. Here, the text is unstructured. First of all, a text is composed by different paragraphs, thus we need to cut the text according to paragraphs, and store each paragraphs in our database solely. Secondly, each paragraph is composed by different sentences, so we then divide sentences by cutting the paragraphs base on some English symbols such as ".", "!", "?", ";" or same symbols in Chinese. Next, we store those sentences in our database solely. Because each sentence is also composed by different short opinions sentences, so we cut the sentence according to "," or separate them by space to obtain several short opinion sentences. In this way, an unstructured text can be decomposed into multiple structured texts.

After above work we need to eliminate some useless (chaos) words. The term "stop word" refers to a word (some words) that is (are) automatically ignored in the information retrieval. In order to save storage space and improve the retrieval efficiency, we need to eliminate those stop words before or after processing the natural language data (or text). Because these stop words have little influence in sentiment analysis, we need to remove these deceptive words from the results of word segmentation. In this paper, we contribute a stop word dictionary to eliminate stop words in opinion sentences.

(2) Sentiment information extraction.

Sentiment information extraction extracts the sentiment information that is valuable in texts. In this paper, we propose to use the sentiment dictionary from HowNet, degree adverb dictionary from Internet, and negative word dictionary by us to obtain sentiment elements in opinion sentences.

In the sentiment dictionary from HowNet, there are many sentiment words with their sentiment score. In the degree adverb dictionary from Internet, there are many adverb words with their degree score. In the negative word dictionary by us, there are many negative words. By using those three dictionaries, we compare words in opinion sentences to confirm the kind of each word and give the word score. Specially, if the word is negative word, the word score is "−1".

(3) Sentiment classification.

The sentiment classification determines sentiment tendencies of the text.

In this paper, we propose an algorithm to calculate text sentiment score. To calculate text sentiment score, firstly we divide a text into paragraphs, then cut a paragraph into sentences, and lastly separate sentences into opinion words. After this, we firstly calculate sentiment scores of opinion words, then compute sentiment scores of sentences, next sum scores of paragraphs, and finally we can obtain the sentiment score of the text. Base on the sentiment score of the text, we can analysis the sentiment tendency of the text. The specific method to calculate the text sentiment score will be proposed in Sect. 4. In general, if the score is greater than 0, the sentiment tendency of the text will be positive. Otherwise, the sentiment tendency of the text is negative.

By using above methods, we can obtain a comment's sentiment score. Generally speaking, the greater of the comment's absolute sentiment score, the stronger of the sentiment tendency of the comment.

4   Proposed Scheme

Base on the way described in the last section, we hereby propose a specific method to calculate a text's sentiment score. Particularly, we concentrate on comments from mobile applications, which is remarkable sources for implying public opinions. We propose several new algorithms that are tailed design for comment data, which present distinct difficulties due to its short and chaos properties.

4.1   Computing Sentiment Values of Opinion Sentences

For a sentiment word, it will be assigned a sentiment value, denoted as S. In general, if a degree adverb appears in front of this sentiment word, that degree adverb is used to strengthen the sentiment value of this word. We assume that the degree is D. If there is a negative word before the sentiment word, then the sentiment polarity of the sentiment word will be reversed. We set the value of the negative word to -1. As the odd number of negative words in Chinese is still negative, but even negative words for the positive state. Thus, we give the following Algorithm 1 to calculate the sentiment value of an opinion sentence.

After above operations, the sentiment value of an opinion sentence is available. If the value is greater than 0, the sentiment tendency is positive. If it is less than 0, the sentiment tendency of the opinion sentence is negative. If it is around 0, it means that the opinion sentence is neutral. The higher is the sentiment value of the opinion sentence, the stronger is the tendency of the opinion sentence.

4.2   Computing Sentiment Values of Sentences

After getting the sentiment value of an opinion sentence, the sentiment value of a sentence is obtained based on the following method:

$$score_{senten} = \sum_{i=1}^{L} \frac{i}{L} * score_{opinsenten} \tag{1}$$

Algorithm 1. Calculate Opinion Sentence Score

---

set $W = 1, Score = 0$;
  for $word \in OpinionSentence$ **do**
    if $word \in degreeDict$ **then**
      set $W = W * D(word)$;
    else
      if $Word \in notDict$ **then**
        set $W = W * -1$;
      else
        if $word \in senDcit$ **then**
          set $Score = Score + W * S(word)$;
          set $W = 1$;
        end if
      end if
    end if
  end for
  return $Score$;

---

where i represents the position of the opinion sentence throughout the sentence; L represents the number of opinion sentences contained in the sentence.

By using method 1, we can calculate the sentiment value of a sentence. The reason is that in Chinese, it is common to state important information at the end of the sentence [10]. We stress that the importance of an opinion sentence is related to its location.

4.3 Computing Sentiment Values of Comments

Different from calculating the sentiment value of a sentence, we analyze the influence of different sentences in the paragraph to it's sentiment value, and propose a method to calculate the value of a paragraph's sentiment:

$$weight = \begin{cases} \frac{L-i}{L} & i < \frac{L}{4} \\ \frac{i}{L} & i >= \frac{L}{4} \end{cases} \tag{2}$$

$$score_{Paragraph} = \sum_{i=1}^{L} weight * score_{sentence} \tag{3}$$

where i represents the position of the sentence in a paragraph, starting at 1; L represents the number of sentences in the paragraph.

4.4 Judging Unlisted Words

The most critical step in calculating the sentiment value of an opinion sentence is to compare the word in the opinion sentence to the word in sentiment dictionary, negative word dictionary, and degree word dictionary, so as to classify the word's kind and get the word's score.

The sentiment dictionary we use to analyze sentiment words is based on HowNet. However, this system has not been updated for a long time, and many words have new implications in recent years, especially in mobile applications environment. Thus, we need to update our sentiment dictionary to detect as much sentiment words as possible to make our system be more useful.

Word2Vec is a software tool developed by Google for training word vector. It expresses a word as a vector form efficiently according to a given corpus. In our proposed system, we use Word2Vec to find out the most similar word to an unlisted word in the corpus. The unlisted word is the word or words which is(are) not collected in the sentiment dictionary, negative word dictionary, and degree word dictionary, but is(are) essential to judge the sentiment tendency of a sentence.

It is very simple to implement the code in Python to use Word2Vec to training the word vector. Firstly we need to obtain the corpus for training. The corpus contains all article's content we have collected, with all the comments of articles, negative word dictionary, degree adverb dictionary, and sentiment dictionary's content.

We use some methods in Word2Vec model to increase the accuracy of the model. We can treat our existing dictionary as a training corpus for the original Word2Vec model, and upgrade to a new model for further training. After the model is updated, we can test its efficiency. By entering "China" for testing, the results are shown in Fig. 1:

我国:0.591204226017	我国:0.591191768646	我国:0.456856787205
我们:0.567599773407	我们:0.567157268524	我们:0.443490803242
骨气:0.454989075661	骨气:0.451166421175	大中华:0.41534230113
咱们:0.442545235157	咱们:0.436943858862	外国人:0.374125093222
团结:0.429398208857	外国人:0.427167743444	大陆:0.345852255821
外国人:0.428709596395	团结:0.425999909639	咱们:0.341952651739
大陆:0.424053996801	伤害:0.421460360289	骨气:0.332326203585
伤害:0.422680199146	大陆:0.420773893595	祖国:0.321983605623
咱:0.403672665358	大中华:0.409728199244	伤害:0.321355491877
大中华:0.40215498209	承担责任:0.397470504045	团结:0.314311623573

Fig. 1. Use Word2Vec model to verify effects of similarity

The function to detect similarity in the model is *model.most_similar*(). The function returns the most similar words in the model to "China" and returns the values of the corresponding similarity. The figures from left to right are the result by using the model of word2vec, word2vec2, word2vec3.

We use the word2vec3 model to search similar word for unlisted words. By using the *model.most_similar* function, we can find the first 10 words that are most similar to unlisted words. In the training model we have dumped all news, comments, sentiment dictionary, negative word dictionary, and degree word dictionary's content into the model file. Thus it is inevitable to find the most similar word in the model file with unlisted words. If an unlisted word is in one of those 3 dictionaries, we enclose the word into the dictionary, and calculate the score of the word. The score of the word is calculating as

$$score_{unlisted} = score_{mostsimilarword} * degree_{similarity} \tag{4}$$

where $score_{mostsimiliarword}$ is the score of the most similar word in the dictionary; $degree_{similarity}$ is the similarity degree of the word, which can be computed by using $model.most\_similar()$.

5   Experiment Results and Analysis

5.1   Analysis About Comment's Sentiment Score

In the experiment, we select 100 comments randomly, and get the scores of those comments. Here we assume that the comment tendency is neutral if the comment sentiment score is less than 1 but greater than −0.3. The comment sentiment tendency is positive, if the sentiment score is greater than 1. The comment sentiment tendency is negative, if the sentiment score is less than −0.3. Then we judge the comment sentiment tendency manually, and give the comment sentiment tendency. The result is shown in Table 1.

Table 1. Machine and manual judgment about 100 comment's sentiment tendency

	Positive	Negative	Neutral
Machine	34	48	18
Artificial	33	50	17

In the Table 1, we state that it is rational to use Algorithm 1 and other two methods to calculate the comment sentiment score. We verify the correctness about those three algorithms by calculate the recall rate R, correct rate P, and F value by using above data. More specifically, correctly rate $P = \frac{A}{B}$, recall rate $R = \frac{A}{C}$, and $F = 2*P*R*(P+R)$ [10]. Here A represents the comment number with the comment is tagged as positive (negative and neutral) comments both by using machine and artificial method. B represents the comment number with the comment is tagged as positive (negative and neutral) comment, only using machine method, and C represents the comment number with the comment is tagged as positive (negative and neutral) comment, only using artificial method.

After analyzing the data in the Table 1, we list the result of P, R, F in the Table 2.

In the Table 2, it shows that it is useful by using Algorithm 1 and other two methods to calculate the comment sentiment score. We also find that it is more useful to detect negative comments by using those algorithms than detect positive and neutral comments.

Table 2. The correct rate P, recall rate R, and F value

Sentence polarity	P	R	F
Positive	$28/34 = 82.35\%$	$82/33 = 84.85\%$	83.58%
Negative	$45/48 = 93.75\%$	$45/50 = 90\%$	91.84%
Neutral	$14/18 = 77.78\%$	$14/17 = 82.35\%$	80%

5.2   Analysis

There are some experiments blow, during the experiment, we have some explanation to the experiment results. The reason why we do those experiments is to get the data statistic's rule from the endogenous data from mobile applications, and to find some user behaviors model in mobile applications.

Comment Number Distribution vs Time

(1) The distribution of comment number in three months.
   Figure 2 depicts the distribution of comments number in 3 months. According to statistics, the number of comments on a topic (e.g., "THAAD") event in Toutiao has a rapid growth pattern in three months from January to March 2017. The number of comments in January was 12520, with 26569 in February and 74568 in March, in which presenting a linear growth per month with the slope of 3. It can be found that, with the fermentation of hot news events, the attention to the relevant events growth explosively.
(2) The distribution of comment number in one month.
   Figure 3 shows the changes about the comment number from February to March in 2017. Both of these pictures show very strongly fluctuations, especially in February. By analysis the news in the peak of comment number in both two months. The peak of the comment number coincides with some hot news happening. From above images, it can be seen that since March, the general public attention to relevant events has been gradually decreasing.
(3) The distribution of comment number in one day.
   Figure 4 reflects the changes of comment number with hour times in a day. It can be clearly seen that the number of comments in one day is perfectly coincident with normal personal spare time in daily life. For example, the number of comments rises gradually between 4 a.m. and 9 a.m. But between 9 and 11, the number of comments goes down or drops slightly. Between 11 and 12, there is another uplift, because it is a time for taking a break (reading news). Between 12 and 14, there is a drop due to lunch time or noon sleep.

Comment Sentiment Score vs the Number of Reply or Clicking Agreement

(1) The relationship between comment scores with the number of clicking agreements.

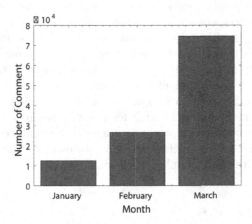

Fig. 2. The relationship between the number of comments with month

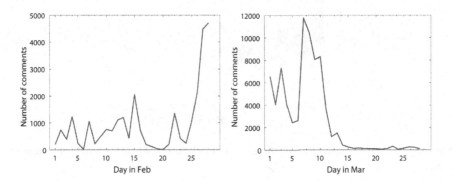

Fig. 3. The relationship between the number of comments with month in February and March

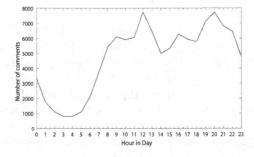

Fig. 4. The relationship between the number of comments with time in a day

Figure 5 reflects the relationship between the score of comments with the number of clicking agreement for the comment. Because the comment score is too small to show in the figure, we expand the score of all comments by a factor as 1000. It shows that the more clicking agreement number of the comment, the comment sentiment tendency is more likely tendency to neutral, whose score is around 0. If a comment score is larger, then the number of clicking agreement is smaller. But in general, the number of clicking agreement for positive comments is more than that for negative comments.

(2) The relationship between comment scores with the number of replies.

Figure 6 is similar to Fig. 5. However, it is obvious that the number of reply is much smaller than the number of clicking agreement.

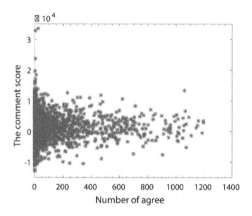

Fig. 5. The relationship between the number of clicking agreement with the comment score

The Relationship Between Comment Sentiment Score's Standard Deviation with Time

(1) The relationship between the standard deviation of comment scores with time lasting in a month.

Figure 7 shows the relationship between the standard deviation of comment's sentiment score with time lasting in February 2017. By analysis the data we can find that the standard deviation of sentiment value tends to be flat or even smaller (As public opinions tend to be same on the same event, for example, from February 16 to February 19, the sentiment value of the comments on the "THAAD" event gradually returned to a neutral position). However, the standard deviation of sentiment score for comments will rise above normal proportion when the same event are renewed after news subsides. It is because new updates are published and they may present different or even opposite sentimental tendencies with the original one (For example, the standard deviation of sentiment scores is very large in February 22. After checking

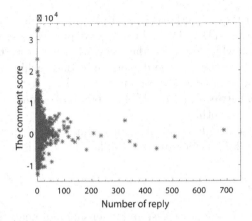

Fig. 6. The relationship between the number of reply with the comment score

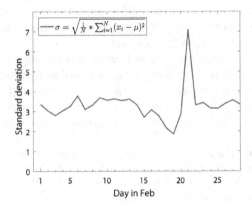

Fig. 7. The standard deviation of comment score with time in February

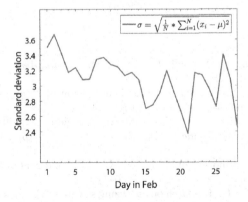

Fig. 8. The standard deviation of comment score with time in March

the news in February 22, we find it is "Rok and US military exercises are in the process, whether THAAD will be able to deploy" and some other relevant news). The reason why we use standard deviation in this part is that standard deviation can reflect the average dispersion of data, which is good at reflect people's sentiment tendency's divergence.

(2) The relationship between the standard deviation of comment scores with time lasting in another month.

Figure 8 shows the standard deviation distribution of comment scores vs time lasting in March 2017, which has the similar characteristics in Fig. 7.

6   Conclusion

In this paper, we propose a novel system for sensing and analyzing mobile application big data such as news comments. We propose a sentiment analysis method based on sentiment dictionary to calculate comment sentiment score and judging the comment sentiment tendency. The extensive experiments and analysis verify the correctness of the proposed algorithms. We also points out some models base on statistics to user behaviors such as replying comments and clicking agreements, and its relation between behaviors and duration time.

From our experiments and analysis, it is possible to predict a large scale opinion trend. Those observations and capabilities can help us to strengthen news recommendation system, create opinion intervention system, sense public opinion implications, and design interactive manners in mobile applications.

Acknowledgement. The research was financially supported by Major Scientific and Technological Special Project of Guizhou Province under Grant No. 20183001, the Open Funding of Guizhou Provincial Key Laboratory of Public Big Data under Grant No. 2017BDKFJJ006, Open Funding of Hubei Provincial Key Laboratory of Intelligent Geo-Information Processing with under Grant No. KLIGIP2016A05, and National Natural Science Foundation of China under Grant No. 61502362. We also thanks for the comments from W. Jiang, S. Lin, Y. Liao, and M. Lei.

References

1. Delan, X., Juming, C., Shengli, T.: Orientation research based on HowNet. Comput. Eng. Appl. **44**(22), 143–145 (2008)
2. Dong, Z., Dong, Q.: HowNet and the Computation of Meaning. World Scientific Publishing Co., Inc., Hackensack (2006)
3. Shi, H., Jia, D., Miao, P.: Improved information gain text feature selection algorithm based on word frequency information. Comput. Appl. **34**(11), 3279–3282 (2014)
4. Yang, J., Lin, S.: Emotion analysis on text words and sentences based on SVM. Comput. Appl. Softw. **28**(9), 225–228 (2011)
5. Fan, N., An, Y., Li, H.: Research on analyzing sentiment of texts based on k-nearest neighbor algorithm. Comput. Eng. Des. **33**(3), 1160–1164 (2012)
6. Popescu, A.M., Etzioni, O.: Extracting product features and opinions from reviews. In: HLT/EMNLP on Interactive Demonstrations, pp. 32–33 (2005)

7. Wei, W., Xiang, Y., Chen, Q.: Survey on Chinese text sentiment analysis. J. Comput. Appl. **31**(12), 3321–3323 (2011)
8. Wu, H.C., Luk, R.W.P., Wong, K.F., Kwok, K.L.: Interpreting TF-IDF term weights as making relevance decisions. ACM Trans. Inf. Syst. **26**(3), 55–59 (2008)
9. Yang, X., Ma, Q., Yu, L., Mo, Y., Wu, J., Zhang, Y.: Gauging public opinion with comment-clusters. New Technol. Libr. Inf. Serv. **32**(7), 51–59 (2016)
10. Yijin, C., Shujin, C., Guihong, C.: Online public opinion mining: user's sentiment analysis. Doc. Inf. Knowl. **6**, 90–96 (2013)
11. Zhou, Y., Yang, J., Yang, A.: A method on building chinese sentiment lexicon for text sentiment analysis. J. Shandong Univ. (Eng. Sci.) **6**, 27–33 (2013)
12. Zhao, Y.Y., Qin, B., Liu, T.: Sentiment analysis. J. Softw. **21**(8), 1834–1848 (2010)
13. Wang, Z., Wu, Z., Hu, F.: Words sentiment polarity calculation based on HowNet and PMI. Comput. Eng. **38**(15), 187–189 (2012)
14. Liu, Z., Liu, L.: Empirical study of sentiment classification for Chinese microblog based on machine learning. Comput. Eng. Appl. **48**(1), 1–4 (2012)

SDVRP-Based Reposition Routing in Bike-Sharing System

Zengyi Han[1] , Yongjian Yang[2], Yunpeng Jiang[1], Wenbin Liu[2],
and En Wang[2(✉)]

[1] Department of Software, Jilin University, Changchun 130012, China
{hanzy15,jiangyp15}@mails.jlu.edu.cn
[2] Department of Computer Science and Technology, Jilin University,
Changchun 130012, China
{yyj,liuwb16,wangen}@jlu.edu.cn

Abstract. Bike-sharing systems have recently been widely implemented. Despite providing green transportation method and a healthy lifestyle, bike-sharing systems also poses problems for system operators: In order to meet the public's demand as much as possible, operators must use multiple trucks to relocate new bikes and repaired bikes from the depot to different stations. Then, the route to minimize the cost for the delivery trucks becomes a serious problem. To address this issue, we first formulate the problem into a split delivery vehicle routing problem (SDVRP) since every station's demand can satisfied by multiple trucks, and use the K-means algorithm to cluster stations. In general, K-means is used to cluster the nearest points without constraint. In this real-world constraint problem, the sum of zones' demands must be smaller than total truck capacity. Therefore, we transform the SDVRP into a traveling salesman problem (TSP) by using a constrainted K-means algorithm to cluster stations with the demand constraint. Finally, according to the context, we use a genetic algorithm to solve the TSP. The Evaluation considers four real-world open datasets from bike-sharing systems and shows that our method can solve this problem effectively.

Keywords: Bike-sharing system · SDVRP
Traveling salesman problem

1 Introduction

Bike-sharing systems, which provide short-term bike rental services with parking stations scattered throughout an urban city, are booming in many cities all over the world. More than 700 large cities [1] including Beijing, San Francisco and Tokyo, have deployed bike-sharing systems. These systems provide a convenient, low-cost, environmentally friendly transportation alternative [2]. In recent years,

Supported by National Natural Science Foundation of China under Grant No. 61772230 and the Natural Science Foundation of China for Young Scholars No. 61702215.

J. Vaidya and J. Li (Eds.): ICA3PP 2018, LNCS 11335, pp. 596–610, 2018.
https://doi.org/10.1007/978-3-030-05054-2_45

a relatively new bike-sharing model, called free-floating bike-sharing (FFBS) [3], has been implemented, especially in China. The FFBS system in China, called Mobike, is shown in Fig. 1. These bikes are equipped with various types of sensors, e.g., GPS, bluetooth, and vibration sensors [4].

Fig. 1. Mobike bike-sharing system

With this new model of bike sharing, customers use their smartphones to locate bikes, and bikes can be locked to an ordinary bicycle frame (or any solid standalone) after use, thus customers do not need to worry about a lack of vacant frames at bike stations when they need to return a bike, and eliminate the need for large number of specific stations [3]. Compared with traditional station-based bike sharing, by reducing infrastructure construction, FFBS saves substantial initial cost [3]. FFBS also protects bicycles from being stolen by real-time tracking of bikes with built-in sensors, and provides excellent conditions for bike relocation. With FFBS, customer satisfaction is improved because obtaining and returning the bikes is more convenient than ever. Additionally, the average walking distance with FFBS is short.

However, despite the significant benefits of FFBS, it remains challenging to relocate bikes in a valid way. After a period of time, many bikes are left broken in locations where they are can not be used again. To increase bike service availability, bike-sharing system operators have to relocate these broken bikes from remote locations to depot in order to repair them, and operators also need to deliver these repaired bikes and new bikes from depot to certain stations to cover more customers' demand, a process that is typically performed by trucks or trailers driving around the city. Then bikes are assigned to station according demand, as shown in Fig. 2. However, system operators have limited resources, which constrains the extent to which relocation can occur.

The regular method used to deliver bikes first determines the demand at each area, which is typically achieved via history data analysis and prediction. Second, truck routes are designed to perform the necessary deliveries to reach the target area. To increase bike service availability and minimize the redistribution

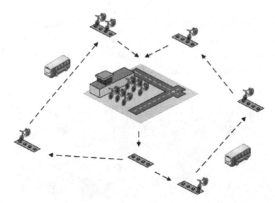

Fig. 2. SDVRP in bike-sharing system

cost, we must determine the optimal route for trucks to deliver bikes from the depot to the certain stations. This problem is an exciting application in the field of computational sustainability. With prediction technology, it is easy to determine the demand of each area. Thus, the assumption of this problem is that the requirements of each area are known in advance and do not change during operation. Therefore, our situation corresponds to a split delivery vehicle routing problem (SDVRP) [5]. Since SDVRP is a complex NP-hard problem, it is very difficult to solve.

Since bike-sharing system always contain many stations, and it will take a lot of time to calculate. In this paper, we use the K-means algorithm to transform the SDVRP into a TSP(traveling salesman problem), which can be solved by various heuristics algorithms and make every problem easy and quick to solve. In this context, we use the genetic algorithm to solve the TSP.

This paper makes the following three main contributions:

- We model the bike-sharing deliver problem as a split delivery vehicle routing problem, and then use a K-means algorithm to cluster the stations that are near to each other. We then transform the SDVRP into a TSP problem and use a genetic algorithm for every cluster to solve the TSP problem.
- To the best of our knowledge, this is the first work that models a bike-sharing deliver system as a split delivery vehicle routing problem.
- We evaluate our model with a real world dataset collected from the *Bay Area Bike-Sharing system* and consider three additional bike-sharing systems. The experimental results clearly show the effectiveness of the proposed methods.

The remainder of this paper is organized as follows. Related work is discussed in Sect. 2. We then present the problem formulation and properties in Sect. 3, followed by the methodology used to solve the problem in Sect. 4, including the K-means algorithm and genetic algorithm. Section 5 describes our datasets and provides an in-depth evaluation. We conclude the paper in Sect. 6.

2   Related Work

In parallel with the spread of bike-sharing programs around the world, and due to the increasing importance of bike-sharing programs, there has been growing interest in the related scientific research, including the history, worldwide deployment, and infrastructure. In [6], Paul provide a history of bicycle sharing. In [7], Shaheen et al. surveys China's Hangzhou Public Bicycle. Pucher et al. [8], conduct an international review of bike-sharing's facilities and programs. Owing to the operational difficulties of managing bike-sharing systems, previous work mainly focuses on four research substreams: rebalancing operations between stations, system planning, demand prediction, and system modeling.

In terms of rebalancing operations, there are two main challenges in the bike rebalancing problem: determining the target station inventory and the large-scale multiple-capacity vehicle routing optimization with outlier stations [9]. In [9], Liu et al. report that rebalancance is not only a necessary mechanism to make full use of the availability of the station, but also a more convenient mechanism to save time and make customers comfortable. To this end, Aeschbach et al. establish mechanisms to incentivize customers to transport bikes among stations [10]. Schuijbroek et al. [11] propose a new cluster-first route-second heuristic method to rebalance the inventory.

System planning includes determining the number and capacity of stations [12]. For instance, Chen et al. [12] solve the station placement problem by estimating the potential trip demand using a semi-supervised learning algorithm and a GIS-based method. Research has also been conducted to optimize the placement of stations in bike-sharing systems. For instance, in [2], O'Mahony et al. analyze bike-sharing system data to determine the optimal placement of bikes to facilitate usage.

Demand prediction involves predicting station status and bike usage with different models. This type of research is mainly focused on predicting the number of available bikes and docks at the station level. For example, in [13] Yang et al. propose a spatio-temporal bicycle mobility model, using mainly historical bike-sharing data, and devise a traffic prediction mechanism on a per-station basis with sub-hour granularity. Chen et al. [14] construct a weighted correlation network to model the relationships among bike stations, and dynamically group neighboring stations with similar bike usage patterns into clusters. Then, they perform Monte Carlo simulations to predict the over-demand probability of each cluster. However, these station-level prediction methods do not consistently yield accurate results due to the impact of adjacent stations [15] and complex environmental factors that affect bike usage (such as weather, temperature, and social events).

With respect to system models, in [16], Chen et al. formulate the trip inference problem as an ill-posed inverse problem, and propose a regularization technique to infer bike trip patterns. In [17], Lin et al. develop a public bicycle redistribution system based on normal VRP. Additionally, they propose an optimization method that considers road conditions, traffic rules, and geographical factors, rather than simply using Euclidean distance. Naturally, the use of actual distance would lead to lower costs in reality [11].

The vehicle routing problem (VRP) [18] and traveling salesman problem (TSP) [19], they are two popular problems in the field of combinatorial optimization. The SDVRP (split delivery vehicle routing problem) is a form of the VRP [20] that allows the same customer to be served by different vehicles if it reduces the total costs [5]. The SDVRP is an NP-hard problem as proved by Archetti et al. [21], that was introduced by Dror et al. in 1989 [22]. The Tabu search algorithm can solve the SDVRP [23,24], but Tabu search effectively handle small situations [25]. The TSP (Traveling Salesman Problem) is an NP-hard problem [26], but several heuristics algorithm for TSP are already known. In this work, we use the SDVRP to model the bike sharing assignment process, and we use K-means algorithm to transform the SDVRP to a TSP.

3   Mathematical Formulation and Properties

The SDVRP can be defined over a graph $G = (V, E)$ with vertex set $V = \{0, 1, \ldots, n\}$, where 0 denotes the depot, the other vertices are stations, and E is the edge set. c_{ij} is the travel cost of an edge $(i, j) \in E$, which is supposed to be nonnegative. Each station $i \in V - \{0\}$ is associated with an integer demand d_i. m is the upper bound on the number of trucks to serve, each with a capacity $k \in Z^+$. Each truck must start and end its route at the depot. The demands of the stations must be satisfied, and the quantity delivered in each tour cannot exceed k. Our objective is to minimize the total distance traveled by the trucks.

Therefore, the SDVRP can be formulated as follows:

$$Min \sum_{i=0}^{n} \sum_{j=0}^{n} \sum_{v=1}^{m} c_{ij} x_{ij}^v. \tag{1}$$

We use the following notations: x_{ij}^v is a Boolean variable equal to 1 if truck v travels directly from i to j and equal to 0 otherwise, and y_{iv} is the quantity of demand of i delivered by truck v.

Subject to:

$$\sum_{i=0}^{n} \sum_{v=0}^{m} x_{ij}^v \geq 1 \quad j = 0, \ldots, n \tag{2}$$

$$\sum_{i=0}^{n} x_{ip}^v - \sum_{j=0}^{n} x_{pj}^v = 0 \quad p = 0, \ldots, n; \quad v = 1, \ldots, m \tag{3}$$

$$\sum_{i \in S} \sum_{i \in S} x_{ij}^v \leq |S| - 1 \quad v = 1, \ldots, m; \quad S \subseteq V - \{0\} \tag{4}$$

$$y_{iv} \leq d_i \sum_{j=0}^{n} x_{ij}^v \quad i = 1, \ldots, n; \quad v = 1, \ldots, m \tag{5}$$

$$\sum_{v=1}^{m} y_{iv} = d_i \quad i = 1, \ldots, n \tag{6}$$

$$\sum_{i=1}^{n} y_{iv} \leq k \quad v = 1, \ldots, m \tag{7}$$

$$x_{ij}^v \in \{0,1\} \quad i = 0, \ldots, n; \quad j = 0, \ldots, n; \\ v = 1, \ldots, m \tag{8}$$

$$y_{iv} \geq 0 \quad i = 1, \ldots, n; \quad v = 1, \ldots, m \tag{9}$$

Constraint (2) requires that each station is visited at least once. Constraint (3) is the flow conservation, which means that a truck cannot stay at a station. Constraint (4) is the subtour elimination constraint. Constraint (5) states that customer i can be served by truck v only if v passes through i. Constraint (6) ensure that the entire demand of each station is satisfied. Constraint (7) ensures that the quantity delivered by each truck does not exceed its capacity.

We now illustrate the two properties of the optimal solutions of the SDVRP. Dror and Trudeau and Liu already proved these properties in 1989 and 2012 [27].

Theorem 1. *If the travel route c_{ij} satisfies the triangle inequality, and there exists an optimal solution to the SDVRP, when the station's demand equals the truck's capacity ($d_i = k$), then this zone should be satisfied by a single truck.*

Proof 1. Assume station B's demand is equal to a truck's capacity, and split route into r_k and r_{k+1}. The depot is O.

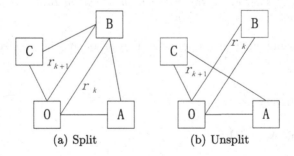

(a) Split   (b) Unsplit

Fig. 3. Situation 1, B is on the right side of AC's attachment

Note that the total lengths of these three split routes are $Z_{split} = d_{OC} + d_{CB} + 2d_{OB} + d_{BA} + d_{AO}$, $Z_{unsplit} = d_{OC} + d_{CA} + d_{AO} + 2d_{OB}$, $Z_{split} - Z_{unsplit} = d_{CB} + d_{BA} + d_{CA}$ (Fig. 3).

In situation 1 and 2, because of the triangle inequality, we know that $d_{CB} + d_{BA} - d_{CA} > 0$. In situation 3, $d_{CB} + d_{BA} - d_{CA} = 0$. Therefore, when station's

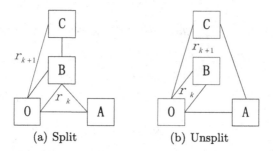

Fig. 4. Situation 2, B is on the left side of AC's attachment

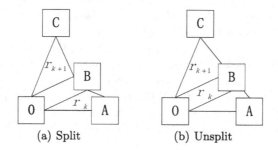

Fig. 5. Situation 3, B is between AC's attachment

demand is equal to a truck's capacity $(d_i = k)$, then this zone should be serviced by a single truck (Figs. 4 and 5).

Theorem 2. *If the travel route c_{ij} satisfies the triangle inequality, then there exists an optimal solution to the SDVRP in which no two vehicles have more than one split customer in common.*

This paper mainly uses property 1. The proof for the property 2, can be found it in the literature [18].

4   Methodology

4.1   K-means Algorithm

The K-means algorithm is a popular machine learning technique for classification, and has been proven to be effective in solving many problems.

We use the K-means algorithm, to cluster stations that are near to each other to be served by one truck. However, owing to the truck's limited capacity, this problem is a constrained clustering problem. Therefore we cannot directly apply the K-means algorithm. During clustering, we consider that sum of each station set demand cannot exceed the maximum capacity.

Algorithm 1. Data Preprocessing

Require: The station's original demand d_i, Truck's capacity k.
Ensure: The station's remaining demand rd_i.
1: **while** $i < n$ **do**
2:     **if** $d_i \geq k$ **then**
3:         $rd_i = d_i - k * \lfloor d_i/k \rfloor$
4:     **end if**
5: **end while**
6: **return** rd_i

When the zone's demand exceeds the truck's capacity, we have proved that we need to meet the demand by truck alone. As in Algorithm 1 does, the remaining demand rd_i is less than the truck's capacity k, so the zone can be a member of the cluster.

Algorithm 2. Constrained K-means Cluster

Require: The zone's remaining demand rd_i, Truck's capacity k.
Ensure: The cluster of zones $c_1, ...c_j, ...c_m \in C$.
1: Select m cluster centroids randomly as $\mu_1, ...\mu_j, ..., \mu_m \in R$.
2: **while** $iteration < N$ **do**
3:     **for** $\mu_j \in R$ **do**
4:         **for** $s \in V$ **do**
5:             $c_j = arg\min_j ||s - \mu_j||^2$
6:         **end for**
7:         $\mu_j = Avg(s_i \in c_j)$
8:     **end for**
9: **end while**
10: **while** $iteration < m$ **do**
11:     **for** $s \in c^j$ **do**
12:         $distance^s_{\mu_j} = ||s - \mu_j||^2$
13:         $Sort(distance)$
14:     **end for**
15:     **for** $s \in c^j$ **do**
16:         $rc_i = rc_i - d_i$
17:         **if** $rc_i < d_i$ **then**
18:             $Split(station)$
19:         **end if**
20:     **end for**
21: **end while**
22: **return** C

Because of the constraint on the limit truck's capacity, the sum of clusters' demand cannot exceed the total capacity. To solve this real-world constraint problem, we use Algorithm 2 Constrained K-means Cluster. We use K-means to initialize the clusters of points. First, randomly select m cluster centroids. Then, for each station s, determine the cluster to which it belongs. After this initiation, we begin to check the limit capacity of each cluster. We need to select one cluster and sort the points according to the distance to the cluster center $distance^s_{\mu_j}$. Then, we add the nearest point to the cluster and calculate the remaining capacity. Next, we check the remaining capacity rc_i: if it is smaller than the current point's demand, we use Algorithm 3 to split the station's demand so that the demand can be satisfied. Because K-means is not certain to converge, we repeat these two calculations to obtain improved clusters until the number of iterations reaches the maximum number N.

When the zone's demand exceeds the truck's remaining capacity rc_i, we split the demand to solve this problem. To use fewer trucks and increase utilization, we use Algorithm 3 to split demand. According to the Theorem 1, we split the station c's demand into two parts, d^1_s and d^2_s, where d^1_s is the remaining capacity that can be met for the former zone by one truck at a time, and d^2_s is the remaining demand that cannot be satisfied. Therefore, the station's demand belongs to two clusters: one is the origin and the other is a newly added center.

Algorithm 3. Split Demand

Require: The zone's remaining demand rd_i, Truck's remaining capacity rc_i.
Ensure: The assignment of demand zone c.
  1: set $c^1_s = j$
  2: set $d^1_s = rc_s$
  3: set $c^2_s = j + m$
  4: set $d^2_s = d_s - rc_s$

4.2   Genetic Algorithm

After clustering, we determine the zones that can be satisfied by one truck, which means we have already transformed the SDVRP to a TSP. Then, we need to solve the TSP.

In the TSP, we have a set of cities (in this problem: stations) and know the distance from each of the different cities. Our goal is to find the ordered route of the stations that minimizes total length.

The genetic algorithm (GA) [28] is a metaheuristic algorithm inspired by the process of natural selection. An optimization problem's candidate solutions will evolve toward better solutions during the calculation.

Fitness function evaluation: The shorter the route, the better, so the fitness function can be the reciprocal of the distance, which in our case is $1/distance$.

A detailed description of the genetic algorithm for our problem is given below:

Step 1. **Initialization:** Randomly generate M routes as a initial population.

Step 2. **Selection:** In each subsequent generation, select a portion of the existing population to pass to the new generation. Individual solutions are selected by a

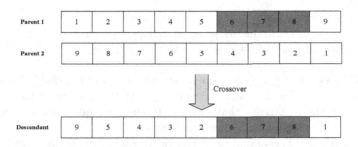

Fig. 6. Crossover

fitness-based process, where it is often more likely to choose an adaptive solution (measured by a fitness function) (Fig. 6).

Step 3. **Crossover:** A genetic operator used to change the component of a route from generation to generation. Crossover similar to breeding and biological crossover. We use three-point crossover: Three-point crossover selects three stations on the parent routes. All station other than the three selected stations are exchanged between the parent routes to generate a child route (Fig. 7).

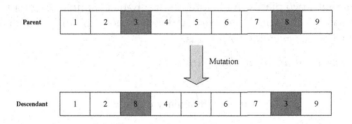

Fig. 7. Mutation

Step 4. **Mutation:** Since in TSP, each station will be visited only once in a route, during mutation, the order of two stations is swapped.

5 Performance Evaluation

In this section, we conduct computational experiments to evaluate the performance of our method. We have tested our implementations on real large-scale datasets from the *Bay Area* and three other bike-sharing systems. The compared algorithms, datasets, simulation configurations and performance are presented in the following.

A. Compared Algorithms

In this paper, we compare the two most related algorithms: the first-fit decreasing algorithm and Tabu search algorithm, with our method.

- First-Fit Decreasing: This is a simple greedy approximation algorithm. First, sort the zone's demands in descending order; then, attempt to assign the demand to the first truck that can satisfy the demand. If the present truck cannot satisfy the demand, then a new truck is used.
- Tabu Search: First, randomly generate one initial route. Create new solutions by swapping the order that two zones are visited in a potential solution, just like in the genetic algorithm. The total travel distance between all the zones is used to judge how ideal one solution is compared to another. To prevent cycles (i.e., repeatedly visiting a particular set of solutions) and to avoid becoming stuck in local optima, a solution is added to the Tabu list if it is accepted into the solution neighborhood. The Tabu search stops when the maximum number of iterations, which we set to 3000, is reached. When the Tabu search stops, it returns the best solution found.

In SDVRP, some zones' demands may exceed the capacity of the truck, so we perform preprocessing step before the calculation. In practice, if the demand for any zone is greater than or equal to the capacity of a truck, then we split the demand into two pieces. As before, we use K-means: first assign a truck that can itself satisfy the zone's demand and leave the remaining demand for the subsequent regular calculation process.

B. Datasets and Simulation Configurations

Table 1. Summary of datasets

	Bay area	Indego	Divvy	CiTiBike
Num of stations	67	119	585	812
Average demand	82	3.2	1	2
Max demand	14	15	17	21

We conduct extensive simulations on four real-world datasets: the Bay Area Bike-Sharing system [29], Indego Bike-Sharing system [30], Divvy Bike-Sharing system [31] and CitiBike Bike-Sharing system [32].

These Bike-Sharing data are collected by bike sensors during several years. To prove the effectiveness, we use only a single snapshot of all the stations' data, as presented in Table 1.

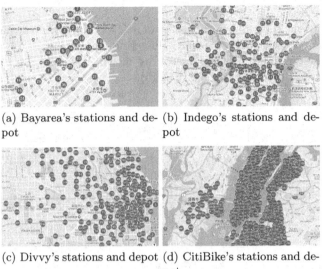

(a) Bayarea's stations and depot

(b) Indego's stations and depot

(c) Divvy's stations and depot

(d) CitiBike's stations and depot

Fig. 8. Depot in four traces (Color figure online)

The bike-sharing systems do not provide their depot locations, so we select the center of the stations as the depot. The green points in Fig. 8 represent the bike-sharing systems' depots.

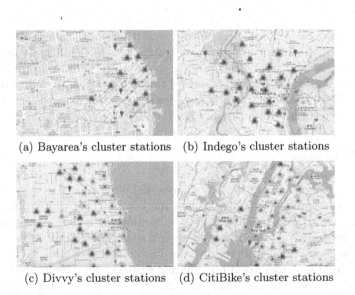

(a) Bayarea's cluster stations

(b) Indego's cluster stations

(c) Divvy's cluster stations

(d) CitiBike's cluster stations

Fig. 9. Clusters in four traces

C. Performance

In the experiment, the number of clusters depends on total zone demand divided by the truck's capacity. The K-means clustering algorithm is applied to determined the clusters for the four datasets, as shown in Fig. 9. The stations in a cluster are served by a single truck (Fig. 10).

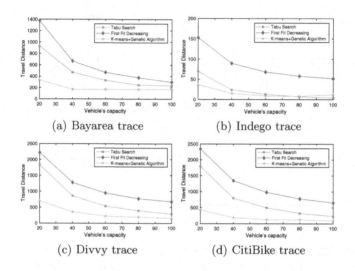

(a) Bayarea trace   (b) Indego trace

(c) Divvy trace   (d) CitiBike trace

Fig. 10. Results of four traces

We evaluate the performances of three algorithms for the above four datasets. We assess these algorithms for different truck capabilities of 20, 40, 60, 80, and 100. The larger the truck capacity is, the lower the total distance traveled.

The experiment results in four traces that have the same change tendency. As seen in Fig. 1, proposed method provides better performance than that of the other two algorithms in most situations.

6   Conclusion

In this paper we formulate the bike-sharing deliver problem as a split delivery vehicle routing problem, and propose a method to solve this problem. First, we use the K-means algorithm to cluster customers that are close together to receive bikes from a single truck. We then transform this problem into a TSP and use the genetic algorithm to solve the TSP. Finally, we evaluate our method with data from four real-world bike-sharing systems. The results show that our method can provide bike-sharing operators with routes to deliver bikes to every area efficiently.

As future work, we intend to improve this study in the following ways. First, in reality, there are lots of good condition bikes also need to reposition to certain parking areas, and this repositioning process can be done at the same time with collecting broken bikes. Overall, this process will improve efficiency, and we can model these process into a new problem. Second, in this study, we use Euclidean distance, but the between areas can not be completely straight lines in reality. Therefore, we need to use Google Maps API to obtain the real distance between areas. Third, owing to the limited data, we have tested our method with only four real datasets. To make our model more robust and accurate, we plan to evaluate our work with more bike-sharing system data from different cities, particularly in China. Finally, we also need to explore the influence of the number of cluster on the truck's travel distance.

References

1. Singla, A., Santoni, M., Bartók, G., Mukerji, P., Meenen, M., Krause, A.: Incentivizing users for balancing bike sharing systems. In: AAAI, pp. 723–729 (2015)
2. O'Mahony, E., Shmoys, D.B.: Data analysis and optimization for (Citi) bike sharing. In: AAAI, pp. 687–694 (2015)
3. Pal, A., Zhang, Y.: Free-floating bike sharing: solving real-life large-scale static rebalancing problems. Transp. Res. Part C: Emerg. Technol. **80**, 92–116 (2017)
4. Zhu, C., Zhou, H., Leung, V.C.M., Wang, K., Zhang, Y., Yang, L.T.: Toward big data in green city. IEEE Commun. Mag. **55**(11), 14–18 (2017)
5. http://neo.lcc.uma.es/vrp/vrp-flavors/split-delivery-vrp/
6. DeMaio, P.: Bike-sharing: history, impacts, models of provision, and future. J. Publ. Transp. **12**(4), 3 (2009)
7. Shaheen, S., Zhang, H., Martin, E., Guzman, S.: China's Hangzhou public bicycle: understanding early adoption and behavioral response to bikesharing. Transp. Res. Rec.: J. Transp. Res. Board **2247**, 33–41 (2011)
8. Pucher, J., Dill, J., Handy, S.: Infrastructure, programs, and policies to increase bicycling: an international review. Preventive medicine **50**, S106–S125 (2010)
9. Liu, J., Sun, L., Chen, W., Xiong, H.: Rebalancing bike sharing systems: a multi-source data smart optimization. In: Proceedings of the 22nd ACM SIGKDD International Conference on Knowledge Discovery and Data Mining, pp. 1005–1014. ACM (2016)
10. Aeschbach, P., Zhang, X., Georghiou, A., Lygeros, J.: Balancing bike sharing systems through customer cooperation - a case study on London's Barclays Cycle Hire. In: 2015 IEEE 54th Annual Conference on Decision and Control (CDC), pp. 4722–4727. IEEE (2015)
11. Schuijbroek, J., Hampshire, R.C., Van Hoeve, W.J.: Inventory rebalancing and vehicle routing in bike sharing systems. Eur. J. Oper. Res. **257**(3), 992–1004 (2017)
12. Chen, L., et al.: Bike sharing station placement leveraging heterogeneous urban open data. In: Proceedings of the 2015 ACM International Joint Conference on Pervasive and Ubiquitous Computing, pp. 571–575. ACM (2015)
13. Yang, Z., Hu, J., Shu, Y., Cheng, P., Chen, J., Moscibroda, T.: Mobility modeling and prediction in bike-sharing systems. In: Proceedings of the 14th Annual International Conference on Mobile Systems, Applications, and Services, pp. 165–178. ACM, 2016
14. Chen, L., et al.: Dynamic cluster-based over-demand prediction in bike sharing systems. In: Proceedings of the 2016 ACM International Joint Conference on Pervasive and Ubiquitous Computing, pp. 841–852. ACM (2016)

15. Li, Y., Zheng, Y., Zhang, H., Chen, L.: Traffic prediction in a bike-sharing system. In: Proceedings of the 23rd SIGSPATIAL International Conference on Advances in Geographic Information Systems, pp. 33. ACM (2015)
16. Chen, L., Jakubowicz, J.: Inferring bike trip patterns from bike sharing system open data. In: IEEE International Conference on Big Data, pp. 2898–2900 (2015)
17. Lin, J.-H., Chou, T.-C.: A geo-aware and VRP-based public bicycle redistribution system. Int. J. Veh. Technol. **2012**, 1–14 (2012)
18. https://en.wikipedia.org/wiki/Vehicle_routing_problem
19. https://en.wikipedia.org/wiki/Travelling_salesman_problem
20. Yun-zhang, L.I.U., Hui-yu, X.U.A.N.: Summarizing research on models and algorithms for vehicle routing problem [j]. J. Industr. Eng. Eng. Manag. **1**, 027 (2005)
21. Archetti, C., Mansini, R., Speranza, M.G.: Complexity and reducibility of the skip delivery problem. Transp. Sci. **39**(2), 182–187 (2005)
22. Dror, M., Trudeau, P.: Savings by split delivery routing. Transp. Sci. **23**(2), 141–145 (1989)
23. Amuthan, A., Thilak, K.D.: Survey on Tabu search meta-heuristic optimization. In: 2016 International Conference on Signal Processing, Communication, Power and Embedded System (SCOPES), pp. 1539–1543. IEEE (2016)
24. Ho, S.C., Haugland, D.: A tabu search heuristic for the vehicle routing problem with time windows and split deliveries. Comput. Oper. Res. **31**(12), 1947–1964 (2004)
25. Archetti, C., Speranza, M.G., Hertz, A.: A Tabu search algorithm for the split delivery vehicle routing problem. Transp. Sci. **40**(1), 64–73 (2006)
26. Gendreau, M., Hertz, A., Laporte, G.: New insertion and postoptimization procedures for the traveling salesman problem. Oper. Res. **40**(6), 1086–1094 (1992)
27. Liu, W.-S., Yang, F., Li, M.-Q., Chen, P.-Z.: Clustering algorithm for split delivery vehicle routing problem. Control Decis. **27**(4), 535–541 (2012)
28. https://en.wikipedia.org/wiki/Genetic_algorithm
29. http://www.bayareabikeshare.com/open-data
30. https://www.rideindego.com/about/data/
31. https://www.divvybikes.com/system-data
32. https://www.citibikenyc.com/system-data

GAI: A Centralized Tree-Based Scheduler for Machine Learning Workload in Large Shared Clusters

Ce Gao, Rui Ren$^{(\boxtimes)}$, and Hongming Cai

School of Software, Shanghai Jiao Tong University, Shanghai, China
{gaoce270863799,renrui,hmcai}@sjtu.edu.cn

Abstract. With widespread applications in image recognition, language translation, computer vision and other areas, deep learning (DL) have been proliferating over the past decade. Practitioners from different business groups in industries train DL models on a shared cloud computing infrastructure for these applications with different priorities. During the model training process, one of the key challenges is to minimize the life-cycle of high priority model training jobs. This paper analyzes the distributed training of machine learning (ML) models and identifies short board effect in the training process: GPU training requires higher network bandwidth compared to CPU training. The key insight motivates the design of GAI, a centralized scheduler for ML workload. It relies on two techniques: (1) tree-based structure. The structure stores the cluster information hierarchically to apply multi-layer scheduling. (2) well-extended priority algorithm. We consider priorities from multiple dimensions for model training jobs comprehensively to support resource degradation and preemption. The prototype of GAI is implemented on top of Kubernetes, Kubeflow, and TensorFlow. It is evaluated using a simulator and a real cloud-based cluster. Evaluations show 28% increase in scheduling throughput and 21% training convergence speedup on DL models.

Keywords: Resource management · Distributed machine learning Centralized scheduling · Resource utilization

1 Introduction

Over the past decade, we have witnessed the era of rapid advances in artificial intelligence, powered by the resurgence of ML, especially DL. DL has become a hot topic for both academia and industries like Alibaba, Facebook, and Google. These DL models exhibit a high degree of model complexity that raises new challenges and opportunities to cluster management.

ML frameworks like TensorFlow [1], MXNet [3], and Caffe [11] allow engineers to set up a one-off cluster to run distributed ML jobs with the support of parameter server architecture [17]. The architecture splits the job into two

© Springer Nature Switzerland AG 2018
J. Vaidya and J. Li (Eds.): ICA3PP 2018, LNCS 11335, pp. 611–629, 2018.
https://doi.org/10.1007/978-3-030-05054-2_46

parts: parameter server and worker. A parameter server maintains a partition of the globally shared parameters. It collects the gradient and updates the parameters over training iterations. A worker server stores a portion of the training data locally to compute statistics such as gradients. The architecture has widely applied in DL model training.

Cluster management systems like Google Borg [2], Apache Mesos [10], Apache Yarn [23] and Daphne [25] now support multiple distributed computing systems which include TensorFlow and other ML frameworks in the same cluster. They greatly simplify the operation and maintenance work for the jobs submitted from different teams or users.

However, there is a problem in most cluster management systems which is limited rack-aware and priority support [26] that causes the difficulties to integrate real ML workload on the systems. None of the existing cluster management systems can efficiently handle ML workload in a large shared cluster. They are usually not able to offer the best hardware accelerators to the highest priority model training jobs. The main cause is lack of design and optimizations for ML workload from the scheduler side. Compared to traditional workloads, ML workload has some unique characteristics: First, distributed ML jobs are getting increasingly diverse both in terms of the size of input/output data and the scale of the models. Second, distributed ML jobs are usually network and computing intensive. Therefore hardware accelerators speed up the training progress significantly [16], and low latency network makes parameter updates efficiently. Last, the priority of ML jobs is more complex than traditional jobs. The distributed model training job usually contains a number of parameter servers and workers, and there are many dimensions, like distribution and the runtime of the job that will affect the priority.

To address these challenges, we propose Gatekeeper for AI (GAI), a centralized scheduler for ML workload on large shared clusters. Some contributions have been made in this paper:

- The system model for scheduling ML model training jobs on a given cluster is formalized in this paper. The formalization shows that the problem of scheduling ML jobs based on parameter server architecture is NP-complete.
- We present the ML workload characterization. Network and computing bottlenecks of ML jobs are verified experimentally. Different hardware devices (e.g. GPU, CPU) and communication modes (e.g. RPC, IPC) are used to train the model like Inception V3 [22], ResNet-50, ResNet-152 [9] and VGG-16 [21]. The experiments show clearly that when the ML training job uses CPUs, computing is the bottleneck; when using GPUs, the network is the bottleneck.
- Based on the key insight, GAI is presented to minimize the lifecycle of model training jobs and support priority for these jobs. GAI schedules distributed model training jobs based on parameter server architecture, on the data center. We offer best effort service and supports resource degradation and preemption due to two features: rack-aware tree scheduling; resource degradation and preemption.

- We implement the prototype of GAI on top of Kubernetes, Kubeflow, and TensorFlow. The evaluation shows that GAI improves the throughput by nearly 28% on a medium-sized cluster with the support of priority and achieves 21% training convergence speedup on DL models. We also demonstrate that the lifecycle of higher priority is shorter by average compared to those lower priority jobs. Then we can see that the overhead imported by GAI and light container-based virtualization is acceptable.

The rest of this paper is organized as follows: Sect. 2 describes the background, Sect. 3 motivates GAI with workload characterization, Sect. 4 presents the main methodologies adopted by this paper. We evaluate GAI in Sect. 5 and conclude this paper in Sect. 6.

2 Background

The design of GAI is related to distributed ML and cluster management systems. Therefore in this section, the parallel architectures of distributed ML jobs and cluster management systems are introduced as preliminaries. There is a discussion on the existing researches after the related work.

2.1 Parallel Architecture of Distributed ML

Distributed ML is an iterative-convergent program which is similar to single-process ML. Based on the property, the researchers proposed a parameter server framework for distributed ML [17]. Parameter server framework separates the system into parameter servers and workers. Parameter servers serve the globally shared parameters while workers maintain the training progress. The framework adopts either data parallelism or model parallelism [12].

Figure 1(a) is the architecture of model parallelism. In the model parallel architecture, the model is partitioned and assigned to different workers. Each worker maintains a part of the ML model and is responsible for updating it. Model parallelism is usually used to train models that require more memory

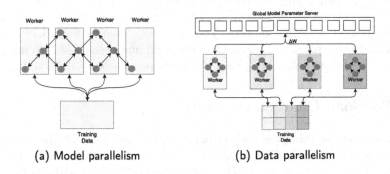

(a) Model parallelism   (b) Data parallelism

Fig. 1. Parallelism architecture

(e.g. image classification). Model parallel architecture introduces a certain amount of overhead, it relies on the good network connection.

Figure 1(b) is the data parallel architecture. Each worker in the architecture of data parallelism has a replica of the model and accepts a portion of training data. After one iteration, the workers push the gradients to the parameter servers and fetch parameters from the servers.

2.2 Cluster Scheduling System

Cluster scheduler plays an important role since hardware resources are allocated to specific jobs through the scheduler. Monolithic scheduler, such as Paragon [5], Quasar [6], Borg [24], Kubernetes [2] and Firmanent [7], uses a centralized single-process scheduler to schedule all kinds of jobs on the cluster. Monolithic scheduler is hard to expand with multiple workloads. Two-layer scheduler, such as Mesos [10] and Yarn [23], introduces application-specific scheduler into the monolithic architecture. The new layer guides the centralized scheduler to make suitable resource allocations for applications. To better concurrency, Shared-state scheduler, such as Omega [20], imports multiple schedulers based on the optimistic concurrency control strategy. It is assumed that the scheduling conflicts are rare, so shared-state scheduler performs high throughput. But there is a significant drop when the conflicts are frequent.

Distributed scheduler, such as Sparrow [19], is the architecture designed for batch jobs. In this architecture, there is no centralized scheduler to maintain the state of the cluster. The scheduler picks up some nodes and schedules the jobs in the subset of the cluster. Scheduling delay in distributed approach is relatively low but it is hard to support online business.

Hybrid scheduler, such as Hawk [4], Mercury [14], and Daphne [25], divides the jobs into long-running jobs and short jobs. It schedules long-running jobs using a centralized scheduler and assigns short jobs to a distributed scheduler. Hybrid scheduler adapts well for multiple workloads, but the complexity is high.

In the conclusion, now the existing researches on distributed ML mainly focus on the optimization from the ML framework side. It works well when the distributed training jobs are running on bare metal servers, while there is an increasing demand to run the workload in the cloud.

The existing cluster management systems usually treat batch jobs or long-running jobs as first-class objects. They are not designed for ML workload. Therefore, in this paper we analyze the workload and design GAI, to minimize the lifecycle of distributed ML jobs and import priority to model training.

3 Workload Characterization

In this section, we formalize the system model to introduce the problem that we hope to solve. Then short board effect of model training jobs on network and computing is presented, which shows the opportunities and challenges of scheduling ML jobs on clusters.

3.1 Problem Formalization

We consider that GAI schedules a set of jobs that contains a set of tasks on a homogeneous data center. To illustrate the process concretely, we take a model training job as an example. As shown in Fig. 2, a model training job has a number of parameter servers and workers. All the tasks (parameter servers and workers) of the job will be scheduled by the scheduler. And they will be placed on some servers. During the training progress, each worker communicates with all parameter servers via remote process call or inter process call in each iteration, and we call this the network cost. Workers execute real training logic using CPUs, GPUs or other hardware accelerators according to the model parameters from parameter servers, and this causes training cost.

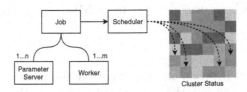

Fig. 2. Scheduling a model training job on a cluster

We assume that the resources in the data center are always strained, which is demonstrated in previous works [18]. Consider a set of model training jobs $J = \{j^1, j^2, \ldots, j^m\}$ running on a set of servers $S = \{s^1, s^2, \ldots, s^n\}$. We define a model training job j^i with j^i_{ps} parameter servers and j^i_{worker} workers, the time associated with the lifecycle of job T^i_j includes waiting time $T^i_{waiting}$, placement latency $T^i_{scheduling}$ and completion time $T^i_{completion}$. $T^i_{waiting}$ is spent when the job is queued to be scheduled. $T^i_{scheduling}$ is caused by the scheduler, which is dedicated to scheduling the job on the data center. $T^i_{completion}$ is the model training time and it can be defined by

$$T^i_{completion} = \sum_{z=1}^{j^i_{worker}} \left(C_{training}(w_z, s_z) + \sum_{k=1}^{j^i_{ps}} C_{network}(w_z, s_z, ps_k, s_k) \right) \cdot N \quad (1)$$

N is the number of iterations. s_z is the server that the worker w_z is performed. $C_{training}(w_z, s_z)$ is defined as the training cost of the worker w_z which is performed on server s_z in one iteration. It can be expressed as

$$C_{training}(w_z, s_z) = \begin{cases} C_{GPU}(w_z, s_z) & \text{If use GPU} \\ C_{CPU}(w_z, s_z) & \text{otherwise.} \end{cases} \quad (2)$$

We call C_{GPU} and C_{CPU} the cost using GPU and CPU. If the server has idle GPUs and the scheduler assign the GPU to the worker, the cost is the running time of training on the GPU. While C_{CPU} is the running time on CPU.

$C_{network}(w_z, s_z, ps_k, s_k)$ in Eq. 1 denotes the network cost for worker w_z on server s_z and parameter server ps_k on server s_k in one iteration. And it is defined by

$$C_{network}(w_z, s_z, ps_k, s_k) = \begin{cases} C_{IPC} & s_z = s_k \\ C_{RPC} & s_z \neq s_k \end{cases} \tag{3}$$

C_{IPC} is the cost using inter-process call (IPC). When the parameter server and the worker are performed on the same server, the method of communication between them is inter-process call. While when the parameter server in the server s_z while the worker in the server s_k, remote process call (RPC) is used to communicate. The cost is defined by C_{RPC}.

The scheduling algorithm for ML workload seeks mappings from tasks of the jobs to the servers with idle resources. The goal of the algorithm is to minimize $\sum_{i=1}^{m} T_j^i$, which has been demonstrated to be NP-complete [13].

3.2   Short Board Effect

As described in Sect. 3.1, computing and network communication are the major cost of a model training job, thus we present a study of the short board effect of data parallel ML training jobs on computing and network. The study demonstrates two main points through well-designed experiments:

- Short board effect is significant at cluster scale.
- ML jobs with GPUs suffer from low throughput network, while jobs using CPUs does not require high bandwidth connection.

Our hardware and software environment for the experiments are shown in the Tables 1 and 2. In 10GB Ethernet networks, we use CPUs and GPUs to train different models (Inception V3 [22], ResNet-50, ResNet-152 [9] and VGG-16 [21]). In the first experiment, we use 1 CPU, 1 GPU, 2 GPUs to train the ML models respectively. As shown in Fig. 3(a), the experiment of GPU based ML jobs yields speedups of 20 times than CPU based jobs. ML jobs using 2 GPUs are 90%–95% faster than the jobs using 1 GPU. And data parallel ML jobs using a mix of GPUs and CPUs does not fully exploit the GPU's performance because of short board effect.

Figure 3(b) shows the result of the training speed of 32 batch-size Inception V3 model in different distributed architectures and different hardware resources.

Table 1. Hardware configurations

Hardware	Configuration
CPU	Intel Xeon CPU E5-2697 v4 @ 2.30 GHz
GPU	Nvidia GeForce GTX 1080Ti
Network card	Intel Corporation 82599 10 Gigabit
Switch	H3C S5820V2-52QF

Table 2. Software configurations

Software	Configuration
OS	CentOS Linux release 7.3.1611
ML framework	TensorFlow 1.4

To demonstrate the universality, We conduct in four architectures: (i) 1 parameter server, 1 worker, (i) 1 parameter server, 2 workers, (iii) 2 parameter servers, 1 worker, (iiii) 2 parameter servers, 2 workers. The result shows that the bottleneck of CPU based training jobs is computing, and the network does not affect the scalability. We place parameter servers and workers in different machines and get 35%–64% speed degradation compared with placing all parameter servers and workers in one machine.

Therefore we summarize the key insights: Network is not always the bottleneck for distributed ML jobs. It affects the training speed of GPU based ML jobs but CPU based jobs do not require high network throughput.

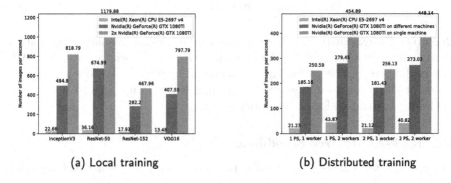

(a) Local training   (b) Distributed training

Fig. 3. Training speed using different configurations

4 GAI: A Scheduler for ML Workload

In the previous section, we show the short board effect of model training jobs. In this section, based on the effect, we propose a tree-based scheduling model, then present a resource preemption and degradation algorithm for better utilization.

Based on the observations and the characteristics of ML workload in the previous section, we propose the goals of GAI:

- Minimize the lifecycle of model training jobs.
- Guarantee the priority of ML jobs. High priority jobs are allowed to preempt hardware accelerator resources to accelerate the training progress.

Figure 4 presents the overview of GAI. The input is a series of distributed model training jobs, and the output is the mappings from the tasks (parameter servers and workers) of the jobs to the servers. GAI relies on two main techniques:

Rack-Aware Tree Scheduling: GAI uses a centralized rack-aware tree scheduling method and maintains a resource tree in memory to place all tasks of the ML training jobs in one machine or in the machines belong to the same rack as far as possible.

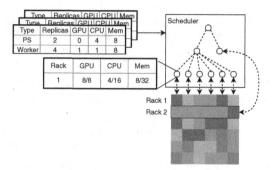

Fig. 4. Overview of GAI

Resource Degradation and Preemption: We present a resource degradation and preemption algorithm for data parallel ML jobs. There are different ML jobs in different priorities similar to traditional workloads. We use a vector to represent the priority and support degrading low priority jobs to release the hardware accelerators for high priority jobs.

4.1 Rack-Aware Tree Scheduling

The previous section shows that GPU based training jobs are network-sensitive applications. Thus, GAI presents rack-aware tree-based scheduling and maintains two different scheduling paths. GAI chooses different paths according to the status of the cluster to keep high utilization.

In a commercial data center, the servers on the same rack share the same Ethernet switch, thus the servers are communicated with each other through a high bandwidth, low latency network. The feature is indifferent to network insensitive applications, such as web services, while it has a significant impact on the distributed training jobs which introduce heavy communication traffic between parameter servers and workers. GAI keeps a multi-level tree structure to organize all the servers in the cluster according to the network conditions between the servers.

ML training jobs usually require multiple hardware accelerators to accelerate the training. Thus, we gather the servers in the same rack into a small cluster, and the resources in the cluster can run at least one distributed ML job at the same time. Figure 5 represents the architecture of GAI scheduler. The resources in the cluster are abstracted into resource tree, where the leaf nodes in the tree represent servers and the second-level nodes represent the racks. The parent nodes in the tree collect and gather the runtime information (e.g. CPU, GPU and memory usage) of all its child nodes.

To preserve the extensibility, GAI supports logical partition in the resource tree. In some application scenarios, there are some servers without GPUs. These servers can be added to the same logical node to indicate that we can not schedule distributed training jobs to the servers. Most extensibility requirements can be supported indirectly through logical nodes.

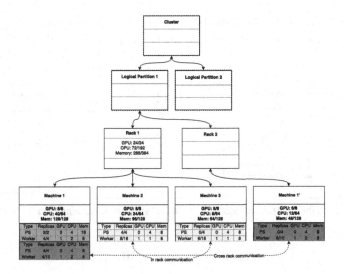

Fig. 5. Resource Tree in GAI

GAI performs multiple validations during scheduling on the resource tree to determine the sub-optimal placement:

- First, GAI checks if the machines in the rack satisfy the resource requirements of the ML jobs. It is executed in rack-level nodes to determine if the sum of the free resources of all the machines on the rack can run the new job.
- After the first step, GAI validates the resource slots of each server to avoid resource stranded problem.

The placement algorithm is executed twice. The first pass is to schedule GPU resources. When there is no idle GPU, we run the resource degradation and preemption algorithm based on priority described in Sect. 4.2. If the cluster still does not have GPUs for the job, the requirement is relaxed and the algorithm is run for CPU again.

GAI implements a short scheduling path when the utilization of the cluster is low. Most of the servers has sufficient resources, then the default scheduling algorithm in GAI takes relatively long time to schedule a training job, so GAI imports randomized method to speed up the scheduling process. GAI randomly selects some secondary nodes and decides which rack to assign the new ML jobs based on the resource usage. GAI uses a random approach as Sparrow [19] does in a centralized manner. The randomized scheduling method reduces the size of potential candidate set and the scheduling delay as well when the cluster is idle.

4.2 Resource Degradation and Preemption

In a commercial cluster, ML jobs have different types and belong to different business groups, thus have different priorities. We design GAI's priority strategy based on priority vector. It is used to perform resource degradation or preemption. We summarize some factors that affect the priority of ML jobs:

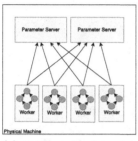

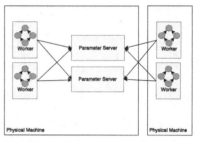

(a) Distributed training job on a single machine

(b) Distributed training job on two machines

Fig. 6. Distribution of ML jobs

The Distribution of ML Jobs. The distribution of ML jobs on the cluster is very complicated. For example, we create a ML job with two parameter servers and four workers. In the best case, all replicas are scheduled to one server which has free resources, as shown in Fig. 6(a), to avoid the short board effect.

Figure 6(b) shows a worse case: two workers are placed on another server, thus the communication between the parameter servers and these two workers is not as good as the other two workers. Such job is in relatively low priority since the training speed is lower than the situation in Fig. 6(a).

Therefore, we design a priority algorithm based on the distribution of ML jobs. The algorithm can be expressed as Algorithm 1. If all parameter servers and workers are placed in the same machine, the job is in highest priority on this dimension. We prefer to preempt or degrade the jobs whose internal communication is cross rack or cross server.

ML Job Runtime. The runtime of ML jobs affects the priority, since the cost of restarting or interrupting an ML job that has been running for a relatively long time.

To determine the distribution of the duration of ML jobs, we analyze the data trace of ML workload in Facebook [8], extract the description and summarize the workload characteristics as described in Table 3.

The training jobs of neural network models such as CNN and RNN are the longest-running jobs and take approximately tens of hours, while GBDT and SVM jobs take less time. We use a power-law-like heavy-tailed distribution to sample the duration of the jobs. In the long-tailed distribution, the vast majority of jobs are completed in a short time. Therefore, we use the logarithm to calculate the priority and ensure that the priority of the job is distributed within a reasonable range. And we truncate the priority if we encounter the situation that it exceeds the threshold (The highest priority for a single dimension is set to 5).

Algorithm 1. Priority algorithm for distribution dimension

$Priority \leftarrow 0$
$MaxPriority \leftarrow 0$
for $ps \in PSes$ **do**
  for $worker \in workers$ **do**
    $MaxPriority \leftarrow MaxPriority + HighPriority$
  end for
  if $isInOneMachine(ps, worker)$ **then**
    $Priority \leftarrow Priority + HighPriority$
  else if $isInOneRack(ps, worker)$ **then**
    $Priority \leftarrow Priority + MediumPriority$
  else
    $Priority \leftarrow Priority + LowPriority$
  end if
end for
return $Priority/MaxPriority$

Table 3. Characteristic of ML workload in Facebook

Model	Resource	Frequency	Duration	Inference relative capacity
SVM	CPU	Every hours	Few seconds	10x
GBDT	CPU	Daily	Few hours	1x
CNN	GPU	Weekly	Many hours	10x
RNN	GPU	Weekly	Many hours	1x

The Type of ML Jobs. We define the type according to multiple dimensions as described in Table 4.

The online model training jobs have the highest priority, so we set the priority of these jobs to 5. And there are two types of research model training jobs: normal training jobs and hyperparameter tuning jobs. Hyperparameter tuning jobs consume more resources and usually are not urgent jobs. The priority of this type is set to a lower value.

Table 4. Priority for types of model training jobs

Type	Training	Hyperparameter training
Production	5	N/A
Research	3	1

The Type of Dominant Resource. In general, hardware accelerators are more expensive, then the utilization of this kind of resource is more critical than other hardware resources. The primary goal of this dimension is to increase the utilization of hardware accelerator resources. It is not an ideal solution to degrade the jobs whose replicas are all running on CPUs since CPU is not the first-class resource for ML jobs. We calculate the priority based on the numbers of GPUs that used by workers. Equation 4 shows the calculation. In this equation, n represents the number of GPUs that workers of the job are using. Sigmoid function is used to determine the upper and lower bounds of the convergence of the function.

$$Priority(n) = \frac{5}{1 + e^{-n}} \tag{4}$$

Number of Preemptions. Starvation occurs when a higher priority job dominate a resource and a lower priority job is blocked from gaining access to the resource. As a result, the lower priority job cannot make progress. To avoid the problem, GAI adds a bias. GAI offers the jobs that have been preempted one or more times the highest priority in this dimension. And the jobs without any degradation are in the lowest priority.

We aggregate the priorities of different dimensions into a priority vector. GAI refers to the predicate-priority model in Kubernetes.

- Firstly, the predicate process is performed. In this process, we find out all the jobs that can be preempted according to the hardware resource requirement of the new job. GAI supports single-job preemption in this process because of the complexity.
- Secondly, GAI determines if the dimension of job type in the priority vector is strictly greater than the preempted job, to ensure that ML jobs in the production environment are not preempted by the ML jobs for research.
- Finally, GAI removes the jobs in the candidate set that are in higher priority than the newly submitted jobs. The distribution of the jobs is a property at runtime, thus GAI sets the dimension of the new job to the highest score by default. While the job gains the lowest score in the dimension of ML job runtime. GAI performs weight-based calculations on the four dimensions of priority, as shown in Eq. 5.

$$Priority_{total} = \frac{\sum_{i=1}^{4} W_i \cdot Priority_i}{5 \sum_{i=1}^{4} W_i} \qquad \cdot \tag{5}$$

5   Evaluation

In this section, we compare GAI with default scheduler in Kubernetes. Evaluations show that GAI improves the scheduling throughput and speeds up the training of ML jobs.

5.1   Methodology

Implementation. We implement the prototype of GAI as a stand-alone scheduler for Kubernetes 1.8.5. GAI can work together with the default scheduler with the help of Kubernetes by design. In that case, GAI schedules ML jobs while

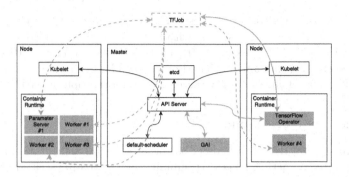

Fig. 7. Architecture of GAI

default scheduler deals with other jobs. We choose TensorFlow 1.4.0 as the framework for running ML jobs. Kubeflow 0.1 is applied to combine TensorFlow and Kubernetes.

Figure 7 shows the architecture of GAI. We build GAI on top of Kubernetes instead of revising the original code of Kubernetes. In the prototype, we register a custom resource definition *TFJob* for distributed TensorFlow model training jobs in the cluster and run an operator to manage the lifecycle of TensorFlow training jobs on Kubernetes. TensorFlow operator from Kubeflow creates informers for *TFJob*, which is TensorFlow custom resource, pod and service which are Kubernetes internal resources. It watches the shared state of the cluster through Kubernetes API server and makes changes the attempting to move the current state towards the desired state. GAI is placed in the master node and it is responsible for scheduling TensorFlow jobs.

Workload. There is no public trace now for ML workload, hence we construct the workload trace mainly based on the description of the internal ML workload in Facebook [8]. In the real cluster, there are some jobs for research purpose which duration and number of tasks per job are shorter than the jobs for production purpose. Thus we also create a trace of ML jobs submitted by researchers. We use a power-law distribution similar to the production environment to generate the trace.

Simulator. We implement a simulator to simulate how GAI behaves in a large shared cluster. Different hardware leads to different training speeds, thus we assume that training jobs using GPUs are 20 times faster than jobs using CPUs according to historical records. The simulator reads trace data as input, run the real scheduling algorithm and assign jobs to virtual nodes. Scheduling and communication delays are set to random numbers which change within a relatively small range. We run the simulator on one 8-core Intel(R) Core(TM) i7-6700 CPU bare metal server. It can simulate the scheduling process in the cluster with 20000 virtual servers.

Real Cloud-Based Cluster. We establish a real cluster based on the cloud. The cluster has 5 8-core CPU servers with hyper-threading enabled and 5 8-core servers with 1 GPU ($10 \times 8 \times 2 = 160$ virtual CPU cores and 5 GPUs in total). Most of the experiments are run based on the simulator approach while we use the real cloud-based cluster to get the real load information of GAI.

5.2   Scheduler Throughput

We run Kubernetes default scheduler as the baseline implementation and GAI, to demonstrate the performance. We submit the workload described above and run the experiments in the cluster with 200, 500, 1000, 5000, and 10000 nodes iteratively. Virtual servers with different hardware configurations are created. 50% servers in the cluster have 1 GPU and 30% servers have 2 GPUs, while the other 20% only have CPUs. To avoid the potential problem that the cluster is full of use, the duration per job is set to 5 s. We disable the preemption and degradation functionality, because the feature is not expected in the benchmark. The corresponding logic about preemption in Kubernetes is also skipped.

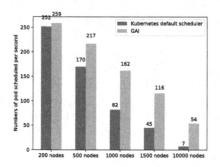

Fig. 8. Scheduler throughput

We implement the benchmark based on the scheduler performance test in Kubernetes and run it for 5 min. Then we calculate the average throughput for the scheduler. As shown in Fig. 8, the throughput of GAI is 27.6% higher than the baseline implementation at medium scale (500 servers), and behaves better at large scale.

GAI maintains a tree-based architecture. When the requests are sent from the control panel, GAI queues the requests in different queues for nodes. Thus the tree-based architecture has good scalability. Kubernetes native scheduler uses a single queue to manage all the resource requests, and it needs to run the predicate and priority processes for each server. The design allows Kubernetes to schedule the traditional workloads well but it also imports some overhead when the cluster size is growing.

5.3   Job Waiting Time

Job waiting time is the time from the job is queued to be scheduled to the job is actually scheduled by the scheduler. In this section, we submit jobs with different priorities. We use the workload above while the training is not actually executed. In order to control the duration of the ML jobs precisely, the jobs only create the parameter servers and workers but it does not train the models. We set the active duration for jobs and kill the training jobs when it is time.

We group the jobs whose priority is larger than 0.7 as high-priority jobs. And jobs whose priority is lower than 0.3 are grouped as low-priority jobs. Because the priority is dynamic, we count all jobs which have come to the threshold at least once valid. We also run the workload in Kubernetes for comparison.

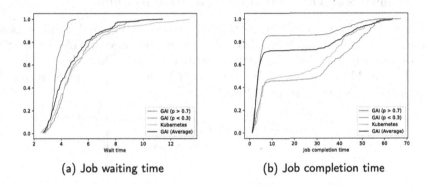

(a) Job waiting time   (b) Job completion time

Fig. 9. End-to-end latency

We run the experiment in the real cloud-based cluster. Figure 9(a) shows the result of the experiment. Jobs whose priority are greater than 0.7 achieves lower waiting time because of the support of resource degradation and preemption. And we can see that the waiting time of the jobs scheduled by Kubernetes default scheduler is slightly longer than GAI. The distribution of Kubernetes is a long-tailed distribution since the jobs are overstocked.

5.4   Job Completion Time

Job completion time is the training time spending on the model. We design an experiment using the real cluster to demonstrate that the high priority jobs are more likely to use GPUs to train. We run simple MNIST model training jobs using CNN and collect the completion time of jobs. The training job usually takes 30–50 s when training based on CPUs and takes nearly 2–4 s on GPUs.

We run this experiment in the real cluster and limit the number of iterations to make the model training process predictable. Figure 9(b) demonstrates that jobs whose priority are greater than 0.7 usually have GPUs to run, therefore the completion time is shorter and 80% jobs finish their training in 8.7 s. Low priority jobs spend more time to do the same mode training task. 80% of low priority jobs finish in 48 s. As shown in Fig. 5, the average training time of GAI is 14.6 s which achieves 21% speedup compared to Kubernetes default scheduler.

Table 5. Training convergence speedup in top k% ML jobs

Top k%	Speedup	Convergence (s)
25	26.1%	2.03
50	22.7%	2.56
100	21.4%	14.59

5.5   Comparison with Native Distributed TensorFlow

GAI runs the ML workload on container-based platforms, and it takes some overheads for the training. We evaluate the convergence speed of GAI on MNIST [15] training job, and GAI with native distributed TensorFlow when training a DNN for the MNIST dataset. We run the DNN with 1 parameter server, 5 workers and 2 parameter servers, 4 workers.

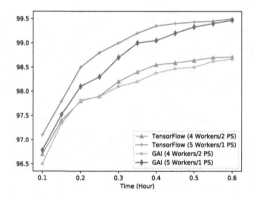

Fig. 10. Model convergence (MNIST)

Figure 10 shows the result. The convergence speed of the jobs scheduled by GAI and run on Kubernetes does not have significant differences compared to native distributed TensorFlow. The jobs running with 5 workers and 1 parameter server converge slower than native distributed TensorFlow since the job is network and computing intensive and the virtualization of containerization (e.g. Docker) uses cgroup and apparmor for isolation and security. These features import overhead for computing.

5.6 Discussion

In this section, we reconsider the design decisions of GAI and discuss the limitations.

We provide more insights on the performance and effect of GAI. GAI's high throughput capability benefits from the tree-based architecture. Experiments demonstrate that GAI provides best effort service for jobs. GAI improves the throughput by nearly 28% on a medium-sized cluster, and achieves 21% training convergence speedup on DL models compared to Kubernetes default scheduler. We also compare container-based solution with native distributed TensorFlow to illustrate the overhead imported by the prototype of GAI is low. Table 6 shows an overview of a selection of orchestration frameworks, their architecture, and features.

Table 6. Comparison with existing scheduler frameworks for ML workload

Scheduler	Architecture	Resource granularity	Rack awareness	Priority preemption	Priority degradation	Gang scheduling
GAI	Centralized	CPU, GPU, Memory	Yes	Yes	Yes	Yes
Kubernetes	Centralized	CPU, GPU, Memory	Partial	Partial	No	No
Mesos	Centralized (Two Layer)	CPU, GPU, Memory	Yes	No	No	Yes
Yarn	Centralized (Two Layer)	CPU, GPU, Memory	Yes	No	No	No
Sparrow	Distributed	CPU, Memory	No	No	No	No
Hawk	Hybrid	CPU, Memory	No	No	No	No

GAI relies on many parameters and thresholds in the scheduling process. Currently, we assign the values to these parameters and thresholds manually, and statically. We can use some ML algorithms about hyperparameter tuning, to choose the optimal values for these parameters. This requires a reasonable model and data set. In addition, GAI should support dynamic parameter adjustment. Under different loads, the weight of each dimension of the priority vector should be adjusted.

The prototype is a scheduler plugin in Kubernetes, and it can work with Kubernetes default scheduler to schedule multiple workloads via different schedulers. The feature is implemented from Kubernetes side, while Kubernetes has no mechanism to handle scheduling conflicts between different schedulers. Therefore we do not evaluate it. It should be supported after Kubernetes has a good support for the feature. Moreover, GAI currently uses container-based virtualization to isolate resources, which is the default option in Kubernetes. We are investigating using hypervisor-based containers for better isolation during model training.

6 Conclusion

The work presented in this paper consists in a centralized scheduler for ML workload named GAI to effectively share a single cluster among different DL applications. To this aim, we propose tree-based scheduling to establish the hierarchical structure of the cluster and the multi-dimensional priority algorithm which considers different aspects of model training jobs to degrade or preempt the resource for higher priority jobs. By hiding the short board effect, we have demonstrated the capability of our approach to support large shared clusters containing hundreds of thousands of servers. We implement the prototype of GAI on top of Kubeflow, Kubernetes, and TensorFlow. Moreover, we create a trace based on the real ML workload in Facebook and evaluate GAI using the trace. The result shows that the throughput of GAI is 27.6% higher than default scheduler in Kubernetes at medium scale when scheduling ML jobs and it achieves 21% training convergence speedup on DL models. Then there is an experiment to demonstrate that GAI imports fairly low overhead to improve isolation compared to native distributed TensorFlow.

The main directions for future work are twofold. The first one we are currently investigating is fine-grain control of hardware accelerator management. GAI currently requires the exclusive use of GPUs. As future work, GAI should import fine-grained scheduling and affinity control to make the most advantage of GPUs.

As long-term future work, We are investigating approaches and methods of improving scheduling and isolation of distributed model training jobs to make GAI production ready. We hope that GAI will inspire more ideas on scheduling for ML workload and ship off practical implementation.

Acknowledgements. This research is supported by the National Natural Science Foundation of China under Grant No. 61373030.

References

1. Abadi, M., et al.: TensorFlow: a system for large-scale machine learning. In: 12th USENIX Symposium on Operating Systems Design and Implementation, vol. 16, pp. 265–283 (2016)
2. Burns, B., Grant, B., Oppenheimer, D., Brewer, E., Wilkes, J.: Borg, omega, and kubernetes. Commun. ACM **59**(5), 50–57 (2016)
3. Chen, T., et al.: MXNet: a flexible and efficient machine learning library for heterogeneous distributed systems. arXiv preprint arXiv:1512.01274 (2015)
4. Delgado, P., Dinu, F., Kermarrec, A.M., Zwaenepoel, W.: Hawk: hybrid datacenter scheduling. In: Proceedings of the 2015 USENIX Annual Technical Conference, No. EPFL-CONF-208856, pp. 499–510. USENIX Association (2015)
5. Delimitrou, C., Kozyrakis, C.: Paragon: QoS-aware scheduling for heterogeneous datacenters. ACM SIGPLAN Not. **48**, 77–88 (2013)
6. Delimitrou, C., Kozyrakis, C.: Quasar: resource-efficient and QoS-aware cluster management. ACM SIGPLAN Not. **49**, 127–144 (2014)
7. Gog, I., Schwarzkopf, M., Gleave, A., Watson, R.N., Hand, S.: Firmament: fast, centralized cluster scheduling at scale. In: 12th USENIX Symposium on Operating Systems Design and Implementation. USENIX (2016)
8. Hazelwood, K., et al.: Applied machine learning at Facebook: a datacenter infrastructure perspective. In: 2018 IEEE International Symposium on High Performance Computer Architecture (HPCA), pp. 620–629. IEEE (2018)
9. He, K., Zhang, X., Ren, S., Sun, J.: Deep residual learning for image recognition. In: Proceedings of the IEEE Conference on Computer Vision and Pattern Recognition, pp. 770–778 (2016)

10. Hindman, B., et al.: Mesos: a platform for fine-grained resource sharing in the data center. In: 8th USENIX Symposium on Networked Systems Design and Implementation, vol. 11, p. 22 (2011)

11. Jia, Y., et al.: Caffe: convolutional architecture for fast feature embedding. In: Proceedings of the 22nd ACM International Conference on Multimedia, pp. 675–678. ACM (2014)

12. Jiang, J., Yu, L., Jiang, J., Liu, Y., Cui, B.: Angel: a new large-scale machine learning system. Natl. Sci. Rev. **5**, 216–236 (2017). https://doi.org/10.1093/nsr/nwx018

13. Jin, J., Luo, J., Song, A., Dong, F., Xiong, R.: Bar: an efficient data locality driven task scheduling algorithm for cloud computing. In: Proceedings of the 2011 11th IEEE/ACM International Symposium on Cluster, Cloud and Grid Computing, pp. 295–304. IEEE Computer Society (2011)

14. Karanasos, K., et al.: Mercury: hybrid centralized and distributed scheduling in large shared clusters. In: USENIX Annual Technical Conference, pp. 485–497 (2015)

15. LeCun, Y., Bottou, L., Bengio, Y., Haffner, P.: Gradient-based learning applied to document recognition. Proc. IEEE **86**(11), 2278–2324 (1998)

16. Lee, D., Mehta, N., Shearer, A., Kastner, R.: A hardware accelerated system for high throughput cellular image analysis. J. Parallel Distrib. Comput. **113**, 167–178 (2018)

17. Li, M., et al.: Scaling distributed machine learning with the parameter server. In: 11th USENIX Symposium on Operating Systems Design and Implementation, vol. 1, p. 3 (2014)

18. Lu, C., Ye, K., Xu, G., Xu, C.Z., Bai, T.: Imbalance in the cloud: an analysis on Alibaba cluster trace. In: 2017 IEEE International Conference on Big Data (Big Data), pp. 2884–2892. IEEE (2017)

19. Ousterhout, K., Wendell, P., Zaharia, M., Stoica, I.: Sparrow: distributed, low latency scheduling. In: Proceedings of the Twenty-Fourth ACM Symposium on Operating Systems Principles, pp. 69–84. ACM (2013)

20. Schwarzkopf, M., Konwinski, A., Abd-El-Malek, M., Wilkes, J.: Omega: flexible, scalable schedulers for large compute clusters. In: Proceedings of the 8th ACM European Conference on Computer Systems, pp. 351–364. ACM (2013)

21. Simonyan, K., Zisserman, A.: Very deep convolutional networks for large-scale image recognition. arXiv preprint arXiv:1409.1556 (2014)

22. Szegedy, C., Vanhoucke, V., Ioffe, S., Shlens, J., Wojna, Z.: Rethinking the inception architecture for computer vision. In: Proceedings of the IEEE Conference on Computer Vision and Pattern Recognition, pp. 2818–2826 (2016)

23. Vavilapalli, V.K., et al.: Apache Hadoop YARN: yet another resource negotiator. In: Proceedings of the 4th Annual Symposium on Cloud Computing, p. 5. ACM (2013)

24. Verma, A., Pedrosa, L., Korupolu, M., Oppenheimer, D., Tune, E., Wilkes, J.: Large-scale cluster management at Google with borg. In: Proceedings of the Tenth European Conference on Computer Systems, p. 18. ACM (2015)

25. Xia, Y., Ren, R., Cai, H., Vasilakos, A.V., Lv, Z.: Daphne: a flexible and hybrid scheduling framework in multi-tenant clusters. IEEE Trans. Netw. Serv. Manag. **15**, 330–343 (2017)

26. Zhang, Q., Zhani, M.F., Boutaba, R., Hellerstein, J.L.: Dynamic heterogeneity-aware resource provisioning in the cloud. IEEE Trans. Cloud Comput. **2**(1), 14–28 (2014)

Data-Centric Task Scheduling Algorithm for Hybrid Tasks in Cloud Data Centers

Xin Li[1,2,3](✉), Liangyuan Wang[1], Jemal Abawajy[4], and Xiaolin Qin[1]

[1] College of Computer Science and Technology,
Nanjing University of Aeronautics and Astronautics, Nanjing, China
{lics,qinxcs}@nuaa.edu.cn, lywangcs@163.com
[2] State Key Laboratory of Computer Architecture,
Institute of Computing Technology, Chinese Academy of Sciences, Beijing, China
[3] Collaborative Innovation Center of Novel Software Technology
and Industrialization, Nanjing, China
[4] School of Information Technology, Deakin University, Melbourne, Australia
jemal.abawajy@deakin.edu.au

Abstract. With the development of big data, a demand for data analysis keeps increasing. This requirement has prompted a need for data-aware task scheduling approach that can simultaneously schedule various tasks such as batched tasks and real-time tasks in a data center efficiently. To this end, we propose a hybrid task scheduling strategy coupled with data migration in data center. Firstly, we translate the task scheduling problem into task selection problem, and give methods of selecting batched tasks and real-time tasks respectively. Then the method for scheduling both batched tasks and real-time tasks is introduced in detail. Finally, we integrate data migration into the hybrid scheduling strategy. Experimental results show that, compared to the traditional FIFO algorithm, the proposed task scheduling strategy greatly improves the data locality and data migration performs very well on reducing the job execution time. Our algorithm also guarantees an acceptable fairness for tasks.

Keywords: Data analysis · Data migration · Batched task
Real-time task · Hybrid scheduling

1 Introduction

With the development of Internet technology, the demand for big data analysis is increasing. Many tasks in cloud computing environment are data-intensive thus making data as the necessary condition for task execution [14]. Many enterprises and organizations need to periodically analyze the latest data, such as the social networking sites like Facebook [2]. Task scheduling is one of the most important problems for data analysis in large systems. For these periodic tasks, or batched tasks, the execution time is an important indicator of decision-making. Less

© Springer Nature Switzerland AG 2018
J. Vaidya and J. Li (Eds.): ICA3PP 2018, LNCS 11335, pp. 630–644, 2018.
https://doi.org/10.1007/978-3-030-05054-2_47

time means more benefits. To reduce system's expected response time, people have proposed different server deployment strategies [6]. The reduction of job execution time is also important to minimize energy consumption of system [16]. In addition to reducing the execution time, some applications for edge computing [10] and smart city [17] demand fast data analysis, and the tasks can be online tasks. Batched tasks are mostly periodic or cyclic and tend to have a longer time for waiting system to respond. In contrast, online tasks (i.e., real-time tasks) require system to respond quickly, usually within a few minutes [7]. Therefore, in order to meet the deadline for real-time tasks, the system needs to respond as soon as possible.

Traditional scheduling methods consider only batched tasks or only real-time tasks. With the popularity of big data, the scale of batched tasks and real-time tasks keeps increasing. In data centers with big data, an approach that is capable of simultaneously scheduling batched tasks and real-time tasks while taking into account data requirements are necessary. There are two cases for task execution: locality mode and remote mode. A task will be called data-locality task when the task and its input data are assigned to the same server. Otherwise, the job will be named as remote-access task. Obviously, the remote mode will consume more time than the locality mode, since the remote-access task needs to read and load data from another server in the network. Since data transfer is time consuming and energy consuming, the core of the problem is to select a proper task to execute when some servers are available. We illustrate the problem of hybrid scheduling with the Fig. 1 as follow.

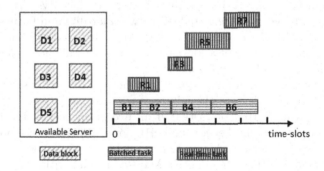

Fig. 1. Hybrid scheduling tasks which required specific data blocks

In this paper, a task scheduling approach that is capable of simultaneously scheduling batched tasks and real-time tasks while taking into account data requirements is presented. We consider the job scheduling under given data placement and introduce a time model for computing the job execution time in two modes based on our previous work [8]. According to the different constraints of response time, we can distinguish batched tasks from real-time tasks and schedule them respectively. The experimental results show that our hybrid scheduling strategy can not only improve the data locality, but also guarantee the fairness of the tasks.

Generally, our contribution can be summarized as follows.

– We propose a hybrid task scheduling strategy for scheduling batched tasks and real-time tasks. It also takes delay scheduling into consideration.
– The strategy combines data migration to improve the data locality of tasks. We propose algorithms to measure the cost and benefits for two job execution modes, and models to evaluate the merit and demerit for data migration.
– We conduct extensive simulations, and the results demonstrate that the hybrid scheduling strategy combined with data migration has significant performance improvements on global job execution time reduction.

The rest of this article consists of the following sections. We review the related work in Sect. 2 and give some preliminaries in Sect. 3. Then, we introduce methods for scheduling batched tasks and real-time tasks in Sect. 4. In Sect. 5, a hybrid task scheduling strategy that combined with data migration is proposed. We evaluate our algorithms in Sect. 6. Finally, we conclude our paper in Sect. 7.

2   Related Work

In recent years, scholars researched on scheduling algorithms mainly on four factors: data locality, fault-tolerance, resource sharing and resource-aware scheduling. The hybrid task scheduling strategy combined with data migration in this paper is proposed to improve the performance of task execution by improving data locality. Data locality is one of the most important concerns that determine the task execution time [13]. To guarantee better data locality, delay scheduling policy [15] is proposed to make a tradeoff between locality and fairness, another important factor [12]. The basic idea is that, when the job should be scheduled, according to fairness, it cannot achieve data locality: it waits for a small amount of time and let other jobs be scheduled first.

In a heterogeneous environment, the exceptions of operating system, kernel, network and so on can lead to the failure of task execution. The default fault-tolerant mechanism in Hadoop is that if an exception occurs, the failed task will be re-performed on another idle node [1]. Some algorithms are proposed for estimating task exceptions such as LATE (Longest Approximate Time to End) algorithm [5] and SAMR (Self-Adaptive MapReduce) algorithm [3].

People have developed many scheduling algorithms to improve the utilization of resources. The Fair scheduling algorithm [11] is a default scheduling strategy of Hadoop. It can ensure that each user in the cluster has approximately equal resources and can satisfy the principle of fairness among various users. The Capacity Scheduler uses a resource-aware algorithm [11], which is also a default scheduling strategy in Hadoop.

The scheduling methods mentioned above are generally designed to schedule batched tasks and methods for scheduling real-time task in MapReduce [4] is not very popular. At present, most algorithms do not consider scheduling both batched tasks and real-time tasks. The majority of existing research has focused on the management of computing tasks and resources because they are widely considered to be expensive. However, the management of storage resources and data movement between the storage and computing resources are becoming more and more important, as the scientific applications are becoming more and more data-intensive [14]. The hybrid task scheduling strategy proposed in this paper is closely related to where the input data is deployed and will greatly improve the data locality.

3   Preliminaries

For a given data center with heterogeneous servers, all tasks share the data and resources. We split the resources and data into multiple uniform resource slots and data blocks respectively. According to the locations of the resource slot and the data block of the task execution, we classify the task execution in two modes: the locality mode and the remote mode. Since the memory capacity is limited for each server, it is hard to guarantee full data locality for all tasks. To minimize the global execution time, we need to schedule tasks in locality mode as many as possible. In this paper, batched tasks and real-time tasks have different execution time when the tasks are executed in the locality mode. The execution time of different batched tasks or real-time tasks is also different.

We assume that there are N servers in the data center and K different data blocks. B_i represents the ith batched task and R_i represents the ith real-time tasks. The time is split into multiple time-slots. For each task, its start time is restricted by response time, which means the system must schedule a task within its response time. For batched tasks, the response time is very long, usually can be hours, while the response time for real-time tasks is only minutes even seconds. We use $response\_time$ to indicate the response time of tasks, and the $response\_time$ of each task is different. We use f_i to identify the wanted data block for task B_i or R_i. $S_j(1 \leq j \leq N)$ is the jth server and $D_k(1 \leq k \leq K)$ refers to the kth data block. It should be noticed that the wanted data block f_i should be some specified data blocks, for example D_k, which means $f_i = D_k$. There are two assignment decisions, one is data-assignment, the other is task-assignment, and the task-assignment includes batched task-assignment and real-time task-assignment. For any assignment decision, it could be represented by the following indicators.

$$\pi(D_k, S_j) = \begin{cases} 0, & \text{there is no replica of } D_k \text{ on } S_j; \\ 1, & \text{otherwise.} \end{cases} \tag{1}$$

$$\pi(B_i, S_j) = \begin{cases} 1, & \text{Batched task } B_i \text{ is assigned to server } S_j; \\ 0, & \text{otherwise.} \end{cases} \tag{2}$$

$$\pi(R_i, S_j) = \begin{cases} 1, & \text{Real-time task } R_i \text{ is assigned to server } S_j; \\ 0, & \text{otherwise.} \end{cases} \tag{3}$$

To describe the task execution mode clearly, we introduce the following indicators.

$$\phi(B_i, f_i) = \begin{cases} 0, & \text{Batched task } B_i \text{ is executed in locality mode;} \\ 1, & \text{Batched task } B_i \text{ is executed in remote mode.} \end{cases} \quad (4)$$

$$\phi(R_i, f_i) = \begin{cases} 0, & \text{Real-time task } R_i \text{ is executed in locality mode;} \\ 1, & \text{Real-time task } R_i \text{ is executed in remote mode.} \end{cases} \quad (5)$$

We use the notation T_0 to represent the task execution time under the locality mode. For the remote mode, we use T_r to represent the task execution time. Here, we have $T_r = T_0 \times (1 + \alpha)$, where α is a constant factor determined by the data center architecture and the networking situation. The networking situation will be worse if the number of tasks executed under remote mode is larger, hence, α will be larger and increase the time cost. For the case with data migration, the migration time $\Delta T = \beta \times T_0$ is another critical factor for hybrid scheduling, and β is a constant factor.

As mentioned above, we take batched task B_i for example, $\phi(B_i, f_i)$ equals to 0 and indicates that the task and its associated data block is placed on the same server. Hence, the task execution time can be represented by the following equation.

$$T(B_i) = T_0 \times (1 + \phi(B_i, f_i) \times \alpha) \quad (6)$$

For each server, the makespan is determined by the workload, including the initial workload and assigned tasks. We use the notation $L^i(S_j)$ to represent the workload of server S_j before task B_i is assigned to S_j. And at the beginning, none of tasks is assigned to S_j, $L^i(S_j)$ refers to the initial workload. Hence, we can use the following equation to represent the total task execution time which is represented as $L(S_j)$ (or normalized workload) for server S_j.

$$L(S_j) = L^i(S_j) + \pi(B_i, S_j) \times T(B_i) \quad (7)$$

4   Hybrid Scheduling

Given a data center that consists of N servers with one resource slot and M storage slots. There are K different data (blocks) with 3 data replicas allocated in the servers with some default settings. We use *start_time* to represent the start time of executing tasks, $B \cup R$ represents the collection of batched and real-time tasks. The problem is to place m batched tasks and n real-time tasks on the servers, such that the global job execution time is minimized and for each task, the start time does not exceed the response time. The number of data replicas placed on each server should not exceed the storage capacity M at any time-slot. The problem can be formalized as follow.

$$min.maxL(S_j), 1 \le j \le N$$
$$s.t. \forall t, \sum_1^K \pi(D_k, S_j) \le M, 1 \le j \le N$$
$$\forall J \in B \cup R, J.start\_time \le J.response\_time$$

It is easy to understand that the problem is NP-hard. In fact, even if scheduling only batched tasks has been proved to be NP-hard [9]. We can regard the problem like this: we need to select some tasks from the queue when some servers are available. If none of tasks can be executed in locality manner, we need to make a tradeoff between remote execution and waiting, and select the one that provides best benefit. Based on this problem transformation and the tradeoff, we propose our algorithms for scheduling batched tasks and real-time tasks as follows.

4.1 Batched Task Scheduling

Assume that there are m batched tasks in the system and they have a longer response time. When scheduling batched tasks, we should minimize the job execution time. Given all batched tasks have arrived in the system. The tasks are sorted in ascending order by execution time. The first step before scheduling is to select a proper task from the queue and is shown from line 1 to line 7 in Algorithm 1.

In Algorithm 1, S_i is idle and request a task. We find all tasks which can be executed in locality mode on S_i and select the one with least T_0 by function $min\_worktime(\cup b)$. If none of tasks can be executed in locality mode on S_i, then select the task which has least T_0 from all batched tasks. Finally, we return the selected task J and schedule it in next step.

Algorithm 1. Batched task scheduling: BatchedTaskSchedule(B_i)

Require: m:the number of batched tasks; $\cup B$:all batched tasks in the queue; S_i:the ith server with available resource slots; S_v:the server which has the minimum load in th cluster.

1: **for** $j = 1 \rightarrow m$ **do**
2:     **if** $\pi(f_j, S_i) = 1$ **then**
3:         $\cup b \leftarrow B_j$;
4: **if** $\cup b \neq \emptyset$ **then**
5:     $J \leftarrow min\_worktime(\cup b)$;
6: **else**
7:     $J \leftarrow min\_worktime(\cup B)$;
8: **if** $\pi(f_J, S_i) = 1$ **then**
9:     assign(J, S_i);
10: **else**
11:     $S_v \leftarrow min_load(\cup S)$;
12:     $T \leftarrow L^i(S_v) - t + T_0(J)$;
13:     **if** $\pi(f_J, S_v) = 1$ and $T < T_r(J)$ **then**
14:         assign(J, S_v);
15:     **else**
16:         assign(J, S_i);

The process of scheduling batched tasks is shown from line 8 to line 16 in Algorithm 1. J represents the selected task which will be scheduled. If the data has been placed on S_i, we assign the batched task J to server S_i. If J cannot be executed on S_i in locality mode, we find out the server with least workload by function $min\_load(\cup S)$ and indicate it with S_v. If the data required by task J is placed on S_v, we should make a tradeoff between two factors. One is the time for J to be executed on S_i in remote mode, i.e. $T_r(J)$. The other is the time for J to wait for S_v to release resources, then executed on S_v in locality mode. The waiting time is $L^i(S_v) - t$, the execution time is $T_0(J)$. We use T to represent the sum. Only when T is less than $T_r(J)$, we assign task J to server S_v, otherwise, J will be executed on server S_i. This method is called delay scheduling.

In addition, we should be aware that there is only one resource slot for each server as discussed in this paper. Actually, it is easy to extend our algorithms to the case that the server contains multiple resource slots. What we need to do is taking the real slot as one server in our work, and the slots in the same host server share the same data. To simplify the description, we still assume there is one slot for each server in this paper.

4.2   Real-Time Task Scheduling

Assume that there are n real-time tasks arrived one by one and sorted by the response time in the queue. It's urgent to schedule real-time tasks as soon as possible due to the small response time. Therefore, the more important factor to consider is that, the start time of each real-time task to be scheduled cannot be over the response time. Also, before scheduling, we should select a proper task from the queue. The algorithm for real-time task scheduling is shown in Algorithm 2.

Algorithm 2. Real-time task scheduling: Real-timeTaskSchedule(R_i)

Require: n:the number of real-time tasks which have arrived in the queue; $\cup R$:all real-time tasks in the queue; S_i:the ith server with available resource slots; S_v:the server which has the minimum load in the cluster.

1: **for** $j = 1 \to n$ **do**
2:     **if** $\pi(f_j, S_i) = 1$ **then**
3:         $\cup r \leftarrow R_j$;
4: **if** $\cup r \neq \emptyset$ **then**
5:     $j \leftarrow min\_responsetime(\cup r)$;
6:     $J \leftarrow min\_worktime(\cup j)$;
7: **else**
8:     $j \leftarrow min\_responsetime(\cup R)$;
9:     $J \leftarrow min\_worktime(\cup j)$;
10: **if** $\pi(f_J, S_i) = 1$ **then**
11:     $assign(J, S_i)$;
12: **else**
13:     $S_v \leftarrow min\_load(\cup S)$;
14:     $T \leftarrow L^i(S_v) - t + T_0(J)$;
15:     **if** $\pi(f_J, S_v) = 1$ **and** $L^i(S_v) < J.arrive\_time + J.response\_time$ **and** $T < T_r(J)$ **then**
16:         $assign(J, S_v)$;
17:     **else**
18:         $assign(J, S_i)$;

In Algorithm 2, if S_i requests a real-time task, we find out all tasks which can be executed on S_i in locality mode and assign the one with least response time by function $min\_responsetime(\cup r)$. If there are more than one task, we select the one with least work time, i.e. T_0 by function $min\_worktime(\cup j)$. If none of tasks can be executed in locality mode on S_i, we find tasks with least response time from all real-time tasks by function $min\_responsetime(\cup R)$ and select the one with least work time by function $min\_worktime(\cup j)$. Hence, we get a proper real-time task J to schedule.

The scheduling method for real-time tasks is different from batched tasks. We introduce it from line 10 to line 18 in Algorithm 2. If the data required by task J is deployed on S_i, we assign task J to server S_i so that the task can be executed in locality mode. Otherwise, find the server S_v which has the least workload in the cluster. If the data required by J is on S_v, we need to judge whether the task J can be executed on S_v and at the same time, meet the constraint that the start time mustn't be over the response time. If task J can be executed on S_v in time, we need to make a tradeoff between two factors. This is as same as what we have discussed on batched tasks before. In general, we choose the method which can provides better benefits.

4.3   Hybrid Scheduling

The hybrid scheduling strategy is to integrate the two scheduling method above together and achieve our purpose to reduce the execution time of all tasks. Also, the strategy must meet the response time constraint. We have discussed the problems on task selection and scheduling for batched tasks and real-time tasks respectively. In this section, the core content we will introduce is to how to deal with the situation that both batched tasks and real-time tasks are in the system at the same time. The scheduling method is shown in Algorithm 3.

Algorithm 3. Hybrid scheduling

Require: t:the global time-slots to complete all tasks; $\cup B$:all batched tasks; $\cup R$:all real-time tasks which have arrived.

1: $t \leftarrow 0$;
2: **for** $i \leftarrow 1 \rightarrow N$ **do**
3:     **if** $S_i.slot > 0$ **then**
4:         **if** $\cup R \neq \emptyset$ **then**
5:             $J \leftarrow Real - timeTaskSelect(\cup R)$;
6:             $Real - timeTaskSchedule(J)$;
7:         **else**
8:             **if** $\cup B \neq \emptyset$ **then**
9:                 $J \leftarrow BtachedTaskSelece(\cup B)$;
10:                 $BatchedTaskSchedule(J)$;
11: $t \leftarrow t + 1$;
12: **return** t;

We split the time into many time-slots and at each time-slot t, check the state of servers. If there is a server S_i is idle, we first check if there are real-time tasks in the system. Because of the small response time, the real-time tasks are always prior to batched tasks. Therefore, only when the queue of real-time tasks is empty or all real-time tasks have already been scheduled, we can schedule the batched tasks.

5   Hybrid Scheduling with Data Migration

In this section, we will add the data migration to the hybrid scheduling strategy to make a further improvement in data locality. Data migration means the process of migrating a data block to a specified server. After data migration, the server which originally can execute some tasks in remote mode, will be able to execute them in locality mode. Although data migration can make a time reduction by improving data locality, it also results in an extra time cost cause migrating data is time consuming. We use ΔT to represent the time of data migration. The process of data migration is shown in Algorithm 4 in detail as follow.

Algorithm 4. Data migration: migrate(f_J, S_v)

Require: J:the selected task; num:the number of replicas of each data; $degree$:the number of tasks which require data f_J as input;S_v:the target server for data migration.

1: **if** $S_v.storage\_space > 0$ **then**
2:     assign f_J to S_v;
3:     $f_J.degree \leftarrow f_J.degree + 1$;
4: **else**
5:     **for** $i \leftarrow 1 \rightarrow M$ **do**
6:         $d \leftarrow min\_degree(S_v.data)$;
7:         **if** $D_d.num > 1$ **then**
8:             replace f_d with f_J;

For the implementation of $migrate(f_J, S_v)$, we should be aware that if there is no enough storage space on S_v, some data may be replaced by f_J. The reason to select D_d in Algorithm 4 but not other data is that the degree of data D_d is minimum among the data on server S_v, where the degree indicates the number of tasks taking the data as their input data so far. However, we have another important principle that there should be at least one replica in the data center for each data. This principle works when the replica of D_d on server S_v is the only replica, and we will select another data within minimized degree except D_d.

Data migration is only added in some specific steps of scheduling batched tasks and real-time tasks and the architecture of the hybrid scheduling strategy doesn't change. We will only introduce the processes of data migration in scheduling batched tasks and real-time tasks in detail, other relevant methods can refer to the previous algorithms we have presented before. It is easy to understand we discuss data migration only in the case that, task J cannot be executed in locality mode on idle server S_i and the server S_v, which has least workload, has no data required by J. The following algorithms we will discuss are all based on this case. Except this, any other situations can find a scheduling method. Task J can be executed either on S_i remotely, or on S_v in a delay scheduling manner. The algorithm for scheduling batched tasks with data migration is shown in Algorithm 5.

Algorithm 5. Batched task scheduling with data migration: BatchedTaskSchedule(B_i)

Require: $\cup B$:all batched tasks; S_i:the ith server with available resource slots;S_v:the server which has the minimum load in the cluster.
1:   $J \leftarrow BatchedTaskSelect(\cup B)$;
2: **if** $\pi(f_J, S_i) \neq 1$ **then**
3:     $t1 \leftarrow L^i(S_v) - t$;
4:    **if** $t1 < \Delta T$ **then**
5:       $T2 \leftarrow \Delta T + T_0(J)$;
6:    **else**
7:       $t2 \leftarrow t1 + T_0(J)$;
8:    **if** $T_r(J) > t2$ **then**
9:       migrate(f_J, S_v);
10:      assign(j, S_v);
11:    **else**
12:      assign(J, S_i);

In Algorithm 5, to decide whether to perform data migration, first we should calculate the time of task J to be executed on S_v in data migration manner. Task J has to wait for S_v to be idle, and the waiting time is $L^i(S_v) - t$, represented as $t1$. If $t1$ is less than T, it means the server S_v will release resources before the process of migrating the required data to S_v is completed. Therefore, the whole execution time is the sum of T and $T_0(J)$. Otherwise, the migration time is shorter than the waiting time $t1$, the whole execution is the sum of $t1$ and $T_0(J)$. We use $t2$ to indicate the whole execution time with data migration on server S_v. Here, we need to make a tradeoff between two factors. One is the execution time on S_i in remote mode, i.e. $T_r(J)$, the other is $t2$. If $t2$ is shorter than $T_r(J)$, we migrate the data required by J to server S_v, then assign J to S_v so that J can be executed in locality mode on S_v. Otherwise, J will be executed remotely on server S_i.

The algorithm for scheduling real-time tasks with data migration is similar and shown in Algorithm 6. In Algorithm 6, we first calculate the time of waiting S_v to be idle and represent it as $t1$. Then we can get the whole execution time with data migration time like procedure in Algorithm 5 and represent it as $t2$. There is another time $t3$, which means the start time of J if J is executed on S_v after data migration. Before making the tradeoff between T_r and $t2$, we need to

---

Algorithm 6. Real-time task scheduling with data migration:
Real-timeTaskSchedule(R_i)

Require: $\cup R$:all real-time tasks in the queue; S_i:the ith server with available resource slots; S_v:the server which has the minimum load in the cluster; t:the global time-slots to complete all tasks.

1: $J \leftarrow Real - timeTaskSelect(\cup R)$;
2: **if** $\pi(f_J, S_i) \neq 1$ **then**
3:      $t1 \leftarrow L^i(S_v) - t$;
4:      **if** $t1 < \Delta T$ **then**
5:          $t2 \leftarrow \Delta T + T_0(j)$;
6:          $t3 \leftarrow t + \Delta T$;
7:      **else**
8:          $t2 \leftarrow t1 + T_0(J)$;
9:          $t3 \leftarrow L^i(S_v)$;
10:     **if** $T_r(J) > t2$ **and** $t3 < J.arrive\_time + j.response\_time$ **then**
11:         migrate(f_J, S_v);
12:         assign(J, S_v);
13:     **else**
14:         assign(J, S_i);

---

judge whether the task J can be executed in time within the response time. Only in the case that $t2$ is less than T_r and the start time of J can meet the response time constraint can we assign J to S_v. It means task J will be executed on S_v in locality mode after data migration and consume less time than on server S_i, J can also be scheduled within the response time.

6   Performance Evaluation

We conduct simulations with varies settings. Based on our previous work in [8] we can set the value of constant as $\alpha = 1.2$ and $\beta = 0.8$. We set $N = 50$ servers and $M = 20$ storage slots for each server. All tasks shared $K = 300$ data blocks with default 3 replicas in the data center. The replicas are placed randomly by the rule that the replicas of the same data block will not be placed on the same server. The task execution time T_0 in locality mode and the input data for each task are given randomly. There are 3 cases of tasks in the system. Case 1: all batched tasks; case 2: all real-time tasks; case 3: batched tasks and real-time tasks. We will analyze the 3 cases by conducting our scheduling methods.

For the first case, we considered 1000 batched tasks that have arrived to the system and are sorted in the order of their ascending execution time. The simulation results are shown in Fig. 2, where the x-coordinate represents the time-slots and the y-coordinate is the CDF value. The CDF value indicates the percentage of the completed jobs for given time-slots. From the results we know that our algorithms perform better than the typical FIFO method. The scheduling method with data migration is also better than without data migration. We should be aware that the improvement produced by data migration is limited

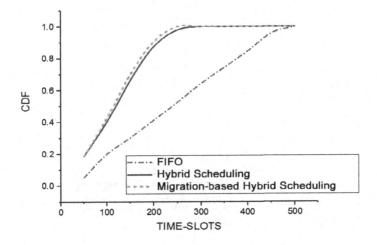

Fig. 2. Scheduling only batched tasks

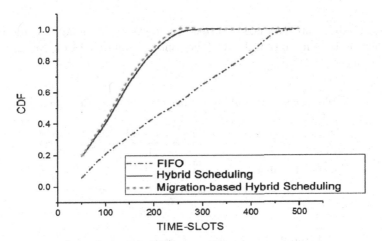

Fig. 3. Scheduling only real-time tasks

because the storage slots are limited and we only migrate data in some specific conditions as discussed before.

For the second case, we let $n = 1000$ real-time tasks arrive in 100 time-slots and sort them by response time in ascending order. The simulation results are shown in Fig. 3 with same coordinates settings. we can see that, for real-time tasks, our algorithms are also better than FIFO. The performance of data migration is similar with scheduling batched tasks. This is because all real-time tasks will arrive after 100 time-slots and the condition will be similar with case 1.

For case 3, we let $m = 500$ batched tasks in the queue and $n = 500$ real-time tasks arrived in 100 time-slots. The simulation results are shown in Fig. 4 with same coordinates settings. From the results we can know that our algorithms

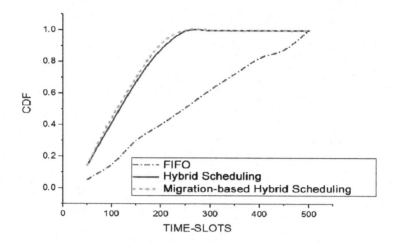

Fig. 4. Hybrid scheduling both batched and real-time tasks

can also schedule batched tasks and real-time tasks at the same time and reduce the execution time more than FIFO. The contribution of data migration is same as the results of the two cases above.

Table 1. Fairness analysis-average waiting time (time-slots)

Algorithm	Case 1	Case 2	Case 3
FIFO	213	169	197
Hybrid scheduling	75	56	68
Migration-based hybrid scheduling	75	56	64

Table 2. The amount of overtime real-time tasks

Algorithm	Case 2	Case 3
FIFO	7	5
Hybrid scheduling	3	2
Migration-based hybrid scheduling	2	2

Fairness is another key factors for task scheduling. We use average waiting time characterize the fairness. We analyze the average waiting time under the above 3 cases. The results are shown in Table 1. From this table, we know that our algorithms not only reduce task execution time, but also provide better fairness than FIFO. We also evaluate whether data migration can meet the constraint of response time for real-time tasks. For case 2 and case 3, we count the number of real-time tasks which can not be executed before response time. From the results shown in Table 2 we know that our algorithms have less overtime tasks than FIFO.

7   Conclusion

In this paper, we proposed a hybrid scheduling strategy for scheduling both batched tasks and real-time tasks, and data migration is taken into consideration to improve the data locality. The delay scheduling is also considered. We formalize the problem and the basic idea is to compare the benefits between instantaneity and data locality for tasks. Simulations show this method can provide better time reduction than FIFO and acceptable fairness. In addition, data migration can also improve the data locality and shorten global time.

Acknowledgment. This work is supported in part by the National Natural Science Foundation of China under Grant 61373015, in part by the Jiangsu Natural Science Foundation under Grant BK20160813 and BK20140832, in part by the National Key R&D Program of China under Grant 2018YFB1003902, in part by the Open Project Funded by State Key Laboratory of Computer Architecture under Grant CARCH201710, and in part by the Project Funded by China Postdoctoral Science Foundation.

References

1. Apache hadoop. http://hadoop.apache.org/
2. Apache pig. http://pig.apache.org/
3. Chen, Q., Zhang, D., Guo, M., Deng, Q., Guo, S.: SAMR: a self-adaptive mapreduce scheduling algorithm in heterogeneous environment. In: IEEE International Conference on Computer and Information Technology, pp. 2736–2743, June 2010
4. Dean, J., Ghemawat, S.: Mapreduce: simplified data processing on large clusters. In: Proceedings of USENIX OSDI, pp. 1–45 (2013)
5. Lee, Y.C., Zomaya, A.Y.: Energy conscious scheduling for distributed computing systems under different operating conditions. IEEE Trans. Parallel Distrib. Syst. **22**(8), 1374–1381 (2011)
6. Li, D., Wu, J., Chang, W.: Efficient cloudlet deployment: local cooperation and regional proxy. In: International Conference on Computing, Networking and Communications, pp. 757–761, March 2018
7. Li, X., Tatebe, O.: Data-aware task dispatching for batch queuing system. IEEE Syst. J. **11**(2), 889–897 (2017)
8. Li, X., Wang, L., Lian, Z., Qin, X.: Migration-based online CPSCN big data analysis in data centers. IEEE Access **6**, 19270–19277 (2018)
9. Li, X., Wu, J., Qian, Z., Tang, S., Lu, S.: Towards location-aware joint job and data assignment in cloud data centers with NVM. In: Proceedings of IEEE IPCCC, pp. 1–8, December 2017
10. Shi, W., Gao, J., Zhang, Q., Li, Y., Xu, L.: Edge computing: vision and challenges. IEEE Internet Things J. **3**(5), 637–646 (2016)
11. Thomas, L., R, S.: Survey on mapreduce scheduling algorithms. Int. J. Comput. Appl. **95**(23), 9–13 (2014)

12. Vavilapalli, V.K., et al.: Apache hadoop yarn: yet another resource negotiator. In: Proceedings of the 4th Annual Symposium on Cloud Computing, no. 5, October 2013

13. Wang, W., Zhu, K., Ying, L., Tan, J., Zhang, L.: Map task scheduling in mapreduce with data locality: throughput and heavy-traffic optimality. IEEE/ACM Trans. Netw. **24**(1), 190–203 (2016)

14. Yu, B., Pan, J.: Location-aware associated data placement for geo-distributed data-intensive applications. In: IEEE Conference on Computing Communications, pp. 603–611, April 2015

15. Zaharia, M., Borthakur, D., Sarma, J.S., Elmeleegy, K., Shenker, S., Stoica, I.: Delay scheduling: a simple technique for achieving locality and fairness in cluster scheduling. In: Proceedings of the 5th European Conference on Computer Systems, pp. 265–278. ACM (2010)

16. Zhou, Z., et al.: Minimizing SLA violation and power consumption in cloud data centers using adaptive energy-aware algorithms. Future Gen. Comput. Syst. **86**, 836–850 (2018)

17. Zhu, C., Zhou, H., Leung, V.C.M., Wang, K., Zhang, Y., Yang, L.T.: Toward big data in green city. IEEE Commun. Mag. **55**(11), 14–18 (2017)

Author Index

Printed in the United States
By Bookmasters